Immanuel Jakobovits

Journal of a Rabbi

LIVING BOOKS

Journal of a Rabbi

by IMMANUEL JAKOBOVITS, B.A., Ph.D.

LIVING BOOKS, INC.
NEW YORK, N. Y.

Dedicated

to my cherished

M O T H E R

"Three partners have a share in man:
the Lord, his father, and his mother."

(*Kiddushin* 30b)

CONTENTS

PREFACE

THE instinct of self-preservation, nature's most powerful urge, manifests itself in diverse ways. It provides trees with barks; it makes birds sing to attract their mates, and it sends salmon up-river to spawn in safety. It animates the physiology of love and hunger and pain to reproduce and preserve and protect life against decay and oblivion.

The drive for self-preservation also makes authors write. This explains why, in the biblical phrase, "of making many books there is no end."

Upon the appearance of this book I shall enter the twenty-fifth year of my pulpit career. With the spoken and the written word serving as the tools of my vocation, my output of sermons, addresses, articles and letters during this period has been considerable. This volume is an attempt to rescue some of these from oblivion, to assign some permanence to speeches which are often ephemeral and "but as yesterday when it is passed," and to writings hidden away in some dusty periodicals.

The implied claim to literary survival and attention lies less in the instrinsic value of my thoughts than in the rather unusual nature of my experience, of my subject matter and sometimes of my way of thinking. My rabbinical activity has taken me to three widely different countries on both sides of the Atlantic—ministering to three distinguished congregations in London, presiding over the religious destiny of Irish Jewry in Dublin, and now guiding an illustrious congregation at the heart of the world's largest Jewish community in New York. The multi-colored strands in the cosmopolitan fabric of such a diverse background cannot but invest the composite picture of my reactions to life's promptings with some uncommon features.

My special interests, too, have been varied and at times off the beaten track. The field of medicine in Jewish law—to which I have particularly devoted myself—has scarcely begun to be cultivated. Also beyond the narrow confines of popular treatment are many other subjects which have engaged my interest, such as the "slavery" legislation of Judaism or the significance of alliteration in biblical exegesis.

Above all, the selections here included address themselves to the great problems of Jewish living and thinking posed by the cataclysmic changes we have witnessed in our generation. The rise of Israel, the explosive expansion of science, the ecumenical overtures from Rome, the ascendancy of materialism and the secularization of society—these and numerous other factors have spawned the most exacting challenges to Jewish spiritual leadership. They call for bold thinking, untrammeled by the die-hard conventions and cliches of past approaches. They demand a critical reappraisal of Jewish thought and Jewish policies.

Some of the contributions within these covers are a modest attempt at discharging this responsibility. Whether in censuring the present trends of rabbinic leadership, of religious Zionism and of Yeshivah education, or in challenging the all but unanimous American-Jewish commitment to the banishment of religion from public life, or in advocating Federal aid to parochial schools—I have never flinched from espousing unpopular minority views when I felt these were called for by the changing pattern of contemporary life or by the loyalties to Jewish teachings and history. In my interpretations of Jewish law and thought, too, I have often preferred untried paths of exploration to mere embellishments of time-worn homilies and anecdotal flourishes.

This *Journal of a Rabbi,* then, recounts the intellectual wanderings and adventures of a rabbi whose commitment to the absolute verities of the Jewish tradition has provided him with answers as well as questions, with assurances no less than perplexities, on the great issues of our times. Born into the twentieth century and exposed to the impact of Western thought and scholarship, I have shared many of the doubts and questionings of my less religiously-committed contemporaries. But ultimately my faith in the truths of Judaism has sustained me in wrestling with the problem of how to merge the two worlds, of an ancient religion and a modern civilization, into an harmonious entity.

This book is not meant to be an autobiography. At most it is a grossly incomplete self-portrayal of a groping mind, harassed as well as stimulated by a busy life of communal service. But the literary products of such a life must necessarily reflect some biographical traces of my pilgrimage. In this book these find expression in my reflections on Jewish life in England, Ireland and America, in my participation at state occasions— from a sermon to mark the inauguration of Dublin's Jewish Lord Mayor to blessing the President of the United States at a White House reception, in my reactions to family joys and sorrows, in my many convention addresses, and in my letters to newspaper editors on current controversies.

In a selection of writings ranging over nearly a quarter of a century individual items are bound to be unequal in style and merit. There may indeed be a few ideas which, from the vantage point of my experience today, I would have expressed differently, or maybe not at all. But on the whole, I have found scarcely anything I wrote one or two decades ago which I would not now reaffirm with equal conviction. Some repetiveness here or there is also inevitable in a collection of this kind, however careful I may have been in my choice from a very large accumulation of material. For these deficiencies I must ask the reader's indulgence.

In conclusion I wish to thank the Directors and staff of Living Books, Inc. for their personal interest in the production of this book and the cheerful understanding with which they handled an assignment involving many exceptional problems. My grateful acknowledgements are also extended to the editors of the various periodicals for their kind permission to reprint items originally published by them.

This publication would have been impossible without the substantial help of my cherished friends, Messrs. Morris Blank, Morris Kavy, Michael Pauker, Henry Richard, Hyman Ross and, above all, Henry Hirsch and Hermann Merkin. To their generosity and friendship I owe far more than this book. I hope that its acceptance by the reading public may in some measure make them gratified partners with me in our joint labors to project an enlightened, forward-looking image of Judaism in the world of today and tomorrow.

IMMANUEL JAKOBOVITS

New York City,
10 Sivan, 5725/1965.

1

The Challenge of Our Times

Jewish Secularism

F EW complaints about our age command more agreement than that religion is declining. Many observers believe that we have reached an unprecedented low ebb in religious faith and observance. Along with other denominations, it is alleged, Judaism, too, is now but a pale shadow of its former massive strength, lacking the popular appeal it once possessed.

Victor Schonfeld Memorial Lecture, published in *The Jewish Post* (London), September 14. 1956.

This gloomy picture, painted by nostalgic memories mixed with present disappointments, is not altogether accurate. The strictly observant element within Jewry has mostly, if not always, been in a minority. Already at the end of our first exile, according to the Midrash, only one of every five Israelites was worthy to participate in the exodus from Egypt.[1] A little later, again, but one of the twelve tribes (Lévi) refused to worship the Golden Calf.[2] Even in talmudic times, the masses of the people were often ignorant and oblivious of their religious obligations. The dispute over the correct form of the *Tephillin* (Rashi and Rabbenu Tam) still testifies to the long periods during which this fundamental commandment was not commonly performed,[3] and the institution of the public reader *(Sheli'ach Zibbur)* in our synagogues— originally to help pray those unable to read by themselves —is a lasting monument to the widespread illiteracy of former generations.[4] In the cherished Middle Ages, too, the religious and moral conditions were frequently deplorable—even by present-day standards. Today, for instance, we could hardly imagine a communal plea for sanction to set up a public brothel, as was addressed to Rabbi Isaac Arama in the fifteenth century.[5]

The confinement of religious observance to a small minority is not, then, a new phenomenon in Jewish history. Indeed, with the exception of the century preceding 1940, it is probably true that, in terms of absolute numbers, there never existed more learned and practicing Jews at any time than today. To this extent, therefore, Judaism is in no greater danger at the present time than at any period in the past; it may, in fact, well be numerically stronger now than almost ever before.

But the problem today is one of quality, not of quantity. The survival of the minority, possibly even in increasing numbers, is not at stake; what is now challenged for the first time is the traditional relationship between the religious minority and the non-observant majority. Up to the Emancipation, the age-old struggle between them always resolved itself into a straight fight between the forces of knowledge and those of ignorance. To be educated broadly meant to be religious. Only "the fool said in his heart: 'There is no

God';"[6] merely "a brutish man knoweth (it) not, neither doth a fool understand this."[7] It was the mark of the *Am ha-Aretz,* the ignoramus, to flout the teachings of Judaism. However numerically inferior the religious element may have been, the masses invariably recognized its intellectual superiority; its claim to the spiritual leadership of the Jewish people was unquestioned. The center of gravity thus always remained the religious core of our people, with the non-conformists being driven to the periphery of Jewish life.

With the Emancipation, there occurred the first major disturbance in this relative balance between the cultured few and the ignorant many. A new factor intruded into Jewish life: Assimilation. Its advent extended the area of conflict into a three-cornered contest, in which the traditionalists were opposed by the dwindling ranks of the indifferent on the one side and the growing number of those consciously promoting their complete absorption in the non-Jewish culture pattern on the other. Thus the battleground for Jewish religious survival gradually shifted from knowledge *versus* ignorance to tradition *versus* assimilation, and education no longer remained the undisputed prerogative of the faithful. Secular learning began to compete with religious learning, and not to augment it as in former ages.

The spectacular and triumphant rise of Jewish secular nationalism greatly accentuated this tendency. To ever larger masses of the Jewish people assimilation has become, not an instrument of individual submersion, but an ideal of national self-expression. The heroic efforts to remain distinct as a unique religious entity have given way to a popular quest for equality as an ordinary national entity. The possession of a Jewish government, parliament, university or police force now often arouses greater pride than the unique creations of the Jewish genius through centuries of incomparable spiritual productivity, than the great religious institutions and acadamies of Jewish learning which distinguish us from others. Paradoxically, we have become extraordinary in our search for ordinary values, for no other nation would betray a similar fascination in accomplishments which all nations display alike.

The tendency to "normalize" Jewish existence and to assimilate it to the common characteristics of other peoples has led to a corresponding shift in the popular recognition of Jewish leadership. This has largely passed from our spiritual guides to political, military and other secular leaders. They are now acclaimed as the custodians of our future, as the legitimate heirs to the historical heritage of the past. On the intellectual plane, too, the religious element as the major ferment in our destiny as a people is all but excluded. For cultural inspiration, more and more Jews now look increasingly to thinkers and scientists whose only link with Jewish traditions is, at best, their use of Hebrew as a vehicle of expression. The secularization of Jewish life, this cutting adrift of our people from its historical anchorage, has gone apace so rapidly and imperceptibly that we are no longer even surprised when fundamental social and educational problems affecting the future pattern of Jewish existence are discussed without any reference to the religious norms which, as our national constitution, used to govern their solutions.

In many respects, these far-reaching developments are due to factors entirely beyond our control. The impact of the Industrial Revolution, with its concomitant materialism, hit the Jews, through their preponderant urbanization, perhaps even more devastatingly than other settled peoples. The emergence of modern nationalism, combined more lately with the desperate Jewish struggle for physical survival, has also helped to place a disproportionate emphasis on the non-spiritual aspects of Jewish life.

But Jewish leadership cannot disclaim all responsibility for these conditions. In some ways, it cannot be denied, it has failed adequately to respond to the challenge of modern thought and currents. We may here point only to two relevant factors which have greatly aggravated the problem of preventing the inroads of secularism.

The most articulate expression of the Jewish religious outlook in our Western lands shows by and large an indifferent, if not hostile, attitude to secular studies. This attitude is particularly pronounced in the main bulwarks of religious learning, the *Yeshivoth,* and is consequently reflected among our leading religious scholars. The reason for this historically astounding fact is quite simple. The chief trends of rabbinic education today are not indigenous to these countries but imported from Eastern Europe. There Judaism had flourished in what was, from the point of view of secular culture, virtually a vacuum. Judaism faced no challenge from outside, and there was no need for the presentation of Jewish teachings in the light of general knowledge. But whenever in the past Jews found themselves planted in a highly cultured society, their religious guides—or at least some of them— always took to secular studies with alacrity. Often they were counted among the foremost exponents of the general culture of their day. Whether we think of the scientific accomplishments of many Tannaim and Amoraim, of the important place occupied by secular knowledge in medieval Jewish philosophy and in the stature of its masters, or of the service to which Samson Raphael Hirsch and his school put their general education — they all realized that Jewish thought could not be preserved in isolation once it was exposed to the allurements and rivalry of other cultures. A refusal to appreciate, and come to terms with, the cultural values surrounding Jewish life was inconceivable at any time.

Today this vital lesson of history is widely ignored, and the price paid for this neglect has been appalling. As a direct consequence, there now exists for the first time in our history a non-religious Jewish intelligentsia—hitherto a contradiction in terms; and our religious society, unable to keep abreast with the advances of modern thought and science has laid itself wide open to the unprecedented charge of obscurantism. The reluctance to countenance a synthesis of religious and secular studies, meant to insulate the religious element from secular influences, has in fact alienated the secular masses from religion.

This, then, is the gravamen of the problem: Either Judaism assimilates secular knowledge as was done in the past, or secular knowledge will continue to displace Judaism as it does at present. If we cannot ensure that our top-ranking thinkers and scientists are religious, we must make sure that those who are religious will be among our leading thinkers and scientists. Every effort should be made to induce ever more alumni of our *Yeshivoth* to take up academic careers and to occupy pre-eminent positions in the realms of arts, science, medicine, and law. We must thus recreate our own religious intelligentsia.

Above all, those charged with guiding the spiritual destinies of our people must combine Jewish with secular excellence if they are to recapture the lost reins of leadership and to command once more the loyal respect of the groping masses.

Another reorientation in the exercise of rabbinic leadership, too, could help to stem the advancing tide of Jewish secularism. Leading scholars throughout the world, it is true, are constantly engaged in re-examining Jewish law and interpreting its application to present-day circumstances. In numerous responsa and other halachic works they continue the dynamic process of extending the sovereignty of Judaism over the ever changing exigencies of life. But, as a rule, their efforts are limited to solving religious problems in the light of modern conditions. What the hour demands even more urgently is to reverse the procedure: to solve modern problems in the light of religious conditions.

Some examples may elaborate this point. The type of perplexities mainly dealt with in practical halachic research are Sabbath observance, *Kashruth, Shemittah,* the *Agunah* problem and similar difficulties created by the demands of Jewish law and aggravated by the social and economic stresses of our time. These are religious problems; they exist only in the eyes of those who already accept the supremacy of Jewish law. To the secularists such problems and their solutions lack any reference to life as they experience it. If Judaism is to have a message for them the chief emphasis ought to be, instead, on the profound moral, social and economic issues baffling our age and how Jewish teaching can help to ease their burden. Contemporary life has thrown up innumerable problems of this kind, such as H-bomb tests, labor relations, strikes, gambling, the treatment of non-Jewish minorities in Israel—to detail only a few at random.

We complain that the rule of Jewish law is being progressively ousted from life and confined to ever narrowing circles of believers. Its scope and appeal cannot be widened unless its guides will go out once again, as did the Prophets of old, into the midst of life, assess the moral dangers and perplexities weighing on mankind as well as on Jewry, and firmly exclaim, "Thus saith the Lord!" In practice this may mean the appointment by every leading rabbinate of commissions to prepare authentic and reasoned pronouncements on the Jewish solutions to the multitude of problems confronting our confused generation.

Judaism demands not the elimination of secular interests but their consecration to the Divine design of life. The alarming encroachments of secularism can be countered only by moving the dividing line between holy and secular into and beyond the territory of the profane, until all "the earth"— even everything 'earthly' and material—"shall be full of the knowledge of the Lord, as the waters cover the sea."[8]

Who Is A Jew?

Reflections on a Crisis

THE serious crisis which has arisen in Israel over the definition of a Jew has dramatically highlighted two almost contradictory developments. Paradoxically enough, the argument now raging over this question indicates both the solution and the creation of the gravest Jewish problems of our time through the rise of Israel.

On the one hand, the widespread and officially supported clamor for broadening the traditionally narrow definition of a Jew is a measure of the revolutionary change in Jewish fortunes brought about by Israel. Hitherto countless Jews sought to conceal their identity in order to appear as, and be accepted by, the non-Jews around them. Now thousands of non-Jews seek to hide their origin or vary their true status in order to be treated as Jews! To have accomplished this historic change is, surely, one of the most momentous achievements of Israel. The Jewish State has thus, after only ten years of existence, reversed the flight from Judaism. It has made it attractive and rewarding to be a Jew. No finer tribute could be paid to Israel.

On the other hand, the crisis has exposed the most appalling danger facing the Jewish people through the emergence

Published in *The Jewish Review* (London), July 18, 1958.

of Israel. By the very act of solving one problem which has bedevilled Jewish life in the past, the State may produce another, even greater perplexity. If the secularists had their way, Israel might well disrupt that very unity of the Jewish people it was established to strengthen. On one side, Israel has removed for the first time in centuries, the barriers between Jew and Jew; whether Europeans, Yemenites, Moroccans or Indians—Israel has made them conscious of the oneness that unites them all. On the other side, the same Israel would threaten to drive a wedge between different sections of our people. There would be "national Jews" (so declared by the State) and "religious Jews" (so identified by history), and the ones would not recognize the others as brothers belonging to a common tribe. The worst disaster that could could strike Jewry would become reality: there would be two unidentical Jewish peoples.

Religious Jews can and will never depart from the age-old legal definition of what constitutes a Jewish person. This definition is hallowed by an unbroken millennial tradition no less than by all the authorities of Jewish law. A person is a Jew only by virtue of either being born of a Jewish mother or of his admission to the Jewish faith as a proselyte according to the requirement of Jewish law. No other manner exists for being or becoming a Jew, and there are legally no half-Jews.

There may, however, be persons of doubtful Jewish status. Under normal conditions, anyone who claims to be Jewish (i.e. either by birth or by formal conversion) is presumed to enjoy the status of a Jew, and no further proof is required.[9] But in some cases, conclusive evidence may be necessary to establish such a claim. Thus, "he who comes from another country—whether man or woman, boy or girl, widower or widow—requires proof that he is Jewish; and even if such persons conduct themselves in accord with Jewish religious law, and speak in our tongue, and are conversant with all the characteristic features of Jews, they must still produce evidence (to be accepted as Jews); accordingly, there was an enactment in Lithuania not to sanction the solemnization of any marriage, unless there is evidence of the Jewish and family origin of the parties."[10]

With the havoc and dislocation in Jewish life wrought by the War some relaxation of these safeguards may conceivably be made as an emergency measure to meet the urgent needs of the many genuine Jews who have lost all documentary or other conclusive traces of their origin. Such modifications are, in fact, operated daily in Israel and elsewhere to overcome the inevitable effects of the Nazi holocaust and mass-migration. But this can only affect persons reasonably presumed to be Jewish. There can be no question, however, of recognizing as of Jewish status people known or suspected to be non-Jews, such as children of a non-Jewish mother, simply because a declaration requesting such status is made before the civil authorities in Israel.

Apart from purely religious considerations, it would be preposterous and utterly chaotic to transfer the prerogative of effecting admissions to Judaism (or Jewishness) from the jurisdiction of competent legal authorities to the arbitrary choice of private individuals. A person may freely choose to embrace another religion, but he cannot on his own render a conversion legally valid. No individual can be left to determine by himself his own (or his children's) religious status any more than his citizenship or nationality. Such matters of personal status are governed by strict laws in every civilized society, and their breach in Israel would be an intolerable affront to the Jewish conscience.

Three important conclusions to be drawn from the present crisis seem inescapable:

1. All incidents of religious friction in Israel in the past were merely minor skirmishes compared with the present conflict. The battlefield has at least moved to the very center of the line dividing the views of religiously-minded Jews from those of the secularists. The stakes now at issue lie at the core of the prolonged tension between them. To that extent the crisis is to be welcomed, for the cause of religious Jewry will for once be united, popular and plainly appreciated by all sections of our people. That could not be said of every past *casus belli* with the secular nationalists.

2. It will now become more and more evident that the ultimate objective of Jewish Statehood, as a factor in unifying

the Jewish people all over the world, cannot be realized unless the state is built on religious foundations. The establishment of Israel may otherwise, in the long run, do more damage than good for the preservation of Jewry and Judaism.

3. As a result of the present conflict, it may now gradually dawn on the Jewish masses everywhere who are the true defenders of Jewish unity and survival, and who threaten to undermine these values. It is bound to become increasingly clear that only religious Jews will prevent the bonds between Israel and the Diaspora from snapping. They alone will ensure that Jews wherever they are dispersed will not be cast off from the House of Israel as inferior or different Jews. Religious Jews will be recognized as the upholders of Jewish integrity in the future, just as they were acknowledged as the champions of the Jewish heritage in the past. Without them there would be no Judaism today and no Jewish people tomorrow.

Jewish–Christian Relations

THE changes in the religious pattern of the world during the past twenty years are no less drastic and epoch-making than those which have transformed the pre-war notions of science and international relations, and it is time for leaders of Jewish religious thought to reappraise the place of Judaism in this new world.

As items of supreme concern to Jews, these historical developments deserve mention.

1. For the first time in two thousand years, Christianity has gone over from the offensive to the defensive. With the emergence of scores of new non-Christian nations, now in the majority at the United Nations, and the liquidation of colonialism by Christian countries, with the persecution of the Church behind the Iron and Bamboo Curtains, and with the suppression of missionary work in Africa and the greater

Extracts from an address delivered at the Convention of the Rabbinical Council of America, June 27, 1963.

part of Asia, the Christian hope of world conquest by conversion or political domination seems now at an end.

2. These pressures have encouraged the present efforts at consolidating the strength of the Church from within—by the new orientation towards Christian unity and an accommodation with other faiths, notably Judaism. The former inter-denominational tensions and rivalries have given way to the spirit of tolerance and co-existence marking the present era of "dialogues." Significant symbols of this shift are the adoption, after years of abortive Jewish efforts, of the Fair Sabbath Law by the New York State legislature with the blessings of the Catholic Church and the spectacular deletion of the reference to "perfidious Jews" in the Good Friday liturgy—a reform which, had it come a thousand years earlier, might have saved millions of Jewish lives.

3. There has also lately been a distinct tendency towards greater emphasis on religious values in public life reflected by American public opinion. A survey soon after the Supreme Court decision on prayers at public schools was said to indicate that no fewer than 80% of all Americans disapproved of the decision, as did virtually all State governors, while a more recent poll credited almost 80% with favoring Federal aid to parochial schools, the increase over the previous poll being heaviest among Protestants. Such a shift is bound to affect most intimately the Jewish community and its relations with non-Jews.

All these dramatic changes challenge Jewish religious leaders with the task of exploring new paths and policies.

1. Since the Jews could be regarded as an obstacle to the universal spread of Christianity, as they were believed to be, only so long as that prospect existed, the time is now opportune to appeal to Christians to eliminate the hoped-for conversion of the Jews from their aspirations and activities. Such a theological "agreement to differ" and to accept as final the survival of Judaism alongside Christianity would in one stroke remove the principal sore in Jewish-Christian relations. As long as the teachings of one faith require the absorption of another through missionary work, there can be no true equality and confidence between them. This

factor, I submit, is today a more serious impediment to Jewish-Christian understanding, and to the elimination of anti-Semitism, than the charge of "deicide."

2. By invariably taking sides with the libertarians in controversies on the role of religion in public life, the Jewish "defense" agencies create a popular image of the Jew as a protagonist of secularism. This is as inconsonant with current religious trends in America as it is inimical to Jewish interests. Jewish religious life could flourish only in a deeply religious society, and the acknowledgement of God in all areas of life by all men remains Judaism's most cardinal tenet. Whatever the justification for Jewish fears in the past, the Jewish religious community must now reconsider its position in the light of the situation as it is today, not as it was in the Middle Ages or at the time of the Founding Fathers. In the gigantic struggle, which will determine human as well as Jewish survival, between the forces of morality founded on religion and of crass materialism fed by godlessness, there can be but one legitimate choice for Jews if they are not to renounce their prophetic heritage as the people who were told "Ye are My witnesses."

3. Through these mutual concessions—Christians abandoning their claims against the Jewish people, and Jews abandoning their dogmatic resistance to manifestations of religion in public life—much bitterness and suspicion would be eliminated. The stage would be set for coordinated action on the great issues facing our age. The voice of religion thus strengthened as a mighty force could then effectively address itself to the moral evils gnawing at the roots of our society: the lust for power, success and pleasure, corruption in government, marital faithlessness, and other vices threatening man's security. Such a voice unencumbered by mutual fears could create an altogether new climate of human dignity and idealism. Religion would no longer be a mere regimen of worship but a universal discipline to regenerate the moral excellence of men and governments joined in serving each other as partners and not as rivals seeking predominance.

The Threat of Calendar Reform

A resolution passed by the Ecumenical Council of the Roman Catholic Church in Rome on October 25, 1963 has once again drawn world attention, and particularly grave Jewish concern, to Calendar Reform. This article will endeavor to present the reasons for the proposed changes in the calendar, a brief history of past attempts to make—and fight—these changes, the attitudes of Judaism and other faiths, and the prospects for the future, including the feasibility of some alternative suggestions.

Our civil (or Gregorian) calendar represents the best and most accurate system so far devised to relate the passage of time to two entirely unrelated astronomical time-units: the daily revolution of the earth around its axis (determining the count of days) and the annual orbit of the earth around the sun (determining the seasons and the count of years). Apart from days and years, the calendar uses two further time-units which have no astronomical bearings: months and weeks. The month, as the name implies, was originally based on the lunar cycle of about 29½ days. But in the present civil calendar it averages about 30½ days and bears no relationship to the phases of the moon; it is simply a convenient expedient to divide the year into twelve more or less equal parts. The week, on the other hand, is a fixed period of seven days unconnected with any lunar or solar phases and therefore reckoned quite distinctly from the count of months or years.

This dual count of accumulated day-units—one based on astronomical data (the year and its sub-divisions of months) and the other by a fixed number of days (the week)—complicates our calendar. For unfortunately the number of days in a year is not divisible by seven, since the earth inconveniently refuses to orbit the sun in an exact number of weeks, taking instead 52 weeks (364 days) plus a little more than a day (altogether 365 days, 5 hours, 48 minutes and 46.069 seconds, to be precise) to complete this annual cycle. Consequently, there is a continual discrepancy between the days of the week

Published in *The Jewish World* (New York), July, 1964.

and the days of the month or year, so that any date of the calendar never falls on the same day of the week in consecutive years.

This discrepancy, which amounts to one day in ordinary years (365 days) and two days in leap years (366 days), results in several awkward irregularities. On the one hand, events and holidays fixed by date, such as Washington's Birthday, Memorial Day and Christmas, fall on a different day of the week every year, and, on the other hand, special days determined by the day of the week, such as Easter, Labor Day and Election Day, occur on different dates every year. For most people these annual variations do not constitute anything more serious than the purchase of a new and different diary each year. But for some limited groups this irregularity may prove costly and a considerable nuisance. Employers of large labor forces, for instance, may incur a good deal of extra work and expense in accounting and in the management of jobs by the need to determine wages and vacation periods on a different basis every year. Organizers of annual exhibitions or sports events must constantly take account of these variations, while astronomers have to contend with additional complications in their calculations of cosmic occurrences.

These groups, notably big business and some leading astronomers, have therefore been in the forefront of the agitation for a reform of the calendar whereby any date will permanently correspond to a specific day of the week. During the past four decades millions of dollars have been poured into a sustained world-wide campaign to effect such a reform by popular propaganda, intervention with governments and churches, and lobbying with national and international bodies.

By far the most publicized and financially best backed proposal is a simple device to overcome the irregularity of the week in relation to the year. In order to ensure that January 1 will fall on the same day of the week (viz., Sunday) every year and thus cause all other dates, too, to correspond permanently to fixed days of the week, the awkward extra day (s) in excess of exactly 52 weeks (i.e. the 365th, and in leap years also the 366th, day of the year) will just be eliminated from the count of the week, as follows: December 30 will be on Saturday; the next day, December 31, will be a "blank day" called "Worlds-Day;" and the day after will be Sunday, January 1. That week, then, from Saturday, December 30, to Saturday, January 7, will in fact have eight days, so that the Sabbath throughout that year would occur on Fridays. In leap years the same procedure would be repeated at the end of June, so that the Sabbath for the following six months would be on Thursdays, and the year after on Wednesdays, etc. Some other minor reforms would at the same time divide the year into four equal quarters of 13 weeks each and also fix the date of Easter (now dependent on the lunar cycle).

Normally any changes in the civil or solar calendar have little or no bearing on specifically Jewish interests. The Jewish Holy Day cycle is in any event entirely unrelated to any civil dates or to any regular pattern of weekdays, and the sole—but quite immaterial—link between the civil and Jewish calendars is the count of the *Tekuphoth* or seasons, affecting the annual date on which one commences saying *Tal u-Matar* (December 5 or, when the Hebrew year is divisible by 4, December 6) and the date, once every 28 years, of *Kiddush ha-Chammah* (April 8).

But this Jewish indifference to calendar reform presupposes the fixity of the 7-day week. Once this is violated—as is now proposed by introducing an 8-day week once every year and twice every leap year, as explained above—the effects on Jewish life would be catastrophic. Since obviously no Jewish or human authority could ever modify the regularity of the Jewish Sabbath every seventh day, as Divinely ordained in the scheme of creation and in the Ten Commandments, Jews must observe the Sabbath at seven-day intervals irrespective of any variations in the length of the week adopted in the civil calendar. Accordingly, the "Blank Day" proposal would inevitably add to the "Wandering Jew" the phenomenon of a "Wandering Sabbath" shifting to a different day of the week once or twice a year.

It requires little imagination to visualize the crippling effects this would produce. The necessity to observe the Sabbath, say, every Wednesday, and some months later every Tuesday, would inflict endless economic hardship on all observant Jews, intolerably interfere with studies at schools and colleges, expose parents to prosecution for withdrawing their children from school one day every week, and above all paralyze the religious life of the community now centered around the weekly Sabbath. It is hard' enough to fill our synagogues for Sabbath services on Friday nights and Saturday mornings; how infinitely difficult it would be to maintain the props of the Sabbath if we were compelled to announce: "The next 'Friday night' services will be held on Tuesday night at 6:30 and the Sabbath morning services on Wednesday at nine!" For most people, Judaism would—sociologically speaking— price itself out of existence through the resultant confusion and the inevitable economic and social disabilities.

Due to the complexity of the astronomical year's precise duration (see the first section above), no practical calendar can ever be perfectly in step with the true progress of time. Changes to correct the accumulated imperfections are occasionally necessary. Our existing civil system is based on the Julian Calendar, itself reformed from the Roman Calendar in 45 B.C.E. by Julius Caesar. This assumed that the average year was exactly 365 days and six hours long; hence it provided for an extra leap day, in addition to the usual 365 days, every fourth year. But actually the precise duration of the year is some 11 minutes less than $365\frac{1}{4}$ days. By the 16th century this discrepancy had accumulated to ten days, prompting Pope Gregory XIII to introduce his reform (the "Gregorian Calendar") whereby ten calendar days were dropped in 1582 and leap years were thenceforth omitted in years ending in hundreds but not divisible by 400, so as to eliminate the error for the future. Even after this change, there is still a deviation from the true astronomical values of about one day in 3600 years.

[Incidentally, the Jewish calendar, calculated and introduced by Hillel II in 344 C.E., is astronomically more accurate than the Julian, though somewhat less so than the Gregorian, despite the far greater complexity of the Jewish lunar-solar system. While the period of the lunar cycle (from one *Molad* to the next) differs from the true astronomical value by less than half a second (29 days 12 hrs. 44 mins. $3\frac{1}{3}$ secs. against

29 days 12 hrs. 44 mins. 2.841 secs.), so that the Hebrew calendar months still follow the phases of the moon quite closely, the divergence between the traditional length of the solar year and the corresponding astronomical figure is more serious, amounting to approximately 4½ days in a thousand years (365 days 5 hrs. 5 mins. 25.438 secs. against 365 days 5 hrs. 48 mins. 46.069 secs.), so that we celebrate *Pesach* nowadays at an average of about eight days later in the year than in the days of Hillel II.]

But neither Gregory's reform nor its adoption by England (1752), Turkey (1917), Russia (1918), and Greece (1923) tampered with the Sabbath. Since the introduction of a civil calendar the continuity of the seven-day week invariably remained intact. Significantly, the only two (ultimately abortive) exceptions were motivated by the avowed aim of destroying Christianity: the introduction of a ten-day week at the time of the French Revolution, and of a five-day week in Soviet Russia some forty years ago.

The suggestion to overcome the imperfections, or rather the inconvenience, of the present calendar by the intercalation of a blank day was originally advanced by an Italian priest, Abate Marco Mastrofini, in 1834. It received the first public support in 1910, from the International Chamber of Commerce, which prevailed on the Swiss Government to begin a study of calendar reform with a view to convening a world conference. This campaign was interrupted by the first World War. Further agitation succeeded in bringing the proposal before the League of Nations in 1923. The proposal was subsequently dropped in 1925, then reintroduced, and finally abandoned in 1931, largely as a result of Jewish opposition, led by Chief Rabbi Dr. Joseph H. Hertz, an episode later brilliantly described by him in a booklet under the title "The Battle for the Sabbath at Geneva: 1924-1931."

Matters remained relatively quiet until after the Second World War and the estalishment of the United Nations to replace the defunct League of Nations. Meanwhile the routed advocates of the "Blank Day" reform regrouped and resumed their militant agitation with the formation of The World Association of Calendar Reform, helped by large funds left by Mr. George Eastman of the Kodak Company, who had previously tried to introduce a calendar reform resolution in Congress in 1928. The renewed campaign led first to the attempt by Panama to bring calendar reform before the U. N. in 1949—a move blocked because no big power gave support —and then to India submitting the proposal to the United Nations Economic and Social Council (ECOSOC) in 1953. (India was motivated by considerations of internal expediency, to counter the confusion resulting from the innumerable calendars in operation on the sub-continent.) Although the proposal was supported by a number of nations (but not by the United States and Britain), it was eventually defeated, again largely through Jewish "lobbying" with governments and churches. In Europe the opposition moves were organized under the leadership of Chief Rabbi Israel Brodie, who convened a conference on calendar reform of twelve European Chief Rabbis, attended also by Chief Rabbi Dr. Isaac Herzog of Israel. This took place in London in November 1954, the first conference of its kind ever held, and from it developed the Conference of European Rabbis meeting biennially since 1957. In America Jewish efforts to maintain the continuity of the week were co-ordinated by the League for Safeguarding the Fixity of the Sabbath, which represented fifty leading American-Jewish organizations of all shades, and which published a Memorandum to the United Nations entitled "The Blank Day Device in Proposed Plan for Calendar Reform" in 1949. This 24-page pamphlet is probably to this day the best summary of the arguments against the "Blank Day" reform.

While Jewish opinion has been unanimous in opposing and fighting the proposal because of the disastrous effects its adoption would have on Jewish life, the attitude of the other faiths has varied from endorsement to indifference, with some isolated instances of active opposition. Most of the Mohammedan countries may be presumed to object to any interference with the seven-day week sacred to Islam (although Egypt supported the Indian resolution in 1953). But they never pressed their case against the "Blank Day," probably partly because they did not wish to identify themselves with the Jewish stand and partly because most Moslems, unlike the majority of Jews living dispersed in Christian lands, would be unaffected by an international decision to adopt the "Blank Day" reform since they reside in self-governing societies that would presumably retain their existing calendars.

Among the Christian denominations only the Seventh Day Adventists and some other minor groups have consistently opposed the reform. The Anglican Church and most other Protestant denominations have veered from apathy to outright agreement. This is not altogther surprising since Christianity once before (at the Council of Nicaea in 325) shifted the Sabbath from the seventh day to the first (as the "Lord's Day"—to finalize the break with Judaism) and thus sanctioned one 8-day week. But this one-time reform is, of course, still a far cry from introducing 8-day weeks at annual or semi-annual intervals and thereby disrupting the continuity of the 7-day week on a regular and frequent basis.

While any decision to adopt calendar reform would obviously be subject to international agreement reached through the United Nations and the votes of national governments (often guided or determined by their respective legislatures), the approval, or at least acquiescence, of the major Churches would be an indispensable condition to such a decision. No reform of the calendar could become a practical reality if it met with religious objections by hundreds of millions of people affected by the change. This confers a special importance on the views of the Catholic Church, as the largest and most powerful single Christian denomination. Governing, as it does, the religious opinions of half a billion people and the votes of numerous governments, the Vatican, by opposing the proposal, would irrevocably doom the fate of calendar reform, though its endorsement or neutrality would not necessarily guarantee the passage of the proposal.

So far the Vatican's attitude has been somewhat equivocal and at times plainly inconsistent. The first clear statement on the matter was made by Pope Pius XI on November 28, 1931 in a published interview with Rabbi Alessandro de Fano of Milan in which, to quote the Rabbi's account as officially approved, "the Pope very cordially pointed out to me that this [reform] could not take place according to the rules of the Church, because the displacing of the Sabbath brought with it also that of Sunday, whereas the traditions established by the canons of the Church are opposed to the change. . . ." Already two months earlier Cardinal Bourne, Archbishop of Westminster, had firmly denied that the Vatican had ever declared that there was no religious objection to the eight-day week calendar.

On the other hand, the Rev. Daniel J. K. O'Connell, S.J., Director of the Vatican Observatory, in a Vatican bulletin published in *Osservatore Romano,* commenting on the "Blank Day" proposal submitted by India to the United Nations in 1953, stated: "With regard to the attitude of the Catholic Church towards proposals for a reform of the Calendar, there are some who think that the Church must necessarily be opposed to all attempt of change. This belief is, in fact, not correct. I think it is true to say that the Church has no reason to oppose in principle a modification of the present calendar . . . under certain conditions. . . ." These conditions, in the statement, did not include the preservation of the seven-day week without interruption.

This imprecise opinion of the Papal Astronomer—no doubt the Vatican's expert and leading authority on calendar matters—is of special interest when read in conjunction with several subsequent statements he made to me in personal communications. In reply to my representations on behalf of the Conference of European Chief Rabbis in 1954, he wrote (in a letter dated November 20, 1954):

> I understand fully your concern at any attempt to interfere with the sequence of the week. I believe that such a proposal would also meet with very strong opposition from so important a part of the population of the world as the Mohammedans, to say nothing of other opponents. I understand also that the Governments of Great Britain and the U.S.A. are very definitely opposed to such a plan. It is hard to see how the United Nations could adopt any plan in the face of such opposition.
>
> As regards the attitude of the Vatican, I have no authority to make a statement. I believe, however, I may safely assure you that the Vatican will not promote or support any proposal that is likely to lead to dissension and confusion.

Subsequently the problem remained quiescent for nearly eight years. Then a bombshell dropped from the least expected quarter. On May 14, 1962, the *Osservatore Romano* indicated in an article that calendar reform, with specific

reference to the "Blank Day" proposal, would feature on the
agenda of the Ecumenical Council then being planned. When
I expressed the consternation of the Jewish community at
this startling announcement, Father O'Connell replied (in a
letter of June 5, 1962):

> The report . . . to which you refer came to me as a complete
> surprise. I have made what enquiries I can. It seems that the
> proposal in question is nothing more than a proposal which was
> submitted to the preparatory Commission for the Ecumenical Council.
> As far as I know it has not even been accepted for discussion at the
> Council.

At a later personal meeting in the Vatican Observatory at
Castel Gandolfo on August 21, 1962 he further assured me
that the reference to the "Blank Day" proposal in the article
was entirely unauthorized and erroneous, that he had strongly
protested "in the highest quarters" against its publication,
and that the Jewish community need have no anxiety whatever in the matter.

Nevertheless, on October 25, 1963 the Ecumenical Council passed a resolution as a special appendix by 2,058 votes
to 9, officially summarized as follows: "The Council is not
opposed to the various initiatives for establishing a perpetual
civil calendar, provided the week of seven days with its Sunday is safeguarded and provided the regular succession of
weeks remains intact—unless most serious reasons would, in
the judgment of the Holy See, persuade otherwise."[11]

This resolution seemed rather ambivalent. Many Jewish
leaders viewed it with the gravest anxiety as sanctioning or
encouraging calendar reform, and the world press specifically
linked the resolution with the Blank Day proposal in feature
articles. Indeed, Miss Elizabeth Achelis, the former President
of The World Calendar Association, in a letter published by
The New York Times on November 5, 1963, immediately
greeted the Vatican announcement as endorsing its agitation
for the Blank Day plan. On the other hand, I felt that the
statement had expressly opposed any interference with the
regular succession of the seven-day week, thus supporting the
Jewish stand—albeit with the crucial escape clause allowing
the Vatican to decide otherwise for "most serious reasons."

I therefore asked the Papal Astronomer for an authentic interpretation of the resolution, indicating that my reading of it definitely committed the Church to oppose the "Blank Day" proposal. He replied (in a letter of November 7, 1963):

> Your interpretation of the decision of the Ecumenical Council with regard to the week is perfectly correct. The council is opposed to any change in the sequence of the weeks. . . . I have now had an opportunity to speak to one of the Fathers of the Council, who confirms this.
>
> Thus you have no reason to be worried about this matter. I agree entirely with you that it would be a very great pity, indeed a tragedy, if the Council were to give any ground for dissension. . . .

There the matter must rest for the moment. In the light of these assurances, I think the Jewish community is justified, and well advised, publicly to associate the Catholic Church with the uncompromising opposition to the "Blank Day" reform, and to exhibit for counter-propaganda purposes the fact that the Church is now officially on record as insisting on the regular succession of the seven-day week. For, after all, the decision of the issue will depend less on what the Vatican has resolved than on what public opinion believes was resolved.

Obviously there is no Jewish objection to calendar reform in principle, so long as the sanctity of the Sabbath every seven days is not violated. Numerous alternative proposals have been advanced which embody all the advantages of the calendar reform plan without any of its disadvantages.

Basically, most of these plans seek to reduce the common year to the convenient length of 364 days, or exactly 52 weeks, so that all dates will be permanently tied to fixed days of the week. But instead of inserting the remaining 365th day as a "Blank Day" every year, thus disturbing the fixity of the seven-day week, these extra days are to be saved up until they accumulate to one or more complete weeks.

Dr. Sidney B. Hoenig of Yeshiva University, for instance, has suggested the adoption of a plan found in the ancient Book of Jubilees. Accordingly, the year would consist of four quarters of 91 days each, totaling 364 days, and the 365th days would be retained for 49 years, when seven extra weeks consisting of these 49 days would be inserted into the calendar. But this is a highly impracticable proposal since it would shift the dates from their true season by as much as over a month and a half every half century, i.e., every 49 years January 1st would occur on what is seasonally November 11, with corresponding discrepancies in the intervening years.

A more reasonable suggestion is to substitute the present leap day every four years by a leap week approximately every five years. (A precise calculation, leading to a practical plan, has been made by Harry A. Augenblick of Microlab, Livingston, New Jersey. It reckons that the average year, to equal the period of the earth's orbit, must contain 52.1775 weeks. This can be accomplished by inserting an extra week every 5.6338 years on average, or in any year that is evenly divisible by 5 but not evenly divisible by 40 except any years evenly divisible by 400.) Other more complex suggestions, involving years of 13 or even 14 months with 28 days each, have been worked out by Joshua Zangen[12] and many others.

It has also been suggested that the blank or leap week might be proclaimed as a "Worlds Week" to be utilized for the rededication of all peoples to the ideals of religion, morality and peace through a universal abstention from work, and the pursuit of spiritual endeavors.

Summary

For the past forty years there has been sporadic agitation to reform the civil calendar by inserting a "Blank Day" at the end of December every year, and another at the end of June every leap year. Such a plan, by introducing eight-day weeks at regular intervals causing the Sabbath to shift to different days of the week every year, would have paralyzing effects on Jewish communal life and impose crippling economic and social disabilities on observant Jews and others faithful to the Biblical Sabbath. Jews have therefore been in the forefront of the fight against attempts to secure the adoption of the proposal. They have been strongly supported by the Seventh Day Adventists, but most other Protestant denominations have raised little or no objections.

Roman Catholic opinion, while equivocal at times, on the whole has been opposed to the change, for practical reasons if not in principle. We may construe the recent Ecumenical Council resolution on the subject as definitely endorsing the Jewish view that the regular sequence of the seven-day week must be safeguarded. There are practical alternative proposals which would meet all claims, such as the accumulation of "Blank Days" to form a blank or leap week every five or six years. Such a "Worlds Week" twice every decade might be dedicated to the universal pursuit of moral and spiritual ideals.

The prospects for the adoption of any world calendar reforms seem to be remote for the time being. Yet the stakes are so high that constant vigilance is imperative.

A concluding word. The "Blank Day" proposal really resolves itself into weighing simplified bookkeeping against religious scruples and humanitarian considerations. In such a balancing the scales are bound to be tipped in favor of those who cherish the Biblical heritage and religious freedom, and who are anxious to ward off the threatened catastrophe of placing millions before the cruel alternative of either abandoning their ideals or facing economic ruin. It would be neither wise nor fair to add further confusion and discrimination to the existing troubles of mankind. Jews will certainly never give up the struggle to preserve the Sabbath, even as the Sabbath has preserved them.

The Jewish Day School

Its Unique Contributions

AMONG all the creative forces lately at work on the American Jewish scene, I regard the Jewish Day School movement as by far the most momentous. With the world's finest and largest Jewish centers of learning sacrificed on the altar of martyrdom in the Nazi holocaust, the spectacular growth in recent years of

Extracts of addresses delivered at the Annual Torah Umesorah Dinner in 1960 and its P.T.A. Convention in 1963.

intensive Jewish day schools here, as well as in Europe and elsewhere, is one of the miracles of contemporary Jewish history. Entire communities that had become spiritually atrophied by a process of slow religious attrition are being revitalized as effective bearers of the Jewish heritage by the sudden appearance in their midst of "children taught of the Lord" and enthusiastically dedicated to Jewish study and observance.

What the rise of Israel has done to regenerate the Jewish people after the shattering catastrophe a generation ago, the emergence of so many Jewish day schools and academies of higher learning has accomplished for the resuscitation of Judaism. And what the Zionist ideal has been to the State of Israel, *Torah Umesorah* has been to America's Jewish day schools.

It may yet be too early to assess the full impact of these schools on the future of American Jewry, or to evaluate their contribution to the enrichment of American life in general. But there can be no doubt that these effects will be wholly positive and constructive. Jewish education knows nothing of the many negative values which so frequently serve as a spur to more and better general education these days, such as the anxiety not to be overtaken by the Russians in the technological race or the concern to prevent children from becoming juvenile delinquents. We believe in education not as a preventive measure, but as an intrinsic ideal. We believe in the totality of the human personality in which the physical and spiritual facets interact as a single unit. To produce this personality, therefore, we require an education in which the religious and secular disciplines are likewise integrated into one harmonious entity.

Moreover, these schools—quite apart from widening the horizons and knowledge of their products—will make for sturdier citizens and more dedicated leaders. There are today probably no groups of children anywhere in America who, in terms of sheer work and hours spent at school, have to bear heavier burdens than Jewish day school students. They must master, in addition to an adequate secular curriculum which they share with all other children, a difficult extra language, a vast and complex literature, a global history extending over 4,000 eventful years, an extremely diversified calendar, a detailed comprehension of innumerable laws and customs, and an often exacting appreciation of religious and moral concepts. To achieve this these children are bound to harness and develop energies which remain latent and untapped in most other children. As a result of being exposed to such severe tests and hardships in their childhood, the Jewish day school products will certainly be equipped with superior tenacity and hardihood to be among the fittest to survive in the event of their encounter with any really grave challenge in life, whether religious, social or economic.

Comparisons and Challenges

When the history of our people during the past dramatic and exciting century will be recorded, perhaps in another 50 to 100 years, four major epoch-making events and developments will, I think, stand out as the most momentous highlights.

First, at about the turn of the century and during the three decades preceding, there was the gigantic mass migration of Jews from the East to the West, notably to the Anglo-Saxon countries in which the principal Jewish communities of the Diaspora are now to be found. That movement, as it turned out, proved to be the *refuah* before the *makkah*. That movement saved the remnant of our people that would otherwise have been lost in the second most fateful occurrence of our lifetime: the gathering of the most tempestuous and devastating storm clouds in our history, which eventually consumed one-third of our people; the fearful holocaust which is less than a generation behind us.   And just as these storm clouds were gathering, there took place the third outstanding feature of modern Jewish history: the regeneration of our national forces culminating in the restoration of Jewish independence and sovereignty in the land of our fathers.

Finally, following that great event in Jewish history of 1948, there occurred a fourth dramatic development which will stand out for all future times in the record of our contemporary annuals: the rise, on a global scale, of the Jewish

Day School movement—a development which, I believe, will have an equal share in importance and significance with the other three events in the influence exerted on the overall course of Jewish fortunes in the present century.

There is something remarkable and unique regarding this spontaneous emergence all over the Jewish world of these schools. While the Zionist movement was motivated and galvanized by a united, co-ordinated effort on an international scale, by a world organization directing the political and other endeavors of Jewish communities everywhere, the Day School movement sprang up simultaneously, with almost mysterious cohesion, in all parts of the Jewish dispersion without any coordinated efforts, without any world-wide organization to stimulate this tremendously significant development. Yet, remarkably enough, the movement has evolved on almost exactly parallel lines in most countries of the Diaspora, as if jointly guided by some unseen mastermind. The parallel is so close that even the present proportion of Jewish children attending these schools is more or less the same in these various countries, certainly if we compare conditions in America and Europe, especially in the countries to which I am to devote my comparative remarks this evening.

In England, for instance, the rate may be slightly higher— I think about 14% of all Jewish children of school age there now attend Jewish Day Schools of one kind or another, as compared with (I understand) roughly 10% in this country —but by and large developments on both sides of the Atlantic have proceeded on remarkably similar lines.

Parenthetically, it should here be emphasized that the proportion of children in religious Day Schools in the Diaspora is only about one-third of what it is in Israel, where well over 30% of all children receive an intensive religious education at the schools of the *Chinuch Atzmai* and the *Mamlachti-Dati* systems. No better indication could be found of Israel's religious superiority over other communities, for there is no more reliable gauge with which to measure the religious temperature of a Jewish community than the ratio of children at full-time religious schools.

Of course, these schools here and in Europe have many features in common and others which divide them. On the negative side, for instance, I would say that what these schools share is that they all struggle. And they struggle hard. In all the countries I recently visited, whether England, France, Switzerland or Ireland, the economic problems faced by these schools are just as back-breaking and heart-breaking as they are here. The repetitious stories of deficits, hardships and financial pressures I continually heard over there nearly made me feel I was once more at home, so familiar were they.

But on the positive side, there is also one feature, and a most important one, which unites these schools. Almost without exception they are sponsored and administered under Orthodox auspices, in Europe as here. This is, in a sense, very remarkable. After all, neither in America nor in Europe are the Jewish communities overwhelmingly Orthodox, not even in terms of the parents or homes from which the Day School children come. The simple truth is that the *mesirath nefesh,* the sense of dedication and sacrifice indispensable for the pioneering and maintenance of Day Schools, is only to be found among people whose religious discipline of life has trained them to persevere in the face of constant disappointments, opposition and hardships.

A crucial contrast between the situation here and that in Europe concerns the intensity of Jewish education. With some limited exceptions, America today is far in advance of Europe regarding the contents and number of hours of religious instruction. In England, for instance, even the best Day Schools provide only between six and, at best, perhaps fifteen hours a week in *limudei kodesh,* apart from one school each in London, Manchester and Gateshead. This is only about one-third or less of the time devoted to religious studies in most American *Yeshivoth* where the periods per week sometimes exceed thirty hours!

Another glaring contrast, of special interest to this PTA Convention, lies in the fact that in Europe, as in Israel, PTAs are unknown. The whole concept of an organizational link through such associations between the school and parents on the one hand, and the community on the other, does not exist there. Altogether, the parents' involvement in the education of their children is far more limited there. They do not concern themselves so much with the administration of the school, the planning of its work, the provision of lunches or indeed with their children's homework after school as is the case here. This is a uniquely American contribution to the totality of the world-wide Jewish Day School picture.

The two principal contributions, then, which American Jewry, and *Torah Umesorah* in particular, can and should make to enriching the Day School movements ·elsewhere are in emphasizing the value as well as the practical feasibility of PTAs and, above all, of the high degree of intensity in Jewish education which has now become the order of the day in the U. S. and Canada. We have to prove to our brethren elsewhere that it can be done and to show them how it can be done.

Now let me come to my second assignment: the challenge before us. One of the most familiar phrases in the context of educational planning these days is "today and tomorrow." This phrase actually occurs in the coming week's Sidrah: *Vekidashtom hayom umachar*—which I might freely render: "And you shall sanctify the today and the tomorrow." What is the meaning of this? It is to sanctify this day, the present, and at the same time already today to sanctify also the tomorrow, the future.

The word *machar*, "tomorrow," plays a significant role in Jewish thought. Let me remind you of one striking instance where it occurs in connection with the parent-child relationship. *Ki yish'alkha binkha machar lemor,* we say at the *Seder* table—"when your child will ask you tomorrow saying . . ." What is the idea of asking tomorrow? The child sits today at the *Seder;* today it goes through all the ceremonies and experiences of *matzah, maror* and the *Haggadah.* Yet today it does not ask any questions. *Machar,* tomorrow, it will ask about yesterday's experiences. That is the Jewish distinction between the today and the tomorrow. Today is *na'aseh*— "we shall do," we shall observe the law as we find it, we sit at the *Seder* and carry out its precepts without questions. Tomorrow, after having absorbed the lessons of yesterday, after the *na'aseh* is over, and our duties are fulfilled, tomorrow is *nishmu*—"we shall hear," we shall try to understand, we shall inquire and ask about what we practiced yesterday. We are to raise our children in such a way that they will not ask critical questions until the today has turned into the tomorrow, until the *na'aseh* is behind them and they can face the challenge of the *nishma*.

All this is, I believe, highly relevant to our situation today. In the Day School movement we have now reached the dividing line between the today and the tomorrow. A decade or more of *na'aseh* is behind us. We have established schools by the hundreds, and we did not ask profound philosophical questions as to where they would lead us, as to what their orientation ought to be. We set out just *na'aseh*, to build and maintain them, to help these schools; that is all that mattered. But now we must begin to think of *machar*, of the tomorrow. We have reached the stage of *nishma*, of *ki yishalkha binkha machar*. The tomorrow has arrived when we must ask questions. We can now face challenges, we can start to become critical, scrutinizing the yesterday and asking the whys and wherefores: what will it lead to? Our task is now *vekidashtom hayom umachar*, to sanctify the tomorrow of questionings as we have sanctified the today of action.

What, then, are these questions and challenges? Number one, I would say, is the urgent need to transmute the concept of Jewish Day Schools from being a matter of private enterprise into a communal endeavor. I think we can now go to the wider community and say: we have pioneered a new idea in Jewish education, we have fought as individuals to set up these schools, indifferent to public reaction and to the lack of public support. It is time now that these burdens, and the indignities involved in bearing them, were eliminated and that the community at large, through its congregations and other agencies, assumed its due responsibilities. In this area Europe has a great deal to teach the American Jewish community, for in Europe Jewish education is largely maintained by communal taxation through the synagogues.

We may not, for the moment, control the Federations and decisively influence their allocation policies. But, as leaders and members of synagogues, we can prevail on our congregations gradually to accept the principle that communal religious organizations are no less responsible to defray and raise the cost of Jewish education than that of congregational worship. Why should not synagogue membership dues and supervision fees for Kosher goods automatically include an education tax? Such a system could eventually take care of our Day Schools and put an end to the present humiliating "charity" collections and the sordid financial state of most of our schools. The whole concept of a *Kehillah,* responsible not only for *Shuls* but above all for schools, must now be brought home with every forcefulness to the wider community. It is primarily up to our PTAS, as the link between the schools and the community, to drive this idea home, to agitate, to plead, to pressure, until the Jewish public, at least its religious element, will come to realize that such historic steps alone will guarantee that there will be worshippers in our synagogues and consumers of Kosher foods in the next generation.

So much on the material aspect of the challenge. Now let me proceed to some questioning on the content of our education, on the orientation or ideology of our schools. Perhaps I may introduce this somewhat delicate subject by a reference to what I believe is the origin in our classic literature to the association between *Torah* and *Mesorah.* These two terms first occur together in the opening Mishnah in *Pirkei Avoth: Mosheh kibbel Torah misinai umesorah liyehoshua* — "Moses received the Torah from Sinai and handed it on *(mesorah)* to Joshua." The *Bartinura* on this Mishnah asks, by implication, a very penetrating question: Why is this statement, dealing with the Sinaitic origin of the Oral Law, made at the beginning of the *Ethics of the Fathers,* a tractate at the end of the fourth division of the Talmud, and not at the beginning of the first tractate, at the head of *Berakhoth,* where the Oral Law starts? He answers significantly that the assertion of Sinaitic authority is needed particularly for the ethical and moral teachings contained in *Pirkei Avoth.* Religious or ritual laws obviously have their origin at Sinai. But ethics can be taught without any religious sanction, too, as found among the ancient philosophers who "invented" rules of good conduct by reference to their "imagination" or conscience. We believe, however, that there can be no true ethics or morality without religion, without reference to the revealed will of God. Hence it is necessary to stress just in connection with our ethical laws that they are part of *Torah* and *Mesorah,* that they are valid and binding only because they derive their authority from Sinai.

We may apply this cardinal teaching to our situation. In our prevailing Day School system the Hebrew and secular departments are still completely segregated and unrelated to each other. There is no trace of any true synthesis whereby Jewish instruction gives a characteristic blend to secular teachings, giving a religious foundation to scientific and humanistic pursuits; and whereby, in reverse, secular knowledge helps to gain deeper insights into an understanding of Judaism in the twentieth century. What the *Bartinura* wanted to emphasize is that *Torah* and *Mesorah* should determine not only purely religious practices as regulated in such talmudic divisions as *Zeraim* (prayers), *Moed* (Sabbath and festivals) or *Nashim* (marriage and divorce), areas in which religious directives are taken for granted. Torah and Tradition should particularly affect our ethical and social conduct, the way we live and fashion our career, the kind of scientists we are, the sort of lawyers or doctors we are—everything we do and study should bear the unmistakable imprint of our Torah convictions.

Through our Day Schools, then, we must aim at producing superior human beings suffused and ennobled by the spirit of Torah; we must turn out people who will ultimately be more upright businessmen, more dedicated physicians, more scrupulous lawyers, more conscientious scientists and even more selfless rabbis than are produced anywhere else.

Only if we now begin to face this challenge with courage and vision can we hope to exploit the full potential of our epoch-making Day School movement for the restoration of our people as moral pioneers to dispel the new paganism rampant in our troubled world, a world which may well depend on the heirs to our Prophets for its salvation.

Government Aid–A Minority View

I N my view, the claim of parochial schools, whether Jewish or Catholic, to Federal aid should be strongly supported by the Jewish Community as a matter of principle, of national interest, of justice and of expediency.

Principle: To us Jews the duty to educate our children, in secular (or vocational) as well as religious disciplines, has been an integral part of the dictates of our faith since times immemorial. Conversely, we have always held religious instruction to form a most vital and indispensable part of general education. To us education without religion is worthless. It may produce technically competent experts but not human beings ennobled by a refined conscience and character—the prime requisite of a civilized society.

Schools which do not provide religious training are career factories, turning out morally indifferent robots; they fail in their principal task to produce upright, idealistic and consecrated citizens of sturdy moral fibre. "The beginning of wisdom is the fear of the Lord," and the foundation of education is character-training based on religious virtues and convictions.

For any Jewish community, therefore, to endorse the divorce of religion from education is a travesty of Jewish thought and history. For thousands of years we have lived and suffered and died to promote the centrality and all-embracing scope of religion in life. That we—sons of our Patriarchs and heirs to the Hebrew Prophets—should now find ourselves publicly on the side of those advocating the rise of a pagan generation is an inconceivable affront to our historic mission as the religious leaven of mankind. For so long as religious instruction is an "extra" to be purchased at a heavy cost, and so long as religious schools are frowned upon as conflicting with the "national ideal" of public education, the vast majority of our future citizens is bound to remain without, or with less than minimal, training in religion.

Published in *The Jewish Forum* (New York), May 1962.

National Interest: America's national interest, too, should dictate public support for parochial schools. It should do so on three distinct counts:

First, what altogether prompts and justifies the Governmen's concern (or the taxpayer's liability) in any education, public or otherwise? Surely the sole reasonable ground for such concern is the recognition that every well-educated citizen is an invaluable investment in the country's future. Taxes are exacted, and allocations made, for educational purposes only because the anticipated returns—in terms of the contributions to society to be made by the products of education—render such expenditures profitable for the country as a whole as a matter of national self-interest.

Now, surely it cannot be argued that the products of parochial schools—the scientists, teachers, artists, industrialists, clergymen or other useful citizens they help to turn out—are going to be less valuable to society and therefore a less profitable investment, simply because they added a comprehensive religious education to their vocational training.

If we accept the principle of spending Federal funds in exchange for the production of men and women who will contribute to the public weal, thus vindicating the outlay, there can be no logical reason for expecting a large segment of the population to "deliver the same goods" of service for the national good free of charge to the public, i.e., to the taxpayer. In other words, the *rationale* for Federal aid (viz., the national interest) is precisely as applicable to parochial schools as to public schools.

Second, the argument sedulously fostered by the opponents of parochial schools that the encouragement of "sectarian" education offends against the national interest seems entirely perverse. Some of the more fanatical antagonists as much as insinuate that it is almost un-American to promote anything but public school education which alone, they claim, can produce integrated citizens out of America's "melting-pot." The reverse is the truth.

In their blind obeisance to conformity and monolithic regimentation, these people would deprive America of its greatest asset: its rich diversity and the dynamic forces generated by its multicultural population. To place all children

into the straight-jacket of a common educational system—
which would perforce be drab and undistinguished, subject
to the lowest common denominator — would stunt their
growth, stifle their potential and inhibit the unfolding of their
full personality.

Parochial schools, far from promoting divisiveness or insular
bigotry, contribute massively to the overall splendor of the
American scene just because they enrich its canvass with
colorful hues of such diversity. They prevent Americans from
becoming a nation of depersonalized numbers and uniform
automatons.

Third, and above all, parochial schools contribute to producing superior defenders of our Western values who are
better able to meet the fearful challenge of atheism and
materialism which today threaten our and our civilization's
very survival. In the end the mortal struggle between East
and West may well be determined by the moral and spiritual
mettle of the contestants more than by destructiveness of their
weaponry or the skill of their diplomacy.

The truly effective competition with the allurements of
Communism lies not in bigger cars and more washing-
machines—the Russians will soon catch up on these luxuries,
too—but in citizens of superior excellence and idealism but-
tressed by religious virtues. Freedom demands the sanctification of religion, as the brotherhood of man requires the
Fatherhood of God. A generation of heathen hedonists,
worshipping the idols of happiness and material success, will
be unable to evoke the herculean strength necessary to contain
the mighty tide of godlessness in the defence of liberty. Furthermore, only children reared in a deeply religious
atmosphere are likely to develop the maximum immunity to
the scourges of juvenile delinquency, dope addiction, loafing
and other vices corroding our society and undermining its
internal as well as external security.

Jewish Day Schools in particular, by virtue of the exacting
demands they impose on their pupils, add another distinct
contribution to the nation's spiritual wealth. There are today
probably no groups of children anywhere in America who,
in terms of sheer work and hours spent at school, have to bear
heavier burdens than Yeshivah students. Complementing

their general studies by up to thirty hours a week in religious instruction, they must master—in addition to an adequate secular curriculum which they share with all other children— a difficult extra language, a global history extending over 4,000 eventful years, a vast and complex literature, a detailed comprehension of innumerable laws and customs, an extremely diversified calendar, and a severely exigent appreciation of religious and moral precepts. To achieve this these children are bound to harness and develop energies which remain latent and untapped in most others. Such exacting mental exercises must produce finer brains, better characters, and greater stamina and hardihood, quite apart from protecting these children from the bane of excessive idleness leading to mischief and perverseness.

Justice: By discriminating against parochial schools, the Government would put a penalty instead of a premium on parents who seek an intensely religious education for their children. They would have to bear not only the additional burden of defraying the extra cost of religious instruction (for which no one claims or advocates Federal aid) but also the onus of paying for the secular education which is mandatory by law. Ironically, then, parents who do not care so much for their children's religious upbringing can claim Federal help, while parents who are religiously more scrupulous cannot; on the contrary, they are forced to pay taxes for the education of other, less religious children without receiving any returns for their own children. There is neither rhyme nor reason in such blatant inequity.

It is often argued that parents who want the "luxury" of parochial education for their children should be prepared to pay for it, just as patients who prefer private rooms to the public wards in hospitals cannot complain if they are denied the benefit of public subsidies available to ward patients. This analogy is altogether fallacious. There is no law of the land to compel people to go to hospitals as there is to compel children to go to school. Public subsidies to hospitals are essentially charitable disbursements, meant primarily for the poor, whereas educational subsidies are obviously not in this category. Parents who enroll their children in parochial schools do so not because they want finer buildings or more costly services than are available at public institutions (as sought by private patients) but because they have religious scruples against rearing their children in non-religious schools. To deprive them of the secular benefits extended to other parents amounts to religious discrimination, not to economic discrimination as in the case of hospitals.

Expediency: Perhaps the most pragmatic argument in favor of Federal aid to parochial schools is that the funds are desperately needed. It is futile and ludicrous to suggest, as many glibly do, that the Jewish community, at any rate, is solvent enough to maintain its own day schools. The fact of the matter is that, with very few exceptions, these schools are not adequately supported by the community, that most of them stagger from one financial crisis to another, with all the attendant evils and indignities of distinguished deans or principals having to spend their time on interminable fund-raising, of teachers being unpaid for months, of buildings being dilapidated, of pupils having no warm meals for ten hours, and of pressing expansion programs being shelved. The truth of the matter is that there are today thousands of Jewish parents who cannot do justice to their religious conscience by sending their children to Jewish Day Schools solely because they cannot afford the high tuition fees for secular as well as religious instruction charged by these schools (and then such fees, even when collected in full, usually meet less than half the schools' operating costs). Even for a fairly comfortable family with three or four children the expense of Yeshivah education is simply prohibitive. Federal aid would not eliminate the heavy burden on conscientious parents, but it might at least halve it, since their payments would be reduced to meeting the cost of religious education only.

Other alleged "dangers": To these principal arguments in favor of Federal aid we should add a refutation of some common arguments against it. Many people fear that Federal aid will lead to undesirable Federal controls. This argument would, of course, be equally valid against Federal aid to public schools. It is also feared that Federal aid would give the Roman Catholics with the largest network of parochial schools, undue strength and influence, or that it would eventually destroy the public school system altogether (as if non-religious schools were sacred and religious schools profane!).

In rebuttal of these charges I can only refer to my Irish and English experience where all Jewish Day Schools are state-aided once they reach a certain standard of secular proficiency. In England and Ireland governmental aid to parochial school has not led to any undesirable interference with Jewish education, has not resulted in preferential rights or status for one denomination over another, and has not eliminated the public school system (this applies to England only; Ireland, with a 93% Catholic population, never had completely non-denominational schools). The Jewish communities in those and other West-European countries have certainly not suffered in the least or compromised any of their rights and freedom because they accepted without argument the government assistance offered to their schools.

As for the constitutionality of Federal aid, I am not qualified to pronounce judgment. This may ultimately be a matter for the courts to determine, and previous rulings on related issues seem to have left us with ample latitude in the interpretation of state-church relations. Meanwhile it is the opinion of many highly competent authorities that Federal aid to parochial schools, in one form or another, would not violate the First Amendment.

A Blueprint for Rabbinic Leadership

THE principal question we are bound to ask ourselves today is: What ails Orthodoxy? Why have we lost our hold on the masses?

The Reform movement, it seems to me, is not our chief problem. It is merely a symptom, not the cause of the general malaise. Reform has not drawn its ranks from the Orthodox camp, but from those already lost to us. The State of Israel has virtually no organized Reform, yet the religious problems there are much the same as they are here.

Address delivered at the First Conference of European Rabbis in Amsterdam, Holland, Nov. 5, 1957.

Our main enemy, I submit therefore, is not Reform, but the secularization of Jewish life. The real challenge before us is not the low proportion of strictly observant Jews—for which there are ample precedents in our history—but the widespread refusal to recognize our spiritual leaders as the true custodians of our national destiny—for which there are only few precedents.

People these days look to rabbis for sermons and the discharge of purely ecclesiastical functions. But for the ultimate realization of the Jewish purpose in history they no longer rely on us or our teachings; for national leadership they look to politicians and other secularist guides.

This unprecedented development is the product of a great variety of factors, some beyond our control. In an age of gross materialism, of the effective separation of Church and State, we cannot help sharing some of the disabilities of religious leaders in general. But to a considerable extent the remedy lies in our own hands. To reassert our historic place in the conduct of Jewish affairs, we must analyze the changed conditions of our times and be prepared to make the necessary adjustment in our basic policies.

In pursuit of this aim I would submit a six-point program, turning from the general and ideological to the particular and practical:

1. *To restore to our people a sense of Divine choice and mission in the world.*

This should perhaps be our foremost long-term objective today.

The contemporary Jewish scene presents a remarkable paradox. For over 3,000 years Israel has not been so much in the center of world affairs as at present. Since Biblical times we have not witnessed such manifestations of Providence as in our times. Yet never before have our people been less conscious of the Jewish role in universal history than now.

In the Middle Ages the humblest Jew was probably more aware that humanity's destiny, the ultimate salvation of all mankind, depended on him and his people than most modern leaders are today. We have all but forgotten the powerful moral lesson taught by our sages when they boldly asserted:

"No punishment comes to the world except on account of Israel,"[13] a statement no doubt designed to imbue Israel with an overwhelming sense of responsibility for the spiritual advance of the world at large.

It is our task, as spiritual leaders who have assumed the heritage of the Prophets, to become interpreters of history. Tremendous events happen around us every day, and we are largely silent on their significance. It ought to be possible for us today to divine some of the marvelous workings of Providence in recent history and thus to demonstrate the link between our extraordinary experiences and the ultimate consummation of Israel's fulfilment.

Today we know that without the pogroms at the turn of the century the bulk of the Jews of Western Europe and America would no longer be alive; that without the Nazi holocaust the unparalleled energies needed for the creation of the Jewish State could not have been generated; that without the military and economic pressures weighing on the young State it would have proved far more difficult, if not impossible, to weld the vast variety of immigrants into a single nation and to retain the unity between Israel and the Diaspora as a common people bound together by mutual dependence on each other. It is up to us to proclaim these facts and to show that the events we are witnessing are an indispensable part of the Divine design leading to our eventual goal.

The time has perhaps also come when we should again address ourselves to the nations of the world as the authentic spokesmen of God's will on universal issues.

I am not sure whether, when the Prophets of old pronounced "the burden of Egypt" or "the burden of Assyria," their kings trembled in their palaces over their impending doom. It may well be that even these prophecies to the nations were primarily meant for the Jewish people, to create within them a worldview and crushing sense of responsibility for cooperating in the realization of the Divine scheme of history.

We must assert ourselves as a mighty spiritual power against which the vague preachings of Reform will appear narrow and insignificant.

2. *To demonstrate the relevance of Judaism to the contemporary world and its problems.*

In the eyes of most Jews, including even many of our own followers, the teachings and observances of Orthodoxy have become irrelevant to the chief perplexities of our times.

It is true, we write numerous Responsa, we give halakhic answers to questions every day. But the questions we answer are usually our own questions, not those of the Jewish men-in-the-street. As a rule, we bend our efforts on solving religious problems in the light of modern conditions. What may be even more imperative today is to solve modern problems in the light of religious conditions, and thus to bring the message of Judaism to bear on our lives.

It has become fashionable to consult medieval Responsa works as source material for Ph.D. theses to reveal the social conditions of the times. One wonders, if some historians of the future—perhaps in four or five hundred years' time— were to read our responsa and other current halakhic literature, how true would their picture be to the realities of our day?

No doubt they would gather from their research that we were struck by a terrible calamity, producing agonizing *Agunah* questions. They might also learn something of our modern household gadgets and the Sabbath problems raised by them. But they would know little about the real issues plaguing us every day. They would find few references to the great moral problems of our times.

We must devote our intellectual energies and apply our learning to such contemporary questions as nuclear bomb tests, literary censorship, the imposition of the death penalty, the treatment of colored peoples and racial minorities, including the Arabs in Israel; we must try to define our religious attitude to euthanasia, sterilization, labor relations, strikes, gambling, etc.; in short, to everything which impinges on the moral consciousness of our age.

Only in this way can we turn our Torah into a "Torah of life" and ourselves into the true guides of Jewish thought in the spirit of the Prophets and their successors.

3. *To eliminate the tendency to indecision in our rabbinic judgments, in matters both of belief and practice.*

We often appear to be hesitant or afraid to give answers with authority and precision. For example, do we, or do we not, really believe—"Except the Lord keep the city, the watchman waketh but in vain,"[14] or the warning in the *Shema* —"Take heed to yourselves, lest your heart be deceived and ye turn aside . . . and ye perish quickly from off the good land which the Lord giveth you," i.e., that a secular Jewish state cannot be viable?

Do we, or do we not, believe—"Oh that My people would hearken unto Me, that Israel would walk in My ways! I would soon subdue their enemies, and turn My hand against their adversaries,"[15] i.e., that the security of Israel, even in a material sense, depends also on religious factors and the fulfilment of its historic destiny?

If we do believe these statements, we must have the courage to say so and to proclaim "Thus saith the Lord!" even if we fly in the face of public opinion.

In halakhic matters, too, we are sometimes reluctant to take bold decisions, particularly at this critical time when some emergency measures may be indicated.

The reasons for our extreme caution are genuine enough. We no longer have the erudition and competence of the earlier authorities who could give firm and final answers, in cryptic terms of yes and no.

But this incompetence as such is no excuse for shunning definite replies. An apparently wrong answer, it seems to me, is better than no answer or a vague answer. On the verse "Thou shalt not turn aside from the word which they shall declare unto thee, to the right or to the left,"[16] our sages comment: "Even if they tell thee of the right that is the left."[17] In other words, we are entitled to appear to be in error and to say "of the right that it is the left."

But we are not entitled to withhold judgment and to refuse to say of the right that it is either the right or the left. Indeed, as the appointed custodians of the law, we have the right to assume that our decisions, however mistaken they appear to others, in fact accord with the truth, "for the spirit of

God rests on the guardians of His sanctuary, and He will not forsake His faithful ones who are ever guarded from error and stumbling."[18]

Our authority today is as great and binding as that of any rabbis preceding us. In every age the people are commanded to repair only "to the judge that shall be in those days;"[19] and "Jephtah in his generation (is due the same respect) as Samuel in his generation, for even the most unworthy person, once he is appointed as a leader over the community, is like the mightiest of the mighty."[20]

This important principle imposes on our followers the obligation to accept our rulings, whether right or wrong, as it imposes on us the obligation to make rulings, whether thought to be right or wrong.

We have no authority to abdicate our leadership and to leave problems we are facing unsolved.

4. *To improve our publicity methods and public relations.*

We must recognize that an entirely new factor has entered into our relationship with the public. For the first time in its history Judaism now has to vindicate itself in a fully democratic society.

Former generations of Jewish leaders could, to a large extent, afford to ignore public opinion; we cannot. Today the success of our endeavours is altogether dependent on carrying the public with us. We can no longer ignore any challenge or any attack on our teachings.

Moreover, we live in a propaganda-ridden age. People these days often buy, not what they need or want, but what psychological advertising campaigns make them buy.

We must, therefore, thoroughly overhaul our methods to fashion and influence public opinion. This has now become a task for experts, and we are not necessarily competent to accomplish it unaided.

We must gather around us highly skilled writers and speakers through whom we can effectively transmit our message and our answers to the people. Every major rabbinate should have attached to it an efficient public relations officer who should act as its spokesman in the press and elsewhere. At the same time he should advise rabbis on policy in matters of publicity.

We should also demand a "Rabbinical Column" to give a regular presentation of our views on current affairs in the Jewish press in the same way as it now features a "Hebrew Column" every week.

Perhaps more imagination, too, is required in our public enlightenment drives. For instance, I can see no reason why we should not follow the example of the Prophets and personally enter the Reform strongholds to preach our message on their own platform. There are surely also ample precedents for rabbinical disputations with the sectarians of earlier generations; why should we shy away from such direct contests between truth and falsehood? And, after all, the Torah was not given for Orthodox Jews only.

We cannot win the battle of the minds unless we are prepared to fight it!

5. *To promote the growth of a religious intelligentsia.*

This is probably our most vital desideratum today.

We have now moved irrevocably into the age of science. The future—who can doubt it?—belongs in great measure to the scientists and technical experts. Their thought will largely govern the public mind—and offer the principal challenge to the religious outlook.

And just at this time, when the need is so acute, we find ourselves virtually without a religious intelligentsia, at least in any organized or corporate strength.

In days gone by, a non-religious Jewish intelligentsia was unthinkable; it was a contradiction in terms. To be without religious faith and learning was a mark of boorishness;[21] today ignorance and non-observance bid fair to becoming essential rungs on the ladder to social distinction. Because we discourage our best talmudical scholars from the pursuit of secular studies, we have—for the first time in our history—laid ourselves wide open to the charge of obscurantism.

It seems to me that with the current trend among our leading rabbinic intellects to discountenance some synthesis of religious and secular values we depart from every historic tradition before us. Of course, there always existed conflicting schools of thought on the attitude to secular avocations in our history. But Jewish studies became exclusive only when the general environment was of a low cultural level and offered no challenge to Jewish culture, such as at the times of Rashi and Tosaphoth, and more recently in Eastern Europe.

However, when planted in a culturally advanced society, Jewish spiritual leaders almost invariably came to terms—often intimate terms—with the thought and scholarship around them, as occurred with such illustrious results in medieval Spain, and later in Italy, Germany and elsewhere.

That this outlook is not shared at most rabbinical academies in Western lands today can only be explained, in my view, as due to the fact that talmudic scholarship is not really indigenous to these countries but more or less recently imported into them from Eastern Europe where the need for finding a *modus vivendi* with secular culture did not exist.

Under our present conditions we need even more than that. We require the accepted concepts and terminology of our age as an instrument with which to present our own teachings.

At the time of the Prophets—a pagan age believing in the supernatural—our seers taught Judaism in terms of prophecy. In the days of the Romans—the masters of legal thought—our sages resorted to law as the principal expression of Jewish doctrine. In the age of Maimonides—when philosophy ruled supreme—our savants turned to that branch of knowledge for the interpretation of Judaism. Now science is in the ascendancy, and we must use its language if we want to be heard.

Our voice does not reach the masses, not because it is too weak, but because it cannot break through the vacuum between our world and theirs.

To overcome this handicap we must have religious scientists, and if we cannot ensure that our scientific scholars are religious we must turn our religious scholars into scientists. We must prevail on our Yeshivoth to encourage some of their finest products to take up science, or medicine, or even some technical career, and special scholarships should be created for this urgent purpose.

We might also consider whether the time had not now come to change the usual secular courses associated with rabbinical training from arts to science.

Religious scientists will be our most powerful commandos of the future!

6. *To reorientate our policy on Reform.*

This is a delicate and difficult subject, and my reflections on it are entirely tentative and offered only as a stimulus to further discussion.

I believe we have to decide whether to write off the Reform movement and its followers as a dead loss, and try to insulate it completely from the adherents of Orthodoxy, or go all out to retrieve what can be salvaged even at the cost of some formal compromise with them.

In the havoc wrought by these dissenters we must distinguish between irreparable damage, which will leave sores festering on the body of our people for generations to come, and purely temporary infractions of the sanctities of Jewish life, causing wounds which can be healed by individual acts of repentance.

Into the former category belong notably the Reform's arbitrary incursions into the spheres of marriage and proselytization in complete disregard of Jewish law, leading to untold personal tragedies and, above all, to the increase of persons who cannot be recognized either as legitimate or as Jewish by the law-abiding majority of our people. To eliminate this appalling evil, gnawing at the very roots of Jewish existence, must be our foremost aim.

It might be worthwhile, therefore, to explore the possibility of offering the Reformers, as an earnest of our anxiety for the preservation of Jewish unity, some kind of truce based on their acceptance of our exclusive jurisdiction in all matters affecting marriage and conversion, even if this meant closing our eyes to their forms of synagogue services and religious education for the time being.

Their agreement to this suggestion would, to my mind, constitute an invaluable gain and possibly pave the way to their eventual return to our fold. On the other hand, if they rejected the offer, we would at least win a substantial moral victory. Their refusal would publicly reveal more clearly than ever before who are the real disruptive influences in Jewish life today. The true causes for disunity and strife would be exposed for all to see.

I still maintain that our chief enemy today is the secularization of our national and even communal life. By our rift with the Reform we are dissipating our vital energies and deflecting our attention from the most crucial struggle ahead of us.

Not since the days of the Flood has the future of all mankind hung so precariously in the balance as at present. The battle between war and peace, between life and death, will not be decided by the advances of science, or by the terror hidden in its weapons of destruction. The issue will be determined by the moral outlook of those controlling these weapons and by the spiritual stature of the nations and their leaders alike.

Our stricken age, stunned by the prospect of total annihilation, is groping for bold leadership to the uplands of universal peace, to be reached along the paths of social justice and moral integrity. As the first and persistent pioneers of these ideals, the Jewish people are bound to play a leading role in providing this guidance. To awaken and discharge such feeling of profound responsibility must, surely, be our supreme charge in this stirring age of challenge and decision.

I am aware that in some of my suggestions and conclusions I may have overstated my case. But, after all, hyperbole is a legitimate figure of speech, employed by the Torah itself.[22] I hope that any recourse to it on my part, though not deliberate, may add to the stimulation of constructive debate.

2

Jews In Two Worlds

The Anglo-Jewish Contribution to Judaism

Tercentenary Reflections

THE first salvos saluting Anglo-Jewry's Tercentenary have been fired. In innumerable speeches
and articles, at special services, exhibitions, and
dinners, the great record of the Jews in Great Britain since
1656 has been portrayed and analyzed, criticized and ap-

Published in *The Jewish Chronicle* (London) , August 31, 1956.

plauded. The fortunes and achievements of British Jews during the past three centuries have been surveyed in much detail, and their contributions in virtually every sphere of public and Jewish life have been sympathetically reviewed. Rabbis, historians, journalists, novelists, educationalists, communal workers, parliamentarians, and scientists—all have applied their searching intellects to the study of Anglo-Jewry's impact on Jewish and British history.

The resultant composite record is, on many counts, truly impressive. It shows that Anglo-Jewry has played a not insignificant role in the advancement of knowledge, of science and the arts, of medicine and literature, of politics and social service, of education and philanthropy, of the struggle for Jewish emancipation and Zionism. Even the contribution to sport and entertainment has been duly noted and evaluated.

Only one field, it would appear, has been entirely omitted in these surveys. Not a single scholar, as far as I know, has tried to assess the place of Anglo-Jewry in the development of Judaism itself. Not that the variations of Anglo-Jewish religious thought and observance have failed to find protagonists as well as critics. But an inquiry into whether British Jews have added any distinctive and permanent values to the many existing facets of Judaism and its religious philosophy has not been attempted.

Throughout Jewish history almost every long-settled community had left some creative mark on the ever-growing variety of Jewish thought. In medieval Spain the foundations were laid for Jewish philosophy and rational exegesis; they have remained part of our cultural heritage to the present day. The great Franco-German communities in the Middle Ages wielded an immense influence on Jewish life through the classic commentaries on the Talmud evolved in their midst. Earlier, in the gaonic era, Jewish liturgy and the responsa literature first took shape, while later, in Italy, the beginnings of the historical school were witnessed.

In more modern times, too, this creativeness never ceased. Eastern Europe has enriched Judaism as the birthplace of Chassidism, the Mussar movement, and the new approach to Jewish learning as developed in the great Lithuanian yeshivot. The Jewries of Germany and Hungary, by founding the *Jue-*

dische Wissenschaft, have opened up entirely fresh vistas of Jewish thought and studies. They have also bequeathed to us the present divisions of Liberal, Reform, and "Neo-Orthodox" Judaism. In the United States the creative urge has found expression in the Conservative and Reconstructionist movements and in other revivalist groups still in the incipient stage. In Israel, too, despite its very brief history so far, new religious philosophies can already be discerned, from the Neturei Karta on the extreme Right to the religious socialism of the Orthodox kibbutz movements.

Moreover, these communities, in addition to the specific trends and movements they have created, have each also left an indelible imprint on the development of Jewish law and custom as a whole. At one time or another they have all produced outstanding religious guides whose views still determine the application of Jewish teachings. Any major rabbinic judgment today must take into account the decisions of Maimonides, who hailed from Spain, of Asheri from Germany, of Karo from Turkey, of Isserles from Poland, and of many other authorities whose rulings constitute the accepted *Halakhah.* To solve present-day religious problems we may also have to consult the responsa works of Moses Schreiber of Pressburg, of Akivah Eger of Posen, of Ezekiel Landau of Prague, of Jacob Emden of Altona, of Benzion Uziel of Jerusalem, of Yekuthiel Grunwald of Columbus, Ohio—to name only a few of the more important authors widely recognized as rabbinic authorities. Again, we owe many religious customs now observed in many parts of the world to various communities in Palestine, Europe, and North Africa which first instituted them.

Can the Jews of these Isles, after a settled and organized life extending over 300 years, likewise claim to have contributed their own strands to the multi-colored pattern of contemporary Judaism? Can they boast of any new religious movement they have created, of any original trend in Jewish scholarship they have initiated, of any immortal halachic celebrities they have thrown up, or of any universal *Minhagim* they have originated?

Anglo-Jewry has, of course, evolved its own characteristic forms of Jewish life. But their distinctiveness rests principally on the institutional level. In many ways unique is the organization of its Rabbinate, its synagogues, its press, and, perhaps, some of its social establishments. But these institutions, valuable as they are, hardly affect the content of Jewish experience. Nor have they determined the outlook and organization of Jews elsewhere to any notable extent. In the realm of Jewish scholarship, too, it is significant that Anglo-Jewry has distinguished itself mainly by the monumental—though essentially unoriginal—work of translating our great classics, the Talmud, the Midrash, and the Zohar.

More to the point at issue here may be the much-lauded Anglo-Jewish predeliction for a "mellow" form of Jewish observance—a moderate, conservative brand of Judaism which, it is claimed, combines the virtues of tolerance and tradition. But even this contribution, which is again unlikely to perpetuate itself as a distinct strain in the fabric of universal Judaism, can scarcely be classified as a movement or a significant reorientation of Jewish thought. Lacking a separate philosophy to inspire it, this typically Anglo-Jewish expression of Judaism is characterized by negative rather than positive qualities. By raising the art of compromise into an ideal, *per se,* it shuns all tendencies of extremism without, however, at the same time finding or emphasizing new values to supplement those modified in the process of accommodation.

In some respects, of course, it is this very absence of originality which has been the strength of Judaism in these Isles. The disinclination to explore and tread out new paths has kept Anglo-Jewry moving, in the main, along the old paths. Consequently, the traditional element has enjoyed a stability hardly found in any other Jewish community. But whether an expanding community, existing in security for three centuries, has paid its historical debt to posterity by merely maintaining some spiritual values without adding substantially to them may be open to question. That, in truth, is the challenge of the Tercentenary.

Why, then, has Anglo-Jewish history proved so singularly unproductive in the field of religion? The answer may lie largely in the hankering after uniformity and centralization peculiar to the Anglo-Jewish communal set-up. Only in a society which promotes, or at least sympathetically tolerates, variety and institutional diversity, can the seeds of independent inquiry, the quest for fresh values really bear fruit. Rigid conformity, on the other hand, is bound to stifle the ambition in search of new paths. Anglo-Jewry is probably more monolithic in character than any other Jewish community, past or present. It has an authorized (Chief) Rabbinate, an authorized (United) Synagogue, an authorized (Jews') College, and an authorized (Jewish) "Chronicle" as well as an Authorized (Singer's) *"Prayer-Book,"* and whoever and whatever is not thus "authorized" enjoys at best some unofficial *de facto* recognition of a partly naturalized alien who will never attain completely equal rights. Another concomitant is the severely practical, if not utilitarian, character of Anglo-Jewry's religious organizations. By and large they all serve a purely expedient end. It is obvious that such conditions do not conduce to spiritual productivity.

One example will suffice to illustrate this point. Prewar Germany, with a Jewish population a little larger than Britain's, possessed three theological seminaries. Apart from training rabbis, each of these academies served as a workshop in which a new link in the long chain of Jewish movements was being forged. From the *Berlin Rabbiner Seminar* emerged the Orthodox synthesis of Jewish and secular learning associated with such names as Hildesheimer and Hoffmann; the *Hochschule* in Berlin became the arsenal of Liberal Judaism, while the *Breslau Seminar* developed the teachings of "Historical Judaism" inspired by Graetz and Fraenkel. Similar conditions obtained in Hungary and elsewhere. The object of these colleges was not simply to supply qualified candidates for ministerial vacancies; it was to contrive a new orientation in the Jewish *Weltanschauung*. Only to the extent that they succeeded in breaking new ground and in creating new types of spiritual leaders did they justify their separate existence—and fulfill the expectations of their founders. These seats of Jewish learning naturally produced leaders who sought to communicate the distinctive outlook of their training to their communities. In this way the seminaries fertilized important popular movements and epoch-making new currents in Jewish history.

London's Jews' College, while staffed with scholars of world renown and of no lesser caliber than graced its Continental sister-institutions, never set itself such aims. Nor was it ever encouraged to develop in that direction. The unchallenged monopoly of the College demands that its orientation shall be focused on the average congregation. The average congregation, in turn, especially in a communal framework of marked uniformity, requires a spiritual guide who shows no pronounced "deviation" from the accepted standards.

How radically different Jews' College is from most other seminaries can be gauged from the recent suggestion that its religious point of view be broad enough for the training of Liberal as well as Orthodox ministers. Such a plan is not likely to be put into effect, for it is hardly conceivable that those trained to guide and strengthen the religious convictions of others shall themselves be educated in a religious vacuum. But the mere fact that such a proposal could be advocated is an indication of the problems to be overcome if the College is to become the training ground and generator of an original, dynamic philosophy of Judaism and thus exert an influence over its alumni to pioneer a religious outlook not presently shared by the majority of the community.

Nevertheless, there are certain signs, as yet still imponderable, which point towards the prospect of some Anglo-Jewish creativeness in the future. The remarkable growth of yeshivot and kindred institutions, which have planted an unprecedented intensity of Talmudic learning in our midst; the increasing popularity of Jewish day schools and youth movements, vitally stimulating the Jewish consciousness of our youth and their search for topical ideals; the establishment of the Institute of Jewish Studies in Manchester, with its novel bias for a mystical approach to Judaism; the recent publication, also in Manchester, of Dayan Weisz's masterly responsa—the first such work to be produced in these Isles for decades; the appearance of Dr. I. Epstein's "The Faith of Judaism," which may be regarded as the first attempt at an Anglo-Jewish "Guide to the Perplexed"; the growing tendency to replace ministers by rabbis, and to decentralize the London and provincial *Batei Din,* with the attendant diffusion of rabbinical authority—all these are potential factors in a process of fermentation which may yet place Anglo-Jewry in the forefront among the great communities that have made an imperishable contribution to the richness of our religious heritage.

Should all these impulses to create fresh concepts of Jewish thought become manifest one day as a powerful element in Anglo-Jewish affairs, it is to be hoped that they will find expression in a movement to enhance and not to diminish the eternal values which have sustained us to this day.

The Jews of Erin

THE individual and organized life of the Jewish communities in Ireland is broadly modeled on the Anglo-Jewish pattern. But this is modified by four important factors. First, Ireland was one of the few European countries not directly involved in World War II. Second, unlike the other two neutral states in Europe, Sweden and Switzerland, Ireland had hardly any influx of refugees before, during, or after the war. Jewish life thus tended to be very conservative, as it was uninfluenced by Continental newcomers. Third, the ratio of Jews to the rest of the population is very low, perhaps the smallest in any English-speaking country. Fourth, Irish Jews live in a staunchly Catholic environment—about 93 per cent of the population belong to the Roman Catholic Church. As a consequence of these factors, Jewish life is marked by a relatively great degree of social isolation and self-containment.

Since the repeal of the External Relations Act and the proclamation of the Republic of Ireland as a sovereign state in 1949, the independence of organized Irish-Jewish life from British Jewry has been increasingly asserted. The chief rabbinate, the administration of the synagogues and of Jewish education, and the organization of Jewish defense had no formal links with Anglo-Jewish institutions, though close un-

Published in the *American Jewish Year Book*, Philadelphia, 1953.

official relations were maintained between the two communities. Only in the spheres of Zionist work and of the youth organizations were the affiliations with London headquarters retained with but few exceptions. Irish Jews thus continued to participate in Anglo-Jewish fund-raising campaigns.

The Jewish population in 1952 is estimated to be 5,400, 95 per cent of whom live in or near the capital. This is an increase of 400 since 1951, when the Jewish segment totaled an estimated 5,000. However, the two decades between 1933 and 1952 have been marked by a steady increase of Jews in Ireland by approximately fifty per cent.

This is mainly accounted for by immigrants from Great Britain who sought to exchange the austerity of that country for the economic opportunities existing in Ireland. The latest figures and estimates also show the strongly centripetal character of the Jewish population movement within the country. The provincial communities are in a state of complete dissolution. Dublin has absorbed almost their entire memberships. Limerick and Waterford, which once had well-organized Jewish communities, have long ceased to count more than one or two Jewish families. At Cork, however, the forty-five remaining Jewish families, amounting to less than one-half of the Jewish population there at its peak a generation ago, continue a successful struggle to maintain their communal life.

Jews both in Dublin and Cork live in more or less compact units covering relatively small urban and to a growing extent suburban areas. In the capital, for instance, over 90 per cent of the Jewish population is still concentrated in less than one-fourth of the city's area. There has been little Jewish emigration from Ireland, the exceptions being the comparatively large number of local girls marrying Englishmen and settling in England. The fairly prosperous and stable economic condition of Irish Jewry has tended to discourage emigration to Israel, even on the modest scale of the Anglo-Jewish *aliyah*, although about half a dozen leading members of Zionist youth societies have joined their English friends in Israel within the past two years.

While Irish Jews suffer no civic or political disabilities, few are to be found in politics or the civil service. A notable exception is Robert Briscoe, whose popularity was again evidenced in the 1951 general election to the *Dail* (Lower House of Parliament), of which he has been continuously a member, representing the Fianna Fail Party for nearly a quarter of a century. He also continues to be the only Jewish councilor on the Corporation of the City of Dublin, in addition to retaining the presidency of the Board of Shechitah of Ireland.

Most Jews are engaged in commerce and industry, though a considerable number has entered the legal and medical professions. A few have reached places of some eminence. Professor Leonard Abrahamson, who early in 1951 was succeeded as chairman of the Jewish Representative Council by Herman Good, a leading Dublin solicitor, continued to be president of the Royal College of Physicians in Ireland. At the University of Dublin (Trinity College) and other university colleges there are about 160 Jewish students, a great proportion of whom have their permanent homes in England.

There has been little evidence of anti-Semitic pressure or agitation. The few and unimportant anti-Jewish publications, particularly the Catholic periodical *Fiat,* which advocates discrimination against Jews on religious grounds, have produced unfavorable effects less in Ireland than abroad, notably Canada, whose section of the World Jewish Congress on February 14, 1950, appealed to the Jewish Representative Counsel to secure some check on the distribution of such literature. There have been no public anti-Jewish manifestations in Ireland since the worldwide Catholic agitation aroused by the opposition of the Vatican to the policies of the Israel government regarding Jerusalem and the Holy Places in 1949, when some mild demonstrations took place in Dublin. The Representative Council and the Defense and Conciliation Committee, established early in 1952 under the Council's aegis, have had only rare occasion to defend Jewish interests on the appearance of some isolated anti-Jewish, or more often anti-Israel, articles in the local press. Generally, however, the attitude towards Jews and Israel has been friendly and sympathetic, though the interests of Catholics in the Holy Land are watched with special concern.

The organization of Dublin's Jewish life is distinguished by a high measure of decentralization. There are seven Orthodox synagogues of varying sizes, all administered as completely independent units. Their combined membership covers over 90 percent of all Jewish families, probably a record for any sizable Jewish community in the Diaspora. The sole organizational link uniting these seven Hebrew congregations are the chief rabbinate and the congregations' representation on the Representative Council and the Board of Shechitah. Since 1947 there has also existed a small Progressive Congregation affiliated with the Union of Liberal and Progressive Synagogues in London. It has functioned without a spiritual leader since the resignation in July 1951 of its minister, Dr. J. J. Kokotek.

Though most synagogues originally employed rabbis of their own, all pulpits have been vacant for some time. These are now occupied in rotation by the Chief Rabbi, assisted in his rabbinical work by Dayan Z. Alony. An important aspect of this work is the supervision of the manufacture of large quantities of kosher meat products for export to Israel (as part of various American, British, and South African gift schemes) and to England.

At Cork the Rev. Shalom Barron, of Stockport in England, assumed his duties as minister-shochet-teacher on May 11, 1952. He succeeded the Rev. Bernard Kersh, who had resigned a few months earlier after fourteen years of service.

Jewish life in Ireland continues on strongly traditional lines. There are no public functions under Jewish auspices which violate the Orthodox observance of the Sabbath, festival, or *kashrut* laws, and it is estimated that over 80 per cent of all Jewish households in the country use exclusively kosher meat.

Approximately four out of every five Jewish children of school-age receive some regular Jewish instruction. Of an estimated total of five hundred children, over three hundred are enrolled with the centrally administered Talmud Torah, an increase of about fifty over the previous years. Private tuition and classes conducted by the Progressive Congregation account for about another hundred children.

Half the pupils educated under the aegis of the Talmud Torah attend Zion Schools, a National School (Jewish) where secular education is provided by the State and where Jewish subjects are taught by the Talmud Torah staff in the mornings. The remainder are instructed by the same teachers in the afternoons and on Sundays at another, newly-acquired center. The period of Jewish instruction at each center averages seven hours a week. The main emphasis is on religious education, and the Ashkenazic pronunciation of Hebrew is maintained in the classroom as well as in the synagogue.

Jewish school education is effectively supplemented by the intensive activities of Dublin's fifteen Jewish youth organizations. These range from various Jewish scout groups and the Jewish Students' Union to a number of Zionist and religious youth societies. Their aggregate membership is about six hundred, of whom about two hundred and fifty belong to strictly Orthodox groups.

There is little interest in or provision for adult Jewish education. The Chevra Gemora attracts about a dozen men to its daily Talmud course, and a mixed group of about twenty members regularly attend a weekly series of lectures on Jewish history by the Chief Rabbi throughout the winter months. Outside the youth societies the study of the Hebrew language is pursued only by a few individuals. With few exceptions, mainly the women's groups, Zionist activity is noneducational in character.

The material needs of Israel still constitute the community's principal single interest. Irish Jewry has always been a Zionist stronghold, and it never counted any active anti-Zionists among its members. But this intense devotion to the Jewish national cause has been expressed almost exclusively in fund-raising efforts in response to the numerous appeals from Israel. While Dublin still has no general Zionist society, some cultural Zionist activities have been sponsored by the Mizrachi and various women's groups, as well as by the Zionist Council, set up in the summer of 1951 to coordinate the work of all local Zionist bodies.

The following describes the major amounts raised during 1951: Joint Palestine Appeal—$27,160; Jewish National Fund —$20,580; Zionist Women's societies (including Dublin Daughters of Zion)—$5,124; Hebrew University—$2,520; Jewish Medical Society—$1,120 (including the cost of a large cotton-wool consignment sent to Jerusalem); Youth Aliyah—

$1,078. The Mizrachi Women's Society dispatched considerable quantities of linen and other articles to Israel.

It is estimated that Irish Jews have also contributed well over $5,600 towards the appeals conducted by the many visiting solicitors from Yeshivot and other educational institutions in Israel and England. Kosher provisions to a number of charitable and educational homes in Israel amounted to $1,400. The total thus raised in Dublin (excluding local charities) exceeded $64,400 during the year. This is scarcely less than the community spent on the maintenance and administration of all its communal, religious and educational institutions.

While Zionist causes command the support of the greater part of the community, there is an almost equal division between those contributing mainly or exclusively to Zionist appeals and those who give first preference to local charities and institutions. Among the latter are the Jewish Board of Guardians, whose income (including bequests) in the 1950's amounted to $15,680. The Home for Aged Jews, which was founded in 1950, raised $49,000 by the end of 1951, though the number of inmates did not exceed ten. Useful philanthropic work is also performed by the Hospital Aid Society, and some Friendly and Ladies' Societies. The Committee of the Home for Aged Jews gave practical consideration to the suggestion to add a Jewish hospital to the home.

In the absence of full-time social workers, most individual social service cases have been handled by the rabbinate.

Virtually the entire Jewish reading requirements of the community are met by British publications, notably the (London) *Jewish Chronicle*, which covers Irish-Jewish news, albeit on a very limited scale. The first Irish-Jewish Year Book (for 5712) was published by the Committee of the Chief Rabbinate in August 1951. Plans have also been completed for the publication of a monthly communal magazine beginning September 1952.

In the social sphere, activities have been more intensive and varied. In addition to Dublin's Jewish communal and Zionist life, which often assumes a markedly social form, there is the Jewish Social and Literary Club, the Jewish Golf Club and the Dublin Maccabi—which inaugurated its sports grounds on May 25, 1952. These attract hundreds of members for regular social and recreational activities. The Jewish Dramatic and Jewish Musical Societies also conduct active programs.

Jews and Irishmen

Some Reflections on an American Lecture Tour

IT was in America that I first appreciated the significance of the story of the three Jews who met somewhere in Europe and discussed their emigration plans. Said the first: "I am looking for comfort and security at last; I have decided to settle in the United States." "My destination is Israel," announced the second, "I wish to be among the pioneers helping to build up the land of my forefathers." "And I am going to Ireland," admitted the third man, rather hesitantly. On being questioned as to the reason for his surprising choice, he explained: "Surely, Ireland must be the last country in the world where the Devil would look to find a Jew!"

It has been my good fortune to find that few qualifications could be more valuable to any foreigner contemplating a lecture tour in America than, apart from the possession of a robust physique, the ability to wear a shamrock together with a Star of David. Jews and Irishmen are commonly enough known in America; but their combination in a single individual, an Irish Jew—let alone an Irish rabbi—seems to be looked upon as a sensational curiosity, almost as a freak, like a fourth leaf on a shamrock. A rabbi from Ireland apparently conjures up the weirdest fancies in the imaginative minds of many Americans. The *Washington Post,* following my appearance in the nation's capital, had to assure its read-

Published in The Jewish Forum (New York), June 1957.

ers that my beard was not green, and the interviewer of the *Toronto Daily Star* confided in his report that he had dancing in his head "visions of cheerful little leprechauns, all wearing green skullcaps" on the afternoon of our press conference. Irish Jewry may be pardoned if they feel a little puzzled why their very existence should call forth so much incredulity in America. Surely they cannot be accused of not having tried hard enough to penetrate into the consciousness of world Jewry. It was from the Emerald Isle that the Yishuv in the Holy Land, twenty years ago, selected the occupant of the highest rabbinical office in the world after he had served as Rabbi of Dublin and later, for seventeen years, as Chief Rabbi of what was then the Irish Free State. But the memory of the Irish-Jewish significance of this appointment evidently soon faded, and the Jews of Ireland had to accomplish something even more spectacular to make their presence known in America. This they did only recently by the dramatic election of a distinguished member of the Jewish community—numbering no more than one-sixth of one per cent in a population consisting approximately of 93% Catholics and 7% Protestants—as First Citizen of the Irish capital.

But the question still remains: Why should Americans find it so much more difficult to believe that there are over 5000 Irish Jews than to accept the existence of, say, New Zealand Jewry or Finnish Jewry—communities certainly no larger than Irish Jewry? And why should my presence have evoked such an extraordinarily intense personal interest, from the White House in Washington to the small but charming community in Savannah, where the audience of over 500 all wore green emblems distributed in my honor by the local Hibernians; from the NBC television interviewers in New York to St. Paul, Minnesota, where the community, on chancing to learn that my birthday coincided with my visit there, greeted me after my lecture with a huge birthday cake complete with shamrocks and *Magen Davids*? When I look at the many presentations given to me by Irish orders and societies throughout the land, or at the magnificent keys presented to me by the mayors of several cities—in some cases the first such presentations ever made—or when I think of the Irish employees who dressed in green when they heard I would be visiting their plant, or of the Italian actress who, on hearing me at the

Catholic Oriel Society's reception, announced she would dedicate her radio program to me the following day . . ., I ask myself, wherein lies the secret of the magic attraction produced by the fusion of Jew and Irishman? The phenomenon was brought conspicuously to the fore with even more pronounced prominence by the Lord Mayor of Dublin, the impact of whose trip to the United States generated more publicity than any other comparable foreign visit to America in recent years.

The explanation may lie, partly at least, in the striking similarities and contrasts which distinguish the two communities from the other diverse nationalities which are being forged into one mighty nation in the fascinating American melting-pot. Most national groups sooner or later shed much of their distinctive individuality in the process of absorption into the fabric of American society. In the course of one or two generations, their national origin usually remains little more than a cherished memory. Jews and Irishmen seem to present by far the most conspicuous exception to this rule.

Though no less fully integrated than others as patriotic American citizens, both groups have retained a remarkable cohesion and feeling of affinity among themselves. Moreover, Jewish and Irish Americans, even after generations of settlement in the New World, have succeeded in maintaining a far more affectionate and practical bond with the lands of their forefathers than the Italians, or Germans, or Swedes, or any other national components of the American people. No national or religious holidays peculiar to minority groups make a greater impact on American life than St. Patrick's Day and the Jewish High Festivals.

This phenomenon is no doubt due largely to the influence of religion. The Irish are commonly identified with the Roman Catholic faith just as the Jews are with Judaism. Both of them, by reason of their intense devotion to a minority faith, have somehow marked themselves off from the more uniform majority as closely-knit communities united by a common religious and historical heritage.

With Jews and Irishmen forming such distinct and religiously-defined groups, it is perhaps not so unreasonable after all, that they should be popularly regarded as incompatible opposites. Little wonder, then, that their combination in the flesh creates something of a sensation to which the nostalgic sentiments of Jews and Irishmen readily respond. Add to this the fact that America harbors by far the largest Irish and Jewish communities in the world, and it will be appreciated why the reaction to an Irish Jew assumes such amazing proportions.

One of the most thrilling experiences of my tour was my visit to the United Nations. I was enthralled not only by that milling humanity in microcosm, speaking a Babel of languages and attired in picturesquely diverse garbs, by the magnificence of the buildings, with their fantastic architecture and bewildering artistry, or even by the touching manner in which Mr. Boland, the Irish Ambassador to the United Nations, introduced me as "my Chief Rabbi" to Ambassador Eban of Israel. The real climax came when, with my own eyes, I saw among eighty national delegations dispersed all over the huge General Assembly hall, seated side by side as friendly neighbors at the same table the delegations of—Ireland and Israel! Their close proximity next to each other may be an alphabetical accident, but to me it signified a far more profound relationship.

Here were seated together the representatives of two young and yet ancient nations whom history and destiny had united by a remarkable series of unusual experiences they had in common. Both are recently reborn nations whose roots reach into antiquity. Both peoples have always felt themselves summoned in a special way to a religious destiny in the world at large—the one as "a nation of saints and scholars," the other summoned to be "a kingdom of priests." Both have been subjected for many centuries to foreign domination and bitter religious persecution. Both have regained their national sovereignty after a long struggle, winning their independence from England in the present century. Both proclaimed themselves republics in the same year 1948, and both their countries are based on partition. Both peoples have made intensive efforts to revive their classic tongues and to fashion them into modern languages. Similar proportions of both peoples now live inside their own territory (about one-seventh), while the remainder are scattered throughout the world, mainly in the United States, in both cases.

These striking parallels may well represent an altogether unique historical analogy between two nations. Indeed, the enigma of the Jewish and Irish peoples' survival and national resurgence is divested of its absolute uniqueness only by the similarity of the two phenomena. The history of both nations has vindicated the incomparable power of national resilience sustained by an invincible religious faith, even when such faith is pitted against greatly superior material and political strength. In both cases it was the separateness of their religious beliefs which prevented the two peoples' submersion in the society surrounding and attacking them through the centuries. The same factor, as we have already noted, accounts for their extraordinary cohesion and resistance to assimilation at the present time.

How far does the actual state of Irish-Jewish relations today reflect this historical affinity? In so far as these relations are exemplified by the treatment of the small Jewish community in Ireland, they are certainly close and cordial. The rights of Jewish citizens as equals among the other denominational groups are expressly recognized in a special clause of the Irish constitution—probably the only Jewish community in the world to be constitutionally protected in this explicit manner. In practice, too, the Jews of Ireland have always felt free from discrimination. In fact, Ireland is one of the very few countries that has never blemished its record by any serious anti-Jewish outrages. Irish Jews are fully integrated into the cultural, intellectual and economic life of the state. If their social contacts with the general population are perhaps not quite so intimate as in some other Western countries, this is undoubtedly due to the all pervasive consciousness of religion in a devoutly Catholic society. With the Jews being similarly devoted to their faith, whatever barriers do exist are, on the whole, mutually raised and mutually respected.

In the international sphere, relations between Ireland and Israel are as yet somewhat more tenuous and less clearly defined. Though the Irish government announced its *de facto* recognition of the Jewish State on the occasion of my installation as Chief Rabbi of Ireland early in 1949, the two republics have still not exchanged any diplomatic representatives. Nevertheless, they carry on some trade with each other. Ireland has also made arrangements for the protection of the comparatively sizeable number of Irish citizens in Israel and for the issuance of visas to Israelis wishing to visit Ireland.

The press and public opinion in Ireland on the whole have been markedly friendly to the Jewish State since its establishment. If the official attitude of the Irish government has been somewhat more wary, we may assume that this is not unconnected with the hesitancy of the Vatican in normalizing its relationship with the Jewish State. Such influence is only natural in a country as loyal to the Church of Rome as Ireland. At first the Vatican's coolness towards Israel was no doubt prompted by genuine concern for the Holy Places in Palestine and for the status of Jerusalem. Deeper theological considerations may also have barred the way to a firm accord between the Roman Church and a sovereign Jewish State resurrected on the soil of the Holy Land. The literal fulfillment, in accordance with the Jewish interpretation, of the Hebrew Prophets' vision of Jews returning in force to their homeland after their long exile, perhaps inevitably led to certain difficulties for those who had seen in the Jewish dispersion evidence for the truth of their faith. But with Christian access to the Holy Places assured, with Jerusalem firmly established as Israel's capital, and with the growing challenge to Christendom by the aggressive and missionary ambitions of Pan-Arabism, there are lately some indications of a shift of Vatican policy in Israel's favor. A similar change can also be discerned in official Irish pronouncements on Israel, particularly at the United Nations.

Among the United Nations, Ireland represents a numerically and militarily insignificant force. Yet there are prospects that her voice will command increasing respect there. Not entangled in any political or military alliances, belonging to no power blocs and having no vested interests in the conflicts of others, Ireland—unlike so many bigger nations—is not under suspicion of seeking to promote her own cause when she advocates a certain policy on foreign disputes. This disinterestedness is bound to give her views a standing not necessarily enjoyed by far greater powers.

These two factors—Ireland's intimate ties with the Vatican and her special position in the United Nations—may eventually invest her attitude to Israel with a significance quite out of proportion to her usual place in international affairs.

The benefit, then, of Ireland's goodwill and support may well be of considerable value to Israel in the future. The Jewish State might also draw some useful lessons from the Irish pattern of the relationship between state and religion. In Ireland, the Church, though disestablished and functioning purely as a moral force, exerts her powerful influence on every sphere of national life, public as well as private. For instance, drafts of parliamentary bills with any bearing on religious or moral issues are generally submitted to the ecclesiastical heads of the recognized denominations (including the Jewish) for comments, so that the legislation will not impugn any religious principles. The adoption of some similar relationship in Israel would ensure that the life of the nation, in all its ramifications, bears the unmistakable hallmark of the Jewish religious heritage.

In return, Israel and her experience could also be of practical value to the solution of Ireland's problems. The Irish Republic is passing through a progressively severe economic crisis, and the resultant unemployment is driving thousands of young Irishmen into "exile" every year. In no countries in the world are the population figures less static than in Ireland and Israel; only, while in Israel the trend shows a constant sharp rise, the population of Ireland is steadily diminishing. Israel's experience in absorbing so many immigrants should help Ireland at least to reduce the loss of so many emigrants. The massive support given to Israel by American Jews—in supplying funds, skills and tourists as well as great moral aid—might point the way to Ireland in harnessing the vast latent goodwill of Irish Americans in the service of their ancestral land. In the expansion of industrial and agricultural projects, too, Israel might provide some useful knowledge. Large-scale afforestation—a great success in Israel and a vital need in Ireland—is a case in point. The Gaelic language revival movement—after so many years of dedicated but unavailing endeavors—might also learn something from the complete restoration of Hebrew as Israel's *lingua franca*.

European civilization is fringed by Ireland at the Western extreme and by Israel at its most Eastern outpost. The two nations, though widely separated geographically and even religiously, have yet so many historical and contemporary features in common. Their respective experiences should not only be of mutual benefit to each other. Their triumphant emergence from centuries of adversity should instill faith and hope into all who are weak or in despair; their devotion to the ideals of friendliness and tolerance should blaze a trail of comfort in a world of enmity; and their heroic perseverance as bearers of human history's richest gifts should inspire mankind at large to blend the imperishable traditions of the past with the accomplishments of the present to secure future harmony and fulfillment.

The U. S. A.—A Visitor's View

A N American lecture tour provides little more than literally a bird's-eye view of the country, usually from a height of some 16,000 feet. But for fleeting moments in between flights (and occasional periods of sleep) one does catch a few close-up glimpses of what goes on down below. Traveling 10,000 miles and speaking in seventeen cities scattered over a dozen American States and two Canadian Provinces, I was bound to gain some impressions of life in that fascinating Continent. Here are a few random samples:

I had my first introduction to one of the more singular features of American Jewish life atop New York's monstrous Empire State Building. "Do you know, rabbi," I was asked familiarly by a Jewish attendant who had recognized me from newspaper pictures, "what are the three most important dates in the calendar for American Jews?" "Rosh Hashana, Yom Kippur . . ." "And the third?" "Well, November 17, of course!" He soon relieved my bewilderment by explaining: "Why, that's the date when the Cadillac model comes out!"

At Cleveland I was shown the new buildings of the Telshe Yeshivah, now one of the leading Torah centers in the world. Rising on spacious beautiful grounds outside the city are enormous air-conditioned study-halls, attractive dormitories

Published in *The Jewish Chronicle*, April 19, 1957.

with modern comforts, busy offices with up-to-date equipment, a huge gymnasium for the Yeshivah's high school, an open-air swimming-pool, and hundreds of young Americans enthusiastically immersed in the "sea of the Talmud."

Outside a Conservative synagogue, I was told, parking meters are provided with notices asking the police to ignore the one-hour waiting limit as the car-owners are attending Sabbath services!

In an unpretentious Brooklyn house, where I spent almost two hours past midnight in audience with the Lubavitcher Rebbe, I saw the nerve-center of an empire over which the sun never sets, a bustling administration controlling 10,000 devout Chassidim and a sprawling network of religious schools and academies in five continents.

In Savannah, Georgia, I visited the local Jewish day school. As I entered the infants' class, a little girl exclaimed: "He looks like Santa Claus!" She had evidently never seen a bearded rabbi before.

At a "Yeshivah" high school in a modern suburb of New York I found a class of twelve-year-old girls (mostly American-born) who had completed Rashi's commentary on the whole book of *Vayikra* (Leviticus) and answered all questions on the subject perfectly in fluent Hebrew.

All these experiences might equally well characterize important phases in contemporary American Jewry. With many synagogues crowded every Sabbath and yet masses of American Jews estranged from all religious observances, with 30,000 children attending intensive Orthodox day schools and yet an alarming high rate of intermarriage, with million-dollar community centers even in some of the smaller cities and yet countless Jews unattached to any Jewish organization, American Jewish life today presents a mosaic of bewildering variety. Large-scale assimilation and militant religious idealism, widespread indifference and an immense awakening of communal consciousness, are all powerful forces in the present process of fermentation.

All this diversity is only natural in a community over ten times the size of Anglo-Jewry—by far the greatest number of Jews ever assembled in a single country. Yet there is more we can expect from such a uniquely blessed community. American Jews not only have the combined strength of unparalleled numbers and unprecedented prosperity; they also enjoy far more freedom than any leading Jewry at any time throughout our dispersion. I was particularly concerned to discover how far American Jews realize their own tremendous potential; how aware they are of the immense challenge imposed by the extraordinary opportunities within and the extraordinary pressures outside; and how conscious they are of the supreme responsibilities thrust on them as (numerically at least) the principal heirs to the Jewish norms and values whose bearers perished in the European holocaust.

Spiritually and culturally the unity of American Jewry is gravely undermined by the often exceedingly bitter strife between the main religious factions. The relative strength of the three major contestants is about evenly balanced, with Orthodoxy probably still slightly preponderant in numbers, and the Conservative and Reform sects in wealth and in influence. But the divisions between them are deeply rooted and increasingly evident in almost all fields of Jewish cultural and social activity. Indeed, it looks as if the fragmentation of Jewish religious life in the New World is approaching the stage when we have to think in terms of different Jewish denominations on the Christian pattern. Already today the rift between an Orthodox synagogue and a Reform temple, with its untraditional officials and form of worship, is as pronounced in the eyes of the respective protagonists as between a Catholic church and its Protestant counterpart.

The strength of the Orthodox camp is further sapped by a good deal of internal disunity. It has three main rabbinical associations (instead of one as among the Reform and Conservative groups); authority over *kashrut* and marriages is left almost entirely to individual enterprise and rivalry. But the main weakness of the Orthodox position seems to stem from its preoccupation with relatively insignificant side issues. In the public mind the principal differences with its rivals concern the use in the synagogue of microphones and English prayers, the separation of the sexes and the height of the partition between them, and often the distance from the synagogue at which cars are parked on the Sabbath. Very few on either side of the conflict have any idea of the real issues at stake; the belief in revelation, the binding character of Jewish law, the place of Judaism outside the synagogue, and the distinction between vague moralistic preaching and a strict moral discipline pervading the whole gamut of Jewish life. The battle is being fought out on largely irrelevant ground—to the greatest disadvantage of the traditionalists.

On the other hand, the keenly competitive element in American Jewish life (as in American life generally) has also produced positive values. If it has severely compromised Jewish unity, it has certainly stimulated Jewish vitality, particularly in the literary and educational spheres. The output of Jewish books and magazines is enormous, spurred on no doubt by the rivals' struggle for recognition. But here, again, the highly practical mentality of most Americans militates against contributions to Jewish thought of great originality and lasting creative merit. Most efforts are bent on strengthening Judaism institutionally rather than philosophically, against the assaults from outside.

A most significant product of the competitive fight for survival is the phenomenal growth of the Jewish day-school movement—now probably the most constructive force in American Judaism. Having lost the allegiance of so many indifferent Jews owing to the allurements of the dissenters, Orthodoxy has been forced to replace attempts at converting the old by enlightening the young. At many scores of modern schools Jewish studies are pursued on a scale and an intensity never before attained in conjunction with first-rate secular education. The idea is proving so popular that such schools can now be found in nearly all communities of importance throughout the country. The rolls often include a preponderance of children from non-religious homes. Lately, even the Conservatives have been induced to embark on a similar day-school program. Of course, conditions in America are exceptionally favorable to this development. The bogy of "segregation" does not unduly trouble people who live among so many diverse nationalities; most Americans work extremely hard, and they do not mind their children being trained to do likewise. At some schools twenty hours a week are devoted to Jewish subjects, in addition to a full secular program; and teachers are fairly well paid, so that the supply of competent Hebrew instructors is reasonably adequate.

The one endeavor in which American Jewry is virtually united is its massive support for Israel. Throughout my seven-week visit, American Jews, as well as Israel, faced a supreme crisis, a situation not dissimilar to that confronting British Jewry during the Bevin era. The attitude of the American administration was distinctly unfriendly. Its proposal to apply crippling sanctions against the Jewish State at first commanded a good deal of tacit approval among the population at large. The abandonment of this iniquitous proposal even before Israel's decision to withdraw behind the armistice lines was, in large measure, due to the determined stand of American Jewry, which aroused public opinion. Speakers on all Jewish platforms throughout the country unanimously and fearlessly denounced the government's policy. At most meetings I addressed the audience was urged to send letters and telegrams of protest to the President, the Secretary of State, and local Congressmen. The vociferous chorus of indignation soon began to turn the tide. The bold resolution of American Jewry, applying the democratic process of pressure, gradually set in motion a chain-reaction of sympathy, transforming the outlook, first of the national press, then of Congress, and eventually of the highest quarters.

Even more staggering is the material assistance rendered to Israel. The fantastic sums raised in America still meet an impressive proportion of Israel's total expenditure. Indeed, all this aid—moral, political, and financial—is so gigantic and indispensable that one may doubt if the Jewish State could exist at all under present circumstances without American Jewry.

In reflecting, then, on the place of the American Jewish community in world Jewish affairs and history, one cannot but be inspired with awe and thankfulness at the wonderful ways of Providence. The year 1492 witnessed the most cruel

blow in medieval Jewish history: the expulsion of the Jews
from Spain; the end of the most illustrious Jewish community
in the Middle Ages. The very same year saw the discovery of
the land destined to encompass the most powerful and prosperous Jewish community in modern times. In our own day
we have grieved over the destruction of the most populous
and creative European Jewries. Out of that agony emerged
the triumph of Israel's restoration to Statehood, itself sustained by American Jewry's rise to greatness just at a time
when its unprecedented strength has become an essential but-
tress to Jewish survival. What an extraordinary vindication of
the Divine design of Jewish destiny!

3

Essays and Studies

A Jewish Community Three Hundred Years Ago

A N extraordinarily interesting picture of the religious and social conditions which obtained
in a leading Jewish community almost three
centuries ago is painted in the records of the Portuguese-
Jewish community at Hamburg which were published early

Published in the *Irish-Jewish Year Book*, 5712 (1951-2).

this century in a German translation of the original Portuguese, and occasionally Spanish, text.* That text represents the actual minutes of the proceedings of the Community Council. This article has utilized numerous entries—sometimes there were over forty meetings a year!—in an attempt at reconstructing the life, hazards, problems and organization of a typical Jewish community in the days of Cromwell.

Those charged with the leadership of their co-religionists occupied onerous and highly responsible positions. They were reminded of their obligations at the swearing-in ceremony which took place every year immediately after Rosh Hashanah following the annual elections of a few days earlier. A characteristic entry, repeated in almost identical terms every year, reads: "Tishri 3rd, 5418 (1657): The newly-elected Council held its first meeting. The oath was taken by the *Tephillin* before the Rabbis. By this oath every member pledged himself to cast his vote on all matters as dictated by his conscience in the interest of the common good and in the service of God. . ."

In many ways the functions and authority of the Council resembled those of a government rather than of a communal organization. Social discipline in those days was exceedingly rigid, and the powers vested in the Council were far-reaching. Severe penalties could be inflicted upon offenders against the Council's rules. These ranged from complete social ostracism, sometimes even expulsion from the community, to the imposition of heavy fines. A serious punishment, too, was to be barred from attendance at Divine Services for a certain period! A minute dated Teveth 24th, 5425 (1665) records that a Benjamin de Rimini appeared before the Council to renew his plea for permission to visit the Synagogue again. "This was granted for Sabbaths, Purim and all Festivals, but otherwise refused."

To go to the synagogue even on weekdays was thus regarded as a privilege. But it also entailed duties. Officers of synagogues today may learn with envy and surprise of the methods

*"Aus dem aeltesten Protokollbuch der Portugiesich-Juedischen Gemeinde in Hamburg," translated and annotated by "J.C." in the *Jahrbuch der Juedisch-Literarischen Gesellschaft*, Frankfurt a/Main, volumes V, VII, VIII, IX, X, XI and XIII (1908-1920).

and effectiveness with which their predecessors three centuries
ago maintained the decorum of the services. At one Council
meeting a considerable fine was imposed on two worshippers
at the Beth Israel Synagogue "for disturbing behavior." Three
years later we find reference to an even more exacting fine,
together with the exclusion from the synagogue for a period of
three months, "for dishonorable conduct." Before Purim,
repeated proclamations by the Council warned the Jewish
population against frolicking in the streets. One Purim
announcement reads: "Since the Council have learned that
the usual excessive and noisy *'Haman-Klopfen'*—whether one's
feet, rattles or other means are used—may disturb our peace,
and since—as our rabbis have declared—there exists no religious obligation for this custom, the Council have decided to
abolish the practice completely and they hereby prohibit
noise-making on Purim or any other occasion. The officers
and teachers are requested to ensure that the boys will obey
this decree and behave as quietly as possible." Another minute
records a decision not to admit children under five years to
the synagogue, unless they were to read the *Haphtorah!* A
few months later, however, the minimum age of admission
was reduced to four years. . . "as long as such children are
seated with the others under the supervision of the officers and
teachers of the Talmud Torah." It was also announced that
a fine would be imposed on anyone bringing a dog into the
synagogue. People indeed looked upon the synagogue as a
home in those days!

With the regular attendance of virtually the entire community, we are not surprised to find the synagogue being used
for secular as well as religious announcements. Thus, requests
for the return of lost property were made from the *Bimah*
whenever necessary. This practice, incidentally, had its origin
in the ancient Temple at Jerusalem.

Much of the time at Council meetings was devoted to discussions relating to the community's officials—and often to
complaints against them. Frequently applications for salary
increases were on the agenda. Usually the applicant had to
prove that he had been blessed with another few children
since the last increase, or that he had to provide for the
marriage of a daughter, before the request was granted. From

different entries it appears that the maximum scale of payments was 650 marks *per annum* for a rabbi, 460 for a *shochet,* 400 for a teacher and 340 for a *chazan.* A *shammas* received 165 marks a year; the value of his gratuities, if any, is not mentioned.

No one could escape the ever-vigilant eyes of the Council's members. On one occasion the *shammas* Abraham Lopez was reprimanded "because he does not carry out his duties with appropriate zeal, refuses to follow the instructions of the *Gabbai,* is not the last to leave the synagogue to shut the door, and permits a non-Jewish maid to enter the House of God unattended to clean up." The minute concludes with the caustic remark: "Lopez promises to improve in all these points." At another meeting, the two *chazanim* were invited to appear. They were told to act as Readers alternately at weekly intervals; to prepare the Reading of the Law in each other's presence, giving a fixed amount for charity for every mistake; to keep the scrolls in good repair and to choose those to be used by lot so that all would be employed alike; and, among other duties, "to get on well with each other, since they were now equals." A year and a half later one of the *chazanim* was asked to dismiss his domestic servant because she was in bad repute.

The teachers, too, were kept under constant supervision. Once it was reported that the children's education was showing signs of deterioration. Thereupon the Council, "in view of its duty to watch over this holy work with great care, since it constituted the greatest *Mitzvah* and since it, more than any other, would ensure our survival in this our exile, resolved to hold a general examination for all pupils every two months in the presence of some prominent members of the community, so that the teachers could be praised or criticized on the strength of the results. May God grant that this pious work will now prosper more happily." On another occasion, the teachers were instructed not to spend the school time on giving children who were under age tuition in the recital of the *Haphtorah.* (For reading this a boy need not be of *Bar Mitzvah* age.) They were also told that the teaching of the special *Bar Mitzvah* prayer and speech must take place outside school periods. At this meeting it was, moreover, de-

cided to spend thirty marks annually for the acquisition of
books to be distributed as prizes every Shavuoth to pupils of
all classes, "to stimulate their zeal."

Particularly strict control was, of course, exercised over
the *shochetim* and butchers. A series of complaints, including
the charge that they weighed the meat before it was "porged"
and that they sold meat slaughtered by Ashkenazim, was once
discussed, only to be referred to the rabbis for their attention
and examination. But even the rabbis themselves were by no
means above or beyond censure. There had been a rule, proclaimed and reiterated at many meetings, whereby the number
of guests to be invited to weddings and *"Berittot"* (circumcision ceremonies) was limited to twenty men and twelve
women, so as to avoid ostentation and annoyance among the
non-Jews. Offenders were subject to very heavy fines. One
day great consternation was shown at a meeting when it was
reported that one of the rabbis had disregarded this regulation
at his daughter's recent marriage. Due to indisposition—
whether in consequence of the excessive festivities is not
stated—he could not appear before the Executive until a week
later. "He expresses his regret," reads the entry, "and is prepared to submit to whatever penalty is imposed on him. It
was decided to inflict some, though mild, punishment on him,
to show that there is no favoring of persons but only strictest
justice, as God commands," continues the account. "But in
view of his financial stress and having regard for his position
and his piety the sentence was reduced to two marks, "which
Moshe de Pinto was to collect." On another occasion a rabbi
and another person were fined because, notwithstanding a
prohibition, they had accompanied an emissary from Jerusalem when he called on private people for subscriptions. Such
appeals, as we shall see, were invariably attended to by the
Council itself on behalf of the community.

But such strictures should not obscure from view the deep
respect and loyalty which the rabbis commonly enjoyed. The
rabbis delivered their sermons fortnightly in the winter and
weekly in the summer, as determined by the Council. The
sermons were received with reverential deference. A minute
of a meeting early in 5426 (1665) reads as follows: "Since our
rabbi has preached several times against the customary ex-

travagance in the dresses of our womenfolk, it shall be announced from the *Bimah:* 'Ladies must not leave their homes without a fitting overcoat except to call on a neighbor. They must not wear dresses of gold- or silver-wrought material. . . Under the same penalty children are forbidden to be adorned with jewelry or golden chains'."

These endeavors to promote modesty and simplicity in female apparel were repeated and sustained. At a meeting held ten days before the New Year 5428 (1667), the rabbi, who attended, referred to his sermon on the previous day and suggested that a directive in these matters regarding chastity should be issued. Failing that, he urged that a decree in any case be published forbidding women to bare their arms to the elbow. But it was decided to leave this matter to the incoming Council. Ten years earlier, the Council had passed the following resolution: "Whereas a ban has been imposed some time ago on dancing at weddings on a penalty of 30 marks, it shall now be permissible—in order to enhance the joy at feasts and weddings—to hold dances at which men and women are separated. Mixed dancing is allowed only among first degree relations, viz., husband and wife, father and daughter, son and mother, brother and sister." The minute closes: "May the Almighty always give His people occasions for joy in His holy service!"

In this connection it is interesting to observe how effectively the Council intervened to prevent marriages against the parents' will. A lady appeared at a meeting in 1663 to protest against the proposed marriage of her son. At her request two prominent Council members are asked to approach the girl's father and to warn him not to induce the young man to court the girl's affections. Eventually the young man declared on oath that he would never marry without his mother's consent, and this declaration was duly recorded.

The Council also enjoyed absolute jurisdiction over rights of residence within the community. Before anyone could settle in Hamburg as a new member the Council's agreement had to be procured upon application. Undesirable elements could be expelled. On one occasion the Council informed the Amsterdam community in writing of a member's expulsion in view of "his continuously sinful conduct."

Our records throw a particularly clear light on the social conditions, and the organization of philanthropy, at the time. About one-half of the meetings were devoted to the dispensing of charity among local and other people in need. In this respect the Council combined with its very many other activities the functions of a Board of Guardians and an agency to assist Jews abroad, especially in Palestine. Though the finances of the community were always described as precarious and very limited, large sums were spent in support of the local poor. The money was raised by direct taxation, but partly also by offerings, special bequests and the collection of fines. Not a penny was distributed without the most thorough investigation into the merits of every individual case, and all disbursements, including the salaries of the paid officials, were subject to annual review by the incoming Council at its first meeting. The general outlook is characterized by extreme discretion and vigilance rather than generosity. On Purim 1661 a poor visitor from Tunis applied for support as he had to provide for his seven daughters. He brought recommendations from the communities of Venice and Livorno. A grant was made on condition that he sets out immediately for Amsterdam. Another applicant was granted eight thalers for his voyage to Amsterdam; two of these were to be given to him on his embarkation, the rest on arrival at his destination. A few days before Pesach 1659 two emissaries appeared from Lublin to describe the terrible experiences of that community. All local synagogues had been destroyed and help was needed for their reconstruction. Following some discussion on the request, it was decided that nothing could be done in this case, since "the present financial difficulties facing our community were due to our frequent charitable efforts in aid of Polish Jewry." But four thalers were allocated to the messengers in respect of their personal expenses. Appeals for Jerusalem were, of course, always given special consideration. On the 1st of Ellul of the same year an envoy from the Holy City delivered letters seeking aid to stem the mounting debts and resultant impoverishment of the community there. It was resolved to remit 150 marks to Venice for this purpose; this amount to include the 126 marks which the Shekel action had realized that year. The rest, as well as 18 marks for traveling expenses, was to be taken from the communal funds. An entry dated Iyyar 1st, 1670, records that a special account was kept for donations to the Holy Land. Four years earlier 1,000 marks had been transmitted. Since then, an additional 1,044 marks had been collected, of which 750 marks were now to be sent there. This sum (which corresponded to an annual average of less than half the rabbi's yearly salary) was to be distributed as follows: Half for Jerusalem, a quarter for Safed, an eighth for Hebron and the remaining eighth for the Portuguese poor. It was decided in future to remit these dues every year, so that those in need would not have to suffer privations owing to delays in dispatching the money. An item which also required regular expenditure was contributions towards the ransoming of Jewish captives. On one occasion such a grant was to benefit a prisoner as far away as Persia.

Finally, reference should be made to a few entries which shed a most interesting light on contemporary events of great historical significance. A minute of the 1st of Teveth, 1665 reads as follows: "We thank the Master of the Universe for the news which has reached us from the Levant, and which has been confirmed from Italy and other regions, that He has vouchsafed His people a Prophet in *Eretz Israel*, the Chacham Rabbi Natan Ashkenazi, and an anointed King, the Chacham Rabbi Shabbatai Zevi, chosen by God to redeem His people from the exile, to honor His name among the nations. . . We trust these tidings because of the many signs and wonders which, as we are informed, have been performed by the Prophet and the King. On this occasion the whole *Hallel* was recited today, with musical accompaniment, as if it was Simchath Torah. A collection for charity realised 405 marks which the Council caused to be distributed by the Treasurer immediately among the poor." Some weeks later the President, following the receipt of further good news from Smyrna, called a few members who lived in his vicinity to a special meeting where it was decided to dispatch envoys to Constantinople to convey the community's homage to "our King, Shabbatai Zevi." Two persons, including the rabbi, were at once elected for this mission. But following complaints by members who had not been invited, that they had not been consulted, the decision had to be rescinded and a full meeting of all members was called by announcement from the *Bimah*. Before this meeting could be held, however, sober thinking replaced the initial enthusiasm. The journey across Europe would take at least three months, by which time "our King" would probably have reached the Holy Land, so that the return of the delegation could not be expected before a year had passed. In these circumstances the Council, at an emergency meeting, felt the great risks and expenses involved were useless, and the planned general meeting was cancelled. A few days later it was decided to reduce the community's debts by offering communal buildings for sale or auction, so as "to prepare for the way which we soon hope to go with the help of God." Nothing further is then recorded of this exciting episode.

Another item of historical interest is reported in the following entry of Cheshvan 9th, 1665: "The Council has learnt that the arrival of Rabbi Sasportas from London is expected every hour. He seeks refuge here from the epidemic which is spreading there. Upon arrival he is to be informed that he and his family must reside outside the limits of the town for at least six weeks, or as long as the Council may determine. Even after that period he must not visit our synagogue without the Executive's permission. May God have mercy upon His people and remove all evil from us!" Two weeks later a meeting was informed that Rabbi Sasportas came to the synagogue on the previous Friday evening, and that he was told to leave and not to visit the community before the lapse of four weeks. A local family that had sheltered the visitor for the night was ordered not to enter the synagogue for eight days. At the same time, a general announcement was made to inform the community that Jews from England, and anyone offering them hospitality in his home, must live in isolation for four weeks.

Of particular interest, too, is a minute of 1658 recording a decision not to call up to the Law, nor to honor with any other "*Mitzvah*" for two years, any person who visits Spain or Portugal, countries which a century and a half earlier had inflicted so much misery upon the Jewish people.

The following entry illustrates the relations with the general local population: "On a date coinciding with Christmas, at the funeral of the late Abraham Senior Teixeira, snowballs and dirt were thrown by the mob at almost all the people in the cortege. Following this demonstration of disrespect and vandalism, a meeting was called five days later when it was resolved to lodge a complaint with the Senate and the Elders, expressing the community's grief and petitioning for protection in the future. . . It was also decided to transmit on behalf of the community twelve loaves of the finest candy-sugar and forty pounds of the best icing-sugar as a gift to the Town Commandant, and as an expression of thanks for arranging for the dispatch of a soldier to restore order among the mob. At the same time it is hoped that he will in future also be ready to defend us. May the God of Israel help us in His mercy and protect us from our enemies."

The years have rolled by with increasing speed since those far-off medieval days. Yet, in comparing our modern communal life with its antecedents three hundred years ago, the similarities seem almost more striking than the contrasts. We may not today limit the number of guests at weddings to thirty-two, but we show the same concern to curb excessive ostentation by those who combine wealth with vanity. Nor would greater modesty in the choice of female dresses displayed at public functions be any less welcome now than it was a dozen generations ago. Lay criticism of communal servants has hardly abated, even if more of it now heard outside the Council chambers than inside. Complaints that the community was exposed to too many appeals continue to this day, but we may be a little consoled to discover that excuses for not giving are not particular to the Jew of the 20th century. We no longer deny the traveler to Spain his *"Aliyah"* in the synagogue, though we might wish that those who survived German beastliness would not now enter into social and commercial relations with the murderers of our people, and forget after one decade what our forbears were expected to remember for fifteen, especially since Spain's crime was dwarfed by the Teutons' satanic infamy.

Thus, Jewish life flows on through the centuries, outwardly ever changing, but fundamentally adhering to the same deathless mold of tradition. Who knows, perhaps if the minutes of our Committee meetings were to be published three hundred years hence, our descendants would look upon our experiences as showing the same pettiness on the one hand and the same greatness on the other, as their own. But, then, we pray the final goal will have been reached long before.

Alliteration in the Bible

B IBLICAL poetry is but rarely characterized by the special features distinguishing verse from prose writings in most modern, and some classical, literatures. Rhyme and metre are replaced by the constant resort to parallelism, either synonymous (by repeating the same idea in similar phrases) or antithetic (by juxtaposing contrasting phrases). A less obvious, but very frequent literary device is to use one or more identical consonants several times in close succession. Such alliterations, which can produce very impressive sound effects, occur with particular frequency in the books of the Prophets, Psalms, and Proverbs, but they are also to be found quite often in almost any other part of Hebrew Scriptures.

The following quotations are among the many more striking examples of this device (the alliterated sounds are underlined):—

פַּחַד וָפַחַת וָפָח (Is. 24:17)

כִּי כְּפָרָה סֹרֵרָה סָרַר יִשְׂרָאֵל (Hos. 4:16)

בֵּרַךְ בָּנַיִךְ בְּקִרְבֵּךְ ... כְּפוֹר כָּאֵפֶר יְפַזֵּר (Ps. 147:13, 16)

אַל תִּלְחַם אֶת לֶחֶם רַע עָיִן ... אַל תִּמְנַע מִנַּעַר מוּסָר
(Prov. 23:6, 13)

Proper names are especially favored as a basis for such alliterative word-plays:

יִשָּׂשכָר חֲמֹר גָּרֶם ... גָּד גְּדוּד יְגוּדֶנּוּ (Gen. 49:14, 19)

שַׁאֲלוּ שְׁלוֹם יְרוּשָׁלָיִם (Ps. 122:6)

קֹהֶלֶת הֲבֵל הֲבָלִים הַכֹּל הָבֶל (Eccl. 1:2)

Published in *The Jewish Chronicle*, August 28, 1953.

Alliterations are met with even in purely legal passages, such as:

שׁוֹפֵךְ דַּם הָאָדָם בָּאָדָם דָּמוֹ יִשָּׁפֵךְ (Gen. 9:6)

וּבְקֻצְרְכֶם אֶת קְצִיר אַרְצְכֶם...וְלֶקֶט קְצִירְךָ לֹא תְלַקֵּט
(Lev. 23:22)

אֲשֶׁר לֹא עָלָה עָלֶיהָ עֹל (Nu. 19:2)

There are also numerous word combinations which have assumed an idiomatic character due, no doubt, to their alliteration. This may explain the almost invariable association of such words as

רֵיחַ נִיחֹחַ, אֶרֶץ מִצְרַיִם, אֲשֶׁר בִּשְׁעָרֶיךָ, וּבְעֶרֶת הָרַע, יַרְדֵּן
יָרֵחוֹ (מִזְרָחָה), חֵלֶק וְנַחֲלָה

to cite a few examples from the Torah only.

While this device serves, in the first instance, mainly of purely euphonic purposes, its detection may sometimes also make an important contribution to the better understanding of the Biblical text. Some expressions, it appears, become fully intelligible only if it is recognised that they were chosen because of the alliterations they contain. Thus, there is only one case in which עברי occurs in a legal context, viz. in the expression עבד עברי which is always used for "Jewish slave." This anomaly has puzzled various commentators (see, e.g., Bachayah on Ex. 21:2). But the otherwise unusual preference of עברי for ישראל or אחיך is easily explained by the alliteration in עבד עברי. A similar consideration may account for the perplexing choice of the verb in the phrase וַיִּקַּח קֹרַח (Nu. 16:1).

In certain instances of alliteration the euphonic element may, indeed, be entirely overshadowed by its exegetical design as a pointer to the deeper meaning of the phrases concerned. A most conspicuous example is furnished by the very opening of the Bible: בְּרֵאשִׁית בָּרָא. Here the word for "created" is not merely alliterated with the expression for "in the beginning," but completely reproduced within it. Clearly this cannot be accidental, and one may assume that it is a striking and deliberate device to indicate that, in the Biblical view, nothing can be conceived "in the beginning" of matter and existence unless the concept of "creation" is literally and essentially an indispensable part of that beginning. The repeated combination of שביעי שבת (seventh . . . Sabbath) may likewise be significant of the identity of association of ideas in the two terms.

In the Song of Moses we find another extraordinary illustration of a similar phenomenon: אמר אויב ארדף אשיג אחלק שלל (Said the enemy; I will pursue, I will overtake, I will divide the spoil). The emphasis here is obviously on the initial א which occurs in five consecutive words. The א as a verbal prefix means "I," and one wonders whether this powerful phrase is not meant to be loudly suggestive of the constant stress on the "ego," the selfishness and vain ambition of the predatory Egyptians in pursuit of Israel. In the English language the tremendous effectiveness of this remarkable alliteration could be recaptured only if it were possible to devise a sentence (with a like meaning) in which five words open with a long "I" without the intrusion of any other initial sounds.

But perhaps the most interesting conclusion to be drawn from the use of alliterated phrases in the Bible concerns the Tetragrammaton. It has often been assumed that the Divine name Y-H-V-H was originally pronounced as it was written, and that the substitution of *Adonai* in its reading was only a later innovation. The following passages show, however, that this hypothesis is untenable and that the traditional practice goes back to the very composition of Biblical texts:

כי יודע א־ד־נ־י דרך צדיקים (Ps. 1:6)

א־ד־נ־י יודע מחשבות אדם חסדך א־ד־נ־י יסעדני (Ps. 94:11, 18)

עיני א־ד־נ־י נצרו דעת (Prov. 22:12)

In all these cases (as also in Ps. 7:18; 8:2; 9:14; and elsewhere)—which occur in contexts containing frequent alliterations—the characteristic rhythm of the verse would be destroyed if the reading of the Tetragrammaton were Y-H-V-H instead of *Adonai* as indicated.

Further researches into this intriguing field would no doubt add much to a fuller appreciation of the Scriptural text and its message. But the few foregoing illustrations and conclusions may suffice to show that by rendering the Bible into a foreign tongue one not merely dims the superb splendor and majesty of the original Hebrew, but completely obscures many of its most effective instruments to stir the reader and to stimulate and fashion his thought.

The Jewish "Eved"* Legislation

A Guide to Treating Social Diseases

THE Jewish laws concerning slavery afford an interesting and illuminating insight into the social system of the Torah. They have aroused a good deal of opposition among its detractors and elicited much apologetic defense among its protagonists. That Judaism should have countenanced the legal subjection of one human being to another grates on the mentality of the twentieth century. On the other hand, that legislation contains many unique and highly progressive feaures. On reflection it may be seen that there are, in fact, few Jewish teachings offering more useful and practical correctives to the social maladies inherent in contemporary society than those laws. A detailed study of this subject, viewed in the light of modern conditions, would therefore merit some serious attention.

Early Suspension of Eved-Laws

While the laws affecting the non-Jewish slave are still technically in force,[1] the institution of the "Hebrew *eved*" was suspended as early as the eighth century B.C.E. The Torah

Unpublished—written in 1945.

*The Hebrew word *eved* and its derivatives are used to denote "service" of God (Nu. 8:19; Deut. 28:47) or man (Jer. 22:13), as well as "subjugation" (Gen. 15:13) or constructive "work" generally (Ex. 20:9; Deut. 15:19). Its precise meaning can therefore only be determined from the context in which it occurs. "Servant" or "slave" as a translation of *eved* may, as will be shown, be almost misnomers; they are here used only for want of a better term in English.

decrees that "he shall serve with you until the Jubilee year;"[2] hence, with the cessation of that observance there ceased also the laws regarding the Hebrew servant, as he was entitled to its benefits.[3] The Jubilee year, in turn, could only be observed as long as it was possible that "every man shall return to his inheritance,"[4] i.e. as long as all Israelitic tribes were in full possession of their land; that observance, and with it the *eved ivri* legislation, therefore lapsed with the exile of some tribes by Sannaherib.[5] That this corresponds to historical fact is attested to by Josephus. He records that Herod introduced a law for the sale of Jewish thieves abroad,[6] evidently since they could no longer be sold as slaves to fellow-Jews, as provided for in the Torah.[7]

Nevertheless, the spirit and lofty principles of these laws which regulated social relations should be observed even today.[8] With this in mind, as well as the added consideration that they form an integral part of the Divine will as revealed in the Torah, is it possible to explain the extraordinary fact —without parallel in the world's legal literature—that many centuries after these regulations had fallen into desuetude were the Biblical commandments concerning slavery fully discussed, greatly expanded and ultimately codified for practical use in Talmudic and rabbinic writings.

Judaism's Opposition to Slavery

In principle Judaism strongly discountenances slavery in any form. "A person does not belong to himself that he may sell himself as a slave,"[9] "for the children of Israel are servants unto Me, My servants. . . ."[10] Anyone who voluntarily enters[11] or extends such enslavement to man is therefore considered a transgressor against this fundamental declaration,[12] and against the Second Commandment, which ordains that "there shall not be unto you any other gods before Me."[13] One's domestic company should consist of poor people rather than of servants, for slavery demoralizes not only the slave, but the master, too.[14] To emphasize the ideal of human freedom the laws protecting the slave head the social legislation in the Torah, just as the promulgation of God as the Liberator of Israel "from the house of slaves" is the first among the Ten Commandments.[15] The enslavement of fellow-Jews was one of the factors which caused the disintegration of the Jewish state and the exile of its inhabitants,[16] and the redemption from Egypt—leading to Jewish independence and sovereignty—aimed primarily at securing the freedom of the individual.[17] This is another reason for the precedence given (among the social statutes in the Torah) to the laws enforcing the release of slaves through the observance of which alone Israel would be worthy of liberation.[18]

The Jewish attitude to slavery is most significantly expressed by the terms used to describe the two main categories of slaves. The Jewish bondman is, throughout the Bible and Talmud, always referred to as *eved ivri,* meaning "Hebrew servant." Nowhere in the legal portions of the Torah and rabbinic literature is a Jew ever called *Hebrew;* he is invariably *Israel.* The difference between the two terms is that the former connotes merely the racial origin and attachment of the Jew, whereas the latter is the name of honor given to the people that accepted the Divine law. A Jew sold into slavery to another cannot be a true "Israelite"; he is simply a "Hebrew."[19] Again, the non-Jewish slave, *"eved" par excellence* in the Torah,[20] is known as *eved k'naani* meaning "Canaanite servant" in the Talmud and rabbinic works. This is all the more remarkable since a racial descendant of Canaan, being among the Holy Land's original inhabitants who were to be completely exterminated,[21] could never be accepted as a slave in a Jewish household.[22] Non-Jewish servants could thus only be bought if they originated abroad, and they had to be other than Canaanites.[23] Characteristically enough, then, the Jewish servant bears the lowest designation for Jew, in the same way as his non-Jewish counterpart is characterized as the "Canaanite," the most debased of the non-Jewish races, doomed to eternal serfdom.[24]

The Jewish opposition to slavery, based on the sovereignty of God and the dignity of man, is carried much further by the actual laws governing the slaves' status and their right to sell themselves as such. As we shall see below, the Torah legislation has, to all intents and purposes, almost completely proscribed slavery of any kind. Such conditions of servitude as it does permit excel the social level and standards presently enjoyed by the average employee in contemporary Western society.

The following is an attempt to summarize the laws concerning the different types of slavery, and to interpret them in the light of the social conditions of our time.

I. The Hebrew Servant

There are three different legal classes that come under the heading of the "Hebrew servant": (a) The person who voluntarily sells himself into slavery because of extreme destitution;[25] (b) the thief who is compulsorily sold into slavery because he is unable to pay compensation for his theft;[7] and (c) the minor girl who is sold by her father because of his extreme poverty.[26]

Conditions of Sale

A person may not sell himself[27] or his daughter,[28] unless he is literally penniless and has no clothing or food whatsoever. The money which he then receives in return must be used exclusively for the purchase of food; it may not serve to pay his debts.[27] If he transgressed the law, and the sale took place under any other circumstances, it is absolutely null and void, even if the would-be servant intended to use the proceeds toward the fulfillment of a *mitzvah*, e.g. to marry.[29]

The only other possibility of a Jew being sold into servitude is that of a thief who cannot restore his theft or its value to the victim; he alone is forced into slavery by Jewish law.[30] But to effect such a sale a number of stringent conditions must be fulfilled. If the thief possesses assets, but is unwilling to pay them, the court may garnish the amount due and turn it over, by force if necessary, as restitution to the aggrieved party.[31] Under such circumstances, his sale as a servant ordered by the court is invalid.[32] Although a thief must normally restore twice the value of his theft,[33] he is sold only to redeem the capital involved; the rest remains as a debt to be paid when he achieves solvency after his eventual release.[34] Hence, if his personal value as a slave exceeds that of the object he stole, he cannot be sold.[35] Nor can he be forced into slavery if he misappropriated possessions belonging to a non-Jew or the Temple Treasury, i.e. national or state property.[36] Finally, he cannot be sold for a second term of servitude if he twice stole from the same Jewish individual.[37] In all such cases he must pay the compensation due as soon as he can afford it.[38] It is evident that these conditions, whether they affect a voluntary or an involuntary sale, are so restrictive as to virtually eliminate the possibility of enslavement altogether.

Objects of Slavery

The institution of slavery among Jews is not designed as an economic expedient at the disposal of the wealthy. Jewish slaves must be treated far more considerately than free employees;[39] it is, therefore, more to the advantage of a potential master to engage the services of an ordinary freeman at a fixed rate of payment than to contract a bond of legal servitude with him. Such a bond, as we shall see, involves all the liabilities of a legal adoption in our days, but only a restricted number of the benefits normally accruing to an employer of labor. If the economy of Jewish society requires bondmen, these should be drawn from the ranks of non-Jews;[40] but even their enslavement is, as will be shown, subject to far-reaching modifications. The laws regulating the conditions, status and treatment of Jewish servants, however, are meant primarily to protect and promote the latters' interests.

Slavery as Punishment

All forms of slavery are regarded as either direct or indirect punishments for specific social offences aiming at the rehabilitation of certain types of criminals. Take, for example, the thief who preys on the public rather than learning and practicing a gainful occupation that would give him the bare necessities of life. Such a person is forced by the court to work his way back to solvency through slavery. On the other hand, economic exigencies compelling a man to sell his daughter or himself in order to eke out a living are considered by our sages to be the result of his own callous disregard (by not leaving his field unoccupied during the Sabbatical year) and exploitation (by charging interest for loans) of the poor.[41] The entire *eved*-legislation is governed by this supreme consideration for the ultimate redemption of such offenders and their rehabilitation as useful members of society.

Combating Poverty

Under normal conditions, every citizen should, through the application of skill, thrift, and industry, be able to provide for his minimum needs. (In abnormal circumstances, i.e. when the Jewish people do not securely occupy their land, these laws are altogether suspended, as we have noted above.) If he cannot, it is more than likely that he lacks the stamina, will, training or know-how to face life constructively. He requires the sympathetic guidance with which his home and environment had failed to provide him. A new home, in which he will enjoy all the privileges afforded to the other members of the family and at the same time be encouraged in the practice of some productive but not oppressive work, would be secured for him. Thus, by balancing rights and duties in a congenial home environment, the Jewish *eved*-legislation had as its object to foster self-respct in the self-indulgent delinquent, to enable him to counteract the corroding effects of his idleness, and the better to rid himself of his anti-social disposition. In short, his social disease must be cured; he must go through a process of reeducation, showing him how best to cope with his economic problems by first learning how to help solve those of others. He must see how a normal, healthy life is led. This, in brief, is the object of his servitude.

The Insolvent Thief and the Self-Sold Slave

Such cure is of use only in the case of persons who are genuinely ignorant of how to earn their living by honest effort. That excludes the thief who possesses sufficient means to meet his needs, yet seeks to enrich himself through crime. He must be punished in a different way. Only he who is genuinely destitute and feels that he is compelled to gain his daily bread by stealing is forced into slavery.

The case of the voluntary slave is not quite analogous. He, too, is quite impoverished. But he could and should have sought better means to get on to his feet again than by sacrificing some of his or his daughter's personal freedom, especially as we assume[41] that he was once perfectly solvent. We, therefore, have less sympathy for him than for the one whose action was, after all, not voluntary but enforced by judicial authority. Hence the latter enjoys more benefits than the self-sold slave, though their treatment is, in most respects, the same. In general, this explains the divergence between the two classes of servants, summarized below.

Status

The personal status of the Hebrew slave is scarcely compromised by his bondage. Unlike his non-Jewish counterpart, he is in no way regarded as the personal property of his master;[42] he therefore possesses ownership rights.[43] If he suffers bodily harm at the hand of his master or anyone else, he must be paid compensation like any other freeman.[44] Altogether, he enjoys complete equality with all Jews before the law,[45] and he must conform to the same observances and injunctions of Judaism, with only one possible exception,[46] which will be dealt with later.

Period of Service

The normal duration of service is for six years or until the advent of the Jubilee year, whichever is the shorter period.[47] The rule applies also, according to prevailing opinion,[48] to the self-sold slave, though he is at liberty to pledge himself for a longer period, so long as it does not extend into or beyond the Jubilee year.[49] An escaped slave must, on his recapture, make up for his absence, unless the Jubilee year intervenes;[50] but he then loses his right to the "parting-gift,"[51] and he must also, according to one view, compensate his master as payment for a debt he owes.[52] In the case of illness, the servant must remain in bondage beyond the period stipulated and make good for the time lost only if he was completely incapacitated for at least four years out of six; otherwise he must be released at the expiration of his term of service, even if he was merely fit for light needlework.[53] If the master died the slave must be set free at once, unless the master left a son. A daughter or a brother cannot inherit him.[54] In the case of a proselyte or a non-Jewish master's death, freedom must always immediately be granted him.[55]

Extension of Service

No voluntary slave, whether male[56] or female,[57] can renew the period of service after its expiration by going through the special ceremony which enables the judicially sold servant to remain in his master's service upon the lapse of the first six years. That ceremony, which takes the form of the master himself piercing his slave's right ear at a door or door post,[58] is meant to be a forceful reminder of the Jewish opposition to slavery. The door post is a "witness"[12] to Israel's liberation from Egypt to make the service of God possible,[59] and the ear is branded as the offending organ which did not listen to the charter of freedom given at Mount Sinai.[12, 13] Even the slave sold by the court can avail himself of this provision, but only under very exceptional circumstances. It cannot be granted unless both master and servant (a) are married and have children, (b) love each other, and (c) are healthy.[60] To prevent any misunderstanding, the slave must address two explicit requests to his master to be allowed to stay. These must be reiterated immediately before the six years have run their course.[61] His servitude is thereby prolonged until the advent of the Jubilee year,[62] or the master's death, the son being in this case unable to inherit the slave.[63] Clearly, this concession is based on the realization that the maintenance of such cordial and mutually affectionate relations between master and servant is to the interest of the latter. For, notwithstanding the fact that he enjoys full health and the company of his own family, he refuses to make himself independent from his master's generosity. Since a servant must, upon his release, be in a position to return to his former station and occupation,[64] this act cannot be performed on a priest, as the resultant blemish would disqualify him from his service in the Temple.[65]

Treatment of Slaves

The relationship between master and slave is summed up in the following significant[66] formula: The *eved* must be treated as a brother, but he should behave as a servant when working.[67] The Torah repeatedly enjoins the master to regard his *eved* as "your brother,"[68] and this consideration permeates the extensive legislation governing his treatment. Thus he must be sold in private and in an honorable manner.[69] Special care must be taken to preserve his personal dignity. He must not be engaged in performing degrading work, such as that of a batman carrying his master's utensils to the bath, or taking off his shoes.[70] Only a free Jew, who acts on his own unfettered will, may be thus employed.[71]

For the same reason,[72] it is also forbidden to impose upon him work which (a) is meant to keep the servant occupied but is not in itself essential or productive and (b) is without a clearly defined time limit. For example, the servant must not be told to "pick grapes until I come."[73] His work also precludes other than domestic labor. For agricultural or skilled labor he is to be paid separately "as a hireling,"[74] according to Rashi.

The treatment of the *eved* as a "brother" implies also his complete equality with his master as regards food, clothing and accommodation[75]—a most revolutionary advance even over modern employment conditions. This goes so far as to require the master to forego his rights to a cushion in favor of his slave, if there is only one to spare between them.[76] The proverbial phrase that "He who buys a Hebrew slave is as if he acquired a master over himself" is expressive of this sentiment.[77] A master is thus fully responsible for the upkeep of his servant and the latter's family. He must not be told to procure his sustenance by his own efforts.[78] If the servant fell ill, all expenses for his treatment and cure must likewise be paid for him, and the master can lodge no claim for compensation, however high his outlay, even after the slave's release.[79]

The Servant's Family

The master's liabilities extend also to the provision of clothing[80] and food for the slave's legitimate wife and children, unless the marriage took place after the sale against his master's wishes.[81] This obligation clearly exceeds that which is legally binding on a husband in normal circumstances.[82] The responsibility for the children's maintenance extends, according to varying authorities, up to the age of six,[83] or twelve years,[84] or even after they have attained their majority.[85] Nevertheless, this duty does not entitle the master to claim the profits of the wife's or children's work. Such earnings go to the slave, not the master.[86] But Nachmanides, against the view of Maimonides, not unreasonably holds that this applies only when the servant's dependents are not maintained by the master.[87]

A judicially sold slave may be forced by his master to marry a non-Jewish bondwoman, in order to produce non-Jewish slaves,[88] provided he already had a Jewish wife and children.[89] But the master cannot compel him to have intimate relations with the bondwoman, if he prefers to live with his Jewish wife; the choice rests with the servant.[90] Since he can remain with the non-Jewess only during the period of his service,[91] he may wish to perpetuate his bondage, against the ideals of the Torah, in view of his natural attachment to her children; that consideration may conceivably explain why he can be given such a bondwoman only in addition to a Jewish wife, thus making it less likely that he will oppose his eventual release and the resultant separation from his non-Jewish partner.[92]

The self-sold slave, however, cannot be so treated.[93] But this restriction applies, in the view of one authority, only to the compulsion, not to the permission, of the servant to live with a non-Jewish bondwoman.[94]

The Parting Gift

Jewish slaves or bondwomen must not be released empty-handed.[95] The master must provide them with a free gift worth at least thirty Shekalim,[96] corresponding to the monetary value of the average slave.[97] It appears that the court can exert pressure, including force if necessary, to compel a master to fulfill this duty.[98] The amount stated is the minimum which must be given, irrespective of the value of the slave's services; but it should be increased according to the benefits which the master derived from those services.[99] As was noted above,[50] the servant loses his rights only, if he had previously escaped. The gift is evidently designed to enable the freed servant to rehabilitate himself. This gratuity must therefore not be used to pay any debts he had incurred,[100] just as "charity"—serving the same purpose of preventing rather than relieving poverty[101]—must not be so expended.[102] In the view of Rashi,[103] however, only the master is absolved from the obligation of satisfying claims made upon his slave by diverting part of the gift to creditors. But the creditors may collect their due from the slave himself, once the assets are in his hand.[104] Whether the self-sold slave is also entitled to the parting-gift is a matter of dispute in the Talmud[105] and among later rabbinic authorities.[106] Two reasons have been suggested for thus putting the self-sold slave at a disadvantage: (a) to discourage people from selling themselves as slaves[107] by putting a penalty on voluntary enslavement,[108] and (b) the fact that the self-sold servant has already received, and presumably still possesses, the equivalent of the gift (i.e. his own monetary value) which he obtained from the master at the time of his sale; whereas the slave sold by the court, who had to pay that amount as compensation to the victim of his theft,[109] would be left penniless upon his release but for the parting gift.[110]

This law, too, is based on the parallel between the freeing of slaves and the liberation of Israel from Egypt;[111] for God also compelled the Egyptians to reward their former slaves upon their emancipation.[112]

Sale of Slaves to Non-Jews

It is forbidden to sell oneself to a non-Jew, though such a sale, if made, is valid.[113] But it is a duty to ransom him, so that he shall not be lost in his non-Jewish environment.[114] This obligation, which is enforced by the court, devolves upon his relatives, precedence being given to the nearest and, in the case of their failure to do so, upon every Jew.[115] Nevertheless, if he is not ransomed, he remains in servitude until the Jubilee year;[116] but his fellow-Jews must ensure that he is not ill-treated or unduly chastised by his non-Jewish master.[117] A judicially-sold slave may under no circumstances be placed with a non-Jew.[118]

Women are not permitted to acquire male slaves, whether Jewish or non-Jewish, so as not to arouse suspicion.[119]

No proselyte can be bought as a slave.[120]

Jewish Bondwomen

A woman cannot be sold for theft.[121] It is disputed whether she can sell herself[122] or not,[123] the Talmud apparently supporting the latter view.[124]

The Hebrew bondwoman mentioned in the Torah is a girl under the age of twelve sold by her father[125] under the circumstances described above.[28] The laws regarding her status (vis-à-vis her master) and treatment are the same as those that apply to the male slave,[126] except for the following provisions. As soon as the father can afford it[127] he must ransom her. If necessary the court may force him to do so against his will,[128] because such servitude is a discredit to her family.[129] The Hebrew bondwoman enjoys all the benefits of the different classes of slaves without sharing any of their corresponding disadvantages. Thus her contract cannot exceed six years,[130] like that of the judicially sold slave,[47] her period of service cannot be extended,[57] in common with the self-sold slave.[56] Nor can she be inherited by the master's son upon the latter's death,[131] as is the case of the servant whose term has been extended.[62] In addition she must also be set free as soon as she reaches physical maturity at the age of twelve.[132] Unlike the self-sold slave,[105] she is entitled to the parting gift,[133] as her father's action in selling her is, in this respect, regarded like that of the court forcing a slave into servitude.[134]

But the chief object of her sale should be her eventual marriage to her master or his son, an obligation which takes precedence over the duty to ransom her.[135] Hence, she cannot be sold to a person with whom or with whose son such a marriage must not be entered.[136] This union must, of course, have her own full consent.[137] Although the ceremony is, in view of her previous contract, somewhat simpler than an ordinary marriage, she requires *chuppah* and thereupon becomes a wife like any other.[138] In fact, a number of important matrimonial laws applying to all marriages are derived from the legislation regarding her treatment as a wife.[139]

Social Significance of Eved Ivri Legislation

The above summary presents a model order of social relations between employer and employee founded on equity, fellowship and mutual service and expressed in highly practical terms. But, as was seen above, the code's main object is the reclamation and rehabilitation of asocial elements. It is this aspect of the law that requires some further elucidation, representing as it does a most significant Jewish contribution to the treatment of criminals.

Here we shall restrict ourselves to the indigent thief. In modern society such an offender is usually sentenced to varying terms of imprisonment. That penalty serves a purely punitive and deterrent purpose, without making any attempt at eliminating those social conditions that led to the commission of the crime. This system necessarily shows five distinct shortcomings: (a) Imprisonment is not likely to improve the moral stance of the criminal, which alone can bring about his regeneration. His criminal environment, his expulsion from a socially healthy community, and his enforced idleness together combine to turn the prisoner into a sullen, hardened criminal who will nurse a perpetual grievance against society. (b) The imprisonment of the breadwinner inflicts unjust punishment and misery upon his family, leading to unfair hardship during his absence and to the possibility of domestic disharmony upon his return. (c) Imprisonment imposes a heavy burden on the law-abiding citizen who, as taxpayer, is forced to contribute toward the upkeep of the criminal. (d) Imprisonment can give little satisfaction to the victim of the crime, whose losses are not thereby made good. And finally (e), the indigent prisoner is, upon his release, left without any financial means to rehabilitate himself. He is thus induced to renew his predatory activities, and the prospects are that he may be more successful in the next attempts, having received expert guidance from his criminal companions during his first term of detention.

The Jewish legal system, is, therefore, free from any imprisonment as a *penal* institution. Jewish law provides for imprisonment only (a) to keep a criminal in custody pending his trial,[140] (b) to protect society from a proven murderer who cannot be judicially executed for lack of direct, non-circumstantial evidence or other reasons,[141] and (c) to protect a murderer from the vengeance of the victim's relatives by confining him, together with his teacher,[142] to a "city of refuge" until the death of the High Priest.[143] But, in view the inadequacy of imprisonment as a means of reform, it is never effectuated as a purely penal measure.

One of the alternatives devised by Jewish law is the offender's virtual adoption by a Jewish family enforced by judicial order. The strict regulations regarding the servant's treatment and the many privileges which must be extended to him presuppose that the master is fairly comfortable (he cannot otherwise afford to keep a slave on equal terms for rather light work only, as demanded by law) and of a kindly temperament. In this way the Jewish legal system avoids the five drawbacks of imprisonment mentioned above. (a) The thief, by being placed in a normal socially healthy and decent atmosphere, is trained in the art of making an honest living as a useful member of society. He enjoys and is shown the advantages of civilized living. (b) During his servitude his family is fully maintained at his master's expense.[80-87] (c) The law-abiding community is not charged with the maintenance of the criminal element in its midst. The expenses incurred by the master are commensurate with the benefits he derives from his slave's services. (d) Judicial enslavement provides the victim of the theft with full compensation for his loss.[109] (e) The servant, upon release, is not left destitute, but must be given the financial means necessary for his rehabilitation.

The *eved ivri* legislation of Judaism thus stands out as the first, uncompromising protest against human slavery as it was known and practiced without any opposition by all nations, civilized or otherwise, until modern times. However much a Jew sins, he remains a Jew;[144] and even the most depraved criminal is still a child of God[145] and must be treated as such. His claim to human dignity is inviolable. The morally weak, more than anyone else, needs to be looked upon as an equal. Only thus can he be taught to regard his fellowmen, not as obstacles curbing his freedom to live on their loot, but as equal partners whose welfare predicates his own. This is the spirit which these laws seek to cultivate.

Poverty and crime are the two most disruptive elements of a healthy society. These evils, gnawing at the roots of social justice and peace, can only be combatted by restoring a feeling of self-respect to the economically dispossessed or the morally degraded. Freedom is a treasured gift, but some will abuse it (the criminal) while others will be unable to utilize its opportunities (the poor), preferring economic dependence—charity. These classes must be shown freedom's assets by temporarily experiencing its partial negation—affecting not their rank but their choice of work. Therein lay the crucial cause of their lapse—the failure to use work as a means of honest self-sufficiency and cooperative betterment of human relations and conditions. Work is not a burden, a painful prerequisite for gain; it is and means a "service" (*Avoda* in Hebrew). That is what the *eved* is to be taught by becoming a "serving" member of society and the human family. Thus only will his six-year ("week-day") period of enforced "service" lead him to the appreciation of true freedom—his "Sabbath."[146]

II. THE NON-JEWISH SERVANT

The *eved k'naani* legislation rests on an entirely different foundation. It serves a reformatory purpose only in a very limited and purely religious sense. Its primary object is, as we have observed,[40] to be found in the economic sphere only. The laws regulating the terms of service of the non-Jew are therefore confined to (a) protecting his interests, and (b) raising his spiritual level. In order fully to understand the disparity between Jewish and non-Jewish slaves, it would be necessary to examine thoroughly the relations between Jews and non-Jews in Jewish law.[147] We are here merely concerned with the social aspect of those relations, and not with the wider issue it raises.

But even the social aspect cannot be considered in isolation from its religio-moral implications. To appreciate the position of the non-Jewish bondman from the Jewish point of view, one must realize that Judaism regards the service of God as the dominant and over-all aim of life. It measures true personal freedom only in terms of the degree to which the individual succeeds in emancipating himself from the grip of his innate passions and impulses by exchanging such slavery to one's lower self for the subjugation to the will of God.[148] "The righteous dominates his passions, the wicked is dominated by them"[149] sums up the Jewish attitude to absolute freedom. Any other encroachment upon a person's freedom is purely relative to this over-riding principle. This conception governs the Jewish approach toward the often conflicting claims of individual liberty and religio-national discipline in the Jewish constitutional theory: Judaism permits no active breaches of the law, social or religious, on the grounds of conscientious objection.

A non-Jew, then, who sacrifices some of his personal freedom in return for rising in moral stature by a more comprehensive submission to the Divine law, is thought to profit considerably by a net gain of real freedom. The partial loss of social freedom must be weighed against the advantage of moral freedom accruing from the more complete observance of the Divine law.

Religious Status

The non-Jewish servant must fulfill the same religious duties as a Jewess, [150] i.e. he must observe all negative commandments and such positive precepts as need be performed within certain limited periods of time.[151] It is further the duty of the master, or, if he fails to do so, the court, to have the slave circumcized;[152] he is then accepted "under the wings of God"[153] in the same way as a proselyte.[154] Like all Jews, he also becomes subject to the penalties laid down in the Torah for offenses committed against the laws of Judaism; but one rabbinic opinion disputes this.[155] The servant cannot be forced to submit to circumcision or any Jewish observances;[156] but if he refuses, he may not be retained for more than twelve months,[157] unless that was expressly stipulated in the original contract.[158]

By accepting the greater part of the Jewish law, the slave becomes an integral part of the family with whom he serves. As such as he is entitled to enjoy the benefits of the Sabbath-,[159] festivals-[160] and Jubilee year-legislations;[161] to have a share in the paschal sacrifice[162] and such other offerings, tithes, etc. as are due to his master.[163] In fact, these benefits were specifically designed to make him feel "like you" an equal.[164] Such slaves are, therefore, considered to be spiritually the highest of the three religious classes of non-Jews (the other two being those who accept and those who do not, the seven basic "noachidic laws" of humanity). The resultant freedom far outweighs the social disabilities to which they are subject.

Personal Status

In contrast to the Jewish servant,[42] the non-Jewish slave is technically regarded as the personal possession of his master;[165] hence he has no property rights and his acquisitions automatically belong to his master.[166] But these possessive powers do not extend to the personality of the slave;[167] he cannot be harmed[168] or killed, by man[169] or beast,[170] with impunity. In fact, the provisions for judicially avenging the blood of free Jews include the non-Jewish servant.[171]

Thus, while the murder of non-Jewish freemen was not originally punished by death at the hands of a court—our relations with them being based on reciprocity,[172] the killing of a non-Jewish slave is so punished, because of his religious attachment to the Jewish people.[173] A master beating his own slave to death is executed, unless death ensued twenty-four hours or more after the assault,[174] as we may assume that there was then no deliberate intention to kill him.[175] But, according to Maimonides, this exception applies only if death was caused by a chastizing rod, not by any other instrument.[176] Anyone else, however, killing a non-Jewish slave is invariably guilty of a capital crime,[177] in common with the murderer of a free Jew. Similarly, if a slave was gored to death the ox must be killed and compensation must be paid at the rate of the average value of a slave, [178] which is the same as that of a Jewess,[179] in view of their common religious obligations.[180]

Regarding the infliction of pain or injuries, the legal position of the non-Jewish slave is, in principle, the same as that of an ordinary Jew. The punishment for hitting a Jewish freeman is thirty-nine lashes with a whip, if the injury sustained cannot be measured in monetary terms;[181] otherwise the compensation which must be paid to the victim exempts the offender from corporal punishment.[182] The same rule applies to striking someone else's slave, though his master receives the compensation due,[183] as he himself has no ownership rights.[166] In the case of a master hitting his own servant, no compensation can be paid,[184] as there is no recipient.[185] Hence there are authorities holding that in such cases the master always suffers corporal punishment, irrespective of the monetary value of the pain caused, since there can never be any exemption from payment of compensation.[186] That would give the slave even greater protection than a freeman. Here again his status is determined by his religious loyalties which mark him as "your brother."[187] Moreover, if a permanent injury was inflicted upon him he must, as will be seen below, be immediately released, since in the absence of possessive rights, there is no other way of compensating him.[188]

Treatment

While it is legally permissible to impose harder work upon a non-Jewish slave than may be exacted from a Jewish bondman,[189] he must be treated with every consideration for his human dignity. The Torah has allowed him to be used for service, not humiliation.[190] Thus, no unduly hard work should be given him, nor should he in any way be oppressed. His food should be like one's own, and served to him before one's own. He should be decently spoken to and a sympathetic ear should be given to his arguments. For cruelty and harshness are not to be found among the children of Abraham whose characteristics are that they are merciful, chaste, and charitable.[191]

Since any neglect of the slave's needs will impair his capacity to work or lead him to escape, which would adversely affect the master's material interests, the latter is not legally bound to maintain him;[192] but in the unlikely case of a master's refusal to feed him, his sustenance becomes the charge of the Jewish community who are bound to look after the needs of the servants in their midst.[193] But in times of economic distress, when the servant cannot count on communal support, the responsibility for his maintenance devolves fully upon his master.[194] That the slave should be treated as a member of the family with whom he serves, entitled to the full participation in all its festivities and privileges, has already been noted.[159-164]

Conditions of Release

In principle it is a positive commandment of the Torah[195] to keep non-Jewish slaves in permanent bondage,[196] though that law has not apparently the same force as other biblical precepts.[197] But there are numerous circumstances which make a slave's release possible or imperative. Thus he can be set free if his freedom serves a religious purpose; for instance, if he is required to make up a congregational quorum (*Minyan*), although that is merely a rabbinical requirement.[198] In the following main cases liberation is enforced by the court: (a) If the slave sustained a permanent, visible and deliberate injury at the hands of his master;[199] (b) if the servant could not otherwise establish a family, such as in the case of a jointly owned slave who is released by one of his masters and who—being partly free and partly enslaved—may thus not marry either a free or a bonded woman;[200] (c) if the master asked his slave to perform an act not incumbent upon non-Jewish slaves, e.g. to wear phylacteries or to read the Law in public;[201] (d) if continued slavery in the case of a non-Jewish bondwoman may lead to immorality;[202] and (e) if the slave was sold to a non-Jewish master.[203] Palestine, even today, occupies a special place in the slavery legislation, and a non-Jewish servant can at any time demand to go there; in that case the master is compelled either himself to take him there or to sell him to someone else who will do so.[204] Hence freedom must also be granted (f) if a Palestinian slave was sold abroad;[205] and (g) if a slave escaped to Palestine.[206] Such a liberated slave has the right to settle anywhere in Palestine,[207] except in Jerusalem;[208] for whilst the Land of Israel is to be shared out among the Jewish and non-Jewish residents alike,[209] Jerusalem should be kept free from strangers.[210] But in every other respect an emancipated slave enjoys the same status and privileges as any other proselyte; in fact, he must be shown even greater consideration in view of his servile mentality resulting from his previous enslavement.[211]

There are, therefore, ample opportunities for a slave's release despite the general ban on such action. In fact, the Talmud records the case of Rabbi Gamliel who was over-joyed when one of the above exigencies occurred giving him a legitimate pretext for liberating his slave.[212]

Judaism and Democracy

Of all the great ideals making up whatever is best in "Western Civilization", it is only democracy which does not derive its entire inspiration from the creations of the Hebraic genius

Published in *Chayenu* (London), December 1947.

and heritage. Social justice, human equality and freedom, the education of the masses; all these first found expression in the literature and history of Israel. Democracy, however, as its name implies, is essentially the legacy of ancient Greece. This admission does not mean that there is no democratic element in the Jewish conception of government, nor does it wish to suggest that Judaism views this vital aspect of human relations with unconcerned neutrality; but it does turn the contemporary notion of democracy into an idea which is largely foreign to Jewish teachings. Perhaps it is, therefore, just in this field that Judaism, especially through its now anticipated return to the political and constitutional arena of world affairs, can make its most significant contribution to modern thought and the solution of present-day world problems.

Jewish History v. Democracy

Democracy, in its simplest and truest analysis, means the rule of the people as determined and enforced by the will of the majority. Judaism and Jewish history predominantly express the ultimate triumph of the minority. It is no chance coincidence that since the emergence of Abraham as the first progenitor of Israel and its faith, leadership was almost exclusively vested in the younger, and thus "minor" or weaker, element. The choice of Isaac, Jacob, Judah and Joseph, Moses, David, Solomon, Judah Maccabeus and many others was invariably made in deference to an older brother or brothers. The Jewish people itself was chosen "not because of their number" but as "the fewest of all peoples."[213] Indeed Israel's perennial survival affords the best illustration for history's choice of a minority destined to vanquish superior numbers and power. We celebrate the deliverance of "the many into the hands of the few," and Jewish tenacity has, as the Midrash already pointed out,[214] consistently defied the principle whereby right is decided by the majority.

The Moral Problem

Judaism sees in the democratic order a certain challenge to fundamental moral principles. Basically, democracy represents a mere extension of the maxim "might is right." What, if not power, necessarily the result of superior numbers, should otherwise give the majority the prerogative for having its views and decisions turned into law and imposed by force upon the minority? There can, in the last resort, be no justification; for "the many are not wise,"[215] that is, wisdom does not inevitably bear any relation to numerical strength. Only might does.

Again, the absolute rule of the majority in an imperfect society must of necessity stifle moral progress. If the masses who are to be raised ever higher towards the ideal level of the moral law, are themselves the ultimate masters and creators of that law, its administration and enforcement, how can any moral advance of the human society be achieved? The mass of mankind under the law ensures their gradual progress towards its standards; the law under the mass of mankind must result in its gradual retrogression towards their standards.

The Religious Problem

Closely related to the moral issue is the religious problem. Albo succinctly expresses this when he says that right and wrong "cannot be determined by the consent of the masses, who will sometimes concur with the perversion of the truth; therefore it is proper that arbitration should be exercised by scholars only, for wisdom is a Divine gift."[216] God and man cannot rule over identical realms—as long, at least, as the Divine and human conceptions of right and wrong are not identical. To quote Albo again: "If we were to assume that we should go after what corresponds to the will of the majority in such matters, we should have to reject the teachings of Prophets and saints alike."[217] These twin issues of the absolute values of morality and religion as opposed to the arbitrary standards of majority decisions determine, as will be shown, the constitutional legislation of Judaism.

The International Problem of Today

Every national majority, under a democratic system, enjoys supreme sovereignty in all matters affecting its external as well as internal conduct. Such a system will ensure law and order within, as it places a potentially insurgent minority at the mercy and under the domination of the majority which controls the unit's legislative and executive organs of government. The minority is effectively disarmed.

It is different in the international arena. Democracy concedes to every nation the right to determine its own code of conduct as decided by popular vote. The average individual, if he were not restrained by national laws backed by police force, would no doubt act primarily on the impulse of self-interest, which would thus largely become the determining factor of his conduct. The popular vote—resting, as it does, on the will of the average individual—is therefore likely similarly to be based on self-interest. And the interests of one national group of people must obviously often be opposed by those of another. But this time the nation is not disarmed; conflicting interests, which must exist, must, therefore, lead to armed contests, which need not exist, if factors other than self-interest were to determine national behaviour. That, in a democracy, is impossible.

Judaism, to solve these problems, provides a unique system of government. It virtually identifies the moral (and religious), juridical and political administration, with regard to place[218] time[219] and personnel.[220] The dispensation of justice, according to the Jewish constitution, is thus no longer part of a government's duties, but the establishment and effective functioning of a government is a part of the duties of "judges," who themselves are merely the administrators, not the creators, of a supreme code of laws which is sovereign because it is Divine. In other words, the stimulus to man's moral progress is not left to the ineffective sermons of the pulpit but placed under the direct control of the legislative and executive organs of government. In this way, Judaism surrenders power to the law, and not the law to power as does democracy. If universally applied, this system would also render wars impossible, or at least less likely, by replacing politicians—pandering to public opinion governed by self-interest—by saints and scholars who, whatever their nationality, will owe allegiance to the same, or at least similar, supreme moral standards of conduct the world over.

The Democratic Element of the Jewish Constitution

While Judaism cannot admit the infallibility of the majority implicit in democracy, it recognises that unrestricted autocracy is bound to lead to tyranny. These difficulties are resolved by the setting up of what we might call a limited democracy. The principle of majority decisions is affirmed[221] but it works on a qualitative, rather than purely numerical, basis; "for it is impossible to say that a small group of scholars should not outweigh a large group of ignorant people, even if it were as great as those who went out from Egypt."[222] On the one hand, eligibility to ruling offices is restricted to morally and religiously qualified persons;[223] on the other hand, the people have the right to select these from a list of candidates thus qualified.[224] Communal appointments are likewise subject to popular consent.[225] Furthermore the people have the right to introduce legislation, especially in the economic field,[226] as long as there is no rabbinic objection.[227] Such legislation then has the same validity as decrees of the Sanhedrin[228] or rabbinic ordinances,[229] and any dissenting minority is forced to submit to it.[230]

The Ideal Democracy

Rousseau has called democracy "a government for gods, too perfect for men."[231] Judaism is inclined to agree with this view, as long as men are imperfect and thus incapable of using their votes with the discretion necessary to prevent the infraction of right. Moral leadership cannot assert itself or its authority through the ballot box until the elector, no less than the elected, is guided by the dictates of righteousness, not expediency. The education of the masses is a prerequisite for the operation of democracy. Moses could never submit to popular clamour challenging his claim to power, unless "all the people of the Lord were Prophets."[232] Meanwhile, just as the British system today agrees to the appointment of judges without popular elections, so does Judaism—which regards its statesmen as executors of justice, not expediency —bestow authority on saintly philosophers, on men who know the law, rather than on the masses who would make it to suit their convenience. And "woe to the generation that would judge its judges,"[233] that would impose the popular will on its leaders! That curse is being visited upon our world today, and it is left to Israel's teachings once more to save mankind from its fury.

By-Paths of Charity

IT is both a challenge and a privilege to be invited to address experts on charity and organizers of charity in the world's greatest citadel of charity. The privilege marks an act of charity on your part; the challenge demands doing justice to the subject—on my part.

It is not my intention to lead you along the well-trodden tracks of the "path of charity." I do do not wish to analyze the unique Jewish concept of charity as the highest expression of "justice" and "righteousness." Nor do I wish to weary you with quotations from Jewish law and legend that depict charity in its widest sense as the cornerstone of Jewish social justice and economic equity. Instead I would like to take you along some of the less explored by-paths in the territory of charity, pointing out some of the most superb vistas commonly hidden from the eyes of travelers in this magnificent terrain of Jewish thought. I want to utilize some more or

Address delivered at the Fifth Annual Assembly of the Commission on Synagogue Relations of the Federation of Jewish Philanthropies of New York on April 24, 1961.

less incidental references to charity in Jewish sources to illumine what I believe to be by far the most significant aspects of this subject.

To my mind the greatest significance of the Jewish charity legislation lies not only in what it actually teaches but in how and where it is taught. Let me first give you just one random example of what I mean by an incidental reference to charity and its significance. The very first *Mishnah* in the talmudic tractate *Shabbath*, introducing the list of actions prohibited as "work" on the Sabbath, defines the ban on moving objects from private or public domain and *vice versa*. To illustrate the application of this law, whereby the offender is not culpable unless he lifts the object in one domain, moves it to the other and then sets it down there, the *Mishnah* portrays as an example a householder inside his home who wishes to hand something to a poor man outside. It lists eight different ways in which the gift may be transferred from the hand of the donor to the recipient, a permutation on the action being performed by one or both of them in terms of lifting and receiving the object. What a wealth of lessons are taught by this ingenuous and unobtrusive method of the Rabbis to enliven a dry and highly technical point of law, itself entirely unrelated to charity, by an idyllic picture of a man standing at the door or window at his home trying to help a poor man outside. How impressively we are here taught that charity, too, constitutes constructive "work" in the legally most basic sense of that term; that supporting the poor should be on our mind even whilst we are engaged in the most legalistic discussions; that the practice of charity is not merely a weekday activity performed by signing checks but should also extend to the Sabbath by personal acts of kindness; that the foremost place for the exercise of charity is the home; that the needy man who comes without letters of credence—for he could not carry them on the Sabbath— is also entitled to our sympathy!

Let me now come to some fundamental teachings expressed in incidental references to charity. Did it ever strike you, for instance, that our solicitude with the poor is especially, and almost exclusively, demanded on occasions of joy? Here are a few examples of this highly characteristic principle:

The Bible enjoins us to contribute agricultural products to the poor. When we rejoice in the fruits of our own harvest, the poor may claim a share of the bounty; a corner of the standing grain in our fields, its gleanings and forgotten sheaves. The same applies to the tithes of the Levites: the liability of fruits to be tithed takes effect only when the work on them is completed.[234] In connection with the contribution of the first fruits, the element of joy as a condition for giving is emphasized explicitly—"And thou shalt rejoice in all the good which the Lord thy God hath given unto thee, and unto thy house, thou and the Levite, and the stranger that is in the midst of thee."[235] The rabbis interpret this passage to imply that the first fruits should be offered to the priests only during the season of joy, the months of the harvest that last from Shavuoth to Sukkoth (Rashi). Of the ten injunctions in the Torah to rejoice on various occasions, no less than six insist that we share our joy with the "have-nots," the orphan, the widow, the stranger and the Levite, "because they have no portion nor inheritance with you."

The most notable occasions for rejoicing are the festivals. In one instance in particular a rabbinical comment gives us remarkable insight into the Jewish philosophy of charity. "And thou shalt rejoice before the Lord thy God," demands the Torah regarding the observance of the Shavuoth festival, "thou, and thy son, and thy daughter, and thy man-servant, and thy maid-servant; and the Levite that is within thy gates, and the stranger, and the fatherless, and the widow, that are in the midst of thee."[236] The rabbis explain: "Four of My guests (the Levite, the stranger, the orphan and the widow) corresponding to your four guests: Your son, daughter, man-servant and maid-servant; if you will rejoice Mine, I will rejoice yours" (Rashi). What an exquisite and touching lesson in which our duty to the poor is brought home to us. The happiness of ourselves and our families is not a bounty to be claimed and taken for granted as a human birthright; it is a commodity to be purchased from God in exchange for giving happiness to those in His charge. The joy to which we are entitled is in exact proportion to the joy we confer on others.

This doctrine finds its practical expression in the constant reminder of Jewish law to remember the wants of the needy and homeless in times of joy. Thus Purim, the jolliest of our feasts, is foremost in requiring us, by law, to consider those less fortunate than ourselves. The biblical mandate of our marking the day with "gifts to the poor" is as strong as the law that we read the *Megillah*.[237] Hence we make a special collection for the poor on Purim, giving them the proceeds of the *Machatzith Hashekel* contributions. Similarly, the *Seder* Service, the happiest home celebration of the year, is the only occasion when we issue a statutory invitation to the hungry to join us in our festivities. And again, it is during Pesach when a special appeal for contributions to the poor is made—the *Ma'oth Chittin* campaign. Our joy is not to be complete or justified unless we share our privileges with the under-privileged.

Perhaps the most beautiful and impressive illustration of this ideal is provided by some traditional customs at Jewish weddings, the occasions of supreme joy in human life. Partly out of consideration for the poor, we strip our brides of all jewelry under the *Chuppah*. All brides are to be equal in the hour when their happiness reaches its climax; and since we cannot expect the poor bride to be as richly adorned as the wealthy, we expect the wealthy to be attired like the poor. In former times this principle was further extended to the bridal dress, too. Based on an ancient Talmudic precedent,[238] no bride, however rich, wore her own dress for the occasion; she borrowed it from a friend, and lent hers in turn to some poor bride, so that no one should be able to say of any bride that her garment put some other, less affluent bride to shame, for everyone knew the dress she wore was not hers.

It is instructive to contrast this attitude with the usual practice prevailing in our own time. In regard to material possessions we insist that they shall be our own property. Nowadays a bride would never wear another's dress simply out of concern for the poor. Yet, when it comes to spiritual possessions we make use of property that is not our own. For example, many people fulfill the precept of the *Arba Minim* on Sukkoth with a *Lulav* and *Ethrog* which belong to the congregation and not to themselves. Or they eat in a *Sukkah* that is not their own, or celebrate the *Seder* at another person's table. Yet just here the law provides "And ye shall take for *yourselves*"[239] that is, these religious requisites "shall be *yours*."[240] Regarding things material, we should rejoice in the happiness of others, and when we rejoice in spiritual adornments they should belong to us. Instead we do the reverse.

The association between charity and joy, so emphatically stressed in Jewish law and practice, is not, however, merely incidental to the duty of philanthropy. It governs our basic outlook on rich-poor relations and on the true ideal of benevolence. The injunction "And thy heart shall not be grieved when thou givest to him"[241] is an integral part of the charity legislation. Help to the poor in its finest form shall be given, not only in *times* of joy, but out of *feelings* of joy.

Moreover, in the imagery of the Torah it is not the poor man who stretches forth his hand begging for alms, but the donor who opens his hand so that the needy may help themselves: "Thou shalt surely open thy hand unto thy poor and needy brother."[242] The initiative rests with the giver, not the recipient.

Here we come to the crux of the subject. The emphasis throughout has been on the donor, his disposition, his feelings and his gestures, rather than on the needs of the poor man. The law stipulates the times and seasons at which those who have are required to give. It does not mention the times and seasons when those who have not are entitled to take. The focus is invariably on giving, not on taking.

The reason for this is that the paramount objective of charity, in the Jewish view, is to help the donor more than the recipient. As stated by an important medieval Jewish source, the ultimate purpose of the laws of charity is to generate in man the qualities of mercy and kindness, not to simply eliminate poverty. If God wished He could eliminate poverty without recourse to human aid.[243]

Charity is meant, primarily, to ennoble the character of the donor. The attainment of this ideal is incumbent upon rich and poor alike. Hence Jewish law rules quite unequivocally that "even a poor man who is supported by charity is himself also obliged to give charity out of what is given to him."[244] This interesting ruling is based on Biblical precedent: The Levites, who lived on the tithes received from the Israelites, were themselves required to pass on one-tenth of that tithe to the priests.[245] If the welfare of the priests had been the main consideration, the Israelites could have given this sum directly to the priests without involving the Levites. The law, then, was not really concerned with meeting the needs of the priests, but with developing the virtues of the Levites.

The priests also were obliged to give something in return for what they were taking from their fellow Jews. It was their function to pronounce the priestly benediction, to give blessings to the people. Let us examine the significance of this obligation. Why was the task of blessing the congregation alloted exclusively to the priests? Why not give this duty to the saints and scholars who, though not of priestly descent, could perform the task with equal skill and efficacy? In what way was their blessing less valuable and even unlawful?

The answer is that it is the priests' dependence on others that qualifies them to bestow their blessing. A blessing, to be effective, must be given with a full heart. Those imparting the blessing must be genuinely concerned with the welfare of those receiving it. And there is no one more sincerely interested in the well-being of the people than the priests whose prosperity is directly related to the prosperity of the tribes they serve. When the priests bless their benefactors, they do so without envy. The more fully their blessing will be fulfilled, the better off they will be themselves.

Similarly, when the poor pray for our health and prosperity in return for the benefactions we bestow upon them, our accounts are balanced. We become equals, for we give them no greater value than we receive in return.

This leads to a final reflection on significant "incidentals" related to the Jewish ideal of charity. Today we often glibly speak about the "brotherhood of man," a notion born out of the Biblical teaching of the common origin of all men and of the Biblical concept of social justice. The Torah, however, interpreted human brotherhood in a far more practical sense. In practice, we all too often refer to our fellow-men and even fellow nations as brothers only when we want something from them. America is "Uncle Sam" to other peoples so long as the "uncle" is rich and liberal with his wealth. We ask other nations to share their scientific and technological riches with us "as brothers" only when they have something to offer that we do not possess. If we have relatives in our family, however distant, who are prosperous or famous we gladly acknowledge our relationship to them; but should a poor beggar approach us for help and claim he is some second cousin, our anxiety to trace the relationship vanishes and we pretend that it does not exist.

The Torah teaches the reverse. It uses several synonyms for "fellow-man." These terms are not used indiscriminately but with utmost consistency. Sometimes he is called "your neighbor:" "And thou shalt love thy *neighbor* as thyself."[246] Or, as at the end of the Ten Commandments: "Thou shalt not covet thy *neighbor's* house . . . , thy *neighbor's* wife . . . , nor anything that is thy *neighbor's*."[247] At other times he is called "your fellow:" "And thou shalt not lie carnally with thy *fellow's* wife."[248] In all these cases our neighbor is independent of us, or has something that we may want. Then he is merely a *neighbor* or a *fellow* human being to us. The Torah calls him "your brother" only when he needs something from us or when he depends upon our support and sympathy: "And if thy *brother* be waxen poor, and his means fail with thee, then thou shalt uphold him."[249] "And if thy *brother* be waxen poor with thee, and sell himself unto thee, thou shalt not make him serve as a bondservant."[250] "If thy Hebrew *brother* be sold unto thee . . . in the seventh year thou shalt let him go free from thee."[251] "Thou shalt not see thy *brother's* ox or his sheep straying. . . ; thou shalt surely bring them back unto thy *brother*."[252] "Thou shalt not see thy *brother's* ass or his ox fallen down by the way . . . ; thou shalt surely help to lift them up again."[253] "Thou shalt not abhor an Edomite, for he is thy *brother*."[254] "Thou shalt not hate thy *brother* in thy heart."[255]

To us the burden of true brotherhood is to claim equality not with our equals or superiors, but with those materially our inferiors. The acid test of brotherhood is how far we are prepared to share what we have with others, enabling them to *become* our equals as brothers. Brotherhood does not mean holding out our hands asking for favors, but stretching them forth offering favors. Brotherhood demands forestalling the grief of taking by the joy of giving. Human brotherhood implies that what unites us all is the common Fatherhood of God to Whom alone "the earth and all that fills it" belongs and over Whose possessions we are to be His faithful custodians, so long as we bear ourselves as His children.

4

Religious Zionism

Israel's Bar Mitzvah

THE history of the twentieth century so far unfolded is not exactly dull. It is packed with enough drama and excitement to fill whole centuries of former times. But alas, it is marked by more tragedies than happiness. Tidal waves of destruction have swept away civilizations and values laboriously built up in long ages of patient human endeavor. And we find only little new construction on the ruins of the past.

Address delivered at the Fifth Avenue Synagogue to mark the thirteenth Israel Independence Day, April 28, 1961.

The earth is soaked to saturation with the blood shed in two world wars and in countless smaller wars and above all in the diabolical slaughter of Jews unparalleled even in our blood-stained annals. What has the world to show in return for these appalling sacrifices?

In the ledger of contemporary history the debit side spills over with red letters of blood recording human losses; by contrast how empty is the credit pages of human gains and advances!

The most outstanding single item on that page, the most constructive event of the century, is doubtless the occasion we commemorate today.

Where in the whole wide world will you find a people, big or small, which in the short span of thirteen years has greater and more epoch-making constructive achievements to its credit than Israel? The list of accomplishments is staggering indeed, and we might well sing an almost endless song of דיינו, recording our thanks to God for His many mercies, in the spirit of the *Hagadah.*

If Israel had been created only to turn the desolation of our ancient homeland into the vibrant, flourishing country it is today, דיינו that would have been enough reason to thank the Almighty.

If Israel had been created only to provide a home for 2,000,000 harassed Jews, דיינו.

If Israel had been created only to justify the hopes, prayers and sufferings of untold martyred generations, דיינו.

If Israel had been created only to make possible the most spectacular vindication of justice in human history by bringing one of our arch-enemies to account for the first time in our experience in a blaze of world-wide publicity, דיינו.

If Israel had been created only to recharge the batteries of Jewish life and communal activity throughout the world, דיינו. על אחת כמה וכמה טובה כפולה ומכופלת למקום עלינו!

At this solemn assembly to mark Israel's coming of age, how fervent, profound and infinite must be our thanksgiving to the Almighty שומר ישראל, the Guardian of Israel, for the miracles which He wrought to restore the people of His choice to the land of His choice!

Let there also go out from this holy convocation a salute to the people of Israel together with its leaders, spiritual and temporal, acclaiming their invincible fortitude in the face of mortal peril; their heroic response to destiny's call for sacrifice in the upbuilding of our land and the ingathering of the exiles; their triumphant struggle for Israel's return to the comity of nations; their splendid example in sharing their skills and experience with under-developed countries; and their massive contribution toward the enhancement of Jewish pride and self-respect the world over, bringing hope to those in despair, the promise of redemption to the oppressed, and new Jewish life to communities threatened by the blight of assimilation and indifference.

But these colossal achievements were not accomplished without bringing grave problems in their wake.

A Bar Mitzvah's passage from boyhood to manhood is accompanied by physical and psychological changes usually presaging a period of crisis and rebellion, the unsettlement of early adolescence. If such manifestations are indeed signs of reaching majority, then Israel is certainly coming of age now.

Israel is presently beset by acute spiritual and political crises. For nearly two years it has had no Chief Rabbi, and for months now it has been without a regular government. The underlying unity of purpose has been undermined by a series of public disputes which have rocked Israeli society and the confidence of the people.

We can only hope that Israel will grow out of its present restiveness and instability as every healthy boy does some time after the crisis following his Bar Mitzvah. But the real problem goes far deeper than these difficulties, which are no doubt merely a passing phase.

Up to the Bar Mitzvah the parents are concerned with the immediate needs of the child: his health, good feeding, adequate schooling, decent manners. These are short-term objectives. So also with Israel. Our main preoccupation so far has been with matters of security, consolidation, economic stability and expansion. These are all problems of the moment.

But after the Bar Mitzvah parents have to think of the boy's future. What career is he to choose? What role is he to play in life? They have to focus their attention on long-term goals. Likewise with Israel. The time is here for Israel to lay the groundwork for greater and long-term objectives. What are to be its historic aspirations? What role is it going to play in the unfolding of God's design in the evolution of the human race? Now we have to concern ourselves with ultimate objectives.

Let us assume that Israel's immediate problems were all solved. Israel would enjoy peace with its neighbors, have a stable government, a prosperous economy, an enterprising industry, and a healthy pursuit of the arts and sciences. Is that to be the sum-total of our hopes? Is that the fulfillment of our Prophets' vision, the compensation for our martyrs' heroism, and the final realization of all our prayers three times a day for countless centuries? Is Zion to be restored merely for the sake of importing persecuted Jews, and exporting oranges, industrial products or even scientific inventions? Is that all for which we have shed our blood and our tears and our sweat during the long agony of our suffering?

Paradoxically enough, in some respects the rise of the State of Israel, the restoration of Jewish sovereignty in our homeland for which we prayed so long, has caused the Messianic vision of Judaism to wane rather than to swell.

Before the establishment of the State, when we exclaimed, "Next year in Jerusalem!", we meant what we said, we expressed our fondest hope with fervor and conviction. Now, when nothing stands between the exclamation and its fulfillment except a call to any travel agency and the purchase of a one-way ticket to Israel, לשנה הבאה בירושלים no longer sets forth our true hopes and yearnings.

Formerly the Prophet Elijah was a welcome guest at our *Seder* tables. We greeted him eagerly as the precursor of the Messiah when he, year after year, reaffirmed the promise of ultimate redemption. Now he is not so welcome; his presence is uncomfortable and even embarrassing. When he reminds us that we and our families will one day be moved to join in the great movement of the ingathering of the exiles,

we remonstrate with him and protest against his interference
with our freedom and security.

There may be people who are unwilling or unable to settle
in Israel for the present. However, many have ceased not
only to pray, but even to hope that they, or if not they then
at least their children or children's children, may one day
witness the personal realization of the ageless Jewish dream.

I hold here in my hand a non-Orthodox *Hagadah* recently
published. The Hebrew text is a completely faithful reproduction of the traditional version; nothing is left out or
added. But the "translation" introduces a few subtle changes.
For instance, our age-old prayer in the Grace-after-Meals
הרחמן הוא ישבור עלנו מעל צוארנו והוא יוליכנו קוממיות
לארצנו which means "May the All-merciful break the
yoke of oppression from off our necks and may He lead
us upright into our land" is rendered ". . . and may He lead
the homeless of our people in dignity to our ancient homeland."* Israel is not for "us," but for "the homeless of our
people." It is to be a land for refugees, a shelter for people
without a haven! What a falsification of Jewish prayers,
what a travesty of Jewish history, what a betrayal of Jewish
blood and tears! Such a perverted reading makes a mockery
of the Jewish destiny as envisaged by our Prophets and of
the suffering endured by the wretched generations whose
only hope justifying their miserable life and their agonized
death lay in their faith of our people's eventual return to
the Promised Land!

Ever since the founding of the Jewish State the historical
significance of the event has been sharply debated in religious circles. Some are convinced that the restoration of
Jewish sovereignty to the Land of Israel marks the first stage
in the fulfillment of the Messianic promise, that we must
look upon this tremendous event—in the words of the late
Chief Rabbi Herzog's prayer for the State of Israel—as
ראשית צמיחת גאולתנו "the beginning of the sprouting
forth of our redemption." Other great religious leaders, equally
devout in their convictions, while not denying the Provi-

Passover Haggadah, compiled and edited by Morris Silverman,
(Conservative) Prayer Book Press, Hartford, Conn., 1950, p. 41.

dential "finger of God" in the miraculous episodes of the past thirteen years, cannot believe that a predominantly secularist state can herald even the beginnig of our Messianic aspirations.

This is an argument which we cannot resolve. Jewish law lays down the important maxim: אין עד נעשה דיין "a witness can never be a judge." Even if the members of the supreme court themselves witnessed a murder, they must not act as judges in the case; they must hand it over to another court, for they cannot be detached enough to render a completely impartial verdict. Similarly, we, as witnesses to the stirring events of Israel's national rebirth, cannot at the same time judge the full meaning of these events and assess their historical significance. We are neither prophets nor the sons of prophets that we should have sufficient introspection into the designs of Providence to pass a final judgment on this issue. It must remain in doubt—*mutal besafek umunach ad sheyavo Eliyahu.*

Whether or not we find ourselves at the threshold of the Messianic age may well depend on what we make of the unprecedented opportunities and challenges now facing us. In the immortal words of Isaiah, *Tzion bemishpat tipadeh veshaveha bitzedakah,* "Zion will be redeemed through judgment and her inhabitants through righteousness." One great judgment is already at hand. Indeed, perhaps the greatest judgment of all times—the most momentous vindication of righteousness in human history. But redemption requires not only the judgment of our detractors and persecutors. We must also judge ourselves in the light of the destiny mapped out for us by our Creator. In the Messianic vision, the enjoyment of peace and decent living standards, the conquest of want and disease are only means to a higher end. The true aims of human existence and struggle are the establishment of God's sovereignty on earth: to acclaim righteousness in place of expediency, the dominion of the moral law in human relations, and the triumph of virtue over wickedness in man's ambitions. To generate and sustain mankind's will to achieve these aims is to be the Jewish national purpose, and the instrument for their fulfillment is to be Zion reunited with her children.

May we, then, in self-judgment, so raise our sights to the Messianic ideal that from Jewish hearts all over the world will pour forth songs of thanksgiving that it was granted to our generation to witness the consummation of the Divine purpose of creation, thanking him *Shehechiyanu vekimanu vehigiyanu lazeman hazeh* "That He has kept us alive, and sustained us, and enabled us to reach this time" of historic fulfillment.

Zionism: Its Promise and Fulfillment

"A king and the public," informs us the Talmud, "are the subject of daily scrutiny." Whereas the behavior of an individual may escape public judgment for a span of time and be subject to review only once a year, the state, because of its great responsibilities and manifold activities affecting the welfare of the community, must necessarily stand up to judgment every day.

Nevertheless, after fourteen years a certain stability sets in. The popular song in the *Hagadah "Echad mi Yode'a"* lists in progression numbers from one to thirteen, attaching a different significance to each number. Up to thirteen, every number bears a different meaning. From fourteen on, a more uniform tendency sets in.

Similar is the life sequence of a youngster.

Until a boy reaches Bar Mitzvah age, his character, mold, and psychological makeup are as yet undetermined. At fourteen, he begins to settle down, and the direction of his life becomes discernible.

That may explain the reason why, according to our sages, certain biblical laws did not take effect immediately on Israel's entry into the Holy Land but only after the first fourteen years of conquest and settlement. Only then did the new Jewish State become sufficiently consolidated to put into effect the special laws related to the soil of the land.

Following this earliest precedent of the original conquest of the land under Joshua, the fourteenth birthday of the re-

Address delivered at the Fifth Avenue Synagogue to mark the fourteenth Israel Independence Day, May 8, 1962.

born State of Israel may afford us a unique and a fitting opportunity to assess its significance and prospects for the future in terms of history and Jewish destiny. After fourteen years of precarious living and struggle, the initial period of Israel's adjustment and consolidation has come to an end. From now on its development may take a steady course. This occasion invites a long-term review of the State's goals and achievements, its shortcomings and disenchantments.

The question to which I address myself is: How far have the designs of history and the workings of Providence fulfilled the dreams of the early Zionist visionaries? To what extent does the reality of Israel's existence correspond to their visions?

In many respects the fulfillment has greatly exceeded expectations. In others it has fallen far short of them. One cannot but marvel at the almost uncanny precision with which Theodor Herzl forecast at the turn of the century that in fifty years' time there would be a sovereign Jewish State. This is perhaps one of the most spectacular prophecies in modern times. Yet how different is this Jewish State from Herzl's *Judenstaat* as he envisaged it.

The early Zionist dreamers sought to "solve the Jewish problem." Jewish statehood, they maintained, would eliminate the "abnormalities" of Jewish existence. By having a country, government, and economy like other nations, Jews would become like "normal" peoples. They would no longer be looked upon as unusual, different people, exposed to all the hatreds and suspicions of the non-conformist.

Leo Pinsker, in 1882, pleaded for Jewish Auto-Emancipation in his famous tract bearing that name. The task of the Jewish people, he declared, was to emancipate itself on a national scale and thus become like other "normal" peoples, an equal among nations. Jewish existence, whether inside or outside the Jewish State, was to be "normalized." That was the object of Theodor Herzl, Max Nordau, and other Zionist leaders no less than of Pinsker.

In 1933, Chaim Weizmann still declared: "If before I die there are half a million Jews in Palestine, I shall be content, because I shall know that this 'saving remnant' will survive. They, not the millions in the Diaspora, are what really matters." Weizmann was wide of the mark on two counts. By the time he died, Palestine had more than twice the number of Jews he had anticipated, while a decade after his death the Jews in the Diaspora still matter very much indeed.

Israel certainly has not "solved the Jewish problem." Jews today are as uniquely different as they had always been. Jews in America are still not like Irish Americans or other "ethnics" who have retained a special bond with their countries of origin. Irish-Americans have no Anti-Defamation League and other defense agencies. The dangers of anti-Semitism today are as great as they were before the establishment of Israel, as witness, for example, the fairly recent world-wide swastika epidemic. The Jewish problem has remained unsolved and will remain so in the foreseeable future. Jewish statehood has not "normalized" Jewish life in the Diaspora.

On the contrary, in some ways Israel has added for Jews many new problems which never existed before. Let me cite a few examples of what I mean.

Soon after I came to Dublin in 1949 to assume my position as Chief Rabbi of Ireland, there were some mild anti-Jewish demonstrations sparked off by the world-wide Catholic agitation on the "Holy Places" at the time. In an effort to prevent any serious outbreaks, I went to see the Archbishop of Dublin, who is primate of Ireland, to reassure him of the protection of Catholic rights and property in Israel and to request his assistance in preserving the happy relations between Jews and Catholics in Ireland. In reply, he asked me to secure for him an official declaration on the safety of the "Holy Places" from the government of Israel. Nothing less would do, said he. He subsequently wrote me, in a personal communication, dated May 26, 1949, in these terms:

> . . . Such a declaration would greatly assist, too, in preventing unfortunate repercussions, such as you stated you fear may arise in Dublin. . . . It would indeed be a grievous pity, if after having safely traversed a period of world-wide and unexampled crisis, innocent people of your Community should now suffer hurt, by reason of the attitude and actions of irreligious members of Israel whose merely political or commercial aims would never be countenanced by the peaceful members of your Community in Dublin.

In other words, Irish Jews were warned that they would be treated as hostages, be subjected to "unfortunate repercussions" and to "suffer hurt" if Catholics were not satisfied with the protection of their interests in Israel. This represents an unprecedented situation in our history. Here is a Jewish community being held accountable and threatened with reprisals for the actions of an independent country, thousands of miles away, for whose policies this community is not responsible and in whose affairs it has no say.

That particular problem concerned only 5,000 Irish Jews. In Russia today there are millions of Jews, who, in addition to the repression to which they are subjected for religious reasons, now have to suffer because current Soviet strategy in the Middle East requires an anti-Israel attitude to appease the Arab states. A vast Jewish community is thus exposed to new forms of discrimination for purely political considerations completely extraneous to the conduct or local relations of that community.

Further problems for various Jewish communities in the Diaspora have been created by Israel's admission to the United Nations. This makes it necessary for Israel to express an opinion on every major international dispute in the world, whether it be the Congo, Algeria, a test ban or racial discrimination in South America. Whenever she votes or even abstains, Israel is bound to antagonize some countries and thereby jeopardize the interests of the Jews in those countries. A grave illustration of this was given only recently, when the government of South Africa saw fit to make some serious unfriendly gestures to the local Jewish community because of Israel's stand in the U. N. vote on apartheid.

New problems arising from the creation of Israel have aggravated the position of many Jews. This is especially true of the Jews in the Arab lands—North Africa, Morroco, Tunisia, and Algeria, where Jews had lived in relative security for many centuries, and where they are now exposed to grave fears and perils.

The solution of the Jewish problem has not been achieved. Israel has provided a haven from oppression for well over a million Jewish refugees. Jewish Statehood has given immense pride and self-respect to Jews all over the world. But as against these accomplishments must be set the new hazards caused by Jewish political independence to many more millions of Jews throughout the world. In this respect, then, the fulfillment of secular Zionism has fallen far short of its expectations.

The religious ideals of Zionism in the broadest sense have also remained largely unfulfilled. The early religious dreamers who supported Zionism had been inspired above all by the Messianic vision of the Hebrew Prophets. The restoration of Jewish sovereignty in the Holy Land was to endow with a sense of realism and urgency the final redemption of a national purpose of the Jewish people.

Yet, paradoxically enough, the reverse has happened. Israel has in fact weakened rather than strengthened our Messianic aspirations. Before Israel, there was still some fervor and conviction in our plea "Next year in Jerusalem"; the longing to witness and personally participate in "the return of the exiles from the four corners of the earth" (and not just from lands of persecution), as expressed in our prayers, was real, at least in the hearts of all devout Jews. Elijah was a welcome guest at our *Seder* tables, but now that Israel exists and the functions of Elijah can be performed by any travel agency issuing one-way tickets to the Holy Land, the prayers for our return to Zion have a hollow ring, and Elijah embarrasses us when he knocks at our door to summon us in preparation for the Redemption. Redemption is now only for the homeless; living comfortably in America or elsewhere in freedom, we feel we are redeemed. We prefer the reality of our contented lives to the dreams of the Prophets. Indeed we have ceased to dream and to hope. Israel, by a strange twist of fate, seems to have knocked the bottom out of our barrel of hope. By gaining political independence, we have climbed to the summit of the foothills, and in our exertions to do so, we have lost sight of the lofty mountains beyond still to be scaled. For 2,000 years and more we clearly saw those soaring mountains of the Messianic ideal from the distance; now, as we got close to them, they seem to have disappeared.

With the rise of Israel, Zionism has become, even for most religious Jews, a very mundane affair. There is no less truth than irony in Koestler's definition of Zionism as "one man persuading another man to give money to a third man to go to Palestine." The bulk of Israel's immigrants are still involuntary exiles, driven there by the pressure of persecutors rather than by the yearning for the restoration of Zion's glory and the fulfillment of its Messianic destiny.

In religious terms, too, therefore, the reality of Israel is remote from the vision of its dreamers.

On the other hand, perhaps even more immediately important are the many successes and triumphs which have exceeded the wildest hopes anyone could have cherished but a few decades ago. In many respects, reality has overtaken the vision and fears in giant strides.

Who would have dared to forecast that the Jews, of all people, could have maintained such stability of government and such national discipline as Israel has displayed during the past fourteen years? Jews have always been great individualists, averse to submitting unflinchingly to any centralized Jewish authority. It is related that when President Truman once reproved the late President Weizmann with the remark, "After all, I am President of 170,000,000 Americans," Weizmann retorted, "But that is nothing: I am President of one million presidents!" That, despite this rugged individualism, Israel has proved to be the only stable democracy in the region, with hardly a change of government and never a challenge to its authority, is an accomplishment of the first order, particularly when in the neighboring Arab States every other Monday and Thursday witness some violent change of government, a palace revolution or a political assassination.

Israel has confounded all prophets of doom with a vengeance. There were those who were convinced that the Jewish State was militarily indefensible against the murderous hostility of the surrounding Arab armies; yet a miracle happened twice, and David defeated the Goliath threatening his life. Then there were those who thought Israel was bound to disintegrate under the weight of economic bankruptcy; but another miracle occurred, and the country, despite its heavy burdens, is in a more prosperous state today than ever before. Again, there were many who believed that the conglomeration of Jews of such diverse backgrounds, colors and cultures from all over the globe would inevitably lead to intense social friction and upheaval; yet, Israel has achieved more integration in little over a decade than America in a century!

In the spiritual and intellectual spheres, too, the false prophets have been discomfitted. It was argued that Jews returning to the soil as farmers and menial laborers would become literally an *Am Ha'aretz,* meaning "ignoramus" and "people of the land" at the same time, that they might soon decline into an ignorant peasantry. Yet in fact, Israel can boast the highest literary standards in the world, enjoying, for instance, a greater *per capita* readership of books than any other country.

Doubts have also often been expressed on the prospects of developing a flourishing religious life in a secular and largely Socialist Jewish State. Yet Israel witnesses today a religious renaissance, an intensity of Torah learning comparable with the spiritually most prosperous periods in Jewish history. In Israel nearly 40 per cent of all children receive intensive religious instruction, compared with only about 10 per cent in America and most other countries of the Diaspora. Israel has already become a supreme citadel of Jewish learning, literally fulfilling "From out of Zion shall go forth the Law," by exporting rabbis, religious teachers and textbooks as well as halachic rulings, guiding Jewish life in the world over.

From every point of view, Israel has retained its uniqueness, both as a people and as a land. It is full of paradoxes, for what is a cause of weakness to other nations is our strength. The ancient prophecy: הן עם לבדד ישכן ובגוים לא יתחשב —"Lo, it is a people that shall dwell alone, and shall not be reckoned among the nations" (Nu. 23:9), is as true today as it ever was.

With all attempts at normalization and international integration, Israel is still the most lonely nation on earth. Situated at the cross-roads of Asia and Africa, it is nevertheless excluded from the Afro-Asian bloc. The only Western state in the Middle East, it is yet not a member of any Western defense alliance, whether NATO or CENTO. A Semitic People in the midst of Arab lands, it is as yet ostracized by the Arab League.

Alone among the nations, Israel belongs to no political bloc, is attached to no ideological camp and has no formal allies. At the same time, this complete isolation—the undoing of other nations—is our source of strength and survival. Through effective integration Israel would have become another insignificant Levantine state. It would be "balkanized" as an inconsequential principality on the Eastern shores of the Mediterranean, eventually to be submerged culturally, economically and perhaps even religiously by the pressure of the neighboring states.

There is probably no country in the world so dependent on outside help, so remote from economic self-sufficiency, as Israel which still relies for a good part of its budget on the financial aid of Diaspora Jewry. To other nations this would have rung a death-knell; to us this is our salvation. The mutual dependence of Israel and the Diaspora—the former counting on the Diaspora's material support and the latter being held to account for Israel's conduct—has forged the bonds between the two Jewries into an indestructible unity.

Without it we might now have two distinct Jewish peoples. Witness, for example, the incipient activities of the separatist fadists, such as the "Canaanities" who seek to break with the historical traditions of Judaism and thus bring about a yawning schism and movement of non-identification with world Jewry. If not for Israel's concern to win favor among the Jewish religious communities throughout the world, who knows what the outcome would have been? Israel might have pursued some independent religious course and experimented with some Judeo-Buddhist form of faith! And world Jewry, in turn, might have been crippled by apathy but for Zionism's vital blood transfusions which render Jewish communal life so vibrant everywhere. How spiritually and socially paralyzed would many communities be today without the ever urgent challenge of Israel's needs.

As we pass now from the fourteen-year period of Israel's consolidation to its more settled stability, we cannot but be filled with thanksgiving and confidence. This epoch-making change is brought into focus once we compare the reality of today with the spirit of desolation pervading Yehuda Halevy's passionate *Odes to Zion* on the one hand, and the *Prophets'* triumphant vision of Zion restored, on the other.

Thus sang Halevy eight hundred years ago:

> O, who may give me wings,
> that I may fly away,
> and there rest from all my wondering
> the ruins of my heart among thy ruins lay?

And again:

> My heart is in the East,
> though in the West I live,
> the sweet of human life no happiness can give
> no joy in sunny Spain mine eyes can ever see,
> for Zion, desolate, alone hath charms for me.

Eighteen hundred years earlier Isaiah spoke these immortal words:

> For Zion's sake I will not hold my peace,
> and for Jerusalem's sake I will not rest
> until her triumph go forth as brightness
> and her salvation as a torch that burneth.
> And the nations shall see thy triumph,
> and all the kings thy glory;
> And thou shalt be called a new name
> which the mouth of the Lord shall mark out.
> Thou shalt also be a crown of beauty in the hand of
>   the Lord,
> and a royal diadem in the open hand of thy God.
> Thou shalt no more be termed Forsaken,
> neither shall thy land any more be termed Desolate
> but thou shalt be called,
> My delight is in her,
> and thy land, Espoused:
> for the Lord delighteth in thee,
> and thy land shall be espoused.
> For as a young man espouseth a virgin,
> so shall thy sons espouse thee;
> and as the bridegroom rejoiceth over the bride,
> so shall thy God rejoice over thee.

(Isaiah 62:1-5)

Mizrachi: A Reappraisal

"MIZRACHI", the name of our movement, stands not only for *Mizrach*—East, the direction in which all our prayers and national aspirations are directed. It also and especially stands for *Merkaz Ruchani*, "Spiritual Center." Mizrachi was conceived as representing a Center, a half-way house between extremes, a bridge between Zionists and traditionalists.

Today this particular bridge no longer serves a primary function in Jewish life. The bulk of religious Jewry acknowledges Zion and the Jewish State. That once vital bridge is now obsolete and survives merely as a great historic monument. It has been left far behind us as we have traveled down the fast-flowing stream of history. That bridge built sixty years ago, now stands over dry land, for the wide gulf of water that once separated religious Jews from Zionism has all but dried up.

Today new bridges are needed further downstream where the rushing waters of division are now creating an ever widening gulf between the two banks.

We have lately witnessed an acute polarization of Jewish life. Those to the right on the religious spectrum have moved further to the right. Never has Orthodoxy been more militant and less compromising than it is today. And those on the left have likewise increased their distance from the center, betraying a hostility to religious values and national sanctities more fanatical than ever. As shown by the recent ugly incidents in Israel and in the United States, tempers are frayed, the gulf has widened, and the two poles are scarcely linked by any common language or ideals. The danger is no longer so remote of it being said to us as it was told to Rebecca: "Two peoples are in your womb, and two nations shall be separated from your bowels."

Address delivered at the Annual Convention of Mizrachi-Hapoel Hamizrachi of America, Winter, 1963-4.

How can we build a bridge between the two and prevent the disaster that once overwhelmed us when our kingdom was divided into two distinct nations?

Above all, in our search for new means of communication, we need greater flexibility, a more tractable frame of mind. We have to beware of monolithic attitudes which admit only one single school of thought.

The Torah describes Jacob as "a simple man, dwelling in tents." On which Rashi comments: "In the tent (Yeshiva) of Shem, and in the tent of Ever." Why was Jacob required to study in two Yeshivoth? Altogether, what need was there for two academies of learning, when there were hardly any pupils? The answer may well be that the intellectual challenge at the time of "Ever" could not be met by the outlook of "Shem" four generations earlier. Hence, as the *Tanchuma Yashan* so aptly puts it, "Jacob left the academy of Shem, and he went to the academy of Ever." Today we likewise need a variety of educational approaches if we are to withstand successfully the cross-currents of our time.

The Mizrachi movement has already begun to play a pioneering role in the creation of a new type of Yeshiva—the Bnei Akiva Yeshivoth, both vocational and high school types of Yeshivoth. It has forged a bridge between religious and secular vocations.

But it must go further and erect many more such bridges to really span the gulf. What we require most urgently, for instance, are modern rabbis, adequately trained to communicate effectively with the youth of today in properly constituted seminaries. Even more desperately, we need a religious intelligentsia, perhaps the most serious desideratum on Israel's religious scene today.

When I recently visited the Holy Land in connection with the highly critical problem of autopsies there, I was appalled to discover that the land now has virtually no religious doctors apart from a few aging immigrants. We are simply not training any religious medical students. Consequently, the whole field of medicine—hospitals, health services, medical schools, etc.—is fast losing the last vestiges of religious influences. The same applies to the fields of law, civil service, arts and other professional areas, with the possible but insignificant exception to science, where some religious elements are still to be found.

If we do not produce religious professionals—and with a high priority on our educational efforts—how can we ever hope to control the keys to the most vital areas of Israel's cultural and social life?

I believe our whole orientation and political propaganda should be thoroughly reappraised in the light of present-day circumstances. I wonder, for example, whether it is wise to place our main emphasis on religious legislation in the Knesset or local government. The fear of Heaven, true religiosity, cannot be legislated. It can only be achieved by persuasion, by personal example, and through intellectual presentation. To my mind, one effective group of Orthodox scientists is worth more than a dozen parliamentary bills.

Again, we must create a more attractive public image than we presently enjoy. We have so far highlighted mainly defensive positions, in opposition to the stand of others. We have opposed *chillul Shabbat,* opposed *treifa* kitchens, opposed pig-breeding, opposed civil marriages. This is bound to put us in an unfavorable light since it makes us appear chiefly as putting on brakes and restraints.

We should place more stress on positive elements and thus put our opponents on the defensive. Why do we not proclaim as our main plank the statistically indisputable fact that in Israel (as also elsewhere) only the religious segments of the Jewish population are practically free from the dreadful and growing scourges of juvenile delinquency, promiscuity, illegitimacy and other vices which corrode the fabric of our society? These are problems which, unlike *Shabbat* or *kashrut,* agitate and trouble the whole world. Where others are vainly groping for solutions, we have somehow contrived to solve these problems. What more spectacular proof than this can we present for our claim that if we do not raise true Jews, we cannot raise good human beings either! Without more religious education and culture, Israel's prisons, already overcrowded with juvenile delinquents and other parasites, will have to be transferred to school buildings, and the danger of moral decay from within will exceed the peril of aggression from without!

Finally, let us raise our sights on our long-term objectives. It is the most baffling paradox of our time that, while we have moved closer to the fulfillment of our prophetic destiny through the restoration of Jewish national sovereignty and the ingathering of the exiles, our Messianic vision has receded more dramatically than ever in our history. Getting nearer to the goal we have lost sight of the goal itself—like a mountaineer who, having climbed the foothills, can no longer see the real peaks beyond, yet to be scaled.

Let us imagine we were to achieve all our immediate objectives; let us assume Israel had peace with her neighbors, a prosperous economy, the highest standards in the arts and sciences and even nation-wide Torah learning and practice; is that the consummation of all our aspirations? Should our imagination not be fired by the urge to see Prophetic vistas far transcending these narrow confines? Should we, as the religious element, not challenge the secularists above all by contrasting the void created by the realization of their aims, with our program of universal proportions yet awaiting realization? Only distant goals can generate ideals and idealism, for a goal reached reduces the ideal into reality, and thus deprive life of its most energizing motive power—idealism.

Herein lies the assurance of our eventual triumph over the secularists. The ultimate test of strength lies in superior idealism, as our history has so amply proved. For the forseeable future our forces may remain in the minority. We should not be daunted by that prospect. History has always been moved forward by the few. It has been our Jewish destiny since the first ancestor to bear the name Israel: *Verav ya' avod tzair*, "And the many shall serve the few." The progress of the masses shall be governed by the minority. But in the end, Jewish destiny is bound to be in our hands. The temporary aberrations of our troubled times will disappear. Dawn will rise on the day that will witness the fulfillment of the promise given to Jacob: "Peoples shall serve you, and nations shall bow down to you, you shall be master to your brothers, and to you will bow down the sons of your mother."

5

Medicine and Judaism

Medicine and Morals

I N the past, the close association between Judaism and medicine occupied an illustrious place
in Jewish cultural history. For many centuries
most of our leading thinkers, rabbis, poets and philosophers
practiced medicine—men such as Maimonides, Judah Halevy,
Abraham Ibn Ezra, and Immanuel of Rome. To this day
Halachic literature is richly suffused with discussions on
medical subjects.

Published in *The Jewish Chronicle*, October 6, 1961.

With this literary and historical legacy, it is all the more surprising that we have not as yet matched the numerous medico-religious manuals produced by other faiths, notably the Roman Catholic Church, by even a single guide-book setting forth in simple practical terms the authentic Jewish answers to the many moral and religious problems raised in modern medical and hospital practice.

An argument frequently encountered by those who advocate the application of Jewish principles to medicine, especially at Jewish hospitals, is: Why not leave medicine to the doctors? By what right can rabbinical writings, extending from antiquity to the present day, prescribe to doctors how to carry out their professional work? The argument is, of course, completely spurious! Certainly, Judaism does not presume to usurp the functions of medicine and its practitioners. Jewish views are strongly opposed to the doctrines and beliefs of those religious systems, such as Christian Science, which repudiate or conflict with medical science and its teachings. No stipulation in Jewish law intrudes into the physician's *medical* prerogative if the basis for his decision is in fact purely medical. Judaism does leave medicine strictly to the doctors.

In truth, the reverse is the case. Modern medical practices often inevitably encroach upon the domains of religion. Jewish law concerns itself with medical subjects only when patients or physicians concern themselves, as they are frequently bound to, with essentially moral or religious problems.

So long as the practice of medicine was rigidly controlled by the Oath of Hippocrates, which guided medical ethics from ancient times up to the present century, the occasions for religious "interference" were relatively few and unimportant. The Oath provided that the honorable physician would limit his art to "healing the sick." Today the area of medicine has extended far beyond this classical definition. Artificial insemination, for instance, already widely practiced by many physicians who would regard themselves as honorable, has nothing to do with "healing the sick." Whether such operations can be justified is plainly a moral, not a medical, issue.

The Oath further required medical graduates to swear that they would not perform euthanasia, abortions and, according to some interpretations, sterilizations, leaving such operations "to those who make a business thereof." Today, two of these practices, if not all three, have become commonplace among some of the most reputable doctors.

We may use abortions to illustrate our point. The number of illegal abortions is so great (estimated in the United States at a million annually, 90 per cent of them performed by physicians, "many of them of good standing in their communities"[1]), that a leading obstetrician recently complained: "The law makes hypocrites of us all."[2]

This is true. But it would be no less true to state: "We all make a mockery of the law." Both these statements, when viewed from different angles, pin-point the crux of the problem at issue here. The question is: Shall the law determine the rights of physicians, or shall the physicians define the jurisdiction of the law?

To the extent that abortions are performed for purely medical reasons as defined by law (i.e. the hazards to the mother's life), the decision properly rests with physicians, as the sole experts competent to pass medical judgments. But in most cases the factors to be considered are much more complex. They usually concern not only medical findings, but also the imperatives of right and wrong. Whether abortions are justified, for instance, in cases of rape or incest, of anticipated psychological disturbances in the mother, or of health risks in the child possibly resulting from German measles in the mother during her pregnancy—all these are problems beyond the professional competence of doctors. The real question, therefore, is: By what right do physicians set themselves up as arbitrators in matters of law, morals, or religion, instead of leaving such matters to those professionally qualified in these disciplines.

One other example may prove instructive: The vexed problem of autopsies. We shall not here deal with the intrinsic Jewish arguments for and against such operations. All that concerns us here is to determine within whose jurisdiction falls the decision whether we have a right to utilize the dead in the service of medical science. We are confronted here, as in so many other medico-moral problems, with two conflicting interests. On the one hand, autopsies are needed on an extensive scale to promote medical progress, a fact which no one disputes. On the other hand, the human body in death as in life is endowed with certain inalienable rights, rights which Jewish law seeks to protect with particular insistence. No consideration, not even the advancement of human health, can *automatically* sweep aside these rights.

That the most urgent medical considerations, even when they might lead to saving countless lives, are sometimes set aside in the face of the inviolable rights of the individual is demonstrated by the horror evoked throughout the civilized world at the medical experimentation on living humans in Nazi Germany. If we were justified in sacrificing but a few individuals on the altar of medicine—by using them for possible fatal tests—we could do doubt amass far more valuable information, and ultimately save the lives of far more people, than by thousands of autopsies on the dead. Yet it is morally wrong deliberately to surrender a single human life, however decrepit, in order to preserve a million others, and no moral person would presume to challenge this ruling.

The comparison between human vivisection and autopsies is admittedly far-fetched in many respects. But the one aspect of the analogy in which we are here interested is perfectly legitimate. In both cases there is a conflict between medical progress and certain personal human rights. In the case of the living, we take it for granted that the individual's claim to life is greater than the claims of society to medical progress. Whether the title of the dead to undisturbed rest is as great as the title of the living to life is a matter of comparative value, subject again to a moral, not a medical, judgment.

In arbitrating on such an issue, a physician is at best like any other enlightened layman. Since he is, after all, an interested party, to leave this judgment solely to him would be to turn the claimant into his own judge. The fact, therefore, that the physician is the medical expert concerned with autopsies weakens rather than supports his demand to decide when the rights and integrity of a human body may be violated. As the technical expert in the field he must obviously provide the medical evidence in support of his claim, but the decision, being of a moral nature, logically rests with moral experts.

Regarding these limitations, physicians are no different from any other professionals. They all must surrender some areas within their general jurisdiction to the superior competence of others. Rabbis cannot claim that, as custodians of Jewish law, they should have the right to decide whether a patient's illness is grave enough to warrant the violation of the Sabbath to avoid any danger to his life. That decision belongs to doctors. Nor can lawyers argue that, because the legal field is their specialty, the dictates of their conscience should determine the laws they administer.

Physicians readily acknowledge the right of a country's official lawmakers to legislate in medico-legal matters. There is no less reason for accepting the jurisdiction of moralists in the solution of medico-moral problems.

Every nontheistic religion embodies within its philosophy and legislation a system of ethics, a definition of moral values. None does so with greater precision and comprehensiveness than Judaism. It emphatically insists that the norms of ethical conduct can be governed neither by the accepted notions of public opinion nor by the whims of the individual conscience. In the Jewish view, the human conscience is meant to enforce moral laws, not to make them. Right and wrong, good and evil, are absolute values which transcend the capricious variations of time, place and environment. These values, Judaism teaches, derive their validity from the Divine revelation at Mount Sinai, as expounded and developed by sages faithful to, and authorized by, its writ. Theirs is the task and prerogative to provide for Jews and Jewish practice authentic answers to all ethical problems in accordance with the principles and precedents enshrined in the inspired writings of Jewish law.

Medicine and Religion—
The Jewish View

JUDAISM'S religious and moral directives in medical practice represent the accumulated wisdom and intellectual labors of millennia, stretching from the Talmud, the codes of Jewish law and their innumerable commentaries, down to the most recent rabbinical responsa work published within the past year—all ultimately inspired by the absolute Divine verities enshrined in the Hebrew Bible, the immutable guide to Jewish conduct. While these laws claim our unquestioned loyalty on the strength of their religious value, as the means to the fulfillment of God's will, they are but the expression of the moral discipline of Judaism. They are founded on the supreme sanctity of human life, on the dignity of man as a creation in the image of God, on the religious precept to mitigate suffering and to heal the sick, on the claims of the sick to spiritual aids in their recovery from illness, and on the rights of patients and physicians to respect for their religious susceptibilities.

In its legislation on medical ethics, Jewish law has the advantage of being heir to a rich millennial tradition of intimate partnership between Judaism and medicine. Many of the principal architects of Jewish law—some of the most outstanding authors of the Talmud, codes, commentaries and other rabbinical writings—were themselves medical practitioners by occupation, some of them making distinguished contributions to medical practice and literature. The literary depositories of Jewish law—from the Bible and Talmud to the vast medieval and modern rabbinical literature—are replete with discussions on religious and moral problems raised in the practice of medicine, and the conclusions they reached frequently reflect their practical experience in medicine no less

This paper served as a draft text for the Introduction to *A Hospital Compendium—A Guide to Jewish Moral and Religious Principles in Hospital Practice,* issued by the Commission on Synagogue Relations of the Federation of Jewish Philanthropies of New York, 1963. In this form, it is reprinted from *The Nu Sigma Nu Bulletin* (University of Wisconsin), Summer 1963.

than their respect for the medical profession and their infinite regard for human life and health inculcated by Jewish teachings.

The Infinite Value of Every Human Life

The first and most cardinal principle in the Jewish approach to medicine is the teaching that the value of every human life is infinite and beyond measure. From this all-important principle flow numerous practical rulings, such as the suspension of almost all religious laws in the face of danger to life, the duty to heal the sick as a religious precept, and the opposition to such acts as suicide, euthanasia and hazardous experimentation on living humans.

To understand the significance and ramifications of this principle some explanation is required. An infinite number is, by mathematical definition, incapable of being reduced or increased by division or multiplication. However often infinity is divided or multiplied, the result invariably remains infinity and therefore identical with the original number.

Two illustrations drawn from Jewish law will enable us to appreciate the practical application of this truth to human life. A child walks at the edge of a skyscraper roof. A wind blows it over the edge, and it hurtles down to its doom scores of floors below. A moment before it is about to crash to its certain death on the ground, a man kills it by shooting or stabbing. He is then deemed as a first-degree murderer, even though he shortened the child's life only by the merest fraction of a second. The reason is quite plain. Since human life is of infinite worth, any fraction of it is of equally infinite value, so that seventy years rate the same as any part of them, whether one year, or one hour or a split second. The crime of murder, therefore—in terms of destroying an infinite value —is entirely independent of the number of years or seconds by which the victim's life is reduced. Infinity is indivisible.

Conversely, the value of one human individual, being infinite, is absolutely identical to that of any number of others, being equally infinite. Accordingly, Jewish law rules that if one hundred people were taken hostage and told to surrender any one of them for execution or else all would be killed, it is forbidden to comply, and the entire group must submit to death rather than have a hand in the killing of a single one. For that one life has precisely the same value as the other ninety-nine combined. Infinity is unmultipliable.

Why is Jewish law so insistent on stressing the evaluation of human life as infinite? Because this is the indispensable foundation of the sanctity of all human life. If a person who has only a few minutes or hours more to live would be worth less than one who can still look forward to seventy years of life, the value of every human being would lose its absolute character and become relative—relative to his expectancy of life, or his state of health, or his usefulness to society, or any other arbitrary criteria. No two human beings would have the same value; they would all be subject to rating according to one or several criteria used. Such a reduction of human values from absolute to relative standards would thus vitiate the equality of all men; it would be the thin end of the wedge dividing mankind into people of superior and inferior value, into those who have a greater and others who have a smaller claim to life. This concept would inevitably lead to justifying the Nazi philosophy of liquidating Jews, gypsies, political enemies, cripples and mental defectives as "inferior" members of society. There can be no stable and defensible line drawn between the Nazi position and the advocates of euthanasia. Either the shriveled patient on his deathbed has exactly the same value and the same title to life as the healthiest and socially most precious individual—because both lives are equally infinite in value—or we open the doors to a system of grading in which the interests of the state, or of health, or other considerations will determine who shall live and who shall die. The moment any human being is toppled from the infinitely high pedestal on which he stands, he drags down with him all others, and the whole fabric of the moral order is bound to collapse.

The Supreme Duty to Save Human Life

It follows from these premises that Judaism can never condone the deliberate destruction of any human life (except in case of criminals or war, when expressly sanctioned by the Creator of Life), whether for the purpose of relieving suffering (suicide, euthanasia) or with a view to saving other human lives (self-sacrifice for the sake of others, possibly fatal experiments on humans).

Another consequence of the supreme and infinite value attached to human life in Judaism is the automatic suspension of all religious laws if necessary to save life. As the Talmud puts it, the ordinances of Torah were given "that man shall live by them, not die by them." The only exceptions to this rule are the cardinal crimes of idolatry, incest (including adultery) and bloodshed. These crimes—constituting the principal offenses against God, oneself and one's neighbor—are the only ones which must not be committed even at the expense of life itself.

Accordingly, the violation of the Sabbath laws, for instance, in the face of danger to life is not only permitted but mandatory. The codes of Jewish law inculcate this duty with every emphasis and urgency. "Whoever is zealous [in the profanation of the Sabbath for the sake of saving life] is praiseworthy." The concession is unconditional and applicable to any threat to life, however remote or doubtful.

Also founded on the supreme regard for human life is the rule of Jewish law raising the healing of the sick into a religious precept. Any person who has the power to save life and does not exercise it, or who stands by idly when a life is in danger, offends against the law "Thou shalt not stand upon thy neighbor's blood." Hence a doctor may never refuse or withdraw his services, even if other doctors are available, unless these are more competent. In legal terms, the religious character of the duty to heal is well borne out by the following law. A person who vowed that he would not accept any benefits or favors from another may still be medically treated by him, because to heal is not rendering a favor but simply performing a religious precept.

The Title to Life Before Birth

In Jewish law the absolute claim to life, based on its infinite worth, takes effect from the moment of birth. This is defined as the moment when the head or the greater part of the body has emerged from the birth canal. From that moment on the right to life of the child is equal to that of the mother or any other persons (provided the child is viable; i.e. it is known to have been carried for a full term or it has survived the first thirty days of life). The destruction of such a child, even before the delivery is complete, is regarded as murder and cannot be sanctioned either to save the mother if she is in danger or to terminate the life of a clearly abnormal child, however deformed.

Before that moment is reached, however, the value of the child is distinctly inferior to that of the mother, so that in the event of a mortal conflict between the two at any stage of pregnancy, it is mandatory to kill the foetus if there is no other alternative to preserving the life of the mother. In other words, Judaism sanctions, nay demands, therapeutic abortions in cases of hazards to the mother's life.

Nevertheless, even the unborn child, inferior as its value may be, does enjoy certain very sacred rights, and to abort it —while not constituting murder—is a most heinous offense except for reasons of the mother's safety.

The Generation of Life

Man has been set into the world to become "a partner with God in creation," in the parlance of the Talmud. From the very inception of human life recorded in the Bible man is charged to "be fruitful and multiply and fill the earth," and this duty marks the first of the 613 commandments the Divine Law enjoined on the Jewish people.

In the Jewish view, the act of procreation is the foremost and holiest fulfillment of man's destiny.

From these fundamental premises derive the detailed Jewish teachings on the moral problems connected with the inception of life, notably on sterilization, contraception and artificial insemination. Since the exercise of man's procreative faculties is a positive and cardinal duty, any deliberate interference with the natural process or organism of generation is a grave offense except when necessitated by overriding medical indications. However, the restrictions imposed on men are far more severe than those on women. Contraception may never be practiced by men, and only the gravest hazards to health can justify operations on them leading to their sterilization. In the case of women the law is more lenient, particularly regarding the conditions justifying sterilization.

Still fewer objections are raised to the employment of oral contraceptives, frequently referred to in rabbinic literature since the time of Talmud nearly 2,000 years ago as a "cup of sterility" or a "potion of roots." Interestingly enough, this drink to prevent conception known to the ancient rabbis could also be used to induce greater fertility, a remarkable anticipation of the present-day hormone preparations which can likewise serve both to promote and to suppress ovulation. Jewish law prefers this means to achieve temporary or even permanent sterility to surgical or other contraceptive procedures on the grounds that it does not directly impair the reproductive organs or constitute a physical impediment to the generative act.

Similar factors account for the rigid opposition of Judaism to artificial insemination, by donor, despite the supreme value and importance the Jewish faith attaches to the blessing of parenthood as the fulfillment of marriage and the achievement of the noblest human task. This abhorrence of A. I. D. is all the more significant in view of the fact that Jewish law, in contrast to the generally accepted rulings of both the Church and civil law, does not brand such insemination as adultery or the child so conceived as illegitimate. This liberal decision is based on another startling talmudic antecedent. By far the first reference in world literature to the feasibility of an impregnation *sine concubito* occurs in the Talmud—some 1,700 years before modern scientific research established the possibility of a conception brought about without any physical relationship between the parents. (The passage concerned rules that a virgin who is pregnant has not thereby forfeited her legal status as a virgin, and it explains the circumstances of her pregnancy as due to her having bathed in waters previously fertilized by a male—a clear case of artificial, albeit accidental, insemination.)

The Inviolability of the Human Body

Man's inalienable right to inviolability extends not only to his life but also to his body, as the bearer of the Divine soul created in the image of God. In the strictly legal sense the body does not belong to us; it always remains Divine property, whether in life or in death.

With the body's decease and its inability to serve the purpose for which it was created, its custody as well as ownership reverts to God and it must be "returned to the earth as it was." The reverent treatment of the dead body and its speedy burial are biblical precepts, and any indignities inflicted on it are branded as "a curse of God" (Deut. 21:22-23). The duty to inter the dead is not fulfilled (and the laws of mourning do not take effect) until every part of the body that can be found has been buried.

The Rights of the Dead

Once the body is dead, however, the only consideration which might override its rights to being buried intact is the prospect that the secrets it holds might help to save another human life in danger at that time. This is the sole basis for any permission to perform an autopsy. But even such permission is not automatic and can never be given routinely, for the claim of the living to life may be no greater than the title of the dead to undisturbed rest.

The far-reaching duties towards the dead enjoined in the legislation of Judaism serve not only to defend the rights of those who can no longer speak or fend for themselves. They are equally designed to promote the highest regard for life and the living. The medical student who treats the dead human body as an indifferent piece of flesh, as an interesting laboratory exhibit, with complete disregard to its supreme dignity as a unique creation that was once endowed with the spirit of God, such a student may later display the same callous indifference to the infinite value of everyone of his patients. His pursuit of medicine will be a profession, not a vocation; a means to lucre and possibly research, not a mission in the cause of the highest ideal of neighborly love.

On the other hand, the medical student who is trained to approach every dead body with an ever-present sense of awe and reverence, whose religious adoration of God is awakened at the sight of the marvelous mysteries revealed in God's supreme creation, such a student will become a better doctor. His heart will bleed with sympathy for every sufferer, and leap with joy every time he succeeds in effecting a cure. A doctor so trained to revere even a dead body will never deal curtly or carelessly with the living, for he is ever conscious of the priceless treasure placed in his trust.

Judaism's Spiritual Aids to the Sick

A meaningful maxim of the Talmud declares: "The Divine Presence rests upon the head of the sickbed." Man is never closer to God than when he lies stricken and helpless on the sickbed. Gone is his arrogance and self-assurance, his air of superiority over others, and his sense of independence of them. Instead he feels chastened by his ordeal, suppliant and mortified. Dependent on others, he pleads for mercy—perhaps he even prays.

For many people divorced from religion as long as they were healthy, serious illness occasions their first profoundly religious experience. In a very literal sense, they discover the Divine Presence on the sickbed. For the first time they begin to probe deeply into their past conduct, searching for reasons to explain their suffering. Shaken by the fear of infirmity or death, they resolve to eliminate their moral vices and religious failings if only God will heal them. Whether they argue with God about the justice of their affliction, or they promise Him their loyalty in future in return for His healing, they are somehow brought nearer to the reality of His Presence. They commune with God face to face.

How can we help these patients—driven, as they are, by fears, doubts, remorse and self-recrimination—to regain their spiritual strength and confidence? How can we prevent their shattering mental experience from worsening their physical condition, or at least from slowing their recovery? How can we insure that the terrible blow of sickness will produce the one constructive result of moral regeneration instead of adding to the physical damage the bane of spiritual disintegration and despair?

Sick people, more than any others, need the reassurance that they do not affront the susceptibilities of God, that everything done by them and for them accords with His will. They know—rationally or by some mysterious feeling, depending on their religious orientation—that their recovery may depend on a Power beyond the skills of the most competent physician, and they do not want to risk alienating that Power in their hour of trial and adversity.

The same consideration applies to the religious regulations on all medical procedures involving grave moral doubts or perplexities. If a mother must have recourse to the abortion of her fruit, the loss of her most precious creation may haunt her for the rest of her life unless she can be absolutely certain that her sacrifice was sanctioned by God Himself, the Creator of all life, that it was demanded by her religious teachings. If a patient in extremity is to endure the torment of his death agony to the bitter end, at least he wants to be convinced that his God tolerates no short-cut to death, that an Agency higher than any human authority is responsible for his fate and for the refusal of his physicians to terminate his misery by inducing death. And when a person approaches the end to be at peace with his Creator, he wants to be assured that his stricken body will find eternal rest and be returned unimpaired to his Maker.

All these religious graces are required even for people whose religious conscience is only awakened by the experience of illness. For those whose lives are always dedicated to their religion these spiritual comforts are even more indispensable to their fortitude in suffering and their faith in recovery. A truly pious person, who spares neither trouble nor expense to uphold the precepts of his religion every day of his life, could be seriously set back if at the time of crisis his spiritual supports were taken from him. To subject him, when he lies prostrate on the sickbed, to violations of the tenets he treasures, or to the sight of others violating them on his behalf, may well amount to sheer cruelty. The mental anguish produced by such subjection cannot easily be appreciated by those who do not know what it means to live and suffer for one's religious convictions. All the more reason for them to go out of their way in the most scrupulous exercise of neighborly love at its finest: cherishing the feelings of others one does not share oneself. To have sympathy with a patient when one is oneself afflicted with illness is easy and natural; but to have the fullest *Mitgefuehl* with a sufferer when one enjoys the best health oneself, that is noble because it demands an effort at identifying oneself with the wants of someone else. Likewise, for religious personnel to respect the needs of religious patients requires little effort or emphasis; to have such consideration shown by those who do not care for it themselves needs stressing an evokes appreciation.

Judaism's Spiritual Aids to Physicians

A famous talmudic saying, which may at first sight appear odd, states: "To hell with the best of doctors!" However, according to the understanding of the ancient rabbis—many of whom were themselves physicians—the true meaning of this statement was far more charitable than a superficial reading of it might suggest. Following one interpretation, physicians are always to see the abyss of hell in front of them. No class of human beings has such power over life and death as the doctors. The slightest error, the least negligence, might easily lead to the premature death of a patient—and to the mortal damnation of the attending physician. "The best of doctors" are those who are constantly aware of the crushing responsibilities vested in them, who are continuously on their guard not to slip from their lofty path by a mere moment's carelessness over the precipice into the hellish depths of capital guilt.

Another equally profound interpretation suggests that those who *consider themselves* "the best of doctors" deserve to be consigned "to hell." There is no room in medicine for pride, conceit and self-confidence. Doctors, who witness all the time the miracle of life and healing as well as the inadequacy of human knowledge, ought to be the first to realize their utter dependence on the guidance and assistance of the Healer of all flesh. By refusing to plead for His support, or to consult with other colleagues, because they trust in themselves, they may condemn their patients to death and themselves to hell. To other people humility may be a virtue; to doctors it is the indispensable foundation for the success of their practice. Lives depend on the physician's awareness of his own frailty and limitations.

How are these vital qualities of responsibility and humility to be so deeply ingrained in the physician's moral outlook that they will dominate all his activities, down to the most trivial procedure, at all times? Neither the fear of malpractice suits for demonstrable acts of negligence nor the urge for promotion based on efficiency can guarantee a sense of consecration beyond the call of duty expected of the conscientious doctor.

For physicians there is only one effective control: a deeply religious conscience generated and constantly recharged by the fear of God. In a beautiful observation our Sages point out that the Bible always joins the duty to fear God with commandments which "are surrendered to the heart," i.e., the conscientious performance of which can be checked by no-one but God. For instance, "Thou shalt not curse the deaf, nor put a stumbling block before the blind, and thou shalt fear thy God; I am the Lord" (Lev. 19:14). In relation to the work of the physician, every layman is usually deaf and blind, unable to catch and prosecute the careless practitioner. Only the realization that God watches him can keep the doctor on his guard at all times.

The supreme contribution Judaism can make towards attaining the highest standards of medicine is to help in producing consecrated doctors. A truly religious doctor is essentially a superior doctor. The absence of a spirit of reverence, humility and complete dedication is no doubt responsible for more suffering and deaths than the mere lack of technical skill or medical knowledge. Lack of experience can be overcome by consultation with experts; deficient devotion and conscientiousness cannot be remedied except by an inner awareness of God's presence and scrutiny. This can be supplied only by a firm religious faith founded on the fear of God and sustained by the ennobling discipline of serving Him in all areas of life.

Judaism also helps to enhance the personal element in the relationship between the physician and his patients. Complaints are often heard these days that the practice of medicine has become depersonalized, that many doctors treat those in their charge as cases rather than as persons, supplying drugs where sympathy and understanding would be more efficacious, and dealing with organs as if they were machine parts to be repaired instead of treating them as live constituents of the total personality made up of body, mind and soul. The specialist in particular may frequently care for the heart or kidney under treatment but care little for the patient himself and the suffering he endures. A doctor suffused with religious idealism as the inspiration for his work cannot act that way. He is never a mere mechanic or technician but above all a human being serving as God's messenger in bringing succor and comfort to his stricken fellow-man. Such a physician grieves with his patient in pain and rejoices with him in recovery. He heals by virtue of sharing the feelings of the sufferer.

Finally, Jewish thought and observance can serve as a powerful antidote against the demoralizing influences to which a physician is necessarily exposed. The constant sight of blood and suffering, the frequent need to jab needles and scalpels into sensitive flesh, and to view morbid cadavers, are bound to harden the most tender heart if not neutralized by refining agents on the opposite scale. Furthermore, while Jewish law does not object to male doctors treating women, it does recognize the moral hazards involved. Altogether, the doctor's ineluctable preoccupation with the physical features of the human being, with the body in its nakedness, makes it all the more vital to redress the resultant imbalance by particularly emphasizing the spiritual and moral counterparts in the human personality. More than anyone else it is the doctor who requires the uplifting aid of religious faith and practice to maintain his moral equilibrium in the face of the many snares and temptations challenging him every day.

Medicine in Jewish Law

Questions and Answers*

T HE classic codes of Jewish law, culminating in
the *Shulchan Arukh* and its commentaries, represent the rules of Jewish life mainly in their
talmudic formulation. The rabbinical responsa define the
application of these rules to the ever changing problems of the
times. The responsa literature thus mirrors the pattern of
contemporary conditions as well as their adjustment to Jewish thought and law. As a result, this literature has been widely used as historical source material to illuminate the social
background of successive ages.

In surveying the sizeable volume of rabbinic responsa published during the past decade we will discover ample testimony to the great strides made by medicine in that period.
I am unaware of a single collection of recent responsa that
does not deal, often at great length, with medical questions
submitted to rabbinic judgment. Many of these responsa
seek to shed new light on old problems, such as the attitude
to autopsies or the saving of life. Others explore the altogether new territory conquered by the thrusts of medical
progress; advances which often raise moral and religious
problems of the utmost gravity. In this category belong new
procedures such as the heterogeneous transplant of human tissue and cosmetic surgery; new medical discoveries and experiences, such as oral contraceptives and the extension of
therapeutic abortion to cases of anticipated foetal deformities;
and new medical arguments, such as discussions on artificial
insemination, and the right to withdraw treatment from hope-
lessly lingering patients.

Authentic Jewish answers to all these problems have become crystalized in recent responsa works, often in the form
of controversial and mutually exclusive attitudes. In fact, on

To be published in the *Israel Brodie Jubilee Volume*, London, 1965.

*For earlier sources on the subjects here treated references are occa-
sionally made to my *Jewish Medical Ethics*, New York, 1959 & 1962 (cited
in the notes as JME).

most of these issues rabbinic debates continue, and what one rabbi is inclined to permit another may prohibit. But these are the indispensable dynamics of rabbinic law-making. The accepted norms of Jewish law emerge gradually from a consensus of rabbinic opinion based on the preponderance of endorsements of one ruling over another. Only after many rabbis have studied, and ruled on, a given problem—bringing to that problem their understanding of the principles, precedents and arguments applicable to it—can a concensus be reached. The law as applied to any new situation is not an abstract absolute but determined "according to the teaching which they shall teach thee, and according to the judgment which they shall tell thee."[3] All decisions, however divergent they may be, are soundly sustained by the closest approximation to the principles and rulings established by earlier authorities.

By limiting the present survey to responsa which have appeared in print within the past decade, it is my object to bring this subject matter up-to-date with the material contained in my book *Jewish Medical Ethics,* first published in 1958. No claim is made at having exhausted all available sources; only a portion of recent responsa works and rabbinical journals have been consulted in the preparation of this study. The range and scope of the subjects and the questions dealt with are sufficiently broad and representative to make this a fairly comprehensive review of the Jewish response to the challenge that has arisen from the inevitable incursion of modern medical practice and research into the realms of religion and morality.

The sources surveyed here are restricted in kind as well as in time. Anything which has not appeared in the form of responsa or is not closely related to rabbinic writings on specific questions has been excluded. Some rabbinic rulings on medical matters are discussed from time to time in other publications. Particularly noteworthy in this connection is *A Hospital Compendium: A Guide to Jewish Moral and Religious Principles in Hospital Practice.* It was prepared by a committee of rabbis and physicians under the co-chairmanship of Rabbi Benjamin Sharfman and the present writer, and issued by the Commission on Synagogue Relations of the Federation of Jewish Philanthropies of New York in 1963.

1. VISITING THE SICK

The ramified regulations on the religious precept to visit the sick as codified in the *Shulchan Arukh*[4] have recently been discussed in great detail and with numerous references to rabbinic sources by two leading Israeli scholars.[5]

a. By Telephone

A novel inquiry treated in several responsa is the question whether the obligation to visit the sick can be fulfilled by a telephone call. While one rabbi asserts that technically one thereby discharges merely the duty of "charity,"[6] others hold that such a call may be regarded tantamount to visiting the sick, provided it is of some assistance to the patient.[7]

b. Visiting Infectious Patients

The question whether the duty to visit the sick extends to visiting patients suffering from an infectious disease was already answered with a qualified affirmative by R. Moses Isserles[8] against the view of some later authorities who questioned the need to expose oneself to the hazard of contagion in the fulfillment of this precept.[9] A recent re-examination of this question reaches the conclusion, based on several talmudic narratives[10]—that the ruling of Isserles applies only to an infection which would not endanger the life of the visitor even if he caught it, such as jaundice, but that one is not required to risk one's life for the sake of fulfilling merely the rabbinical precept to visit the sick;[11] nor can anyone be compelled to serve such patients.[11a]

c. Hospital Visits by *Kohanim*

The law barring Jews of priestly descent (*Kohanim*) from defiling themselves to the dead by sharing a common roof with a corpse presents, of course, a special problem to priestly visitors to hospitals. This problem has recently been restudied at length[12] with the conclusion of generally confirming earlier rulings[13] in favor of permitting such visits unless it is definitely known that a dead person is there at the time. But two authorities are against such visits for fear that modern hospitals may be presumed to contain preserved organs or embryos causing defilement.[14] At the same time, permission was given to a priestly patient to visit a surgery containing a skull since its capacity to confer defilement was subject to a two-fold doubt.[15]

2. LAW-SUSPENSION TO SAVE LIFE

With the bulk of the Jewish regulations on medicine dealing with the conditions under which religious laws may be set aside or modified in the face of hazards to life or health, it is not surprising that many of the references to medical matters in recent rabbinic literature are devoted to this important field of Jewish medical ethics, particularly in view of the growing complexity of Sabbath and dietary problems in modern medical practice. Several major studies, including an entire book, have lately been devoted to an analysis of the highly diversified rabbinic sources on the subject and to defining in modern terms the conditions listed in the Talmud and codes as constituting possible risks of life and thus warranting the suspension of religious laws.[16] Into this rubric also falls the ruling that in deciding on the degree of dangers to justify violations of the law the majority of physicians' opinions prevails.[17]

a. Sabbath Observance

Most of the questions on Sabbath observance deal with possible conflicts between the Sabbath laws and medical requirements. One novel decision, for instance, deems any patient with a temperature of 102° F. or over as being potentially in danger and entitled to otherwise forbidden services on the Sabbath.[18] Another asserts that, while writing (e.g. prescriptions, hospital admission forms, etc.) for a patient on the Sabbath is obviously prohibited (being of no direct therapeutic urgency), even a moderately sick person may repair to a Jewish doctor although he writes prescriptions on the Sabbath.[19] For a seriously ill person it is also permitted to have x-rays taken on the Sabbath.[20] But a question of whether massages as medical treatment could be sanctioned on the Sabbath is left unresolved.[21] The same author does, however, permit the use of a toothbrush on the Sabbath provided it is not used with toothpaste which is forbidden like soap.[22] The only recent contribution to the vexed problem of violations of the Sabbath for non-Jewish patients[23] is the assertion that the requisite restrictions are even more applicable to the treatment of non-observant Jews.[24]

Several responsa have lately appeared on the use of electrical hearing-aids on the Sabbath. One decision permits the carrying of these aids, provided the apparatus is set and sewn to the clothing before the Sabbath.[24a] A disabled person may push his carriage on the Sabbath by himself; but this work must not be done by another person,[24b] except in a place which is not technically "public domain," when a non-Jew may perform the service.[24c]

b. Dietary Laws

New questions have also arisen on the use of medications containing animal susbtances. Thus derivatives of blood have been permitted on the grounds that their chemical treatment reduces the prohibition to merely rabbinical status and that, moreover, such medication is usually not "eaten" in a conventional manner.[25] Sick persons may also be fed on raw liver.[26]

3. SURGICAL OPERATIONS

a. Consent

In Jewish law the consent of a patient is not required for any operation medically deemed necessary for his health. Indeed, even if he wished to avoid the operation and submit to danger as a means to penitence through suffering, he should be forced to undergo the treatment against his will if necessary.[27] This is particularly so in the case of an infectious disease, where a hazard to others may also exist. The patient is compelled to submit to any treatment required to prevent the spread of the disease, including the marking of his house, and when an epidemic strikes those not affected should be urged to escape.[28]

b. Submission to Surgery

On the other hand, surgical operations should be undertaken only if their efficacy is known to the surgeon; in that case they may be carried out even to prevent merely acute pain, provided the patient is expected to stand the operation.[29] Preventive surgery is to be avoided if the prospects of the condition to be forestalled are remote; but innoculation against infectious diseases is permitted even if the operation entails some danger.[30]

c. Organic Transplants

Many responsa in recent times reflect the acute ethical problems created through the increasing recourse to grafting operations as one of the newest and most promising accomplishments of modern medicine. But while non-Jewish moralists, among both physicians and theologians, have concentrated their debate on the right to use heterogeneous transplants taken from living donors, Jewish authorities are mainly concerned with the utilization of tissue removed from the dead. The right of a person to donate an organ in an attempt to preserve the life of someone else is determined by the controversial view on whether one may, or must, generally risk one's own life or limb to save another's,[31] an issue so far scarcely discussed in the context of graft donations. But the problem of removing and using parts of the dead for such operations, especially for corneal transplants, has received much attention, in recent responsa.

Regarding eye grafts, most authorities have endorsed the now classic argument by the present Chief Rabbi of Israel[32]—that any tissue from the dead grafted to a living patient, by being literally restored to life, loses its forbidden character as a part removed from the dead and may therefore be utilized.[33] Only one scholar rejects this reasoning, although he still allows the operation on the ground that saving a person from complete blindness, which may make him more easily liable to fatal accidents, is tantamount to saving his life.[34] This argument is mentioned by others, too. Hence, and because of further considerations on the rights of the dead, it has been suggested that, in making the necessary provisions during his life-time, the donor should stipulate that his eye be used for a person suffering from, or threatened with, blindness on both eyes,[35] and that the disused part of the eye after the cornea has been removed be disposed of by burial only.[36] One rabbi also urges informing the donor that the gift of his eyes, however meritorious, may compromise his atonement after death by reason of the deliberate mutilation of his body.[37] Another rabbi, however, insisting on the inviolability of any Jewish body after death, is prepared to sanction post-mortem transplants to the living only if taken from non-Jews.[34]

While some of these authorities have extended the permission to donate and use eyes to other parts of the dead, too,[38] others assert that the right to perform such operations[39] or to transfuse blood from the dead[40] requires further study.

d. Cosmetic Surgery

The increasing vogue of resorting to plastic surgery for purely cosmetic purposes has lately aroused a good deal of moral questioning among professional and theological experts.[41] To date the only Jewish contribution to this subject is a discussion of the relevant sources with the tentative conclusion that such operations can be justified only if the defect to be corrected was caused by an accident of illness, thus turning the procedure into a therapeutic measure; if the deformity may lead to serious psychological ill-effects; or if it may cause a grave impediment to marriage or domestic happiness in women.[42]

e. Blood Donations

The donation of blood for life-saving operations is almost literally the fulfillment of the precept "Thou shalt not stand upon the blood of thy neighbor,"[43] rabbinically interpreted as making it an offense to stand by idly when another's life is in danger.[44] Yet blood donations, though constituting a religious obligation, cannot be enforced since they may involve an element of risk for the donor.[45] They may be given for payment, and they do not contravene the law against self-mutilation, since they may be compared to venesection permitted in the Talmud as a normal health measure.[46]

f. Operations on Parents

The severe ban on wounding, or causing any loss of blood to, parents even for medical purposes has led to many discussions on whether children may even give injections to their own parents.[47] Recently these restrictions have been fully re-examined again,[48] and one opinion holds that insulin shots, for instance, should not be administered on parents unless they cannot afford to engage professional help for this service.[49]

g. Disposal of Amputated Parts

Many authorities insist that any limbs or organs removed in surgical operations must be disposed of by burial.[50] But a recent responsum argues that legally interment is not required for such parts severed from the living and that any disposal, even by incineration, is in order so long as they are not treated in a disrepectful manner.[51]

4. THE GENERATION OF LIFE

a. Semen Sampling

Whether, and how, a husband whose marriage has proved barren may procure a sample of his semen for a fertility test is a question that has often been discussed in rabbinic writings.[52] The latest responsa generally permit this, provided the sample is not obtained by a manual manipulation but by the husband's use of a condom during regular intercourse or by *coitus interruptus*.[53] A biopsy taken from the testes for a similar purpose does not disqualify a man from maintaining his marriage as one "maimed in his privy parts."[54] But one rabbi objects to all such tests for both religious and social reasons; for such tests are futile whatever the result, and if they establish the husband as the cause for the sterile marriage, they may possibly lead to marital disharmony, unless new medical advances will find a cure for sterility after being ascertained by these tests.[55]

b. Artificial Insemination from the Husband

This procedure involves much the same problem and solution as semen testing,[56] and it should not be resorted to except in cases of extreme urgency.[57] Some rabbis object to this operation being performed while the wife is in a state of menstrual impurity, even if medically indicated;[58] but others are prepared to disregard that state if necessary,[59] or at least to reduce the period of impurity from twelve to eleven days if by making the insemination one day earlier the prospects of success are enhanced.[60] One opinion also holds that a child so conceived should never be circumcized on the Sabbath (similar to a child born by caesarian section), although the mother should observe the laws of impurity in the same way as following a natural birth.[61]

c. Artificial Insemination from a Donor

To the sizeable literature on this subject[62] a few new responsa have been added in recent years. With one surprising exception,[63] they confirm the unanimous condemnation and abhorence of this practice by earlier authorities.[64] An individual opinion holds that a child born under such conditions may have to be regarded as illegitimate (*Mamzer*), or at least be subject to the disabilities of a foundling.[65] A similar verdict was also reached by American court decisions in 1954 and 1963.[66]

d. Contraception

Turning from artificial methods to bring about conception to artificial means to prevent it, we find little new to augment the voluminous responsa on this subject found in virtually all rabbinic writings of the past two centuries.[67] Usually the only indications countenanced for the practice are grave hazards to the mother feared from renewed pregnancies.[68] But one scholar also permits the use of chemical spermicides, which he legally compares with the "sterility potion" mentioned in the Talmud,[69] to a mother who had previously given birth to two abnormal children and whose husband had already fulfilled the duty of procreation, but the permission is granted for two years only.[70] In fact a much closer parallel to the oral sterilizing agent so permissively treated in the Talmud and the codes[71] seems to be the contraceptive pill recently discovered (or rediscovered). The religious attitude to its use is only beginning to be discussed in rabbinic literature.[72] While the pill certainly represents the least objectionable method of birth-control, since it involves the least interference with the generative act and organs, it should not be used if it causes risks of irregular bleeding or other dangers.[73]

A tragic responsum of the war period allowed women in the Nazi ghettos, whose lives were doomed if found pregnant, to resort to birth-control, especially since any child she might conceive would also be doomed and could thus be regarded as inviable.[74]

e. Sterilization

Jewish law judges the sterilization of females more leniently than of males.[75] Nevertheless, since such an operation even on women constitutes a biblical offense, it should not be performed unless there is some danger to the woman. Even then she should rather use contraceptives than submit to sterilization if the danger feared would result from a pregnancy.[76]

The sterilization of males occurs most frequently as an all but inevitable by-product of operations on the prosthetic gland, raising a serious problem often discussed rabbinically in the past.[77] More recent rulings have permitted an operation to lower a testicle to its proper place, even though this occasionally results in its loss,[78] and even the complete excision of the testicles in cases of great pain, although this may render the patient into one "maimed in his privy parts."[79] But this disqualification does not ensue from such surgery if these parts had previously been impaired "by the hand of Heaven," that is, for natural causes.[80]

f. Abortion

An altogether new problem of the most tragic proportions which has lately aroused much public debate, and some rabbinic expressions of opinion, concerns the recourse to "therapeutic" abortion, not because of a threat to the mother's life, but the fear that her child may be born deformed, due to the mother having either caught German measles (rubella) or taken a drug (especially thalidomide) suspected to be injurious to the embryo during the first few weeks of pregnancy.[81] The Jewish view unanimously affirms that the title of an unborn child to life is not compromised by any physical or mental abnormalities, however crippling, even if such defects were definitely ascertained before birth.[82] The deliberate killing of such a child therefore constitutes "an appurtenance of murder," although foeticide is not technically regarded as a capital offense in Jewish law.[83] The destruction of a deformed child after birth, for which a mother was acquitted in the celebrated Liege trial of 1963, is deemed as plain homicide, of course.[84] The only indication for an abortion in these circumstances, would be, as in all cases, the concern for the safety of the mother. Any genuine fear of psychological disorders which might lead to a risk of life would be considered in the same way as any physical threat to her life resulting from her pregnancy.[85]

g. Defloration

The increasingly widespread recourse of virgins to physicians—a practice certainly frowned upon by Judaism except when really essential—also found an echo in a recent responsum. This permitted a young wife to disregard the bleeding caused by the artificial defloration, since the talmudic ordinance of impurity following virginal bleeding was enjoined only if resulting from the natural act.[86]

5. THE TERMINATION OF LIFE

a. Euthanasia

Euthanasia proper, that is, an attempt to relieve suffering by actively and deliberately hastening death, is of course condemned as sheer murder by all authorities.[87] To doctors who practice "mercy-killing" may be applied the talmudic dictum "To Gehennah with the best of physicians," a reference—according to one commentator—to those "who kill the patient"[88] out of misplaced compassion.[89] One questionable source appears to justify suicide as a means to end suffering,[90] but this has been rejected as completely alien to Jewish law which rates suicide as even worse than murder, as there can be no atonement for self-destruction by repentance.[91] A patient must not refuse religiously proscribed services or foods if necessary for his healing; how much less may he refuse treatment to escape from physical suffering.[92]

Far more complex and controversial is the problem of indirect euthanasia, when the patient's death is merely the result of either some medication given only to relieve pain or of the withdrawal of treatment. With the constant development in modern medicine of powerful pain-killers and of ever new devices and drugs to prolong lingering life, this problem has now become particularly acute and engaged the attention of several rabbis as well as moralists of other faiths.

On the use of analgesics administered solely to mitigate acute pain, though often resulting also in shortening life, a

permissive opinion has recently been expressed.[93] Sanctioned
by the same authority is the removal from a dying patient of
medications or machines designed to prolong life, supported
by the talmudic account[94] of the martyrdom of R.
Chananya ben Tradyon who permitted his executioner to assuage his
suffering by increasing the flames and removing the wool
placed on his body by his torturers to slow down his demise.[95]
Some years earlier a similar sanction to withdraw artificial
means to sustain a lingering life was also justified on ground
that the physician's duty to heal is limited to cases when he
may hope to "restore" the "lost" health of the patient,[96] and
that removal of an artificial impediment to the onset of
death is expressly sanctioned in the *Shulchan Arukh*.[97] Any
such sanction would not, however, extend to the withdrawal
of natural means of subsistence, such as food (even if intra-
venously administered) and probably also blood and oxygen.[98]

Opposing these two views are two others which will not
tolerate any relaxation of efforts, however artificial and ultimately hopeless, to prolong life. In defense of this opinion
it is argued that no prognosis of impending death is ever
certain;[99] that the patient's consent is quite irrelevant, since
the doctor is not his agent but God's in the exercise of healing;
and that the withdrawal of medication cannot be compared to
the *Shulchan Arukh's* permission to stop a clattering noise
or to remove from the patient's tongue salt holding up his
demise in the final phase.[100]

b. Autopsies

Under the mounting pressure of the medical profession for
ever more human bodies to serve training and research purposes, the Jewish religious objections to autopsies now constitute the most bitter bone of contention between rabbis and
physicians, especially pathologists. A survey conducted in 1959
by a committee composed of rabbis and doctors has revealed
that at Jewish hospitals in New York City, in which the
average rate of autopsies is about 50%, religious qualms are
an important factor in the refusal of relatives to give their
consent for such operations, and that the resultant low autopsy
rate at kosher hospitals threatens their continued accredita-

tion as teaching institutions.[101] In Israel, again, about the only civilized country where the law does not require consent from the family, the rate of autopsies at public hospitals is as high as 70% or more—a situation which has provoked continual protests from the religious community, sometimes erupting to violence and even cabinet-crises.

The impact of this clash between religious and medical claims has of late produced many re-examinations of the rabbinic attitude to this explosive subject, and it featured prominently at the 1963 Congress on the Oral Law held in Jerusalem.[102]

On the whole, little new has been added in all these rabbinic discussions and writings to the classic formulation of the halakhic attitude by R. Ezekiel Landau of Prague two centuries ago when he permitted autopsies only if the life of another patient then at hand might thereby be saved.[103] A leading scholar reaffirmed this statement without further qualification or elaboration but a few years ago.[104] Only one responsum has argued against the "at hand" condition as applying merely to the violation of the Sabbath by acts for the sick which could be left to a weekday if the danger to life were not immediately present; medical science, on the other hand, could never be advanced to save countless lives if autopsies could only be performed when patients who might benefit from the findings happened to be "at hand" immediately. The author is therefore inclined to permit the operation, provided the person had given his consent in his lifetime.[105] Some other authorities have also liberalized the "at hand" restriction, but only to the extent of requiring patients with symptoms similar to those of the deceased to be available at that time though not necessarily at that place, since the speed of modern communications enables a patient in one part of the world to benefit immediately from new discoveries in another.[106]

It has also been suggested to broaden the definition of autopsies performed directly for life-saving purposes by including post-mortems to ascertain the effects of new drugs or treatments, as well as to correct suspected errors of diagnosis made while the patient was alive.[107] Another argument in favor of a more lenient interpretation is that any operation on the dead carried out for an essential purpose cannot be regarded as a "disgrace" to the dead.[108]

On the other hand, several scholars have emphasized that relatives may halakhically prevent, but never sanction, any autopsy since they have no rights over the body of the deceased, and since the onus of his immediate burial rests primarily on them.[109] Certainly it is forbidden to surrender for research the body of a person who died without relatives (an "unclaimed body"); his interment is a special precept incumbent on the whole community *("met mitzvah")*.[110]

Further restrictions recently stressed in several responsa are that, when autopsies have been performed, the laws of mourning cannot be observed until all parts of the body have been interred and that priestly members of the family may not defile themselves to their dead if any part of the body is missing at the burial.[111]

Among the practical proposals made to solve the problem of autopsies with due regard for religious as well as urgent medical demands are the training of competent rabbis in medicine and anatomy, so that they themselves can determine each case on its merits,[112] and the establishment at Jewish hospitals of special boards consisting of two (preferably religious) physicians and one rabbi who should unanimously approve of every post-morten operation and arrange for a chaplain's supervision when requested by the family.[113]

6. CIRCUMCISION

a. Anaesthesia

A frequently discussed question in recent responsa concerns the use of anaesthetics for circumcisions. According to one decision, a general anaesthetic is not to be given to an adult proselyte, since he requires consciousness "in entering the sanctity of Israel," nor even to a Jewish infant, "as he would be like a stone, and one cannot establish a covenant with a stone; moreover, the removal of the foreskin from a sleeping child would be regarded by people as a mere operation and not as an initiation into the Covenant of Abraham." But the decision permits a local anaesthetic, against the view of an earlier authority.[114] Other rulings, however, sanction general anaesthetics even for proselytes, "since their circumcision is not a religious precept (which might require conscious intention) but merely a condition" to their admission as Jews,[115] and since in any event the obligation to perform the rite rests on the circumciser, not the subject whose consciousness is therefore immaterial.[116]

b. Hypospadias

With the modern method to use the foreskin in plastic operations usually carried out at the age of three or four years to correct congenital hypospadias, two rabbis have ruled in favor of postponing the circumcision in such cases, so as to make the operation possible and prevent the child from becoming sterile later on.[117] Strangely, neither of these responsa raised the question of the permanent reattachment of the foreskin after its removal, or considered alternative methods to rectify the deformity without using the foreskin.

c. Medical Impediments

If a child is jaundiced, the circumcision should be delayed in accordance with the expressed instructions of the Talmud and the codes, even if the doctors deem the child well enough to undergo the operation on the eighth day.[118]

A non-Jew whose life may be endangered by his circumcision cannot be admitted to Judaism as a proselyte, for it is an indispensable *condition* to his conversion, not a religious *duty* devolving on him which, if it were so, could be set aside for urgent medical reasons as it is for a Jew under such circumstances. In fact, one should not allow such an applicant to submit to the operation, since any fatal outcome might result in a *Chillul Ha-Shem*.[119]

7. PROFESSIONAL ETHICS

a. Secrecy

A physician summoned to court as a witness must give testimony on the illness of his patient even without the latter's consent; for any person is required to submit evidence in his possession if demanded in the interest of justice. This rule is set aside only if the physician had sworn to his patient that he would not reveal his professional knowledge without the patient's agreement; in that case any testimony given in violation of the oath is invalid.[120]

b. Liability

A physician who killed in error is guilty before the Heavenly tribunal, and he requires atonement if he caused the death of his patient by a mistaken treatment; but if the error consisted of mixing up a medication with a poison, the act is considered as homicide.[121]

The "sanction of the ecclesiastical court *(Beth Din)*" mentioned in the codes as exonerating physicians from certain liabilities[122] is not to be understood as a formal license to practice medicine granted by the court (which is outside its competence) but as an affirmation of the public's acceptance of their medical qualification, whether successful in individual cases or not.[123]

8. EXPERIMENTATION

a. On Animals

Two rabbinical studies have recently again confirmed that Jewish law raises no objection to the use of animals for research conducive to medical progress, provided that all reasonable steps are taken to avoid the infliction of any unnecessary suffering.[124]

b. On Humans

In 1963 a bulky volume was published under the title *Clinical Investigation in Medicine: Legal, Ethical and Moral Aspects.*[125] It reports in great detail on the growing incidence of medical experimentation on human beings currently practised—and widely debated. The section on "Religious Statements" lists the views of two Christian theologians as well as a lengthy and profound address by Pope Pius XII on "The Moral Limits of Medical Research and Treatment," whilst the "Jewish" attitude, inexplicably, is represented by an Israeli Professor of Medicine who does not make a single reference to any religious, let alone Jewish, principles.[126] This unfortunate contrast dramatizes the peculiar omission of this important challenge to moral guidance in rabbinic writings. The massive subjection of volunteers, prisoners, patients and other groups—with and sometimes without their consent—to often hazardous experiments raises ethical problems of the utmost gravity. Their solution in the light of Jewish teachings remains one of the most crucial desiderata in the rabbinic treatment of medico-moral issues.

c. Priorities

A somewhat related problem has, however, been treated authoritatively in response to the following enquiry: An observant Jew had a limited quantity of a certain new drug (in the aureomycin family), and he asked whether he may hold a part as a reserve in case he may one day need it for himself; whether it was better to supply one patient with several dosages as required for his complete cure, or to give several patients one dosage each to ensure their temporary relief; and whether he was entitled to give precedence in the distribution of the drug to his relatives or friends, or was he forbidden to discriminate between one person and another in the saving of life. The verdict given was that the questioner had no right to refuse aiding those who were in immediate and certain danger because he might perhaps himself become a victim of their affliction in the future and then need the drug; that a sure cure of one person is to be preferred to temporizing for many; and that in the saving of life no priorities other than those listed in the Talmud[127] could be recognized.[128]

9. *KOHANIM* STUDYING MEDICINE

Whether Jews of priestly descent, in view of the restrictions on their contact with the dead (cf. above 1, c.), may take up a medical career involving practical work in morbid anatomy poses a problem which has generally been resolved in the negative.[129] But two recent studies of this problem are inclined to adopt a somewhat less rigid attitude, tentatively permitting young *Kohanim* to fulfill their ambition to study medicine provided they do not themselves engage in dissection but merely study the subject by observation; however, the final rulings are reluctant to make even this concession (in any event probably of little value in practice) because it may easily lead to forbidden acts of touching the dead in the course of time.[130]

10. PSYCHIATRY

The most neglected field in the development of Jewish law on medical subjects is no doubt psychiatry. There are scarcely any responsa dealing with the many moral and religious problems in this specialty. The reason is not far to seek. The treatment of mental disorders as a strictly medical discipline exists only since comparatively very recent times, and the classic sources of Jewish law yield few clues to the religious attitude to, for instance, psychoanalysis or to the treatment of insanity in general. While the legislation of Judaism on the insane distinguishes itself from other ancient and medieval systems by its compassion and humaneness,[131] it makes understandably little reference to any therapeutic measures.

In the past, the main rabbinic concern in this area has been to determine whether the Sabbath laws may be violated for insane persons as for other gravely ill patients, a question often discussed and usually resolved in the affirmative.[132]

Recently a novel argument has been advanced to justify such leniency. Among the reasons for the suspension of laws in the face of danger to life is the rationale "Profane one Sabbath for a person, so that he may observe many Sabbaths afterwards."[133] This reasoning, it is argued, applies with equal force to the insane: since their incompetence exempts them from the performance of religious duties, their treatment may help them to fulfill these duties later on and therefore vindicates the temporary disregard of laws interfering with their healing.[134] On this basis, then, serious psychiatric disturbances, even if they involve no risk of life, would override religious laws in the same way as grave physical diseases. On similar grounds another responsum permitted a father to commit his insane daughter to a non-Jewish institution; for such a person is even less bound to any religious obligations than a minor and, moreover, in this case, any other course might have endangered the father who suffered from a cardiac condition.[135]

The Dissection of the Dead in Jewish Law

MORAL autonomy or moral automation—that is the most fateful choice confronting mankind today. As long as the moral law reigns supreme, the spectacular advances in science and technology will be effectively controlled by the overriding claims of human life and dignity. Man will be safe from the menace of his own productions. But when the quest for knowledge and power is unhemmed by moral considerations, and the fundamental rights of man are swept aside in the blind march to mechanical perfection, the ramparts protecting mankind from self-destruction are bound to crumble. Today the struggle between science and religion is no longer a competitive search for the truth as in former times. It is a battle between excesses and controls, between the supremacy of man's creations and the supremacy of man himself.

Published in *Tradition* (New York), Fall 1958.

In the past, the human inventive genius served mainly to aid nature in the amelioration of life. Now it bids fair to supplant nature replacing it by an artificial, synthetic existence in which the deepest mysteries of creation are not only laid bare but subjected to the arbitrary whims of mechanized man. The push of one button can now exterminate life by the million; psychologically waged advertising campaigns can determine the eating habits of whole nations; chemical drugs can curb or release human emotions at will, and break down the most determined will-power to extract confessions. The control over man's conscience, over procreation and extinction, over human existence itself, is being wrested from nature and surrendered to scientists and technicians.

In this new dispensation the physician, too, is playing an ever more vital role. Human life, which he can artificially generate out of a test-tube and terminate out of a syringe-needle, is now at his bidding. Psychiatry may soon bring even human behavior under his sway, almost like a robot plane guided by a remote radio operator. But who will control the physician and the growing army of other scientists? That is the crux of the moral dilemma of our times.

There can be little doubt that, of all applied sciences, it is pre-eminently medicine with which Judaism, historically and intellectually, enjoys a natural kinship, and to which Jewish law is best qualified to address its reasoned, pragmatic rules of morality. For many centuries rabbis and physicians, often merging their professions into one, were intimate partners in a common effort for the betterment of life. The perplexities of our age challenge them to renew their association in the service of human life, health, and dignity. Indeed, they challenge Judaism itself to reassert its place as a potent force in the moral leadership of humanity.

I.

Jewish law has insisted from the beginning that the physician may practice his art only by virtue of an express sanction granted to him by God.[136] The control over health, life, and death is essentially a Divine prerogative.[137] It cannot be exercised by man except in so far as he is delegated by the

Creator to do so. Even the setting aside of religious precepts for the preservation of life is not a natural right but a scriptural mandate.[138] For in the Jewish view man's claim to any inalienable rights, whether in life or in death,[139] derives primarily from his creation "in the image of God."[140] In other words, man is the recipient of rights and God the giver; He alone can confer and define those rights.

In accordance with these basic principles, Jewish legislation has always asserted its right to intrude into the domain of the physician (no less than of the rabbi).[141] Its provisions include precise regulations on the doctor's duty to heal, his professional charges, his legal responsibilities, and his title to ignore certain religious laws in his medical work. But above all it sets out to define and circumscribe his rights in cases where human life and dignity may be at stake. Hence the detailed laws on such operations as artificial insemination, sterilization, contraception, abortion, and euthanasia.

Since the biblically assigned rights of a person, as we have mentioned, extend beyond death, Jewish law must obviously also concern itself with the problem of dissection. The subject occupies considerable and constantly growing space in current rabbinic literature. The final verdict is still a matter of debate. We shall here atempt to trace the origins and development of that debate in its historical and comparative context, from antiquity to the present day.

II.

In the Talmud, the ultimate source of Jewish law, the dissection of human corpses *for medical ends* is not mentioned. This is not surprising. At the time of the Talmud, anatomical experiments on humans were entirely unknown. There had been some occasional excursions into this field in ancient times, but all these early steps into human anatomy were soon abandoned, usually because of religious restraints in one form or another. The first dissections in China are ascribed to the legendary physician Pien Ch'ioa many centuries before the Alexandrian exploits in this branch.[142] But these operations came to be regarded as incompatible with religious piety and were, with rare exceptions, discontinued until modern times.[143] In ancient India, where medicine and surgery had developed to a high standard, the dissection of the human body was opposed on religious grounds,[144] even if some non-surgical methods for exposing the internal organs were very occasionally tolerated.[145] The Syriac Book of Medicines has a few references to human dissection,[146] due no doubt to the impact of the Alexandrian school where the author had studied in the 2nd century B.C.E.[147] In Greece, the classical home of medicine, the study of anatomy may go back to Aristotle[148] or even earlier savants.[149] But any sustained advances were rendered impossible not only by the failure to appreciate its importance for medical purposes, but also by social and religious prejudices,[150] particularly the insistence on immediate burial.[151] Even in Egypt, where it had long been customary to disembowel and embalm the dead, anatomical science failed to gain from the experience because of religious scruples. Although the Bible expressly states that Jacob's body was embalmed by "the physicians" in Egypt,[152] the belief that it was an act of gross impiety gradually militated against the employment of doctors. Consequently, the operation was left to special functionaries, the "Paraschite," who became an object of popular execration.[153]

The only real break in this deep-rooted antagonism to dissection in antiquity occurred at Alexandria in the 3rd century B.C.E. At that Egyptian outpost of Hellenistic culture the new anatomical science flourished for a time virtually unhampered. But even that interlude was of short duration. By the time Galen commenced his medical education in 146 C.E. the practice of human dissection had already ceased everywhere for half a century.[154] From that time even the faintest scientific research into the human body was not initiated again until over twelve centuries later.

The earliest Jewish reference to the practice is a remarkable statement, generally overlooked by medical historians, by the Alexandrian philosopher Philo. He speaks of ". . . physicians of the highest repute who have made researches into the construction of man and examined in detail what is visible and also, by careful use of anatomy, what is hidden from sight in order that, if medical treatment is required, nothing which could cause serious danger should be neglected through ignorance."[155] This passage may, of course, reflect local influences rather than Jewish teachings, but its unqualified endorsement of anatomical dissection is nonetheless notable.

III.

In talmudic times, then, the whole problem was no longer acute, since dissection for medical research had fallen completely into disuse. There is no foundation for the allegation[156] that the Babylonian Talmudist Rab of the 3rd century "bought cadavers and dissected them,"[157] nor do any facts justify the claim by the medical historian Baas that "dissection in the interests of science was permitted by the Talmud."[158] Yet there is some evidence to support the assertion by some historians[159] that dissections and autopsies on humans were carried out by the authors of the Talmud, albeit only very occasionally and never for medical purposes. In fact, the Talmud records several significant references to the subject, all of them of importance to our problem.

In one passage[160] the Palestinian teacher of the 1st century, Rabbi Yishmael, relates that the Ptolemaic Queen Cleopatra once delivered her female slaves, following their execution for treason, to the king for anatomical investigations; he opened their bodies and studied the stages in foetal development.[161] In a more important statement,[162] the Babylonian sage-physician Samuel records that the disciples of the same Rabbi Yishmael[163] once boiled[164] the body of a condemned prostitute to ascertain the exact number of bones in human beings.[165] Practical researches must also be presupposed for the detailed list of human bones given in the Mishnah,[166] particularly since the figure given is at variance with the less accurate number listed by the Greek physicians.[167] In other places the Talmud speaks of "hands soiled through (handling) blood, foetal growths and placentas" for ritual enquiries;[168] of one sage who had kept the skull of King Jehoiakim in his home;[169] of another who had held up a bone of his tenth son to comfort mourners;[170] and of a third who admitted that "he used to bury the dead and to observe their bones," whereby he studied the osteological effects of alcoholism.[171]

None of these statements deals specifically with anatomical experiments for purely medical ends.[172] They therefore hardly imply an unconditional sanction of human dissection. But it is noteworthy that no voice of protest was raised against these practices, a fact all the more remarkable since Jewish law in general rigorously upholds the inviolability of the human body in death as in life. It condemns any undue interference with the corpse as an execrable offense against the dead. Though never explicitly set forth in the Talmud, the prohibition to disgrace or disfigure the dead was always assumed as a logical extension of the biblical ban[173] on allowing even a criminal's body to remain unburied overnight.[174] The prohibition itself, and the question whether it can be waived for legal purposes, is mentioned in two discussions on the right to defile the dead for procuring evidence in litigations— the one criminal and the other civil. The outcome of both discussions is not altogether conclusive. The circumstances in the first case (a murder charge) were such as would in any event render the findings of an autopsy, had it been permitted, irrelevant to the conviction of the suspected offender and insufficient for his complete acquittal.[175] But the trend of the argument suggests that the Talmud would not rule out postmortem examinations for forensic purposes if the results might yield crucial information to the court.[176] In the other case permission for an exhumation to ascertain the age of the deceased (in support of legal claims by his relations) was refused as an unwarranted sacrilege, but only on the additional grounds that the features might have changed after death; moreover, it is argued that the obligation to accept financial loss rather than disturb the dead may apply to the relatives only.[177] Altogether, the Talmud rules "whatever is done in honor of the living does not constitute a disgrace to the dead,"[178] but the context in which this occurs deals merely with delays in carrying out the burial.

To the extent, then, to which these talmudic sources are relevant to our problem, Jewish law became heir to a rather tolerant attitude to dissection. But it must be emphasized, before applying these arguments to medical needs, that the cases in the Talmud just mentioned deal only with very minor infringements of the peace of the dead. Furthermore, there was generally a sharp distinction between legal autopsies and scientific dissections. The anatomical experiments at Alexandria, and later at Bologna and elsewhere, were quite independent of medico-legal dissections which developed as a separate discipline and not as a branch of scientific anatomy.[179]

We may here digress for a while to look at the corresponding development within Christianity. While the decline of anatomy in the 1st century of the Common Era can hardly be ascribed to the as yet quite insignificant influence of the new faith,[180] the Christian tradition of disapprobation was set quite early. Already in about 400, St. Augustine had declared: "With a cruel zeal for science, some medical men who are called anatomists have dissected the bodies of the dead, and sometimes even of sick persons who have died under their knives,[181] and have inhumanly pried into the secrets of the human body in order to learn the nature of the disease and its exact seat and how it might be cured."[182] Tertullian, two centuries later, is said to have "hated dissection."[183] Although the early Church never issued a formal ban on anatomy, the idea of dissection must have outraged Christian sentiment.[184] It was regarded as a violation of man's dignity and an incompatible with the belief in bodily ressurection. Even the dissection of animals was not always possible since the student was in danger of being taken as a magician.[185]

IV

As we enter the second millenium, we find little change in this outlook. The progress of anatomy was slow and tortuous. At the School of Salerno in the 11th century, often described as the first university, the ape used by Galen was replaced by the pig,[186] because it was thought to resemble man internally—a belief already found in the Talmud.[187] But human corpses were still excluded, probably because of the opposition of the Church.[188] Scientific interest in the human cadaver did not begin to revive until the 13th century. In 1238 Frederick II ordered that a corpse should be dissected every five years for study purposes[189]—the first mention of dissection as an established practice,[190] even if the instruction was purely nominal.[191] At Bologna dissections were intro-

duced later in the same century.[192] The first clear reference
to a post-mortem examination dates from 1286, when a physician at Cremona investigated the cause of a pestilence then
raging in Italy, and the first "modern" work on anatomy was
published by Mondino de'Luzzi in 1316, following public
dissections at Bologna University.[193]

Thenceforth, the renewed interest in dissection spread only
in small stages. It was officially sanctioned—with certain safeguards which usually restricted the subjects to criminals—at
Venice in 1368, at Montpellier in 1375, and at Lerida in
1391.[194] These experiments, still of little scientific value,
generally served to illustrate ancient medical texts rather
than foster independent research. The public displays of
"anatomies" often turned into academic feasts, to which the
civil and ecclesiastical authorities were invited.[195] Anatomical demonstrations did not commence in Paris, Vienna, and
Prague until the 15th century,[196] while at Padua the study of
anatomy was not included in the elaborate medical curriculum in the middle of that century.[197] Even in the 16th century dissections were not common.[198] Paracelsus still "de-
spised anatomy and failed to see how any knowledge could be
gained from the dead body."[199] Only some years later was
the entire outlook changed by the great pioneer in anatomy,
Vesalius.[200] In Italy, Holland, and France dissection as a
means of teaching anatomy began to be quite frequent only
in the 17th century; in Germany and England it was introduced later still.[201] At most European universities regular
anatomical instruction on cadavers was not initiated until
the beginning of the 18th century.[202]

Throughout this tedious progress of the new science, the
religious prejudice against dissection faded only very gradually and then often reappeared. By an extraordinary coincidence, it happened twice—in 1300 and in 1737—that the Christian and Jewish authorities made pronouncements, quite independently of each other and yet on strikingly similar subjects,
with an important bearing on dissection; in both cases the
two religions adopted opposing viewpoints. In 1300 Pope
Boniface VIII issued a Bull which banned the practice of
boiling human corpses (presumably of crusaders who had
died far from their homes) to facilitate their removal to conse-

crated burial grounds.[203] Medical and social historians are about equally divided in their views on the Bull's relevance to anatomical studies. While some discount the influence of the Bull,[204] many others aver that, even if the edict was not specifically directed against anatomists, it certainly fortified the public abhorrence of dissection and was, in fact, largely responsible for delaying the progress of anatomy.[205] It is certain that some pioneers in anatomy were hindered in their work by theological considerations[206] or opposition,[207] that religious prejudice was mainly responsible for the objections to dissection until its introduction at the various universities,[208] and that the practice often required ecclesiastical sanction,[209] sometimes to be obtained from the popes as an indulgence.[210] Gradually the resistance eased. In 1556 Charles V received the following reply to an enquiry from the theological faculty at the University of Salamanca: "The dissection of human cadavers serves a useful purpose and is therefore permissible to Christians."[211] But the undercurrent of theological misgivings did not finally disappear until Prospero Lambertini, later Pope Benedict XIV, expressed the official attitude of the Catholic Church as favouring the practice for the advancement of the arts[212] and sciences in unequivocal terms in 1737.[213] Since then the Church has raised no objection to medical dissection.[214]

The stagnation of medieval anatomy and surgery has also been attributed to the "superstitious horror of mutilating a corpse" among Jews and Arabs,[215] and to "the Jewish tenets, adopted by the Mohammedans, [which] compelled students to be satisfied with making their observations on the carcasses of brutes."[216] Among the Arabs religious opposition to dissection was certainly explicit and sustained.[217] The Koran itself expressly forbids the opening of a corpse, even if the person should have swallowed the most valuable pearl which did not belong to him.[218] This was always applied in support of the ban on anatomical dissection at Turkish,[219] Persian, and other Mohammedan universities.[220] In 1838 the law was amended to permit the dissection of Christian and Jewish bodies, though not of Moslems.[221] But in practice the religious prohibition of dissection was usually upheld even in very recent times.[222]

It is clear from our records that the Jews, too, did not actually make any significant contributions to the advancement of anatomy in the Middle Ages. But it is highly questionable whether this was due to any religious inhibitions, as has been claimed by even so knowledgeable a master of Jewish medical history as Harry Friedenwald.[223] There is absolutely no substance in the charge, first made by Jean Astruc[224] early in the 18th century and later often repeated,[225] that the laws of ritual defilement militated against the dissection of human bodies. These laws do not prohibit the touching of a dead body (except to Jews of priestly descent); they merely lay down the conditions of impurity resulting from such contact and the procedure to be adopted to regain ritual cleanliness.[226] True, the duty to inter all human remains is reinforced by the fear lest some unburied parts might cause a priest to be unwittingly defiled.[227] But this consideration would hardly prove a greater obstacle to autopsies than the biblical law of immediate burial itself.

The evolution of the Jewish attitude almost exactly reversed the chronological pattern of the development within the Church. As we shall now discover, the papal edict *against* reducing a corpse to its bones coincided with a rabbinic ruling *sanctioning* a similar operation. As long as Christian theologians occasionally *condemned* the dissection of the dead, the Jewish authorities remained *silent;* and at the moment when the Church finally *ended* the argument by a clear statement in favour of the practice, the Jewish discussion was *opened* by a decision against dissection. We may now review these stages in some detail.

In about the same year as Boniface VIII promulgated his Bull against the mutilation of corpses to facilitate the transportation of the remains, the Jewish savant R. Solomon Adret gave a ruling permitting placing quick-lime on dead bodies to hasten their decomposition in order to ease their removal elsewhere in accordance with the wishes of the departed[228]— a decision also codified in the *Shulchan Arukh*[229] and later often mentioned as an argument in favour of medical autopsies[230] (just as the Bull was mentioned to support the opposition). A similar practice was sanctioned by the 16th century scholar R. David Zimra for speeding the admission of the soul to Heaven (which, according to early sources,[231] must await the body's decomposition), but he nevertheless advised against such interference with the ordinary course of nature.[232] By a curious reversal of effects, Adret's ruling (used by some to promote anatomy) was utilized by R. Isaac Elchanan Spector, a leading scholar of the 19th century, to foil the anatomists; he counselled a questioner from America concerned with the pilfering of cemeteries to bury the remains with lime in order to render them unfit for anatomical dissection.[233]

During the time when Christian protests against dissection were occasionally heard, there is no record of any Jewish objections to the practice. Indeed, there is some evidence to the opposite effect. While the claim that Maimonides himself made practical tests in anatomy[234] can probably be dismissed as conjectural, clear proof exists of the participation in dissections by Jewish or Marrano doctors. Thus the celebrated physician Amatus Lusitanus—in whom his parents had "implanted . . . an attachment to Jewish religion, tradition and customs"[235]—performed twelve dissections at Ferrara to confirm his discovery of the valves in the azygos veins in 1547.[236] Again, it is said of Abraham Zacutus, the Marrano who joined the Jewish Congregation at Amsterdam in 1625,[237] that he "deserves special praise for the frequency with which he made autopsies at a time when they were rare . . . As a result he published post-mortem findings in the plague, in affections of the heart, malignant tumours, renal and vesical calculi, etc."[238] The famous rabbi-physician of the 17th century, Jacob Zahalon, also appears to have at least condoned autopsies; he refers with evident approval to a post-mortem examination carried out by a Gentile doctor on a Jewish victim of the plague in 1656 to discover if death was due to a bubo or an intestinal hernia.[239] Interesting, too, is an anatomical illustration in Tobias Cohn's *Ma'asei Tuviah,* a popular medico-religious work first published in Venice in 1707; it depicts the body of (what appears to be) a Jew opened to expose the internal organs and compares them to the divisions of a house.[240]

These few instances are obviously far too isolated to admit of any general conclusions on the Jewish religious attitude at the time. More significant may be the complete absence of rabbinic protests prior to the 18th century. Jewish leaders can scarcely have been unaware of the problem. Practical studies in anatomy, as we have shown, began to be well established at many European universities in the 17th century or even earlier, and the many Jewish physicians and medical students of that age are bound to have been confronted with the need from time to time to witness, or even to participate in, autopsies and the "anatomies" regularly performed at the medical schools. In fact, Jews were particularly concerned with this problem for another reason. Their corpses were often especially favoured by the anatomists. An anonymous tract of 1829 informs us that, "as the Jews bury early, their cemetery formerly produced the best and freshest subjects, equal in freshness to the body sent to the venal undertaker . . ."[241] The problem distressed the Jewish community in Padua already in 1680, when the students at the famous university demanded all Jewish corpses for their anatomical institute.[242] Jews certainly objected to this wretched "body-snatching" no less bitterly than their neighbors, but there is no record of any condemnation of dissection itself in the prolific rabbinic literature of those centuries.

V.

It was not until 1737—the very year when the Christian debate finally concluded in favour of dissection—that the Jewish arguments against the practice first began. In that year a medical student at the University of Goettingen asked R. Jacob Emden whether he could participate on the Sabbath in the dissection of dogs used in the absence of human material. The rabbi, one of the leading authorities of his age, replied that such operations on the Sabbath involved many prohibitions, where they were performed on humans or animals. Moreover, in the case of human corpses, whether of Jews or not, it was in any case forbidden to derive any benefit from them.[243] Within the same century the question was treated again by R. Ezekiel Landau, the renowned scholar who died in Prague in 1793. He was asked on behalf of the rabbinical authorities in London whether they might accede to a request for an autopsy on a Jew—who had died after an operation for calculus in the bladder—to ascertain the proper treatment for similar cases in the future. The reply, while not adverting to the ban on benefitting from a human corpse, stated that such a post-mortem examination was an act of gross indignity to the dead, strictly prohibited in Jewish law. This consideration could be set aside only if there was a reasonable and immediate prospect of thereby saving a human life. But with no patient at hand to gain from the experience of the autopsy, its object was too remote to warrant the act. Moreover, "even non-Jewish doctors do not make anatomical experiments on any corpses except those of executed criminals or of people who gave their consent whilst alive; and if we were—Heaven forfend!—to be lenient in this matter, they would dissect all our dead in order to study the arrangement of the internal organs and their function so as to determine the medical treatment of the living."[244]

Since the beginning of the 19th century, the problem has engaged the attention of almost all leading rabbis in numerous responsa. As the practice became more widespread and the religious difficulties it created more pressing, a number of new elements were introduced into the discussion. The great respondent R. Moses Schreiber, in a judgment dated 1836, accepted the position taken up by Emden and Landau; only he thought the ban on benefitting from the dead might not apply to the bodies of non-Jews in accordance with their own views and their religious teachings. But he emphatically agreed that the remote possibility of saving life could not override the certainty of desecrating the dead; by the same token all work involved in medical studies would suspend the Sabbath laws on the assumption that a human life might thereby be preserved at some future date. Hence he regarded it as reprehensible for a Jew to bequeath his body for anatomical research.[245] In 1852, R. Jacob Ettlinger, a famous German rabbi, further argued that the duty to save life could obligate only the living, not the dead who were free from this as from any other religious obligation.[246] Also, as the saving of life at the expense of one's neighbor's possessions or dignity was in any case questionable,[247] one would not be justified in disturbing the dead even for the immediate cure of a patient with a similar complaint. But he sanctioned the operation if the deceased had sold or allotted his body for that purpose in his lifetime.[248] Both opinions were later opposed by R. Moses Schick, an eminent Hungarian rabbi. He concluded from the Talmud[249] that no-one could renounce the respect due to his body. On the other hand, he held that the talmudic rule whereby all laws (except idolatry, bloodshed, and incest) must give way to the saving of life[250] also applied to the prohibition of disgracing the dead; hence autopsies were warranted if the lives of other existing patients might thereby be preserved.[251] Two leading German rabbis at the time also expressed this view.[252]

In the present century opinions have varied widely. With the growing and direct benefits accruing to medical science from studies on human corpses, some rabbis strongly favoured permitting the practice. The British Chief Rabbi Dr. Hermann Adler, in a memorial address in 1905, lauded the late Frederic David Mocatta for having directed that, if he died from an obscure disease, a post-mortem examination be performed at the expense of his estate "for the advancement of medical science."[253] While Chief Rabbi Abraham Isaac Kook advised the purchase of non-Jewish bodies for anatomical studies,[254] Rabbi Benzion Uziel, another Chief Rabbi of the Holy Land, saw no objection ot the dissection of Jewish bodies, provided it was carried out with due care and respect; but he disapproved of persons selling their bodies before death.[255] Another rabbi even suggested a popular campaign to persuade people to grant their written consent for the dissection of their bodies after death.[256] In favor of the sanction it was argued that to study anatomy by observation did not constitute a forbidden "benefit" from the dead;[257] that any intrinsically prohibited act performed for study purposes was altogether exempt from the original prohibition;[258] that there was no disgrace to the dead when the welfare of the living was at stake;[259] that a ban on anatomical studies would "close the door to medical science";[260] and that, with hospitals everywhere full of patients actually awaiting the findings of anatomical research and with the speed of modern communications, the objections raised by Ezekiel Landau no longer applied.[261]

Nevertheless, many rabbinic authorities remained implacably opposed to any general sanction of dissection, particularly on Jewish bodies. The American scholar Rabbi Yekuthiel Greenwald has listed an impressive array of rabbis who were adamant in their refusal to countenance autopsies, let alone anatomical experiments, on human bodies. He himself caustically suggested that those desiring their sons to study anatomy or advocating the use of Jewish bodies should bequeath their own bodies for dissection. He would not allow even Jewish suicides and criminals to be delivered to the anatomists, since the Bible stressed the respect due to the dead specifically in regard to executed persons.[262] Exceptions might be made only in cases of people afflicted by some hereditary disease if an autopsy could help in the proper diagnosis and thus benefit the descendants.[263] A London rabbi, too, advised relatives not to give permission for post-mortem inquests, though they need not resist the demand for autopsies required by law.[264] Even a scholar as modern in outlook and secular learning as Dr. David Hoffman, the late Rector of the *Rabbiner Seminar* in Berlin, was not prepared to go beyond the restrictive position taken up by Ezekiel Landau nearly two centuries earlier.[265]

The opposition became especially bitter when rabbinical authorities were faced with the problem on a communal scale. For instance, when the "Prosectorium" in Warsaw demanded the supply of Jewish bodies for anatomical studies in 1924, the local rabbinate fiercely resisted the demand.[266] Many rabbis insisted on the ban even if it meant the exclusion of Jews from medical schools or even their estrangement from the Jewish faith, unless that attitude might provoke measures against the Jewish community in general.[267] The actual delivery by the Warsaw Burial Society of a Jewish woman's corpse for dissection led to a great upheaval at the time.[268] When the question was raised by a tuberculosis hospital in Denver, U. S. A., the leading American rabbis likewise maintained an uncompromising stand against the supply of Jewish bodies for dissection.[269]

Among the arguments to justify these objections—widely upheld right up to the present—were that dissections involved a proper "benefit" from the dead since they included acts and

not merely observation,[270] and since they directly promoted
the doctors' material interests;[271] that the motive for disgracing the dead was not the honor of the living but their
physical advantage;[272] that all concessions on those grounds
were in any case limited to keeping the dead unburied for a
maximum of twenty-four hours;[273] that in Jewish law all
parts of the body required burial which could not be assured
after its dissection;[274] that the indiscriminate renunciation of
Jewish bodies would publicly shame the Jewish name;[275] and
that any general sanction would lend itself to many abuses
which could not be controlled.[276]

The problem became really pressing with the foundation
of the Hebrew University at Jerusalem and the planned establishment of a medical school there. Already in 1924 the difficulties were widely discussed in rabbinical circles.[277] But for
two decades religious objections to dissection remained an
insuperable obstacle to the realisation of the project. The
University simply had to carry on without a medical school,
just as had been the case at several Moslem universities and
as was still the case in the State of New Jersey, where anatomical experiments continue to be banned to this day.[278] But
with the rise of Israel as an independent state the pressure
became so great that an adequate compromise between religious and medical claims had to be found.

Negotiations ensued between Chief Rabbi Dr. Isaac Herzog, acting on behalf of the Chief Rabbinate of Israel, and
Dr. Yaski of the "Hadassah" University Hospital at Jerusalem,
leading to an agreement whereby post-mortem examinations
were sanctioned when (1) they are legally required, (2) the
cause of death cannot otherwise be ascertained, on condition
this is formally attested by three physicians (as designated in
the agreement), (3) they may help to save the lives of other
existing patients, on condition a similar certification is produced, and (4) they are required in cases of hereditary diseases to safeguard the health of the surviving relations; provided always, among other stipulations, that the hospital
authorities will carry out the autopsies with due reverence for
the dead, and that they will deliver the corpses and all parts
removed therefrom to the burial society for interment after
use.[279] Regarding the use of bodies for medical teaching pur-

poses, Dr. Herzog further issued the following statement: "The Plenary Council of the Chief Rabbinate of Israel . . . do not object to the use of bodies of persons who gave their consent in writing of their own free will during their lifetime for anatomical dissections as required for medical studies, provided the dissected parts are carefully preserved so as to be eventually buried with due respect according to Jewish law."[280] In 1953 similar provisions were embodied in the Anatomy and Pathology Law passed by the Israeli Parliament.

In the discussions which led to these decisions, it was emphasised that there could be no distinction in Jewish law whereby "the body of an honored or rich person must not be dissected, whereas that of a poor or forsaken person could be so used; the sole foundation of a sanction could only be the saving of human life, and in that consideration no difference could be made between one or another."[281] This attitude, as has been observed,[282] is in direct contrast with, for example, the English Warburton Anatomy Act of 1832 which released for anatomical study all bodies which were unclaimed and which civil law therefore regarded as *res nullius*.[283] In Jewish law it is, on the contrary, the body of a person left without relatives whose burial imposes a special obligation upon the whole community; even the High Priest—otherwise forbidden to defile himself even for his closest next-of-kin—must ignore his sanctity by personally attending to the immediate burial of such a person![284]

With the concordat reached between the highest religious and medical authorities in Israel and in operation the problem was by no means finally resolved. The argument over those who can no longer speak for themselves continues unabated. The traditionalists charge that the official agreement, itself of doubtful merit, is being abused; far more bodies are subjected to indignity than is really essential and the dissected parts are not always treated and eventually interred as required by law. The agreement, it is alleged, is being used as a subterfuge to allow the anatomists to lay their hands and knives on the dead with utter disregard to the rights of the deceased and the feeling of their relations.[285] Indeed, the agreement itself is attacked as an excessive surrender to the profanation of Jewish values.[286] The devotees of anatomy, again, complain that popular prejudice and religious opposition still hinder the proper scientific exploitation of the secrets revealed by every dead body for the advancement of medical science.

Lately several religious doctors have also joined in the theological debate, though often in a spirit of polemics rather than of sober enquiry. Friedenwald has listed five medical articles on "Post-mortem Examinations among the Jews" written between 1914 and 1939.[287] To this list a few further contributions could be added.[288] More recently the extreme views of the two camps have been zealously defended by Dr. Sussman Muntner and Dr. Jacob Levy, both of Jerusalem. The two doctors claim that the main debate is now only of academic interest: the former because he believes the rabbinical opposition to be at an end, and the latter because he considers the medical need of bodies at an end. To Dr. Muntner it appears that, in regard to autopsies, "all arguments have already ceased and everyone has now been reconciled to the sanction even from the religious point of view."[289] Virtually all the talmudic and rabbinic sources he has collected lead him to the conclusion that there never existed any objection to anatomical dissection; if some Jewish scholars did express a contrary opinion, it was only "because they wished to introduce the heathen concept of the honor of the dead and the ban on dissection into our literature."[290] For Dr. Levy, on the other hand, "the star of anatomy is now sinking." The present tendency is for the science of anatomy —the important findings of which are already known—to be replaced by various physical methods in the diagnosis and treatment of disease. Thus, three most recent and revolutionary advances in medicine—the discovery of penicillin and other antibiotics, heart operations and polio vaccinations— owe their development to biological, chemical, and X-ray research, not to dissection.[291]

In respect of medical training, Dr. Levy admits, some facilities may have to be sacrificed in order to maintain the highest moral and religious standards in the Holy Land. But he suggests that practical anatomy can now be studied on drawings and plastic models, on tissue removed in live operations

or imported from abroad, and—if necessary—by a short course
at a foreign university.²⁹² For, in practice, the conditions
under which even the more lenient authorities approved of
dissection simply cannot be carried out: there can be no respect
for the dead in the anatomy room (often there is levity instead!), and it is impossible to ensure that all parts of the
corpse are ultimately buried.²⁹³ Dr. Levy denounces the
Anatomy and Pathology Law—which permits the dissection of
any corpse on medical certification without regard to the
wishes of the deceased or his family—as an affront to the
freedom of conscience, unparalleled in any other civilised
country. In Israel, he protests, 90% of all who die in public
hospitals are subjected to autopsies, as against only 30% at
the famous Columbia University! Even with this wholesale
violation of the dead, he argues, no commensurate advantages
either in prestige or in scientific discoveries have accrued to
medicine in Israel which would vindicate the disregard for the
sanctities of Jewish law.²⁹⁴

VI.

And so the debate continues. There are no doubt weighty
considerations on both sides. The many complex technical
arguments advanced in the different rabbinic rulings must
not obscure from our view the profound moral issues behind,
and embedded in, these discussions. Let us summarize the
main principles involved. Were it simply a matter of choosing between life and law, Judaism would require the latter
to give way without question. But the issue is not so simple.
The conflicting interests are really between those of life and
those of the dead. The living are free agents, and as such
charged with the supreme duty to preserve life at all costs.
Not so the dead. Their bodies are not our property, and
*their title to undisturbed rest may be as great as the claim
of the living to life.*

The subjective element, too, is of paramount importance.
To reduce the human corpse to the utilitarian function
of a text-book from which the pages are torn out one by one,
and to ransack the body by wanton raids on its scientific treasures is as irreverent to the dead as it is degrading and spirit-

ually hebetating to the living. Those training to bring succor to the sick and the suffering may themselves lose their regard for the dignity of man—the first prerequisite in the practice of the healing art. That loss may well outweigh the gain in medical knowledge. One is reminded of Johnson's scathing attack on animal vivisection two hundred years ago, when he castigated "the anatomical novice . . . [who] prepares himself by familiar cruelty for that profession which he is to exercise upon the tender and the helpless . . ." and condemned "these horrid operations, which tend to harden the heart, extinguish those sensations which give man confidence in man, and make the physician more dreadful than the gout or stone."295

As against these considerations, it seems clear that some of mankind's worst scourges, such as cancer and coronary thrombosis, will not be conquered without the most painstaking studies on thousands of victims from these dread diseases. Modern communications have made the world shrink into a single parish, so that we may consider the revelations of an autopsy in America to be potentially of immediate benefit to a sufferer in Asia. It must also be accepted that a certain experimentation in anatomy is indispensable in the training of competent doctors.

How can these clashing interests be reconciled in conformity with Jewish law? All Jewish religious authorities agree that any sanction of dissection can be contemplated solely on the grounds of its immediate, if only potential, contribution to the saving of life; that the number and extent of autopsies must be limited to an irreducible minimum; that a sense of reverence must be preserved during and after the operation; and that all the remains must be buried as soon as possible with due respect. Prior consent for every autopsy should also be obtained from the subject during his life-time or his family Ideally all operators should themselves be God-fearing and fully conscious of the dignity with which every human body is endowed as a creation "in the image of God." In their absence, the proposal by Dr. A. H. Merzbach of Israel to establish a council of three religious doctors at every major (Jewish) hospital to determine the necessity of post-mortem examinations296 is worthy of consideration. Alternatively, hospital chaplains or visiting rabbis might be appointed to sanction and supervise all autopsies in compliance with Jewish law.

Far more perplexing is the problem of dissection for teaching purposes. Happily the aids produced by modern science are often such as help to solve the very problem it creates. It ought now to be possible gradually to replace normal anatomy by the use of artificial models, combined with the experience gained from animal dissections and attendances at surgical operations.

The Mishnah concludes with the significant words: "The Holy One, blessed be He, found no vessel holding greater good for Israel than peace."[297] Every major prayer in the Jewish liturgy concludes with the craving for peace. Life itself concludes with peace, "for the latter end of man is peace."[298] Life may be worthless if sustained by means of disturbing that peace.

Jewish Views on Plastic Surgery

THIS symposium is probably unique. I do not think that the religious attitude to cosmetic plastic surgery has ever before been the subject of a joint Christian-Jewish discussion, certainly not under such distinguished medical auspices.

Speaking for the Jewish side, I doubt whether the moral and religious problems involved, if any, have so far altogether received any practical consideration among our religious guides. Frankly, your kind invitation to participate in this symposium presented me with quite a challenge. For, although Jewish medical ethics happens to be my own specialty—having done my doctorate thesis for the University of London on this subject—I could not find any direct reference to our theme in the voluminous rabbinic literature, particularly the responsa (that is, published rulings in answer to

Transcript of a contribution to a Symposium on "Religious Views on Cosmetic Surgery" before the American Society of Facial Plastic Surgery, published in *The Eye, Ear, Nose and Throat Monthly* (New York), February and March, 1962.

questions submitted to rabbinical judgment) dealing with medico-moral matters.

I surmise that the reason for the absence of any discussion on this subject in rabbinical writings to date may be—quite apart from the fact that cosmetic surgery is a relatively new department of medicine—that those who seek such operations will not generally submit questions to rabbis, while those who seek advice from rabbis are less like to submit to cosmetic surgery.

I have therefore tried myself to explore the original literary and legal sources which might guide us in our attitude to this subject. Let me preface the presentation of my findings by just two historical comments.

First, as you know, the medical profession has been governed in its ethical outlook for thousands of years by the Oath of Hippocrates, which may go back to the fifth century B.C. This Oath provided, among many other stipulations, that the physician restrict his work to "helping the sick." Perhaps it is an indication of the Oath's obsolescence in our own day that helping the sick is now no longer the only domain of the physician. He performs a vast variety of operations which have nothing whatever to do with helping the sick. Artificial inseminations, for instance, bear no relation to helping the sick; nor do the many abortions for reasons other than possible hazards to the life or health of the mother. The same applies of course to purely cosmetic operations. For I very much doubt that the psychological stress, resulting from the facial mal-formation to be corrected, will outweigh and neutralize the health and other risks involved in the operation. In other words, the chief indication for such surgery, I suspect, is cosmetic pure and simple and not medical.

All these non-therapeutic activities therefore present the medical profession with a completely new set of moral issues which the ethical tradition of medicine, as reflected in the Hippocratic Oath, neither covers nor sanctions.

Second, I want to refer to an historical precedent of which you may not be altogether cognizant, but which is mentioned in all the standard histories of medicine. Your first predecessor in plastic surgery was a certain Italian pioneer by the name of Gaspare Tagliacozzi who lived in the sixteenth century. He is known as "the inventor of rhinoplasty." But he suffered a rather cruel fate for his pioneering efforts. He had carried out some daring operations on people with deformed faces. This was condemned by the Church as an unwarranted "attempt to improve upon the work of the Almighty." After his death the protests against his innovation led to his exhumation from the church cemetery in which he had been laid to rest and to his reburial in unconsecrated ground as a mark of shame.

The issue before us, then, as a religious problem, is a fairly old one. In fact, following the opposition voiced against plastic surgery for theological reasons, such operations were not revived until the nineteenth century.

I mentioned these two historical aspects in order to obtain some orientation on the whole question as to whether cosmetic surgery can conceivably constitute a religious and moral problem.

From the Jewish point of view, I would say that we find here, as in most medico-moral problems, a conflict of interests. There are arguments, and some of them weighty arguments, heavily in favor of such operations under certain circumstances. But there are also some very real difficulties and perplexities which have to be considered as counter-arguments. It is therefore the task of moralists, in our case of rabbis, to put these arguments on both sides unto the scales and to see which side ultimately outweighs the other.

Let me begin with the possible conflicts that may arise with certain principles of Jewish law. It would appear to me that for us three distinct problems might present themselves.

The first is the insistence of Jewish law that a person is not permitted to endanger his life, however slight or remote the risk, except when necessary for some overriding reason. Now, since obviously every operation involves some risk of life—and I understand there are patients who undergoing plastic surgery have died on the operating table—we are here faced with a problem: Is it lawful to submit to such risks, however small, for cosmetic reasons, for reasons not necessarily connected with any medical or therapeutic considerations? Would

cosmetic considerations in themselves be a sufficient ground
for warranting this exposure to danger? This is the first
problem that would have to be resolved.

Problem number two is our extremely insistent objection
to any mutilation of the human body. We regard it as a
grave religious offense for a person to inflict an injury not
only on others but equally on himself. One is not permitted
to make even a small incision in one's own body unless there
are weighty medical reasons requiring such an operation.
The explanation for this attitude is based on a significant
Jewish principle. We maintain that the human body is divine
property. We do not own our bodies; we are merely their
custodians. The body was given to us to perform certain
functions set out for us by our Creator, but we can never
assume a possessive right over it either in life or in death
(which accounts, incidentally, for our restrictive attitude to
autopsies). According to an important medieval Jewish
authority, even as beneficial an operation as circumcision
may be regarded as a mutilation and is sanctioned only because God has commanded it to us. This reasoning has been
suggested to explain why Abraham, although he is said to have
observed other moral and religious laws in his earlier years,
did not circumcize himself until he received a divine order to
do so at the age of ninety-nine years.

Hence, since any plastic operation constitutes a mutilation—involving incisions, grafts, *et cetera* impairing the integrity of the body—we must ask ourselves: Are cosmetic
considerations urgent enough to entitle the patient and the
doctor to ignore the strong Jewish objection to any mutilation,
whether self-inflicted or caused by someone else?

Third, I might mention a problem of a more theological
nature that could possibly be raised. We believe of course that
our world is governed by divine Providence. God is not only
our Creator, but the ultimate Authority for all lawful human
activities, especially when these may involve changing the
order of things as He created them. The question therefore
is: By trying to improve on God's work and create a human
being other than He had created or intended, do we not
attack the scheme of Providence?

Now, this problem of course exists in all medical operations. If we believe that there is a divine Providence at work which, let us say, causes or wills illness, then what right do we humans have to flout the will of God and cure a person? This question was already posed in the Talmud, the encyclopedic depository of Jewish law and thought, dating from the beginning of the current era and to this day the principal guide to rabbinical judgments. The answer given in the Talmud is that the Bible itself provides physicians with an express sanction to pursue their calling. In connection with the wilful infliction of injuries the Bible stipulates that the attacker "shall surely cause him (i.e. the victim) to be healed" (Ex. 21:19) — that is, he shall be liable to pay the medical expenses. Hence, reasons the Talmud, it is indicated that "permission was given to the physician to heal."

However, this "permission" may well be restricted to healing, so that the physician's therapeutic work, since it enjoys divine sanction, would thus not be regarded as an unauthorized interference with Providence. But whether such sanction goes beyond "healing" to include also acts of surgery dictated by purely cosmetic considerations, is a question which would still require a great deal of careful thought.

So far, then, I have listed the three possible objections or limitations which could be found in Jewish law in relation to cosmetic operations. Now let me mention briefly the considerations in favor of cosmetic treatments as reflected in Jewish thought.

The notion of cosmetics, as you may well know, is not exactly foreign to the Bible. Time and again it refers to the physical beauty and attractive features of many of its leading heroines, evidently with complete approval. As a matter of fact, everyone of our principal matriarchs—Sarah, Rebeccah and Rachel—is recorded as having been "beautiful in appearance" (Gen. 12:11; 24:16; and 29:17). You may also recall that Esther, in preparing herself to appear before King Ahasuerus as his potential Queen, spent six months on one course of cosmetic treatment and then six months on another (Esth. 2:12). Perhaps we should regard it as merciful if today we can manage with just one operation and not have to spend an entire year on cosmetic preparations for the enhancement of our physical beauty!

Rabbinical writings go even further in extolling the virtues of feminine attractiveness. In an early work going back to Talmudic times known as the Midrash, a very incisive comment is made on a question which evidently troubled the minds of our rabbis. They asked: Why was it that our matriarchs were kept barren for such a long time? Sarah did not conceive until she was ninety years old, Rebeccah was forty; and there were many years of agonized prayer preceding the fulfillment of their craving for maternity. Rachel was driven to exclaim in her distress: "Give me children, or else I die" (Gen. 30:1). Why did God inflict so much mental anguish on these virtuous women? One of the answers our rabbis gave —something like eighteen hundred years ago—was that God wanted to preserve the beauty of these women in the eyes of their husbands, so that they should not lose their attractiveness by early pregnancies. This is a remarkable statement, indicating the lengths to which Jewish homiletical teachings go in encouraging the esthetic appearance of women for the preservation of happy marriages. The anxiety to prevent wives from "being repulsive to their husbands" also accounts for several religious concessions in Jewish law, such as the right of a married woman to use cosmetics while in mourning as an exception to the usual rule forbidding all other mourners to beautify themselves for thirty days following the death of a close relative.

On the other hand, the Bible also singles out two men for their extraordinary beauty—Joseph and Absalom—and both eventually came to grief because of their vanity, according to rabbinic exegesis. In the case of Joseph, his handsome features are mentioned immediately prior to the incident with the wife of Potiphar (Gen. 39:6 ff.) which led to the charge of seduction against Joseph and his subsequent incarceration. On this juxtaposition our sages comment: Joseph was punished because he was so vain and self-conscious about his physical attractiveness. They similarly censured Absalom about whom it is written: "Now in all Israel there was none to be so much praised as Absalom for his beauty"—especially of his hair (2 Sam. 14:25-26). Hence he found his end by being suspended from a tree by his hair (*ib.*, 18:9).

Thus, while in the case of women, the ambition to enhance one's physical attractiveness by cosmetic means is tolerated and even encouraged, in the case of men this is frowned upon as vanity liable to lead to trouble.

As for the argument mentioned before that we must not submit to any risk of life, certain circumstances may also entitle us to disregard this regulation to some extent. For instance, Jewish law permits people to travel overseas or through deserts—despite the hazards involved, at least in ancient times—if such traveling was rendered necessary for business reasons to maintain one's livelihood.

I would therefore conclude that our objections to cosmetic operations could be set aside if the deformity to be corrected is serious enough (1) to make it difficult for a woman to find a matrimonial partner or to maintain a happy relationship with her husband, or (2) to prevent a person from playing a constructive role in society, and in particular from pursuing his calling with a view of maintaining himself and his family in decent comfort.

In the case of men, then, I cannot possibly see any sanction for such operations in Jewish law except in cases where they could not otherwise earn enough for themselves and their families. In the case of women, there would be the additional consideration of eliminating anything which might adversely affect their chances of marriage or the relationship between them and their husbands. Should these considerations not apply, I believe Jewish law may be hesitant in granting a sanction for operations which would encounter all the three objections I have mentioned.

Finally, I want to emphasize that, in view of the fact that no formal ruling on this matter has as yet, to my knowledge, been issued, whatever I have said must be of a somewhat tentative nature. I have merely been thinking aloud, trying to present to you some of the considerations which I have come across in Jewish sources and which may be relevant to our problem.

But I have no doubt that as a result of the stimulus which your meeting has given to me and which I, in turn, will pass on to some of our sages, some firm opinions may ultimately be expressed on what is, after all, a concern of medicine, if not necessarily of healing.

Problems of Jewish Family Life

With Special Reference to Birth-Control and Artificial Insemination

I AM deeply sensitive to the great honor done to me in being asked to deal at this Conference with the Holy of Holies of Judaism, with the Jewish home and family. We are living through stirring times. Our attention has for years been focussed on the spectacular rebirth of our people's national glory. In the more domestic sphere our interest is absorbed by synagogal and Jewish educational affairs. In our preoccupation with communal and national Jewish problems, little do we seem to realize that the foundation of Jewish life is slowly decaying in our very midst. Thousands of Jewish homes have been turned into luxurious lodging places, adorned with the latest labor-saving gadgets, but not with books of Jewish, or indeed general, cultural interest. To find even a Hebrew תנ״ך at a Jewish home has become as rare as to discover people who spend their most enjoyable time at home. "To have a good time" is now almost synonymous with "to go out". In the absence of religious home ceremonies and educational pursuits, domestic attractions have been displaced by the cinema, the dance-hall and the club.

Take away the strict observance of the Kashruth laws, and every restaurant can replace one of the most important functions of the home, and often of the wife and mother with it. Take away the שבת and יום טוב and the most delightful feature of home life is gone together with at least a weekly opportunity for husband and wife to belong to each other

Address delivered at the Ninth Conference of Anglo-Jewish Preachers, London, May 17, 1951.

exclusively and jointly to rejoice with their children whom they hardly see during the week. Take away our purity regulations guiding marital life, and you weaken, month by month, the most powerful bond holding husband and wife together; for over-indulgence and lack of regular renewal will eventually wear off their natural attraction for each other. But how many young people realize this inter-relation between the three pillars of Jewish home life, שבת טהרה and כשרות, and the stability of marital existence? How many of them are made to realize that these divine rules cannot be violated with impunity, that there is an inevitable connection between increasing divorce rates and decreasing holiness in life?

Our generation has witnessed an alarming rise in Jewish marriage problems and failures. It may surprise you to hear that the proportion of Jews applying for help to the National Marriage Guidance Councils is, according to my information, about ten times as high as the corresponding percentage among non-Jews. This appalling fact is a challenge to the entire Jewish ministry, for there can be little doubt that among the many causes for this sad state of affairs is the waning influence we have on those in our spiritual charge.

The minister as a synagogue official deals almost exclusively with only one aspect of marital life—with its happy beginning under the *Chuppah*. But only a tiny fraction of those who later meet the serious domestic problems come to consult him. Perhaps a partial remedy could be found by decentralizing at least some of the Beth Din's work. If דיני תורה affecting domestic disputes and certain work in connection with גטין could be entrusted—under the direction of the Beth Din—to the growing number of ministers holding the Rabbinical diploma, such ministers would gain enormous and most valuable experience. As a result more and more people would turn to them for the solution of such marital problems as do not require expert medical or other specialized treatment. As it is, however, this vital work is not given the attention and patient care it deserves, and our people are driven to seek guidance in non-Jewish quarters.

In this connection I should like to make a remark on divorces—most unhappily an increasingly topical subject. I am not in possession of statistical figures, but it is common knowledge that there are a great number of Jewish people who obtain a civil divorce without subsequently applying to the Beth Din for a גט. The remarriage of such divorcees cannot be a rare phenomenon, and one shudders to think how many ממזרים are born and reared in our communities every year. I know that it is a difficult subject, but I wonder whether more could not be done to dam this fearful flood of bastardy which threatens to engulf and sweep away the last vital stronghold of Jewish religious life. Any measure, however radical, would be justified if it would prevent the birth of only one bastard. A suggestion that might be worth further consideration is to devise some tactful means whereby applicants for marriage at a synagogue would be required to give a written undertaking that, should their marriage unhappily fail, neither party would remarry before the religious marriage (חופה) has been dissolved by a religious divorce (גט). If such a declaration became an accepted part of the marriage ritual—perhaps as part of the כתובה abstract—sentimental objection would be raised against this no more than against the inclusion in the כתובה of provisions in case of the husband's death. The possibility of securing the more effective cooperation of the civil authorities in this matter, if necessary through new legislation, might also be explored.

After גטין comes קדושין. I am very glad that, thanks to the efforts and inspiration of the Chief Rabbi, his office will soon distribute to those registering for marriage at synagogues a booklet giving an attractive and intelligible presentation of some of Judaism's marital and domestic legislation. In this respect we are only now doing what other denominations accomplished long ago in a sphere which should see Jewish thought and teachings lead the way for others. Another venture, which some synagogues have already adopted with great success and which should be extended to all congregations, is to distribute Orders of the Wedding Service among those attending synagogue marriages. This helps to enhance the impressiveness of what should be one of Judaism's most inspiring ceremonies and thus to leave a deep religious imprint on the newly-weds. But these measures should be augmented, wherever possible, by personal contact before marriage. In congregations where marriages do not occur by the score every year, the minister ought to meet beforehand those whom he is to marry, preferably at a family occasion, for instance as guests on a Friday night. The young partners should be made to feel that a wedding ceremony is not a formality but essentially a family event in which the minister has a personal share. He should not, therefore, be a stranger to them until he sees them under the *Chuppah*. Their presence at a true Friday night celebration at the minister's home should also prove of the greatest value in creating in the young couple an appreciation of Jewish home life. Where the minister cannot carry this out, a rota of carefully selected *Ba'alei Battim* should undertake this very useful obligation. No amount of literature can equal in effectiveness the practical example. There are countless young people that will never even have seen the charms of Jewish home life if it was not shown to them on such an occasion.

Before I turn to the two special subjects which I have been invited to treat in this paper, I must say a few words on the moral and social havoc wrought by the growing lack of premarital and marital chastity in wide circles of our society. This awful evil gnaws at the roots of our existence. Moreover, it is usually the source of marital disaster and the attendant wreckage of domestic peace and happiness. Few can doubt that the cheap and smutty entertainment offered to our youth has done much to blunt their sense of decency and refinement, and to break their will and ability to resist temptation. A particularly grievous consequence has been the almost complete eradication of that modesty and moral bashfulness whereby Jewish female virtue used to distinguish itself so nobly. We cannot, of course, control or even influence the moral standard of the films or fiction literature. But at least we can exert ourselves to ensure that social activities under Jewish auspices, especially in synagogue halls, should counter rather than strengthen these unholy influences.

בראתי יצה"ר ובראתי לו תורה תבלין There is only one effective antidote to immorality, and that is religious culture! Young people, whether married or unmarried, who spend one or two nights a week at pictures and another two at dances would have to be very exceptional if coarse sensuality did not gradually dominate, and ultimately demoralize, them. It is probably impossible under present circumstances to reimpose the rigid moral discipline of our Rabbis whose צניעות legislation has been so much maligned, but whose wisdom and deep insight into human psychology is only now becoming apparent when we see the results of the present-day liberalism in these sacred matters. However, there is no justification for the existence of youth and other societies whose almost exclusive function is to provide cheap and vulgar entertainment. Some of our fund-raising bodies are also not free from blame in this depressing state of affairs. It is our duty to infuse a religious and cultural spirit into these activities, and if we cannot do that, it is wrong to lend our or the synagogue's support to organizations or functions which, however unintentionally, contribute to the disruption of our most cherished heritage.

According to Jewish law and ethics, it is no answer to suggest that if we did not promote such entertainment, our youth would seek it among non-Jews. The renowned fifteenth century commentator and philosopher, R. Isaak Arama, mentions in his celebrated עקידת יצחק that he ruled on several occasions that it was wrong for a community to condone even the slightest evil, however much it was hoped thereby to prevent far worse excesses by individuals. The problem he faced arose out of a suggestion to tolerate prostitution and brothels for single people as long as such publicly controlled institutions would reduce or even eliminate the capital crime of marital faithlessness which was then rampant. Arama's unequivocal answer was

טוב ומוטב שיכרתו או ישרפו או יסקלו החטאים ההם
בנפשתם : משתעקר אות א' מהתורה בהסכמת הרבים

It is surely better that individuals should commit the worst crimes and expose themselves to the gravest penalties than publicly to promote or even condone the slightest compromise with the moral code of the Torah![299] Those who have had occasion to see the commonness, vulgarity and sensuality dragged into so many of our homes that were meant to be sanctuaries will not fail to understand that the application of this ruling has more than sheer prudery to commend it!

I now come to the two special subjects to which I have been asked to give some attention. They concern the religious problems raised by the practice of artificial human insemination (A. I.) and birth-control. As I will demonstrate below, both subjects are exceedingly complex, and I deal with them rather reluctantly and *only on the strict understanding that nothing I say will be used* להלכה למעשה , *unless it is confirmed by* גדולי ההוראה . I must make this explicit reservation with all the emphasis at my command, particularly since I am not aware that the first subject has ever been treated outside purely halachic literature, whereas even the second theme has received only the scantiest attention in non-technical works of rabbinic scholarship. While I cannot, of course, do full justice to such vast subjects in the limited time at my disposal—quite apart from the even more severe limitations of my knowledge—I will endeavor to sketch some aspects of the historical development and treatment of these perplexing problems; define the chief halachic principles involved; and, for purposes of perspective and comparison, give you some indication of the attitude of other religious and legal systems.

Artificial Insemination

A. I. is of fairly recent origin. A legend tells us that it was employed on horses by Arabs as early as the fourteenth century,[300] yet the first scientific research on A. I. in domestic animals was not carried out until late in the eighteenth century.[301] Experiments on human beings followed very soon afterwards, but no successful case was reported before 1866 when the first test-tube baby appeared in the United States.[302] Since then rapid and enormous advances have been made in this field. There are today, especially in America, tens of thousands of human beings who were conceived as well as born in a clinic and whose fathers are known only to God and the physician.[303] In this country A. I. is not practiced on a very wide scale,[304] though accurate statistics cannot, for obvious reasons, be procured. In fact, it appears that in regard to A. I. as well as euthanasia,[305] physicians prefer their own limited judgment to the law more often than we are led to believe. The true number of births and deaths caused by their deliberate intervention will never be known. These matters cannot be regulated by the State only. Without a deeply religious and moral conscience absolute control can never be exercised over the arbitrary generation and termination of human life.

The legal position relating to artificial human insemination is rather obscure and undefined. As far as I know, the subject is not covered by any explicit legislation either in Europe or in America. This is somewhat strange and significant when we consider that Jewish law, as we shall see, pronounced on this problem as early as 1930. The present legal issues can, therefore, be determined only from a few, isolated judgments given in some celebrated law-suits. Thus the Supreme Court in Ontario ruled in 1921 that A. I. with donated semen (A. I. D.) constituted adultery.[306] A similar conclusion appears to be indicated by Lord Dunedin's judgment in a British case which occurred in 1924,[307] but no American court has decided the issue—at least not until 1947.[308] In 1945[309] the then British Minister of Health (Mr. Willink) told Parliament that he was advised "that it would be a breach of the law to register as legitimate a birth that occurred as a result of this operation when the husband was not in fact the father of the child." As the law stands, therefore, there is little doubt that A.I.D. involves both the wife and the donor in an act of adultery and renders the child born in this way illegitimate.[310] But the law does not say anything about the legality of the operation itself. On the other hand, A.I.H. (i.e., if the husband's semen is used) is not touched by the law at all, and the resultant child enjoys the same legal status as if born after normal intercourse.[311]

Before I deal with the Jewish attitude I also wish to make a few remarks on the Christian views regarding this problem. The first Roman Catholic pronouncement was made in a Holy Office decree of 1897.[312] This has been followed by innumerable discussions and rulings in the many works and periodicals on Catholic moral philosophy and medical ethics. These make it clear that A.I.D. is definitely immoral, "because it is a violation of the natural law which limits the right to generate to married people, and which demands that right to be exercised personally and not by proxy."[313] This reasoning is significant and considerably at variance with the Jewish point of view, though the conclusion is similar to it. In regard to A.I.H., however, Catholic opinions vary. But the margin of difference is being narrowed down by a tendency among Catholic theologians within recent years to favor the stricter view which considers every form of A.I. as intrinsically unlawful except "assisted insemination in the wide sense," i.e. if it is applied after normal intercourse between husband and wife as an aid to the natural process—by forcing the semen through artificial means into the wife's tract which it should have entered through the natural act, but was unable to enter owing to some physical impediment.[314] But there is practical unanimity among Catholic moralists that the husband may not procure the semen, either for medical examination in cases of suspected infertility or for A.I. into his wife, by any method which involves masturbation or other forms of *coitus interruptus*.[315]

The Protestant attitude is far less final and more flexible. In the *Report on Aritificial Human Insemination of a Commission Appointed by the Archbishop of Canterbury* (published in 1948), all but one of the 13 members agreed that A.I.D. involved a breach of the marriage, was wrong in principle and contrary to Christian standards.[316] They recommended that, in view of the evils involved, early consideration should be given to the framing of legislation to make the practice criminal offense. Regarding A.I.H., all members with one exception agreed that even masturbation by the husband may be justifiable, if there is no other practicable alternative to bring about the successful insemination of the wife.[317]

Our Halakhah, while it may arrive at similar conclusions, views such problems from an entirely different angle, and it was with this in mind that I summarized the Christian viewpoints to stress these differences in moral and legal thought. Jewish law does not, as does Roman Catholicism, recognize any essential relationship between the "natural" character of an act and its legality. Nor can Judaism solve such problems, as other Christian denominations do, on the basis of some vague and general principles of morality. The practical Halakhah is guided solely by the directives of earlier authority, whether biblical or rabbinic, and it is to the literary sources of Jewish law that we must look for the compatibility between human conduct and the will of God.

In what is perhaps one of the most startling testimonies to the exhaustive comprehensiveness of its legislation, the Talmud in a legal discussion mentions one of the main halachic principles involved in A.I. some seventeen hundred years before scientific research made its application in all but accidental cases possible. I refer to the question put to Ben Zoma whether a High Priest is permitted to marry a virgin who is pregnant, notwithstanding the biblical insistence upon her absolute virginity.[318] This is answered in the affirmative, and the circumstances of her pregnancy are explained as due to an impregnation through water in which she bathed and which was previously fertilized by a male.[319] The possibility of such generation *sine concubito* has apparently not been recognized by the Greeks or other nations of antiquity, and Jewish literature is certainly the first to give it recognition in a legal context.[320] The second important source is a late Midrash which is repeated in several medieval works, both historical and halachic. It reiterates the belief that Ben Sirach was conceived in this way, the father having been the Prophet Jeremiah, and the mother, according to some sources, the Prophet's own daughter.[321] Strangely enough, despite the general maxim אין למדין הלכה מן האגדה,[322] this Midrash, even more than the Talmudic reference, has been used much to determine the Halakhah in cases where conception occurred without any physical contact between the parents. This Midrash, incidentally, is also quoted as "a legend of the Rabbis" by the famous sixteenth century Marrano physician Amatus Lusitanus to clear a nun from the suspicion of fornication after a miscarriage.[323]

Halachically, various medieval authorities utilize this Midrash to establish the important principle that a man whose semen accidentally fertilized the female ovum by indirect contact through water is regarded as the legal father of the child so produced and is, in fact, considered as having fulfilled the religious duty of procreation in respect of that child.[324] Moreover, R. Isaak Lampronti, the early eighteenth century rabbi-physician, proves in his monumental *Pachad Yitzchak* from the account of Ben Sirach's conception that such a child is not a ממזר, even if his father and mother would have committed an incestuous act had they had normal relations with each other.[325] These rulings, which are disputed by some authorities,[326] are of course of the greatest importance to our subject of A.I.D.

A further halachic precedent to our problem is first mentioned by R. Peretz ben Elijah of Corbeil (thirteenth century) in his הגהות סמ"ק. He rules that a woman must be careful with the use of linen on which a man other than her husband had lain, lest she become pregnant and the resultant child, not knowing the identity of the father, marry the latter's daughter, i.e. his own sister. Yet R. Peretz agrees that this offspring would not be regarded as born of an adulterous union, though the father is not the mother's husband. This ruling, which is also repeated by various later authorities,[327] once again vindicates the principle that the relationship between father and child is not necessarily dependent on physical intercourse between the parents, and that, on the other hand, the legal consequences of incest illegitimize a child only if the forbidden union between the parents was natural.

But there are פוסקים who do not agree with these rulings, nor indeed with the literal interpretation of the Ben Zoma passage in the Talmud and the traditional account of Ben Sirach's conception. Thus R. Judah Rozanes of Constantinople, the eighteenth century author of the *Mishneh Le-Melekh,* doubts that an impregnation through water can ever be effective.[328] Several eminent rabbis, even to the present century, have shared this view.[329] The historicity of Ben Sirach's birth through a conception *sine concubito* has likewise been denied centuries ago, e.g. by the chronicler R. David Gans in his *Tsemach David,* first published in 1592.[330] But the rather bold refusal of Rozanes and others to believe in the literal meaning of a Talmudic passage has been heatedly contested by such scholars as R. Chaim Joseph David Azulai[331] and R. Jonathan Eybeschitz[332] in the first and second half of the eighteenth century.

I have surveyed some of the discussions and conclusions on which the present-day treatment of our problem is based in some detail in order to show not only how the essential principles have been laid down in the classics of Jewish law long ago, but, above all, to indicate the complexity of the considerations, the importance of tracing the sources and the difficulties in the way of reaching finality in such matters. I will now turn briefly to some of the modern responsa dealing with the subject, before giving a short summary of the halachic position to date. I believe that our problem was first dealt with in a responsum by Rabbi J. L. Zirelsohn in reply to an inquiry from Budapest in 1930.[333] He was concerned with a case of A. I. D., and he regarded it as constituting plain adultery. Disregarding the earlier arguments on impregnation through water as apparently irrelevant, he finds support for his ruling in the literal meaning of the text: ואל אשת עמיתך לא תתן שכבתך לזרע לטמאה בה.[334] Hence the wife involved, as an adulteress, is אסורה לבעלה following the operation, and the child produced is a ממזר —the result of an adulterous conception under normal circumstances. Incidentally, it seems to me, that scriptural support for this opinion can rather be found in the use of the word תבל for incest. Rashi,[335] according to one interpretation, derives the word from בלל, to mix, and he explains: מבלבלין זרע האב בזרע הבן, there is a mixture of semen from the father and the son (in case of a man who has illicit relations with his daughter-in-law). This appears to imply that the mere mixing of the seed, as distinct from physical intimacy, constitutes תבל or incest.

But this extreme view, to my knowledge, was not confirmed in any of the numerous responsa, which subsequently treated the question, except for a contribution which the South African Rabbi Abraham Lurie made to a protracted discussion on A. I. It appeared in the Tel Aviv halachic periodical *Ha-Posek* a year ago.[336] Thus the Sephardi Chief Rabbi of Israel, in his *Mishpetey Uziel*,[337] regards the child as legitimate in the halachic sense, and not as a bastard, but the wife would not be allowed to have relations with her husband during her pregnancy resulting from the insemination, since she must be looked upon as a מעוברת חברו. Rabbi Uziel also declares as illicit any unnatural act to procure the semen for such a purpose. The former principal of the Berlin Rabbiner Seminar, Dr. J. Weinberg, in a very recent responsum (private), claims that such questions cannot be decided by direct reference to the wording of the Torah. He avers that no

adultery of incest can occur unless the offending parties had
been in physical and intimate contact with each other. He,
too, therefore concludes that the resultant child is not a bastard. But, in common with all authorities on the subject, he
vigorously condemns A. I. D. as מעשה כיעור ותועבת מצרים
because it opens the door to many dangers and abuses.
Since only the mother, her husband and the physician are
likely to know that the putative father is not, in fact, the
child's father at all, the mother—upon the death of her husband—might be unlawfully freed from יבום וחליצה on
the mistaken assumption that the deceased husband left a
child. On the same assumption the child might be regarded
as legal heir to an inheritance which, by law, is due to someone else. The legalization of A. I. D. would also pave the way
to far more disastrous forms of promiscuity, as a wife, guilty
of adultery, could always claim that the pregnancy which the
husband did not, or was unable to, cause, was brought about
by A. I. D., when in fact she had adulterous relations with
another man.[338] Dr. Weinberg concludes his opposition to
any form of A. I. D. on the additional ground that, should a
child be so conceived and be born, he would have to be regarded as a שתוקי, whose mother is known, but whose father
cannot be identified. As such, he might have to be debarred
from marriage.[339] R. Hillel Posek, in his periodical *HaPosek*
likewise denounces the practice of A. I. D. which he considers
as אביזרייהו דג"ע, as the appurtenance of incest.[340] He
urges that such childless parents should adopt orphaned
children instead. Other authorities cited in the אוצר הפוסקים
are also unanimous in their unconditional opposition to
A. I. D.[341]

So much for A. I. D. Regarding the permissibility of A. I.
H., however, rabbinic opinions are very much more divided.
The problem has often been discussed, especially in relation
to the question whether a husband is allowed to produce a
sample of his semen in order to have it medically tested, if
necessary. The root of the problem is to determine the exact
definition of הוצאת זרע לבטלה. There is an obvious connection between this and the controversy to which I have
already referred—whether a man whose semen produced a
child *sine concubito* has thereby fulfilled his obligation of

פרי' ורבי'. Yet there are some who hold the act of masturbation of this purpose to be unlawful even if he should
thereby fulfill the first commandment, because לא התירו
אסור שבות בשביל קיום עשה.[342] But others refute this view,
claiming that such an act performed for the sole purpose
of making the eventual birth of a child possible can never be
regarded as הוצאת זרע לבטלה, whether the מצוה of פו"ר
will thereby be technically fulfilled or not.[343] Although the
greater weight of opinion in this controversy seems to favor
the more lenient view,[344] it is clearly quite impossible to
issue a general היתר of this practice. I think we might be
prepared to encourage the adoption of two methods advocated
by some Catholic theologians and physicians, viz. the use during normal intercourse of either a perforated condom[345] or,
better still, a special instrument which has been designed in
America for this particular purpose, the "cervical spoon."[346]
Both appliances make it possible to obtain a sufficient quantity of semen for examination or insemination purposes without seriously interfering with the marital act or its natural
effectiveness, and I believe little or no halachic objection can
be raised against their use when medically indicated.

In summary, then, Judaism condemns A.I.D. in any form
as an utter abomination, though we are less concerned with
the intrinsic immorality of the practice than with the abuses
to which it lends itself. Such human stud-farming exposes the
society to the gravest dangers which can never be outweighed
by the benefits that may accrue in individual cases. As Jewish
spiritual leaders we should therefore in common with others,
denounce this immoral practice or any suggestion to legalize
it. On the other hand, the consensus of halachic opinion disagrees with the law of the state and the church as it now
stands in regarding the offspring produced by A.I.D. as
illegitimate and the operation itself as adulterous. Such an
offspring, according to Jewish law, is the legal child of the
donor (that is, if he can be identified with absolute certainty); the child cannot inherit his putative father nor
free his mother from יבום וחליצה in case of her husband's death. There are weightly reasons for imposing marriage restrictions upon such a product of A.I.D. No final
opinion can be expressed on A.I.H. or the procuring of

semen for examination purposes; but there is every probability that, under certain circumstances and with suitable safeguards, a היתר for this practice can be found in individual cases.

Birth-Control

In contrast to A.I., the history of birth-control is very ancient indeed. So also is the religious and moral opposition to it. Thus the Midrash, quoted by Rashi (on Gen. 4: 19, 23), attributes this practice to the depraved humans before Noah in prehistoric times.[347] According to these sources, some contraceptive potion[348] was given to wives in those times "in order to preserve their beauty," in one case, and to prevent children from being born into an age of destruction, in another. The only explicit biblical reference to this practice is in the story of Er and **Onan** who practiced birth-prevention by *coitus interruptus,* and were punished with death for their crime.[349] It is wrong therefore to associate Onan's offence with masturbation as implied by the conventional meaning of the term Onanism.[350] The term should properly be used for the practice of birth-prevention on the part of the male. In ancient Rome this evil was particularly widespread, so much so that the Emperor Augustus, alarmed at the unfavorable population rates, is recorded to have chastized the offenders as traitors of the fatherland and as "cruel murderers of those whom they should conceive and bear."[351] Many ancient and medieval collections of popular medical recipes included assortments of magical mixtures designed to prevent conception.[352] But it should not be imagined that, even among the pagans, no moral voices were raised against this growing evil. The ordinances of a heathen shrine of the second century B. C. discovered at Philadelphia in Asia Minor mention an oath taken by those who entered it by saying that "they would neither turn to nor recommend to others . . . to have a hand in . . . contraceptives."[353]

The Roman Catholic Church has waged unremitting and uncompromising war against birth-control. It condemns it under all circumstances, medical or otherwise. Her theologians, who counsel continence as the sole licit means to prevent births,[354] are, however, in some doubt in regard to the application of the Ogino-Knaus method, popularly known as the "safe period" calculation and the legality of disseminating information on this method,[355] about which I will say more presently. The Anglican Church shared this opposition to birth-control which it denounced as "dangerous, demoralizing and sinful," at various Lambeth Conferences before 1930.[356] But in that year a resolution was carried with a large majority which suddenly adjusted the concepts of morality and sinfulness to permit the use of methods other than abstinence "where moral obligation to limit parenthood is felt."[357] As one critic has observed, since then the purveyors of contraceptives "welcome with eagerness the Church as an ally."[358] Just how widespread the employment of contraceptive methods was just before the Second World War can be gauged from a revealing survey which has been conducted by the American magazine *Fortune* in 1938. It estimated that approximately 200,000,000 dollars were spent annually by American women on some of the 636 different contraceptive products available in that country.[359] How many children thus unborn could otherwise be maintained in comfort with this astronomical sum of money!

The Jewish attitude to this staggering social and moral problem has, as I have already indicated, received only very little attention in non-rabbinic literature. This is all the more surprising if one bears in mind that there is an almost inexhaustible halachic literature on the subject. There are few responsa works of the last century or two which do not raise and answer this question. But as far as I know, there are only two printed pronouncements made in this country in English on the subject.[360] Both appear in non-Jewish books and both are quite inadequate and perhaps even misleading. The first is quoted by Professor A. M. Carr-Saunders in his *World-Population*[361] as an "authoritative account of Jewish teaching by Lauterbach," to the effect that the woman is certainly allowed to use any kind of contraceptive after her husband has fulfilled the duty of propagating the race, having had two children. The second statement is by the late Chief Rabbi Dr. Hertz. It is given as a comment on Lauterbach's teaching in the form of a personal communication to the well-known Catholic doctor and writer, Dr. H. Sutherland, who reproduces it in his book *Control of Life*.[362] Dr. Hertz there describes the statement cited by Carr-Saunders as "not incorrect, but not quite complete" and adds that "the moral obligation, if not the commandment, still rests upon him (i.e. the husband) of propagating the race when he has already two children." Dr. Hertz concludes: "Contraceptives permitted to women are only allowed in cases where considerations of health make such action necessary." Even this cautious statement over-simplifies the position. With some variations it might be accepted for practical purposes, had its author added the overridding proviso that under no circumstances can the practice of contraception, in whatever form, be sanctioned by Jewish law, unless the conditions prevailing in each individual case have first been successfully submitted to rabbinic judgment.[363] The factors involved are so intricate and delicate, and the stakes—concerning, as they do, capital judgments—are so grave and sacred, and the danger of misinterpretation is so real and serious, that no general ruling can be given. Every single case must be judged on its own merits by a rabbi on the basis of the medical information vouchsafed from a professionally reliable physician who should himself be God-fearing and conversant with the gravity of the religious and moral considerations involved.

The factor which should be emphasized above all others is the positive attitude of Judaism towards large families.[364] Unlike Roman Catholicism, Jewish law regards the procreation of children as a cardinal duty, in fact as the first divine commandment given to man.[365] People who refuse to put at least a son and a daughter into the world and thus replace themselves are looked upon as social pariahs who reduce the glory of God and contribute to the extinction of His human creatures.[366] The Torah stresses the fact that every one of our matriarchs craved to be blessed with children after an agonizing period of barrenness[367] so as to perpetuate this outlook from the very birth of our people. Moreover, the one- or two-children-system has proved destructive of the delights and attractions of true Jewish home life. This suicidal system has helped to displace the home as the center of Jewish life and to promote selfishness among parents and children alike, because neither is trained to sacrifice things for other members of the family and society. Even more vital, perhaps, is the demographic factor. Few realize what scale of human reproduction will be required gradually to replace the disastrous losses inflicted upon our people through its threefold decimation within the last decade.[368] In terms of sheer survival no service to the Jewish cause can even remotely rival that rendered by the Jewish mother, and no money is more fruitfully invested than in the rearing and education of a large family.

Whether the religious duty to procreate applies to women as well as to men is the subject of a controversy in the Mishnah.[369] Various suggestions have been offered to explain why, according to the view which was eventually codified as law,[370] this duty is not, at least technically, incumbent upon the female.[371] I think the reason may be that the woman, as modelled on חוה, the "mother of all life,"[372] has the desire for the creation of new life and children so deeply implanted by instinct, that there was no need to reinforce her natural impulses by divine legislation. Whatever the reason, this view has obviously important bearings on our subject.

In this case I have deliberately anticipated the discussion of the halachic principles involved by a brief statement of the general approach of Judaism towards this problem. This cannot be viewed in the right perspective unless the overall attitude of Jewish law is always born in mind and not lost in a maze of detail and largely academic argument. On the other hand, no rabbi can presume to guide a questioner on this subject if he has not thoroughly familiarized himself with the wealth of literary sources, particularly the opinions of the ראשונים, which determine the Halachah.

The Talmud mentions our problem only once in a legal context;[373] that is when R. Meir permits, and, according to some ראשונים [374] commands, contraceptive precautions to a minor wife, and to women during pregnancy and lactation, because a conception under those circumstances may have fatal consequences upon the mother or the existing embryo, or the suckling respectively. The חכמים, however, counsel reliance upon divine protection even under those conditions.

Whichever of the many interpretations of this much debated argument we accept, it is clear that the validity of none but medical considerations is admitted. I need not say that Judaism rejects the cosmetic argument mentioned earlier. It opposes the eugenic argument with equal force. It is not for men to determine who is fit to survive and whose life and birth should be prevented.[375] But Judaism is also emphatic in condemning the economic argument as a valid indication for contraception.[376] If our ancestors, who faced far worse economic and social conditions than we do, had ever recognized the legality of artifically limiting their increase out of a desire to spare their potential progeny the prospect of destitution, suffering and slaughter, none of us or our people would exist today. The responsibility to sustain life once it it is created ultimately rests upon the משביע לכל חי , not ourselves.

This explains why nearly all of the innumerable relevant responsa raise the question from the medical point of view only. The question is: May a woman whose life is certified to be in grave danger if she became pregnant employ contraceptives, and, if so, in what form? Motives other than these were not even worth considering. Yet, the very fact that the subject has been discussed so frequently and at such length proves that Judaism is very far from the dogmatic attitude of the Catholic Church in this matter. None of the responsa contemplates complete continence as the answer to the problem.[377] Such a course is considered as not only highly impracticable but, indeed, as contrary to Jewish law which demands of the husband that he fulfill his marital duties at regular intervals.[378] This duty is quite distinct from the obligation to beget children; it is the inviolable birthright of every married woman. Even she can renounce it only occasionally, and then only if מצות פרי' ורבי' has already been fulfilled.[379] Hence Judaism would advise divorce rather than a marriage which demands total continence either for religious or medical reasons.[380]

This leads me to a word about the "safe period." Independent investigations by Professors Ogino in Japan (1924) and Knaus in Austria (1929) have shown what Jewish legislation appears to have anticipated by three and a half thousand years; namely that the fertility of the normal woman varies in regular cycles, and that there is a monthly period, lasting about seven days, during which conception is not likely or altogether impossible.[381] More recent research has all but perfected the methods to calculate that agenic period, but it is generally admitted that this calculation, to be reliable, must be made by a doctor, and that even then no absolute guarantees can be given.[382] Some Catholic books give various graphs and tables to assist those who wish to restrict their marital relations to the infertile period.[383] I do not think that the question of the "safe period" has received unfavourable treatment in any of our modern responsa, and it would not seem wrong to advise young people to seek medical guidance along these lines in circumstances which morally and religiously justify such negative precautions.[384]

Concerning the application of positive means to prevent conception if this may endanger the mother's life, opinions vary widely. The most lenient view is first put forward by the famous sixteenth century author of the *Yam Shel Shlomo,* R. Solomon Luria.[385] He permits the insertion by the wife of a tampon before intercourse, and so do many authorities who agree to this action if conception might prove dangerous.[386] R. Akivah Eger, on the other hand, almost two centuries later, leads those who will not tolerate any impediment to operate during intercourse, holding that the wife may only afterwards, according to his interpretation of the Talmudic passage, remove the semen as best she can.[387] The *Chatham Sofer* also agrees with this view.[388] There is unanimity on the unlawfulness of anything done by the husband to render his act ineffective.[389] Should the danger of conception to the wife's life be permanent, she should be advised to submit to X-ray or surgical treatment, as other devices requiring constant use must not be employed in such cases.[390] The degree of danger to life can, of course, only be determined by a physician. Any serious doubt regarding her ability to survive a pregnancy is regarded as placing her in such danger. But the possible, or even certain, impairment of health, if this is not likely to lead to fatal consequences, is not a sufficient indication for the use of contraceptive precautions.[391] Thus the artificial spacing of children for considerations of the mother's health cannot justify contraceptive action except when she breast-feeds her child and in other special circumstances.

It is not for me, certainly not on this occasion, to rationalize these regulations. Their moral and social value, quite apart from their paramount religious worth, should be apparent to every Jewish social worker who has seen the low level to which Jewish family life has sunk. The danger to civilization originates, in the last resort, not from the Kremlin, but from the laboratories and workshops of mass destruction, whether by atom-bomb or the much more destructive spermicide which every day exterminates germinating human life by the million. In a remarkable passage the Talmud[392] tells us that Amram, Moses' father, one day decided to divorce his wife. "What is the use of procreating children," he said, "if they are liable to be drowned by the command of Pharaoh?" But he was answered; "You are worse than Pharaoh— for, unlike him, you decree death not only in this world, but also in the next!" He thereupon reversed his decison—and produced a Moses! A Moses is born neither by accident nor by planning, but only as a product of an act of faith.

This passage also teaches another lesson. Why did not Amram, intent on having no more children, practice birth-control instead of divorcing his wife? Though the practice, as we have seen, was well known in antiquity, that thought never occurred to him and his wife. To have the pleasures of marriage without its burdens was inconceivable to them. And that is precisely what so many young people of our times want. They desire the delights of marriage, but not its hardships. More children usually mean less luxuries and comforts. Parents often have to decide whether to have larger families or larger cars—and the cars generally win.

The popularity of contraception has opened the door wide to immorality and marital faithlessness, to the eradication of all traces of sanctity, refinement and self-control from life, and this on a scale which even the ancient heathens probably never knew. Man has become a brutalized addict to selfishness and convenience, and he forgets that, in the end, he has to pay a far higher price for his failure to maintain the ideals of a moral and ennobled life than would be incurred by co-operating with God in the normal generation of life. And perhaps we might also remind our members that the arrival of an unwanted child is always a happier event than the non-arrival of a wanted child! We ministers, as the spokesmen of God's word, have a heavy responsibility in these matters; only a bold and fearless stand by the dictates of our halachic guides can justify our election to the spiritual leadership of our people.

6

Jewish Law and Its Administration

Notes on Rabbinic Legislation

Biblical Sanction

I T is regarded as axiomatic in Talmudic[1] and Midrashic[2] literature that all rabbinic teachings are derived from the revelation at Sinai. The Torah expressly sanctions the legislative rights of the Rabbis and enjoins submission to rabbinic laws in the words: "According

Published in *Chayenu* (London), July-August, and September-October, 1952.

to the teaching which they shall teach you, you shall do; you shall not depart from the word which they shall tell you to the right or to the left."[3] Obedience to the Rabbis is thus decreed as both a positive and a negative commandment.[4] The judges are likewise empowered to rule in matters of dispute or difficulty concerning the laws of the Torah: "If there arise a matter too hard for you in judgment, between (one kind of) blood and (another kind of) blood, between sentence and sentence, between plague and plague, matters of controversy within your gates, then shall you arise and go up to the place which the Lord your God shall choose; and you shall come to the priests, the Levites, and to the judge that shall be in those days, and enquire; and they shall tell you the sentence of judgment; and you shall do according to the word which they shall tell you from the place which the Lord shall choose; and you shall observe to do according to all that they shall teach you."[5] Thus all rabbinic laws are based on the commandment "you shall not depart."[6] Consequently benedictions recited over the fulfillment of positive rabbinic laws include the same formula as those for biblical laws: ". . . . who has sanctified us through His commandments and commanded us to . . ."[7] But opinions differ in the Talmud as to whether the Divine sanction determining this form of benediction derives from the passage quoted above,[8] or from the verse "Ask your father and he shall tell you, your elders and they shall say it to you."[9]

There is, however, a far-reaching controversy among later authorities regarding the implications of that sanction. According to Maimonides, every offence against laws ordained by the Rabbis automatically constitutes a transgression of a positive and negative Torah commandment.[10] Such laws are (a) by rabbinic tradition part of the original oral revelation at Sinai (הלכה למשה מסיני), (b) deduced from the Torah through the accepted hermeneutical rules of interpretation, or (c) purely rabbinic legislation. Against this view, Nachmanides agrees only regarding the first two categories (a and b) which have full biblical status, but argues that purely rabbinic laws can never involve their transgressor in Torah offences, as rabbinic ordinances are expressly stated to be in many ways inferior in status to those commanded in the Torah.[12] R. Simon b. Zemach Duran, supporting Nachmanides,[13] further disproves Maimonides on the ground that rabbinic laws are excluded from Israel's oath to observe the Torah taken at Sinai and embracing all its laws.[14] Later authorities, in support of Maimonides, have refuted these arguments; the former (i.e. that of Nachmanides) because the Rabbis, in ordaining their laws, may themselves have vested them with an inferior status in order to differentiate them from Torah laws;[15] and the latter because such laws, since they are not specifically mentioned in the Torah, are not included in the oath, even though their observance is expressly enjoined in the form of positive and negative commandments.[16] Nevertheless, Nachmanides who knew but rejected the above refutation of his argument,[17]—whilst he does not regard every rabbinic law as constituting a positive and negative Torah decree—obviously still considers obedience to the Rabbis as divinely decreed in the form of a law like all other laws in the Torah.[18]

On the other hand, the rift between his view and that of Maimonides is further narrowed down by vital qualifications in the latter's attitude. Accordingly, only such rabbinic laws enjoy in principle the status of a positive and negative biblical commandment as have been ordained by the Supreme Court in Jerusalem[19] and thus have permanent and universal validity[20]—qualifications strongly supported implicitly by Maimonides himself,[21]—and then only if the transgressor was motivated not by considerations of expediency or convenience, but by the desire to demonstrate his opposition to the Rabbis.[22] Laws so ordained by the Supreme Court may in fact be on exactly the same level as biblical laws, except where they clash with the latter. In this way the difficulties raised by Nachmanides would be entirely removed.[23] Whilst decrees and ordinances issued by a court cannot be abrogated by later authorities except under certain limited conditions, the Torah (in the second passage cited at the beginning of these notes) gives every court—though its members may be less learned than earlier[24] or contemporary but unauthorized scholars[25] whom they oppose—complete autonomy in rulings affecting interpretations or decisions of the Divine law even when these conflict with previous rulings.[26] Apart from the two passages quoted above, the Torah specifically sanctions and enjoins the Rabbis to promulgate "fence"-legislation to protect the law of the Torah.[27]

Scope of Rabbinic Legislation

In addition to the clearly defined right and duty of the Rabbis to issue special ordinances and decrees to safeguard the religious and social interests of the people, and to add to, adjust or modify biblical laws under certain circumstances, the Torah accords to courts of law and to the Rabbis far-reaching autonomy in three particular fields: (a) the fixing of legal standards, (b) disposal of private property, and (c) marriages.   Regarding (a), whilst the minimum standard measures (e.g. the volume of food forbidden in the Torah) making a person liable to punishment are fixed by the Oral Law given at Sinai,[28] it is left to the Rabbis to determine such standards as are otherwise undefined.[29] Thus we often find the phrase "Scripture entrusted (the formulation of a particular law) into the hands of the Rabbis" in the Talmud[30] and rabbinic literature generally.[31] In this way the Rabbis are authorised to determine what constitutes prohibited "work" on the intermediate days of festivals,[32] certain details regarding oaths,[33] the validity of evidence by normally unqualified witnesses,[34] the comforts forbidden to be enjoyed on the Day of Atonement,[35] the ban on adopting non-Jewish practices,[36] the removal of leaven before Passover,[37] and the conditions an *Ethrog*, etc., must satisfy before it can be used on Sukkoth.[38] According to a late rabbinic responsum, however, the Torah grants to the Rabbis such authority to determine the details of the law only if the relevant scriptural texts would otherwise appear to be contradictory and thus in need of rabbinic interpretation to decide the law;[39] but this view is not generally accepted.[40]

In regard to (b), an important rule in rabbinic legislation provides that "the court's confiscation (i.e. declaration to be ownerless) of money or other private assets is valid."[41] Such confiscation has Torah status[42] and it can be ordered by any court, even if it is not fully qualified, or by the recognized lay authorities of the community.[43] The application of this rule must, however, be guided by the desire to prevent serious social or religious evils, at least when its operation affects a commandment of the Torah, such as the law to release all debts in the Sabbatical year.[44] Some authorities,[45] apparently including Maimonides,[46] hold that this rule grants the court power not merely to confiscate private property but also to transfer it to the possession of another individual; others oppose this view.[47] There are also opinions which limit such power to the greatest authority of the generation.[48] In any case this right must not be exercised except with the utmost discretion.[49]

Again (c), the Rabbis can declare a marriage contract null and void with retrospective effect on the principle that "he who betrothes a woman, does so (on condition that he acts) in accordance with rabbinic law,"[50] as he must expressly state "according to the law of Moses and of Israel" when reciting the marriage formula.[51] This power to annul a marriage can be exercised even without the express reservation in the marriage formula, when the act of betrothal conflicts with the *manner* prescribed by the Rabbis,[52] such as a marriage forced upon the bride.[53] This rule, whereby the validity of a legal act is dependent on rabbinic consent, applies only to marriages, not divorces,[54] or any other legal deal.[55] Yet even in the case of marriage the act is invalidated only if a rabbinic objection arises subsequently, not if the betrothal itself offended against the law of the Torah or the Rabbis.[56] But from the exceptions to this rule[57] it appears that it operates only in cases expressely mentioned in rabbinic literature.[58]

Status of Rabbinic Legislation

"Whatever the Rabbis enacted they ordained as though it were a Torah law."[59] Thus the same regulations apply to the tithing of vegetables—instituted by the Rabbis—as to the tithing of corn, wine and olive oil—commanded in the Torah.[60] Similarly, a husband can inherit his wife, though he is only rabbinically entitled to do so, on the same terms as a son.[61] According to one view in the Talmud, this rule applies only to enactments which are based on Torah laws, representing an extension of them.[62] Any but tannaitic ordinances are in any case also excluded from this rule,[63] which is not without exceptions.[64] The Rabbis therefore generally protected their own enactments by decreeing the manner of their observance to be on the same lines,[66] often even on more stringent lines, that is, more stringent than the Torah lays down for its own laws.[67] The reason is that "the laws of the Torah require no strengthening, but those of the Rabbis do,[68] as people may otherwise treat them lightly and despisingly.[69] Thus, for example, whilst if someone vows to fast on a Sabbath or festival the oath is valid and must be carried out, such a fast must not be kept on Purim or Chanukah which are rabbinically ordained[70] in order to bring home the importance of rabbinic laws.[71] But opinions differ as to whether such stringency applies only to enactments which represent a mere extension of a Torah law, e.g. the right of a husband to inherit his wife,[72] or only to laws which are in no way based on the Torah, as only such require special strengthening.[73] A third view holds that even rabbinic laws which find some support in the Bible have their authority thus reinforced.[74] The Rabbis granted their own laws more protection than is afforded to Torah laws only in cases where it is proper to impose special penalties on the transgressor[75] and the occasion for which occurs frequently;[76] such protection is then regarded as an "extraordinary measure" for checking lawlessness in the same way as the observance of a rabbinic law may sometimes justify the breach of a biblical injunction with which the former conflicts.[77]

Often, however, the Rabbis decreed no such "strengthening for their words;"[78] they could, in fact, ease the practice of their own laws on the principle that "what they have instituted they can modify" as they deem right,[79] as long as the authorities making and modifying the law are identical.[80] In view of the varying degrees of severity with which different rabbinic laws are thus vested, only the Rabbis' own express ruling can decide to which of these categories any of their laws belong.[81]

The Talmud frequently emphasizes the relative superiority, in some ways, of the Oral Law over the Written Law;[82] the above indicates that this applies also to their observance. In

some respects greater zealousness is expected for the fulfillment
of rabbinic laws than for Torah commandments.[83] Accordingly, "he who transgresses the words of the Rabbis commits a
capital offence,"[84] that is, an act which may lead to the death
penalty, such as in the case of a "rebellious elder."[85] A person
who actively[86] disregards a rabbinic law "is called wicked"
and therefore rabbinically disqualified from giving evidence at
court,[87] though—according to some views—only if such a transgression was motivated by a lust for money.[88]

Lenient and Stringent Rulings

Whilst obedience must be shown towards the Rabbis' restrictive enactments, the individual should not go beyond
what is decreed in the Torah[89] and rabbinic law.[90] Such self-
imposed laws may easily lead to encroachments of rabbinic
authority in other cases[91] and thus to heresy.[92] One should
therefore adopt the more lenient as well as the stricter rulings
of any one school of thought, and it is regarded as "folly" to
accept only the more restrictive practices of differing authorities,[93] unless one is in doubt as to which authority to accept.[94]
Rashi, however, holds that everyone is free to impose the more
stringent decisions upon himself.[95] It is always easier to rule
strictly (which even an unscholarly person can do to evade
doubts); the expression of a more lenient view, however, testifies to a more certain tradition (which alone can account for
such leniency); in recording contrary opinions preference is
therefore given to the latter.[96] Hence it is the more stringent
ruling which requires special proof.[97] But in view of the
ordinary people's laxity in the observance of the law, it is
sometimes necessary—even today—to withhold certain lenient
rulings from the public and to teach them more severity than
the law itself actually requires.[98]

Mistaken Rulings

As a rule the Ashkenazi schools of learning—being more
scrupulously zealous in their religious observances[99]—tended
to incline more towards rigid decisions of the law than their

Sephardi contemporaries,[100] except in matters where the social and economic pressure of their environment forced them to certain modifications which the Sephardim were not compelled to share.[101]

The words of the Torah "You shall not depart from the word which they shall tell you to the right or to the left"[102] imply that the decisions of the Rabbis must be accepted even if they appear to be wrong,[103] though not of necessity if they are actually mistaken.[104] The accounts of Rabbi Eliezer's submission to the majority view although his opinion was really correct,[105] and of Rabbi Gamaliel's order to Rabbi Joshua openly to desecrate the day which the latter had calculated to be the Day of Atonement,[106] despite the fact that the prevailing view was in both cases not absolutely correct, seem to prove that the individual must bow even to a mistaken decision of the Rabbis.[107] Whilst the second proof is accepted by many,[108] it can be refuted, as the Torah specifically declares the fixing of the calendar to be dependent on the Rabbis even if their calculation is wrong; the case of the Day of Atonement would thus constitute an exception, expressly provided for in the Torah, to the general rule.[109] But opinions differ in the sources cited[110] as to whether the Rabbis must be obeyed even if one knows their ruling to be definitely erroneous, or only if they *appear* mistaken—which seems more logical.[111] In any case, the entire principle involved is certainly based on the desire to maintain the religious discipline of the people and on the realization that it is better to once act wrongly in unity than rightly in disunity.[112]

A generally accepted exception to this rule is the case of a member of the Supreme Court disputing a decision of his colleagues;[113] he must submit to the majority ruling only if he was overruled whilst actually sitting with them; otherwise he must act according to his conviction, once he knows their decision to be wrong,[114] as the principle of majority decisions does not apply in such cases.[115]

Usually, then, the responsibility for mistaken rulings rests with the Rabbis who make them and not with the people[116]— nor, according to some, even with the individuals[117]—who carry them out. Legally, however, many conditions must be fulfilled before the Rabbis' guilt is technically established.[118]

The Rabbis are responsible for errors of judgment only if (a) the Supreme Court[119] in the presence of its head and the absence of any unqualified judges[120] issued a unanimous[121] and express[122] ruling, (b) the majority of the Jewish population or tribes in the Holy Land acts on their error,[123] (c) the people acted solely because they relied on the Court's pronouncement,[124] (d) the erroneous judgment was not due to a mistaken appraisal of the facts,[125] and (e) the ruling would involve not the transgression of a full biblical law but only a part of its not expressly mentioned in the Torah.[126] Even Maimonides who, against the view referred to above,[117] holds an individual responsible if he acts on a mistaken judgment of the Rabbis,[127] makes a distinction between a recognised scholar who acts accordingly knowing the ruling to have been erroneous, and other people doing so, as the latter's knowledge" in such matters "is not considered knowledge."[128] All cases mentioned under the above heading deal only with errors committed by the Supreme Court at Jerusalem[129] or at Yavneh,[130] though the latter Court is excluded from the legislations concerning the "rebellious elder."[131] Mistaken rulings of other courts or of individual Rabbis are treated separately.

Fallibility of the Rabbis

Judaism never claimed infallibility for its spiritual leaders. Moses himself,[132] in common with other biblical heroes[133] and the Rabbis of the Talmud[134] as well as such outstanding later authorities as, for instance, Rashi,[135] often committed or admitted errors or ignorance in certain matters, "for there is not a righteous man on earth who does good (only) without (ever) sinning"[136] and "all men pervert the truth (occasionally)."[137] Thus Alfasi[138] and Maimonides[139] sometimes attribute mistakes even to the Geonim despite the latter's high authority.[140] Even the Supreme Court, as we have seen in the previous paragraph, can err, and we must always take into consideration the possibility that any rabbinical court's opinion may be mistaken[141] in certain cases. Generally, however, we assume that the Rabbis are fully familiar with the details of the case before them,[142] and the Talmud[143] and

Codes[144] rule that we need not usually[145] reckon with the possibility of mistakes, except when we have reason to fear that the judges are not fully conversant with the details involved in particular cases.[146] Yet no Rabbi is expected to have all halachic rulings in his head,[147] and having committed an occasional error does not disqualify him from acting as judge.[148] The enormous power vested in the rabbinic legislators—the heirs of the Prophets[149]—derives from their extraordinary single-minded devotion to the study and practice of the Divine Law[150] which practically guarantees their freedom from error and falsehood.[151]

The administration of Jewish law also requires immense scientific and general erudition[152] which the supreme legislators must master.[153] The Talmud[154] and some Codes[155] in fact regard the acquisition of such knowledge as a positive commandment on its own, quite apart from the desirability to study science in order to appreciate the greatness of God and His works.[156] For halachic purposes the Rabbis often made thorough observations and investigations into nature,[157] and if necessary they would consult expert opinion to establish the scientific data required for the Halakhah.[158] In such matters they even relied on non-Jewish sources[159] on the assumption that all knowledge was once in Jewish hands, though it was later transmitted to others whilst we lost many parts of it.[160] But scientific opinion cannot be accepted when it opposes the teachings of the Torah[161] or the Halakhah of the Talmudic Rabbis,[162] and any apparent conflict between science and Jewish law should be resolved in favour of the latter,[163] as our inability to harmonize them may be due to our lack of understanding.[164] But it is recognised that such conflicts exist.[165] Even nature itself submits to some extent to the dictates of the Halakhah,[166] as many authorities confirm.[167] Thus the ripening of plants,[168] as far as that affects the law,[169] the duration of pregnancy,[170] and the various stages of puberty[171] can be influenced by the Court's determination of the calendar, as all these occur on certain dates or after a fixed number of years or months (the length of which is decided by the Rabbis). The incidence of the seasons is not, however, affected,[172] since that would be of no legal consequence.[169] The Torah itself mentions two instances of interference with nature in its legal procedure, viz. the effect of the "bitter waters" in establishing the guilt of the "faithless women,"[173] and the divine administration of capital punishment for certain offences even though its operation may not be apparent to us today.[174]

But in matters which have no bearing on the Halakhah we find certain imperfections in the Talmud and other rabbinic works acknowledged by later authorities. There are, for instance, many examples of inaccurate quotations from the Bible.[175] These may be due (a) to the occasional unfamiliarity of the Rabbis with the full scriptural text,[176] (b) to uncertainties about the correct reading,[177] (c) to the Talmud opposing certain versions of the Masoretic texts,[178] or (d) to the desire to express the meaning or gist rather than the full text of a verse,[179] since in any case—as Maimonides points out—the Rabbis' qualifications require them to be proficient scholars, not scribes.[180] It also appears that some Amoraim were occasionally not fully familiar with earlier rabbinic writings, including perhaps even the Mishnah.[181] Again, we sometimes find grammatical errors in rabbinic literature.[182] These have been condoned by some authorities as being of no consequence,[183] though others have stressed the importance of studying grammar, as long as it is not turned into a major subject at the expense of Torah learning.[184] Rabbinic works also contain a number of unscientific etymological explanations.[185] But in general no special reliance need be placed on writings[186] or opinions[187] which are not based on ancient tradition, and the Talmudic Rabbis, who were really interested in science only as far as it concerned their understanding of the Torah and its laws,[188] were not so careful and meticulous in their research into science and history when it did not affect that understanding.[189] Hence they sometimes uncritically borrowed from their non-Jewish contemporaries certain imperfect scientific or historical data, which we are free to reject as representing not authoritative traditions, but the general knowledge of their age.[190] But in the interpretation of the law such lapses were impossible.[191]

In principle, therefore, it seems that, while no intrinsic infallibility attaches to the Rabbis of any age, only their purely non-halakhic statements can be questioned or rejected. But

even the finality of the halakhic legislation, within the limits
set out by the law itself, derives less from the inherent verity
of all the Talmud's teachings than from the fact that later
generations of scholars unanimously agreed to accept them as
final.[192]

Contemporary Rabbinic Periodicals

THERE are today probably little more than half a
dozen periodicals devoted exclusively to rabbinical studies. About equally divided between Israel
and America, they are all published in Hebrew and at intervals varying from one to six months. Their contents may be
subsumed under two principal headings: academic dissertations on talmudic themes (*Chiddushei Torah*) and practical
Halakhah, usually in the form of responsa to topical questions
on Jewish law (*Teshuvot*). The distinction is similar to that
between pure and applied mathematics in the realm of technology. But unlike modern scientific literature, the present
tendency in rabbinical journals is to tip the scales overwhelmingly in favor of purely or mainly theoretical discourses. Of
twenty-five articles in the latest issue of *Hadarom* (the Torah
journal published by the Rabbinical Council of America), for
instance, only two original contributions seek to supply specific
rulings on practical issues (Rabbi J. J. Weinberg on whether a
coffin temporarily used for one dead person may afterwards be
used for another; and Rabbi S. Hibner on the earliest time
in the evening for *Sefirat ha'Omer*). It may be surmised,
parenthetically, that this unequal ratio between theoretical
and practical rabbinics is related to the very small proportion
of professional rabbis among the alumni of rabbinical colleges nowadays. "Pure" talmudic research seems to prove far
more attractive than "applied" work among rabbinical masters and students alike.

This item and the remainder of this chapter are extracts from the
"Review of Recent Halakhic Periodical Literature," a regular department
of *Tradition* (New York) edited by the author since Spring 1961.

The all too scanty preoccupation with current halakhic problems in rabbinical periodicals does not, of course, exhaust the contemporary output of practical Halakhah. Far more important are the responsa collections now appearing in growing number (Rabbi Mosheh Feinstein's massive four-volume work *Igrot Mosheh* is an invaluable addition of this genre). But even these works again constitute only a small fraction of present-day rabbinical books. Our reviews, being limited to periodical literature, will therefore occupy itself with but a small part of the literary halakhic productions of our day.

Interestingly, articles of halakhic interest now also appear increasingly in non-rabbinical journals. These halakhic studies in scientific and even popular periodicals are generally of a more historical or analytical nature, as some of the samples included in the following reviews will indicate.

The Dynamics of Rabbinic Law-Making

W E will introduce the present review by some reflections on the characteristics of rabbinic law-making as a prime feature in the evolution of Jewish law.

In the jurisprudence of Judaism, the legislature and judiciary are fused together. Rabbis are charged to determine as well as to administer the law. They serve as judges in applying the rulings of existing laws to cases in doubt or under dispute; and when faced with situations lacking any precise precedents, they act as legislators by issuing new rulings.

In the exercise of both functions, rabbis are subject to a "constitutional" system, as presently practiced, which is altogether unique. Unlike any other national or religious legal system, Judaism does not vest the authority to make or adjudicate laws in any clearly defined individual or group. It has neither a supreme court nor a hierarchy, neither a chief justice nor a supreme pontiff to lay down the law with finality, In fact, there is no formal office or official appointment at all which would automatically authorize its incumbent to demand universal submission to his rulings. Even a Chief Rabbi of Israel—tenant of the highest ecclesiastical office in Jewry—may readily defer to the judgment of some superior scholar who holds no official position altogether, and any duly qualified rabbi may presume to challenge a decision rendered by others if his interpretation of the law conflicts with theirs.

How then does the juridical process of Judaism operate? Under such conditions of apparent licence and individual independence, how can order be joined to law? By what methods do rabbinical rulings eventually command the assent of rabbis and religious laymen the world over? Who and whose decisions enjoy final and binding authority?

In contrast to all other legal systems, whether on a state or church level, the administration of Jewish law is highly decentralized and yet subject to universal sanctions, and it is uniquely democratic whilst at the same time acknowledging the supremacy of individual authority. Thus it operates on three principal levels:

1. *Local Autonomy.* The authority of the local rabbinical head (the *Mara d'Atra*) of a congregation or community (e.g. the chief rabbi of a city or country) is traditionally binding for the members of such congregation or community, and it cannot be challenged by any other rabbinate, however superior its rank or area of jurisdiction. But such authority can only be exercised on a strictly local level; it does not extend beyond the confines of the individual rabbi's official jurisdiction.

2. *Consensus of Opinion.* When the principles of Jewish law have to be applied to new problems, a verdict one way or another is not usually accepted as authentic until it is endorsed by a number of leading rabbis constituting the majority of those consulted. As a rule, such problems are submitted quite independently to the judgment of various rabbinical authorities. As the replies accumulate, often in the form of printed responsa, a trend of opinion gradually becomes crystalized, and this is then accepted as the binding norm of the law, against any minority views of dissent, by virtue of the numerically superior weight of its endorsement.

3. *Individual Authority by Popular Acclaim.* A rabbinical ruling may also enjoy unquestioned validity by reason of the supreme excellence of the scholar who issued it. Such authority is quite informally, and solely as an expression of religious public opinion, bestowed on one or more of the *gedolei ha-dor* —the Sages of the Generation—purely because of the popular recognition of their pre-eminent scholarship and saintliness. Their word is law, but it is their public esteem which makes it unchallenged and absolute.

With the exception, then, of the first category, which is strictly limited in scope and therefore immaterial as a general guide to rabbinic law-making, all new decisions of law derive their validity ultimately from their implicit or explicit assent by the majority. This system insures that:

1. the development of Jewish law, by virtue of its strongly democratic direction, will always be a dynamic and organic process commanding the indispensable sanction of public endorsement;

2. by vesting authority with duly qualified individuals rather than impersonal offices, legislative power will never be abused or exploited by unscrupulous and unworthy persons seizing control of such offices by political manipulation or the patronage of vested interests; and

3. the door is left open to individual dissent, based on a scholar's conscientious objection to the consensus of the majority, thus allowing for the possibility of the law's constant re-examination and revision in the continuous study and debate among scholars.

The Letter and the Spirit of the Law

THE previous two introductions provided a general survey of the halakhic literary output in our times and a brief discussion of the dynamic processes in the contemporary methods of rabbinic lawmaking. Anent several responsa reviewed below, this

introduction is devoted to some general characteristics of
Halakhah, its employment as an instrument for the expression
of Jewish thought, and the relationship between the letter
and the spirit of the law in Judaism.

In common with most oriental systems of legislation, Jewish law is generally defined in terms of concrete illustrations
representing the rules and principles to be expressed. For
instance, the *Mishnah,* in dealing with the Sabbath laws, does
not speak of the ban on carrying an object from one domain
to another; it speaks of a householder who seeks to hand a
gift from within his home to a poor man outside. Jewish law
draws pictures, as it were, of personal and actual experiences
to convey the abstraction of legal rules. This contrasts with
Western legislation which is phrased in abstract terms; its
laws appear as disembodied, impersonal ideas and principles.
The Jewish tendency to represent abstract concepts by the
symbolic use of concrete things or acts is also reflected in the
characteristic trait of Hebrew etymology in which abstract
words are derived from concrete roots; e.g., *rachamim* ("compassion") from *rechem* ("mother's womb," the object exempli-
fying the most complete empathy or attachment of one human
being to another); or *chet* ("sin") from *chata* ("to miss the
mark," "overshoot the target").

This feature is indeed symptomatic of Judaism in a more
general sense. As a Halakhah-centered system, it employs laws
to convey and inculcate concepts in much the same way as
the artist uses his material for the communication of his
notions. The ideas, feelings and attitudes which he expresses
in terms of poetry, music, painting or other arts we portray
primarily in the form of "do's" and "don'ts." The practical
regulations governing Jewish conduct define our theology, our
philosophy, our ethics and our attitude vis-a-vis any intrinsically abstract subject or problem.

While the Halakhah, then, speaks in terms of action, it
bespeaks a line of thought. Looking at rabbinical responsa,
we often see purely technical arguments, with predominantly
ritual and legalistic undertones. The concrete letter of the law
is more apparent than its abstract spirit. But that is the way
Jewish law operates. It abhors the vacuum of abstractions;
instead it aims at their definition by erecting a legal structure

around them. We may compare it to a building. Only the
concrete walls and floors are visible; yet these exist only for
the sake of the empty space encompassed by them, the "abstract" shelter provided in the building's rooms which in
themselves contain no tangible matter. The room as such is
space *minus* the walls, etc.

Usually in halakhic dissertations and decisions there are
visible only the legalistic bricks with which laws are constructed, i.e., the letter of the law. These indispensable features
of the halakhic edifice exist for the sake of forming Jewish
attitudes and convictions—the spirit of the law. But one can
no more generate that spirit without the letter than one can
create a room without a floor, a ceiling and walls.

It is not always easy, or even possible, to extract the spirit
from the law, at least not with any degree of precision and
certainty. Being abstract, the spirit may be too intangible
and elusive; it may defy all attempts at clear definition. Indeed it may be capable of diverse definitions to different
people or at different times, just as a great masterpiece of
art may suggest different notions to different viewers. "While
several biblical verses can never convey one meaning, one
verse can convey several meanings."[193] In its religious, economic, social, and philosophical significance, the Sabbath, for
example, no doubt meant something different to the generations of Moses or Hillel or Maimonides from what it means
to us today. The spirit of the law can vary; the letter cannot.
But imbedded in the concrete structure of every law is an
abstract idea.

An instructive example of this fundamental feature of
Jewish law may be found in the discussions on liturgical and
synagogue usages reviewed below. Placing the *bimah,* from
which the Torah is publicly read, in the center of the synagogue is obviously meant to emphasize the centrality of the
law in Judaism—an abstraction suggested by a concrete regulation.

Of more profound significance, and serving as a most far-
reaching illustration of this principle, may be the decisions
on the use of microphones in synagogue worship.

The use of microphones on the Sabbath or for trans-
mitting the sound of the *Shofar* and the *Megillah* raises ques-

tions concerning the activation of electrical currents and discharges, the need to perform religious precepts by a human agency, the distinction between a natural echo and artificial amplification, etc.,—all questions of a more or less technical and physical nature. Yet the composite idea which emerges from these concrete particulars deals with the attitude towards the increasing mechanization of life—one of the foremost moral problems besetting our age.

With the advancing tide of technology, man is today threatened by the very machine his genius has created. Human life is in danger of being reduced to an artificial, synthetic existence in which he delegates his work, often his thinking, and sometimes even his generation to mechanical devices. This process, if unchecked by some controls, is bound to stifle the free development of man's personality, his sense of responsibility and moral judgment.

Science is of necessity impersonal and undemanding. It is uncritical of man, for it deals with life *as it is,* not as *it should be,* thus nursing a spirit of complacency. By seeking to eliminate work and to exchange the struggles and hardships of life for prefabricated pleasures, it tends to make human life mechanical, materialistic, soulless, and hedonistic.

True religion works in the opposite direction. It is personal and exacting. It offers constant criticism, pointing up the gap between actual and ideal life. Far from making life easier, it calls for ever more sacrifices and self-imposed privations. It posits service, not comfort and amusement, as the highest ideal, and it promises rewards for effort rather than for success. It aims to maintain the supremacy of man's dignity and unique personality by insuring that the machine will be his servant, not his master.

How can our religious experience promote the attainment and constant awareness of these ideals? Judaism, true to its aversion for credal or philosophical abstractions unrelated to rules of conduct, can do so only in terms of laws.

Many was created to harness and exploit the forces of nature — to "subdue the earth and have dominion over . . . every living thing . . ."[194] To exercise such mastery over the universe and its immense forces is man's privilege. But only within limits. In two areas — one, of place and the other, of time — the Jew must renounce the assertion of his mastery over nature and return it to God, to be reminded that there is a Master above him after all. By proscribing for the Jew the operation of machines on the Sabbath — the sancturary of time — and in the synagogue — the sanctuary of space, Judaism seeks to secure one impregnable refuge from the tyranny of automation.

We do not object to easing the drudgery of life by utilizing the mechanical aids provided by science. On the contrary, Orthodox Jews are probably the greatest beneficiaries of such wonderful gadgets as time-switches, electric shavers — and fully automatic elevators. But in the contemporary struggle for the heart and mind of man between the worship of science and the science of worship, religion must preserve the spiritual area from mechanization and artificiality if it is not to surrender its function as the guardian of the Divine in man. Worship must be purely personal; it cannot be replaced by push-button devices. The medium of microphones may vitiate the personal element in worship. (Moreover, we would compromise the indispensability of synagogues if we could fulfill our religious duty by listening to services on phonographs or loudspeakers, which can be installed at home.) On the Sabbath and in the synagogue we are to be creatures, not creators; for once we are to be servants, not masters, so that we shall remember always to subordinate the scientific urge for mastery to the religious urge for service. Thus the Sabbath and the synagogue are to remind us that the highest achievement of the human intellect lies in our ability to create less than in our knowledge how to control our creations and preserve our supremacy over them. On such knowledge, as we now know, the survival of mankind will ultimately depend.

Abstracts of Recent Halakhic Decisions

Adoption

UNLIKE many ancient legal systems, particularly Roman law, the classic sources of Jewish law did not provide specific legislation on the adoption of children. Thanks to the rigid moral standards of Jewish home life, the pronounced sense of family relations, and the highly developed social conscience for the welfare of orphans as a communal responsibility among Jews, the problem was evidently never acute enough to necessitate any formal enactments regulating the private care for homeless children. But with the more recent flood of orphans created by the ravages of war, and especially of children born out of wedlock, combined with the apparent growing infertility rates in modern times, Jewish adoptions are now fairly common.

The many halakhic problems raised by this practice have therefore lately received much attention. Excellent rabbinical studies on adoption include several chapters (especially on the adoption of non-Jewish children and their conversion) in Rabbi G. Felder's volume *Nachalat Tzevi* (New York, 5719) and three articles in the latest issue of *No'am* (vol. iv. Jerusalem, 5721). But being here concerned with periodical literature only, we will confine ourselves to the illuminating series of four articles on the subject by Rabbi Mordecai Cohen which have just appeared in the popular religious Israeli weekly *Panim el Panim* (January 1-27, 1961) and also in *Sinai* (Dec. 1960-Jan. 1961).

The principal sources on which the attitude of the Halakhah to adoption is founded are:

1. The biblical references to the quasi-adoptions of Moses by Pharaoh's daughter;[195] of five sons by Mikhal, Saul's daughter;[196] of Obed by Naomi;[197] and of Esther by Mordecai.[198]

2. The statement in the Talmud, on the basis of these precedents in the Bible: "Whoever raises an orphan in his home is credited by Scripture as if he had born him."[199]

3. The ruling by Isserles in the *Shulchan Arukh* that a legal document featuring the name of an adopted person as the child of the adoptive father is valid,[200] though greater precision may be necessary in marriage and divorce deeds.[201]

4. The important responsa on problems of adoptions by Rabbi Moses Schreiber[202] and Rabbi Benzion Uziel.[203]

The most fundamental conclusion to be drawn from these and many other sources is, as Rabbi Cohen emphasizes, that adoptions in the sense in which the Romans and most modern legal systems understand them do not exist in Jewish law at all. In Roman law it is the law which establishes the facts; hence the courts have the power to transfer the rights and duties of natural parents to others in their relations to adopted children, in the same way as the courts establish or grant marriages and divorces. In Jewish law, however, the facts determine the law; the courts merely supervise and regulate personal relations into which the parties have entered by their own action. Just as marriages and divorces are executed solely by the parties to them, with rabbis or religious courts acting only to insure that such acts are lawfully performed, legal adoptions in the Jewish view merely represent obligations which the parties involved have agreed to assume, implicitly or otherwise. Such obligations may also result in some privileges, as defined by the courts. But no court can create the full equivalent of natural family relations or replace them.

Following these basic considerations we may briefly sum up the main rulings listed in Rabbi Cohen's article:—

Name: An adopted child may legally assume the name of the adoptive family and use it in legal documents. However, he obviously retains his native status as a *Kohen, Levi,* or *Israel;* therefore he should be called up to the Torah by the name of his natural father, unless the latter's identity is completely unknown, when the adoptive father's name may be used to avoid embarrassing the son. The same applies to his *ketubah.* But a *get* should designate either his natural father's name or none at all in addition to the adopted person's own name.

Circumcision and Redemption: Normally the duty to have a child circumcized rests upon the father or, in his absence, the *Bet Din.* In the case of an adopted Jewish boy, therefore, this duty is transferred to the adoptive father, acting on behalf of the *Bet Din.* He may also recite the usual blessing, preferably as *sandek.* If the boy is the firstborn to his natural mother, the adoptive father may perform the *Pidyon ha-Ben,* omitting the statutory blessing but reciting *Shehechiyanu,* since the latter benediction marks his personal joy at the event.

Honoring Parents: An adopted child owes the same respect to his new parents, albeit only rabbinically, as to his natural father and mother (his bonds with them, being created by nature, remain of course indissoluble, and he continues to owe them every honor in death as in life). Upon the death of his adoptive parents he may recite *Kaddish* for them, though natural children saying *Kaddish* enjoy precedence over him. But the mourning laws apply only following the death of natural relatives.

Testimony: Since adoptions can only establish relationships based on affections and legal commitments but not on consanguinity, an adopted child remains disqualified from giving evidence for his natural family, whilst he may act as a witness for his adoptive family, just as two brothers, even if they are estranged like Jacob and Esau, can never testify for each other, whereas the most intimate friends may do so.

Marriage: For the same reason an adopted person may enter into a marriage with a member of his adoptive family (based on the consensus of rabbinical opinion permitting marriages among step-children having no blood relations), but not with the forbidden degrees of his natural relatives.

Material Obligations: By virtue of their consent to adopt a child, the new parents assume the same responsibilities to their charge as they would to a natural child, obligating them to provide for his sustenance, medical needs, and his religious and vocational training. By the same token, adoptive parents, if they have fallen on hard times, are entitled to support from the child they have adopted, if he can afford it, as a prior claim on his charity.

Inheritance: Whilst an adopted child may claim a maintenance allowance from the estate of his deceased adoptive parents, he does not automatically inherit them unless they made a specific bequest for him in their will or so stipulated before their death. Provisions for such a bequest can legally be made part of the original adoption agreement, as is usually done in the court's adoption order. But such a legacy does not compromise the right of an adopted person and his natural next-of-kin to inherit each other.

Renunciation: An adoption constitutes a legal agreement which has the force of a solemn pledge, if not a formal vow. Accordingly, the adoptive parents cannot renounce their charge without the adoptee's consent, unless they show that they had assumed their obligation under duress. Also, an adoption cannot be annulled on the part of the adopted child except by agreement with his new parents and the court. But since adoptions are to serve primarily to promote the welfare of the child, his commitment is less binding than that of the parents. On reaching adulthood, or possibly even the age of sufficient understanding, therefore, he cannot legally be restrained from rejoining his natural family and from reassuming their name. As a human being endowed with an inalienable right to freedom, this option cannot be denied to him, though morally such an act may be regarded as an expression of gross ingratitude towards those who so liberally expended their love and their means on his upbringing. On the strength of these regulations, concludes the author, the "Adoption Law" passed by the Israeli Parliament—while it may look unduly Western in its form and phrasing, a defect which should be corrected to give it a truly Jewish traditional appearance—is certainly in general harmony with the dictates of the Halakhah.

The Eichmann Case

Say unto God: "How awe-inspiring is Thy Work"[204]
—those killed kill their killers and those impaled impale
their impalers!—*Esther Rabba*, end.

THIS quotation introduces an exhaustive legal
study on "The Judgment of the Jew-Oppressor
in the Halakhah" by R. Moshe Zevi Nehriah
published in the almanac *Shanah be'Shanah* (Jerusalem,
5721). This concise and well-documented article, written by
one of Israel's outstanding halakhists of the younger generation, seeks to supply and analyze the halakhic answers to problems raised by the dramatic capture of the arch-Jew-baiter,
his abduction from Argentina, and his forthcoming trial. It
may serve as a model for the application of Jewish judicial
principles and rulings, as propounded in rabbinic law, to
modern legal and moral problems of great complexity.

One of the main concepts germane to our case is the biblical
law of the "blood-redeemer."[205] This provides that the next-
of-kin of a murder victim, while he is neither obliged nor
entitled to strike down the offender before the trial, is not
culpable if "in the heat of his heart" he does so avenge his
relative's blood.[206] Only when a manslaughterer, before or
after his sentence to exile in a "city refuge," deliberately
escapes, is the "blood-redeemer" given the duty—or, according
to the accepted tannaitic opinion, merely the right—to slay the
killer,[207] because by his escape "he exposed himself to
death,"[208] or because his life is legally protected only within
the limits of such cities.[209] Moreover, after a murderer's conviction by a court of law, his execution is to be carried out
by the "blood-redeemer,"[210] as expressly stipulated in the
Torah: ". . . and they shall deliver him into the hand of the
redeemer of blood, that he may die."[211] While Maimonides
does not list this duty as a distinct commandment (but includes it as part of the general law on the execution of
murderers), Nachmanides treats it as a separate precept where-

by it is incumbent on the "blood-redeemer" to "seek out the murderer, to pursue him and to avenge his crime, so as to bring him before a court and have him executed according to law, or to slay him if the court cannot prevail over him, and in the absence of an avenging relative the court shall appoint a person to pursue the murderer and to act as the avenger of the victim's blood."[212]

Accordingly, the concept of the "blood-redeemer" is to insure that no act of murder shall remain unpunished. This obligation thus devolves not only on the next-of-kin—whose "heart is hot" by nature—but also upon the public which must not stand by idly without bringing a murderer to justice.

The duty to redeem the innocent blood of murder by apprehending the killer and having him tried respects no national boundaries. The first murderer already pronounced his own sentence: "Whoever findeth me shall slay me."[213] The deliberate killer forfeits his title to life and to the protection of society. Even the Temple is to offer no sanctuary: "And if a man come presumptuously upon his neighbor, to slay him with guile; from off Mine alter shalt thou take him, that he may die."[214] On the contrary, the presence of a murderer within the confines of a country places an obligation upon that country—the obligation to try and to execute him. This duty is so severe that, if it is not carried out, the government of that land is itself guilty of a moral offense. As Maimonides explains: ". . . therefore all the inhabitants of Shechem[215] were liable to death; for Shechem had been guilty of robbery, and they [his fellow-citizens] saw and knew it but did not try him."[216] Scripture itself confirms this: "And saviors shall come up on mount Zion to judge the mount of Esau."[217]

Rabbi Nehriah adds: "This argument, in our case, that a country in which the murderer is found is also entitled to judge him, and that through his removal from its borders its title is vitiated—this argument is refuted by the fact that that country ignored for years the presence of the murderer in its territory and the duty devolving on it to bring him to justice . . .; and thereby this title lapses and is transferred to whoever first claims it."

Nor is there any justification in the principal defense submitted by the war-criminals, viz. their acting under orders from above. Even when the order to commit a crime is given by a king, one is obliged to rebel against it and not to carry it out.[218] A command to shed blood must be resisted even at the cost of one's own life. This is a universal rule (applicable not only to Jews who are enjoined to lay down their lives for the "Sanctification of the Divine Name"), since it is based, not on any biblical mandate, but simply on the logical reasoning: "How do you know that your blood is redder than his?"[219], i.e. that your life is worth more protecting than that of your threatened victim. The plea of ignorance is equally inadmissible: "And similarly if he killed and he did not know that it was forbidden to kill . . . he is executed, and this is not considered an unwitting offense, for he should have learned [the law] but did not learn."[220]

Again, the criminal in our case may argue that he merely ordered the killings without performing them himself and that he should therefore be freed from capital guilt by virtue of the usual rule "There is no deputy for an illegal act,"[221] i.e. the responsibility for a crime cannot be shifted by the deputy to his employer. This rule, however, is not applicable to a Noachide who commissions a murder, for it is written: "He who sheds the blood of man *by man,* his blood shall be shed"[222]—"*by man* [that means even] through a deputy."[223] Moreover, the rule is invalid if the person who commissions the crime may presume that his order will be carried out.[224] The case is then identical with the culpability of one who causes a fire by the hand of an idiot or a minor.[225] There is no doubt that the opportunity to persecute Jews by official order was greeted with enthusiasm by those charged with the ghoulish task.

The responsibilities for issuing such instructions is all the greater if they are reinforced by government sanctions. Thus the Prophet Nathan branded King David as the killer of Uriah the Hittite[226] although the King had not personally slain him, "because being a king he would be defied by no one, and it is as if he did the killing; similarly when Saul ordered the slaughter of the men of Nob, the city of the priests, it is as if he killed them. For even though no one

may execute a king's order under such conditions . . . , not
every person bewares of this . . . ; hence the punishment is on
the king."²²⁷ In such cases, therefore, he who gives the order
and he who carries it out are alike guilty of murder.

Also pertinent here are the significant words of Maimonides:
"While there may be offenses even more serious than bloodshed, none involve the destruction of civilized society as
bloodshed does . . . , and whoever is guilty of this offense
is a wicked man throughout and all the precepts he fulfilled in
his entire life cannot outweigh this crime or save him from
judgment, as is written: 'A man that is laden with the blood
of any person shall hasten his steps unto the pit; none will
support him.'²²⁸ You can learn this from Ahab the idolator,
regarding whom it is written: 'There was none like unto
Ahab.'²²⁹ Yet when his sins and his merits were arranged
before the God of the Spirits, no sin was found sentencing
him to destruction, and nothing whatever which could be
weighed against it, except the blood of Naboth [he had shed],
as is written: 'And there came forth the spirit, and stood
before the Lord'²³⁰—'that is the spirit of Naboth [whom he
had slain]'²³¹ . . . , although this evil-doer did not kill him
by his hand but merely caused his death."²³²

As for Jewish capital jurisdiction, normally restricted to the
Sanhedrin and subjected to so many judicial safeguards as
practically to abolish the death penalty, Jewish law provides
the state and the courts with special powers in exceptional
circumstances. To quote Maimonides again: "And regarding
all these murderers and their like who [for technical reasons]
are not liable to execution, if a Jewish king desires to execute
them by virtue of his royal power and in the public interest,
he is free to do so; similarly if a court sees fit to execute
them as an emergency measure, because of the exigency of the
hour, it has the right to do as it deems proper."²³³ In the absence of a king, these rights are vested in the nation as such
and may be exercised by any duly appointed judge.²³⁴

A further relevant consideration may be the law on pursuers
and informers who can be put to death, as an act of self-
defense, to protect the community from threatened or repeated
dangers. This law operates in our time, too.²³⁵ For to exact
punishment from such criminals is not a matter of sheer vin-

dictiveness, as R. Joseph Engel well put it: "It should be explained that a judicial execution, apart from the atonement [it confers upon the sinner], also serves to make sure that neither he nor others shall commit such a crime in the future (as they might if they saw that the crime went unpunished), in accordance with the warning [following the infliction of the due penalty]: 'And those that remain shall hear, and fear, and shall henceforth commit no more such evil. . .'[236] . . ., so that there is an element of saving life in the execution of a murderer, to prevent people from being killed."[237]

The article appropriately concludes with the quotation: "Whoever is merciful with the cruel will ultimately become cruel with the merciful."[238] We might add the verses: "The righteous shall rejoice when he seeth the vengeance . . . And men shall say: 'Verily there is a reward for the righteous; verily there is a God that judgeth in the earth'."[239]

Workman's Compensation and Severance Pay

The November-December 1961 issue of *Sinai*, which is almost entirely devoted to ethical and legal subjects raised in the talmudic division "Damages," features a valuable study on "The Problem of Compensation in the Halakhah" by Rabbi Samuel Tanhum Rubinstein. The article seeks to determine how far Jewish religious law insists on the payment to employees of (1) severance pay and (2) compensation for death or injury.

According to the *Mishnah*,[240] the extent of the employer's obligations to his workers depends on "local custom." But Asheri (*a.l.*) restricts this ruling to "a custom established by the local sages," while the Mordecai (*a.l.*) applies it only to "a custom observed by the ancients, whereas a custom for which there is no support in the Torah is to be regarded as an error in judgment." The verdict of the *Mishnah* may therefore be inconclusive as a guide to our problem.

Chief Rabbi Benzion Uziel held that the worker's title to severance pay was based on the verse "That thou mayest walk in the way of good men, and keep the paths of the righteous,"[241] a verse used in the Talmud[242] to award some negligent porters the payment to which they laid a moral, though not legal, claim.[243]

Rabbi Rubinstein, however, considers the teaching derived from this verse to establish merely a moral obligation which cannot be enforced by a court.[244] He, therefore, prefers to resolve the problem by analogy with the "parting-gift" which the Torah assigns to a Hebrew slave on his release.[245] The biblical law of the Hebrew slave passed into desuetude with the suspension of the Jubilee Year legislation[246] during the First Temple period; yet even "nowadays . . . anyone who hires the services of a fellow-Jew, whether for a long or even short period, should give him a parting-gift when he leaves him . . . ," for the law is meant to implant "noble and desirable virtues in our souls . . . that we should have compassion over him who serves us, giving him of our possessions by way of lovingkindness, in addition to what we agreed to give him as his hire."[247] This opinion in itself may not suffice to compel an employer legally to provide his worker with severance pay, but since it supplies a biblical basis for the present-day practice to exact severance pay from employers, the "custom" may be regarded as enjoining the legal sanction of the Halakhah in accordance with the Mordecai's view stated above.

In 1945 Rabbi Uziel[248] concluded that the courts could not enforce such payments because the practice had not yet been accepted throughout the land and was common only in certain cases. But since then the award of severance pay has become "a daily occurrence," having been accepted by arbitration boards and official bodies dealing with conditions of employment. On this basis, such awards have been endorsed by rabbinical[249] as well as civil courts[250] which have ruled that a) severance payments in different forms accepted in the industry are to be considered as part of the worker's wages, payable on the day he leaves his employment, and b) such payments to a discharged worker do not deprive him of the right to enter into another fixed employment even on the following day.

The second question concerns the right of labor unions to demand of employers that they insure their workers against accidents, and the liability of employers in cases where they failed to provide such insurance in compliance with the law and where no accident compensation was stipulated by contract.

A parallel may be found in the following judgment. Asked whether a person is liable to pay for losses sustained by his messenger in the course of his errand, Nachmanides[251] ruled that the principal is not responsible for losses suffered by his agent, particularly if the latter was paid for his agency. This is based on the verse "In the same day shalt thou give him [i.e. the hired servant] his hire . . .; for he is poor, and he setteth his heart (lit., his life) upon it,"[252] which is interpreted in the Talmud to mean that a hireling incurs any risks of death or loss on account of the wages he receives.[253] This responsum, which is also cited by Karo,[254] implies that an employer is not liable for accidents sustained by his worker except by prior agreement.

But another opinion[255] regards the relationship between a principal and his agent as analogous to that between a borrower and the object loaned (the agent or employee being "on loan" to the principal), and in the latter case the borrower is responsible to compensate the lender for an accidental loss only if the loan was free; but if the borrower paid for the hire he is not liable. This difference of opinion is also recorded in the *Shulchan Arukh*.[256]

R. Moses Schreiber,[257] however, resolves the conflict by suggesting that the Mordecai's ruling—holding the principal liable by analogy with a borrower—applies when the loss or accident is unrelated to him (parallel, e.g., to the death from natural causes of a hired animal), while the decision of Nachmanides—exempting the principal from liability—refers to a case in which the loss occurred as a result of the performance of the agency or hire (e.g., the animal's death on account of its work); this is then the agent's or lender's risk.

Accordingly, we should make a distinction between a paid worker, whose employer is not liable for compensation for his injury or death because such hazards are assumed in return for the payment received, and an unpaid worker who may claim compensation provided the accident cannot be attributed to a reasonable working risk.

Interesting, too is the conclusion of Rabbi Uziel,[258] based on earlier authorities, that since both the employer and employee are motivated by self-interest, a worker's death cannot impose on the employer either a financial obligation or a duty to atone for the mishap by fasting. Nevertheless, he adds, in view of the frequency of industrial accidents under modern conditions, an employer is obligated to insure his workers against death and injury in fulfillment of the law ". . . thou shalt make a parapet for thy roof, that thou bring not blood upon thy house . . .".[259] The same law also imposes a moral, not a legal, obligation on the employer to pay compensation for accidents to his workers if he failed to insure them (as an "established custom," however, this can be enforced nowadays). But in that event the amount of the compensation due need not necessarily be the same as that payable under an adequate insurance policy; instead, it may be determined at the discretion of the court, depending on the circumstances of the accident and the means of the employer and the worker.

The Present-Day Status of Jerusalem

I N an exceptionally interesting and exhaustive article on "Jerusalem at the Present Time in the Halakhah" published in the splendid Israel army journal *Machanayim* (no. 58), Rabbi Mordecai HaKohen deals with three questions: (1) Does Jerusalem still enjoy a higher sanctity than the rest of the Land of Israel? (2) If so, is it still a *mitzvah* to live in Jerusalem rather than elsewhere in the Land? And (3) does this *mitzvah* apply even to the new city outside the walls of the original Holy City?

Among the restrictions to Jerusalem on account of its holiness are the following prohibitions listed by Maimonides: To keep a dead person overnight in it or to pass human remains through it; to have any graves (except those of David and

Huldah which were there from the time of the early prophets);
to sow, plough, or plant trees, gardens and orchards, lest they
may decay (except rose gardens which also existed at the time
of the early prophets); to maintain dunghills for the deposit
of refuse, on account of the vermin; and to build furnaces,
because of the smoke.[260] To what extent these and other restrictions need still be observed nowadays appears to be a
matter of dispute among some medieval savants. The omission of any reference to them in the codes of Alfasi and Asheri,
and the accepted practice to plant willows for the *arba minim*
inside of Jerusalem, would seem to indicate that these prohibitions are no longer in effect, being limited to the period
of the Temple only. On the other hand, R. Eshtori Haparchi,
the famous Italian traveler and scholar of the early 14th century, quotes the rulings of Maimonides and argues that accordingly any *Lulav* taken from a tree planted in Jerusalem
would be disqualified for use on *Sukkoth*.[261] But he adds that
these restrictions probably continue to be valid only insofar
as they derive from the intrinsic sanctity of Jerusalem, while
the laws connected with the ritual of the city, conditioned
as they were by the Temple and its worship, may be suspended
at the present time.[262] On these grounds R. David ibn Zimra,
the renowned North-African halakhist of the 16th century,
also excused his contemporaries living in the Holy City for
not observing all its special regulations.[263]

Jerusalem, then, like the Land of Israel on a lower level,
is invested with two types of sanctity: an intrinsic holiness
which, since it derives from the choice of God and the more
manifest dwelling of the Divine Presence, is unchangeable
and eternal; and a contingent holiness which, as the product
of the Jewish people's exercise of spiritual sovereignty, is
dependent on circumstances. To the latter kind only is related
the talmudic discussion on whether the original sanctification
of the Land is everlasting or temporary,[264] affecting, for example, the continued validity of the agricultural laws in the
Torah peculiar to the Holy Land. But the superior sanctity
of the Land and of Jerusalem as such—as the "inheritance of
the Lord"—is unconditional and undisputed.

We therefore apply to this day the mishnaic law: "All
may be compelled to go up to the Land of Israel (or thence

to Jerusalem), but none may be compelled to leave it."[265]
Accordingly, either partner in a marriage can force the other
to move their residence to the Holy Land, or from any place
there to the Holy City; and should the wife refuse, her
husband can divorce her and she loses her marriage portion,
while in the case of his refusal to follow her she can claim
a divorce together with the payment of her marriage portion.[266] The only legitimate grounds for such refusal may be
the hazards of the journey,[267] but this does not apply to
moving within the Land to Jerusalem. Thus the *Chatam
Sofer* wrote that he urged a rabbinical friend on departing
for the Holy Land to settle only in Jerusalem, for even Safed
with its many graves of immortal saints could not compare
with the sanctity of Jerusalem;[268] indeed he believed that
the terrible earthquake which struck Safed in 1836 was a
punishment from Heaven for the inhabitants' rejection of
Jerusalem and their preference of Safed.[269]

Jerusalem is to attract the dead as well as the living. With
the destruction of the Temple the interdict against the burial
in Jerusalem was removed (see above), and since then countless lovers of Zion have sought to have their remains interred
in its sacred soil, whether they had lived in the Diaspora or
elsewhere in the Holy Land. This yearning is supported
by many aggadic and halakhic passages, some of which are
quoted by the author, including one responsum by Maimonides[270] and another by David ibn Zimra.[271]

Regarding the extension of Jerusalem's sacred status to the
new city, the author makes the same distinction. The limitation of its sancity to "within the walls"[272] and the provision
that no territory may be added to it except by royal or prophetic decree, through the *Urim Vetumim* and the Sanhedrin,[273] apply only to such ritual laws as the consumption
of sacrificial meat or the second tithe. But its holiness in other
respects, including the *mitzvah* to live there, extends to any
area, whether metropolitan or suburban, incorporated in it.
While the author does not cite any halakhic statements in
support of this view, he corroborates it by several aggadic passages (which may be used to determine the law as long as
they do not conflict with express ruling of the Halakhah) as
well as by the argument that the religious duty to reside

in parts of Jerusalem outside the original walls has long
been upheld even in times when there were no prophets or
Urim Vetumim to sanction additions to the Holy City.

Finally, the article discusses the present-day application of
the law to tear one's garments (*"keriah"*) on seeing the cities
of Judea, and again on seeing Jerusalem, and again on seeing
the Temple site "in their destruction."[274] Why is this regulation, though included in all our codes, not generally observed
today? According to Joseph Karo, the words "in their destruction" may be interpreted in two ways: either in the sense that
these places are completely destroyed and not populated at all,
so that on finding any settlement there, even if under non-
Jewish rule, one need not tear *"keriah"*; or places which,
while populated, are in non-Jewish hands.[275] Karo himself
prefers the latter interpretation and so do the commentators
on the passage in the *Shulchan Arukh.*

Consequently, in our day when we have been vouchsafed
to witness the return of Jewish sovereignty to much of Jerusalem and Judea, anyone on approaching Jewish cities, and
especially Jerusalem, in their restored glory, far from having
to tear *"keriah,"* should call forth in song and thanksgiving
to the Redeemer of Israel for having returned the captivity
of His people and His land. On the other hand, the redemption is still incomplete, and many parts of the Land, headed
by the Old City of Jerusalem, are still desolate and indeed
inaccesible to Jews. It is therefore the duty not only of
Jewish tourists from abroad but of those settled in the Land
and particularly in Jerusalem itself to go up to Mount Zion
or other high places, to look at the Old City and the Temple
site and then to tear their garments and weep for the desolation of our most holy possessions, as required by law. Similarly, one should still observe those tokens of mourning (such
as leaving a corner of one's house and table undecorated,
and putting some ashes on the bridegroom's head) which
were expressly enacted "to remember Jerusalem."[276]

Bat Mitzvah Celebration

A REMARKABLE responsum on a highly controversial subject made its appearance in a rather unexpected quarter when *Hapardes* published an endorsement of *Bat Mitzvah* celebrations, albeit with some important reservations, by Rabbi J. J. Weinberg, one of the foremost rabbinical authorities of our age. Following two previous installments featuring a learned discussion on the sources and intent of the prohibition against adopting non-Jewish customs (*"chukkat ha-goy"*), the Nisan 5723 issue sets forth the author's practical conclusions with daring forthrightness.

If one were to forbid *Bat Mitzvah* festivities on the ground that they imitated the non-Jewish practice of confirmations, one would also have to oppose *Bar Mitzvah* celebrations because non-Jews confirm boys, too. Indeed, we should no longer tolerate prayer; for non-Jews also pray. Such conclusions are plainly ludicrous. The object of *Bat Mitzvah* celebrations, even among Reform Jews, is obviously not to introduce a non-Jewish form of worship, but "to strengthen in the heart of a girl reaching for age of *mitzvah* a feeling of love for Judaism and its commandments and to arouse in her a feeling of pride in her Jewishness and her belonging to a great and holy people." Consequently, the fact that the Gentiles too confirm their boys and girls is entirely irrelevant.

A parallel could be found in a ruling by a leading 14th century sage who refused to condemn the practice to visit the cemetery within the seven days of mourning as a forbidden imitation of a non-Jewish custom, even though the practice was common among Moslems; by the same token eulogies should be disapproved as being common among non-Jews, too.[277] This view is also confirmed by the *ReMa*.[278]

Equally untenable was the argument that *Bat Mitzvah* functions should be disparaged as improper innovations, unknown to earlier generations. In the past, argues Rabbi Weinberg, it might have been unnecessary to stress the Jewish education of girls. They grew up in an atmosphere imbued with Torah and piety; they imbibed the spirit of Judaism with their very mothers' milk. But lately great changes had occurred. The influence of "the street" extinguished every spark of Jewishness from the heart of Jewish youth. Girls were being educated at non-Jewish or secular schools with complete indifference to Jewish values and virtues. Under such conditions it was "almost imperative to celebrate the attainment of the age of *mitzvot* for girls also. Moreover, the discrimination between boys and girls regarding the celebration of their reaching maturity would gravely offend the human feelings of the maturing girl."

While approving of *Bat Mitzvah* celebrations, therefore, the author nevertheless objects to holding such functions in synagogues. They should be celebrated at home or in a congregational hall, "and on condition the rabbi gives the celebrant an instructive address, urging her from that day onwards to cherish the principal commandments . . . , such as the Sabbath, Kashrut, family purity, Jewish education, and the obligation to support and encourage a husband in Torah study and observance as well as her eventual determination to set her eyes on a learned and God-fearing man."

It would also be quite wrong to compare *Bat Mitzvah* functions with the playing of organs at synagogue services which leading rabbis had prohibited on weekdays as well as on Sabbaths and festivals as a non-Jewish form of worship.[279] That innovation was introduced by the Reformers as a deliberate imitation of musical embellishments employed at church services; as such this was inadmissable in the synagogue, quite apart from the desecration of the Sabbath which the introduction of organs usually involved.

Daughters Saying Kaddish

ANOTHER question related to Jewish observances by women is also discussed in recent issues of *Hapardes*. May a daughter, especially in the absence of any sons, recite *Kaddish* for a deceased parent? In the Adar 5723 number, the venerable Rabbi H. E. Henkin had published his opinion in favor of a daughter saying

Kaddish in the synagogue's women's quarter together with the men doing so. The following number (Nisan 5723) then featured a contribution by Mr. Th. Preschel, warmly endorsing Rabbi Henkin's responsum and listing several authorities who had previously dealt with this question. Six months later (Tishri 5724) almost exactly the same authorities are quoted again by Rabbi S. J. S. Rubin-Halberstam (the Zeschinover Rebbe), this time to challenge Rabbi Henkin's ruling.

He refers to the law requiring the presence of ten male Jews for the recital of *Kaddish*[280] as an argument against permitting a woman to say it in the women's part, since he regards this division of the synagogue as a separate domain. He then quotes R. Yair Bacharach, the first to mention this question: "While one may assume that a daughter's *Kaddish* also brings aid and comfort to the soul of the deceased, for she is his offspring, nevertheless one should fear that Jewish customs would be weakened thereby. . ."[281]

Further sources cited by Rabbi Rubin-Halberstam show that the permission to make a special *Minyan* to enable daughters to say *Kaddish*[282] in fact applies only to a daughter's son;[283] that R. Jacob Reischer allowed a four-year old girl to recite *Kaddish* as requested in her father's will;[284] that a woman should fulfil her father's wish to say *Kaddish* after him only by attending services and responding *Amen* to every *Kaddish* she hears;[285] and that there was a custom in Prague of very young girls reciting *Kaddish* in a synagogue's vestry where old people would gather in the mornings to read Psalms.[286]

The Sabbath and the International Date-Line

THE problem of fixing the line where "East and West meet" to determine the local incidence of the Sabbath at all points on earth has occupied Jewish scholars from the middle of the 12th century to the present day. It raised a particularly lively controversy with the flight in the summer of 1941 of a remnant of Yeshivah scholars from Lithuania (overrun by the Nazis) through Siberia to Japan and their inquiry from the rabbinate in Jerusalem as to the day on which they should observe the Sabbath and the fast of Yom Kippur. With the growing Jewish addiction to globe-trotting and the increasingly frequent travels of observant Jews on the trans-Pacific route, the problem has now assumed popular and highly practical proportions.

The voluminous and complex literature on this question has now been summarized in an excellent survey by Rabbi Samuel Hibner in the latest issue of *Ha-Darom* (Nisan 5722). The first to discuss this matter was the poet-philosopher Yehudah Halevi in his *Kuzari*.[287] Dealing with the supremacy of the Holy Land as "the center of the inhabited earth"* and adverting to a talmudic parallel in connection with the fixing of the New Moon,[288] Halevi regards the Sabbath as being determined by the position of the sun at midday over Palestine which is practically on the same meridian as Sinai, or rather Alush,[289] where the Sabbath law was originally proclaimed. That time corresponds with sunset in China, at the extreme Eastern end of the inhabited world 90 degrees to the East of Palestine, and with sunrise at the Western extremity of the inhabited world 90 degrees to the West. Consquently, since the Jewish reckoning of the day begins and ends at sundown, the commencement of every Sabbath extends from a line along the 90th meridian East of Palestine until the same line is reached 270 degrees West of Palestine 24 hours later. This would fix the dateline close to the 125th meridian East of Greenwich (Palestine, being about 35 degrees East of Greenwich). This opinion was also held by Halevi's younger contemporary, E. Zerachyahu Halevy Gerondi.[290]

---

*That Palestine is at the center of the world was already asserted in the Talmud. Thus one passage states that the Holy Land was the first part of the world to be created (*Ta'anit* 10a), the remainder following progressively around the center. Another holds that "the Land of Israel is higher than all other lands" (*Kiddushin* 69a). On this an interesting explanation is offered by R. Samuel Edeles: since the world is spherical "like an apple," and Palestine is in the center of the world, it must be the "highest' point on the globe (Maharsha, *a.l.*) . Even geographically, it is significant that in the hemisphere showing the maximum land (i.e., inhabited) surfaces, Palestine does in fact appear at about the center, so that it is closer to the "top" of the populated half of the world than any other part.

Over a century later this verdict was somewhat amended by R. Isaac Ha-Israeli, a disciple of Asheri, in his *Yesod Olam*.[291] He argued that it was unreasonable to assume a single line dividing the East from the West whereby relatively near-by people on opposite sides of that line would observe different days in the calendar. He therefore eliminated the line altogether, holding instead that the East begins at the extreme Eastern end of the inhabited world and the West reaches up to the Western shores of the land surface, these points being separated by the ocean covering the lower half of the globe. Since that part was uninhabited, there was no need to have any precise line between East and West within it; we were not required to legislate for the fish in the sea.

But later authorities found this view quite untenable since human settlements (not to speak of ships) were in fact to be found on the antipodal side of the earth. Precedents for closely-situated communities varying in their reckoning of days were already mentioned in the Talmud,[292] just as national boundaries were clearly demarcated, sometimes even within a city, such as in Acco of which only a part belonged to the Land of Israel.[293] Accordingly, there was nothing absurd in a dateline dividing between East and West; the laws of nature themselves, after all, necessitated such a line.[294]

While the 16th century Italian scholar R. Obadiah Seforno justified the local variations of the Sabbath, despite the obviously fixed time of the original Sabbath, with the verse "It is a sabbath unto the Lord *in all your dwellings*,"[295] i.e., varying according to your habitations,[296] his contemporary R. David ibn Zimra reached a similar conclusion on the basis of a talmudic law which stipulates that a wanderer in the desert who lost the count of days should allow six days to pass and then sanctify the seventh as the Sabbath.[297] Since one is not required to abstain from work on each day as being possibly the true Sabbath, it is evident that the incidence of the Sabbath may be determined in relation to purely local circumstances. Ibn Zimra held, however, that the maximum variation in the commencement of the Sabbath between East and West could not amount to more than twelve hours, so that he too (like the *Yesod Olam*) apparently disputed the existence of a single dateline.[298]

The actual problem of those who travel around the world, losing one day if they go West and gaining one if they go East, is first mentioned by R. Jacob Emden in the 18th century. He ruled that such a traveler should observe the Sabbath according to his own regular count of days and switch the Sabbath only on reaching a settled community keeping the Sabbath on the preceding or following day.[299] In conformity with this opinion, the rabbi-mathematician Joseph Schwartz of Jerusalem contemplated the possibility of three persons in the same place observing the Sabbath on three different dates: one having circumnavigated the world eastwards, the other westwards and the third not having moved at all.[300] These and other authorities[301] thus discount the dateline for travelers.

The first to fix a dateline the crossing of which would determine the Sabbath was R. Chaim Selig Slonimsky, the genial 19th century Russian scholar who excelled in rabbinics, mathematics and astronomy alike. He considered the zero meridian as passing through Jerusalem, so that the dateline would be exactly opposite, 180 degrees from Jerusalem. He interpreted "It is a sabbath unto the Lord in all your dwellings"[302] to mean that the 24 hours of the Sabbath as observed in the Holy Land must at least in part coincide with the Sabbath anywhere else; this can be achieved only if the beginning of the Sabbath is not removed by more than 12 hours (or 180 degrees) in any part of the world from its commencement in Jerusalem. Jews throughout the world would thus always celebrate the Sabbath simultaneously with those in the Holy Land at least 12 hours. This would put the dateline along the 145th degree West of Greenwich (180 minus 35), i.e., to the East of Alaska and Hawaii. On the other hand, R. Samuel Moholiver, the pioneer of religious Zionism and friend of Herzl, thought the dateline was wherever the first East and West travelers originally met; for they established a presumption of the law (*"Chazakah"*) which remained binding. Accordingly, Jews in Alaska (sold by Russia to America in 1867 and thus transferred from the Eastern to the Western hemisphere) must retain the Eastern Sabbath. But this opinion was generally rejected as quite impracticable, particularly since historical research could never determine with certainty the original meeting places of migrants from East and West.

Lately the controversy has been narrowed down somewhat to the following principal views regarding the location of the dateline:

1. *Along the 125th meridian east of Greenwich* (i.e., 90 degrees east of Jerusalem, following the Kuzari). This view was upheld by R. Isaiah Meir Schapira of Czortkow (*Ha-Maggid*, 1872) and notably by the *Chazon Ish* in our time. The latter qualified this ruling, however, by including in the East any land-surface which lies astride the 125th meridian. Hence the entire Asian and Australian mainlands belong to the East, with the West commencing only off their Eastern coasts. This places the island of Japan in the West, and the *Chazon Ish* accordingly advised travelers from China to Japan to switch their Sabbath from Saturday to Sunday on leaving the Asian mainland. This opinion is also endorsed by R. Chaim Zimmerman of Chicago against the attacks on it by many others.

2. *Along the 145th meridian west of Greenwich* (i.e., 180 degrees each of Jerusalem, following Slonimsky). R. Yechiel Michael Tukczinsky, advocating this view, argued that the dateline is bound to be determined by a center or zero line on the opposite side, and just as the international community had accepted the meridian passing through Greenwich as the starting point, it was only natural that Jews should take Jerusalem as the center and point of departure for the division between East and West.

3. *Along the international dateline on the 180th meridian* (i.e., 145 degrees east of Jerusalem) and across the Bering Strait separating Asia from America in the North. This view is supported by R. David Schapira (*Benei Zion*) and especially by R. Menachem Kasher, who has written extensively on the subject, as corresponding to the most natural division between East and West. They refute the opinion of the *Chazon Ish* as illogical, because it would place Australia (as part of it is west of the 125 meridian) in the East and the island of New Guinea, though within the same longitudes as Australia,

in the West (as no part of it is west of the 125th meridian), and because the criterion used is quite arbitrary; for one might equally well say that any land-surface protruding beyond the 125th meridian to the West belongs to the West.

The international dateline has also been endorsed by the rabbinate in Jerusalem in its reply of 1942 to the inquiry received from the refugees in Japan. Following the consensus of rabbinical opinion, Rabbi Hibner reaches these conclusions:

1. The division between East and West in Jewish law corresponds to the international dateline.

2. Those traveling across the dateline need not adjust the days of the week and vary the date for observing the Sabbath until they disembark on land, and then only if Sabbath-observing Jews are to be found there.

3. In order not to lose a Sabbath, travelers from the West to the East (i.e. from America to Asia or Australia) should be careful to arrange their journey so as not to cross the dateline on Friday (in view of #2 above, this applies presumably only to air travelers who might leave the West on Friday and arrive in the East on Sunday, or to any travelers from the West who would reach their destination in the East on Sunday, irrespective of the day on which they crossed the dateline. —I.J.).

Deformed Babies

RECENTLY rabbinic discussions on the problem of the deformed babies tragedy appeared in two current periodicals. Both articles, while partly divergent in their arguments, arrive at similar conclusions.

The first is a learned contribution to the latest number of *No'am* (vol. vi; Jerusalem, 5723) by Chief Rabbi I. J. Unterman of Tel Aviv (who has previously written extensively on related issues, especially in his book *Shevet Miyehudah*). He deals with the question of abortion in cases where an expectant mother contracted German measles (rubella) during her early pregnancy and where it is feared that her child may be born with serious physical or mental abnormalities as a result.[303]

Rabbi Unterman's unconditional objection to abortion in such circumstances is based primarily on his reasoning that even the killing of an unborn child constitutes "an appurtenance of murder" because, conversely, the saving of such a child's life justifies the violation of the Sabbath and other laws.[304] The rule of suspending these laws in the face of danger to life in the case of an embryo is invoked, against a minority view,[305] by most authorities,[306] even if the embryo is below the age of 40 days when it is otherwise regarded "as mere water" (following RaMBaN's interpretation), Furthermore, argues Rabbi Unterman, even when the destruction of an unborn child is permitted in order to save the mother's life (therapeutic abortion), the sanction is granted only because the child, in its mortal conflict with the mother, is deemed "a pursuer" and may be struck down like any other aggressor in pursuit of someone else's life.[307] Without the element of "pursuit," therefore, the killing of an embryo would be unconditionally forbidden,[308] even though the offense—by a scriptural decree[309]—does not carry the death penalty like the murder of born persons. Consequently, any abortion of a human fruit for fear that it may be born deformed must be condemned as tantamount to murder. This prohibition would stand even if it were certain (which is scarcely possible) that the child would be born deformed, just as it is forbidden to kill a crippled person. Likewise, there can be no justification for killing a deformed child already born even by indirect means (such as starving it to death). For "this very thought appears to me as opposing the outlook of the Torah on human life, whereby even in the hardest moments it is forbidden to sacrifice life for any reason whatever other than the sanctification of the Divine Name (martyrdom) or the saving of the mother's life."

A note here adds that if fears of abnormal births were to be taken into account, one might also consider a possibility weighing in the opposite direction, i.e. the fear that an artificial interruption of the pregnancy might permanently impair the mother's fertility (and health—*I.J.*), as Professor Asherman of Tel Aviv advised the author.

Further elaborating the view that the prohibition of killing applies even to an embryo under 40 days old, Rabbi Unterman resorts to an original argument. Unlike the Noachidic law of murder which expressly includes the killing of an embryo—based on the verse "He that sheddeth *the blood of man in man* . . ."[310]—Jewish law exempts the killer of an unborn child from the death penalty by stipulating "He that smiteth *a man* . . . shall surely be put to death;"[311] yet the destruction of a human fruit is deemed an offense against life because "in matters affecting life we also consider that which is going to be [a human being] without any further action, following the laws of nature." Accordingly, while in the Noachidic dispensation of abortion during the first 40 days of a pregnancy would not constitute murder (the embryo having yet no distinct blood and organs), Jewish law extends its opposition to abortion even to that period since it is concerned with a potential human being as well as an existing one.

Thalidomide Babies

THE second contribution on this subject deals with the recent thalidomide problem (which is in principle the same as the German measles problem). It appears as an article by the present reviewer in *The Jewish Review* (London, November 14, 1962). In contrast with Rabbi Unterman's dissertation which axiomatically assumes that there is no distinction between normal and abnormal persons or embryos in their right to life, the latter article is mainly concerned with corroborating this point as well as defining the circumstances in which resultant hazards to the mother may justify the abortion of a thalidomide baby. To these ends the article refers to some respona and other more recent rabbinical writings not cited by Rabbi Unterman.

In what may be the only classic responsum on the status of malformed humans, Rabbi Eleazar Fleckeles of Prague dealt with the question raised by the birth of a grotesquely misshapen child in 1807. Challenging his questioner's argument that such a child might be destroyed on the grounds that it could not be classed as human following the Talmud's exclusion of such monster-births from the ritual laws normally applicable, R. Fleckeles reasoned that this exclusion applied only to the laws of purity (i.e., the mother's impurity after the birth or miscarriage of a baby in human shape). But however deformed a child, once it is born of a human mother and lives, it enjoyed all human rights and must not be destroyed; even starving it to death would be unlawful as homicide.[312] Already in the 12th century the *Sefer Chasidim* (ed. Zitomir, 1879, no. 186) referred to a ruling against terminating the life of a child born with teeth and a tail like an animal, counselling the removal of these features instead. Mental abnormalities, too, do not abrogate or affect the title to life; even for an idiot the Sabbath laws may be violated to save his life like any other, and to kill him is punishable as murder.[313]

While these cases deal only with malformed persons already born, they clearly establish the principle that physical or mental defects in no way compromise the claim to life, and once there is no distinction between normal and abnormal persons in the laws of murder applicable after birth, it follows that no such legal distinction can be made in respect to foeticide before birth either. Moreover, in regard to the destruction of an unborn child suspected possibly to be deformed, there is always the chance that a potentially healthy child may in fact be destroyed. And in matters of life and death the usual majority rule does not apply; any chance, however slim, that a life may be saved must always be given the benefit of the doubt. Hence, even if the abortion of a definitely deformed foetus could hypothetically be sanctioned, the possibility that a normal child might be destroyed would militate against such a sanction.

The only legitimate indication for an abortion, therefore, is a threat to the safety of the mother, based on the explicit directive of the *Mishnah*[314] in favor of an embryotomy when there is no other way to save the mother's life. Such a contingency includes psychological as well as physical hazards, provided they are of a genuinely grave nature. Thus, a 17th century responsum permitted an abortion in a case where it was feared the mother would otherwise suffer an attack of hysteria imperiling her life,[315] just as a mental patient who may endanger his life by suicidal tendencies is considered like any other dangerously sick person.[316]

On the strength of these rulings the *Review* article reaches the following conclusions—with the warning, however, that in such capital judgments, involving decisions on whether a human life is to be or not to be, every individual case must be adjudged by the most competent rabbinic experts:

1. A physically or mentally abnormal child, whether before or after birth, has the same claim to life as a normal child.

2. Whilst only the killing of a born (and viable) child constitutes murder in Jewish law, the destruction of the foetus too is a crime and cannot be justified except out of consideration for the mother's life.

3. Consequently, the fear that a child may (or will) be born deformed is not in itself a legitimate indication for its abortion, particularly since there is usually a chance that the child might turn out to be quite normal.

4. Such an abortion may only be contemplated if, on reliable medical evidence, it is genuinely feared that allowing the pregnancy to continue would have such debilitating effects (whether psychologically or otherwise) on the mother as to present a hazard to her life, however remote such danger may be.

7

State Occasions

Dublin's Jewish Mayor

> *Venishbata chai Hashem be'emeth bemishpat
> uvitzdakah vehithbarkhu vo goyim uvoh yitthal-
> lelu.*
>
> "If thou wilt swear, as the Lord liveth, in
> truth, in judgment and in righteousness; then
> shall the nations be blessed in him, and in him
> shall they glory."
>
> (Jeremiah 4:2)

I T is not granted to every individual, nor even to every community or society, to inscribe their names in indelible letters in the permament record of human history. Most of us pass our lives as more or less insignificant particles of mankind, playing but a modest part in the unfold-

---

Address delivered at the Civil Service in the Greenville Hall Synagogue, Dublin, to mark the election of Councillor Robert Briscoe as Lord Mayor of Dublin, July 8, 1956.

ing of the major dramas of human achievement, and remaining unsung and unknown in the consciousness of future generations.

Only few are privileged to witness history in the making at close range, and fewer still to participate in the making of history.

Indeed, as worshippers at the first Jewish religious service ever to be held in the presence of Dublin's Lord Mayor, we all actually participate in the making of history.

What, then, is the significance of this service, and of the occasion prompting it?

Being Jewish citizens of Dublin, we are gathered here for a twofold purpose: As the Lord Mayor's fellow-citizens, we seek to invoke God's blessings on our First Citizen and his labors. As his coreligionists, we desire to give thanks to the Almighty for the supreme honor bestowed on him and through him on our community.

His charge is onerous no less than honorable. Without divine assistance his work cannot prosper. In our prayers for his success, we are sustained by the knowledge that he brings to bear to his high office the experience of a life-time of distinguished service to this City and to this country, an experience fortified by a rare capacity for leadership, great resources of character and judicious judgment, and an unflinching public loyalty to his faith. His work is, moreover, shared and supported by a helpmate of great charm and dignity who will lighten his burden and help to guide his steps into history.

The Lord Mayor is not merely Dublin's First Citizen; he is probably also Dublin's busiest citizen. To him we can truly apply the rabbis' comment relative to the appointment of judges to rule over the people:

"When I appointed them I said unto them: Now it is not as in the past; in the past you were under your own control, now behold you are subservient to the public" (Rashi, Deut. 1:17).

The Lord Mayor's chief tasks may be summarized under three headings: Firstly, his leadership of the City Council. He is called upon to direct and preside over the deliberations of our City Fathers. What motto could be more appropriate to his responsibilities in this capacity than the charge assigned by the Bible in this week's *Sidrah* to judges in the passage to which I have referred:

"Hear the causes between your brethren, and judge righteously between a man and his brother, and the stranger that is with him. You shall not respect persons in judgment; you shall hear the small and the great alike; you shall not be afraid of the face of man; for the judgment is God's" (*Ibid.* 1:16-17).

We pray with assurance that the Lord Mayor, in his government of this Capital City, will prove bold and fearless, that he will serve the cause of truth and justice without favor, that he will defend and promote the rights of the humblest citizen no less than that of the mighty or the rich, and that the interests of the native and the stranger will be equally close to his heart; for—as all leaders of man—it is to God that he is accountable.

Secondly, he is expected to represent the citizens of Dublin at home and probably also abroad. Whether at the opening of a new hospital to bring healing to the sick, at the laying of the foundation-stone of a new school to educate our children, at the inauguration of a new housing block to shelter those in want of homes, or at state occasions here or elsewhere, the Lord Mayor will represent his fellow-citizens and convey their greetings to many worthy enterprises within the City and often without. We are confident that, with God's help, he will discharge with great honor and distinction the trust placed in his hands, enhancing the fair name of Dublin; that we may say of him, in the words of Isaiah: "That in you we glory."

And thirdly, as Dublin's principal host to visitors, he will have more opportunities than any other citizen to practice one of the finest Jewish ideals and Irish traditions, the display of hospitality to strangers. To his official mansion will file dignitaries and statesmen from foreign lands, official deputations and plain tourists, visiting teams and participants in international conferences. The warmth and cordiality of his receptions will set the tone to their welcome among our citizens: they will enhance Dublin's reputation for true Irish hospitality. We pray that—like the tent of our Father Abraham and of the Lord Mayor's own father Abraham—the Mansion House will witness the forging of many new friendships and radiate brotherly love from its historic walls.

Finally, a few words on our proud and happy feelings as Jews on the singular honor to which destiny has elevated one of the sons of our community. By his election, he has not only raised himself to a stature of world repute, to be the most prominent Jew ever born within these shores. He has also uplifted our standing, and turned the attention and regard of Jewish communities throughout the world to Irish Jewry. Not since my illustrious predecessor was called from Dublin to assume the highest spiritual office in Jewry as Chief Rabbi of the Holy Land has our community featured so conspicuously in the Jewish press in Israel, in the United States, in England, and in virtually every other land of our dispersion.

But there attaches a deeper significance to this historic event which has been greeted with such unprecedented interest and acclaim in Jewish and Irish circles, indeed throughout the civilized world.

By a striking coincidence, it is almost exactly a hundred years ago now—in 1855, to be precise—that the first Jewish Lord Mayor of London was elected. It may be of special interest to us, incidently, that during Sir David Salomon's Mayorality a century ago the inscription on the London monument attributing the City's Great Fire of 1666 to the Roman Catholics was removed. It was thus through a Jew that a cause for intolerance to a religious minority was eliminated.

But what is more significant at the moment is that Sir David, like our Lord Mayor, was also returned as a Member of Parliament. Yet, though elected to the British House of Commons in 1851, he could not take his seat until 1859 after the alteration of the Parliamentary oath, since he refused to take it "on the true faith of a Christian" as previously required. Our Lord Mayor has been a Deputy of the Dail for over a quarter of a century. It is to the abiding credit and glory of our young State of Ireland that such discrimination has never been practiced here.

Tonight, therefore, we Jewish citizens of Dublin join with our Lord Mayor in giving thanks to the Almighty for His mercy and loving kindness, that He has planted us in a land within which, though small in numbers, we are granted full freedom—the most cherished of all human possessions—to play our part as loyal citizens to advance the welfare of the State and to work shoulder to shoulder with our neighbors for the betterment and prosperity of all citizens.

May there go out from this holy House of God tonight a stirring, visible message of goodwill and true human brotherhood to the whole world, particularly to the darkened parts where racial intolerance and religious persecution still assail the inalienable rights of man; may there go forth from this noble temple, together with our thanksgiving, our devout prayers for the peace and well-being of our beloved Capital City, for the happiness and security of its growing population, and for Divine grace and blessing upon the heads of our esteemed First Citizen and his gracious Lady. Holding, as he does, a position on which the attention of many nations will be focused, may be vouchsafed to fulfill the great prophesy of Jeremiah:

Venishbata chai Hashem be'emeth bemishpat uvitzedakah vehithborakhu vo goyim uvo yithallelu "If thou wilt swear, as the Lord liveth, in truth, in judgment and in righteousness; then shall the nations be blessed in him, and in him shall they glory."

John Fitzgerald Kennedy— In Memoriam

NEVER in the long, tormented and blood-spattered history of mankind have the words horror, shock and grief been spoken and printed so often, never have so many eyes been wetted with tears, and never have so many national flags all over the world

Address delivered at the special Memorial Service at the Fifth Avenue Synagogue on the day of the late President's funeral, November 25, 1963.

been flown at half staff, as on the occasion of this supreme tragedy of our times, and, in some ways, of all times.

Our *Sidrah* this week opened *Vayetze Ya-akov,* "and Jacob went away," Jacob departed. Our Rabbis, commenting on these words, remarked that there are some righteous men, some outstanding leaders, *ose roshem* "who make such a mark" on their environment, who leave such an imprint on their age, that with their departure *panah hadah panah zivah panah hadarah* "its glory departs, its splendor departs, and its beauty departs." How much glory there was in this mighty nation being led by a young, dashing, vibrant and dynamic leader! Now, *panah hodah,* this glory has departed with him. How much splendor there was in the greatest democracy on earth being ruled by a man of a minority faith! Now, *panah zivah,* this splendor has passed with him. And how much beauty there was in this being a land in which law and order, the security of our leaders, were taken for granted! Now, *panah hadarah,* this beauty, too, has gone away with him.

We are still petrified with horror by the sheer poignancy of the tragedy. Here the free world's leader, at the prime of life and at the pinnacle of success, having risen to greatness by ballots, is felled down by bullets, resting his mortally wounded head in the lap of his wife, turning the nation's first children into little orphans and all the world into mourners. In our Sidrah Jacob prayed, on leaving his home pursued by the wrath of his brother, *veshavti veshalom el beth avi,* that "I may return in peace to the house of my father." How tragic it is for a child, having been away from his home for some time, to return there and not to find his father there any more. How much more tragic it is for parents to go to their son's home and not to find him there any more, or for a son to be called by death to Heaven and not to find his parents there, for a child to predecease his father and mother!

By a strange coincidence, it was only last Monday at our weekly Talmud Class that we learned the passage which describes how Nadav and Avihu, the two young sons of Aaron, promising leaders, were struck down by lightning bolts out of the blue in the prime of life, to be buried by their old father and uncle. *Heinu de'amrei inshei . . . . ,* adds the

Talmud, "Thus do people say proverbially: Many an old camel is laden with the hides of younger ones" (*Sanhedrin* 52a) slaughtered before their time. What a tragedy when a young man dies and his burden is carried by an older man succeeding him!

But we are moved not only by the utter tragedy of the event. We are also outraged with dismay by the social conditions which made this tragedy possible. We associate such ghastly crimes of violence with near-by republics in backward Latin America, or a distant land like South Vietnam, or the unstable Arab countries where revolutions by assassination are commonplace. We thought it could not happen here, in this civilized country. But it did happen!

How many of us, how many leaders of nations, now exclaim the desperate plea of Jacob: *Hatzileni na miyad achi miyad Esav*, "Save me, I plead, from the hand of my brother, from the hand of Esau!" *Ki yare anochi otho pen yavo vehikani em al banim*, "for I fear him, lest he come and strike me down, (bereaving) a mother with her children." Why this duplication "from the hand of my brother, from the hand of Esau"?, asks Rashi. *Miyad achi she'ein noheg immi ke'ach ela ke'esav harasha*, "from the hand of my brother, who does not conduct himself as a brother but as Esau, the wicked." Though delivered from the same womb, Esau defied the brotherhood of Jacob. We are horrified to find ourselves in a society in which violence is rife, and a man can strike down his brother in cold blood, in which men do not conduct themselves as brothers but as Esaus. What has become of the brotherhood of man in our society when the leading brother in the nation could be slain so cruelly?

But to our grief and dismay we must also add a note of confidence and thanksgiving. In many another country the assassination of the head of state may well be liable to spark off revolution and widespread bloodshed. Here at least we are safe from such a nightmare, thanks to the extraordinary foresight and wisdom of our Founding Fathers, who provided constitutional safeguards for the continuity of government and the smooth transfer of power in critical times as these. We live today literally *bizekhuth avoth*, "by the merit of the Fathers" of the nation. How thankful we should be that we are blessed to live in a land where, following the murder of a president, we can still walk securely and without terror in in the streets of our cities! As Jews we have particular reason to thank God for living in this blessed land, for in times of national turmoil and insecurity, as our experience elsewhere has so tragically proved, Jews are always the first to suffer, the principal target of rioting mobs.

A little while ago, the man who could never rest or tire in his lifetime has been laid to eternal rest. The very earth whose leading ruler he was now covers his stricken mortal remains. The champion of peace is now at peace forever. During these three days of mourning, the world has stood still. The clattering news media were muffled, for there was no news outside the one event. The creaking wheels of business, the garish noise of entertainment, the loud cheers of music and sports—all were muted. In these three days of silence we have had the time for contemplation, we have been in the mood for remorse and self-criticism, for thinking about the state of the world and man. For three days political sparring and international differences have been forgotten; the parties and nations have been united in peace. Is it too much to hope that this unity and peace shall continue to prevail, that our awful awakening to the horror of crime will expunge crime from blotting—and entertaining—our society in the future, that our chastened spirit of contrition will hallow the new age ahead of us? Would it be too much to hope that, after this catastrophe which has struck us, we resolve to realize these high ideals of our late beloved President, to complete his unfinished business, so that he may accomplish in death what he was not spared to see fulfilled in his life?

Today it is dark and sombre in our hearts. The lights have gone out all over the world. But this is a time for faith and rededication. Later this month we shall celebrate our festival of *Chanukah,* the festival of lights and rededication. However dark it is today, the lights will go on again one by one until the whole *Menorah* is ablaze with light, and cheerfulness returns to our hearts and homes. After Jacob's majestic dream in the night, when he saw the ladder linking Heaven and earth and received the promise of God's protection, we are told: *vayasem otha matbeva vayitzok shemen al rosho,* "and he set up a memorial stone, and he poured oil upon its head." As we now set up a *matzevah,* a memorial stone, a monument to the gallant life of our President, let us too consecrate it with oil, the fuel for light, so that the flame of his ideals may burn forever. Let us rally around our new leader in brotherhood and unity, praying that God may inspire him with vision, strength and courage to guide the destinies of America and the world. May the Almighty comfort the sorrowing widow—now a symbol of fortitude—and her orphaned children; may He comfort us, America and all the world in mourning. And may the memory of our President, who has now joined the holy ranks of martyrs, be a blessing everlasting.

A Tribute to Sir Winston Churchill

F OR the past 32 years this date, January 30, has been the most infamous day and anniversary in all history. On January 30, 1933 the most evil tyrant in the annals of man came to power. Perhaps it is a not altogether insignificant coincidence that on this very same date 32 years later the man primarily responsible for breaking that tyranny is being laid to his eternal rest. In 1933 on this date the earth erupted in blazing volcanos, raising mountains of ashes and destruction from which flowed rivers of blood and tears over many lands, and today on this same date the earth is once against opened up to receive the mortal remains of the man who, promising nothing but blood and sweat and tears, caused these rivers of blood and tears to cease.

This coincidence provides us with a classic study in the contrasts and comparisons between good and evil, and in the principal men who governed these forces. Both men exercised extraordinary power by their matchless gift of speech. Through their oratory, they were able to mesmerize the masses, to sway the thoughts and actions of millions. One used that

Sermon delivered at Fifth Avenue Synagogue on the day of Sir Winston Churchill's funeral, January 30, 1965.

power to crush the conscience and discernment of the people, to turn them into a vast army of regimented robots serving blindly to sustain the most brutal tyranny ever known, whilst the other used that power of speech to galvanize the courage and determination of free men to break that tyranny and to remain free.

Both leaders hypnotically manipulated the minds of their people at their bidding. But the one debased and prostituted the language to wield it into a vile instrument of intimidation and maniacal hysteria; and the other ennobled and sublimated the language into a majestic vehicle for transferring his supreme gallantry and resolution to millions of others.

I was there to witness the effect of both. In the 30's I lived in Germany as a child. I will never forget what terror gripped us every time a speech by that evil man was announced. Whenever he spoke, he aroused his hordes to a frenzy of mad inhumanity. Announcing some new extension of his diabolical plans, every speech would send a fresh shudder of horror through the world, and particularly among the Jews under his sway.

Later I was in embattled England in its finest hour. The German war machine had savagely broken down all obstacles in its path of conquest. France lay prostrate under the Nazi jackboot. Only the thin strip of the English Channel separated the gloating enemy from his final triumph. How well I remember the atmosphere of fear and despair rampant in those terrible, yet heroic days, and how the feeling of gloom and foreboding was dispelled by the buoyant confidence the great British leader exuded in his rousing speeches. Every time his booming voice came over the radio, he transfixed his people, turning fear into faith, the experience of terror into dogged determination, and grim adversity into shining courage.

The contrast between these two contestants in history's most fateful battle is well expressed in the Psalm dedicated to the Sabbath—*Mizmor shir leyom ha-shabbath.* Both the righteous and the wicked grow and die like an organic plant. But, *biphro'ach resha'im kemo esev, vayatzitzu kol po'alei aven, lehishamdan adei ad,* "when the wicked sprout forth as grass, and all the workers of iniquity flourish, it is only that they may be destroyed forever." True, evil-doers, too, shoot up from the ground and prosper. But their growth only leads to their own utter destruction. When the grass dies, it withers and decays; nothing of it survives. Not so the righteous. They are also but plants. Their growth and prospering are described by the same verb *yiphrach* as the *biphro'ach* of the wicked, but with a difference; *Tzaddik katamar yiphrach ke-erez balevanon yisgeh,* "The righteous man flourishes like a palm-tree, growing great like a cedar in Lebanon." A mighty tree, like a palm or cedar, even when it is felled and dies, continues to be useful; from its timber one can construct a Temple to the glory of God and build homes to shelter people.

Of course, the wicked and the righteous alike often prosper —*biphro'ach*. But the wicked man, when his life's work of evil is done, decomposes in the earth like rotten grass; he faces everlasting destruction and oblivion—*lehishamdan adei ad*—like dying weeds on a foul dunghill. His achievements in life generate in his death only the sickening loathing of a putrid compost-heap. His works become the garbage of history. The righteous man also grows and dies. But when he is felled down, something survives which is immortal and indestructible like the hard wood of a cedar-tree. Out of his life's accomplishments countless lives can be rebuilt and inspired long after he is dead. He continues to provide the material for the construction of temples and homes erected *lehaggid ki yashar ha-shem,* "to declare that God is upright . . ." In the end, good outlives evil.

This is the imperishable glory of the mighty man we honor today. There is hardly another man, if any at all, of whom it may truly be said that he was individually responsible for saving the whole of mankind. Of him who immortalized the phrase during the crucial Battle of Britain "Never have so many owed so much to so few" we may indeed say: "Never have so many owed so much to one man!" We Jews have particular cause to record our eternal gratitude. But for this one man, every one of us here might today be reduced to smoke and ashes in the ovens of Auschwitz and other death factories that devoured the lives of six million of our brothers and sisters. But for his resolute defiance of the evil tyrant and his gangster hords, the "final solution" might have been the epitaph to us all, and the flickering lights of freedom might have been snuffed out all over the world.

He not only prevented our extinction; he also played a major part in lighting our most brilliant beacon in post-exilic times. While he was largely responsible for severing from our ancestral homeland the part East of the Jordan which was later to join our sworn enemies, he made an indispensable contribution to the rise of the Jewish State and the national independence our people in Israel enjoy today.

At the same time we should never forget the long years of the gathering storm when his brave and prophetic voice cried out in the wilderness. Had his impassioned warnings been heeded in time, we would not have had to mourn the annihilation of one third of our people, and the world might have basked in the sunshine of a Warm Peace instead of shivering in the freeze of a Cold War.

January 30, then, will for ever remain a date of supreme fame and infamy. In 1933 it marked the beginning of humanity's lowest depths and Jewry's most agonizing ordeal; in 1965 it marks the end of mankind's finest hours and the era of Israel's greatest triumph.

At this very moment, when the mortal remains of this immortal man are being borne to their final rest, and his sojourn on earth makes way for his journey to life and fame everlasting, we pray in the words of our Sidrah which we still recite whenever we set out on a journey: *Hineh anokhi shole'ach mal'ach lephaneikha lishmorkha baderekh velahavi'akha el hamakom asher hakhinothi.* "Behold, I send an angel before you, to guard you on your way, and to bring you to the place which I have destined for you"—that God's protecting angel may accompany him on his journey to the immortal place of honor which destiny has carved out for him.

Blessing the President

MR. PRESIDENT. At our Synagogue services every Sabbath we recite a prayer for your welfare and Divine guidance. This prayer opens with the words: "May He Who giveth salvation unto kings and dominion unto princes, bless the President of the United States, Lyndon B. Johnson." We have now come to convey these blessings in person to you.

By an ancient Jewish law, we are required in the presence, or in the sight, of a head of state to recite a special benediction—a blessing many of us say only once in a life-time. I will now ask my fellow-visitors to recite this with me, first in Hebrew and then in English: *Barukh shenatan mikhvodoh levasar vadam.* "Blessed art Thou, O Lord, our God, King of the universe, who hath given of His glory to flesh and blood."

Mr. President. There is no man, nor has there ever been any man in history, who has ruled over more Jews than you do. Not even the President of Israel can speak on behalf of five-and-a-half or six million Jews, nor could Moses or David, King of Israel. On their behalf and on behalf of the Jewish people throughout the world, of whose freedom you are the principal defender, we invoke the blessings of the Almighty, in the words of the prayer to which I have already referred: "May God preserve you in life, guard you and deliver you from all trouble and sorrow, that you may uphold the peace of the realm, advance the welfare of the nation, and deal kindly and truly with all the House of Israel."

Spoken before President Lyndon B. Johnson at a White House reception to a group of Orthodox Jewish leaders, March 10, 1964.

The Pursuit of Justice—
A Charge to District Attorneys

A SIGNIFICANT Biblical law in the Book of Deuteronomy reads: "Judges and officers shall thou make thee in all thy gates," that is, in the courts located in the city-gates. By this Divine command the obligation was imposed upon the people to set up officials to adjudicate and enforce the law in all districts, thus investing the delegates to this Conference with Divine sanction and authority. At no period in America's history has the judicious exercise of this authority been in greater demand than today, when law and order are being challenged by rising crime rates and by ever more widespread outbreaks of lawlessness and disorder. In these perilous times the charge to bring law-breakers to book becomes an indispensable service not only to the triumph of justice but to national security and survival as well. We pray, therefore with anxious hearts that these deliberations may be inspired and uplifted by the constant awareness of the Divine injunction and awesome responsibilities devolving upon this distinguished assemblage.

Justice, as Disraeli once put it, is truth in action. Expanding on this thought, we may say that the pursuit of justice requires not only *reaction* to crime but *action* to forestall and prevent it. Even as the doctor must train his patient to promote health as well as to fight illness, and as the clergyman must encourage his flock to seek good as well as to depart from evil, so must the guardians of the law transcend their role as *reactors* to crime by being also leading actors in man's epic struggle to make reverence for truth and justice supreme, by turning the conscience of every citizen into his own law-enforcement agency. For, like parents and teachers, the task of prosecutors is to render themselves superfluous by reason of the very success of their labors.

Invocation delivered at the Conference of the National District Attorneys Association in New York, August 19, 1964.

In invoking, then, the blessings of God, the Sovereign of Justice, upon the organizers, leaders and participants of this Conference, we pray that He may speed the day when, in the words of an ancient Hebrew prayer recited on the forthcoming Jewish New Year, the Days of Judgment, "iniquity shall close·her mouth, and all wickedness shall be wholly consumed like smoke, as the dominion of arrogance passeth away from earth;" the day when the quest for justice shall rank in the ambitions of every citizen at least equally with the quest for wealth, comfort and amusement; the day when the finest human brains and resources will be dedicated to discovering and applying the elusive formula on how to build two homes, and two nations, next to each other, so that happiness rules inside them and peace between them; the day when the pursuit of justice will in fact be our ultimate national and human purpose.

8

Family Joys And Sorrows

To My Son Joel

Address on the Occasion of His Bar Mitzvah
April 20, 1963

> "I will make mention of the mercies of God,
> the praises of God, according to all He has
> bestowed on us."

M Y dear Joel!
In opening with this Thanksgiving to God
our Creator, I am overwhelmed by an emotion
of great joy. I would tell you, as Jacob told his son Joseph
when he blessed him: "The blessings of *your* father are

mightier than the blessings of my parents." As Rashi explains: *Ha-b'rakhoth shebayrakhni Hakadosh Barukh Hu gavru v'halkhu al hab'rakhoth shebayrakh et horai.* The favors with which God has blessed us, your parents, are greater than the bounties with which He blessed our parents. We have been granted a life of more ease and security, of greater freedom and opportunity, than our parents ever knew. We brought you into a world in which you never experienced the tragedy of war. You have never known what it means to be a refugee, and you have never known the terror of persecution or want. Compared to our parents, who had to face much hardship and sacrifice in their lives, we have lived a sheltered and comfortable life, filled with many undeserved joys and successes. Never forget for a single day what we owe to God for these extraordinary favors.

But in another sense, too, "the blessings of your father are mightier than the blessings of my parents." You are heir to double the tradition which I have inherited. In addition to what has been bequeathed to you by the Jakobovits family, your heart and mind have been enriched by the superb qualities and reputation of your mother and her parents. Together with my dear mother, we are honored to greet them as the crowns of our *Simchah* today.

My dear Joel, your ship of life has been safely pulled from the harbor of your birth by two powerful tug-boats. Now the lines have been cast off; you must take command and sail under your own steam through the ocean of life. Today we are handing over our command of your vessel to you. You are on your own now. We will try to help you chart your course, and we will continue to supply you with some fuel for your voyage. But the responsibility for piloting your life is yours.

You may ask us, your parents, who are responsible for bringing you into the world: What kind of passage am I going to have? Will the sea of my life be calm or stormy? Will my voyage be comfortable or full of dangers and sickness? Will I reach my destination in safety or drift aimlessly in the vast ocean ahead of me? I wish, my dear son, that I could answer these questions. But I cannot. You remember

Rashi's remarks describing how Jacob called his sons to bless them: "And Jacob called his sons, and he said: Gather together, and I will tell you what will happen to you in the end of days." Rashi comments, "Jacob sought to reveal the end, but the Divine inspiration departed from him, and he began talking about other matters . . ." Every father and every mother want to tell their children what the future has in store for them. But a veil is drawn over our vision of the future. My dear child, I cannot tell you what is in store for you, and I must speak to you about "other matters."

As your father, however, I can bless you. I can help to chart the course which is most likely to see you safely and happily through life. What blessing can I give you on this supreme day in your young life?

As you know, your birth was greeted with special joy and excitement by us and our family. You were not merely our firstborn; you were the first boy to be born in our family following the passing of my sainted father Joel זצ״ל and you are the first child to bear his name.

Of all my childhood memories and impressions of my father, one event always stands out in my memory. It is not any one sermon that he preached to his congregation with so much love and fire; it is not even the *Seder* at which he presided with majesty and radiance in the white *kittel* he has now worn for over sixteen years and still wears today . . . No. It is the memory of the blessing he would give me, and my brothers and sisters after me, every Yom Kippur Eve, just before the start of the great fast and before leaving our home for *Kol Nidre*. I did not hear his words. I just felt his hands on my head, and I saw a tear or two drop into the *sefer* (book) in which he was looking. Only later did I discover the beautiful and moving words of this blessing, and ever since you made me into a father, I have bestowed this blessing on you every year on Yom Kippur Eve.

Today I give you this blessing, a father's blessing, in public. No words of mine could more adequately express what we, your parents, wish and pray for you in the inner recesses of our soul. This is the text of the blessing, taken from the

Jewish code of law called *Chaye Adam, "The Life of Man:"*

ויהי רצון מלפני אבינו שבשמים שיתן בלבך אהבתו ויראתו ...

"May it be the will of God, our Father in Heaven, that He may put into your heart the love and fear of Him; and may the fear of God be upon you that you may not sin, that you be ever aware of God's presence, that He is with you and watches you wherever you are.

"May your passion be to learn Torah and to perform Gods commandments. Let your eyes look forward, your mouth speak the words of wisdom, your heart meditate on the mysteries of God and His law, your hands be busy in the exercise of good and noble deeds, your legs run to perform the will of your Father in Heaven with zeal. May He one day grant you the joy of having righteous children who will be busy with learning Torah and practicing *Mitzvoth* all their days. May He secure for you a livelihood with His law, with ease and abundance from His open hand and not by the gifts of flesh and blood, a vocation which would still leave you free to serve your Creator."

Today, then, I say to you, my dear son, as Moses said to his brother Aaron in your *Sidrah: K'rav el hamizbe'ach*—"come near to the altar!" You know that living a Jewish life means living a life of constant sacrifice. You cannot have all the enjoyments that others have. While other boys, who care little about Judaism, play, watch TV or loaf, you often sit and learn Torah. You cannot eat, work, or live as you would wish. As a *Shomer Shabbath* many careers which are open to others are closed to you. And once you earn your own living, a good share of your earnings will be apportioned to religious and charitable causes rather than to luxuries afforded by others. *K'rav el hamizbe'ach*—"Come close to the altar," symbolizing as it does a life full of sacrifice. For there is nothing finer, nobler and more wonderful than a Jewish life consecrated to God, as you have already begun to discover.

When Moses asked his brother to come forward to the altar, Aaron hesitated. As Rashi states: *Shehayah Aharon bush vayerah lageshet. Amar lo Mosheh, 'Lamah atah bush? Lekhakh nivcharta!*—"Aaron was bashful and afraid to come near. Said Moses to him: Why do you shy away? You have been chosen for this role." And so I say to you: Don't shy away. Plunge into the study of Torah with unbounded enthusiasm however much others may ridicule or reject it. Whatever the choice of your career, be it a doctor, a lawyer, a cobbler, or even a rabbi, remain a *Bar Mitzvah*, a practicing Jew, and become a *Ben Torah*, a learned Jew. Ascend the altar with pride and courage, conscious that *lekhakh nivcharta*, that for this purpose you have been chosen, for this reason you are the bearer of your grandfather's name, Joel.

A long time ago, the first Jewish father also took his beloved son to the altar. As Abraham and Isaac went on their journey to the sacrifice on Mt. Moriah, it was said of them, *Vayelkhu sh'neyhem yachdov*— "and the two of them went together." And as Rashi comments, *B'lev shaveh*— "with a common heart." Joel, today you become my equal in the congregation of Israel. Let it be said of us, too, "and they both went together." Let us both share together our problems, our worries, and our triumphs. As long as God grants us life, let us journey together, *B'lev shaveh*, moved by common ideals and aspirations.

And now I have two especially happy tasks. One is to present to you, as I do to all other Bar Mitzvah boys, this *Siddur* on behalf of our congregation. I know you have received many wonderful *s'farim* (books). But, I hope, this *Siddur* will occupy a special place of honor on your shelves. For it bears the inscription and good wishes of the Congregation in whose midst we have found so much happiness and friendship. This synagogue has been your second home. Here our many friends have watched you grow up. And here, through the years, you have prayed to God that He may grant you health and strength to fulfill the high hopes set on your future. Cherish this *Siddur* accordingly!

Secondly, I have given you a father's blessing as a *"birkhath hedyot."* I now have the joy and privilege to ask your revered grandfather to bestow upon you the *"birkhath kohanim,"* a blessing which you should treasure for the rest of your life. It is given by an illustrious personality who combines the sanctity of the priesthood with scholarship and piety in the tradition of the great rabbis.

Hesped Mar—A Memorial Tribute

To my beloved sister, Lotti Schonfeld, who passed
away on Tish'ah B'Av 5719, 1959.

מורי ורבותי, לא אליכם כל עברי דרך הביטו וראו אם יש
מכאוב כמכאובי אשר עלל לי אשר הוגה ה' ביום חרון אפו

> "Let it not come unto you, all you that pass by
> the way. Behold, and see if there be any pain
> like unto my pain, which is done unto me,
> wherewith the Lord has afflicted me in the day
> of His fierce anger" (*Lam. 1:12*).

THIS plaintive question baffled us on *Tish'ah
B'Av*, and today, four weeks later, we still ask *im
yesh makhov kemakh'ovi*, "is there any pain
like unto my pain?" And we still have no answer. On that
terrible Friday following *Tish'ah B'Av*, when we brought the
mortal remains of our beloved sister to her final resting place
and saw the earth open up to receive her stricken body, I
kept asking, *"mah lekohen b'veth hakvaroth"*—what does this
priestly soul do in a cemetery? How did Lotti—always so full
of life and vigor, who never knew misery or worry, replete
with understanding and compassion for others, bringing them
smiles and succor—how did she come into a *beth olam*, how
can she be eternally at rest? Our *sh'loshim* have now passed,
and we are still stunned, bewildered, and without a response
to our questions.

And yet, since then we have moved *"baderekh,"* along the
highway of life—*habitu kol ovrei derekh!* Yesterday, we
passed a new spot *baderekh,* along the same highway. Thus
we read in the *Sidrah:*

כי יקרא קן צפור בדרך... והאם רובצת על האפרחים או על
הבצים לא תקח האם על הבנים. שלח תשלח את האם ואת
הבנים תקח לך.

> "If a bird's nest chance to be before you *in the way* . . .
> and the mother is sitting upon the young or upon the eggs,

you shall not take the mother with the young; you shall surely send the mother away, and the young you shall take for yourself." On this the *Mishnah* in *Berakhoth* comments: *Ha-omer al kan tzippor vagi'u rachamekha . . . meshathkin otho.*—"If one says, 'Even to a bird's nest reaches Your mercy, O God,' one silences him," because it implies turning Divine laws meant to be absolute decrees into mere indications of God's compassion. But Rashi comments: "He who says *in his prayer*," to which the *Tosaphoth Yom Tov* adds: We silence him only if he refers to the law of the bird's nest in the course of his prayer, but by way of interpretation or practical application one is permitted to use this law. We *are* entitled to exclaim with anguish: God's mercies extend even over a lowly mother bird, a dumb creature, sitting and protecting its young ones; and here we had *ha-em rovetzeth al ha-banim,* a human mother rearing and defending her children, spreading her wings over her family. And this loving mother was torn from her little ones in the prime of life—*shalach teshalach eth ha-em*—sent away for ever, *ve-eth ha-banim tikkach lakh,* and we are asked to take her children and to bring them up without the care of their mother?!

Indeed, *im yesh makh'ov kemakh'ovi,* where else can one find such a tragedy, a young woman snatched away in the full bloom of youth, leaving a bereaved mother grieving for her cherished daughter, a widowed husband sorrowing for the beloved wife of his youth, young children turned orphans, brothers and a sister mourning for the heart of their family, a community robbed of its pride and glory? Even the *Tanakh* which recounts so many melancholy events does not record a misfortune of the kind that befell us.

Yes, as we scan the varied experiences recorded in our holy writings, we may find only one parallel. It too occurred *baderekh,* "on the way": *vatamoth alay Rachel baderekh,* "Rachel died on the way." Here too was *ha-em rovetzeth al ha-banim,* "a mother sitting upon her young" *baderekh,* being snatched away, leaving her children to others. Our Rabbis tell us Rachel died in her 37th year, and like Rachel, Lotti was also 37 years old when she was taken from her nest, her home and her community.

It is most remarkable that there is no mention of any mourning for Rachel. Even when Jacob merely feared he had lost Joseph, his sons came to comfort him, while here, at the death of his beloved wife, none offered a word of comfort or consolation to the young Patriarch in his grief. Why? Maybe there can be no comfort in the face of such adversity. There are no words of consolation to mitigate such pain. The text of the Torah itself, as it were, is rendered mute in the presence of such a blow; it pays its tribute to Rachel's short life and to the suffering of Jacob and his children in a silence more eloquent than any words could evoke.

Yet, the death of Rachel evoked a consolation more lasting and of a different kind: ויצב יעקב מצבה על קבורתה היא מצבת קברת רחל עד היום "And Jacob set up a memorial upon her grave; that is the memorial of Rachel's grave unto this day." Rachel became much more than a mere memory. She became a symbol to future generations, she was to mean more then even Sarah or Rebecca, the first mothers of our people. Upon the grave of Rachel, who had died so young, Jacob erected a monument which was to last for all times, for she was destined to become, more than any other woman in Israel, the incarnation, the personification of "mother of our people." Rachel, who had to part physically from her young husband and small children so early in life, Rachel would live on to share the sorrows and hopes of her beloved children, to comfort and inspire them for all generations. Whenever they be in trouble, *Rachel mevakkah al baneiha,* Rachel would weep over her children, as they visit her grave, *baderekh,* "on the way," as pilgrims seeking strength from their mother. There she would rise to lighten their burdens and inspire them with faith and hope in their future: *Ki yesh sakhar liph'ulatekh . . . veyesh tikvah le'acharitekh,* "For there will be a reward for your labor, and there will be hope for your latter end."

For the loss of Lotti, too, we may find no comfort, and words of consolation are meaningless. Indeed, if we cry for the suffering inflicted on those dear to her, how much more must she weep, she who loved life so intensely, who lived for her children with every fibre of her being. No one could feel the bitterness of this blow more than she whose happiness depended on the happiness of others. Our Rachel, Lotti our beloved, *mevakkah al baneiha,* she surely weeps for her children, her eyes are overfilled with bitter tears for the husband she adored so much, and her devoted heart is certainly bleeding for her precious mother. She truly feels the ache of her dear friends here and in so many parts of the world. She cries with us.

But Lotti will not remain just a fond memory to us. Upon her name will go up an everlasting monument; her life, her deeds, her love and friendship will inspire others for generations to come. We, her family, and you, her congregation, will build a home and a shrine in which her spirit and memory will be perpetuated. That home and this synagogue will become places of pilgrimage for those who have known and loved Lotti to find comfort and inspiration. Here we shall complete a monument to her greatness for which she herself laid the foundations with so much zeal and happiness. Those burdened with cares and frustrations will be cheered by the echo of Lotti's sweet voice forever ringing within these walls: כי יש שכר לפעלתך... ויש תקוה לאחריתך "There will be a reward for your labor, there will be hope for your latter end."

Lotti was so indispensable to all of us, so much part of our lives, that the future without her looks dim and bleak. When I awoke from a dazed bout of slumber on the first morning following her passing, I could not understand how the sun could rise again, how the world around us could look bright and sunny when there was so much darkness within us. But as the brother who was closest to her in age and nearest to her throughout her life, I know that, even if she now weeps with us, she will become our eternal mother of comfort. I know that she would, with all the certainty and enthusiasm of which she was capable, endorse the confident reassurance which Isaiah, the great prophet of comfort, expresses in next week's *Haphtorah:* לא יבוא עוד שמשך וירחך לא יאסף כי ה' יהי' לך לאור עולם ושלמו ימי אבלך "Your sun shall no more go down, neither shall your moon withdraw itself, for the Lord shall be your everlasting light and the days of your mourning shall be ended."

9

Sermons

Reflections on the Jewish Concept of After-Life

"This world is like an ante-chamber before the world-to-come; prepare yourself in the ante-chamber so that you may enter the main hall!"[1]

T HE theme for our reflections this morning is certainly the most difficult religious subject of all. How can one explain our belief in the world-to-come, in after-life or the here-after, to modern thinking people in our sophisticated age? Perhaps even the belief

Sermon preached before *Yizkor* on Yom Kippur 5723, October 8, 1962, at the Fifth Avenue Synagogue, New York City.

in God is a more rational concept and easier to accept than the belief in after-life, in the immortality of the soul. Surely this is purely a matter of faith. It cannot be discovered in test-tubes, proved by mathematical formulae or philosophical reasoning. There is no historical evidence for the existence of "the next world;" no one has yet returned from heaven and told us what to anticipate there.

And if this is a matter of sheer faith or blind belief, why even try to explain it? Those who believe require no convincing, and those who do not, how can they be convinced?

The problem is not unlike that of mourners stunned and perplexed by a terrible bereavement. As the sainted Chofetz Chayim once put it, for those who have faith there are no questions, and for those who have no faith there are no answers.

Yet the belief in the here-after is undoubtedly one of the cardinal teachings of Judaism, enunciated as an integral part of our faith in the Talmud and by all leading Jewish philosophers. It is implied in numerous biblical passages, such as when Balaam exclaimed: "May I die the death of the righteous, and my latter end be like his;"[2] and when Abigail told David: "And the soul of my master will be bound up in the bond of life (after his death)."[3] This phrase has become the key-note in our memorial prayer for the departed. The belief in a here-after is also taken for granted by the Preacher when he cries out ". . . And the dust returns to the earth as it was, but the spirit returns unto God who gave it;"[4] and in elegiac prayer of the Psalmist: "For You will not abandon my soul to Sheol."[5]

This belief has been derided by the ancient pagans as well as by the modern skeptics. It is related of the Greek cynic philosopher Diogenes that he instructed his students to cast his body unto a field after his death. "But ravens will consume your flesh," declaimed his disciples. "Then place a stick in my hand so that I can drive the ravens away," he answered. When the disciples argued that one cannot move after death, Diogenes retorted: "In that case what difference does it make, what do I care if the ravens eat my flesh?"

This is the same attitude that our moderns have adopted toward cremation after death. The same attitude prevails among those who advocate unlimited autopsies on the dead. For them death is the final end, denying as they do the belief in a here-after for body and soul.

I.

In my attempt to find some explanation for the here-after, I searched and found in a recent rabbinical work* an exposition which is simple and yet profound, rational and at the same time poetic in its beauty and power.

Imagine an unborn child in the mother's womb who is endowed with a fully developed mind and senses. As it lies there crouching its head between the knees and feeding on the mother's sustenance, it would doubtless regard its dark, confined space within the mother as its entire world and the period of its foetal growth as its span of life.

Now imagine there were twins, who were speculating on their fate to be. "What is to become of us after we leave the womb and depart from our universe?"

From what they see and feel around them, they could not possibly have the slightest notion of life after their separation from the mother.

Now imagine one twin has faith and claims some knowledge of a future life after leaving the mother, while the other is a skeptic, believing only what his senses and mind can perceive—only in "this world."

The first argues: "I have faith—sustained by a long tradition passed on to me—that on leaving the womb, we will enter a new life of much broader dimensions." And he tells what tradition has taught him; that on their departure, they would eat by mouth, see with their eyes, stretch out their legs and walk on the face of a vast earth, which features seas and mountains, plants and beautiful skies above.

But the other twin scoffs at this "simpleton." "Only a fool can believe all these fairy tales which the mind cannot grasp." "And according to you," asks the child of faith, "what will happen to us after we depart from the womb?" "That is simple," answers the "enlightened" skeptic. "When we depart

*See Y. M. Tucatzinski, *Gesher Ha-Chayim* (*Bridge of Life*). Jerusalem 1960, part 3, pp. 5 ff.

from this world of ours, our food supply will be cut off and we will drop into the abyss from which there is no return."

As they talked, the womb opened. The "simpleton" departs first. The "rational" twin, still inside, trembles with shock and grief at the "misfortune" that befell his brother. He cries and mourns: "Brother, where are you? Woe is me for your destruction!" As he bewails the loss of his brother, he hears a terrible shriek from his fellow-twin just outside the womb. The brother inside shakes with terror and exclaims: "Woe, this is his final agonizing death-cry as his life is snuffed out."

While this yet unborn twin grieves and wails over his brother's "death," there is rejoicing and festivity in the home of the new-born. The parents and relatives celebrate and greet each other: *"Mazal Tov, Mazal Tov—a son is born to us!"*

What a powerful illustration, this, on one hand, for our inability to grasp life beyond this finite world and, on the other hand, for the infinite life in store for us. If there is such a difference between the world of the womb and our universe, how much vaster must the difference be between our physical world and the spiritual life the soul enters on leaving the confinement of the body!

Just as the "enlightened" brother who remained in the womb could not visualize that the brother who departed from the mother did not die but, on the contrary, ventured forth into a wide world from a miniature one, so can the wisest man on earth, applying pure reason, have no conception of the soul's life after it is freed and delivered from the body at a new birth. Anyone who therefore mocks at the idea of a here-after, who maintains that the death of the body is the end, and that nothing more vast, more perfect and infinite awaits him, is like the cocksure and defiant twin inside the womb who mourned the departure of his brother from his world.

The exit from the womb is the birth of the body; and the exit from the body is the real birth of the soul. Hence the Preacher's statement, "Better . . . is the day of death than the day of one's birth."[6] This gives a rather different twist to Mark Twain's witticism: "Why is it that we rejoice at a

birth and grieve at a funeral? It is because we are not the
persons involved."

II.

Let us now venture one step further in our exploration,
not of outer space but of what is beyond it. What kind of
future existence does Jewish tradition hold forth for us? What
joys await us that moved our sages to say: "Better one hour
of blissfulness in the world-to-come than all the life in this
world"?[1]

Maimonides[7] illumines our understanding of this abstract
subject with a penetrating analogy. The blind cannot visualize colors and the deaf cannot imagine music, just as a fish
cannot have any concept of fire. Hence (elaborating the
thought of Maimonides), the joy of a connoisseur in beholding a beautiful painting of a great master can never be experienced by the blind, and the thrill of a music-lover listening to a wonderful symphony is inaccessible to the deaf.

Now, in this world our common joys are mainly physical:
delectable food, elegant clothes, material success, marital delights and the like. All these joys are non-existent in the
world-to-come which has only purely spiritual joys to offer.
As the Talmud asserts: "In the world-to-come there is no eating, no drinking, no trading, no sensual pleasures; but the
righteous sit, with their crowns adorning their heads, and
enjoy the splendor of the Divine Presence."[8] The only pleasures available, then, are the infinite joy of perceiving the
majesty of the Divine truth, justice, mercy and harmony—
the beholding of the ultimate perfection. But these pleasures
can be enjoyed only by those who have trained themselves
in this world to appreciate such joys, to be sensitive to purely
spiritual delights. To develop such sensibility requires constant intellectual and spiritual exercises on earth; it comes
to those who in their life-time have learned the supreme
fascination of religious studies, the thrill of witnessing the
triumph of right over might, the utter joy of bringing succor
to the weak and the needy, the perfect contentment springing
from faith and hope, and the happy ecstasy of contemplating
the attributes and wondrous works of the Creator.

Think of visitors to an art gallery or a concert hall. Those who have cultivated an appreciation of the arts through years of study and artistic pursuits will derive the fullest enjoyment from what they see or hear, whilst those who never indulged in such pursuits but limited their interests to idle or mundane pleasures will feel bored and lonely. So also in the world-to-come where our spiritual self will be what we have made of it while on earth. The spiritually cultured souls will reap the reward of susceptivity to the entrancement with the Divine glory around them, whilst the others will be condemned to unmitigated boredom, loneliness and disgrace for all eternity.

Yom Kippur gives us a foretaste of these purely spiritual joys in store for us. On this day we are close to the sublime state of angels. We mortify our flesh by denying ourselves our common physical pleasures. As in the world-to-come, there is today no eating, no drinking, no trading, no marital relations. The sole fascination offered by this Holy Day lies in our extraordinary religious experience, our immersion into the world of prayer and godliness, our thrill at ridding ourselves from our feelings of guilt, and our contentment at being at peace with ourselves, our neighbors and our God.

III.

There is of course also another form of immortality, one which is perhaps more easily understood than the spiritual existence in the here-after of which we have been speaking until now. It is this second expression of immortality on which we are to reflect now, as we are about to remember those dear ones who, released from the confinement of this *Alma dishikra*, "world of falsehood," have been borne into the eternity of the *olam ha'emeth*, "the world of truth," in the language of our rabbis.

Literally, it lies in our power to make our parents and ancestors immortal. My sainted father ז״ל often used to say: "Whenever I have to make an important decision in life, I ask myself: 'what would my father counsel me to do in this situation, how would he want me to act?' And so my father, though long departed, still lives and guides me just as he did when he was still among the living." By setting up our deceased parents and forebears as our constant mentors and advisors, by acting always in harmony with their way of life and wishes, we not only preserve their spirit alive, but we make them instruct and lead us from the grave as they did while on earth. They are thus no more dead than is the influence they continue to exert on us.

In this sense we also have it within our power to make *ourselves* immortal. To this day in countless Jewish homes and houses of learning one can hear such phrases as "Rashi says," "the Rambam rules," or "the *Chofetz Chayim* holds." These creative giants of the spirit still talk to us, still govern our conduct, though they left this earth long ago. The work of their lives has never ceased. They are all immortal. Likewise our life will be great and imperishable to the extent that our wisdom will inspire men, our munificence will help the poor and the sick, our vision will enlighten our successors, even after we have departed from this world.

Some of us may still exercise an influence twenty-five years after our departure, perhaps through a hospital we helped build to heal sick bodies, or a synagogue we helped erect to repair sick souls. The great among us may still be active among the living fifty years after death, perhaps through a book we wrote or children we helped to educate. The greatest in our midst may radiate their brilliance hundreds of years beyond their passing, maybe by creating a powerful movement to affect the course of history or by composing a classic work of art or literature.

But all of us, whether endowed with exceptional talents or not, the humblest as well as the mightiest, can—if we but want—become immortal and leave an indelible mark on history through the contribution of our means and energies, whether great or small, towards ridding the world of evil, substituting virtue for vice, and our indispensable share in speeding the day when the Kingdom of God will be brought down from the next world to the reality of this world when the Prophetic vision will be realized: "He will destroy death forever; and the Lord God will wipe away tears from off all faces, and the reproach of His people shall He remove from all the earth."[9]

THE CHALLENGE OF CRISIS

1. The Blessings of Fear

(Rosh Hashanah—First Day)

"Shall the Shofar be blown in a city, and the people not tremble?
"Shall evil befall a city, and the Lord hath not done it?
"The lion hath roared, who will not fear?"[10]

THIS Rosh Hashanah we need no *Machzor* to remind us that a great judgment is at hand—that the fate of humanity is in the balance. In former years we may have required some imagination or pure faith to believe that on these Days of Awe all mankind, every human being, is being judged for life or for death. Today our daily newspapers report the awful warnings of doom and destruction found in our sacred liturgy:—"And Thou openeth the Book of Remembrance, and it reads by itself." The records are open, the facts proclaim themselves. Looking down at our stricken planet threatened with a calamity of universal proportions, "even the angels are terrorized, seized by fear and trembling."

At this supremely critical moment no faith is needed to convince us that right now decisions are being made not merely on the issue of peace or war, but *mi yichyeh umi yamuth,* on the very survival or extinction of man; *mi ba'esh,* whether by the searing fire of atomic radiation, *umi bamayim,* or by hydrogen blast, *mi bara'ash,* whether by the artificial earthquake of a multi-megaton bomb, *umi bamagephah,* or by the plague of bacteriological warfare.

These are grave times. Charged to proclaim the word of God and to offer you His guidance in this period of peril and

Five addresses on the fundamentals of Judaism, delivered at the Fifth Avenue Synagogue during the High Holy days 5722–1961, when the Berlin Crisis, and the resultant tension between East and West, was at its height.

perplexity, I face a crushingly heavy responsibility. In the poet's stirring words we heard this morning in our *Shacharith* service:

"My heart grows hot the while I muse and pray,
'Tis kindled as a fiery glowing coal;
Doubts, like a tempest, agitate my soul;
For terror hath invaded us this day."

This is not the time for entertaining sermons. On these Days of Judgment, I propose not to preach, but to reason with you. The time at my disposal on a single day is too short to develop the momentous subject of man's judgment. Consequently, I will divide my talk into two parts, dealing today with the challenge, and tomorrow and on Yom Kippur with our response. During the precious hours of our devotions before God we have some hard work to do together, you and I. My task is to guide you in this work; yours to respond and cooperate with me.

I stand, as some of you may, utterly perplexed before one of the greatest riddles of all times. Here the world's leading statesmen glibly and almost casually brandish the threat of thermo-nuclear warfare, which could well reduce one half of mankind to charred bone fragments, and the other to demented cripples. Here we live at the brink of history's deepest abyss, at the capricious mercy of some power-drunk leader, who cares neither for God nor for human life, who would willingly and without any scruples sacrifice hundreds of millions on the altar of his political ambitions, and who need only order the push of one button to obliterate, minutes later, a super-city like New York so completely, that the lava-strewn ruins of ancient Pompey would look like Paradise by comparison. And yet with such diabolical devastation and universal agony staring us in the face—tomorrow or next year or the year after—we somehow remain unperturbed, relatively indifferent to our fate.

Outside the most ominous and tempestuous clouds of war ever to appear on earth are visibly gathering, while inside us there is calm, not like the calm before the storm, but in truth the calm in the hurricane's eye.

I feel this uncanny contrast within myself, and I am shocked by it, and I see it in others around me. We all carry on our lives more or less as if we were on a pleasure cruise on some distant planet.

But this is not the whole point of my riddle.

Imagine the proposed target of a devastating attack were not the whole of humanity nor even all of the United States, but just the Jewish people. Imagine some gangster with the most powerful forces at his command would threaten to drop bombs on all Jewish centers, wipe all Jewish areas, shoot at Jewish families wherever they were found.

What consternation, what an outcry, what terror there would be!

Would we not, if we could do nothing else, proclaim fast-days and hold special services of intercession which would be packed to capacity from morning to evening every day? Would there be a single Jew who would not readily give up his business or pleasure any hour of the day or night to storm the barriers between us and God and plead for mercy? Would that not be a natural instinctive reaction of a people to a fore-warning of impending slaughter?

But once the assault is aimed at all citizens of the world, not just at one selected community, we seem composed and little agitated.

Let me develop this question one step further.

Imagine you or I had a child that was very sick, and the doctors said it might die or remain a cripple for life. Could we forget that worry for a single moment? Would not the very contours of our faces betray our grave anxiety and despair?

And even if the doctors had given up hope and we ourselves could give no medical aid to our stricken child, would we not at least pray, and pray with utter devotion for the child's safe deliverance, so that we would have the satisfaction—if nothing else—of at least having done something to stave off such a tragedy? And when, under the burden of such a peril, we prayed for our child, would we not weep bitterly until our faces were swollen with tears and all other thoughts banished from our mind? Would that not be a perfectly normal reaction?

Yet, when this tragedy threatens not only some child—yours or mine—but all of us, it leaves us comparatively unaffected.

Should one not expect at a time like this that **rivers** of tears would flow in our synagogue, that frantic screams for help would accompany our prayers, that a stampede of worshippers would crush the very walls of our houses of worship?

Should one not expect that, stirred and chastened by the experience of having such a ghastly fate hanging over our heads, everyone of us, you and I, would become a little more serious and responsible in our daily conduct, that this overwhelming pressure on our conscience would find some constructive outlet and produce some tangible changes in our lives? Would you not be entitled to expect of a person like myself to study a little more every day, of how our Prophets and sages faced up to disaster, so that I might be more inspired by their lessons and inspire others as well? Would I not be entitled, conversely, to expect of individuals who might hitherto have been somewhat indifferent, to our dietary laws, for example, to resolve in this supreme emergency to uphold the Divine laws of *Kashruth* in and outside the home; or others who might have spent more on entertainment than on charity, to decide in future to respond to the cries of the needy according to their means? In short, should we not expect in these terror-ridden times that everyone would feel the urge to eliminate some of his shortcomings and to demonstrate some token of genuine repentence, even if only on the off-chance that perhaps a return to God might avert the evil decree?

It is credible, then, that in fact nothing of such a spirit of contribution is to be seen, that on the contrary some people seem to worry more about what synagogue seat is allocated to them than about the prospect of themselves and their seat being blown to bits? Is it thinkable that while threatened with such a ghoulish massacre anybody can still give a thought to petty trifles?

Now let me ask: If you saw parents whose child was critically ill, and these parents faced the prospect of the child's death or mutilation with complete abandon and equanimity—

would you not say that such parents were unfit to have the child, and deserving of what was coming to them?

Shall it be said of our generation that, if we are so unconcerned with our fate as to carry on life as usual, if in facing danger we still refuse to seek God and to pray to Him every day, that we deserve what is coming to us?

For *one* life in danger our heart would bleed, and for *millions* in danger our heart is impervious to all feelings. How can one explain this? Have we really become so callous, have we already lost our senses, our humanity, so completely that we care less about the destruction of all mankind, including ourselves and our children, than the loss of a single child? What is the answer to this riddle?

Evidently the magnitude of the threatened disaster simply staggers the human mind, stuns our senses and blunts our feelings. A Hebrew proverb says: *Tzaroth rabbim chatzi nechamah,* "Trouble shared by many is half the consolation." Perhaps, therefore, *Tzaroth kulanu kol nechamah,* "Trouble shared by all is the whole consolation."

I can find no other explanation for this inconsistency except that it is one of the most distressing limitations of our mind and heart, apparently a failing with which we are born.

Maybe this explains the Jewish emphasis on individuals, on single lives, in the creation both of humanity and of the Jewish people. Had Judaism taught that God created millions at the beginning, human life would have been without value: "Therefore a single human being was created at first," says the Mishnah "to teach you that whoever destroys one life is as if he destroyed a whole world."[57]

The same applies to the origins of our people. Our history, in contrast to that of other peoples, did not begin with the emergence of a whole nation, nor even a tribe, but with single individuals, with the Patriarchs. Their example has set the values and inspired the lives of the Jewish people throughout our history for the very reason that our attention is focused on single personalities and not on a multitude.

That was also the greatest value of the Eichmann trial. The tragedy of six million dead moved us less, with all the harrowing stories and pictures in the newspapers, than the personal accounts of a few wretched survivors who reduced the tragedy to individual persons in the witness box. Millions mean little to us; individuals mean everything.

Our first task, then, is to think of the *Olam maleh,* "the whole world," in terms of *nefesh achath,* "a single life," to individualize the danger facing us. Then we may begin to feel the pain and the agony and the terror of the situation.

For pain and adversity, too, may be a blessing. If decaying teeth would not ache us, we would never go to the dentist, to have them repaired. If acute appendicitis were painless we would never consult the surgeon and have the diseased organ removed before it bursts with its lethal contents. Instead of living with pain, we would die without pain. Pain saves lives.

Maybe if we really felt some excruciating pain from the disaster hanging over us, we would turn to the Healer of all flesh and still save our lives.

We are about to hear the shrill sounds of the *Shofar,* the siren that served as a warning signal in the far past. "Shall the *Shofar* be blown in a city, and the people not tremble?" Let it shake us out of our lethargy, let it make us tremble in fear and awaken us to reality of our situation. The fear of danger is the greatest protection against it. "When the lion roars, who will not fear?"[10] The man who is not afraid of lions will much sooner be mauled and devoured than the one who fears its violence.

But pain and fear are merely negative reactions. Today we have dealt with the challenge. *Machar yihyeh ha'oth hazeh*—tomorrow we shall begin to discuss our response to it.

Meanwhile let me conclude with Hillel's immortal counsel: "If I do not care for my own life, who will? And if I care only for myself, what am I? And if not now in this supreme crisis, when?" *Yehi ratzon shetithchadesh alenu shanah tovah umethukah,* "May it be God's will to renew unto us a good and sweet year."

2. "With All Thine Heart"—
The Meaning of Prayer

(Rosh Hashana—Second Day)

"And repentance and prayer and righteousness
avert the evil decree."

(High Festival liturgy)

YESTERDAY we considered our reactions and feelings
in the face of the present grave threat to the peace
of the world and to the survival of mankind.

You may now ask: Of what use and advantage is it even
if we are aware of the danger? What can we do, when we are
so completely impotent and defenseless? We cannot even
build an ark like Noah to ride over the waves of destruction.
The only really effective defense against modern warfare—as
against cancer or heart-attack—is prevention.

As Jews we cannot contribute atom-bombs or rockets to
the defense of peace. "Some trust in chariots and some in
horses; but we will make mention of the Name of the Lord
our God."[11] Our principal weapon is prayer. When Jacob
rescued his children from danger "with my sword and with
my bow,"[12] the *Targum* renders these words *Bitzlothı
uvera'uthi,* "with my prayers and my supplications."

So long as we believe that the world is not governed by
some blind forces of mechanical determinism, so long as we
do not surrender to the idolatry of fatalism but affirm that
there is a God who rules and guides our destiny, we must
believe in the supreme power of prayer.

If you did not believe in the efficacy of prayer, you would
not be at synagogue today. As soon as one abandons the belief in prayer, religion becomes an empty pretense, Judaism
collapses. The synagogues would then better serve as temples
of truth if converted into laboratories of science, and our
Holy Arks should be filled with test-tubes rather than with
sacred scrolls.

But the power of prayer depends upon the energy we put into it, just like the strength of a battery corresponds to the electric energy with which it has been charged. Can we supply this invincible power to our prayers?

Let me read to you the following pertinent observation of my revered father-in-law in the very opening sentences of his book *The World of Prayer:*

> "Modern man has lost the capacity to pray. Rare indeed are the individuals who can free their souls from the paralyzing apathy of our days . . . from the disastrous spell of rationalism and material-istic thought, to pray with deep devotion for the realization of the ultimate purpose in life. The worshipper is conscious neither of the comforting and purifying power of prayer nor of its elevating and ennobling effects, for prayer fell victim to a culture estranged from God and became degraded to an act of mere habit."[13]

Real prayer requires anguish, a feeling of inadequacy and nothingness in relation to God, a shaken soul, a bleeding heart. "The Lord is near unto them that are of a broken heart, and such as are broken in spirit He saves."[14] Thus the Psalmist speaks of "The prayer of the poor man."[15] This aspect of prayer is so vital that Jewish law, in a truly poignant regulation, requires of the *Chazan,* of the reader who leads the congregation in prayer, "that he shall be married and have children, so that he shall [know how to] pour out his heart and offer supplications from the depth of his heart."[16]

Perhaps our lives today are too easy to appreciate the essence of prayer. Thank God, we do not know what it means to suffer hunger, to worry whence to take tomorrow's bread for our children, to run to the synagogue on *Shabbath mevorkhim* preceding the new month and cry out for a *chayim shel parnasah,* "a life of sustenance."

We must learn again how to *daven,* how to pray properly.

There is a story of a Chasid in distress who went to his Rebbe and asked him to intercede with God on his behalf. "Rather than ask me to pray for you," countered the Rebbe, "why don't you ask me to teach you how to pray, so that you can address your pleas to God yourself?"[17]

Alas, I can neither pray for you nor teach you how to pray, I have to learn that great art myself. Let us try together, then, and study how to pray from the teachings of our faith.

Adversity itself is the best teacher. A remarkable Midrash on our biblical Rosh Hashanah readings says: "Why were our Matriarchs, the mothers of our people, barren for so long? Because the Holy one, blessed be He, desired to hear their prayers."[18] Did our rabbis really mean to suggest that God inflicted the agony of childlessness on these righteous women simply because He loved to hear them cry and plead? What sort of pleasure did God have in seeing Sarah wait desperately for the blessing of maternity until she was ninety years old, or Rachel utter her anguish *cri de coeur* "Give me children, or else I die,"[19] or Hannah weep sorely "in bitterness of soul"[20] for the gift of a child?

No, the meaning of the Midrash is that God wanted to teach them how to pray. He yearned for the kind of prayer which can come out of the depths of affliction. Moreover, our sages averred that it was on Rosh Hashanah that these three women received the promise of motherhood.[21] For it was on Rosh Hashanah, our rabbis surmised, that their prayers reached their climax. Historic men in Israel like Isaac, Joseph and Samuel are born only to parents who pray for their children with the soul-stirring fervor and desperate urgency shown by these women. That is what God craved for.

But to reach that climax in prayer on Rosh Hashana is possible only after long and regular practice. These noble women had prayed on other days, too. They had pleaded with God every day of the year, even if He answered them only on Rosh Hashanah.

A man who uses his legs only three times a year will find that he cannot walk properly even then, for his muscles will waste for lack of exercise. Similarly, he who prays only on Rosh Hashanah and Yom Kippur may find his prayers limping even on these days. Prayer requires constant exercise to be effective.

Next, prayer needs intense concentration. In the beautiful words of the Talmud, "A man's prayer is not heard unless he offers his soul with it."[22] The great Rabbi Nachman of Bratzlav, grandson of the founder of Chasidism, paraphrased these words thus: "Man must lose himself in prayer and forget his own existence."[23]

Our sages spoke of prayer as *avodah shebelev,* as "a service or labor of the heart."[24] Prayer to them meant hard work and heart-work; and a heart operation is a most delicate operation. Now imagine a heart-surgeon bending over his patient during a cardiac operation and thinking not of his work but of the fees due him the day before which did not come in. Similarly the worshipper who, while attending a Divine service, puts his mind on business matters instead of on his prayers in single-minded devotion. As a famous seventeenth century Polish preacher expressed it so felicitously: "Is this a service of the heart, when the body is in the synagogue and the mind in the market?"[25]

Prayer must spring from, and produce, a mood of ecstasy. Listen to this meaningful analogy drawn by the Baal Shem Tov: "When a person is drowning in a river and he struggles with violent motions to save his life, surely his onlookers would not laugh at him. So also, if a man prays and shakes his body whilst doing so, one should not ridicule him, for he tries to save himself from the turbulent waters of distraction which seek to divert his mind from his prayers."[26]

True prayer enlists the heart more than the brain; even the illiterate can pray with the deepest devotion. The story is told of a simple peasant who appeared before the Baal Shem Tov (the founder of Chasidism) soon after the conclusion of Yom Kippur grief-stricken that he could not join the congregation in prayer on the holy day. In weeping tones he told the great Rebbe that, as he was about to close his little store and go on his way on the eve of Yom Kippur, he was held up by some officials who engaged him until nightfall, forcing him to spend the holy day in his village which had no *Minyan.* He had no *Machzor,* nor could he read anything except the letters of the *Aleph-Beth.* Thus he sat all day broken-hearted going over the Hebrew alphabet and hoping that God would order his disjointed letters into prayers. How could he now atone for his absence from the synagogue on Yom Kippur? After listening to his tale of woe, the Baal Shem Tov placed his hands on the head of his petitioner and exclaimed: "For the past ten years no prayer as beautiful and pure as yours has ascended to Heaven."[27]

This, then, is the road of prayer. Where does it lead? What will it achieve?

To begin with, prayer strengthens us to bear our burdens and to persevere in adversity. In the touching words of the famed Yiddish writer Peretz: "Prayer sometimes dulls the hunger of the pauper, like a mother's finger thrust into the mouth of her starving baby."[28]

But prayer does more than act as a palliative. Genuine prayers are answered, too. Who has not had some experience, at one time or another, of a miracle being wrought by prayer? Let me relate my own personal experience. During my ten years in Ireland, there were three occasions, and only three occasions, when we publicly recited *Tehillim* (Psalms) for desperately ill patients. The first time it was an old man, devout and beloved by the community. He was sinking fast, and the doctors had given up all hope for his recovery. One morning, in our despair, we called the congregation together and implored God in readings from the Psalms to spare this wonderful man's life. From that very day the tide began to turn; he rallied and recovered miraculously.

Another occassion concerned a young girl, a pupil of our Talmud Torah. She had been struck by a severe attack of polio. Placed in an oxygen tent, her life ebbed visibly. The doctors told the grief-stricken parents to be prepared for the worst. Once more the congregation gathered to say *Tehillim*. Defying the medical prognosis she suddenly regained her strength and she was back at our school a few months later.

The third time it was my own child, then a few months' old baby. Dehydrated and emaciated to her little bones, she was rushed to the hospital in a pitiful state. The doctors' hopes faded as she would not respond to treatment. At the height of the crisis my friends joined in a heart-rending plea for mercy by reciting *Tehillim* together at the end of our *Shacharith* Service. The child, snatched from the Angel of Death by prayer, is in your midst today to tell the happy ending of this story.

I am by training and temperament too much of a rationalist to be usually given to mystic beliefs, and I would not relate such incidents to you if I had not been a personal witness to them.

Prayer can save not only individuals but also vast cities. The final biblical lesson we shall read on these Days of Awe is the Book of Jonah. It tells the story of an historic deliverance by prayer so topical, so exciting and so dramatic that I shall read the account of its climax to you.

"And the word of the Lord came unto Jonah the second time, saying: 'Arise, go unto Nineveh, the great city, and make unto it the proclamation that I bid you.' So Jonah arose, and went unto Nineveh, according to the word of the Lord. Now Nineveh was an exceeding great city, of three days' journey. And Jonah began to enter into the city a day's journey, and he proclaimed, and said: 'Yet forty days, and Nineveh shall be overthrown.'

And the people of Nineveh believed God; and they proclaimed a fast, and put on sackcloth, from the greatest of them even unto the least of them. And the tidings reached the king of Nineveh, and he arose from his throne, and he laid his robe from him, and he covered him with sackcloth, and he sat in ashes. And he caused it to be proclaimed and published through Nineveh by the decree of the king and his nobles, saying: 'Let neither man nor beast, herd nor flock, taste anything: let them not feed, nor drink water; but let them be covered with sackcloth, both man and beast, and let them cry mightily unto God; yea, let them turn every one from his evil way, and from the violence that is in their hands. Who knows whether God will not turn and repent, and turn away from His fierce anger, that we perish not?'

And God saw their works, that they turned from their evil way; and God repented of the evil which He said He would do unto them; and He did it not."29

The present-day Nineveh covers the entire world, all men and all beasts. To avert our doom let us Jews, as the Prophets of mankind and the Kingdom of Priests, arouse humanity to cry mightily unto God, to plead for peace with every ounce of our strength we can muster, so that our Father of mercy may have pity over His creatures and turn away from His fierce anger to grant us the supreme blessings of life and tranquility.

3. "With All Thy Mind"— Our Belief in God

(Yom Kippur—Kol Nidrei)

"And you shall love the Lord, your God, with all your heart, and with all your mind, and with all your means."[30]

UNDER the mounting stress of the present turbulent times I resolved this year to devote my addresses on these Days of Judgment to some of the fundamental teachings of Judaism rather than to any homiletical pleasantries. On Rosh Hashanah we discussed prayer which, together with repentance and righteousness, "averts the evil decree." Prayer is our response to the first call of the *Shema*—to love God with all our *heart*. On Rosh Hashanah we labored with the heart; we exercised our emotions.

Tonight, at this most solemn service of the year, we shall deal with the first requirement for salvation; repentance, return to God, as our response to the second call of the *Shema*: to love God *bekhol nafshekha*. This word in biblical Hebrew does not mean "your soul" as it is usually rendered. It actually means "your mind." Thus the Book of Proverbs speaks of a *nefesh* without knowledge: *Gam b'lo da'ath nefesh lo tov*, which can only mean: "Also, that the mind be without knowledge is not good."[31] Again, the commandment to wear the *Tephillin* upon the arm and upon the head is introduced with the words: "And you shall place these My words upon your heart (that is, facing the arm-*Tephillin*) and upon your mind." *Nafshekha* must denote "your brain" rather than "your soul."

According to Jewish law, the *Tephillin* of the head are more sacred than those of the arm or heart.[32] Paradoxical as it may sound, the heart of Judaism lies in the head. We rate Jewish thinking and Jewish knowledge even higher than Jewish feeling. Worse still than to be confined to a hospital is to be an inmate of a mental institution. There is no more precious possession than the health of the mind. Hence its spiritual welfare comes even before that of the heart in Judaism.

And so tonight we will put our brains to work; we will flex the muscles of the intellect, the mind, leaving the consideration of the third element, "righteousness," performed "with all our means" for tomorrow.

Return to God, that is to accept and love Him "with all your mind," means above all to acknowledge Him, to believe in Him. Now, the belief in God is by and large taken for granted, certainly among synagogue worshippers. What, then, is there to discuss on this subject?

But frankly, how deep and how widespread is this belief really today?

Let us first survey the belief in God on a universal scale. As God reviews this day the place of man on earth, let us review the place of God on earth. How has God's conquest of the human mind fared over the ages to the present time? The results of such a survey are not too reassuring.

There is taking place this day not only the opening of the General Assembly of the United Nations, a convocation of the leaders of peoples, but also a general assembly of all individuals populating the world to be mustered before God. As we shall read again tomorrow, "And all that come into the world pass before You as sheep to be counted."

In this "general assembly" there are more than three billion people, divided almost equally into three camps; the religiously developed, the underveloped and the maldeveloped. Perhaps just over one billion people profess the monotheistic faiths of Judaism, Christianity and Islam. Another billion, spread over vast lands in Asia and the greater part of Africa, are religious neutrals, uncommitted, neither acknowledging nor rejecting God. Their religion differs from the primitive notions of pagan antiquity.

And nearly another billion, alas, are in militant rebellion against God. Behind a curtain of iron they have built for themselves a mighty empire of science and materialism soaring into outer space, a gigantic edifice which makes the ancient Tower of Babel look puny by comparison. For the first time in history we have not only individuals but powerful states dedicated to the overthrow of all religion, states that seek to eradicate the belief in God from the hearts and minds of man as a matter of national policy. Such a *Memsheleth zadon,* such "a dominion of arrogance," is entirely unprecedented in the annals of the human race.

Worse still, what the Western world refuses to recognize and what we Jews, who brought religion into the world, should be the loudest to proclaim, is that this is the crux of the ideological struggle between West and East. Instead of fighting phantoms—social doctrines or economic systems—we should above all attack the barbaric Godlessness of our adversaries.

What we should never tire to consider is that Communism as such teaches a lofty doctrine of human equality and brotherhood; a doctrine not entirely unrelated to our Prophets' passion for social justice. How can we explain, then, that Communism has been perverted into such a diabolical instrument of oppression, that it has led to the rise of prisons engulfing almost whole continents, to the brutal destruction of all freedom, to the degradation of man into a soulless machine? How can fine ideals produce such a ghastly reality?

The answer is quite simple, apparently too obvious to be noticed: There can be no brotherhood of man without the Fatherhood of God. It is only as children of a common God that we humans are brothers. Take away the link, and the chain of human fraternity and understanding disintegrates. Dethrone God, and the dignity of man created in His image is bound to collapse. That is the true cause of all our present-day terror in the world.

Let us next examine the strength of the belief in God nearer home, in our own vaunted Judaeo-Christian civilization.

History appears to evolve in strange, uneven waves, in periodic cycles of ups and downs. The famous philosopher Whitehead asserted that the sum total of knowledge Europe had in the year fifteen-hundred was less than that possessed by the Greek scientist Archimedes in 212 B.C.E.[33] We may similarly discover that even in the West people know and care less about God in the twentieth century than they did five hundred or 1,000 years ago.

In the past few centuries God has been on a massive, unparalleled retreat—and so has, not incidentally, human happiness and security. With all the rash of beautiful new synagogue and church buildings springing up everywhere, God matters less in modern society than ever before. People resort to religion as they do to tranquilizers—to drown their anxieties. They consult clergymen as they do a psychologist—to soothe neurotic minds or to eliminate deep-seated complexes. Religion has become another hunting ground for fun, happiness and entertainment or even fashion, instead of being the inspiration for the moral discipline of life it is meant to be.

Even here, in the very country which has as its motto "In God We Trust," we live in an intellectual and cultural climate distinctly unfavorable to the healthy growth of religious beliefs and practices. Most American children spend more time every week in front of corrupting TV screens than on ennobling religious instructions; they know more about the ephemeral stars of Hollywood than about the immortal heroes of the Holy Land. Comics and science-fiction are their new Bible.

The blame for this drift has often been laid at the door of science. It is alleged that in the light of our modern knowledge about the age of the world, the evolution of man, the insignificance of our planet in the vastness of space, one can no longer believe in a Creator, in Providence, in a Divine Law. How true is this charge? How objective are the findings of science, how unprejudiced its teachings and researches?

Listen to the illuminating words of one of the most eminent scientific writers of our country. Dealing with the unsolved riddle of evolution and discussing whether life could originally have created itself, he writes:

> "The beginning of the evolutionary process raises a question which is as yet unanswerable. What was the origin of life on this planet? Until fairly recent times there was a pretty general belief in the occurrence of 'spontaneous generation.' It was supposed that lowly forms of life developed spontaneously from, for example, putrefying meat. But careful experiments, notably those of Pasteur, showed that this conclusion was due to imperfect observation, and it became an accepted doctrine that life never arises except from life. So far as actual evidence goes, this is still the only possible conclusion. But since it is a conclusion that seems to lead back to some

supernatural creative act, it is a conclusion that scientific men find very difficult of acceptance. It carries with it, what are felt to be in the present mental climate, undesirable philosophical implications. . . . For that reason most scientific men prefer to believe that life arose in some way not yet understood, from inorganic matter in accordance with the laws of physics and chemistry."[34]

"Undesirable philosophical implications"—there's the rub! What a devastating exposure of unscientific science! Scientific evidence honestly analyzed, it is admitted, points to God as the only reasonable and logical conclusion, yet it is "difficult of acceptance," for no other reason than giving some comfort and support to religious beliefs!

Where, then, I ask, is the real prejudice to be found today: with those who affirm the existence of God, and who have for so long been taunted with the charge of obscurantism and intellectual bias; or with "scientific men," who, while confessing that the conclusion of their observation leads to God, reject that conclusion because it does not fit into their preconceived notions of a Godless and soulless and meaningless nature?

Should we not, on the contrary, with all the awe-inspiring wonders and infinite marvels revealed by scientific researches, have a far more profound appreciation of God than the ancients?

Abraham had neither a telescope nor a microscope to peer into the mysteries of nature; yet he made the greatest discovery of all times, giving sense to life, meaning to existence, and purpose to history. He gazed at all the stars merely with the naked eye; yet of him it is written, "And He (God) brought him outside and said: 'Look now toward heaven, and count the stars. . .' And he believed in the Lord."[35] The Rabbis added a remarkable comment: "God took Abraham outside the orbit of the world and lifted him above the stars" (Rashi), that is, Abraham's vision transcended the bounds of the finite universe to recognize the infinite God beyond.

Today we can increase our vision of nature by countless millions not only above us but also beneath. We are able not only to see galaxies at the unimaginable distance of 2,000 million light years and endorse with millions of proofs the proclamation of the Psalmist: "The heavens declare the glory of God."[36] We can also see the glory of God revealed in a tiny pin-head, with its considerably more than a million, million, million atoms, each of them a universe of its own.[37]

Why, then, does science fight shy of drawing the logical conclusion from its ever growing accumulation of marvels? What accounts for its prejudice against religion? Why does science gain ever more devotees among our finest brains and religion lose them? Why do statements by leading scientists evoke greater respect than those of religious leaders?

The answer is simple: Science is impersonal and undemanding. It deals with things as they are, with life as it is; it wants nothing from us.

Religion, on the other hand, postulates ideals. It deals with things as they should be, with life as it ought to be lived; it points up the gap between what we are and what we should strive to become. It issues a personal challenge; it is exacting.

It is far easier to practice the religion of science than the science of religion. Science, it is hoped, will one day—if it does not destroy us before then—provide us with a life of perfect comfort and ease, rid us of all hard work and responsibilities. All we shall have to do is push buttons while sitting back in idleness to enjoy the pleasures of life in leisure unlimited. Religion asks for the hard way, offering constant criticism and never permitting any self-satisfaction.

No wonder people prefer to worship the idol of science rather than the God of religion!

We have now surveyed the belief in God among humanity at large and society in general. Let us finally turn to ourselves.

To the Jewish people, after all, this belief is the very essence of our existence. In the celebrated words of Saadya Gaon, the first ranking Jewish philosopher: "Our nation is a nation only by virtue of its Torah."[38]

To begin with, our entire concept of the belief in God is different.

There is a story of a grandson of the famous Rabbi Akiva Eger—a pillar of the *Mithnagdim*—who was "converted" to Chasidism. To imbibe the teachings of the new movement, he spent some time on a visit to the *"Chiddushei Harim,"* the renowned founder of the Gerer dynasty. On his return his father asked him: *"Nu,* what did you learn from the great

Rebbe?" "That there is a God," was his cryptic reply. "That even our non-Jewish maid affirms." "The difference is this," he explained, "she believes there is a God; I now know there is a God."

The very term "belief" is alien to Judaism. Our sacred writings speak of *d'aath Elokim,* "the knowledge of God."

To believe implies some doubt; to know is to accept a certainty. Religious belief is gained by intuition; knowledge by learning. Hence the Jewish emphasis on study, on constant learning. The way to the faith of Judaism leads primarily through the brain, not merely through the heart.

What sort of a God, then, is it we acknowledge and worship? Is it a God who is sovereign, independent, free and transcendent or a slave to the whims of man, subject to the dictates of our conscience?

We have today some large and powerful pseudo-religious movements founded on the premise that not everything in the Torah is Divine and eternal. Their theologians arrogate to themselves the right to discriminate between the laws of the Torah, picking and choosing what appeals to them and rejecting what they dislike. Ethical laws are fine and popular; these they accept as Divine. Ritual commandments are not attractive to their minds; these are consigned to the limbo of history as man-made and obsolete.

In other words, *they* decide what shall be law, not God. Their conscience makes the religion and dictates to God what shall be His will, using Him merely as a rubberstamp to confirm their notions of right and wrong. If the decision as to what our religion requires of us rests with them and not with God, why do they need God altogether? Their worship of the human conscience is idolatory, not religion; for their God is made in the image of man. He is a puppet whose strings are pulled by humans.

Our Prophets teach us to the contrary: "*He* declared unto you, o man, what is good and what the Lord seeks from you: Only to practice justice and the love of mercy, and to walk humbly with your God."[39] It is God who defines "what is good," not man.

The crux of our understanding of the knowledge of God lies in the last phrase, usually rendered "to walk humbly with God." Literally the phrase has an entirely different meaning. The Hebrew word *hatzne'a* has the same root as *tzni'uth,* which denotes something hidden or secret. *Hatzne'a lekheth im elokeikha* really means, therefore: "To walk with your God even when you are in secret, quite alone with Him."

The supreme test of our faith in God is not when we find ourselves assembled in the synagogue, but when we are alone with Him, when no one else watches.

In moments of grief and adversity, when we feel lonely and forsaken on the brink of despair, when we have been bereaved of a precious life near dear to us, *then* to be comforted by His Presence and by His promise "There will be hope for your future,"[40] *then* to vindicate His justice by proclaiming "The Rock, perfect is His work"[41] and by reciting the *Kaddish* "Sanctified and magnified be His Name. . .," thus "to walk in loneliness with God"—that is *da'ath elokim,* "the knowledge of God."

In times of temptation, when we find ourselves in secret places with the doors locked to the prying eyes of onlookers, on the verge of surrender to lust and sin, *then* to resist the overtures of passion, *then* to feel the heavy hand of shame lest we pollute ourselves, realizing that God is present—that is *da'ath elokim,* "the knowledge of God."

When we are in business, and the opportunity knocks for some gain through a little fraud or dishonesty, even if no one could ever find out, *then* to be held back by the fear of Heaven —that is *da'ath elokim,* "the knowledge of God."

The Hebrew word *da'ath* means more than mere intellectual knowledge. It also describes the most intimate relationship between husband and wife, as we read of the first humans: *Ve'adam yadah eth chavah ishto vatahar vateled,* "And Adam *knew* Eve, his wife and she conceived and gave birth."[42] Hence the Prophet speaks of the relationship between God and Israel in terms of: *Ve'erastikh li . . . veyada'ath eth Hashem,* "And I will betrothe you unto Me . . . and you shall *know* the Lord."[43] We are to be bound to God with the same bonds of love and intimacy as unite married partners. And if a man really loves his wife, he will not be faithless to her even if his infidelity cannot be discovered; he will be loyal to her in secret as well as in public. That is what the true "knowledge of God" requires of us.

That love, too, is mutual. God seeks our love: "And you shall love the Lord, your God with all your heart . . ." In return He assures us of His love even before we recite the *Shema: Ahavah rabbah ahavtanu,* "With abounding love have You loved us . . ."

On this supreme night, therefore, we plead with greater fervor and confidence than ever: "As a father has compassion over his children, so may You, o Lord, have compassion over us!"

4. "With All Thy Might" Ethics and Religion

(Yom Kippur—Musaph)

"Is such the fast that I have chosen, the day for a man to afflict himself, is he to bow down his head like a bulrush, and to spread sackcloth and ashes under him? Is not this the fast that I have chosen:

To loose the fetters of wickedness, to undo the bands of the yoke, and to let the oppressed go free, and that you break every yoke?
Is it not to deal your bread to the hungry, and that you bring the poor that are cast out to your house;
when you see the naked, that you cover him, and that you hide not yourself from your own flesh?"44

NOWHERE in the vast storehouse of the world's literature, religious or secular, is there a nobler definition of man's duty to man than in these exquisite lines from this morning's Haphtorah. What a superb introduction this is to the third fundamental requisite for "averting the evil decree"—*tsedakah,* "righteousness" and to the third faculty with which we are to love God: *bekhol me'odekha,* "with all your means."

Repentance and prayer are the indispensable foundations of Judaism. But without *tsedakah,* righteous conduct, these virtues are like a strong substructure sunk into the ground with nothing built on it. Our fasting, our religious exercises, our reconciliation with God are meaningless, unless they lead to righteous deeds.

What then is *tsedakah?* This unique Hebrew word has two meanings: Righteousness in the widest sense, and charity in the narrower sense. These two meanings are distinctly mentioned by the Prophet—". . . To loose the fetters of wickedness . . ." and "to deal your bread to the hungry . . ."

These two meanings correspond to the two major symbols of Yom Kippur: Fasting and white clothes.

"The reward of fasting is charity," says the Talmud.[45] The fast makes us feel the pangs of hunger. It makes us experience the distress of want. For once we share the pain of hunger with the poor. If tonight with the conclusion of our fast we should fail to think of those who suffer hunger because they have nothing to eat, we would have been merciless beyond words. For nothing can excuse or mitigate the cruelty of him who, having experienced what it is like to go without food for one day, does not care to help those who have to go without adequate food every day. Hence the Talmud adds "Anyone who defers the distribution of charity overnight following any fast day is as if he was shedding blood."[46] That is the plain message of Yom Kippur on the subject of simple charity.

The white clothes we wear on Yom Kippur, as the High Priest did when he made atonement for the people in the Holy of Holies, consist of the *Kittel,* the garment that will one day serve as *Takhrichim,* the shrouds accompanying us in the grave. Yom Kippur is to remind us of the time when we shall all have to accept what Judaism regards as the noblest form of charity in the wide sense: *Chesed shel emeth,* "loving kindness of truth."[47] For services to the dead are rendered without any self-interest. The dead cannot repay the kindness of the living. There can be no expectation of plaques or honors, or of services in return. Of such disinterested performance of "righteousness" in its truest sense Yom Kippur is to remind us.

Why, you may ask, does the Jewish concept of ethics, of noble conduct, require any religious support and motivation? Why can we not espouse a secular morality, like scientific humanism or ethical culture? Why is Judaism so implacably opposed to divorcing *Tsedakah* from *Teshuvah* and *Tefilah;* to isolating *Gemilath Chasadim,* the practice of good deeds, from *Torah* and *Avodah,* from religious learning and worship? Can there be no goodness without God? Do we not all know many people, Jews and Gentiles, who have warm hearts and noble souls, who liberally support good causes and who are upright in all their dealings, without worshipping God formally or even acknowledging Him?

There are three principal answers to these questions:

Firstly, absolute standards of ethics cannot exist without God. The ancient Greeks believed that it was right to expose crippled children to die in the woods so that they would not be a burden to society. To the Eskimos it is a virtue for children to kill their own parents when they become too old to maintain themselves. Many Nazis were no doubt sincerely convinced, in all conscience, that they were rendering a meritorious service to mankind by wiping out Jews and gypsies as "subhuman races" plaguing society. The Communists treasure the interest of the state more than individual freedom.

Our sense of justice condemns all these attitudes as diabolically evil. But if we affirm that good and evil are values to be determined by the arbitrary whims of one's conscience, by what right can we condemn the ethical aberrations of the Greeks or Eskimos? On what basis can we brand as immoral the murderous practices of the Nazis and Communists? Perhaps they are right and we are wrong. Have they not as much right to determine what is ethical as we do?

Human consciences are as capricious as they are diverse. What appears ethical to one may be immoral to another. The recent controversy over the Newburgh welfare code is a striking example of how human opinions based on mere conscience can divide on matters of right and wrong.

Judaism insists, therefore, that there must be a Higher Authority than man's fickle conscience to define what is ethical, that the absolute standards of right and good can be determined only in relation to the revealed will of God.

Secondly, secular ethics is inferior in quality to religious ethics.

Many great philanthropists will gladly write out checks for deserving causes; yet should some wretched beggar or *Meschulach* knock at the door of their home or office, he will be told by the maid or secretary that they are not in. Charitable people who fear God do not behave that way.

There are businessmen who enjoy the highest reputation for integrity and yet will have no qualms to treat their employees with exacting harshness, address them crudely and hurt their feelings. Truly religious persons do not behave in this manner. They know that all humans are brothers, equally created in the image of God, and they will treat the lowliest subordinate, the most menial servant, with the same kindness and consideration as they treat a millionaire friend.

How often does one hear otherwise fine and decent men say: "I am a good Jew," or "I give so much charity." This too is a flaw in a man's ethical make-up. Deeply devout people never indulge in self-praise. A refined sense of humility is their hallmark. When ethics is combined with religious faith, pride gives way to modesty, and self-esteem surrenders to self-criticism in the constant search for higher ideals.

Thirdly, and most important, secular ethics is degrading; it robs life of a supreme goal and purpose. By making success instead of service the highest aim in life, we often confuse means with ends. Life itself is subordinated to the enterprises necessary for making a living.

A well-known writer has with justice asked: "It is not possible that man will learn to conduct business without being dominated by Business? May not the future leadership in business undertakings belong to those whose vision is not limited to business success?"[48]

That surely is the deeper meaning of the witty remark made by a great eighteenth century rabbi: "Some people think of business when they are in the synagogue; is it too much to ask them to think of God when they are at business?"[49]

In the Jewish view, integrity of character is an integral part of religious piety. The practice of ethics is ennobling only if it belongs to our worship of God. For *Tsedakah* implies that the motive for all our endeavors, whether occupational or charitable, is the urge within us to serve and help each other. True *Tsedakah* calls on me to rejoice in my neighbor's success as much as in my own, for we are both engaged in promoting the common good in compliance with God's will.

We are about to intone the *Yizkor* Service. In that hallowed memorial prayer for the departed souls we make a peculiarly worded pledge. The text reads: *Yizkor Elokim eth nishmath avi mori. . . . shehalakh le'olamo ba'avur she'ani noder tsedakah ba'ado . . .,* "May God remember the soul of my revered father . . . who has passed on to his world, *by virtue of my pledge to give charity for his sake. . ."*

What is this, a commercial transaction? Does God need our reminder to remember?

No, God's remembrance requires neither a cue nor payment. Charity is meant to bring God to us. As the Talmud puts it: "He that gives a penny to the poor merits to greet the Divine Presence, as is written: 'As for me, I shall behold Your Presence in righteousness (or through charity)'."[50]

Every time we perform a good or charitable deed on earth God remembers our parents who gave birth to us and trained us to do good. By reciting *Yizkor* (lit. "He *will* remember") after making a pledge to donate charity we merely *state* that our act of kindness will redound to the credit of our father and mother in the eyes of God.

As we remember, then, our beloved kinsfolk, we are to rededicate ourselves to a life of righteousness, consecrated by religious faith, which is grounded in the Prophet's sublime promise in our *Haphtorah*: "Then shall your light break forth as the morning, and your healing shall spring forth speedily; and your *righteousness shall go before you,* the glory of the Lord shall be your reward. Then shall you call, and the Lord will answer; you shall cry, and He will say: 'Here I am'."[51]

5. The Hour of Decision

(Yom Kippur—Ne'ilah)

"And it shall come to pass, that at evening time there shall be light."[52]

I N our previous four addresses we surveyed the principal features of the edifice of Judaism. I tried to take you on a guided tour through the magnificent structure of Jewish thought, and to discover how to enter this palace through the portals of our heart, our mind and our might.

Now at the climax of the day, in this hour of *Ne'ilah,* this brilliant edifice will be floodlit in all its resplendent glory for the last time. In but a short while, the lights will go out, *Be'eth ne'ilath sha'ar,* the gates will be shut, barring entry and exist.

Shall these gates of the sanctuary of Judaism be locked before or behind us? Shall we stay within or without for the rest of the year? That vital decision we must make now, within the next hour, while the gates are still open.

Shall the palace we have seen, the sanctuary we have visited today, be a museum or a residency? Shall our prayers and observances, the religious insights and inspiration we have gained, be archaic exhibits or part of real life?

This is the challenge of this holy *Ne'ilah*-hour.

I am not an evangelist to prompt you into a declaration of faith in God by coming forward from your seats. That decision must be made inside your heart. But decide you must, here and now, before the gates are shut and the lights extinguished.

Conscious of the grave responsibilities resting on me as the spiritual pilot of our congregational ship in these tempestuous, perilous times, I tried my best to pass on to you, my crew and passengers, the basic life-saving rules on how to prevent our ship from foundering. Some may disembark this evening, but the cruise of this ark of life goes on. I shall remain behind on its bridge. I shall be here in our precious synagogue, God willing, more or less every day—every Festival, every Sabbath, every weekday. And should there be any vacant seats, the blame will be mine. Pointing at those unoccupied seats, God will hold me to account: "Perhaps you did not preach forcefully enough on Rosh Hashanah and Yom Kippur when you had the chance of the year. Maybe your arguments did not carry sufficient conviction, or your own enthusiasm was not impassioned and contagious enough." So long as I am your spiritual guide, I am responsible and held to account for your religious shortcomings. I have enough shortcomings of my own; I plead with you, therefore, do not let these charges be added to my already overdrawn account.

But far more than my own fate before the judgment of Heaven depends on your response. The fate of all mankind is at stake.

Let no one say, what difference can one little congregation, or even a few individuals, make to the fortunes of the world. On account of one man, Jonah, who abandoned his Divine mission and slept in a moment of extreme danger, a whole ship with all its passengers was brought to the brink of disaster. And thanks to that same one man, an entire vast city was eventually saved from utter destruction. So many owe so much to so few!

Maimonides expresses this thought in striking fashion: "A person should always look upon himself as if he were half innocent and half guilty. Similarly, he should regard the whole world as evenly balanced between merit and guilt. Hence, if he commits a single sin, he tips the scale of guilt for himself and for the entire world, bringing about his and its doom. But if he performs a single good deed, the scale of merit is overbalanced and he causes salvation and deliverance for himself and for mankind."[53]

Never has this profound moral teaching been truer than today, when the fate of mankind literally hangs so precariously in the balance. Who knows whether our resolve to place a little extra virtue into the scale of merit may not be decisive in securing a verdict of survival for the whole human race? Never before in history may so much depend on so few!

The great day is now about to close in a crescendo of the spirit. During the hours of contemplation on Rosh Hashanah and Yom Kippur we have tried to learn *Mah Hashem doresh mimkha*—"what the Lord seeks from us." But religious experience is meant to be a perpetual dialogue between God and man. In addition to what God demands from us, we have also articulated our demands from him.

And so, for the past ten days, we have listed our needs and pleas in the *Avinu Malkeinu* prayer addressed to "our Father, our King." In this prayer we ask God for forgiveness, for a good new year, for the removal of evil, enmity and suffering, for health, for life, for sustenance, for national redemption and for the acceptance of our prayers. Finally, at the very end of the prayer we plead: "Our Father, our King! be gracious unto us and answer us, for we have no good works of our own; deal with us in charity and kindness, and save us." This last note, because it refers to us as undeserving, is customarily recited in silence.

The Maggid of Dubno relates the following story to explain this *sotto voce* custom: A man once went to a large store where, going from counter to counter, he picked a great number of precious and expensive items he wished to own. Having collected his big assortment of beautiful wares, he asked for the manager. Embarassed at his inability to pay, he whispered to the manager, "I want these articles, but I am afraid I have no money to pay for them. Will you please extend to me sufficient credit so that I can purchase them."

Similarly, said the Dubno Maggid, we first place a tall order for God's gifts. There is not a blessing for which we do not ask. Then, at the very end we tell God in a whisper: "But I am afraid I have no good deeds to pay for these blessings; so please, God, be charitable and extend me some credit."

Of course, our merciful Father will grant us credit. But He takes us on trust, confident that, even if we are now unworthy of receiving all the blessings we asked for, we will endeavor by good deeds and piety to merit the life, health, peace and happiness He bestows on us in the meantime.

That is why we are to rejoice, as Yom Kippur dismisses us to our daily pursuits in the weeks and months ahead. The atmosphere of solemnity and grave anxiety of the Days of Judgment gives way to feelings of confidence, triumph and jubilation. The laws of Yom Kippur, with all their exacting regulations about praying, fasting, and self-denial, themselves conclude on this cheerful note, "One should eat and drink and rejoice at the conclusion of Yom Kippur, as the Midrash[54] avers: When Yom Kippur ends, a Heavenly voice goes forth and proclaims: 'Go, eat your bread with joy, and drink your wine with a merry heart; for God has already accepted your works'."[55]

THE GREAT REVOLUTIONS OF OUR AGE

1. The Human Rights Revolution

(Rosh Hashanah—First Day)

AMONG the convulsions that have changed the face of our post-war world few are more thrilling and dramatic than the revolutionary movements in quest of human equality.

Throughout history, mankind has been divided into ruling peoples and subjugated peoples, empires and colonies, masters and slaves.

Now, within only twenty eventful years, all this has radically changed. The drive for equality has become the most potent social and political force of our times, perhaps of all times.

Scores of nations, even in the world's darkest and longest-dominated regions, have suddenly thrown off the shackles of colonialism and have been raised to independence, ranking as equals in the family of nations with countries as powerful as the United States or Great Britain.

At the same time, our country is astir with the cries of millions of disenfranchised citizens demanding equality in status, in opportunity, in education and in jobs.

Five addresses delivered at the Fifth Avenue Synagogue during the High Holy days 5724-1963.

These momentous developments may well mark one of the most decisive and constructive turning points in the history of human relations.

To Jews this historic turn of events should occasion special rejoicing and gratification, and particularly on Rosh Hashanah, man's birthday. For the subject of equal rights for all men as children of God created in His image is the historical significance and major theme of this festival. We celebrate today the 5724th anniversary of the brotherhood of man!

It was, after all, our Prophets who proclaimed thousands of years ago the doctrine of the unity of man, when it was still unheard of among the peoples of the earth: "Have we not all one father? Hath not one God created us? Why do we deal treacherously every man against his brother, profaning the covenant of our fathers?"[56]

We have recently witnessed the March on Washington, the first mass demonstration for human equality ever held. We Jews have marched on our synagogues for countless centuries, every year, every Rosh Hashanah and Yom Kippur, to hold demonstrations for human equality. Our people, our saints and our sinners, men, women, and children, have for millennia past dreamt and prayed for the day when, in the exalted words of our festival liturgy: ". . . all humans shall form one band to perform Thy will with a perfect heart." We have proclaimed annually for many centuries at our most solemn services: "And all believe that He is soft to reconcile, the Great Leveler Who renders equal the small and the great."

What is happening today represents the greatest and most universal consummation of Jewish ideals, the most dramatic realization of Jewish teachings, brought to the world by a hundred generations of Jewish history and cultural pioneering.

We can appreciate how distinctly Jewish this concept is when we contrast conditions here with those in Israel. More has been achieved in one decade in Israel to integrate the most diverse cultural elements—white with colored, untutored with highly educated immigrants, than has been accomplished here in a century! In Israel no police force is required to secure the admission of dark Yemenite or Moroccan children to schools; no citizen is debarred from houses of worship, or denied his right to vote. None is segregated in public or private places because of his color; whereas here and in South Africa, governors and governments, churches and universities are still in the forefront of the losing battle to maintain segregation and apartheid.

But why travel so far across the nation to the Deep South, or across the Atlantic to a distant land? Right here, next door, in my own apartment building, and presumably in many others in the neighborhood, colored people are still forbidden to ride in the front elevator, unless saved from their degradation by the company of a white child!

The great revolution, then, has only begun, and it may yet take decades or generations until it is completed. For this is necessarily a slow and painful process which cannot be successfully accomplished overnight in the face of eons of prejudice, ignorance, hatred, and cultural cleavages.

What is needed is infinite patience no less than vision and fortitude until all men will appreciate and cherish the supreme meaning of this day, expressed so profoundly in the Mishnah dealing with of the worth of every individual human being: *Lephikkakh nivrah adam yechidi . . . shelo yomar adam lechavero abba gadol me'avikha,* "Therefore was man originally created as a single being . . . that no man should say to his fellow 'My father is greater than yours'."[57]

This classic statement epitomizes the characteristic difference which still distinguishes the Jewish position from that of our civil rights movements and from the popular attitude in general. Our ideal is that no man should say to his neighbor "My father is greater than yours." It does not state that only one human being was created as the progenitor of all mankind in order that every man may claim "My father is *as great as* yours," but rather that people shall *not claim* "My father is *greater than* yours."

In other words, it is not the one who feels *inferior* who shall *claim* equality, but the one who feels *superior* who shall *grant* equality. The emphasis is on respecting the equal status of your neighbor, and not on his right to demand equal status with you.

In Jewish thought, we never speak of human rights, only of human duties. We list the teachings of Judaism as *Mitzvoth,* as commandments, not as *zekhuyoth*, as rights. We put the onus of righteousness on the giver, not the taker. We teach people not to think in terms of what they may *demand from others*, but of what they *owe to others*. Here lies exposed one of the main curses afflicting our age: people talk more of rights than of duties; they are concerned more with what they can get out of life than what they have to put ino life. Even in Jewish congregations there are many who are interested more in what the synagogue should do for them than in what they should do for it.

Judaism teaches that we cannot enjoy any privileges until we first attend to our obligations, that human rights will not be a universal reality until we first think and act on our human duties.

With all our enthusiastic espousal of human equality, however, we must recognize that there is also a negative side to this ideal. To exaggerate the scope of equality is as dangerous as to minimize it. Indeed, a distorted over-emphasis on human equality may well be the cause of some of the great problems facing our society.

The very Mishnah which posits the equal status of all men as the reason for the creation of a single human being in the beginning, also utilizes this fact to teach the infinite variety of men: ולהגיד גדולתו של הקב״ה שאדם טובע כמה מטבעות בחותם אחד וכולן דומין זה לזה, ומלך מ״ה הקב״ה טבע כל אדם בחותמו של אדם הראשון ואין אחד מהם דומה לחברו. "(And therefore man was originally created as a single being) . . . to tell the greatness of the Holy One, blessed be He; for if man strikes many coins from one die, they are all equal to each other, but the King of Kings molded all humans from the die of the first man (Adam), and yet not one of them is like his fellow." While man-made articles mass-produced from a single prototype are all alike, God's creatures, though reproduced from a single individual, are all different. No two human beings are identical. The descent of all men from one common ancestor thus testifies, on the one hand, to the equal status enjoyed by all and, on the other hand, to the incomparable uniqueness of the Creator in making mankind so infinitely diverse that out of the billions of humans no two are alike.

There is no contradiction here. The two statements complement each other. All human beings *have* basically equal rights and equal duties. But they *are* not equal, nor are they meant to be. On the contrary, the miracle of creation is that no two people are alike. We are all different in looks, in disposition, in character and in intellect. The same applies to nations. No two of them are the same in their national characteristics, achievements and purposes.

This endless diversity is precisely the spice of life. Ludwig Boerne once said: "Where only equals meet, boredom will soon preside, and stupidity will serve as secretary."

It is this diversity which, in our misplaced overexuberance for human equality, is bound to give way under the inexorable pressure of the steamroller of uniformity. Such misguided addiction to equality expresses itself, particularly in America, in many forms—from such trivia, say, as fashions, to fundamentals, as school education.

Let some celebrity start a new fad or fashion, and everybody will want to copy it, until all look alike like a row of ninepins.

Again, at the other end of the scale of values, many of our most powerful personalities and organizations are committed to the shallow principle that all American children should be educated alike, that only the uniform type of public schools should be deemed legitimate and deserving of state support.

Instead of giving people equal rights and duties, they want to *make* everyone equal, shape them all alike, put them all in the Procrustean bed of conformity and dull monotony.

A passage in the Talmud declares: לא חרבה ירושלים אלא בשביל שהשוו קטן וגדול, שנאמר כעם והי' כהן וכו' "Jerusalem was destroyed only because they made equal the small and the great, as it is written 'and it is like people, like priest'."[58] This perverted doctrine of equality—seeking to level out all differences, making alike the great and the small, priest and people, leader and follower, saint and sinner, one religion and another—was responsible, according to our sages, for the decline and fall of Jerusalem!

A society raised along one pattern is as prone to collapse as a building erected on a single pillar, and as useless as a machine made only of equal parts.

Scientific support for this fundamental point was only recently discovered and underscored. At the International Congress of Genetics an outstanding scientist-philosopher urged that greater attention be paid human genetic diversity than to human equaliy. The report continued:

> "As our understanding of genetics increases, we shall, I believe, see that society is freest in which opportunity for acting according to one's genotype (hereditary makeup) is maximized."
> He declared that no attempt had yet been made under either capitalism or socialism to place people in society so that they would be happiest and most efficient. One reason for this failure, he suggested, has been the preoccupation with asserting racial or national homogeneity and neglecting the fact of intrinsic human inequality.[58a]

As Jews we have a special stake in seeing the desire for human diversity maintained and encouraged. We cannot preserve our identity and religious distinctiveness except in a society which looks on diversity not as a bane but as a boon, not as an impediment to national greatness but as an enrichment of national life.

We cannot be creative in an environment which regards swimming against the stream as unpatriotic. The right and willingness to be different are the very warp and woof in the fabric of Jewish survival.

We have already sacrificed millions who defected from traditional Judaism on the altar of conformity. We *want* equal obligations and privileges, but we do *not want* to *be* equal.

These two aspects of human equality and diversity make up the content of this festival's most superb prayer, the *Aleinu,* a prayer so fundamental and exquisite that it has been borrowed from the Rosh Hashanah liturgy to accompany us every day of the year as the concluding climax of all our services. This is the prayer with which countless Jewish martyrs throughout our history have gone to their death because they were denied equal *rights* and because they yet refused to *be* equal, insisting that to live a life like others was not worth living.

This noble prayer begins, *Aleinu leshabe'ach la'adon hakol,* with "our duty to praise the Master of all," to render thanks to Him *Shelo asanu kegoyei ha'aratzoth velo samanu kemishpachoth ha'adamah,* "for *not* having made us like the nations of other lands, and *not* placed us like unto others in the human family on earth," acclaiming our Creator, *Shelo sam chelkenu kahem*, "for *not* having set our portion like theirs," *Vegoraleinu kekhol hamonam*, "*nor* our lot like that of their multitudes." For this favor we bend our knees and bow and thank God today and every day. We are happy and grateful for being different and distinct.

But at the same time *nekaveh lekha . . . lir'oth meherah*, "we express the hope . . . that we may soon see" the acknowledgement by all men alike of their common duty *Lethaken olam bemalkhuth shaday*, "to establish the world under the Kingdom of the Almighty," *Vekhol bnei basar yikr'u bishmekha*, "when *all* the children of flesh will call upon Thy Name," *Yakiru veyed'u kol yoshvei tevel ki lekha tikra kol berek tishava kol lashon*, "when *all* the inhabitants of the world shall recognize and know that unto Thee every knee must bend, every tongue must swear."

Then and only then, through diversity of life and unity of purpose, will the day dawn when *Vehayah Hashem lemelekh al kol ha'aretz bayom hahu yiheyeh Hashem echad ushemo echad*, "the Lord shall be King over *all* the earth, in that day shall the Lord be One and His Name be One."

2. The Scientific Revolution

(Rosh Hashanah—Second Day)

O F all the massive upheavals rocking our age, the scientific revolution is certainly the most spectacular. In historical perspective it may not prove to be the most momentous. The political, social and religious spasms of our time may well leave more lasting effects on the future history of mankind. Yet the exploits in science have captured our imagination most.

Characteristically enough, ours is an age designated, not by a political or social name, but by a scientific name. It is not called the Age of the United Nations, or the Age of Human Rights. The name it bears is the Atomic Age, the Space Age, or the Nuclear Age.

Our entire economy and social thinking are geared to science. We have crash programs not to train wiser statesmen or better politicians, but to produce more and better scientists. We do not engage in international competitions to reduce crime or divorce rates, but in a race to the moon.

Some have compared the exploits of our age to the vainglorious pyramids the Egyptians built, and our astronauts to the gladiators of old, turning our world into a huge and expensive circus in which governments display breathtaking shows and all humans are the thrilled spectators. And who knows whether, like the ancient pyramids and gladiators, our modern artifacts and actors will not also deal death and house the dead rather than assure and beautify life?

To religion, and to Judaism in particular, the spectacular rise of science is a matter of special concern.

There is no day more appropriate for discussing our relations with science, the study and exploitation of nature, than Rosh Hashanah. For *Hayom harath olam*, "this is the anniversary of the universe," the birthday of nature, no less than *Hayom ya'amid bamishpat kol yetzurei olamim*, the anniversary of man's birthday and his common origin, about which we spoke yesterday.

As Jews we have never shied away from scientific inquiry or shunned the study of man and the universe. On the contrary, for us the pursuit of science became a religious precept: *Minayin shemitzvah al adam lachashov tekuphoth umazaloth, shene'emar ushmartem va'asithem ki hi chokhmathchem uvinathchem le'einei ha'amim*, "whence do we know that one is religiously obliged to conduct astronomical research? From the verse, 'For this is your wisdom and your understanding in the eyes of the nations'."[59] We value science so highly that we are required to recite a special benediction at the sight of an outstanding scholar or scientist, be he Jewish or non-Jewish: *Barukh . . . shenathan mechokhmatho liberiyothav*, "Blessed be He . . . Who gave of His wisdom to His creatures."[60] Nature study is part of our religion, for it is the means by which to appreciate the grandeur of the Creator, even as we know the artist by his work: *Hashamayim mesaprim kevod el*, "The heavens declare the glory of God."[61]

But modern science attempted more than just investigate the laws of nature and harness them at the service of man. It became a rival and antagonist of religion. It pontificated on the origin and destiny of man with cock-sure confidence; it eliminated God, reduced man into a freak product of chance, and enthroned reason as the supreme deity. It spoke in accents of arrogance and with a finality and infallibility which even the most inspired prophets never used. "Science says" became the new dogma, replacing "Thus sayeth the Lord."

As a new philosophy of life, this worship of rationalism promised the millennium. In this vaunted age of rationalism, so its early devotees believed with a faith worthy of better causes, science would answer all questions; there would be no more wars, and the brotherhood of man would be a reality. Psychoanalysis would even rid us of all feelings of guilt and anxiety. Peace would rule inside and outside us.*

Alas, it did not work. The promises remained unfulfilled.

In a phrase we repeat constantly during this penetential season we say: *Sarnu mimitzvotekha umishpatekha hatovim velo shaveh lanu,* "we have departed from Thy commandments and good laws, and it hath not profited us." The flight from religion did not pay off.

Science has not removed the specter of war, it has not reduced the divorce rate, it has not decreased crime and juvenile delinquency, it has not contributed to human happiness or security. Science has not proved a substitute for religion.

Perhaps this is just as well. If science had succeeded in making true its exaggerated claims as the panacea for all our ills, religion would have ceased to exist in the hearts of man.

Instead, religion has made an amazing come-back. Many of the 19th and early 20th century apostles of science, who

*A week after delivering this sermon, I found some of these thoughts re-echoed in "Skeptical Look at 'Scientific Experts'" by David E. Lilienthal, *The New York Times Magazine,* September 29, 1963: "The evidence increases that we are in the midst of a crisis in the scientific community. . . The crisis of confidence has its roots in concern that scientists and other experts . . . have more and more been seeking to use methods applicable to the physical world in areas of the world of men that are beyond the reach of such methods: human goals and purposes. . . Many of the most noted of these experts and specialists have departed from their own fields of competence with a cocksure confidence that they can find answers—out of their scientific or technical knowledge or intuition—to what cannot be finally and firmly answered at all. . . ."

poured such scorn on religion, would turn in their graves if they knew how many of their dogmas have been debunked and how powerful religion is again after all its tribulations in the past one hundred years.

Today science speaks in more humble tones. It knows it produced more questions than answers. What were once laws have become theories, and theories have turned into hypotheses. The ultimate mysteries of life and its meaning have not been unraveled; the limitations of science are today better realized than ever before.

The relationship between science and religion, between God's creation of matter and spirit, is well illustrated in a fascinating Midrash. When God created the world with words *Bereshith bara elokim* ("In the beginning God created"), starting with the letter *"Beth"*—the second letter of the Hebrew alphabet, the first letter, *"Aleph,"* complained: "Why did You pass me over, creating the universe with the second letter instead of beginning the creation with me, the head of all letters?" But God reassured the *"Aleph"*: "By your life, your time will come; I have reserved for you an even greater act of Divine creation. For when I will reveal Myself at Sinai to proclaim the Ten Commandments, I will start with you: *Anokhi Hashem,* ("I am the Lord, thy God").["][62]

What is the meaning of this apparently childish dialogue between God and a letter of the alphabet?

The Midrash teaches that the creation of heaven and earth, the wonders of nature with all its mysteries and unfathomable forces, the vastness of the universe and the marvels of the countless myriads of atoms composing it—all this is merely the "B" of Divine creation. Greater and more wonderful still than any material creation, the "A" and the primary demonstration of God's creativity, is what occurred at Sinai, when He proclaimed the purpose and meaning of everything He had called into existence, when He laid down the moral law which was to govern His creatures and make their lives worth living. Heaven and earth and all that fills them are only the means, the laws of nature reveal merely the secondary aspect of God's glory; the ultimate end is the fulfillment of God's will, the primary revelation of His majesty lies in the

Torah, in the laws epitomized by the Ten Commandments, for the sake of which everything else was called into being and sustained in life.

Let us apply this supreme lesson to our own situation today. Let us translate this penetrating Midrash into contemporary terms.

We marvel today with boundless admiration at the ingenuity of the human intellect for its capacity to devise and construct a little sphere, hurl it into space and there make it travel on its predetermined orbit, girdling the globe at an incredible speed for hours, days or even years. If we marvel at that—as we should—what shall we say of an entire people which, over three thousand years ago, launched into the space of history ideas and ideals which continue to this day to orbit the earth, bringing not the threat of destruction, but inspiration, comfort, decency and holiness into millions of homes in every civilized country throughout the world, what shall we say of such a colossal achievement? We admire man's stupendous scientific and technological strides; but what are these compared to the gigantic efforts of a whole nation, through centuries of pioneering and martyrdom, to sustain and spread the ideals of morality, social justice and universal brotherhood, to devise and implement the one formula which has eluded all our scientists and technicians so far—how to build two homes next to each other so that peace will rule between them and harmony inside them?

What is demanded of our generation, if it is to restore its sense of values, is that in our dazzling admiration for our material and physical accomplishments we cease to be blinded to the incomparable achievements of the spirit, that we honor our saints and thinkers at least as much as our scientists and entertainers, that we recognize the primacy of the Ten Commandments in securing human peace and happiness over the countdowns of our rocket-launches.

This true relationship between spirit and matter, between man and machine, between moral power and physical force, is symbolized by the *Shofar* we are about to sound.

This *Shofar* is, admittedly, an ancient instrument. It is plain, natural and unsophisticated. There is nothing artificial about it. Nor has its shape or sound changed for millennia.

Yet this simple little instrument has the power to summon more people together than all the greatest orchestras in the world combined. This humble *Shofar* can stir the conscience, move hearts, arouse us to our duties, more effectively than the most refined musical instrument invented by science.

What is the mystic power of the *Shofar?* What is its magnetic appeal outlasting the ages?

Its secret, like the secret of Judaism, is that it brings us the sounds of eternity.

It is the same ram's horn which marked the beginnings of Jewish history when Abraham substituted for his son on the altar a ram caught by its horns in the thicket. It is the same *Shofar* that our ancestors heard at Sinai to herald history's most momentous event. It is the same *Shofar* whose sounds rang through the halls of the Temple in Jerusalem. It is the same *Shofar* that sounded a warning signal whenever our people were in danger. It is the same *Shofar* which for thousands of years and for untold millions of Jews has given a foretaste of the *Shofar gadol,* the great horn, which would proclaim the time when והי' ביום ההוא יתקע בשופר גדול ובאו האובדים בארץ אשור והנדחים בארץ מצרים והשתחוו לה' בהר הקודש בירושלים "And it shall come to pass on that day, that a great horn shall be blown; and they shall come which were lost in the land of Assyria, and they that were outcasts in the land of Egypt; and they shall worship the Lord in the holy mountain at Jerusalem."[68]

3. The Religious Revolution

(Yom Kippur—Kol Nidrei)

HAVING considered the human rights and scientific revolutions, we will now turn to the religious and moral upheavals of our contemporary society.

The businessman who may remain indifferent to the upturns and downturns in enterprises other than his own, will doubtless become intensely interested and personally involved in the security values affecting his own stock.

Our Jewish national business is religion and morality. They are the bread and water of our very existence. As we read in our prayers tonight and every night: "For they are our life and the length of our days." We should follow the fortunes of religion anywhere as we follow the ups and downs of stocks we own, for all our national wealth is invested in religion.

If to others, therefore, the religious revolution of our time may be of secondary interest, less exciting than the adventures in space and the crises in race, to us Jews the epoch-making changes in the past twenty years in the affairs of religion in general, and Judaism in particular, must be the most dramatic and important events of our age.

These changes are certainly no less drastic and unprecedented than those which have swept away the pre-war notions of science and human relations. They are no less revolutionary.

Let me illustrate some of the most significant aspects of these changes by relating two stories of R. Levi Yitzchak of Berditchev, the great Chasidic Rebbe of the 18th century who was a saint in his lifetime and became a legend in his death for his daring arguments with God in defense of Israel. The first story is based on the rabbinic law making it a special *Mitzvah* to eat and drink festively on *Erev Yom Kippur* just as it is our duty to fast on Yom Kippur.

It was on the Eve of the Holy Day. The congregation was assembled in the synagogue, awaiting to hear the solemn chant of *Kol Nidrei*. R. Levi Yitzchak was not in his customary seat. Holding a lit candle, the Rabbi was seen moving from bench to bench, as if in quest for something he might have lost . . . The worshippers, startled at this activity, asked their leader: "Rabbi, what are you doing?" "I have been looking for one inebriated Jew, but I find none." Thereupon he ascended the pulpit and exclaimed: "Lord of the Universe, who is like Your people Israel, chosen and holy? Where else would you find a people which, commanded to eat and drink, to feast a little more than usual, would not yield a single drunkard? Yet the ruling that an extra portion of food and drink should be consumed on the Eve of *Yom Kippur* yielded not one Jew who was soused. All partook of extra portions of food and beverages, after which they hastened to the synagogue. Not one Jew is drunk or fatigued. All are sober and holy. All are ready for the pains of hunger and the privations of this sacred fast, willing to confess their sins before You and repent with a contrite heart. Surely they are worthy of Your forgiveness and to be inscribed in the Book of Life!"

If we had a R. Levi Yitzchak today, he might under different circumstances exclaim: Almighty God, take a look at Your unique people of Israel. Consider the immensity of the tragedy they had endured in the past generation. They were struck by the greatest of catastrophies ever to overwhelm any people. They lost six millions in history's worst slaughter. One-third of their entire people perished, the segment which represented our people's most fertile seed. With their death, the reservoirs of Jewish learning and piety were dried up and the strong-holds of Jewish tradition wiped out.

Any other nation would have turned into an army of cynics and desperate radicals under the stress of such fearful blows. They would have lost faith in Divine justice, rebelled against a God Who betrayed them, and turned their back on a religion which should have disintegrated with the blood of its finest sons.

Yet the remnant of this people is tonight assembled by the millions in Your sanctuaries. There is not a Jewish community anywhere without a service to Your glory this night. What a people, what an indomitable faith, what a miracle of religious might!

And R. Levi Yitzchak might have continued: Look at the Jewish people in the Western lands, especially in affluent America. Never before have Jews lived in such comfort and security. Never in history have they been exposed to such temptations to give up their ancient rituals and traditions, never have they been subjected to greater pressures of assimilation and conformity.

From within, dissident movements have been gnawing at the roots of the old tree, ready for the kill, confident that Orthodoxy could not survive. Already in 1924, a Reform Jewish magazine had declared: ". . . Orthodoxy in Judaism is something like snakes in Ireland. . ."* They were convinced that the remnants of Torah Judaism would be swept

*CCAR Year Book, 1924, p. 238.

away for good with the slums of the Lower East Side, especially once the supply of traditionalists immigrants from Europe was cut off for ever.

And now, look at the miracle of revival that has taken place. These "doomed" traditionalists have made a fantastic comeback with a vengeance. Today Orthodox Jews are installed on Fifth Avenue hitherto a preserve for Reform Jews. They control virtually all Jewish day schools throughout the country. They raise tens of millions of dollars annually to sustain the most comprehensive system of Jewish education ever known in modern times, superior to anything seen even in pre-war days. Today more than 60,000 American-Jewish boys and girls study Torah more intensively and for longer hours than any group of students pursue their professional studies at any university. We now have flourishing organizations of Orthodox scientists and Orthodox college students, units that scarcely existed ten or twenty years ago. Kosher meals are served increasingly in elegant hotels and to travelers on planes and ships—and, one hopes, soon even in Jewish hospitals. Despite our terrifying losses in Eastern Europe, the proportion of observant and learned Jews in the world today is probably as great as it ever was in modern times.

Two events during the past year highlight this amazing resurgence of traditional Judaism. One was the biggest mass-demonstration in tribute to a single Jew ever seen in America. Tens of thousands of Jews, mostly young, massed in the streets of New York to bid farewell to the mortal remains of Rabbi Aaron Kotler זצ״ל, the foremost rabbinical sage of our time. No Jewish leader, no Jewish statesman, philanthropist, nor the most popular Jewish celebrity or most outstanding Jewish scientist, ever received such honors. It was a manifestation of Orthodox strength which percolated into the daily press in long reports and impressive pictures the like of which had never been seen before.

The second event happened recently in Israel, where well-organized groups of young "activists" staged simultaneous demonstrations in three cities against the missionary schools luring Jewish children from destitute homes away from our people and religion. We may or may not agree with the methods used, though we now know that, contrary to the tendentious newspaper reports, there was no violence of any kind. Nor was the action undertaken by "fanatics," as alleged. Mainly these were moderate students from the Zionist-oriented Yeshivoth. In any case, there is no Jew harboring a spark of Yiddishkeit who did not leap with joy and pride that we still have in our midst doughty young Jews for whom *shemad,* apostasy, is the most horrifying word in the vocabulary, whose hearts bleed with grief and outrage at little Jewish children who, after having escaped from the clutches of persecution to find refuge in the Holy Land, are torn from their faith. It is a grim case of distress, poverty and ignorance being exploited for the purpose of spiritual kidnapping in their own land. We hear so much these days of the lost generation, about young Jews who do not care for the sanctities and beliefs of their people, who do not care for any Jewish values, and for whom neither intermarriage nor even *shemad* evokes any more the terror it did in the past. How great should be our joy, then, that we once more have young men who militantly defend our most precious possessions, and expose themselves to prosecution and humiliation in order to arouse the conscience of our people.

With the world-wide statistical increase of Orthodox Jews— resulting from a relatively high birth-rate, a low assimilation rate, and their massive conversion of other Jews—at many times the rate of the assimilationists, a new R. Levi Yitzchak of Berditchev might soon take a candle in hand and crawl under the pews of our synagogue on Yom Kippur in a vain search for a non-observant Jew! Another fifty years, and with God's help we will be there!

This upsurge is not, of course, happening in a vacuum; it should be seen as part of the revolutionary changes in the religious patterns of society beyond our Jewish confines.

If it is one of the miracles of modern Jewish history that Judaism, instead of being smashed on the anvil of suffering and succumbing to the allurements of assimilation, has experienced a remarkable rebirth, it is no less of a miracle, in a world shaken to its foundations by two world wars, challenged by the new worship of money and science, assulted by mighty empires of godlessness, that religion has survived altogether. It has survived, nay, it has even gained in strength. In past periods of such turmoil, history witnessed the rise of new religions, and the splintering or decay of old ones.

The opposite has now happened. Surprisingly, there are no signs of any new faiths and no further disintegration of the existing religions. Instead the old ones are drawn together; unity and dialogue are the great watchwords of our time. Different religions have begun to talk to each other; they seek common ground instead of battling one another. This is an altogether new phenomenon in the history of religion, a revolution if ever there was one.

Equally significant and epoch-making is the sudden end, in but twenty eventful years, of one religion as the dominant faith. After occupying for nearly 2,000 years a central and constantly expanding place in the political and cultural history of civilization, its dream of world conquest now appears at an end, following the liquidation of colonial empires and the suppression of missionary work in Africa and the greater part of Asia, not to mention the reverses behind the Iron and Bamboo Curtains. This, too, is a development of historic proportions, and with consequences to Jewish fortunes which are already beginning to be felt in the relaxation of 2,000 year-old tensions.

Following the old adage *"Wie es christelt sich, so juedelt's sich,"* we Jews have a vital stake in the religious loyalties of our non-Jewish neighbors. We are gratified, therefore, that religion in America, far from declining as a force in our national life, has lately come ever more to the fore. Where formerly religious items would be relegated to the back pages of our newspapers, they have recently often been front page news. Whether dealing with court decisions on religious issues or with reports on religious councils, they give a welcome indication that religion again begins to matter in the consciousness of the nation and the concern of its thinkers.

Our task is to nurture this consciousness and concern until the service of God will become the supreme pursuit of every human being as the fulfillment of our messianic aspirations. And the more devoutly religious our neighbors are, the more will Jews take their Judaism seriously.

But alas, this religious ferment also contains many bubbles of air. Let me now relate the second story of R. Levi Yitzchak of Berditchev which, I believe, will illustrate the negative aspects of this religious awakening.

It happened one Rosh Hashanah. The Rebbe prepared himself for the blowing of the *Shofar*. He put on his *Kittel* (white gown), recited the stirring Psalm *Lammnatze'ach* seven times with the congregation, lifted the *Shofar*—and then suddenly stopped. The people waited, but there was no *Berakhah*, no *Shofar* sound. The uncanny silence became oppressive as the perplexed worshippers fixed their gaze on their motionless Rebbe. After a very long pause, he finally explained:

"There, near the door, sits a Jew who all his life lived among non-Jews. And he cannot read Hebrew. When he saw the whole congregation standing in prayer, he was seized by a feeling of envy. He began to cry and sobbingly said: 'Father in Heaven, You know all prayers, their source and meaning, and I only know a few letters of the alphabet. Here, I offer you *aleph, beth, gimmel, daled* (the first four letters of the Hebrew alphabet), and You, in Your great mercy, arrange these letters into prayers'!" "Now," concluded the Rebbe, "God is busy ordering the letters of that devout man; hence we must wait before we can blow the *Shofar*."

In this story is reflected the religious tragedy of our times.

We have, in our synagogues, not just one solitary Jew who cannot read Hebrew properly and follow the congregation in prayer; we have many. But who cries? Who feels anguished and heart-broken because of his illiteracy? If Judaism were really as close to us as it should be, ought there not be rivers of tears flowing from the eyes of those who, perhaps through no fault of their own, cannot even read and understand the language of their people? Would we not expect our children to cry if, on occasionally visiting us, they could not speak and comprehend our language; should we not then weep grief-stricken when we are unable to read and understand God's word the holy tongue of our Torah and Prophets?

This humble Jew in the story, who was overcome by shame and envy, certainly made sure that the following year he could join the congregation by learning some Hebrew in the meantime. If some of our congregants would have this feeling of inadequacy, they might well be able to follow our services next year; for they would feel the urge to overcome their handicap in the intervening months by studying Hebrew.

But this applies also to those who can read and understand their prayers. Are there any with lachrymose eyes at our services? Recall the fervor and feeling that welled within the hearts and eyes of our parents and grandparents when they cried before God יהי רצון מלפניך שומע קול בכיות שתשים דמעותינו בנאדך להיות "May it be your will O God, Who hearkens to the voice of weeping, to store our tears in Your flask..."

Do our prayers really touch us, grip our heart, seize our soul, penetrate our innnermost depths?

Our inability to cry in an outpouring of prayer is symptomatic of the shallowness of present-day religion. The stream of religion today, as has often been said, is one mile wide and one inch deep. Our religious devotion is external, formal, conventional, even fashionable, but it has not conquered our heart and mind. Yes, we go along with religious practices and other good deeds, but often our heart is not fully with us. The *Weltschmerz* does not touch us sufficiently. When we see a Jew violating the Sabbath, or hear of one guilty of unethical or immoral conduct, does our heart really bleed as if pierced by a dagger? When we see a poor man and cannot help him, do we inwardly weep with compasion? When Yeshivoth or synagogues or other vital institutions struggle under the burden of debts inhibiting their progress, how many of us are really distressed and bothered to the point of torment, as we would be for lack of means to feed our own children?

These failings are all manifestations of a religion that leaves us cold and without passion. This religion without tears may explain the paradox of our present condition: While the religious revolution has moved forward in giant strides, morality has declined. To this baffling problem we will turn our attention next time.

As we now plead, then, for the blessings of life and health and peace, let us remember the saying in the Talmud: "From the day the Temple was destroyed, the gates of prayer were shut; yet the gates of tears were never closed."[64]

In this spirit let us pray with redoubled fervor and earnestness: *ya'aleh kolenu me'erev, veyavo tzidkenu miboker, veyera'eh pidyonenu ad erev,* 'May our voice ascend this evening, leading to our righteous conduct in the morning, so that our redemption may appear as night concludes this holy day."

4. The Moral Revolution

(Yom Kippur-Musaph)

AMONG the most striking features of the entire Yom Kippur services is the choice of our Biblical readings for the day. Out of the four—two from the Torah and two from the Prophets—three do not mention Yom Kippur at all. Only this morning's Torah reading actually referred to the Day of Atonement, setting forth the ritual in the ancient Temple. The other three readings from Scriptures focus attention on a different subject altogether.

Our *Haphtorah* of this morning gave us Isaiah's stirring plea for righteousness. The fast God delights in, he proclaims in this majestic message, is not just our abstention from eating and drinking, wearing sackcloth and ashes, or indulging in religious rites; it is rather the abstention from fraud and oppression, depriving ourselves of bread to give to the hungry, opening our homes to the poor and clothing the naked.

For *Minchah* this afternoon our Torah reading concerns forbidden marriages and the rules of sexual morality, whilst the *Haphtorah* relates the story of Jonah, the most dramatic story ever told of a city condemned to destruction because of immoral and unethical practices and eventually saved from its doom by repentance.

The religious inspiration of Yom Kippur, then, like Judaism itself, wants to make of us not only better Jews in the narrow ritual sense, but also better human beings. The Biblical messages of Yom Kippur are primarily concerned with moral failings—not just our own but also those of the non-Jewish world, as exemplified by the story of Jonah's mission to pagan Niniveh.

Clearly, then, in selecting the most significant passages from the Bible for reading on this supremely holy day, our Sages placed the main emphasis on our moral regeneration.

All the revolutions we discussed so far on these Days of Awe have propelled man forward with a mighty thrust. The freedom movements have brought independence to more nations and the hope of equal treatment to more individuals in a single decade than a millennium in the past. The scientific revolution has suddenly rocketed us forward to the most thrilling adventures in outer space and into the mysteries of the tiny atom, adding more to our knowledge of nature in twenty years than had previously been accumulated since the beginning of time. The religious revolution has transformed bigotry into understanding, and given religion an uplift, status and respectability it has not enjoyed in a hundred years.

But morally, we seem to be slipping back into the barbarism of antiquity, to the garish ostentation of ancient Rome, to the body-worshipping cult of the Greeks, to the obscene perversities of the pagans, and to the shameless immodesty of the primitive jungle.

Applying the Isaiah passage from our *Haphtorah* to our times, we might well say that, instead of abstaining from fraud and oppression, we have turned crime into our major entertainment on the screen and in the news; instead of depriving ourselves of bread to give to the hungry, we deprive ourselves of bread to slim, and we waste our grain in giant silos when millions starve in the world; instead of opening our homes to strangers. we are often strangers in our own homes, having our good time elsewhere; and instead of clothing the naked, we display nudity and semi-nudity on beaches, in magazines, and sometimes even in more familiar places.

These charges require no substantiation for readers of our daily newspapers and weekly magazines. Every issue now features sickening stories of low life in high places, graft in government, fraud in big business, shameful divorces among popular celebrities, sordid murders in fashionable apartments, and a staggering increase in crime, vice, juvenile delinquency and dope addiction.

Perhaps you will say: Only the exceptions reach the news-paper columns, like air-crashes.

But, if over one marriage in every four ends in divorce, that is no exception. If 13,000,000 American children today come from broken homes, that is no exception. If 85% of all marriages among college students involve pre-marital pregnancies, that surely is no exception. And if two billion dollars are lost annually through employee thefts of money and merchandise, and if the United States is short each year of five billion dollars by income-tax cheating, and if another two billion dollars are contributed annually to the new Temples of Paganism called funeral parlors, then we might with justice state that our moral order has, by and large, collapsed.

Now, you may ask, what is *our* role in this melancholy, revolting picture? And to the extent we are not personally involved, what is there that we can do to help clean the very air we breathe from its smutty pollen?

Everyone wears an air of self-righteousness. Drawing a blind over one's own affairs, one loves to gossip about the scandals of others.

Gossip itself is one of the greatest evils. Trading in scandal makes scandal a marketable commodity, and where there are sellers there are buyers.

Nothing so horrified our ancient Rabbis as evil gossip. It ranked, in the language of the Talmud, as worse than bloodshed, idolatry or even incest.[65] For an evil tongue helps to circulate the poison of wrongdoing in the bloodstream of society, killing its entire organism. Hence our Rabbis constantly warned us: Beware, shut your lips tight to evil speech, and close your ears to those assaulting you with it!

Shunning gossip like the plague is only one of the virtues stressed by Judaism in its unrelenting fight against evil, though this virtue is little respected or mentioned today.

Another value in Judaism is modesty or bashfulness. When Jeremiah castigated his contemporaries for their moral lapses and excesses, he listed their evil deeds and lashed out at the great and small alike: "For from the least of them even unto the greatest of them, everyone is greedy for gain; and from the prophet even unto the priest, everyone dealeth falsely."[66] His denunciation reached its climax of fury in the words: "They are not even at all ashamed; neither know they even how to blush."[67]

Just as religion requires tears to flourish, so does morality require the capacity to blush. But we blush with shame in the face of evil no more than we weep from the heart's depths in prayer.

How much less immorality would there be today if, instead of unashamedly looking at indecent figures or pictures we would turn our eyes away in disgust. What woman would dare to profane the House of God by immodest attire, disporting herself as she might in an opera-house or dance-hall, if she knew her fellow-congregants would sink their blushing faces in shame at the sight of her? What Jew would publicly violate the Sabbath in front of any traditional synagogue by smoking or using a car, if he sensed that his brethren would be outraged and disgraced by his profanity? Who would dream of besmirching the innocence of youth with early dating, of soiling the purity of adolesence with pre-marital adventures, of demolishing the sanctity of marriage by adultery, or of debasing the glory of old age by salacious pleasures, if our society still had the horror born of shame for these evils, a horror which our forefathers cultivated so carefully?

Tz'ni-uth or bashfulness, an inborn shyness or reserve, used to be the hallmark of Jewish refinement. A sense of shame is one of the characteristics by which, according to Jewish law, one can determine whether a person belongs to the seed of Abraham.[68] Jews often have been guilty of many petty offenses, but immorality was as rare as was murder among them.

Today, we wantonly expunge these noble traits from our hearts and the hearts of our children. Parents are impatient if their sons and daughters have not begun to learn the art of courting and consorting at an age when their courts should still be schools and their consorts books. But these same parents are shocked and shattered if, after driving their children to be premature adults, they later behave as adults with the irresponsibility of children, getting involved in mischief and unhappy marriages.

Perhaps the worst of all the allies of evil is the connivance with it by silence. The silence of the Germans and the nations was the great scourge which sent six million Jews to the gas-chambers, and silence is the fertilizer which helps the weeds of evil to grow today.

One of the principal precepts in the Torah's code of holiness commands us: "Thou shalt surely rebuke thy neighbor, and not bear sin with him."[69] It is our religious duty to denounce evil wherever we find it. When we see our fellow-man committing a wrong, we have no right to stand by idly in silence. By failing to protest, even if our protest will be unheeded, we become accomplices in crime.

The majority of people are still happily honest and decent. But by our acquiesence or passivity we encourage the growth of vice.

Recently the abomination of our current funeral practices, "the American Way of Death," was widely publicized—at last. Are we not all guilty in raising this grisly monster? When we are invited to participate in the pagan custom of viewing the dead, do we wince? When we are offered, instead of the traditional plain pine box costing a few dollars, an ornate casket costing hundreds or thousands, with all the blood-curdling trimmings of embalming, dressing and other benefits, do we argue? When this death-tax helps to pour fortunes into private pockets instead of filling the coffers of the community for education and social service, as it ought to do and as it always did in Jewish communities in the past, do we cry out with indignation?

If we ask, then, how is it that we witness today at the same time a low ebb of morality and a rising tide of religion, there is but one answer: Where religion is not shallow and superficial but really taken seriously, moral standards are in fact secure. Among people who faithfully observe the Sabbath and *Kashruth*, who learn Torah intensively and cherish its ideals, you will scarcely find illegitimate or delinquent children; in their homes you will see no obscene literature and hear no vulgar speech. Truly religious people do not gamble or defraud; they do not visit dens of vice, nor disport themselves indecently dressed.

The best proof for the moral effectiveness of a religious discipline can be found in Israel, where the geographical boundaries between religious and irreligious circles are often more clearly drawn than anywhere else. During my recent visit there I was told by a high government official that in the religious quarter of Mea Shearim, for instance, not a single case of juvenile delinquency had come to the notice of the Police! In Beer Sheba a leading municipal official advised me that the social and moral difficulties widely encountered among Oriental children were incomparably reduced among the students of religious schools. The moral laxity and promiscuity so notorious in certain Kibbutzim simply do not exist in any religious Kibbutz.

Much of the blame for the moral decline of our times rests on our religious leadership, rabbis not excluded. We were meant to be the heirs of the Prophets: "From the day the Temple was destroyed, prophecy was taken from the Prophets and given to the sages, to rabbinical scholars."[70]

The Hebrew Prophets did not preach sermons in synagogues or temples. They went out to challenge evil where it was to be found. They assailed corrupt kings in their palaces, castigated the wicked in their dens, denounced greed and exploitation in the market place, and passionately cried out against immorality near the hiding-places of vice.

By confining our preachments to our sanctuaries, we preach largely to the converted. By limiting our public pronouncements to the banalities and platitudes acceptable to newspaper editors, we reduce the message of God to trite cliches and glib slogans.

Perhaps we ought to consider, following the Prophets' example, challenging corrupt politicians on their own platforms, attacking crooked business practices inside the citadels of commerce and finance, and proclaiming the wrath of God against the seducers of vice and immorality in marches on Hollywood, on night-clubs, music-halls, gambling dens and other cesspools of evil. We ought to cry out loud, likes Moses, until *Ha'azinu hashamayim vethishma ha'aratz*, "the heavens will listen and the earth will hear." By such dramatic demonstrations of God's ire, we may arouse the public conscience to feelings of shame and remorse, and to the danger of our civilization, like others before it, collapsing under the weight of its own moral turpitude.

We do not know how successful the Prophets were. Sometimes their warnings were heeded and the impending doom was averted, as in the story of Jonah who saved a mighty city by his effusion of God's anger.

On most occasions, their exhortations were spurned, and their prophecies of doom came to pass, as was the case with the destruction first of the Kingdom of Israel and then of the Kingdom of Judah.

The Prophets were lonely and unpopular people, hated by the men of power and wealth, ignored by the masses, and often persecuted by their temporal rulers.

But what difference does it make today whether they failed or succeeded at the time? The targets of their fury, the once mighty kings and princes, the iniquitous priests and exploiters, are dead and forgotten, while the Prophets, lonely and isolated at the time, are still immortal today and for all times. Their words are studied and proclaimed wherever we find civilized men, their ideals are to this day upheld as guideposts to perfection. Their message is not dimmed by the passage of time.

Is not the *Yizkor*-prayer our own effort to secure for our beloved kinsfolk a similar immortality beyond death? *Yizkor* means remembrance in the future. Is not everyone of us yearning, in the words of the Psalmist, "that at his death he shall not take everything (down to the grave), that his glory shall not descend after him."[71]

We can make ourselves and our forebears immortal, we can ensure *"Yizkor,"* that God and history "will remember," were we to aspire to be the Prophets of mankind and bring the ideal of Moses, the Father of Prophets, to realization: "Would that all the people of the Lord were prophets."[72] For in the end, truly immortal are only those who have had a share in bringing about the ultimate days when, in the glorious words of our festival prayer, "Then shall the just see and be glad, the upright shall exult, the pious shall rejoice in song, and iniquity shall close its mouth, and all wickedness shall be wholely consumed like smoke, when Thou causest the dominion of arrogance to pass away from the earth, . . . speedily, in our days!"

5. The Revolution Within Us

(Yom Kippur—Ne'ilah)

I N a little while the lights which have shone so brilliantly here all day will go out, and this House
of God now so bright and radiant will be dark.
For many Jews, alas, the lights will go out not only in their
synagogues, but in their hearts, too. With the end of Yom
Kippur the flame which illumined their souls on this holy
day will be extinguished, not to be kindled again until next
Rosh Hashanah. For the rest of the year they will go to
sleep, religiously speaking.

Yom Kippur is a kind of alarm-clock, awakening us to our
duties. Some people, when they hear the alarm sound in the
morning, wake up for a moment, turn around on their bed,
and when the bell has stopped ringing go back to sleep again.
Others use their alarm-clocks to wrest themselves from their
slumber, jump out of bed and brace themselves to the tasks
of a new day. So also is Yom Kippur. Some people are aroused
just for a moment, but their inspiration is like a flash. As
soon as the prayers cease and the last *Shofar* has been sounded,
they relapse back to sleep, and they hibernate for the long dark
winter ahead. Others are awakened by Yom Kippur and
they stay awake. They know that the lights extinguished here
tonight will be put on again tomorrow and every day for
services, that this House of God will be as bright and radiant
as it was today on the lovely festival of Sukkoth, only five
days away, and on every Sabbath.

The challenge Yom Kippur poses is how to keep awake
during the year to come, how to refrain from falling back
to sleep after the rousing spiritual symphony of Yom Kippur
is all over, after the alarm has stopped sounding.

The problem of keeping awake faces not only ordinary
mortals; it confronted even the High Priest, our supreme
spiritual leader. And it faced him on Yom Kippur itself. He
was required to officiate at exacting ritual exercises by day,

and also to stay awake for the entire night of Yom Kippur, lest he might render himself impure while asleep and unfit for his sacred duties by day. However tired he felt, he had to be kept awake for twenty-four hours. How was this achieved?

The Mishnah relates that "they would read to him; and what books did they read? From Job, Ezra, and Chronicles"[73] —"for these subjects draw the heart of the listeners, so that sleep will not snatch them" (*Bartinura*).

There are three ways to keep a Jew religiously awake, to rouse him to his Jewish duties even during the months of the winter. The first is symbolized by the Book of Job. This Book speaks of tragedy in life. Job was struck by misfortune, bereavement and hideous disease. In a series of terrible blows, he lost, first, his possessions, then his family, and finally, his health.

Job's trials represent one way to bring Jews back to the synagogue even when it is not Yom Kippur, to awaken them on ordinary weekdays. When misfortune befalls a man, when death turns a happy family into mourners, when the anxiety of grave illness calls for prayer, the urge to go to the synagogue is suddenly felt—to plead for mercy, to say *Kaddish,* or to offer a prayer for healing.

If one does not want to read the Book of Job, there are two alternatives. One is the Book of Ezra. Ezra, the Scribe, was the great national hero who organized and led the return of the Babylonian exiles to the Land of Israel. He was also a great religious pioneer who dissolved all mixed marriages and restored Torah learning and observance.

Ezra provides us with the second method of how to keep alert for the whole year: Become active in the great Jewish movements of our time. Join in the historic return of our people to Zion; share in the upbuilding of our land; become an active worker in organizations toiling for the welfare of Israel. Or else, work for your congregation and the development of its religious life; spread Torah learning by helping Yeshivoth to flourish and expand; give your talents and energies and resources to some cause dedicated to the revival of the Jewish spirit. If you read and follow Ezra, you will not fall asleep.

Finally, there is a third method to stay awake, applicable to those who lack the capacity or means to be active in the exciting work of rebuilding Jewish life: read the Book of Chronicles. This book records the history of our people, the lives and achievements of our great leaders. If you do not want to be a Job and you cannot be an Ezra, turn to Chronicles. Study our unique history, learn the superb writings of our Prophets and Rabbis, familiarize yourself with Jewish philosophy and literature. Join some classes of Jewish study, attend lectures and debates of Jewish interest, seek enlightment and inspiration from the chronicles of the past and the present. If you read and study Chronicles, you will stay awake.

We have devoted ourselves during these High Festivals to the epoch-making revolutions which have stirred our age. Today a great spiritual transformation has taken place within us. Through the impact of our services, our prayers and our repentance, we are different today from what we were yesterday. *Yom Kippur* summons us to keep on riding on the crest of the revolution wrought inside our hearts, to retain for the whole year the spiritual alertness to which we have been aroused today.

May the three great books which kept the High Priest from falling asleep keep us awake, too. In this solemn *Ne'ilah* hour we pray that we may not be exposed to the trials and vicissitudes of Job, that we may be spared, by the mercy of God, from misfortune, illness, and sorrow. But if we are to be tested by fate, may we have the strength and fortitude to triumph over the blows of Satan as Job did. We pray that we may raise a new generation of Ezras to consummate the ingathering of our exiles and the return of our people to its religious heritage. We pray, finally, that we may be granted to write a new and glorious page in the chronicles of Israel, adding another creative and creditable chapter to the eternal history of our nation.

THE CHALLENGE OF LABOR

1. "For Man is Born to Labor"

(Rosh Hashanah—First Day)

"For man is born to labor . . ."[74]

THE unusual plethora of empty seats this Rosh Hashanah proclaims the early timing of the festival and its rare coincidence with Labor Day, a coincidence which has not happened since 1937 and which will not occur again for the rest of this century. This combination not only deserves a sermon; it is a sermon in itself.

For us every Rosh Hashanah is Labor Day. The Hebrew *avodah,* "labor," also means "service," "worship." Celebrating the completion of God's labor in creating the world, we turn to the challenge of man's labor in perfecting the Divine order.

Judaism is particularly fond of this term *avodah,* work, labor, service, and its derivatives *eved,* "servant," "worker," and *avad,* "to labor," "to serve."

At the very beginning of human history God placed man "into the Garden of Eden to work and to guard it."[75] In the Jewish view, even paradise is a place for work. The only fit place for idleness is the cemetery.

The highest rank that the Bible can confer on man is *eved Hashem,* "servant of the Lord." It was applied to Moses and to the people of Israel. And the holiest ritual in the Temple at Jerusalem was called the *avodah,* "the service," "the act of labor."

Indeed, Jewish thought views the relationship between God and man as that of master and worker, employer and employee, as expressed in the famous pasage of *Pirkei Avoth,* which may well represent the message of Rosh Hashanah: "The day is short, and the work is much, and the laborers are sluggish and the reward is great, and the Master of the house is urgent."[76]

Five Addresses delivered at the Fifth Avenue Synagogue during the High Holy days, 5725-1964.

Rosh Hashanah is the day when our contract with God, our Employer, comes up for renewal. What are the terms of this contract which we negotiate every year at our High Holyday services?

First, "the day is short." Our working hours are all too short. We often wished they were longer. We ask for overtime: *zochreinu lechayim,* we want more life, longer employment. But at least while we are employed, time is the one gift we all share equally. During the year we may have had different earnings, we may have experienced varied fortunes or misfortunes; but time we all had in the same measure. Everyone of us is exactly one year older since last Rosh Hashanah. No one had one hour more or one hour less than anybody else.

Where we differ is how we have used this time, what we have accomplished during the year, what improvements we have made on ourselves and the world around us since last Rosh Hashanah.

The second clause in our contract provides, "the work is much," the tasks allocated to us are great indeed. God demands a full day's service every day. He has laid down duties to Him and to our family, to our fellow-Jews and to society at large, at home and in the synagogue, at work and even at leisure. He insists that we shall serve Him in all our activities. When we eat and drink, our motive should not be simply to gratify our appetite like the brute but to strengthen our body for the service of God, and when we go to sleep we are to think of bracing ourselves for the tasks of another day. Even when we enjoy the delights of marriage, our principal intention should be to become partners with God in the creation and perpetuation of human life.[77]

Our contract assures us "the reward is great." What other employer provides you with an income, with the air you breathe, the health you enjoy, and the very life that animates your body? What other boss can guarantee you, as part of your wages, peace of mind and happiness in life, the promise of immortality and a share in the making of history? Who else can give you the gift of children and the blessing of intelligence?

But, alas, "the laborers are sluggish." So many of us want to have a "good time" rather than a useful time in life. We want more than lunch and coffee breaks during our working hours; we want to have time off from our duties to God in the evenings, on Sundays and other occasions. Sometimes we are not really at work even while attending services in the synagogue, but interrupt our spiritual labors by talking or just idling.

The contract states: "the Master of the house is urgent." He presses, He is in a hurry. He wants us to complete His plan for universal perfection. He needs our labor urgently. He has already waited over 5,000 years. Yet the job of achieving universal peace and human brotherhood is far from finished.

Think of the frustration of an architect who draws up a magnificent blueprint and provides all the materials for an architectural masterpiece, but whose workers are lazy and delay the execution of his plan from year to year.

Never for a single moment are we to forget the unfinished task of liberating the oppressed, of refining the conscience of man, of banishing violence and hatred, and making the pursuit of truth and virtue the highest ideal and fondest ambition of man.

We believe in collective bargaining. We belong to unions called congregations. We emphasize the value of collective worship. We have come here today for public prayer, because we are convinced that the effect of an individual pleading with God on his own cannot be compared with a whole congregation pouring out their hearts together. Far more can be accomplished by collective supplication than by individual negotiations with God.

There is only one restriction: We cannot go on strike against God, our Employer. We can demonstrate, by all means. We can "sit in" at His dwelling places, the synagogues, and unite to present our demands for "a good life, for adequate sustenance, for redemption and salvation." We can cry together, sing together and make all the noise we want to make our claims heard. As unions we can band together and appoint a spokesman, the *sheli'ach tzibbur,* the public reader or messenger, who will plead and negotiate for us. But we cannot strike, lay down our tools, and allow human progress to come to a standstill.

Nor do we need to resort to strikes. For our Employer has promised to meet our demands if we fulfill His. As a labor union of workers in the vineyard of the Lord, we are even assured fringe benefits. We are to receive not only sickness benefits, but health insurance: "And it shall come to pass, if ye hearken to these ordinances, and keep them, that the Lord thy God shall keep for thee the covenant and the mercy which He swore unto thy fathers . . . and the Lord will take away from thee all sickness . . ."[78]

There is also the promise of superannuation: "To love the Lord thy God, to hearken to His voice and to cleave to Him, for it is thy life and the length of thy days."[79]

We are guaranteed not only holidays with pay, but holy-days with joy: "And thou shalt rejoice in thy festival."[80]

Above all, our Employer has consented to let us, as His workers, share in the profits accruing to us from a moral, peaceful and happy world established according to His instructions.

In renewing, then, our contract with God today, let us pledge to carry out His assignments willingly and conscientiously, so that He, in turn, will inscribe us "in the book of good life."

2. Our Debt for the Labor of Others

(Rosh Hashanah—Second Day)

"As others toil for me, I toil for others."[81]

R osh Hashanah is traditionally the anniversary of creation, the birthday of man. But the creation of man was not a single event, isolated in time. Man's evolution is never at a standstill; it is an ongoing process.

At every marriage—the basis of creating new human life— we recite a blessing praising God, *Yotzer ha'adam*, "Who *createth* man," not *Yatzar ha'adam*, "Who *created* man."

In this continuous process of creation, man was invited from the beginning to become a partner with God. *Na'aseh adam,* "Let us—I, God, and you, man—make man together." God on His own can make perfect plants and animals. He cannot create a perfect man without human cooperation.

The Talmud relates of the sage Bcn Zoma that, when he saw a crowd of people, he recited a special blessing, *Barukh shebara kol eleh leshamsheni,* "Blessed be He Who created all these to serve me," and he would explain: "What labors did Adam have to perform until he won his bread! He ploughed, sowed, reaped, bound the sheaves, threshed, winnowed, selected the ears and ground them, sifted the flour, kneaded the dough and baked it, and only then did he eat, while I rise in the morning and find all this prepared for me. And what efforts did Adam make until he found a garment to wear! He had to shear the wool, wash and comb it, spin the thread, weave the material, and only then did he find a garment to wear, while I get up in the morning and find a ready suit to wear."[82]

How easy life is made for us by the labors of others!

But think also, how far man has advanced by his own ingenuity, how much he has progressed by the contributions of former generations.

God merely created a primitive world. Man had to forge his way ahead by dint of his own brawn and brain, searching for means to master and harness nature at his service, exploring, discovering, inventing, and adventuring.

We should be grateful for the patient efforts and hardwon advances of our forebears for all the comforts and conveniences we enjoy today! Compare, for example, the time and energy that formerly went into producing a flame or a light, with that of today. Today we strike a match or flick a switch and achieve in a split second what used to take hours. How much inventiveness and research, how many generations' accumulated experience, have gone into making such simple articles as paper and pens and books, such common gadgets as eye-glasses or watches, not to speak of such modern facilities as airplanes, telephones or electric shavers.

Should we not, especially on this anniversary of creation, recite a blessing *Barukh shebara kol eleh leshamsheni,* thanking God for making man His partner in the evolution of civilization, in the expansion of creation?

But Rosh Hashanah recalls not only physical creation of matter and energy. It brings to mind even more emphatically spiritual creation and man's contribution to it.

All our Scriptural readings these Rosh Hashanah days deal not with the story of Genesis but with the genesis of the Jewish people. The heroes of this festival are not Adam and Eve, but Abraham and Isaac, Sarah and Rachel, Hannah and Samuel—the creators of the Jewish people and the architects of the first Jewish kingdom, the original discoverers of God and the makers of the God-serving state.

To their gigantic spiritual labors must be added the religious creations of generations of prophets and rabbis, of philosophers, mystics and writers of great originality who together make up the colossal spiritual heritage we enjoy today.

How many centuries of spiritual exploration and religious inventiveness, of literary labors and poetic skills, of despair and ecstasy have gone into the composition of our matchless prayers! Today all we have to do is to open a *Machzor* or *Siddur,* and all these prodigious compositions—the product of millennia of inspired labor—are readily in front of us! How many generations of scholars and thinkers have labored day and night to erect the massive structure of Jewish law and philosophy, to interpret the Torah and define its principles, to pioneer the pathways of Jewish thought and practice! Today we merely have to consult a few encyclopedias or reference books or law codes, and the entire panorama of Judaism opens up before our eyes through the efforts of others!

On this day of spiritual creation should we not recite a blessing, *Barukh shebara kol eleh leshamsheni,* thanking God for making man His partner in the evolution of the human spirit, in the expansion of our understanding and vision of Him and His will?

Yet there are many who argue that religion ought to be based not on tradition but on personal inquiry and the search of the truth. These people do not want our children "indoctrinated" with Jewish beliefs before they can think for themselves. They want their children to grow up without any "prejudice" or "bias," so that later in life they can decide for themselves whether to believe in God and accept Judaism.

These people refuse to acknowledge the authority and religious decisions of earlier generations. They want us to work out our own salvation, discover God by ourselves, build up Biblical scholarship by our own efforts, untrammeled by the traditions of the past.

What a preposterous reversal of human progress, what an arrogant denial of religious evolution, what a fantastic retrogression to the primitive beginnings of man's spirit!

You might as well tell a child that he must never use matches or electric switches until he invents them; that he must not study the laws of Euclid or Newton until he discovers them on his own. You might as well tell our contemporaries to burn all libraries, so that we can produce our own literature, without drawing on the wisdom of the past; to discard all social and political experience accumulated from former times, so that we can work out our own salvation without prejudice; to destroy all the gadgets and implements produced by past scientists, so that we can create a technology based solely on our own efforts.

If we could not utilize the creative work of the past on the specious grounds that they prejudice us, but expected each generation to build from scratch its own thought and science, its religion and technology, its art and literature, where would we be?

Man would return to the cave and the jungle—hunting for food, and praying to the sun or some piece of rock. Man would live in a physical and spiritual straightjacket, relapsing in every generation to where he began, and never moving forward on the road which leads through history to human excellence and perfection.

That, essentially, is the burden of our dispute, as Orthodox Jews, with the non-Orthodox and the secularists. We do not quarrel about the need for progress, to move constantly on in the evolution of Judaism. Every day leading Orthodox rabbis the world over expand and develop Judaism by making new decisions, by applying its principles to new situations brought on by the advances in science, in medicine, in social relations and in other spheres of modern life. Every day Orthodox

Jewish thinkers are at work in expanding the frontiers of Jewish philosophy, applying new methods of research to Jewish scholarship, giving new interpretations to the Bible, the Talmud, the codes and other Jewish classics.

The need for meeting the challenge of new insights and modern conditions is not at issue.

What does divide us is our acceptance of the authority and spiritual creations embodied in the wisdom amassed by past tradition.

We are not prepared to discount the gigantic labors of the past—to do the work of Abraham in discovering God, of Moses in communicating His law, of the Prophets in defining human and Jewish objectives, of the Talmud in erecting the massive edifice of Jewish thought and conduct, and of the countless other thinkers who contributed to the interpretation of Judaism, all over again. We are not prepared to start from scratch, and to become spiritual cave-men and religious primitives once more. We are not willing to turn the wheel of history back to its starting-point.

We are not content to feed our children on crumbs of ignorance at Sunday schools or Hebrew classes a couple of hours a week. Instead we insist on an intensive Jewish education ten, twenty or even thirty hours a week in order to pass on to our children an adequate understanding of the vast treasures of our language, literature, religion, and history accumulated over the millennia. We want to ride on the backs of the giants to enlarge the horizons of the truth with each generation, and not remain pigmies stunted in our growth because we negate the labors lavished on our development in the past.

Rosh Hashanah summons us to make sure that future generations will say to us, as we say of past generations: *Barukh shebara kol eleh leshamsheni,* "Blessed be He Who created all these to serve me." What we owe to the past we must pay to the future, even as a child repays his debt to his parents only when he one day has to toil and provide for his own children. Ours must be the determination to make certain that in the final reckoning which history will accord to our generation, we shall not be found wanting nor fall behind our forebears in faithfully preserving the rich heritage of the past, contributing to the treasures of the present, and ensuring their transmission to the future. Then the generaions to come shall no more say of us that we have lived in vain than we have reason to say of the generations before us.

May we prove worthy to have others thank God for the gift of life to each and every one of us, as they will proclaim: *Barukh shebara kol eleh leshamsheni,* "Blessed be He Who created all these to serve me!"

3. The Burdens of the Rabbi's Labor

(Yom Kippur—Kol Nidrei)

I F THERE is a divine service that is unique, it is certainly *Kol Nidrei.* It is the only time when we wear a *Tallith* at night. The *Kol Nidrei* prayer itself is without parallel in our liturgy. And the solemnity of our melodies and atmosphere tonight make this service altogether incomparable among the year's religious experiences.

It is also distinguished for one less obvious feature contributing to its uniqueness: It is the only service of the year at which the rabbi serves in a specifically rabbinical capacity.

We open the service with a declaration by the rabbi, joined by two other elders, formally constituting a rabbinical court: *Biyeshivah shel ma'alah uviyeshivah shel mattah . . . anu matirin lehithpalel im ha'avaryonim.* "At the session of the Heavenly court above, and at the session of the earthly court below . . . we grant permission to pray with the sinners."

This probably is a flashback to the time of the Marranos, or crypto-Jews, who during the Spanish Inquisition had outwardly surrendered their Jewish faith to preserve their lives, but who wished to rejoin their brethren on Yom Kippur to demonstrate their secret attachment to Judaism. Since they had undergone conversion to another faith, their admission required the formal sanction of an ecclesiastical court.

In contrast, then, to all other services of the year, when the rabbi is essentially an ordinary worshipper like anybody else and without any distinctly rabbinical functions, tonight is the only occasion in our synagogue ritual when the rabbi exercises a rabbinical prerogative, at least nominally.

This may be a suitable occasion, therefore, to depart from the usual practice and devote our reflections on *Kol Nidrei* night not to the ideals, duties and shortcomings of the congregation, but to speak instead of the rabbi's ideals, duties and shortcomings. Tonight I shall tell you of the rabbi's labors, lead you into the inner sanctum of the rabbi's conscience and work-motives, his stresses, despairs and rewards, his frustrations and compensation.

The Talmud tells of a sage who, on ordaining two young rabbis, sounded this note of caution: "Do you really think that I give you dominion over others? No, servitude I give you."[83]

Never was this more true than today, when spiritual leadership is confronted with unprecedented challenges and opposition. More than ever before, countless rabbis are subjected to cruel anti-religious pressures, to organized attempts battering their conscience into submission to breaches of their faith and convictions. The past year in particular has witnessed ugly and widely-broadcast efforts to coerce the conscience of some of the world's leading rabbis, including the Chief Rabbis of Israel and of England, to modify religious rulings they issued under vicious pressures of government and press campaigns.

This night, then, is an opportune time for an appraisal of the functions and burdens of the rabbinate.

The modern rabbi in Western lands is indeed a far cry from his classic counterpart of the past.

He is charged with the conduct of services. He has to be an organizer, administrator, fund-raiser, after-dinner speaker, marriage counselor, sick visitor, funeral official, all in one. Often, especially in America, he functions also as a news commentator, political analyst, book reviewer, film critic, freedom rider, ghost writer—and sometimes, amidst all other tasks, as a spiritual leader and teacher.

Formerly, the rabbi was, as the Hebrew term *rabbi* implies, principally a teacher, a judge, an authority on Jewish law. His main preoccupation was to *pasken sha'aloth*, to give religious rulings on questions submitted to him and educate people to ask such questions.

The difference is perhaps best illustrated by the varied usages of the rabbi's place of activity. To describe his area of jurisdiction, and competence, one used to speak of a rabbi's *kiseh harabbanuth*, a "throne" or "seat of the rabbinate." He ruled, he *sat* and learned. Now we speak of a rabbi's pulpit— he *stands* and talks.

There is a story of one congregation's officers who engaged a new rabbi. When he stipulated that he wanted enough time and opportunity to learn for a couple of hours every day, they told him: "We don't want a rabbi who still has to learn; we want a rabbi who has his studies behind him and who knows."

With all the multifarious duties and activities of the modern rabbi, one is reminded of the legend about the great and saintly Rabbi Levi Yitzchak. When he was about to be born, Satan complained that if that great soul were to descent on earth, it would reform the world, and his own power would come to an end. But the Holy One, blessed be He, comforted Satan, and said: "But he will be a rabbi, and he will be too occupied with communal affairs."

Complaints *against* rabbis, sometimes spiced with pungent cynicism, are not new. Over 150 years ago the outstanding Chasidic master, Rabbi Nachman of Bratzlav, berated the rabbis of his time with biting wit, saying: "It was hard for Satan alone to mislead the whole world, so he appointed prominent rabbis in different localities."

But much older and more persistent are complaints *by* rabbis against those in their charge.

The very first rabbi in history, *Mosheh rabbenu*, Moses our Rabbi or Teacher, already cried out in despair: *Eikhah essa levadi torchakhem umasakhem verivkhem,* "How can I bear by myself your troubles and your burdens and your strife.[84] *Eikha essa levadi,* "how can I bear by myself," alone. What oppressed Moses about carrying out the burdens of his office was above all his loneliness. A true rabbi often suffers terrible loneliness.

These days we frequently hear of the loneliness of an American President in his awesome office. But his is neither a social nor an intellectual isolation. He can freely share with his friends their ideals and their pastimes—even their jokes. He can dance with other people's wives, let alone with his own, he can eat at any of their homes, and he can even make a little fortune on the side like anyone else. He is lonely only when he makes decisions of state, and then for no more than eight years; otherwise he lives completely in the world of his friends.

Not so the rabbi. Though he attends more wedding parties and crowded dinners than most people, he is often very lonely indeed. Having to practice what he preaches, and preaching much that is unpopular, he lives a life apart. To him many of the pleasures and concerns of his closest friends are out of bounds. He must be above politics and beyond the temptation of business speculation. In fact, he often lives in a different world from those surrounding him.

His worries are scarcely theirs—how to influence people and make friends for Yeshivoth or *Mikvoth,* or how to unravel a knotty halackhic problem. His thrills are not always theirs —such as when he has succeeded in winning a Jew for Sabbath observance or for attendance at daily services in the synagogue. His scale of values in rating and respecting people has to be different. To him, a humble, kindly, pious person tucked away on some backseat may be a really great and distinguished man compared to some big name whom everybody honors although his possessions hardly include rectitude, piety or scholarship.

The rabbi even judges his own sermons differently. When his congregants look for a message that is timely, up-to-date like the latest newspaper, he may search for what is timeless, imperishable like the Bible, as topical today as it was centuries ago and as it will be for all future times because it expresses eternal verities. When his listeners react "I enjoyed your sermon" he may prefer them to say: "I cannot say that I enjoyed your sermon; but you have convinced me that your plea is right, and I will try to change my ways accordingly."

The rabbi is lonely in his working hours when he broods over a sermon. He is lonely in his leisure hours when he studies. Sometimes he is even lonely when he prays in the synagogue while others talk or idle, or when he conducts a class and only a handful of people attend.

Innumerable are the occasions when he exclaims with Moses: *Eikhah essa levadi,* "How can I bear alone . . ."

Moses then referred specifically to three anxieties that beset him: *Torchakhem umasakhem verivkhem,* "Your trouble and your burden and your strife."

According to Nachmanides, *Torchakhem,* "your trouble," refers to the trouble Moses experienced in teaching the laws of the Torah to Israel. The rabbi's foremost effort must be to teach, to instruct.

How difficult it is to teach laws regarded by so many as obsolete or too hard; to preach that man's aim should be not to have a good time but to make the times good! How much trouble one encounters to explaining the primacy of the spirit in an age of materialism, the joys of goodness and decency in an era of cheap pleasures, the virtue of humility and self-sacrifice in times of self-advertisement and material ambition! How much hardship a rabbi invites by constantly swimming against the stream, by advocating a religious discipline which demands daily expenses and restraints, by setting a premium on feelings of guilt and a penalty on a life of ease. "How can I bear your trouble . . ."

Umasakhem, "your burden" is a reference to Moses's prayer for the community. The rabbi's second chief task is to plead and intercede for his congregation and its members.

His greatest "burden" is to feel the sufferings of the poor, experience the grief of the bereaved and the anguish of the sick, to have the fullest of empathy that parents possess for their young, to cry out to God for the welfare and health of his flock as he would for his own children. He has to pray hard, for he knows that he will be held to account for the failings of his congregation. As its leader he is responsible for the religious education and conduct of each individual in his charge. "How can I bear your burden . . ."

Lastly, concludes Nachmanides, *Verivkhem,* "your strife," refers to the duties of Moses as a judge in litigations and disputes. This represents the third of the rabbi's main tasks.

It is the rabbi's function to make peace where there is argument or strife, to reconcile enemies, to dispense justice in quarrels brought before him for arbitration. This, too, is hard. How embarrassing it often is to tell a person "You are wrong, or selfish," "you must apologize, or pay compensation." Nothing is more thankless than to be a judge over other people's conduct. Yet that is the task of the rabbi, and he cannot evade it. In fact, Jewish law insists that disputes among Jews must not be brought before non-Jewish courts; they should be referred to a rabbi or a *Beth Din,* a rabbinical court, for settlement at a *Din Torah,* a religious arbitration in accordance with our own rules of justice and equity. Not so long ago such *Batei Din* existed in every Jewish community, and the discharge of this responsibility belonged to the rabbi's most exacting preoccupations however difficult and often unpleasant an assignment it was. "How can I bear your strife . . ."

We acclaim God every day in the *Shemoneh Esreh* as *Rofeh ne'eman verachaman,* "a faithful and merciful Healer." This contrasts with a human doctor who heals either with *emunah,* with "faith," or with *rachmanuth,* with "compassion." If he is faithful, he cannot be guided by pity; he must be firm and sometimes even cruel. He may have to sink a knife into the tender flesh of his patient, he has to jab needles, prescribe bitter pills, and insist on rest and diet without mercy. And if he is *rachaman,* "compassionate," he cannot be *ne'eman,* "faithful" to the dictates of medicine. He must make his choice, for only God is a Healer who can be *ne'eman* and *rachaman* at the same time.

Similarly the rabbi, the human healer of souls. He too must often choose being either *ne'eman* or *rachaman,* between giving people what they need or what they want. If he is faithful, he must be firm and sometimes harsh. He must prescribe strict rest on Sabbaths and a rigid diet of *Kashruth* every day. He may be called upon to break up the love between a Jewish boy and his non-Jewish girl friend, or to reprove his own friend for moral or religious lapses without pity. And if he is soft, guided only by "humanitarian" feelings, or by the desire to please and flatter, he cannot be faithful to the dictates of Judaism. If he preaches a religion of comfort, a Judaism without tears and hardship, without discipline and restraints, he betrays his faith and abdicates his function. Only God can combine *ne'eman* and *rachaman; midath hadin,* "the rule of justice," with *midath harachamim,* "the rule of mercy." But human judges are commanded: *Ani verosh hatzdiku,* "do justice to the afflicted and the destitute,"[85] on which the Midrash comments: *Terachemu eino omer, elah hatzdiku,* "It does not say 'have mercy' but 'do justice.' "[86]

Of course many rabbis, even the best and most sincere among them, are often tempted, like Jonah, to take the line of least resistance and flee from their divine calling. Frustrated and discouraged, they choose to escape because they cannot bear up under the load—to proclaim unpleasant truths to unwilling listeners, threaten punishment to those who rebel against God or resort to unethical practices against their fellow men. How can a rabbi be frank with a solitary patient whose pains become acute as he lies in bed and he feels puzzled and cruelly abandoned to his fate? Would it answer his questions on why he suffered if he were told that perhaps he had defied God's law and desecrated the Sabbath? Frankness would require the rabbi to pursue his mission with a touching faith. How could he sit calmly by when spouses seek to consult him on their unhappy marriages? How could he venture a judgment that perhaps they had failed to uphold the Jewish family laws which are calculated to ennoble husband-wife relations? What explanations could a rabbi offer to parents whose sons turned against them by marrying out of faith? How could he summon the courage to tell them that maybe the fault was theirs, having failed to instill Jewish loyalties in their child? Perhaps they had cared more for giving him music and dancing instructions than Hebrew lessons in his childhood and adolescence. How could a rabbi encourage people to be severe in judging their own faults and failings, and be charitable in criticizing others or complaining against God?

These are all challenges to daunt the stoutest heart, assignments to make even a prophet flee and a Moses exclaim: "How can I bear. . . ."

But for all these burdens and frustrations there are also great compensations.

Greater even than the joy of a doctor who has helped to restore his patient to life or health is the joy of a rabbi who has succeeded in bringing some comfort to a broken heart, in inducing a smile on a face worn with cares and worry, in opening the eyes of a worshipper to the splendor of our faith, and restoring a distraught soul to religious life and spiritual health.

Greater than the thrill of a politician who wins an election landslide is the delight of a rabbi who wins a congregation to religious fervor and piety.

Greater than the elation of a captain of industry who has brought off a big and profitable deal is the elation of a rabbi who has prevailed on a member to invest his profits in the service of Jewish education or charity.

And greater than the satisfaction of a laywer who has won a case in court is the satisfaction of a rabbi who has won a case for God and goodness in an argument with a perplexed soul.

A rabbi never labors in vain, so long as he preaches and practices the word of God. In the lovely analogy of the Prophet Isaiah: ". . . Just as the rain cometh down and the snow from Heaven, and returneth not thither, except it water the earth and make it bring forth and bud, giving seed to the sower and bread to the eater, so shall My word be that goeth forth out of My mouth; it shall not return unto Me empty, except it accomplish that which I please and make the thing whereto I sent it prosper."[87]

No doctor or lawyer can ever share with all his patients or clients his professional interests and activities for a complete day, or indeed at any time. No man of any calling or profession can have the soul-stirring happiness experienced by a rabbi on Yom Kippur, when for a full day his world is completely identical with the world of those he serves. He has the high privilege to guide an entire congregation in effecting atonement before God and reconciliation among men. He can operate on a hundred hearts without shedding blood and inspire countless homes without passing their threshold. He is empowered to announce to his flock seeking repentance in truth on behalf of their Creator and Judge: *Salachti kidvarekha,* "I have pardoned according to your request."

4. Collective Labor

(Yom Kippur-Musaph)

IF *Avodah,* meaning "labor" and "worship," is our general theme on these High Festivals, then we are reaching its very heart with the *Musaph* service about to begin. It contains a part simply called the *Avodah,* the act of worship *par excellence,* describing the elaborate ritual of atonement performed by the High Priest in the Temple at Jerusalem.

In the course of this service we shall ourselves participate in a most unusual act. Three times, in addition to once during the *Aleinu*-prayer, we shall go down on our knees and prostrate ourselves before God, as we reenact the impressive Temple service of old, when "the priests and the people . . . hearing the ineffable Name pronounced by the High Priest in holiness and purity, knelt and prostrated themselves . . . and fell on their faces . . ."

Normally the Jew never kneels, neither before God nor before any mortal. Mordecai refused to kneel before the king in the Purim story, and Hannah of the *Chanukah* story had her seven sons slain rather than allow them to bow down before an idol even just to pick up a ring. Through the ages, Jews have always gone down to martyrdom rather than to their knees. Even in worshipping our God, kneeling, as a rule, is strictly forbidden. On the contrary, when reciting specially holy prayers, such as the *Shemoneh Esreh, Kaddish* or *Kedushah,* we are to stand erect and at attention before God, like soldiers inspected by their Commander-in-Chief.

We even object to Jews ever kneeling casually in the course of work. Kneeling is both alien and abhorrent to the Jew, whether for a religious or any other purpose.

The sole exception is Rosh Hashanah and especially Yom Kippur. For once our ritual expects us to break the rule, to go down on our knees and prostrate ourselves in prayer. For once we are to return to the posture we had in the mother's womb before we were born, crouching on our knees in utter impotence and humiliation.

Does not this singular act symbolize the whole meaning of these Awesome Days? "Thou turnest man back to dust (lit. a crushed state) and sayest: Return, ye children of man."[88]

Unlike the animal, man is created to walk erect, to hold his head aloft, reaching for the skies above. Normally man strives and labors, thinks and creates, to raise himself, to climb the ladder of success, to reach out for wealth and power, to walk upright with pride and assurance through life.

Not so on these Days of Judgment and Atonement. Today we are to bend our knees and cringe, to recognize in utter humility the nothingness of man compared to the infinite and eternal majesty of God our Judge. Today we are to return to the embryonic state of pure innocence, to bite the dust in contrition and complete remorse. Today we are to kneel and lie prostrate before God, in humility and self-effacement.

The significance of this act goes even deeper.

What is the exception today will become the rule at the end of time. The time will come, as the Prophet has it, when "every new moon and every Sabbath all flesh will come to bow down before Me, sayeth the Lord;"[89] and when, as we pray daily in the *Aleinu*-prayer, "all inhabitants of the world will recognize and know that unto Thee every knee must bend and every tongue swear."

Rosh Hashanah and Yom Kippur, then, give us a foretaste of things to come. What we do, what we feel, what we aspire as a small people and as an exception today, will become the universal rule in the future. The time will come when every day will witness for all peoples the spiritual grandeur and complete submission to God we experience today.

These Days of Awe have other features, too, which for once bring close, and to the center of our attention, experiences that otherwise still belong to the end.

For instance, the *Aleinu*-prayer itself, placed at the end of all services throughout the year, is on these days put right at the center of *Musaph*, the central service of the day. Similarly, we wear today the *Kittel*, to be used as shrouds at the end of life to clothe our mortal remains after the departure of our immortal soul.

Our kneeling, our *Aleinu*, our *Kittel*, our complete dedication to God—all are exceptional and central today, but will become universal and the rule in the future. The atmosphere, the solemnity, the earnestness, the humility and faith of Rosh Hashanah and Yom Kippur will eventually be the common experience of all men every day. Man's corporate labor will be to worship and serve God in unison.

These are our objectives. What are the means to achieve them?

Time and again on this holy day, we have bent our heads and beaten our hearts while reciting the great confession of our sins: *Ashamnu, bagadnu, gazalnu. . .* "We have been guilty, we have dealt treacherously, we have robbed. . .," and *Al chet shechantanu lephanekha begiluy arayoth, bzilzul horim umorim, bemasa umatan . . .,* we have asked for forgiveness "for the sin we have committed before Thee by immorality . . ., by despising parents and teachers . . ., by dealings in business . . ."

Have we really committed this entire alphabetical catalogue of sins? Have we all been robbers, or shamed our parents and teachers, or been guilty of dishonest business practices? Or are our lips saying something our heart denies, turning us all into hypocrites and liars?

The answer is, of course, that Judaism holds us all corporately responsible for every crime committed in the society in which we live.

Man has rebelled against this notion from the beginning of history. The first question asked by man ever recorded in the Bible was: *Hashomer achi anokhi,* "Am I my brother's keeper?" And man has kept on asking this ever since.

We want to be individualists, to care only for ourselves, without bearing the burdens of others. We want to be left alone. But we cannot. *Lo tov heyoth ha'adam levado*, "It is not good for man to be alone,"[89] the world can never be good if man lives merely for himself alone, without any commitment to others.

Just as our personal life is influenced by the society and environment in which we live, so do we influence society around us. If there is stealing, or immorality, or disrespect for parents, or business dishonesty in the world today, we are all to blame and each one of us must beat his heart and say *Al Chet.* We all belong to a collective labor force, as it were— as members of a community, of a nation, and of humanity; we are all our brothers' keepers, all responsible for one another.

On Rosh Hashanah we discussed how each of us benefits from the labors of others, how our lives are made better and easier through the creations and inventions and services of our neighbors and ancestors. But, to balance the account, we must also share in the blame for the faults and sins of others; we are degraded by the depravity of our neighbors.

Do you know which is the biggest business in America today? No, it is not General Motors or any of the other industrial giants. Crime is the largest business in the country today —a two hundred billion dollar per year business!

And we are all partners in this business, even if it may bring us more losses than profits. Crime needs a social climate in which to breed, and we all help to create that climate. Every time we look at a film glamorizing crime without protest, we encourage the popularization of crime and the vulgarization of life.

The other day our newspapers carried a heart-warming story about a man in Long Island who returned to its owner a precious dog he found and who refused a huge reward offered to him, arguing that he had only done what was right. For every such story of virtue in our papers there are fifty stories of crime and vice. If the ratio were reversed, we would soon secure a climate of moral health in which crime cannot become rampant.

Why is not the ratio reversed? Because we like to read about crime rather than about virtue; it is more exciting and entertaining. And the demand creates the supply.

Every time we allow ourselves to be entertained by crime, every time we buy a toy gun for a child, every time we are not too particular about business ethics, every time we offer a little graft, every time we act unkindly with workers or tenants, we encourage the rise of crime and become accessories to it.

The same goes for immorality, marital faithlessness and all the other vices so widespread today. By tolerating indecent exposure, by seeing films betraying the sanctity of marriage, by reading smutty literature, by ogling other men's wives, we help to corrode the fabric of our society and contribute to the loose morals of our age.

The same applies nearer home, to Jewish values.

For the first time in our history we now hear constantly talk about the "vanishing Jew." When persecution and slaughter decimated our people, no one ever spoke of the vanishing Jew. Throughout the Middle Ages, when the total number of Jews scarcely exceeded one million and whole communities were often bleeding to death or exposed to starvation, no Jew ever worried about the survival of his people. There was a wandering Jew, a suffering Jew, a martyred Jew, but never a vanishing Jew. And today, in our affluent and free society, where few Jews suffer hunger and none violent persecution or forced conversion, we lose them by the hundreds of thousands, through assimilation, mixed marriages and sheer indifference, combined with a record low birth-rate.

Orthodox Jews, it is true, who not so long ago were the vanishing tribe in America, are now probably the only segment of the community that, far from vanishing, increases through a relatively high birth-rate and a low assimilation rate. Nevertheless, we are all guilty partners to the crime of national suicide.

At present about 60,000 children attend Jewish day schools in America, while many times that number get no Jewish education at all. If these figures were reversed, the American Jew would not vanish!

If all Orthodox Jews—and not only the really charitable ones and the poor among them—were to tax themselves and spend 10% of their incomes on better Jewish education, we could accomodate in our day schools hundreds of thousands of children and give them enough education to ensure that they would not vanish. Our schools would not be dilapidated and overcrowded buildings disgracing the community, but palaces of learning; and our teachers would not suffer the hardship of going for months unpaid but, by earning a decent living, attract to their ranks men and women of the highest caliber now often lost to more lucrative pursuits.

Aval Anachnu chatanu, "but we have sinned." We nibble at the problems of our time instead of laboring at them.

Our first order of the day, therefore, must be to restore our traditional sense of collective responsibility.

The criminal languishing in prison, the wretched partners to a broken marriage awaiting their release in a divorce court, the ignorant college student courting a non-Jewish girl and Jewish self-destruction—are all our brothers, and we are their keepers.

Yom Kippur wants to arouse in us this feeling of collective guilt, so that it paves the way to our collective happiness and security. Today we are sharing everything together, sinners and saints. No one has eaten better food than anybody else, no one has spent the day in more luxurious surroundings or enjoyed better entertainment than anyone else. We have all recited the same prayers, confessed the same sins, expressed the same hopes and pleaded for the same blessings.

But Yom Kippur is not an end in itself; it is but a guidepost to the future. What is an exception today is to become the rule tomorrow.

Let us learn today how to bend our knees before God in submission, how to wear the garb of death in the fullness of life, how to beat our own hearts for the sins of others. Then we may seen see realized the triple program for the future outlined in the three-fold prayer characterizing these Days of Awe: First the brotherhood of man: "And impose Thine awe upon all Thy works . . . that they may fear Thee and all creatures prostrate themselves before Thee, that they may all form a single band to do Thy will with a perfect heart . . ." Second, turning the vanishing Jew into the vanquishing Jew, jubilant in his spiritual triumph: "And give glory unto Thy people, praise to them that fear Thee, hope to them that seek Thee ... joy to Thy land and gladness to Thy city . . ." And third, the victory of righteousness and the extinction of crime: "And the righteous shall see and rejoice . . . while iniquity shall close her mouth, and all evil shall be wholly consumed like smoke . . . ," *Bimherah beyameinu*, "speedily, in our days!"

5. The Pangs of Labor

(Yom Kippur — Ne'ilah)

"It is the day of atonement; a holy convocation shall it be unto you, and ye shall afflict yourselves."[90]

O UR most exacting spiritual labors of the year, which began on Labor Day, are about to be concluded. We have traced the concept of labor from our service to God to the services of others to us, from the labor of the rabbi to the collective labor of the community.

Now, as the pain of hunger begins to torment us in these final moments of the fast, we shall turn to the pangs of labor.

Suffering is the inevitable concomitant of all service and creation.

When the first man and woman were created and placed in the Garden of Eden to work and guard it, they sinned. They and all their descendents after them, were punished for what they had done in opening the floodgates of sin to the entire human race. Adam was told: "Cursed be the ground for thy sake; in pain shalt thou eat of it . . . thorns and thistles shall it bring forth for thee . . . In the sweat of thy face shalt thou eat bread. . ."[91] And Eve was told: "I will greatly multiply thy pain and thy travail; in pain shalt thou bring forth children. . ."[91]

Both of them would suffer the pangs of labor in bringing forth new creation: the man outside in laboring to produce bread, and the woman inside in laboring to deliver children. From the beginning, then, it was ordained that nothing would be created by man or woman without sweat and pain. Neither the life of a new plant sustaining human existence nor the life of a new child propagating the human race could be produced without suffering. There could be no true creation without travail.

Is not this one of the great lessons of Yom Kippur?

Today we have endured affliction; we have denied our hungry and thirsty bodies the balm of food and drink. That is surely the very reason why we were creative today. Our personalities are reborn in the pangs of labor, the pain of self-affliction.

If any day of the year changes us, makes some difference to our character, it is surely this day. We are purged of the burden of sin, morally and spiritually regenerated to assume a new and more meaningful life. This refining process can no more be accomplished without suffering than metal can be refined without heat or children be born without pangs.

Is this not also one of the great lessons of Jewish history?

When a son was born to Joseph in Egypt—the first Jew to taste the experience of exile from his homeland—he called him Ephraim, explaining *Ki hiphrani hashem be'eretz anyi,* "for the Lord hath made me fruitful in the land of my affliction."[92] Affliction made him fruitful and creative. And when later all his family went down to Egypt and they experienced the first blows of persecution in our history, we are told of the nascent Jewish people: *V'kha'asher y'anu otho ken yirbeh v'khen yifrotz,* "and the more they oppressed it, the more it multiplied and spread."[93] Oppression made Israel prolific.

And so it was throughout our history. Suffering produced an irresistible will to create new life and immortal monuments to the human genius. We became at once the most suffering and the most creative people on earth.

"If there are ranks in suffering," wrote the great German-Jewish scholar Zunz in a celebrated passage quoted by George Eliot in *Daniel Deronda,* "Israel takes precedence of all nations; if the duration of sorrows and the patience with which

they are borne ennoble, the Jews can challenge the aristocracy
of every land; if a literature is called rich in the possession of
a few classic tragedies—what shall we say to a national tragedy
lasting fifteen hundred years, in which the poets and the
actors were also the heroes?"

Compare the number of Jewish prophets and philosophers, of Jewish Nobel Prize winners and other world-renown-
ed benefactors of mankind, to the number produced by any
other people of the same size, and the lesson becomes indisputable.

Is not this also one of the great lessons of life itself?

According to a famous talmudic witticism *Asya dimagen
b'magen, magen shavya*, "a doctor who heals for nothing is
worth nothing."[94] Indeed, anything you get for nothing is
worth nothing. Only what is won the hard way is truly
treasured.

Just as a mother loves her child all the more because she
bore it with pain and sacrifice, and as a man will cherish his
accomplishments all the more dearly if he achieved them
by the sweat of his brow, so does our appreciation for anything
in life rise in proportion to the hardship we endured in
gaining it.

Children do not appreciate food or candies if they do not
occasionally hunger for them. A student will not feel the thrill
of passing an examination if he did not sweat for it. A person
will not really be attached to a charity, to a hospital or a
Yeshivah or any other noble cause, unless it has meant a sacrifice of time and money to him, nor will he love his synagogue if he obtained its services for nothing. For this reason
the Torah insists that pilgrims visiting the Temple "shall not
appear before the Lord empty," without offerings.[95]

Yom Kippur would not pull our heart-strings if we had not
fasted and afflicted ourselves, and the Prophet Jonah would
not have addressed Nineveh with such passion if he had not
experienced the terror of the storm at sea on his way there.

And so it is also with religion in general. A religion which
demands nothing is worth nothing.

How else can we explain that Orthodox Judaism, which is
so hard to practice, loses far fewer Jews than non-Orthodoxy,
which is so much easier to non-practice.

What you work hard for you love, and out of travail you create. Modern Israel, so uniquely creative, is an unmatched example of pioneering in the world for the very reason that it was born and raised in the torment of fire and sweat. "Those who sow in tears will reap in joy."[96]

True happiness is catapulted from the stresses of effort and struggle. The forthcoming festival of Sukkoth would not be "the season of our joy," if it were not preceded by the exertions of Rosh Hashanah and Yom Kippur.

Our sages state that when Yom Kippur terminates one should rejoice and be of good cheer. In anticipating the conclusion of this great day, let me close our series on labor in a lighter vein, with a story on today's biggest labor problem—domestic labor.

A letter was once published in the advice-giving column of a newspaper from a woman with a problem. Her husband snored all night, and she could not sleep. Otherwise, she admitted, he was kind and considerate. He even provided her with two maids to help her with housework. But his snoring irritated her, resulting in her loss of sleep. And she was nervous all day. What, she asked, should she do?

The columnist replied: "My dear woman, send away the maids and do the housework yourself. You will then be so tired at night that your husband will not disturb your sleep."

Some of us have a similar problem in a spiritual sense. They have the labor of Judaism performed by maids, by others who keep the household of God running all year round, while they themselves take it easy. They let their synagogues organize adult classes and services, but they want others to attend them. Then, through the snoring voice of their conscience, they are unable to find peace of mind, and when they awaken to the brilliant day-light of Rosh Hashanah and Yom Kippur, and attend services, they tend to become nervous, fumble in the *Machzor,* and are unable to follow the services. What should they do?

The answer is: Work hard at Judaism by yourself, and not by proxy, all the year round. Make an effort to keep a truly *kosher* home, sanctify the Sabbath, come regularly to services, give up at least one night a week for Jewish studies. You will then be so preoccupied that the snores of your conscience will be silenced at night and you will not be in any state of nervousness in the presence of God by day.

"When thou eatest the labor of thine own hands, happy shalt thou be and it shall be well with thee."[97] May our exacting labor today and our Jewish work throughout the year ensure for us a year blessed with every happiness and well-being!

10

The Festivals and Their Significance

Some lesser-known Facts and Explanations

PESACH

NAME

THE Festival which we know as *Pesach* ("Passover") is never so called in Torah; it invariably uses *Chag Hamatzoth* ("The Festival of the Unleavened Bread"), while *Pesach* describes the day preceding the Festival (which we call *Erev Pesach*) when the pascal

Published serially in the *Bulletin* of the Fifth Avenue Synagogue, 1960-1964.

lamb was sacrificed. The explanation for the two names, it has been suggested, is to be found in the verse of the *Song of Songs:* "I am unto my beloved, and my beloved is unto me." God (speaking through the Torah) lauds Israel and its perserverance by referring to "the bread of affliction," while Israel praises God Who "passed over" the houses of the Jews and saved their first-born *(Kedushath Levi)*.

* * *

The name of the festival, *Pesach,* and its English equivalent *Passover,* is derived from the same root in the verse, "And the Lord will pass over *("uphasach")* the door, and will not suffer the destroyer to come in unto your houses to smite you,"[1] a reference to the sparing of Jewish homes during the plague of the death of the first-born in all Egyptian homes. The root *pasach* also means "to limp," "to walk haltingly;"[2] hence the adjective *piséach* meaning "lame."[3] *Pesach* thus points to the most characteristic feature of redemption as a danger passing over, as the destructive force of history and nature by passing the redeemed and leaving them providentially unscathed, though such deliverance comes haltingly and only to those who wait in faith. The principal significance of the festival's message, then, lies in Jewish survival against the usual odds of national decline and extinction, a survival assured by patience and hope.

CHAMETZ

Chametz literally means "oppressive," as *chamotz,* "the oppressor,"[4] and *chometz,* "the violent man."[5] In the immediate sense, therefore, chametz refers to the violence done to the dough by the process of fermentation which oppresses it and turns it sour. But in a figurative sense the enjoyment of freedom demands the removal and destruction of all *oppression* which *sours* human society. Often the attainment and preservation of liberty requires action in *haste* before the grain of order goes to seed and *ferments* into *violence* and *oppression.*

* * *

Among the reasons advanced for the omission of the blessing *"Shehechiyanu"* ("Who hast kept us alive")—usually recited when performing a religious duty for the first time in a year—over searching the *Chometz* and counting the *"Omer"*, is that both duties lack joy because they involve an element of destruction: burning the bread and remembering the martyrs of Israel during the "Omer" mourning period.[6]

MATZAH

Matzah means not only "unleavened bread" but also "strife."[7] Just as *lechem*, "bread"—from *lacham, milchamah*, meaning "to fight,"—"war"—refers to the struggle in earning a livelihood,[8] so *Matzah*, replacing bread on *Pesach*, characterizes the same fight for sustenance. Only bread is a universal quest ("war" fight between nations), while *Matzah* involves a struggle limited to one people ("strife"—fight between individuals). *Matzah* is also connected with *matzatz*—"to squeeze," "to suck out" perhaps a hint at the leaven which is "squeezed out" and eliminated. *Matzah*, then, as the "bread of affliction," symbolizes struggle combined with poverty, hardship deprived of wealth, as the essential ingredient of salvation.

*   *   *

One of the most celebrated, prolonged and violent rabbinic controversies during the past century concerns the propriety of *Matzoth* baked by machine (first invented in Austria in 1857). The numerous responsa and indeed whole books written in opposition to, and in defense of, the innovation could nearly fill an entire library shelf. Among the arguments advanced for banning such *Matzoth* was that the machine would deprive the poor of an annually-expected income; that the baking should be supervised by an adult, intelligent Jew who could not be replaced by a machine lacking intelligence; and that there was danger of the dough leavening before being baked by interruptions in the constant kneading and by the heat of the machinery prematurely warming the dough. Others rejected these arguments as unfounded, but to this day many pious Jews insist on using only hand-baked *Matzoth* for the *Seder* or even for the whole Festival.[9]

EREV PESACH

On *Erev Pesach* two "legal fictions" are customarily observed: The completion of a talmudic tractate (*"Siyum"*) for the first-born so that they need not fast, having attended a religious festivity (*"Se'udath Mitzvah"*), and the sale of *Chametz* to a non-Jew, whereby it is technically no longer in Jewish possession, as required by the Torah. As regular customs, both practices are less than 400 years old, and both have been attacked as unwarranted evasions of the law by many rabbis.[10]

THE SEDER

The Seder (like *Siddur* meaning "Order of Service") is the only "service" with a complete liturgy for use outside the synagogue. The main test of the *Hagadah* goes back almost unchanged to the days of the Mishnah (2,000 years ago) or even earlier. It thus belongs to the oldest parts of our liturgical literature. No Jewish book has been published in more editions and inspired a greater variety of artistic talent than the *Hagadah*.

* * *

The home festivities on the first two *Pesach* nights, it has been suggested, are called *Seder*, which literally means "order,"[11] because the miracles of the Exodus recounted at the *Seder* are themselves part of the "order" of nature and history devised and planned by Providence from the beginning.[12] Another interesting reason given is that *Pesach*, which commences with the *Seder*, determines the "order" of all other festivals in the year. Thus *Shavuoth* always falls on the same day of the week as the second day of *Pesach*, *Rosh Hashanah* and *Sukkoth* correspond to the third day, *Simchath Torah* to the fourth day, *Yom Kippur* to the fifth day, etc.

* * *

This may also explain the conspicuous role played by the number "four"—the most regular and "orderly" of all figures (cf. the complete symmetry of a square with its four equal sides)—in connection with *Pesach*: The "four" special Sabbaths preceding the festival; the "four" cups of wine; the "four" questions; the "four" sons; and the "four" precepts observed at the *Seder* (two biblical: eating *Matzah* and telling the story of the *Hagadah;* and two rabbinical: eating *Maror* and drinking four cups of wine). According to another opinion, the number "four" corresponds to the "four" categories of persons who must render public thanks to God (*bensh gomel*) for deliverance from danger—sea voyagers, desert travelers, released prisoners and people who have recovered from sickness. The deliverance from Egypt symbolizes rescue from all these four hazards (*Gaon of Vilna*).

*   *   *

On the first two Festival nights no *Kiddush* is recited after the service in the synagogue[13] because even the poorest are presumed to have a *Seder,* with four cups of wine, either on their own or as guests elsewhere.

*   *   *

The wine cup used for *Kiddush* and the *Arba Kosoth,* of which the greater part should be drunk each time, must hold a minimum of a *"reviyith,"* literally a "quart" of a log or 86 grams (a little over 3 ounces), corresponding to the numerical value of the Hebrew letters in *kos* (20+6+60). But the *Chazon Ish* insists that the proper measure of a *"reviyith"* is 150 grams (over 5 ounces).

*   *   *

The "Four Questions" in the *Mah Nishtanah* may correspond to the "Four Sons." They all ask: "Why is this night different from all other nights?," but each one is stuck by some feature at the *Seder* characteristic of himself. The Wise Man notices the most significant religious distinction of *Pesach:* the *Matzoth* replacing *Chametz.* The Wicked Man is not concerned with religious symbols; all he sees at the *Seder* is *Maror.* For, to him Judaism is "only bitter" and burdensome, offering no delights as it does to his companions. The naive Simpleton, again, is not roused by anything unusual at the *Seder* until he discovers that on this night we dip food in a liquid twice, that for once we all seem to behave like children. He is interested only in the playful parts of Jewish life, its games and socials, not its serious work. And finally, there is the indifferent, who is not concerned to ask any questions at all. His sole concern is his comfort and convenience; all that strikes him at the *Seder* table is that on this night everybody reclines comfortably on his cushion as he does all the year round.

The Seder—The Jewish "Order" of Life

The *Hagadah* is the only special Order of Service for use exclusively at home. All other liturgical collections (e.g., the *Siddur, Machzor, Selichoth, Kinnoth*) are mainly for synagogue services. Hence, while all other prayers are focused on the community, the *Hagadah* addresses itself to the family and its components. The text of the Hagadah is arranged in a set "order" (Hebr. *Seder*). This represents the "order" of life, or the "stages of man," from birth to life's end, from being a product of the family, to becoming a producer and head of a family, as follows:

KADESH—When a Jewish child is born, the first task of parents is to consecrate its life to a holy purpose, just as any Holy Day is inaugurated by *Kiddush*. Only if parents begin their work of education with *kadesh,* will the lives of their children be a constant *Yom Tov,* a perpetual source of delight.

URECHATZ—In infancy the child is still helpless; it cannot wash itself. It is up to the parent to free it from all impurities, by washing himself and setting an example of purity and noble conduct.

KARPAS—Now the child starts to enjoy pleasures. This is the time to learn *bore peri ha'adamah,* that there is "a Creator of the fruit of the earth," that all gifts and joys come from God, and that one must bless Him before every pleasure to deserve it.

YACHATZ—Next, the responsibility for training the child is "broken up" between parents and teachers, paving the way for—

MAGGID—Education, "relating" to the child the origin and meaning of Jewish existence. The long process of

Maggid precedes the meal at the *Seder,* just as intensive education must come first if life is to be meaningful later on. Following this lengthy stage, adolescence sets in with—

ROCHTZAH—renewed "washing" of impure temptations, this time by oneself. At this stage the battle of life begins in earnest, and it starts with warding off the overtures of lust and lewdness. For at this age the hazards of immoral lapses are greatest.

This is also the time to learn a new blessing. One no longer lives on *peri ha'adamah,* the ready-made "fruit of the earth", prepared by others, but on *lechem min ha'aretz,* "bread from the earth" won through many labors and much toil (*lechem,* from *milchamah*—"battle"). Yet even for hard-won enjoyments one must bless God as

MOTZI—"the One Who brings forth" bread and supplies every means to sustain life. He and His laws are to be remembered not only when we are children, but above all when we have entered the real struggle of life. However, "man does not live by bread alone." Besides his material needs, he must have—

MATZAH—unleavened, spiritual bread, symbolizing the privations and the sobering effects of a religious discipline of life. Only with such religious convictions can one bear in fortitude—

MAROR—the bitter elements of life, and even bless God for them as one blesses Him for good fortune. For in life, both good and bad fortune, must be—

KORAKH—"wrapped together," so that the sorrows of life may be balanced by its joys. Only after these preparatory conditions are met can we proceed to—

SHULCHAN ARUKH—to the "prepared table" of our own, to the establishment of home and family in the festive spirit of achievement. Now—

TZAFUN—the "hidden part" (*aphikomon*) set aside at the *Yachatz* stage—school education—can be given full scope and application. Then the afternoon and evening of life will prove—

BAREKH—"blissful" and "graceful," like the blessings of grace following the meal;

HALLEL—a poem of "praise," an orderly and beautiful life without discord; and—

NIRTZAH—"acceptable" to God and man alike. Thus does the *Seder* exemplify the Jewish "order" of life

HAGADAH

Hagadah means "telling," "story," and is of course derived from the *Pesach* command, "And thou shalt tell (*"vehigadta"*) thy son, in that day, saying: It is because of that which the Lord did for me when I came forth out of Egypt."[14] Related to the root *gadad,* which means "to attack,"[15] "to intrude"[16] or "to make incisions,"[17] "thou shalt tell" suggests relating the story until it leaves an indelible mark on the listener, until it intrudes into his consciousness and attacks any prejudices opposing (Hebrew *neged,* "against," also from the same root) it. In other words, *Hagadah* is more than the narration of a story; it is the reenactment of an experience, the re-living of a story told so realistically that it is cut permanently into one's memory and outlook.

* * *

By the year 1900, there were 1000 different editions of the Hagadah, 200 of them illustrated, printed in 93 places.[18]

PRAYER FOR DEW

The beautiful Prayer for Dew (*"Tephilath Tal"*), solemnly sung on the first day of *Pesach* for *Musaph,* was composed by Eleazar Kalir, the most illustrious and prolific of all Jewish liturgical poets. Although over 200 of his superb poems are known, many of them among our best-known Festival-and Fast-prayers, very little is known of the life of this author. The period in which he lived has been variously placed from the seventh to the eleventh centuries, or even to the tannaitic era of the Talmud at the beginning of the Common Era, and his assumed country of origin ranges from Babylonia or Palestine to Italy. Thus does this inspired poet transcend the fixed bounds of time and space.

CHOL HA-MO'ED

On *Chol Hamo'ed* the *Tephillin* are removed before saying *Hallel*, except on the first day of *Chol Hamo'ed Pesach*, when they are to be worn until after the reading-of-the-Law, because on that day the reading includes the first two portions inscribed in the *Tephillin*.[19] Thus this is the only occasion on which we can wear the *Tephillin* while actually reading about them in the Torah.

LAST DAYS

The last two night of *Pesach* are the only *Yomtov* nights when *"Shehechiyanu"* is not said for kindling the lights or at *Kiddush*, because they are the only Festival days in the year which do not constitute a new *Yomtov*.

CHAMETZ AFTER PESACH

Chametz which remained in Jewish possession over *Pesach*, even accidentally, without being sold to a non-Jew, must not be eaten or otherwise used or turned into money after *Pesach*. It remains permanently prohibited and must be destroyed (whatever the loss) as a penalty, so that the sinner shall not benefit from his offense or negligence.[20]

COUNTING THE OMER

The date for commencing the Counting of the *Omer*—"from the morrow of the Sabbath"[21]—sparked off some of the most devasting secterian schisms in Jewish history: first between the Pharisees and Saducees and later between the Rabbis and the Karaites. The traditionalists, who accepted the authentic interpretation of the Oral Law, held that "the

Sabbath" here, as occasionally elsewhere, referred to the Festival, so that the count was to begin on the second day of Pesach, while the dissidents, who rejected the Oral Law, interpreted "the Sabbath" in its usual sense and began the count on the Sunday following the 15th of Nisan.[22] Perhaps this is a further reason why the *Omer*-period became a time of mourning in the Jewish calendar, in addition to the other sad events associated with that period, viz., the death of 24,000 disciples of Rabbi Akiva and the fearful ravages caused by the first Crusade in 1096.

* * *

Neither the Talmud nor even Maimonides mentions the custom to observe in certain mourning rites (no weddings, music, haircuts, etc.) during the *Sefirah* period between *Pesach* and *Shavuoth* or the semi-festival of *Lag Be'omer*. The Talmud merely relates that 24,000 of Rabbi Akivah's disciples perished in a plague[22a] at the time of the Bar Kochba revolt. The mourning custom is first mentioned by the German talmudist Rabbi Jacob Molin of the 14th century,[23] and since then the season has been associated with many bloody episodes in Jewish history, such as the massacres of the First Crusade in Germany (1096) and the Chmielnicki pogroms in Poland (1648). The observance of *Lag Be'omer* as a festive day—the last special day to be introduced into the Jewish calendar, apart from Israel Independence Day of our own time—is attributed to the tradition that on Iyar 18 (*Lag Be'omer*) the plague of Rabbi Akivah's pupils abated,[24] that the mystic Rabbi Shimon Ben Yochai revealed his esoteric secrets before his death,[25] and that the Manna began to fall in the wilderness.[26]

SHAVUOTH

NAME

The usual name for this Festival—*Shavuoth*—literally means "weeks", or "seven-day periods", a reference of course to the seven weeks (*shiv'ah shavuoth*) to be counted between the beginning of *Pesach* and *Shavuoth*. But *Shavuoth* can also

denote "oaths"; hence the talmudic tractate dealing with
oaths is called *"Shavuoth"* (the connection between "seven"
and "oath" is that both bear the stamp of sanctity: the Sabbath
and the solemn word). The name of the Festival, therefore,
reminds us of two "oaths": God swore that He would never
forsake Israel, and Israel swore to uphold His law.[27]

* * *

We refer to *Shavuoth* as "the time of the Giving of the
Torah" and not "the time of the Receiving of the Torah"
because the Torah was given at Mount Sinai, but the time
for receiving it is every day.[28]

* * *

The festival is also called *Yom Ha'Bikkurim,* "Day of the
First-fruits,"[29] since "the bread of the first-fruits," i.e., of
the first wheat, was offered on that day.[30] From the same root
we have the word *bechor,* "first-born". The Hebrew letters of
the root (*b, ch* and *r*) are the only letters in the alphabet whose
numerical value is double the preceding letters (2, 20 and 200,
following the letters representing 1, 10 and 100), perhaps an
intimation of the double portion due to the first-born. While
Pesach represents the deliverance of the first-born, individually
and collectively in the sense of "Israel, My first-born son,"[31]
Shavuoth recalls the double inheritance (two tablets of the
Ten Commandments, two Laws—Written and Oral) bequeathed to God's first-born. At the same time the festival
denotes the first "ripening" or "maturing" (*bachar*) of Israel;
through the giving of the Torah the purpose of Jewish history
began to come to "fruition."

DATE

Shavuoth is the only Festival for which no date is given in
the Torah. It simply states that the Festival is to be celebrated
on the fiftieth day after beginning the count of the *Omer* on
the second day of *Pesach.*[32] Hence, while the Hellenists called
it *"Pentecost"* ("fifty" in Greek), the Rabbis named it
"Atzereth" ("concluding feast"), suggesting that the relationship between *Pesach* and *Shavuoth* is the same as between
Sukkoth and *Shemini Atzereth.* In the Jewish view the free-

dom of Passover is meaningless if cut off from its source of God's Law given on *Shavuoth.*

* * *

The absence of a date for the "Season of the Giving of the Law", as well as the *Torah's* conspicuous omission of a precise date for the Revelation at Sinai itself,[33] stresses the timelessness of the Torah, which is to be topical in all ages and which can never be dated.[34]

IN THE TALMUD & CODES

Unlike *Rosh Hashonah, Yom Kippur, Pesach, Sukkoth* and even *Purim, Shavuoth* has no tractate in the Talmud, neither in name nor in theme. The *Shulchan Arukh* devotes only one chapter[35] to its laws, as against 62 for *Pesach* and 35 for *Sukkoth*. By way of compensation, the whole Talmud and the whole *Shulchan Arukh* are dedicated to the Festival's message—the *Torah*.

DAIRY FOODS

Among the reasons for the custom to eat dairy foods on *Shavuoth* (probably also due to the desire to avoid heavy food at the very late evening meals on the Festival nights in the Summer) is that the Torah is compared in its wholesomeness to milk[36] and that the Israelites on the day they received the Torah had to dispense with meat, as it took some time to prepare it in accordance with the newly enacted *Shechitah* and dietary laws,[37] especially following the tradition that the Revelation took place on a Sabbath when animals could not be slaughtered.[38]

FLORAL DECORATIONS

Since medieval times it became customary to decorate synagogues and homes with green plants on *Shavuoth*[39] as a reminder of the green pastures which covered Mount Sinai[40] according to one opinion,[41] and of the Divine judgment over trees on that day[42] according to another.[43]

But the Gaon of Vilna attacked the custom as an imitation of non-Jewish practices.[44]

*　　*　　*

The following interesting reason is given for the custom to decorate synagogues with plants on *Shavuoth*. When Moses was born, his mother "hid him three months; and when she could no longer hide him, she took for him an ark of bulrushes . . . . and laid it in the reeds by the river's brink."[45] Since the birthday of Moses was traditionally on the 7th of Adar, the date on which he was placed among the river-plants, three months later, was the 6th of Sivan which is the date of *Shavuoth*. Hence, on this festival we bring plants into the synagogue to remember the miracle of the survival of Moses (Gaon of Vilna).

TIKKUN

The custom of spending the first night of *Shavuoth* learning Torah till dawn (*"Tikkun leil Shavuoth"*), so as to prepare oneself for "receiving the Torah" and Ten Commandments read in the morning, is of ancient origin and is first mentioned in the *Zohar*.[46]

AKDAMUTH

The beautiful *Akdamuth* poem,—composed of 45 Aramaic stanzas by Rabbi Meir ben Isaac of Mayence (ca. 1060), contemporary of Rashi, in honor of the Torah—became the cause of a long rabbinical controversy. The earlier practice of singing *Akdamuth* after completing the first verse in the Reading-of-the-Law was heatedly opposed as an unwarranted interruption in the reading of the Torah; it should rather be sung before the *Kohen* says his blessing over the Torah. Notwithstanding this opposition, the earlier view prevailed in most communities.[47]

TEN COMMANDMENTS

In the days of the Temple the Ten Commandments formed part of the statutory Service, being recited daily before the *Shema* by the priests.[48] The practice was later abolished "because of the seditious talk of the heretics (i.e. the Judaeo-Christians), that it should not be said these (Ten Commandments) alone were given to Moses at Sinai."[49] For this reason Maimonides objected to the custom of standing up during the reading of the Ten Commandments, unless one always stood during the Reading-of-the-Law, "since this may lead to compromising our faith through the erroneous idea that one part of the Torah excels another," i.e., that the Ten Commandments are more important than other laws.[50]

* * *

The text of the Ten Commandments is the only part of the Hebrew Bible to have a dual system of cantilation ("*tropp*"). The "*ta'am ha'elyon*" (literally "upper accents," so called because most of the musical marks are above the words) is used for public readings in the synagogue. This follows the literary text ("*kethiv*") in which there is no division of verses; instead each paragraph, corresponding to a complete commandment, is read as a unit. The "*ta'am hatachton*" (literally "lower accents," with most marks below the words), on the other hand, follows the massoretic reading ("*keri*") to be used for private recitation. This system divides the text of the Ten Commandments into 14 verses (instead of 10 paragraphs). While the Fourth Commandment, for instance, is thus made up of four verses, the 6th to 8th Commandments are combined as a single verse, since in the massoretic text no verse should have less than three words.

* * *

The Ten Commandments are never so called in Hebrew, perhaps because the first of them ("I am the Lord . . .") is not really phrased in the form of a commandment, either positive or negative, but is simply a statement or declaration.[51] The Decalogue is described as *asereth hadevarim* in the Torah itself[52] and as *asereth hadibroth* in rabbinic literature (the latter being the common Hebrew usage). Both mean "the ten words" or "things." But the root *davar* is also used in the sense "to drive," "to guide," or "to subjugate,"[53] so that the Hebrew term for the Ten Commandments is suggestive of their purpose as a "guide" to our life through our "subjection" to the will of God.

*   *   *

In place of the Ashkenazi custom of reading the Ten Commandments before the chanting of the *Akdamuth* (poem composed about 1060 in Germany), the Sephardim recite *Azharoth* (a poetic enumeration of the 613 commandments composed by Solomon ibn Gabirol at about the same time in Spain) either after *Musaph* or before *Minchah*. Some Sephardi congregations also recite a poetic *"Kethubah"* describing the "marriage contract" between God and Israel and their mutual obligations contracted at Mt. Sinai.

The Symmetry of the Ten Commandments

Out of the 613 *Mitzvoth* given to Israel at Sinai the Ten Commandments are selected for special pronouncement. Yet they are chosen neither because of their universal application (e.g. the Sabbath law is not incumbent on all men, while the duty to administer justice—as one of the Seven Noachidic Laws—is) nor for their overriding moral importance (e.g., the Tenth Commandment not to covet is surely a less fundamental moral law than is to love one's neighbor as oneself, or not to pervert justice, and numerous other basic laws, not included in the Ten Commandments). How does one account, then, for the choice of these "Ten Words," as they are called in Hebrew?

Saadyah Gaon, cited by Rashi,[54] and Ibn Ezra,[55] found all the 613 commandments incorporated in the Decalogue. In other words, he regarded the Ten Commandments as a summary of the entire Torah legislation. It has also been suggested that the Ten Commandments correspond to the ten synonyms for *Torah* and *Mitzvoth*, used in the 119th chapter of Psalms,[56] so that each would represent a distinct body of laws,—ritual, social, moral, symbolic, religious, etc. On the other hand, several authorities found the Ten Commandments included in the *Shema*,[57] in the holiness code of the nineteenth chapter of Leviticus[58] and, actually in the order of the Decalogue, in the Sidrah *Mishpatim.*[59]

* * *

Moreover, it was assumed that the Ten Commandments were divided into five on each of the two tablets, with the first group listing our duties towards God and the second towards man, and that the five laws in one group were exactly parallel to those in the other.[60]

The First and Sixth Commandments (i.e. the first on either tablet) deal with the acknowledgment of the unity of God on one side and of man on the other. The recognition of one God implies the common origin of all men and hence their equality. This makes the murder of any man, created as he is, in His image, into a capital crime. (Contrast this attitude of the ancient Greeks with that of the Hebrews. The former protected the lives of their own nationals, calling all others "barbarians," on the ground that they belonged to a different species of the human race, created by a different god.)

The Second and Seventh Commandments proscribe faithlessness to our Divine partner in the first tablet (the Prophets often describe Israel's idolatry as adultery toward God) and to our human partner (by adultery), in the second.

The Third and Eighth Commandments share in the ban on the misuse of the property of God and of man. By swearing falsely or idly one violates the "Name" of God, His most inalienable possession, just as stealing violates the sanctity of human property.

The Fourth and Ninth Commandments command truthful testimony—by observing the Sabbath testifying to God's act of creating the world in six days and resting on the seventh, and by not bearing false witness against one's neighbor.

Finally, the Fifth and Tenth Commandments are addressed to our sentiments, impulses and feelings, the former in bestirring love and honor toward our parents as God's partners in our creation, and the latter in curbing our passions, appetites, and acquisitive instincts for possessions not our own.

Thus, the Ten Commandments represent the headings of the five main categories of laws defining our duties, respectively, towards God and man, regarding: (1) the acknowledgement of their unity and integrity, (2) the sanctity of our exclusive and intimate bonds with them, (3) the inviolability of their property, (4) the affirmation of the truth, and (5) the control of our emotions, or the sanctification of (1) life, (2) pledge of faith, (3) property, (4) truth, and (5) feelings.

MUSAPH

All additional offerings (*"Musaphim"*) on festivals include a "sin-offering to make atonement." But on *Shavuoth*, alone among the festivals, the Torah omits the word "sin-offering" (*"chatath"*)[61] because, in the words of the Talmud, God told Israel: "Since you accepted the yoke of the Torah, I account it for you as if you had never sinned in your days."[62]

SECOND DAY

The second day of *Shavuoth* may enjoy a greater sanctity than the other second Festival days observed in the Diaspora. In the case of all other Festivals, the second *Yom Tov* day had originally been added to the first outside the Holy Land because the precise date of the new moon, and hence of the Festival's commencement, could not be communicated in time from Jerusalem where it was proclaimed by the Sanhedrin. But no doubt ever existed, even in the Diaspora, about the true date of *Shavuoth*, since its incidence depended not on a calendar date but on the count of fifty days following the second day of *Pesach* (by which time all communities would know when the count started). We must therefore assume that the second day of *Shavuoth* was originally enacted not because of any uncertainty about the date but on account of its intrinsic importance.[63]

RUTH

The reading of the *Book of Ruth* on *Shavuoth*—which originated in geonic times over a thousand years ago[64]—is explained as due to its reference to the harvest (*Shavuoth* being the "Harvest Festival"), to the Bible's most outstanding proselyte (*Shavuoth* celebrating Israel's conversion to Judaism)[64a], and to Ruth as King David's ancestor (*Shavuoth* being the anniversary of his birth and death).[65]

*   *   *

Among the many explanations given for our practice to read the *Book of Ruth* on *Shavuoth* is the numerical value of the Hebrew *Ruth*. This amounts to 606 (200+6+400), corresponding to the 606 commandments to which Israel submitted at Sinai, in addition to the 7 Noachidic commandments, which had already previously been incumbent on them, as on the whole human race, since the days of Noah, making a total of 613 commandments.[66] Likewise, Ruth herself, following her conversion to Judaism, acknowledged 606 new *Mitzvoth* (Gaon of Vilna).

*   *   *

Ruth—the name of the Biblical book read on *Shavuoth* and of the book's heroine—is probably derived from the Hebrew *re'uth,* meaning "friendship," "companionship" (Gesenius). In a pun on the name, the Talmud explains that Ruth was so called "because she had the merit that from her descended David, who delighted (*rivahu,* from *ravah*—"saturated," "refreshed") the Lord with songs and hymns"[67] through his authorship of the *Psalms.* But the Midrash states that "she was called Ruth, because she looked to (*ra'atha,* from *ra'ah*—'to see') the words of her mother-in-law"[68] and accepted her guidance. Ruth thus represents "friendship" both with God and her fellow-humans—the ideal of the Torah revealed on *Shavuoth.*

YAMIM NORA'IM

ELUL

As a prelude to the Days of Awe, the *Shofar* blown daily at the end of the morning service throughout the month of Elul summons us to our spiritual preparations. The forty days from *Rosh Chodesh Elul* to the tenth of Tishri correspond to the period Moses spent on Sinai pleading with God to forgive Israel's sin for the Golden Calf and culminating, on the original Day of Atonement, in the Divine pardon.[69]

SELICHOTH

As the Days of Judgment draw nearer, the tempo of our penitential exercises is to be accelerated through the daily recitation of *Selichoth* (propitiatory prayers), commencing on the Sunday preceding *Rosh Hashanah* (or a week earlier if the festival falls on a Monday or Tuesday) according to the Ashkenazi rite, and from the beginning of Elul according to the Sephardi rite.[70] These beautiful poetic prayers are made up of three main types: *"Tokhachah"* (admonitions to consider the meaning of life and the value of repentance), *"Akedah"* (poetic variations on the theme of the sacrifice of Isaac) and *"Techinah"* (supplications for Divine blessings). Among the most famous authors whose compositions are included in our *Selichoth* are: Saadyah Gaon (Egypt, 892-942), Rabenu Gershon (Rhineland, 960-1028), Solomon ibn Gabirol (Spain, 1021-1058), Rashi (France, 1040-1105), Eliezer of Worms (Germany, 11th cent.), Judah Hechasid (Germany, 12th cent.) and Leon of Modena (Venice, 1571-1648).

* * *

Selichoth are "penitential prayers," originally consisting mainly of Biblical passages to be recited on *Yom Kippur* and, since the Middle Ages, also of poetic compositions for the entire penitential season from the Sunday preceding *Rosh Hashanah* until *Yom Kippur*, as well as for all other fast-days. The term derives from the Biblical *salach*—"to forgive"—used throughout the Bible only for God's pardoning of sins against Him. In the Torah the word is never associated with *Yom Kippur*, but it is used especially in connection with the prayers of Moses seeking Divine forgiveness for the sins of the Ten Spies[71] and the Golden Calf[72] for which atonement was traditionally granted on *Yom Kippur*. Both pleas are preceded by the "Thirteen Attributes of God,"[73] which form the kernel of our *Selichoth* prayers to this day.

* * *

The confessional prayer in our *Selichoth* and *Yom Kippur* liturgy is recited in the plural: *"ashamnu"*—*"we* have sinned". It expresses the idea that all Jews are collectively responsible for each other. We confess and seek forgiveness for sins even though we did not personally commit them, since we are co-responsible for the failings of our neighbors. All Israel is like one body of which every individual Jew is an organic member (Ari). The listing of our sins, both in the *"ashamnu"* and *"al chet"* confessions, in alphabetical order indicates that our shortcomings range over the whole gamut of wrongs "from A to Z."

UNIVERSAL SIGNIFICANCE

Rosh Hashanah and *Yom Kippur* are the only festivals in the Jewish calendar which are not of national but universal in significance. This is reflected in the prayers peculiar to these days, emphasizing God's role as "King over all the earth" (*Amidah*). Unlike the three "foot-festivals", *Rosh Hashanah* marks not an event in Jewish history but the creation of the world, the birth of man. At the same time it is the Day of Judgment. These two aspects are interrelated. Man is responsible to God only because he was created and must thus serve the purpose envisaged by the Creator. Were man the product of mere chance, not of choice, he could not be held accountable to anyone. This is expressed in the New Year liturgy: "This day the world was called into being: (therefore) this day Thou causest all creatures to stand in judgment" (*Rosh Hashanah Musaph*).

HEAD OF YEAR

Why is the Penitential Season placed at the head and not at the end of the year? So that the beginning of the year, like the first-born and the first-fruits, shall be especially consecrated to God. Instead of the English "all is well that ends well", our sages said "all beginnings are hard;"[74] if you master them and venture forth on the right path, the rest will be easy. "All is well that *begins* well."

CREATION

The first of Tishri, as the date from which the years are counted, is already mentioned in the Talmud.[75] So is the era reckoned from "the creation of the world," now generally accepted in the Jewish calendar.[76] But its use did not become common until the fifth century. Before then—and among oriental Jews up to modern times—Jewish documents used mainly the "Seleucidan era" starting in the year 312 B. C. E. Incidentally, among the non-Jews, too, it was not until the 12th century (in Spain and Portugal some five hundred years later) that the "Christian era" generally replaced the count of years by Emperors or Consuls.[77]

REJOICING

On *Rosh Hashanah* and *Yom Kippur* we omit the phrase "appointed times for gladness, festivals and seasons for joy," because only the three pilgrim-festivals are called *"mo'adim,"* a reference to the "assembly" of all Jews in Jerusalem and the attendant joyful festivals. But even on these solemn days the joy of seeking and obtaining atonement from God is real enough to warrant the *duchaning* by the priests—a ceremony reserved for days of joy since blessings can only be bestowed out of feelings of happiness.[78]

SHOFAR

Shofar, commonly mistranslated "trumpet," really means something "pleasant," from the Biblical *shafar*—"to be good-looking," "beautiful"—hence "round." (In the Talmud *shefofereth* means "tube"). In the Torah, the *shofar* is employed to announce the New Moon and solemn feasts,[79] to proclaim the Jubilee year,[80] and to prepare the giving of the Ten Commandments,[81] as well as to mark *Rosh Hashanah*.[82] The "round," curved nature of the ram's horn is to symbolize the "bent," contrite posture of penitence.[83]

*   *   *

The question of whether to blow the *Shofar* on *Rosh Hashanah* coinciding with the Sabbath became the subject of a celebrated controversy in Jerusalem just over a half a century ago when a famed scholar[84] argued that the rabbinic interdict against using the *Shofar* on the Sabbath (for fear the *Shofar* may be carried in public places on the Sabbath) did not apply to the Holy City, just as—according to the Talmud[85]—the restriction never applied to the Temple.[86]

REMINDERS OF MARTYRDOM

The two most solemn prayers of *Rosh Hashanah* and *Yom Kippur*—*"Alenu"* and *"Kol Nidrei,"* respectively—are both intimately associated with Jewish martyrdom in the Middle Ages, and both are recited three times in the High Festival liturgy. The former—proclaiming the spiritual majesty of Israel and the ultimate triumph of the Kingdom of God— was sung by the martyrs while they were burnt at the stake for the sanctification of His Name, and the latter—asking for the absolution of vows—may have been invested with such solemnity by the crypto-Jews (Marranos) when they secretly recited it on the holiest day to renounce their promise to change their faith exacted under duress.

ROSH HASHANAH MUSAPH

The longest *Amidah* of the year is recited on *Rosh Hashanah* for *Musaph*. Its main body consists of ten scriptural verses, followed by a special benediction, in each of the three sections called *"Malkhuyoth"* (Divine kingship), *"Zikhronoth"* (Remembrance) and *"Shofaroth"* (Shofar-blows). The first section opens with the sublime *Aleinu*-prayer which was eventually (from the fourteenth century) taken from here and placed at the end of every congregational service throughout the year. It was edited by the Talmudist Rav in the third century, but an old tradition ascribes its composition to Joshua on his entrance into Canaan.[87]

An Interpretation of the Musaph Amidah

The *Amidah* recited for *Musaph* on *Rosh Hashanah* is quite unique among our great prayers. It is by far the longest *Amidah* of the year, and alone among the Sabbath and festival *Amidoth* it has nine instead of the usual seven benedictions. It is distinguished by the blowing of the *Shofar* interspersed in its repetition by the reader (and, in some congregations, also during its silent recital), and it has bequeathed to every service of the year its incomparable *Aleinu*-prayer.

Above all, this *Amidah* (devoted mainly to a recital of the "additional offerings" in the Temple of old on all other occasions) is unique in its structure and superbly majestic contents. Its principal body develops three major themes, each introduced by an exalted statement of the Divine relationship and communication to man, supported by ten Scriptural verses (four from the Torah, three from the Prophets and three from the Writings), and concluded by a plea and blessing in the form of a final benediction. These three themes are known as *Malkhuyoth, Zikhronoth* and *Shofaroth.*

Malkhuyoth proclaims God's "Kingship" in the universe and looks forward to the recognition of His Sovereignty by all men. It corresponds to the chief name of the festival, *Rosh Hashanah,* literally "Head of the Year," and its significance as the anniversary of His creation of the world and thus His "Headship" of it.

Zikhronoth affirms God's "remembrance" of His creatures and their works. It recalls some highlights of history when He rewarded (e.g. the "Binding of Isaac," the "merit of the Patriarchs") and punished (e.g. the Flood) men for their deeds and "remembered" His promises. It corresponds to the liturgical name of the festival, *Yom Ha-Zikaron,* "Day of Remembrance."

Shofaroth refers to the *Shofar* sounded when "Thou revealed Thyself . . . to Thy holy people, to speak with them from Heaven . . ." through prophecy, particularly at the Revelation of the Torah on Mt. Sinai, and it prays for the "great *Shofar*" to be sounded at Israel's ultimate redemption. This part corresponds to the festival's biblical name, *Yom Teru'ah*, "Day of Blowing the *Shofar*."

We may see reflected in these three themes the three cardinal beliefs of Judaism:

Malkhuyoth postulates the *Existence of God* as the Prime Cause of the universe (Creator) and its Ruler ("King").

Zikhronoth asserts the doctrine of *Retribution*, of *Reward and Punishment* which, even if not exacted immediately, is "remembered" for generations. It holds out the fulfillment of His "promises" to the righteous and wicked alike. It emphasizes the meaning of the festival as the "Day of Judgment" when all creatures are "remembered" by their deeds before Him.

Shofaroth declares the belief in *"Torah min Ha-Shamayim,"* in *Revelation*, whereby God communicated His will at Sinai and later through His Prophets. The *Shofar*, as the symbol of the immediacy in God's relation to man used in Temple worship as well as in Revelation, also heralds Divine deliverance—God's intervention in history to assert His Sovereignty. Thus the cycle is complete.

The same three themes also find expression in the three paragraphs of the *Shema*—the Jew's daily declaration of faith—and the three pilgrimage festivals.

The *Existence of God* is proclaimed in the first paragraph, setting forth His unity, and our duty to love Him, to study His words, and to consecrate our bodies (*Tephillin*) and homes (*Mezuzoth*) to Him. It also is symbolized by *Pesach*, recording God's wonders and signs "that ye shall know that I am the Lord."

The doctrine of *Reward and Punishment* is defined in the second paragraph showing the consequences of hearkening to, and of defying, the laws of God. It is also represented by *Sukkoth*, the symbol of Divine Providence—"for He will shelter me in His *Sukkah* on the day of evil."

Finally, the *Revelation* of the Torah from Heaven is recalled by the third paragraph dealing with *Zizith*, including the sky-blue thread "that ye shall remember all the commandments of the Lord" as coming from Heaven. This is also the meaning of *Shavuoth,* the anniversary of the Giving of the Law at Sinai.

ROSH HASHANAH CUSTOMS

The custom to eat some apple dipped in honey on *Rosh Hashanah,* with a prayer that the new year may be "good and sweet," is first mentioned by the German rabbinic scholar Jacob Molin of the fourteenth century.[88] He is also the first to record the observance of *"Tashlich,"* the custom to walk to a river with fish and recite various verses, especially "And Thou wilt cast (Hebr. *'Vethaslich')* all their sins into the depths of the sea."[89] The *Minhag* has been explained as a reminder of the *"Akedah."* According to the Midrash[89a] the Satan, in order to prevent Abraham from sacrificing Isaac and fulfilling God's will, threw himself across their path in the form of a river. Both, nevertheless, plunged into it until the water reached their necks.[90] The custom is also interpreted as symbolic of man's plight, which may be compared to "the fishes that are taken in an evil net;"[91] and as a visible reminder of creation, which saw its genesis in "the depth of the sea" (Isserles).

*   *   *

The custom of *Tashlich* (which is of late medieval origin and not mentioned in the *Shulchan Arukh*) is observed on the second day of *Rosh Hashanah* if the first day falls on the Sabbath because it is feared that people may carry books with them to the river.[92]

FAST OF GEDALYAH

The Fast of Gedalyah, which commemorates his assassination on the first of Tishri, is always postponed to the third (or, if that falls on a Sabbath, the fourth) of the month on account of the festival preceding it. Gedalyah was Governor of Judea, appointed by Nebuchadnezzar after the destruction of the first Temple in 586 B. C. E. With his death the Jews lost the last vestiges of independence and the fate of the first Jewish commonwealth was finally sealed.

DAYS OF PENITENCE

"During the ten Days of Penitence everyone should search and examine his deeds and do repentance for them. A sin about which one is in doubt requires more penitence than a definite sin, for one is more remorseful if one knows what one did than if one does not. For this reason the sacrifice offered (in ancient days) for a doubtful offense had to be more precious than the ordinary sin-offering."[93]

* * *

True repentance consists of three elements: the confession of one's sins, genuine remorse, and the resolve not to repeat past offenses. "What is complete repentance? If one had the occasion again to commit a sin one had committed before . . . and one yet desisted and did not commit it on account of penitence and not out of fear or weakness . . . that is real repentance."[94]

EREV YOM KIPPUR

"Whoever eats and drinks on the Ninth of Tishri is considered as if he afflicted himself (i.e. fasted) on the Ninth and Tenth."[95] An interesting variety of reasons has been advanced why one is duty-bound to eat on the eve on *Yom Kippur*: (1) That man will be strong enough to fast on the following day,[96] (2) that by eating on the eve of *Yom Kippur* he will feel the pangs of hunger more acutely on the day following,[97] and (3) because on the eve of the holiest day of supreme judgment, the Jew, engrossed as he is in thoughts of penitence and pleas for life, would hardly have any natural desire for food. Hence, by yet forcing himself to eat on the eve of that fateful day, he is serving God as much as he would by fasting on other days.[98]

YOM KIPPUR: NAME

Yom Kippur—"Day of Atonement"—comes from the root *Kafar*—"to cover" (note the close relationship between the Hebrew and English words which doubtless have a common origin); hence *Kapporeth*—the "lid" or "cover" on the holy ark. Atonement therefore literally means a "covering up" (of sins). Sins cannot be eradicated completely; repentance merely renders them invisible by placing a "lid" over them. The word is also related to *Kofer*—"ransom". By means of penitence, guilt is exchanged and our debt to God is paid and liquidated. The same root may also signify "to wipe out," "to deny," or "to ignore"; *Kefirah* is "heresy" or the "denial" of the truth, just as *Kapparah* is "atonement" or the "denial," the "wiping out" of the untruth, of sin.

MORTIFICATION

Under the heading of "self-affliction," the principal prohibitions on *Yom Kippur* are eating and drinking, washing (other than eyes and fingers), anointing, wearing leather shoes, and conjugal intercourse.[99] If a person is too weak to fast *and* go to synagogue, he should rather spend the day at home in bed than break the fast, as fasting is a cardinal biblical law,[100] while worshipping with the congregation is not. But if a doctor determines that fasting may be a grave health hazard, it is then a religious duty to eat, subject to rabbinic approval. A seriously sick person should even insert the *Yomtov* formula of *"Ya'aleh veyavo"* in the Grace after Meals,[101] since "to him the Day of Atonement is as ordinary festivals are to us."[102] But, wherever possible, he should not consume more food than the size of a small egg and more drink than the fill of his cheek within ten minutes, so that the total volume will not constitute the biblically forbidden amount.[103]

SCRIPTURAL READINGS

The Torah- and Haphtorah-readings on *Yom Kippur* (other than those dealing with the Day's worship[104]) present

Judaism's three supreme themes: sexual morality, the sanctity of the Sabbath, and the duty not to shirk the Jewish mission to be God's messengers (relations with peoples of the world).

YIZKOR

Originally *Yizkor* was recited only on *Yom Kippur,* based on the interpretation of the verse: "Grant atonement to Thy people Israel whom Thou hast redeemed;"[105] "*to Thy people Israel*—these are the living, *whom Thou hast redeemed*—these are the dead."[106] Hence, it has been suggested that the usual rabbinic name "*Yom Hakippurim*" in the plural denotes atonement for the living and atonement for the dead.[107] The extension of the custom to other Festivals is more recent. It is not mentioned in the *Shulchan Arukh* and is unknown in most Sephardi communities to this day.

SHOFAR

The reason for blowing a single *Shofar* sound at the conclusion of *Yom Kippur* is to remind us of the *Shofar* sounded at the commencement of the Jubilee year on *Yom Kippur*[108] and to mark the departure of the Divine Presence ascending back to Heaven, as it is written. "God is gone up amidst shouting ('*Teru'ah*'), the Lord amidst the sound of the horn ('*Shofar*')."[109]

SUKKOTH

NAME

The word "*Sukkoth*" is used for the first time in the Torah as the name of a place East of the Jordan, so called by Jacob because he there "built himself a house and made *booths* for his cattle,"[110] possibly as a "shelter" to protect him from Esau.[111]

*   *   *

Sukkoth occurs originally as a place-name, so called by Jacob because he built there "booths for his cattle."[112] In one other biblical passage the term is again used as a "shelter" for animals, i.e. in Job 38:40, where it refers to a lion's den. In using the word for a human home, therefore, the emphasis is not on its comforts and decorations, or even on its durability ("homes" for animals lack all these), but simply on the protection it affords. In fact, the root *sakhakh,* from which *sukkah* is derived, means "to protect." A particularly vivid illustration of this word's employment in that sense is in reference to the Cherubim *sokhakhim bekhanfehem*—"protecting with their wings" the lid covering the Holy Ark.[113] The wings of angels which symbolize the Divine shield guarding His Law are analogous to the function of the *Sukkah* in standing guard over Israel's spiritual blessings.

DATE

In the main Torah passage dealing with *Sukkoth*[114] the insistence that the Festival shall be celebrated "in this seventh month" is mentioned three times, while the requirement to celebrate it "for seven days" is repeated no less than six times. This is to emphasize that the joy of *Sukkoth* is to be seven times as long as *Rosh Hashanah* and seven times as long as *Yom Kippur.* Moreover, *Sukkoth* brings the festival season to its culmination with the rejoicing before God in the "Sabbatical" or *seventh* month of the year.[115]

*   *   *

"The reason for observing *Sukkoth* at the time of ingathering, when plenty fills your houses and granaries, is to remember that God housed the children of Israel in booths for forty years in the wilderness when they possessed nothing they could call their own, so that you will render thanks to Him Who has given you possessions and filled your homes with all good things, and that you should not say 'My might and the strength of my hand have brought me all this wealth'."[116]

*   *   *

The duty to dwell in tabernacles during the festival is mentioned only once in the Torah,[117] where the reason given is "so that your generations may know that I made the children of Israel to dwell in booths, when I brought them out of the land of Egypt."[118]   The festival is fixed for the month of

Tishri during the Fall season because the Israelites in the
wilderness then began feeling the cold and started to build
shelters for themselves,[119] or to emphasize our dependence on
God by leaving our homes filled with the harvest's bounties
at that time when we might otherwise attribute our wealth to
our own labors and strength,[120] or because the farmer then
rests and is free from pressing labors.[121]

SEASON OF JOY

Jewish law defines the commandment to rejoice on *Yom Tov*
—stressed particularly in connection with *Sukkoth,*[122] "the
time of our rejoicing"—as dividing one's time equally between
the synagogue and feasting at home, buying sweets for one's
children and clothes and jewelry for one's wife, and extending
hospitality to the poor.   But one should beware of the joy
degenerating to gluttony and levity.   It was to curb such
excesses that the religious courts were required to appoint
special officials who were charged with the responsibility of
protecting men and women from gathering together in frivo-
lous assemblies.   And at home, too, the feasting must not be
jarred by any unseemly merriment or drinking incompatible
with the sanctity of the occasion.   To enhance the enjoyment
of the festival, divine service should start later than usual
(on weekdays) and finish at least by midday.[123]   Therefore one
should rebuke *Chazanim* who unduly prolong the prayers with
excess singing "half of which belongs to neither God nor to
you[r enjoyment]."[124]

SUKKAH

The verse "They shall go from strength to strength"[125]
is applied to those who go from the performance of one
Mitzvah to another, particularly as it concerns those who,
as soon as *Yom Kippur* is concluded, start with the building
of the *Sukkah.*[126]

*   *   *

The commandment to believe in God is mentioned only
once, namely among the laws of *Sukkoth,* in Jacob ben Asher's

great law code *Arba Turim* (on which Joseph Karo's *Shulchan Arukh* was later based). The context reads:

> "That your generations shall know that I caused the children of Israel to dwell in booths when I took them out from the land of Egypt"[127]—Scripture relates the *Mitzvah* of *Sukkah* to the Exodus ... to testify to the truth of the existence of the Creator... for the booths mentioned are the clouds of glory with which He surrounded and protected them from attack and heat."[128]

*   *   *

The *Sukkah* serves as a token of peace ("Tabernacle of peace") perhaps because it is a symbol of moderation and compromise: It must be a temporary abode (*"dirath ar'ay"*) and yet be used like a permanent home (*"k'eyn taduru"*); its covering must be thick enough to provide more shade than sunshine inside and it should yet be loose enough to allow the stars to be seen through it; the covering material must be of plants "grown from the earth" and yet be detached from the ground; the *Sukkah* must be at least ten handbreadths high and yet no more than twenty cubits (appr. 3 feet and 37 feet respectively); it must accommodate a person and yet need hold only his head and the greater part of his body; it must be specially built for the Festival (at least in part) and may yet be left standing from year to year. Moderation and compromise are the ingredients of peace.

*   *   *

The principal duty of "dwelling" in the *Sukkah* is to eat and sleep in it.[129] However, "the present custom not to sleep in the *Sukkah*, except for those who are particularly devout, has been explained by some as due to the cold elements, for sleeping in cold places would involve physical distress. But to me it appears [that the reason for the relaxation is] that the precept of *Sukkah* is given to every man and his home, that means a man with is wife, just as he would be dwelling for the rest of the year, and where it is impossible to retire with his wife because he has no *Sukkah* of his own, he would therefore be free [from the obligation of sleeping there]; hence if he can have a *Sukkah* for his own exclusive use, it is proper that he reside there with his wife as he does all the year round."[130]

* * *

A *Sukkah* must not be higher than 20 cubits, approximately 37 feet, but no lower than 10 handbreadths or 36 inches. It may be erected atop an animal, but not under a tree.[131]

ARBA MINIM

With the exception of the *Aravah* ("willow"), none of the names we use for the *Arba Minim* is found in the Torah. It describes the *Esrog* (probably from an aramaic root *"tarag"* meaning "to be bright") as "a fruit of a goodly [Hebr. *"hadar"*] tree,"[132] so called because of the Esrog's pleasant fragrance and appearance,[133] or because the fruit dwells (reading: *"ha-dar"*) on the tree from year to year, or because it grows on water (Greek: *hydor;* cf. hydro).[134] The word *Lulav,* called "branches of palm-trees" in the Torah, is derived from *"lavlev,"* meaning "to sprout," while the name *"hadas"* for myrtle, described as "boughs of thick trees" in the Torah, is of biblical origin[135] and may be connected with an Assyrian word meaning "bride."[136]

* * *

Although the festive wreath consists of four species (*"Arba Minim"*), the benediction only mentions the *Lulav* (*"al netilath lulav"*), because it is the largest of the four.[137]

* * *

The *Esrog,* which is the only fruit among the four plants making up the festive wreath, is also mentioned in rabbinic literature as the fruit of the forbidden tree from which Adam and Eve ate in the Garden of Eden;[138] hence the name "Adam's Apple."

* * *

Maimonides cites the universal Jewish practice of using an *Esrog*[139] as proof of an unbroken oral tradition going back to Sinai and handed down through the generations side by side with the Written Law.[140]

* * *

One need not spend more than one-fifth of one's possessions on the purchase of a *Lulav* and *Esrog,* or on the performance of any other positive commandment; but to avoid the transgression of a negative precept (such as not to eat *terephah* food, or not to work on a *Yomtov*), one must sacrifice one's entire fortune, if necessary.[141]

SIMCHATH BETH HA-SHO'EVAH

Special balconies for women were introduced in the Temple at Jerusalem on the occasion of the "Rejoicing of the Water Libation" on the second night of *Sukkoth,* when water was drawn and poured on the altar amid scenes of wild jubilation. The purpose of the enactment was to prevent frivolity during the celebrations. On that night of rejoicing disused priestly garments, soaked in oil, were burned, putting the Temple court in a blaze of leaping torches which lit the whole of Jerusalem. The masses would sing: "Happy our youth that it has not put to shame our old age."[142]

CHOL HA-MO'ED

The references in the Torah to *Pesach* and the Exodus from Egypt are far more numerous than to *Sukkoth,* which is mentioned only in the general listings of the festivals and the sacrificial order of service. Hence, while on *Pesach* a different portion of the Law is read on every day and two scrolls are taken from the Ark even on the *Chol Hamo'ed* days (one for reading about Passover and the other about the statutory offerings for the day), on *Sukkoth* we read the same portion on the first two days and we use only one scroll on *Chol Hamo'ed.*[143]

HOSHANA RABBA

*   *   *

Hoshana is a compound of *hosha—*"save!", and *na—*"I pray," corresponding to the *Hallel's hoshi'ah na.* The word was then transferred to the festive wreath, and especially to the willows in it, because of their association with the liturgical poems in which *"Hoshana"* is the constant refrain. The stress on "save!" and "salvation" in the *Sukkoth* ritual is due to the fact that festival follows immediately on the solemn Days of Judgment and thus represents the final chance for forgiveness and salvation, or that—having obtained atonement—we can pray for Divine deliverance with greater confidence than at any other time. This "final chance" climatically concludes on *Hoshana Rabba,* "the great salvation." This name for the last *Sukkoth* day does not occur in the Bible or even in the Talmud, which mentions it merely as the "Day of *Hoshana"* or the "Day of Willow."[144]

*   *   *

The custom to stay up and study part of the night of *Hoshana Rabba* is of medieval origin (*Shevilei Haleket*), going back to the much earlier belief mentioned in the *Midrash* and the *Zohar* that the day marks the final sealing of the Divine judgment on *Rosh Hashanah* and *Yom Kippur.*

*   *   *

To prevent *Hoshana Rabba* from ever falling on a Sabbath (when the custom of beating the willow could not be observed), the first day of *Rosh Hashanah* was made never to occur on a Sunday in the fixed calendar introduced by Hillel II in 360.[145]

SHEMINI ATZERETH

Shemini Atzereth, the eighth day of *Sukkoth,* is a designation not yet found in the Talmud (where the day is called *atzereth shel chag*—"the concluding of the festival"). It is really a disjointed phrase lifted from the verse: *bayom hashemini, atzereth tiheyeh lakhem*—"on the eighth day, a concluding (festival) shall be unto you."[146] *Atzereth* itself means "holding back," "closing up," as in the phrase from the *Shema:* "and He will close up (*ve'atzar*) the heavens." Thus *atzereth* is a *"concluding* festival." Biblically it refers to the final day of the *Rosh Hashanah-Yom Kippur-Sukkoth* festive season, while rabbinically *atzereth* is used for *Shavu'oth* as the conclusion of the *Pesach* season. In modern Hebrew, *otzer* means "curfew" (literally "holding back").

* * *

Shemini Atzereth combines the prayer for rain *("geshem")* and the remembrance of the dead *("yizkor")*, just as the reference to rain *("mashiv haru'ach")* in the daily *Amidah* during the winter is to be inserted in the passage on God's reviving of the dead *(". . . mechayeh methim . . .")*.[147] For rain brings life to nature as the resurrection revives the dead.[148] In this festival day, with its special emphasis on physical and spiritual rejoicing, matter (Hebr. *"geshem"* or *"gashmiyuth"*) and spirit (Hebr. *"ru'ach"*) are thus united, as they are symbolically in the phrase *"mashiv haru'ach* (wind or spirit) *umorid hagashem* (rain or matter)."

* * *

Like *Shavuoth*, which occurs 50 days after *Pesach*, *Shemini Atzereth* (being a separate festival) should have been fixed 50 days after *Sukkoth*. But the Torah put it forward to follow immediately after *Sukkoth* in order not to trouble the people with a pilgrimage to Jerusalem in the midst of the rainy season in the winter.[149]

SIMCHATH TORAH

Simchath Torah—"Rejoicing of the Law"—as a term for the second, exilic day of *Shemini Atzereth* has come into use only since the Middle Ages. Strangely, and significantly, both words have basically a similar meaning: *Simchah*, from *samach*—"to rejoice," is related to *zamach*—"to sprout forth," "to grow," whilst Torah comes from *harah*—"to conceive," "to be pregnant." *Simchah* is "creative" joy, happiness "sprouting forth" like a plant from the seed of a joyful event, and Torah is the highest "concept," or man's spiritual energy "generated" by God Himself.

* * *

When a group of men is called to the Reading-of-the-Law on *Simchath Torah*, one person should recite the blessings for all and the others should pay attention. *"Duchaning"* is omitted on *Simchath Torah* because we fear the priests may have had a drink beforehand, which would disqualify them from performing this sacred office.[150]

Thoughts on the Conclusion of the Festive Cycle

. . . and the feast of ingathering at the turn of the year.[151]

Sukkoth marks the culmination both of the cycle of the three pilgrimage festivals and of the series of the holy days in Tishri. With its celebration we reach the climax of "the season of our joy," for its meaning sets the seal of completion on the symbolism of the Jewish calendar and "gathers in" the finished product of our festive experiences.

The entire universe expresses itself in a kind of dualism. There is heaven and earth, summer and winter, fire and water, life and death, male and female, matter and spirit. All the dynamics of movement, of power, and of growth are created by the interplay of opposite forces. Positive and negative currents generate electricity and magnetism in the realm of physics. The combination of male and female is the source of all organic life, and the interplay between body and soul galvanizes and sustains human existence.

The Torah, too, is compared to the most basic physical opposites—to fire and to water.[152] Fire and water are natural enemies. Water extinguishes fire, and fire evaporates water. Yet in proper combination, they are the source of all energy and growth. From the steam engine to hydrogen fission, from the blade of grass, which needs heat and moisture, to the sustenance of every human cell—all are energized by fire and water.

The dynamics of Judaism are likewise the product of contrasting forces.

Rosh Hashanah and *Yom Kippur* represent fire—purging heat, and rising flame. They assist in the *ascent* of man to Heaven, when he leaves his home for the higher plane of the synagogue. On the Day of Atonement, man becomes like a ministering angel, only spirit, without eating or drinking. On this day the High Priest "shall take a censer full of coals of fire"[153]—a symbol of fiery fervor.

Again, *Sukkoth* emphasizes water; the willow of the brook in the festive wreath, the libation of the water festival on the second night, and the prayer for rain on *Shemini Atzereth*. It features matter (*"gashmiyuth"*) brought down from Heaven as rain (*"geshem"*) to nourish the earth. It calls for the *descent* of the Jew from his home in skyscrapers above to the *Sukkah* below. It stresses physical pleasures, eating and drinking— "the season of our joy."

Both fire and water are organic parts of the Torah. It expects us at times to wrest ourselves from the earthly material life below and soar to the heights of Heaven above like fire, and at other times to bring the message and inspiration of Heaven above down to earth below and fructify our mundane existence like water.

Judaism sanctions neither complete asceticism nor gross materialism. It demands a judicious mixture of both ingredients to power human progress.

The moment we separate the body from the soul, or matter from spirit, we have death. *Sukkoth* can bring no more joy without the antecedent of *Rosh Hashanah* and *Yom Kippur* than the Days of Awe can effect atonement without the culmination of the Festival of Joy.

The purpose of *Yizkor* is to renew the mutual interplay between the living and the dead. By remembering death we give new urgency to life. The energies released by fusing the thoughts of life and death, of spirituality and happiness, generate the forces of true creation.

CHANUKAH

NAME

Chanukah, though a post-Biblical festival, bears a Biblical name. In this form the word occurs only once, in connection with the consecration of the walls of Jerusalem by Ezra and Nehemiah: ". . . to do the dedication (*Chanukah*), with gladness, with thanksgiving and with singing . . ."154 As a noun in the construct state (*chanukath*) and as a verb (*chanakh*) the term is used for the act of dedicating the altar,[155] the House of God or Temple,[156] and any private house.[157] It also occurs in the modern sense of "education" (*chinukh*): "Train a child in the way he should go."[158] We thus conceive of "education" as the "consecration" of life. Education is not primarily the cramming of knowledge into a child's mind, but the "training" conducive to a "dedicated" life. Just as the "consecration" of a building or Temple adds nothing to its physical features but merely sanctifies it for a noble purpose, so does true "education" consist of giving a person high ideals and a hallowed purpose in life rather than mere knowledge. *Chanukah,* then, recalls the event which restored the purpose and sacred aims of Jewish existence through the "consecration" of the Temple and what it stood for.

* * *

The Hebrew word *Chanukah* means both "dedication" and "education." To educate a person means to dedicate him to life. The name of the Festival is also interpreted as *"chanu"* ("they encamped," i.e., came to rest) *"kah"* ("on the 25th" of Kislev, the date of the Festival's first day).[159]

* * *

The first to call *Chanukah* the "Festival of Lights" was Josephus in his *Antiquities of the Jews.*[160]

HISTORY

Chanukah and *Purim,* although they both celebrate significant Jewish victories over oppression, are observed in a characteristically different fashion. The distinguishing feature of *Chanukah* is the recitation of *Hallel,* psalms of praise to God, while that of *Purim* is feasting and merriment. The reason for the distinction is that *Chanukah* marks primarily a religious victory, for Jews in Maccabean times were offered the alternative of apostasy and assimilation to Hellenism; hence our celebration assumes a mainly religious character, marked by the singing of hymns to God. The Jews threatened by Haman, on the other hand, had no such alternative; the miracle then was their sheer physical survival. Hence we commemorate the event by physical joys.[161]

* * *

Chanukah, celebrating an event connected with the priesthood and the purification of the Temple, appears ancient and Biblical. *Purim*, with its account of anti-Semitism, persecution, intrigues and banquets, has a modern ring. Yet the story of *Chanukah* (165 B.C.E.) occurred well over two hundred years after the story of *Purim* (probably early in the fourth century B.C.E.). In fact, while *Purim* is the last Biblical festival, *Chanukah* is the first post-Biblical one.

* * *

The festival commemorates two events: the victory over the Greeks and the miracle of the oil. In our prayers (*Al Hanissim*) we mention the first and not the second, while the Talmud refers to the second but hardly the first. The reason may be that when we speak to God, to Whom miracles are natural, we thank Him for human victories; when Judaism speaks to us, it emphasizes the Divine or supernatural aspect of the Festival.

* * *

The name *Hasmonean* may be a title of honor or nobility. It is so used in Psalms: "Noblemen (Hebr. "*Chashmanim*") shall come out of Egypt"[162] and in the *Targum Yerushalmi* on the verse: "The bows of the mighty men are broken, and *they that stumbled* are girded with strength."[163] Or it may be a family name, taken from the place "*Cheshmon*" mentioned in the Book of Joshua.[164] In a context unrelated to *Chanukah* "the sons of the Hasmoneans" are cited in the Mishnah,[165] the only reference to the Hasmoneans in the Mishnah.

IN THE TALMUD

The Mishnah does not mention *Chanukah* at all, except only incidentally—to free a storekeeper from damages if his light, placed outside his store in the street, set a passing haycart on fire, provided it was *Chanukah*.[166] This glaring omission, and generally the talmudic tendency to play down the Maccabean victory, is probably a protest against the Hasmonean combination of priesthood with kingship, or—as we would say—of religion with politics.[167]

* * *

According to a midrashic source, *Chanukah*—recalling the rededication of the Temple by the priests and the valor of the priestly dynasty of the Maccabees—was instituted to compensate the tribe of Levi for their exclusion from the festivities at the consecration of the original Tabernacle in the wilderness.[168]

* * *

In the Talmud the reference to the origin and meaning of *Chanukah* is limited to the following passage: "What is *Chanukah?* On the 25th of Kislev (begin) the eight days of *Chanukah* . . . For when the Greeks entered the Temple they defiled all its sacred oils, and when the rule of the house of the Hasmoneans prevailed and vanquished them (the Greeks), they (the Hasmoneans) searched and found only one cruse of oil bearing the seal of the High Priest (confirming its purity); this was sufficient for but one day. But a miracle occurred, and they lit the lights from it for eight days . . . ."[169]

THE MIRACLE

Following this account, the question has often been asked: With the oil from the cruse sufficient for one day, the miracle really lasted only seven days; why then was the festival celebrating the miracle extended to eight days? Several answers have been given, among them:

1. The first day, too, witnessed a miracle since, after pouring the oil into the *Menorah,* miraculously enough oil remained in the cruse for the next day; or since they used only one eighth of the cruse's contents for each night, including the first, it yet burned for a full day.[170]

2. God performs the miracle of providing supplies only by increasing a substance already in existence not by creating it *ex nihilo,* as proved by the Prophet Elisha's question to the

poor woman he sought to help: "What have you in the house?" and the subsequent increase of the little oil she possessed.[171] Hence, here, too, the oil which burned from the second to the eighth day could not have been newly created but must have been added to what miraculously was left over on the first day.[172]

3. Even with the seven days' miracle of the oil a special day of festivity had to be set up to commemorate the Maccabean victory and the miracle of finding one cruse of pure oil.[173]

All these explanations are designed to show that we can expect the assistance of Providence only if we add our own efforts: " (Heaven) assists him who comes to purify himself", or as the English proverb has it: "God helps those who help themselves."

*   *   *

Nissim means "miracles" in post-Biblical Hebrew. In the Bible the word occurs only in the singular *nes* and is never used in the sense of "miracle".[174] There it stands for a "banner",[175] a "high pole",[176] or a "flag".[177] The word is no doubt related to *nasa*—"to lift," "to raise on high." The "miracles" we recall, then, are really "banner" events, "high" points of history, or sudden "rises" in the otherwise straight line indicating the regularity of the laws of nature. As such, "miracles" betoken a "flag" around which we gather for national consolidation. All the "miracles" we celebrate in the Jewish calendar serve the purpose of stimulating our national consciousness and idealism as the people chosen by God to be His religious pioneers.

". . . and the many into the hands of the few . . ."

Chanukah celebrates not only a single miracle or a single Jewish victory over twenty-one centuries ago. That victory in itself marked one of the most crucial turning-points in the history of man. If the Maccabees had not triumphed at that time, Judaism would have been submerged in the sea of Hellenism and ceased to exist as a distinct religion. Consequently, Christianity would not have emerged 165 years later, nor would the stage have been set for the rise of Islam in the seventh century C.E. The entire history of religion and civilization for the past two thousand years was made possible by that small band of Jews from little Modin who pitted their valor against the might of Antiochus and his hordes. Never before or after that epoch-making victory have so many owed so much to so few!

But *Chanukah* means more. It epitomizes the continuous miracle of Jewish history. From the beginning the Jewish people has been destined to be among the smallest nations. "Not because ye were more in number than any people did the Lord set His love upon you, and choose you, but because ye were the fewest of all peoples. . . ."[178] From the time Abraham left the community of mankind "on the other side" (*ivri*) as a minority of one, and little David challenged mighty Goliath with a pebble and sling, to the time Jews lived as tiny minorities among the empires and mass-religions in their dispersion, and the State of Israel ultimately arose as one of the smallest nations in one of the smallest lands, Jewish history has been an unending battle of the few against the many, the weak against the strong, and right against might. It has been an unceasing vindication of the triumph of the spirit over the power of numbers and force. What Pharaoh merely saw in a dream—lean cows consuming fat cows, and withered ears swallowing up full ears—became the reality of Jewish experience.

In nature, this capacity of the small to engulf the big and of the few to prevail over the many is manifested only by the power of fire. The tiniest flame, a mere spark, can kindle the most gigantic torch or set whole cities ablaze.

The flame of fire is therefore the symbol of *Chanukah*. Starting with a single light, it does not end until the entire *Menorah* is ablaze. From little beginnings come great ends, and from the heroism of the few the many are inspired. This will remain the challenge of Jewish history to the end of time.

MEHADRIN MIN HA-MEHADRIN

The phrase *"Mehadrin min Hamehadrin"*—nowadays applied especially to those most meticulous in *Kashruth* observance—is taken from the talmudic reference to households where each member kindles an additional light every night of Chanukah.[179]

    *   *   *

The practice to kindle an additional light on the *Menorah* every night of the Festival for each member of one's household is demanded in the Talmud[180] of people who are *"Mehadrin min Hamehadrin"*—most meticulous in the observance of the law. The reason why popular custom has in this case adopted the manner reserved by the law for the most pious may be that the miracle of *Chanukah* was itself a result of the people's extreme piety. According to the strict law, there was no need to search for pure oil sealed by the High Priest, since the laws of defilement are in abeyance when the public is involved. But as the Maccabees and their followers nevertheless did not want to rededicate the Temple with impure oil, which would have been legal but not pious, and they thus rendered the miracle necessary, we also commemorate the event by going beyond the strict letter of the law and acting as *"Mehadrin min Hamehadrin."*

MENORAH

The *Menorah* is the oldest emblem of the Jewish people, predating by many centuries the *Magen David,* which was not generally used as a Jewish symbol until the fifteenth century.

    *   *   *

Menorah in the Bible is used exclusively for the seven-branched "candlestick" in the sanctuary. The word is derived from *nur*—"to shine," hence *ner*—"light," "lamp." As the symbol of Chanukah, the *Menorah* represents the same relationship to education as "light" to "enlightenment." The candlestick re-lit by the Maccabeans was plundered by the Romans at the time of the destruction of the Temple 235 years later and carried by them to Rome, where its image was engraved on the Arch of Titus standing to this day. From there it was copied to form the emblem of the State of Israel.

    *   *   *

The *Chanukah Menorah* has eight arms, while the *Menorah* in the ancient Temple had seven. Because of its use in the

Temple, we must not today reproduce any candelabrium with seven arms, of whatever material or form.[181]

LIGHTS

The lights are meant to "publicize the miracle"; hence they should be placed at the door facing the street or near a window overlooking it.[182]

* * *

Even the poor man who lives on charity must pawn his shirt to buy oil for the *Chanukah* lights.[183]

* * *

The *Mitzvah* of the *Chanukah* lights is performed by kindling them; hence, if they accidentally went out even before they burned the minimum time, the required time being one-half hour, one is not obliged to light them again.[184] Yet the usual practice is to rekindle them without reciting the blessing again. The former law is reflected in the wording of the blessing: ". . . Who has commanded us *to kindle* the light of *Chanukah*."

* * *

The duty to observe *Chanukah* and light the *Menorah* is merely a rabbinic enactment, being of post-Biblical origin. What is the justification, then, for our attributing this *Mitzvah* to God in our benediction ". . . . Who has sanctified us by His commandments and commanded us to kindle the Chanukah lights?" The same question applies to the blessing over such other rabbinic observances as the reading of the *Megillah* on *Purim,* the Sabbath lights and the washing of hands before meals. The Talmud replies: Since God bids us in the Torah to act "according to the law which they (i.e. the rabbis) shall teach you" and "not to turn aside from the word which they shall tell you,"[185] or to "ask your father, and he will declare unto you, your elders, and they will tell you,"[186] it follows that in performing any rabbinic enactment we fulfill a Divine law.[187]

* * *

On Friday night the *Chanukah* lights should be lit before the Sabbath candles, since with the lighting of the latter the Sabbath has set in and one may no longer kindle any lights.[188] Yet, if one cannot afford to purchase both *Chanukah* and Sabbath lights, the latter take precedence, because "the peace of the home" is more important than "the publicity of the miracle."[189]

* * *

The *Chanukah* lights serve only "to publicize the miracle"; hence, as the *Haneroth Halalu* song has it, "we are not permitted to make any use of them, but only to see them."[190] The Shabbath lights, on the contrary, should be taken advantage of; for they serve to insure "the peace of the home": Where darkness reigns, there can be no harmony, whereas light leads to peace and understanding.

* * *

While one need generally spend only up to one-fifth of one's possessions on the performance of a *Mitzvah*,[191] the provision of *Chanukah* lights (and of the four cups of wine on *Pesach*) constitutes an exception to this rule: "Even a poor man who lives on charity must borrow money or sell his clothes to buy oil for lighting,"[192] because of the importance of "publicizing the miracle."[193]

MA'OZ TZUR

The *Chanukah* song *"Ma'oz Tzur"* was written by a poet named Mordecai (ben Isaac Halevi of the thirteenth century?). The tune is German in origin (at least five-hundred years old) and has often been adapted as a Christian hymn.[194]

GAMES

According to several ordinances enacted by medieval Jewish communities, games of "hazard" (including cards) were permitted as an exception on *Chanukah*, provided they were not played for money.[195]

PURIM

NAME

Purim means literally "lots," a reference to *pur* in the verse: "In the first month, which is the month Nisan . . ., he cast *pur*, that is, the *lot*, before Haman from day to day, and from month to month, to the twelfth month, which is the month of Adar."[196] According to one explanation, Haman chose the month of Adar for the destruction of the Jews because Moses had died in that month; but he did not realize that Moses was also born in that month. However, it is more likely that Providence deliberately made the lot cast at the beginning of the year (Nisan) to defer the threat of extinction to the end of the year (Adar) so as to give the Jews the maximum time to repent.[197]

* * *

Purim, plural of *pur* ("lot"), is a word that occurs only in the Book of Esther. It is probably of Assyrian origin (literally meaning "urn") and is several times translated into the Hebrew *goral* (the usual word for "lot") in the Biblical text itself.[198] It refers to the lots cast by Haman to determine the date for the extermination of the Jews. In the choice of this word for the name of the festival[199] the irrationality of anti-Semitism is emphasized: The blind hatred of Jew-baiters is as arbitrary and capricious as a "lot" drawn from an "urn."

HISTORY

Purim, being fixed to fall on the fourteenth of Adar, celebrates not so much the defeat of Haman and the destruction of his henchmen, which occurred on the 13th day of Adar, as the calm and peace enjoyed by the Persian Jews on the following day.[200]

* * *

The identity of King Ahasuerus of the Book of Esther has never been established with absolute certainty. Already the *Septuagint* and Josephus regarded the name as a mutilation of

Artaxerxes, and historically he is nowadays generally identified with the Persian King Artaxerxes II (404-361 B.C.E.).[201]

* * *

The question how Esther, a Jewess, could be married to the non-Jewish king Ahasuerus—particularly since it was assumed that she was Mordecai's legal wife at the time[202]—is already discussed in the Talmud. The answer is that her conduct was necessary in the public Jewish interest of survival and thus became a matter of *"Kiddush Hashem";* moreover, a woman's passive submission to *force majeure* does not constitute a breach of a cardinal law requiring martyrdom.[203]

FAST OF ESTHER

The Fast of Esther on the thirteenth of Adar which—unlike the other four statutory fast days in the Jewish calendar—is not mentioned in the Talmud, is first recorded in an eighth century work *(She'eltoth);* its observance is therefore less stringent than the other public fasts, and exemptions may be granted more easily for reasons of pain or even slight ill-health.[204]

SEVEN LAWS

The observance of *Purim* is the second of the seven rabbinical laws added to the 613 commandments of the Torah. *Purim* itself also has seven main precepts: (1) the reading of the *Megillah;* (2) sending presents to one's neighbors and (3) gifts to the poor; (4) the reading about the battle against Amalek from the Torah; (5) the insertion of *"Al Hanissim"* in the *Shemoneh Esreh* and the grace-after-meals; (6) the festive *Purim* meal; and (7) the prohibition to fast and deliver eulogies at funerals.[205]

IN THE TALMUD

Unlike *Chanukah* which is scarcely mentioned in the Mishnah,[206] *Purim* has an entire Tractate of the Talmud *(Megillah)* devoted to the feast and its observance. Above all it deals with the reading of the *Megillah,* but in this context it also details the laws on the readings from the Torah and Prophets generally.

BOOK OF ESTHER

Esther, as the title of the Book, is of course named after its principal heroine. She received this honor not because her contribution to the final deliverance was any greater than Mordecai's, but because it was her order which "confirmed these matters of *Purim;* and it was written in the book."[207] She had requested the sages of that time to have the book written and added to Scriptures (Rashi). Her name was Haddassah ("myrtle") as well as Esther.[208] The Talmud records various opinions to explain these names. Either Hadassah was added to her original name Esther "because the righteous are called myrtles,"[209] or she was later named Esther because she "concealed" her origin from Ahasuerus, or else because the non-Jews called her Esther,[210] a Persian word meaning "bright star" (cf. the sound of "star" and "Esther" in English), for she arose to "shine" to Israel in a dark hour of doom.[211]

*   *   *

Esther is the only Biblical book not to contain a single mention of God, unless some of the 187 references to "the King" are (homiletically) applied to Him.[212] Among the many reasons given are that Mordecai, when writing the book, deliberately omitted the Divine name because he feared that the Persian copyists would substitute the names of their idols[213] or that the book was originally copied from heathen sources.[214] Another reason may be that, while the battle against the Egyptians who had some cause for their hostility[215] was to be left to God ("The Lord will fight for you, and ye shall hold your peace"[216]), the fight against Amalek ("And Joshua discomfited Amalek . . . with the edge of the sword"[217]) and Haman, whose aggression was quite unprovoked, was properly a human responsibility. God must arbitrate only when one human interest conflicts with another; but when others are subhuman, it is enough for us to be human.

*   *   *

Megillah ("scroll"), from the root *galal* ("to roll"), is used several times in the Bible to denote a rolled book or document.[218] Is not mentioned in the Book of Esther itself. There it is called *iggereth*, "letter;"[219] hence the custom to fold the scroll "like a letter" for public reading.[219a] But in the Talmud the Book of Esther is invariably called *megillah*, "the scroll," since—in contrast to the other four *megilloth*—Esther must always be read from a scroll of properly prepared parchment.

READING OF MEGILLAH

The duty to hear the reading of the *Megillah* takes precedence over any other religious obligation, even over the study of Torah (which itself is so important that one must not interrupt the teaching of Torah to children even for the building of the Temple of Jerusalem[220]). The sole exceptions are the supreme duties owed to the living and the dead: One need not attend the reading of the *Megillah* if prevented from doing so by either having to care for a gravely sick patient or by being engaged with the burial of a person who has no relatives.[221] Following one opinion, even a circumcision may be put off to the ninth day if one cannot otherwise hear the *Megillah* on *Purim;*[222] but this view is not accepted in practice.[223]

* * *

In contrast to the Torah, the *Megillah* may lawfully be read in any language one understands by and for a person who knows no Hebrew,[224] provided it is handwritten in that language on parchment in accordance with all the laws applicable to a Hebrew *Megillah*.[225] But nowadays the *Megillah* is never publicly read in any translation even for the benefit of women,[225a] since it is assumed that at least the men understand some Hebrew.[226]

* * *

Also in contrast to a *Sepher Torah*, a *Megillah* is *kosher* even if the text is vocalized and provided with cantillation marks for readers who cannot otherwise recite it, though such additions to the text should preferably be avoided.[227]

* * *

The principal obligation of reading the *Megillah* is by day,[227a] partly because the verse insists "And these days should be remembered and kept throughout every generation . . ."[228]

* * *

Women too are obliged to hear the reading of the *Megillah,* although they are normally exempt from the performance of duties restricted to particular times,[229] because the miracle of *Purim* was brought about by a woman.[230]

* * *

It is forbidden to talk during the reading of the *Megillah,*[231] for one has not discharged one's duty if one has missed hearing even a single word of it.[232]

* * *

The names of the ten sons of Haman, which always occupy a full page in the Scroll of Esther (and are therefore written in very large letters), should be read "in one breath" because they all lost their lives simultaneously.[233]

* * *

The origin of greeting the mention of Haman in the reading of *Esther* with noises produced by rattling *"gregars"* (lit. *grzegarz,* a Polish word) and stamping with one's feet was to fulfill literally the commandment to "blot out the memory of Amalek;"[234] this was done by writing the name of Amalek or Haman on pieces of wood or one's shoe-soles, and then knocking them until the name was completely wiped out. Later the writing disappeared, while the noise-making remained.[235]

NO HALLEL AND HAPHTORAH

According to one opinion in the Talmud, *Hallel* is not recited on *Purim,* as it is on *Chanukah,* because the miracle did not take place in the Land of Israel.[236]

* * *

At the morning service on *Purim,* as on *Rosh Chodesh* and *Chanukah,* no *Haphtorah* is being read following the reading of the Law so as not to detain worshippers unduly, as these are legally working days.[237]

GIFTS

It is a religious duty to donate half of one's country's current coin (here 50 cents) to charity before *Purim* (as a reminder of the half *Shekel* collected for the Temple at this season) and to present gifts of at least two items of food each to two poor persons (*Shalach Manoth*) on Purim.[238]

* * *

The reason for deferring the collection of the *Machatzith Hashekel* until *Purim*, although the appeal for *Shekalim* in Temple times was made at the beginning of Adar fourteen days earlier,[239] is to insure the maximum response, since more people are likely to attend services on *Purim* than on *Rosh Chodesh* Adar.[240]

* * *

One should donate the amount of *Machatzith Hashekel* three times, corresponding to the three offerings ("*Terumah*") mentioned in the Torah,[241] and hand this over to the poor,[242] in addition to the "gifts to the poor"[243] one is obliged to give on Purim.[244]

FEASTING

The day should be celebrated by a festive meal at home (*Se'udath Purim*), which must be commenced before *Purim* concludes at nightfall, and by merriment and drinking "until one does not know the difference between 'cursed by Haman' and 'blessed by Mordecai';" but others hold that one need not drink to excess and that instead one may sleep a little whereby one will also become oblivious of the difference between Haman and Mordecai.[245]

* * *

Inordinate drinking, normally frowned upon, is legally encouraged on Purim,[246] because the salvation celebrated by the festival was itself brought about by drinking parties.[247]

SHUSHAN PURIM

Cities known to have been walled at the time of Joshua observe Purim on the 15th of Adar, the date when the Jewish victory was complete in Shusham (the Persian capital) itself.[248] This enactment was made as a tribute to the Land of Israel, so that its ancient cities should not appear to rank lower than Shushan.[249]

*   *   *

Thus in Jerusalem *Purim* is celebrated on the 15th of Adar. In Prague, where it is not known for certain whether the city was enclosed by walls in Joshua's times, *Purim* is observed on both the 14th and 15th of Adar and the *Megillah* is read four times (both evenings and mornings) to this day.

11

Controversy: Letters To The Editor

O F the great controversies which have aroused
world-wide Jewish debate during the past
quarter-century there are few in which this
writer did not participate—on one side or the other. Some of
these polemics are reprinted elsewhere in this volume, such
as the articles on Who is a Jew—Reflections on a Crisis, and
Government Aid to Parochial Schools. This chapter is limited to a selection of letters published in newspapers and
magazines. Each item is introduced by a brief account of the
argument which prompted the intervention.

Suffering and Punishment

In April 1947 the Chief Rabbi of the Holy Land, Dr. Isaac Herzog, issued a Passover message in which he related the terrible sufferings experienced by the Jewish people to its religious and moral failings. This thesis immediately aroused a storm of protest and debate. *The Jewish Chronicle*, in the issue following the publication of the message (April 11, 1947), printed several "rejoinders" from Dr. I. Maybaum and others, and it published the letter below on April 23, 1947.

To the Editor of THE JEWISH CHRONICLE:

It is remarkable, and sadly symptomatic of our drift from historic Judaism, that Dr. Herzog's now famous pronouncement should have been greeted with such amazement. Was he not, after all, reechoing . . . the cry which the Prophets and savants of Israel always raised when suffering overtook the Jewish people, . . . expressing what marks the most significant Jewish contribution to the interpretation of history?

Whatever the explanation of the unprecedented misery in which the Jewish people and the world find themselves alike today, there can be no doubt about the Jewish traditional attitude as reflected in all strata of our vast and varied literature. Had we been the true spiritual heirs of the Hebrew Prophets, we would find nothing novel or startling in the assertion that national suffering on the part of Israel and the nations is the inevitable consequence of moral and religious decline. "And I will punish the world for (their) evil, and the wicked for their iniquity."[1] "Grievously hath Jerusalem transgressed, therefore is she become an abomination."[2] The Jewish State fell, according to our Rabbis,[3] not because of the might or wickedness of her enemies but through her own spiritual collapse. Dr. Maybaum's fundamental fallacy in his argument against this doctrine lies in his confusion of individual with national suffering. The Book of Job and the Talmudic conception of *Tsadik vera lo* deal exclusively with the problem of the former. This clear distinction is often reiterated.[4]

The Jewish religious philosophy of history has nowhere been stated more succinctly than by our greatest and most rational of philosophers:

"And this is part of the Jewish concept of *Teshuvah:* viz., that when trouble comes . . . all should know that suffering derives from their evil deeds, as is written: 'Your iniquities have withholden good things from you'.5 And that will cause the calamities to abate. But if they will not remorsefully turn to God in prayer, but say, our misfortunes have happened by mere accident, then they will cruelly persist in their evil deeds and cause further misfortunes to fall upon them. That is the implication of the words in Lev. 26:23, 24: if, when I cause you suffering so that you penitently return to Me, you claim it as an 'accident,' then I shall also bring to the full fury of further 'accidents' upon you."6

Our age, and our people in particular, would do well to ponder these challenging teachings. It is a unique phenomenon in our history that the unparalleled disasters which have recently been inflicted upon our people were in no way associated with the equally unparalleled secularization and religious disintegration of the Jewish masses; that our costly failures and catastrophies should have produced just indictments against others, but no *Selichoth* and no reawakening of the Jewish religious genius. Our position in the world would have been slightly different had we represented a cohesive and powerful moral force for the Divine solution of the staggering social and political problems of our time. Instead we are considered a "nuisance" wherever we are, and a perpetual problem which the nations of the world are not unnaturally eager to liquidate once and for all time.

If the matchless sacrifices of our heroic pioneers in our Homeland are merely to add one more sovereign people to the already too numerous variety of disunited nations, we can hardly expect their help or even sympathy in our efforts. Only if we recapture our lost sense of Divine choice and toil to build an exemplary state *unlike* any other would we be able to justify our *raison d'etre* into triumph over the threat of extinction otherwise long overdue. Only thus could we build the *"Gottesstaat,"* "a light unto the nations" in quest for a moral order. Only then will our descendants be able to point to our vicissitudes and exclaim in unison: That was their finest hour! This is the Jewish doctrine of national reward and punishment, this is the way to resuscitate the glory that is Israel!

London E.1.   (The Rev.) I. JAKOBOVITS

The Bible and Medical Aid

The letter below, which appeared in *The Jewish Chronicle* of August 15, 1952, was written in reply to a medical correspondent who had taken issue with the statement, made in a lecture on "The Physician in Jewish Law," that the consulting of doctors had never been regarded as wrongful in Jewish religious classics.

To the Editor of THE JEWISH CHRONICLE:

Mr. Romy Fink (in your issue of last week) is quite right in emphasizing the significance of the Biblical criticism of the Judean King Asa, who, in his disease, "sought not to the Lord, but to the physicians." This important reference was not, of course, omitted in my lecture, even though there was no mention of it in the necessarily condensed report which appeared in *The Jewish Chronicle*. In fact, both the chairman of the meeting and I discussed at some length the problem raised by this apparent objection to medical aid.

Perhaps more instructive than the passage itself are the interpretations given to it by the Jewish commentators. Most significantly, the early rabbinical classics appear to ignore the stricture upon Asa altogether; that particular verse in II Chronicles 16 is one of the very few to which no reference at all seems to be made in the Talmud and Midrashim. On the contrary, the Aggada unreservedly lauds Asa as a good and pious king. Indeed, the Biblical narrator himself records with obvious approval the honors bestowed upon the dead king at his funeral (II Chronicles 14). The medieval commentaries also reflects a general, though admittedly not unanimous, refusal to regard the passage as implying some opposition to the consulting of physicians. Isaac Abarvanel, for example, considers Asa's behaviour stupid rather than irreligious, because—being stricken with so serious an illness at the age of 80—he should not have relied on medical help. He ought to have realised that only a Divine miracle could save him. Similarly, Leon de Modena explains that it was futile to believe that the incurable disease from which the king suffered could be healed by human means. The great Halachist, Joel Sirkes, likewise recognizes the weakness of Asa's conduct only because of his failure to combine faith in God with reliance on physicians. The remark in the book of Chronicles is thus in complete harmony with the Biblical and post-Biblical view of Judaism, which looks upon the physician as a Divine agent whose knowledge and skill should be utilized for the relief of human suffering, provided God is acknowledged as the Ultimate Healer.

Your correspondent's own thesis is ingenious and interesting, but historically quiet untenable. To justify the objection to Asa's recourse to medical aid in the eighth century B.C.E., when ancient medicine was well advanced and often employed perfectly rational cures (including a variety of surgical operations, as mentioned in much earlier Egyptian papyri), on the grounds that medicine in those days was identical with magic as evidenced by the discovery of trephining scars on neolithic skulls in prehistoric times, is clearly a glaring anachronism. A like disregard for the facts established by medico-historical research is betrayed by the suggestion that "vast strides must have been made" in the brief interval of less than two centuries separating Asa from Jeremiah, who admittedly "thought it right to consult the physician, and to use the balm he prescribed." Actually, the "vast strides" from demonic to rational medicine spanned millennia, not centuries!

But even if Mr. Fink's assumption were correct and Asa was criticized merely because he resorted to magical medicine-men, the Biblical reprimand would only confirm, not invalidate, my contention (which I had, in fact, qualified in my lecture) that "the consulting of (rational) physicians was never regarded as wrongful." Maimonides follows this line of reasoning in his commentary on the Mishna which relates with approval the hiding of the Book of Medicines by King Hezekiah. That ancient work, Maimonides claims, prescribed purely magical and astrological cures, and their use thus offended the Torah.

Your correspondent cannot, surely, be correct in his assertion that "the Pentateuch makes it quite clear that the only illness which is sent as a punishment from Heaven is leprosy." Has he forgotten the sixth of the Ten Plagues,[7] the repeated warning that various diseases (other than leprosy) will visit those who disobey the Divine law[8] and the promise that submission to His law will be rewarded by the banishment of all bodily afflictions.[9] These and other passages indicate beyond doubt that the Torah considers every illness as a punishment from Heaven, though its mitigation by medical intervention is sanctioned at the same time.

This misunderstanding of the Biblical attitude may have led Mr. Fink to make the entirely unwarranted statement: "The treatment *(sic)* of the leper is set out in great detail in Leviticus, but for all other diseases the sufferer was not called upon to attend the priest and, presumably, he was permitted to consult the physician." No, any patient, including the leper, was "permitted" to repair to the physician. Leviticus does not deal with medical treatment but with the priestly task to diagnose and, if necessary, to isolate the leper.

May I conclude with a plea which is germane to this discussion? It is regrettable that so few of our modern scholars and Jewish academic institutions in Israel, America, and England devote themselves to researches into Jewish medical history and, more particularly, into the attitude of Judaism to the great moral and religious problems set by medical science and practice in our own day. Perhaps the World Congress of Jewish Physicians held this week at Jerusalem will help to intensify and popularize these important studies and lead to the long overdue establishment of a Chair in Jewish Medical History and Ethics, at least at the Hebrew University. There are few fields of scientific and historical knowledge to which Jewish thought and experience could make a more valuable contribution than to the spiritual and physical betterment of man and his life.

33, Bloomfield Avenue,   I. Jakobovits.
S.C. Road, Dublin.   (Chief Rabbi)

The Jews and World Power

The following letter, kept anonymous at the editor's suggestion, was published in Ireland's leading Catholic magazine, *The Standard,* on November 21, 1952. It was written in reply to an isolated, but vicious anti-Semitic attack by an anonymous correspondent.

To the Editor of THE STANDARD:

Your readers have, surely, seldom been treated to a grosser concoction of bigotry, untruths and hate-mongering than in the letter which you published over the initials "J.F.L." last week. In his wild allegations your correspondent speaks of "Jewish tyranny" and the Zionists' "wish for world power," and as evidence he offers "a few particles of fact" which, like all half-truths, distort the full and real facts.

"J.F.L." harps on the by now stale canard that the Bolshevick Revolution in Russia was engineered by Jews as part of their plan for world domination. To be sure, some Jews actively—though never as prominently as your contributor suggests—participated in the movement to overthrow the tyranny of the Czar. Little did they foresee that they would pave the way to an even more brutal tyranny in which the Jews, as usual, could again be the worst sufferers. Your ill-informed correspondent need only glance at the Jewish press today to convince himself of the cruel fate to which Jews are subjected behind the Iron Curtain. The Jewish religion and Zionism are ruthlessly proscribed, and recent purges in Soviet-dominated countries have been particularly directed at the elimination of Jews from positions of power or influence.

Your letter-writer must, no doubt, know from his evident researches into the identity of Communist supporters that during the post-war years no countries in Western Europe had a more active and powerful Communist party than France and Italy—the two most overwhelmingly Catholic States in free Europe outside Ireland. It would be no more preposterous to deduce from this fact that Catholics seek world power through Communism than to argue that the participation of Jews in the Russian Revolution proves their wish to use Communism as an instrument for world domination.

Your readers may now judge for themselves whether a State machine, which mercilessly crushes Jews and Judaism alike, is a "Jewish tyranny" or a tyranny over Jews; whether a movement which roots out Zionism exists "thanks to Zionism's support," and whether a people recently decimated by the Satanic forces of a totalitarian regime and now bent on the realization of its age-old national aspirations in one of the world's smallest countries, is likely to suffer from the insane delusion of world domination!

Dublin   JUSTICE

Music on Israel's Independence Day

The letter below, published in *The Jewish Chronicle* of May 1, 1953, contains an official decision on the Chief Rabbinate of Israel on the controversial question of music on Israel Independence Day, which always occurs during the *Sephirah* mourning period when music is normally banned.

To the Editor of THE JEWISH CHRONICLE:

The publication in your last issue of the report, and a correspondent's letter, on the rabbinical ban on instrumental music at the Independence Day celebrations in Liverpool prompts me to communicate to you the undermentioned correspondence with the Chief Rabbinate of Israel.

When, late in 1950, the local J. N. F. Commission approached me with a proposal to hold the blue and white ball on the anniversary date of Iyar 5, I submitted their request for a ruling to my predecessor, Chief Rabbi Dr. I. Herzog, stating, *inter alia;*

> ". . . I have informed them that while I have no authority to allow the *Sephirah* regulations to be disregarded on this occasion, I would address this request to you, so as to ensure that we act in conformity with the other communities in world Jewry. . ."

On Marcheshvan 29, 5711, Rabbi S. A. Shazori, the Chief Secretary of the Chief Rabbinate, replied as follows:

> "Your letter has been considered at a meeting of the Chief Rabbinate of Israel, and in accordance with its decision we are to inform you that we are unable to sanction instrumental music and dances on this day which occurs during the *Sephirah* period."

I might add that in Dublin our annual Independence Day celebrations on Iyar 5 lost none of their dignity and impressiveness, because, acting upon a verdict from Jerusalem, we refused to ignore the sacred memory of the Jewish martyrs, whose suffering and sacrifice—recalled by our mourning at this time—made Israel's rebirth possible.

33 Bloomfield Avenue   I. JAKOBOVITS
S. C. Road, Dublin   Chief Rabbi of Ireland

Reform Judaism and Jewish Unity

In November 1957 the first Conference of European Rabbis was held in Amsterdam. Among the items discussed were the inroads of Reform Judaism into the mainly Orthodox communities of Europe. Reports of this historic Conference elicited a sharp attack against the participants by a Reform correspondent from Dublin, charging that in their opposition to Reform they were sowing the seeds of Jewish disunity. The following letter was written in reply to this charge and published in *The Jewish Chronicle* on November 15, 1957.

To the Editor of THE JEWISH CHRONICLE:

It appears that the spokesmen for "Progressive" Judaism now seek to become the apostles of Jewish "unity" in much the same way as the Communists have appropriated the plea for "peace" as their watchword. The logic, let alone the justice, of the Reformers' argument is really hard to see for any fair-minded person. First they break away from the historic traditions of our people, assault the unity of our Torah and the integrity of our law by choosing what they like and rejecting what they do not understand, sow bitterness and strife by their secession from our established communities and their propagation of unlawfulness, and then have the audacity to pontificate to the loyal element on the dangers of disunity!

If your correspondent from Dublin (who wrote last week) and his fellow dissenters are really as concerned to heal the breach which they have created as they profess to be, let them demonstrate their avowals of unity by deeds, not words. Let them cease to solemnize marriages which contravene Biblical and rabbinic law, let them stop disrupting the unity of our people by issuing "admissions" to Judaism which no law-abiding Jew can conscientiously recognize, let them join with us in our hard battle for the unconditional submission of all Jews to the Divine Law. Let them show at least some respect and understanding for those who, in the face of constant provocation and denigration, genuinely labor day and night to "salvage our Jewish heritage."

Your correspondent's unworthy imputation that our conference at Amsterdam was called with the "avowed intention to accentuate differences" scarcely merits a reply. While, in our relatively few but heavy-hearted references to the Reform movement, we sometimes differed on how to meet its inroads into communal and national unity, the single-minded aim which animated us all was how to restore the continuity and integrity of Jewish life on the basis of its time-honored sanctities. How often at our deliberations did we hear the agonizing cries of the many heart-stricken people who, because of the Reformers' disregard of Jewish law, found themselves rejected by Jews and non-Jews alike, or who were debarred from Jewish marriage because their parents had entered into a union condemned by the Torah.

These tragedies, together with the continued captivity of our brethren behind the Iron Curtain, cast a deep and painful shadow over our conference. But we were profoundly heartened at this otherwise most inspiring gathering by the indications reported to us from all the communities represented that a new spirit of religious enthusiasm is beginning to sweep through the ranks of our youth everywhere, that the demand for more intensive Jewish education and for more intelligent practical observance is growing every day, and that there is greater solidarity than ever before among the guides of our religious destiny.

Cheered by this enthralling experience, we are fortified in our unshakable confidence that the eternal values of "Orthodox" Judaism will eventually triumph and again unite our people, even as they have prevailed over all heresies and false interpretations of our faith in the past. How infinite will be our joy when the oneness of Israel will once again proclaim the Oneness of our Creator to a world pushed to the brink of disaster because it chose to flout the sovereignty of His law and to subvert His moral order. In this spirit of unity, founded on common ideals, we stretch forth our hand to all our brothers and invite them to help in achieving the massive task before us for the betterment of Jewish and human life.

33 Bloomfield Avenue   I. JAKOBOVITS
S.C. Road, Dublin   (Chief Rabbi of Ireland)

Deep Waters

Ever since the rise of modern Israel, the place of religion in the Jewish State has been the subject of a sharp, and often violent, debate. At times the battle between the traditionalists and the secularists was fought over the strangest issues. One such *cause célèbre*, symptomatic rather than characteristic of the "Kulturkampf," was the controversy aroused by the proposal to establish a mixed swimming-pool in Jerusalem over the vehement objections of its Orthodox population. The endorsement of these objections by sixty-three British and Irish rabbis was attacked in an editorial in *The Jewish Chronicle* on June 27, 1958, which two weeks later printed the following reply.

To the Editor of THE JEWISH CHRONICLE:

Your leader on the Jerusalem swimming-pool controversy has raised issues far deeper than the pool's waters. There may be some justice in your comments on the call for an amnesty for those found guilty of a breach of the peace, if indeed the word amnesty, as used here, "means declaring to those who after fair trial have been shown to contravene the law were in the right after all." What is open to question, however, is your challenge of the right of rabbis in the Diaspora to proclaim the moral teachings of Judaism, and to protest against their public violation, particularly in the Holy Land, even if these teachings do not command the respect of the majority of members in the rabbis' own communities.

Granted that, in referring to "a deep breach in the holiness and purity of Jerusalem," the 63 signatories of the protest expressed themselves "in rather extravagent terms." One appreciates, of course, that words like "holiness" and "purity" do not easily fit into the common pattern of the journalistic vocabulary and editorial parlance of our times.

I also concede that the language used by the signatories may appear "intemperate." The same criticism was no doubt leveled, with the same justice, at the Hebrew Prophets when they so violently denounced very similar evils in their days.

I further admit that your opinions on mixed bathing are probably shared by most of your readers. There are precedents in our history for such conflicts between Jewish law and Jewish life, too.

On the other hand, you will not deny that the moral revulsion against mixed bathing is founded on good Jewish authority. Because of such "abominations" the Torah warned us (rather "intemperately") in the verse: "That the land vomit not you out also, when ye defile it, as it vomited out the nation that was before you." Significantly enough, your leader appeared just at the time when the part of the *Shema* which we recite twice daily was repeated twice at the end of the Sidra of the week, containing these "extravagant" words: "And ye shall not seek after your own heart and after your own eyes, after which ye used to go awhoring . . . and ye shall be holy unto your God." The context deals with the sanctification of human dress through the *tsitsit!*

The problem you now have posed is: What are conscientious rabbis to do when "practices common to Western life" clash with the moral code of Judaism? Can they exercise the right, which they claim is theirs and which you evidently deny, to make public pronouncements on moral and religious issues, following the lead of the Prophets and classic teachers of Judaism? Or must they forbear to preach these ideals, and to protest against their blatant defiance, until the "majority" of Jews in Western lands will "dream of accepting" them? In that event rabbis should abdicate their spiritual leadership in favor of politicians and journalists who are certainly far better equipped to feel the pulse of public opinion.

In this particular case the problem is further complicated by the fact that the argument concerns the public Jewish standards of morality in the Holy City of Jerusalem, a fact completely overlooked in your editorial. Jerusalem probably has a greater proportion of strictly Orthodox Jews than any other city in the world. Many of them have chosen to live within its hallowed confines just because they wanted to escape from the mundane and unholy influences found everywhere else. If some Israelis insist on disporting themselves semi-denuded in promiscuous bathing, is the Mediterranean not big enough for them? Must they affront the moral feelings of tens of thousands of pious Jews in Jerusalem, and the sensibilities of countless other Jews—and Christians—who cherish the supreme sanctity of the holiest city on earth? And should Jewish religious leaders be reproached for rallying to their cause, and for demanding nobler standards of moral integrity for the "Faithful City" than for London, Paris or New York?

Jerusalem is holier than any synagogue. To it all our prayers are oriented. Surely, you, Sir, or any reverent person, would not tolerate or defend indecorous behavior in a house of worship, however many people would condone such conduct. Why, then, should you acquiesce in the desecration of the Jewish people's, nay mankind's, Holy of Holies? And true holiness is to be found in consecrated human conduct, not in consecrated buildings. In its inhabitants lies the sanctity of Jerusalem!

One final point. You speak of the "Neturei Karta in Mea Sh'arim and their sympathizers," as if to imply that the signatories of the poster belong to this group. The inclusion of several leading Mizrachi rabbis alone should refute such an imputation. The signatures were obtained and given on an entirely non-political basis. (In fact neither I nor presumably many of my colleagues who signed the protest knew that it would be distributed by the Agudas Israel!) We are not concerned with the fanatics who might exploit the dispute for their own partisan ends, but solely with the *cri de coeur* of those who genuinely grieve over what they regard as an unwarranted profanation of their sanctuary. In this stand we are united with all sincere rabbis throughout the world and with our devout brethren who struggle for Israel's spiritual (and therefore material) security, whether they signed this particular protest or not.

33 Bloomfield Avenue　　　　　　　　　　I. JAKOBOVITS
S. C. Road, Dublin　　　　　　　　　(Chief Rabbi of Ireland)

"Red or Dead?"

Addressing itself "to one of the most agonizing ethical dilemmas ever faced by man," the Spring 1962 number of *Tradition* presented a symposium on the "Red or Dead?" debate then widely discussed throughout the Free World. As the first comprehensive Jewish inquiry into this subject, the authors sought to bring the sources of Jewish law and thought to bear on determining whether, and to what extent, a surrender to Communist rule might ever be preferred to mutual annihilation in a nuclear conflict, if no other alternative existed. The symposium consisted of an article by Rabbi Maurice Lamm and two rejoinders, the first of which is reproduced below.

The hesitation of the leading spokesmen of religion to pronounce on the "Red or Dead" issue, regrettable as it may be, is understandable enough. On the one hand, the alternatives to be weighed are of such cataclysmic proportions— affecting, as they do, every human life on earth—that a feeling of personal inadequacy and lack of qualification to express an opinion on this supremely fateful question may be a mark of one's realistic sense of responsibility rather than an abdication of one's duty. For such a super-decision the world really requires super-saints and super-scholars, equipped with a wisdom far exceeding even Solomon's. On the other hand, the problem itself is so completely unique and without parallel that even the most learned master of religious knowledge may be excused if he finds his search for reliable guidance in the literary storehouse of his faith unavailing. How can there be precedents for a situation which is so unprecedented?

This perplexity is particularly acute for the teachers of authentic Judaism. Unlike many other moralists or religious thinkers, they cannot resort to some vague and loosely defined system of ethics or to the dictates of their conscience for authoritative answers to any moral questions, let alone to a question of such fearful dimensions. The Judaism of the Torah can determine ethical conduct only in terms of exact and compelling laws, and these in turn can enjoy the sanction of classic Jewish teachings only if they are conclusively founded on principles and practices enshrined in the established corpus of Jewish religious legislation.

Granted these premises, then, the problem would appear wellnigh insoluble.

Yet the challenge must be met, however unequal to the task both the judges and the laws they administer may seem to be: for the "Red or Dead" issue is clearly of a purely moral nature. True, before judgment can be pronounced, a great many political, military, psychological and other factors have to be most carefully ascertained and analyzed. The decision first requires an accurate expert assessment, for instance, of the political developments likely to ensue from either verdict, of the feasibility to deter an atomic aggressor by the threat of atomic retaliation or defense, of the chances of human survival after an atomic holocaust, of the ability of one country (however unassailable militarily) to subjugate a hostile world for long, and of a host of other questions on which presumably no one but the nation's top political and military leaders has any reliable information. Such data are indispensable in considering and adjudging the issue before us, and this information (however strictly classified for security reasons) should be made available (confidentially if necessary) to those charged with helping to reach a decision and to guide public opinion. But whatever the part played by expert evidence in providing the facts on which the decision must be based, the decision itself is the prerogative of the most competent moral authorities. And since we believe the revealed will of God to be the only absolute arbiter of moral values, we must needs look to the spokesmen of religion for the ultimate judgment and for securing its public acceptance by recourse to every publicity device at their disposal. In this grave challenge Jewish spiritual leaders, as the heirs of the original moral law revealed to man, face a special responsibility which they cannot ignore or delegate to others.

Of the two problems mentioned in the first paragraph, that of our competence is the more simple to resolve. According to the Torah, no judicial perplexity is so great that it is beyond the adequacy or authority of the spiritual guides of any age. "Jephtah in his generation is as (authentic as) Samuel in his generation,"[10] for jurisdiction is always conferred on "the judge *that shall be in those days.*"[11] Those charged with religious leadership must never claim that their relative insufficiency renders them unequal to a contemporary challenge.

They have no right to shirk the responsibility of making even the most fateful decisions required in their time, for their authority is as great and absolute as that of the most outstanding visionaries in any other age. Our leading rabbis today are the Moses, or Isaiah, or Hillel, or Maimonides of our time.

More formidable is the question of how to find any instructive precedents to guide us in our present dilemma. The Talmudic parallels adduced by Rabbi Lamm—on the religious classification of wars, on the limits of voluntary martyrdom, on the superiority of life over law, etc.—are all relevant and valid as far as they go. Yet they all touch only on more or less insignificant aspects of the problem, for none of these parallels envisage the enslavement or annihilation of the entire human race! The difference between the "Red or Dead" issue and the rabbinic precedents cited is not just in degree but in kind: the difference is the same as between amputating a limb or an organ of a person and killing him altogether. The fact that both acts have the destruction of living tissues in common is, of course, quite immaterial to the principal distinction between the acts. Similarly, the rulings on wars or martyrdom—dealing merely with the sacrifice of a part of humanity or a people—may be quite inconclusive as a guide to decisions involving all members of the human or national society.

On the other hand, Jewish law itself does equate the life of a single individual with that of all mankind. "Whoever destroys a single life is regarded as if he destroyed the entire world, and whoever preserves a single life is regarded as if he preserved the whole world."[12] This is not a merely homiletical or aggadic statement; it is of equal significance as a practical ruling of the Halakhah. Equating the worth of one with any number of human beings as identical, it postulates that every individual is of infinite value and infinity multiplied or divided by any number still remains the same infinity. Accordingly, it is forbidden deliberately to sacrifice one human being even in order to save thereby a hundred or a million others,[13] just as a person who has only a few more moments to live (i.e. a tiny fraction of life) enjoys precisely the same infinite worth as another who can still look forward to seventy years of life.[14]

We are therefore halakhically justified in drawing some analogy between the fate of one or more individuals whose life is at stake and that of the whole of humanity, however un-precedented the latter contingency may be. To that extent Rabbi Lamm's inferences from the teachings on limited threats to human life he quotes are valid in the strictly legal sense, or at least in theory. But in practice it may well be that, just as the law distinguishes between an individual and the public in regard to martyrdom and certain moral values (as recog-nized in Rabbi Lamm's article), it also evaluates the rights and duties of the entire human society differently from those of a more confined public. In other words, the applicability of rules affecting individuals or the public to the conduct of humanity at large must still be proved.

Turning now to the essence of the problem at issue, I think an analysis of the most fundamental question involved should yield a somewhat different approach from Rabbi Lamm's in our search for halakhic guide-lines. The underlying question in the "Red or Dead" issue, as it confronts us at the moment, is not whether we choose the one or the other. Naturally we prefer neither. The actual question *now* is whether (a) the free world should continue its atomic build-up—both as a deterrent to prevent an attack and as a means to "massive retaliation" in the event of an attack—even at the risk of universal destruction ("Dead") or (b) it should disarm uni-laterally to avoid the alternative of global annihilation even at the risk of eventual enslavement ("Red"). In moral terms the problem is reduced primarily, I believe, to the question of whether the unquestioned right of self-defense (surely the only justification for war or its preparation) includes the threat (deterrent) or act (retaliation) of destroying one's own life together with that of the aggressor. So long as wars were limited and it was likely that the belligerents would survive and one would emerge victorious, the basic right to arm and to wage war was clearly asserted by the law of self-defense, whether what was to be defended were lives or moral values. But if both the lives and the values to be defended may, as now appears possible, themselves be destroyed together with the aggressor in the exercise of self-defense, the right to resort to it is questionable.

Halakhically this question may be defined in relatively simple terms. A major source in the Torah for the law of self-defense is the provision exonerating from guilt a potential victim of robbery with possible violence if in self-defense he struck down and, if necessary, even killed the attacker before he committed any crime.[15] Hence, in the words of the rabbis, "if a man comes to slay you, forestall by slaying him!"[16] Now this law confers the right of self-defense only if the victim will thereby *forestall* the anticipated attack and save his own life at the expense of the aggressor's. But the defender would certainly not be entitled to frustrate the attack if this could be done only at the cost of both lives; for instance, by blowing up the house in which he and the robber encounter each other. Presumably the victim would then have to submit to the robbery and even to death by violence at the hands of the attacker rather than take "preventive" action which would be sure to cause two deaths.

In view of this vital limitation of the law of self-defense, it would appear that a defensive war likely to endanger the survival of the attacking and defending nations alike, if not indeed of the entire human race, can never be justified. On the assumption, then, that the choice posed by a threatened nuclear attack would be either complete mutual destruction or surrender, only the second alternative may be morally vindicated.

Once the recourse to atomic warfare even in self-defense (retaliation) is eliminated, the threat to resort to it when attacked (deterrent) also would naturally have to be abandoned. A threat is effective, and can be justified, only as long as the possibility to carry it out exists. It would be futile, in order to scare off robbers, to equip one's home with a powerful bomb if one has no intention, or right, to explode it when actually challenged by a robber.

The law of self-defense (i.e., the right to kill an attacker in anticipation of an act of violence on his part) does, of course, also extend to preventing (though not to retaliating) a moral assault, but the exercise of this right is restricted to preventing rape constituting adultery or incest;[17] this is therefore inapplicable to our problem.

With the exclusion of self-defense as a valid argument in favor of the "Dead" plank, the only major consideration that remains is the martyrdom theme (developed at length by Rabbi Lamm), i.e., whether the moral values to be preserved transcend the worth of life itself, so that we are required to defend them to death. I cannot altogether agree with Rabbi Lamm's reasoning on this matter. Dealing with the individual's choice between "Red or Dead," he rightly concludes that the suppression of moral values resulting from the "Red" alternative would not be such as to justify or demand their defense at the cost of life. If he nevertheless finally opts in favor of "Dead" in the light of Jewish teachings it is because he regards the defense of Judaism and of the Land of Israel as a *casus belli* for an Obligatory War *(Milchemet Mitzvah)* to be fought even at the risk of total annihilation.

This argument seems completely irrelevant to me. Surely we are not asked or meant to express an opinion on whether Jews or Israel should choose "Red or Dead," but on what we, as Jewish citizens, would urge the free world to decide on the basis of our religious teachings. We could scarely determine such a choice by the obligation which *we*, as Jews, owe to our own faith or to the national interest of Israel.

Nor are the principles governing Obligatory Wars necessarily applicable to the nations of the world. The *religious duty* to defend Israel's borders and Judaism, imposed on us by Divine law, is obviously limited to the people of Israel. Moreover, even for Jews I doubt if the laws relating to the Obligatory Wars, or to collective martyrdom, can be applied in the present circumstances. According to Maimonides, the duty to surrender to death rather than to the cardinal sins of idolatry, incest, and bloodshed (i.e., the three supreme offenses against God, oneself and one's neighbor) stems itself from the concept of the "sanctification of the Name"[18] on the basis of the verse "And I shall be sanctified in the midst of the children of Israel."[19] This implies that the martyrs will be survived by other Jews who will be inspired to similar heroism by such a test of faith, or who will at least continue to uphold the sanctity of the Name. But if the alternative to surrender is the destruction of the whole Jewish people, the sacrifice lacks all meaning, since God can no longer "be sanctified in the midst of the children of Israel."

This explains, no doubt, why—the regulations on Obligatory Wars notwithstanding—Rabbi Johanan ben Zakkai and his party opposed the Zealots' plan to fight the Roman aggressors to the finish, choosing instead to surrender to their godless conquerors rather than to risk the extinction of the Jewish people. And the Romans, after all, were at least as "Red"—in terms of the enslavement and moral degradation inflicted by their conquest—as the Communists are ever likely to be. Yet Rabbinic Judaism never censured Rabbi Johanan ben Zakkai for his fateful decision against "Dead." It is absurd to defend Judaism by risking the liquidation of the last Jew to uphold it. History has triumphantly vindicated the profound wisdom and justice of this historic decision. It would likewise be utter folly to fight for the preservation of our Western ideas at the expense of the human element able to transmit them to future generations.

No human group has been confronted more often by the tragic choice between the loss of freedom and the loss of existence than the Jewish people. Its attitude, in broad principle, has always been exemplified by the Psalmist's jubilant cry of thanksgiving: "The Lord hath chastened me sore; but He hath not given me over unto death."[20] The Jew has ever preferred life with indignity and servitude to death with glory. With every fibre of his being he clung to life even under the most miserable conditions, holding out, in patient submission to suffering, for the dawn of freedom to break, if not on himself, then at least on his descendants.

We believe that, in the final analysis, the only really effective protection of mankind, as of the Jewish people, from the calamitous peril of both "Red" and "Dead" lies in strengthening our moral and religious defenses.

"Oh that My people would hearken unto Me,
That Israel would walk in My ways!
I would soon subdue their enemies,
And turn My hand against their adversaries.
The haters of the Lord should dwindle away before Him;
And their punishment should endure forever"[21]

IMMANUEL JAKOBOVITS

Circumcision, Ritual or Surgical?

The following letter, published in the July 1962 issue of *Jewish Social Studies*, rebutted charges against *Mohalim* and ritual circumcision as traditionally practiced, which had appeared in an article featured in the January 1962 number of that journal.

To the Editors of JEWISH SOCIAL STUDIES:

Lovers of Judaism and objective scholars must have been utterly dismayed, as I was, to read the highly tendentious contribution by Dr. Charles Weiss entitled "A Worldwide Survey of the Current Practice of Milah (Ritual Circumcision)" which you saw fit to publish in your January 1962 issue.

Far from being a "survey," this piece is an undisguised plea for the abolition of ritual circumcision. It is but the latest outburst in the long history of attacks on this hallowed institution by the detractors of Judaism. Ritual circumcision means, by definition, a circumcision performed in accordance with ritual requirements, that is in our case, with the provisions of Jewish law. Since the author advocates ignoring the most essential of these provisions—such as the performance of the operation by a religiously qualified official—the proposed practice would lose its ritual character and thus defeat its avowed purpose.

Dr. Weiss supports his plea by a series of specious arguments, many grossly selective and misleading quotations, and—worst of all—the omission of any references to facts belying his prejudices.

The type of sources used is demonstrated in the very first paragraph of the article which cites some obscure French writer of 1847 for the view that "Abraham circumcized himself merely to cure an obstruction of the urethra which had made him infertile." Evidently it did not occur to either "scholar" that Abraham's infertility did not prevent him from begetting a son thirteen years prior to his circumcision and that this therapeutic "motive" for the operation made nonsense of the circumcisions performed "on the same day" on his young son and on the members of his household[22] and later on his infant Isaac![23] Or did Ishmael really show symptoms of infertility at thirteen years and Isaac at eight days? This must be a unique case of hereditary infertility!

The author's sharpest invective is reserved for the *Mohalim*, especially if they are "pious" as required by law. To corroborate his canard that *Mohalim* are, as he implies, irresponsible charlatans, and that there had been "many cases of severe hemorrhage, infection and other 'mishaps'," including "several tragedies . . . following *milah* during the past few years," he mentions the alleged experiences of two doctors and refers to the Quarterly Cumulative *Index Medicus* which lists an assortment of reports on six isolated cases ranging over three countries in Europe and Australia since 1929! But he dismisses as "misleading the simple" the official statistics of the New York City Health Department which indicate that there had been only one death from circumcision out of over half a million cases (including surgical operations) from 1939 to 1952 in a city which contains the largest Jewish population (and presumably the greatest number of *Mohalim*) in the world! Dr. Weiss discounts these records on the extraordinary grounds that "*Mohalim* are usually not required to sign hospital charts," as if that would make any difference to their liability for any deaths caused by them.

That there are some incompetent *Mohalim* no one will deny. But all the available evidence suggests that their comparative number is certainly no greater than that of incompetent doctors. Your readers might like to compare the indictments against *Mohalim* scattered throughout the world assembled by Dr. Weiss with the following instances of "mishaps" in circumcisions performed by physicians collected at random from medical periodicals appearing in the United States alone during the past few years.

The *Southern Medical Journal* (Feb. 1949, pp. 288-90) records a case where the penis was denuded and partially amputated by an M.D. due to the use of electrocautery at a circumcision. The same *Journal* (Aug. 1949, p. 657) reports cases of high frequency current used by physicians which resulted in the complete sloughing of the external penis. Dr. Winston S. Pugh, in *Surgical Clinics of North America* (April 1935, pp. 461-70) states: "I have seen many misfortunes by a lack of good preparation . . . I have been personally responsible for some . . . Poor techniques by a doctor (resulted) in an enormously swollen penis, black as coal . . . profuse bleeding 24 hours later . . . severe infections . . . If you possess any of the newfangled clamps, place them on your museum shelves . . ." Another doctor, in the *Journal of Pediatrics* (May 1941, pp. 657-8), describes a baby circumcized by an obstetrician on the eighth day which six weeks later had its skin denuded, edema around the corona, and the shaft swollen. The *Virginia Medical Monthly* (April 1941) quotes a doctor who has had to transfuse quite a few children for an obstetrician who routinely circumcized males at birth, while the *U. S. Naval Medical Bulletin* (Jan.-Feb. 1949, p. 120) lists numerous disabilities, including sterility, impotence and chordee, caused by the shortening of the frenum and amputations following surgical circumcisions by poor doctors.

Dr. Weiss's remedy—the employment of doctors instead of *Mohalim* for Jewish circumcisions—is even more hazardous than the disease he seeks to cure, it would seem. The same applies to his fantastic suggestion that all babies be given a general anesthetic during the operation because, among other reasons, " (its absence) is likely to leave traces of some kind on the personality." These "traces" on the personality of the Jew, evident for thousands of years, have surely been altogether beneficial. One would hardly be justified in exchanging these traces for the deaths that would ensue from subjecting all Jewish eight-day male infants to the hazards of a general anesthetic!

No, *Mohalim* know better than that, fortified as they are by four thousand years of uninterrupted experience in this specialty. Little wonder that to this day countless physicians entrust their own sons to the superior skill of *Mohalim* in preference to doctors, often for reasons entirely unrelated to religious considerations.

How false, therefore, is Dr. Weiss's recourse to a passage in my book *Jewish Medical Ethics* to sustain his statement that "some orthodox rabbis are opposed to professional personnel. . ." On the contrary, the only competent professional personnel concerned with ritual circumcisions are *Mohalim*; hence we insist on their employment.

Of course there are negligent and irresponsible *Mohalim* as there are negligent and irresponsible doctors. But the facts bear out as more objective and fair than Dr. Weiss's "survey" the recent judgment of a reputable physician: "The Jewish professional circumsizer, although not a doctor, is required to meet definite standards and is usually very skillful" (Edward T. Wilkes, in *Parents' Magazine*, February 1959, p. 50).

New York, New York   DR. I. JAKOBOVITS

"A Matter of Elevation"

Early in 1959 an automatic elevator, operated by a time-switch set in advance, was installed at the Fifth Avenue Synagogue to avoid the need for any manual operation on Sabbath and festivals. A rather facetious editorial piece on this automatic elevator—the first installation of its kind— appeared in *The Jewish Observer and Middle East Review* (London), which published the following reply on July 3, 1959.

To the Editor of
THE JEWISH OBSERVER AND MIDDLE EAST REVIEW:

A friend has just drawn my attention to the derisive comment on my Synagogue's automatic elevator you saw fit to publish recently under the heading "A Matter of Elevation."

So far you certainly have been always consistent in your anti-religious zealotry and your constant denigration of Orthodoxy. But now, I fear, your readers may detect some strange inconsistency in your attacks.

You never tire of complaining that Orthodox leaders are out of tune with the times and that they have failed to adjust Judaism to the conditions of our age. Yet when the occasion presents itself for you to acknowledge an effort to facilitate Jewish observance by the use of the most up-to-date of modern scientific advances, you do not like it either, and you turn from smear to sneer in order to beat your favorite Orthodox whipping-boy.

It looks as if the specter of religious Jews in twentieth century garb, equipped with electric shavers and automatic lifts to prove the compatibility of their faith with contemporary civilization, is even more objectionable to you than the sight of ear-locked Jews in medieval schtreimels and kaftans.

Could it be, perhaps, that in your rabidly anti-religious fanaticism you fear that your notion of Jewish religious obsolescence may itself become obsolete? Are you disturbed that your condemnation of Orthodoxy is belied by your anxiety that traditional Judaism's resurgence as exemplified by the rise of an ultra-modern synagogue has "invaded" the "ritziest" section of New York? Maybe you are right; the boot of antiquity will be on the other foot after all, and your secularist bigotry will be as archaic as the Karaite heresy, while Orthodox Jews will live happily with the times in New York—and Jerusalem.

Fifth Avenue Synagogue   Dr. Immanuel Jakobovits
5 East 62nd Street   Rabbi
New York 21, N. Y.

The "Jacobs Affair"

Late in 1961 a religious conflict began to erupt in Great Britain which eventually rocked Anglo-Jewry and sent its shockwaves all over the Jewish world. Sparking the bitter controversy was the refusal of Chief Rabbi Israel Brodie first to appoint Rabbi Dr. Louis Jacobs as principal of Jew's College, and later, in 1964, to approve his reappointment as minister of London's New West End Synagogue. In both cases, the Chief Rabbi argued Dr. Jacobs had rendered himself unfit for both these Orthodox positions because of the heterodox views he had expressed in speech and in writing, notably his denial of the traditional belief that the entire Torah was of Divine origin. While the Chief Rabbi received the overwhelming support of Orthodox rabbis and scholars everywhere, the worldwide reports and comments on the conflict in the press were heavily slanted in favor of Dr. Jacobs, largely through the partisanship of the influential *Jewish Chronicle* which, as Dr. Jacobs' principal protagonist from the beginning, embarked on a sustained campaign to turn public opinion against the Chief Rabbi. The letter below, published in the *Congress Bi-Weekly*, on February 5, 1962, was prompted by an article on the controversy.

To the Editor of the CONGRESS BI-WEEKLY:

Mr. S. J. Goldsmith's report on the Jews' College crisis in London, published in your January 22 issue, shows a lamentable departure from your usual standards of objectivity, fairness and accuracy.

It is quite untrue that "most of the members of the council of the College resigned" with Dr Louis Jacobs. The truth is that only the officers resigned after being defeated by a vote of 14 to six at a council meeting which favored the Chief Rabbi's request to postpone a decision until his return from Australia in April.

It is equally untrue that "Dr. Jacobs has the support of the Jewish community." The truth is that at least half of the community side with the Chief Rabbi, as revealed in the correspondence columns of the *Jewish Chronicle*—the principal protagonist of Dr. Jacobs. Almost the entire faculty of Jews' College itself is opposed to the appointment of Dr. Jacobs. So were twenty ministers of the United Synagogue in London as against only thirteen who favored his appointment, according to a poll taken by the *Jewish Chronicle*. Orthodox rabbis and leading Orthodox organizations, such as the Mizrachi, are virtually unanimous in their rejection of Dr. Jacobs as a suitable candidate for the principalship of Jews' College.

Above all, it is completely false and misleading to describe the conflict as one between the Chief Rabbi's "fundamentalism" and the alleged tendency of Dr. Jacobs "to be too much inclined towards inquiry." The Chief Rabbi is himself a modern-type rabbi trained at Jews' College. In common with men like Dr. I. Epstein (the retired principal of the College) and Dr. Belkin (of Yeshiva University) as well as other leading Orthodox scholars throughout the world, the Chief Rabbi disagrees with Dr. Jacobs while yet favoring intelligent inquiry, the cornerstone of all Jewish scholarship.

The real issue lies elsewhere, despite the bombastic claim of Dr. Jacobs in his letter of resignation that "no reputable scholar in the world has an approach that is basically different from mine," a claim as patently absurd as it is immodest. To quote the *Jewish Review*, the principal rival of the *Jewish Chronicle* in England, "Dr. Jacobs believes that the Torah contains higher and lower teachings, parts which are eternal and parts which are ephemeral. This concept clearly abandons the Orthodox religious position." The journal continues: "No wonder that Rabbi Jacobs' attitude has been received with open arms by the Liberal Jewish community (corresponding to the American Reform—I. J.). The Rev. John D. Rayner in a review in the *Liberal Jewish Monthly* of his book *Jewish Values,* writes: 'The present work, though it does not always go quite as far as we would like, is almost completely non-controversial from a Liberal point of view. Naturally one cannot help wondering how a scholar of such liberal mind can continue to identify himself with the Orthodox establishment'."

But the essence of the battle between the Chief Rabbi and his detractors goes far beyond a conflict of personalities. Its outcome will determine whether the religious leadership of Anglo-Jewry shall remain basically Orthodox, as it has always been, or be pushed into the camp of Conservative Judaism (with which the *Jewish Chronicle* and Dr. Jacobs have been flirting more or less openly for some time past).

Fifth Avenue Synagogue,   Dr. Immanuel Jakobovits
New York City   Rabbi

Prayer in Public Schools

The historic U. S. Supreme Court decision of 1962, banning the recitation of the New York State "Regents Prayer" at public schools, was greeted with an outburst of enthusiastic applause from national Jewish organizations and leaders. Only very few Jewish voices were raised in dissent. Among the first of these was the following letter, published in *The New York Times* on July 4, 1962.

To the Editor of The New York Times:

Lest it be thought that all rabbis concur with the recent statement by the New York Board of Rabbis praising the Supreme Court decision on prayer at public schools, I wish to express my dissent from, and utter dismay at, this strange alliance between teachers of Judaism and the spokesmen of atheism or secularism who secured and applauded the verdict.

As spiritual leaders of the people that gave birth to the immortal vision of the days when "the earth shall be full of the knowledge of the Lord as the waters cover the sea," we can scarcely, I submit, be jubilant about outlawing the acknowledgment and worship of God from any area of life, least of all from schools, which pre-eminently fashion the outlook of our future citizens, without making a travesty of Jewish thought and history.

For many centuries devout Jewish parents have taught their children, long before they could read or even speak properly, to include in their simple morning prayers the verse from the Hebrew Bible: "The beginning of wisdom is the fear of the Lord," so as to instill in them the conviction that knowledge or education without a religious foundation is worthless.

The United States is now probably the only country in the world outside the Iron Curtain to brand as an offense the public acknowledgment of God in schools. How can rabbis, heirs to the Prophets of Israel, rejoice over this?

Freedom cannot be maintained without religion, just as the brotherhood of man requires the Fatherhood of God. A generation of heathen hedonists, worshipping the idols of happiness and material success, will be unable to evoke the herculean strength necessary to contain the mighty tide of godlessness in the defense of liberty. Futhermore, even statistics show that only children reared in a wholesome religious atmosphere are likely to develop the maximum immunity to the scourges of juvenile delinquency corroding our society and undermining its security.

"The wall of separation" between state and church must be constructed with ample gateways to prevent the divorce of education from religion if that wall is not to lay siege to our civilization and starve it to death.

These are purely my personal views, but I have no doubt that they are shared by many of my colleagues, whether they are members of the Board of Rabbis or not.

New York, July 1, 1962   (Rabbi) IMMANUEL JAKOBOVITS

Whither Orthodoxy?

In the Winter 1964-5 issue of *Midstream* (published by the Jewish Agency in New York) the Editor, Mr. Shlomo Katz, delivered a withering attack on Orthodox Jews in an article under the above heading. The attack was directed particularly at the Chief Rabbinate of Israel, and it referred to several of the most bitter controversies between the religionists and their opponents which made news during 1964. The reply below appeared in the Spring 1965 issue of the same journal.

To the Editor of Midstream:

On reading your article unencumbered by any knowledge of the facts one must indeed feel profoundly moved by the terrible plight of the poor, oppressed non-Orthodox Jewish masses in their heroic but losing battle against the tyrannical might of the brutal, immoral, arrogant and disruptive assault of Orthodoxy on the unity, morals and security of the Jewish people. And the treachery of it all! To be "creeping up on us" innocent and persecuted Jews "while we were unaware," to scheme this attack behind our backs in secret intrigue—how dastardly!

But Orthodox readers of this haunting article may be pardoned if they rub their eyes in incredulity and ask whether there is not here some confusion between the pursuer and the pursued, between fact and fiction.

You complain with obvious anguish that the growing power recently regained by Orthodoxy (*regained,* for you admit that "most Jews today . . . are only a generation or two removed from Orthodox ancestors") was at first "acquiesced to" and then "resented" as "concession after concession was made to Orthodoxy." One wonders what these numerous "concessions" are. Rabbinical control of marriages, for instance, merely represents the *status quo* inherited by the Jewish State from the Mandatory administration. And to whom were these "concessions" made? To the Orthodox or to traditional Judaism? One wonders even more whether history is not here presented in the reversed image of a distorted mirror. Was it not the Orthodox who at first lamely "acquiesced to" the inroads made by the secularists and other non-observant Jews into Jewish life and who only lately began to "resent" the suppression of everything hallowed by our millennial existence and martyrdom? After all, who has wrested power from whom? Which segment of our people has broken faith with the traditions of our past and sown the seeds of Jewish disunity, the Orthodox or the non-Orthodox?

Your reference to the recent *Shalom* scandal illustrates your squinted perspective on current events. In lambasting an Orthodox leader (and a moderate one at that) for threatening a boycott if the Zim Shipping Company persisted in its plan to make its new ship the first national Jewish unit to serve *trephah* food, you escalated this threat to risking "the destruction of Israel . . ., including the probable extermination of a couple of million Jews . . ., if only the fine points (*sic*) of halachah . . . were observed" (you really do attribute some invincible might, not to speak of sinister intentions, to Orthodox Jews!). Now, with these admittedly catastrophic consequences ensuing from such a boycott, would it not be at least equally true to charge that the Zim management were quite prepared to have not only the *Shalom* put out of commission (as it was 30 miles out on its first *trephah* cruise) but Israel torpedoed, etc., etc., in a gallant fight for the right to serve *trephah* food on a Jewish vessel?

In your frightening catalogue of Orthodox sins *versus* non-Orthodox piety and suffering, the Bene Israel controversy naturally features prominently. Regarding this "exotic community," this "romantic case . . . of fine people, diligent, honestly earning their living . . .," you state: "But now a problem arose (more correctly, was raised). . . . The Rabbinate in Israel raised the question of intermarriage with them . . ." How wicked, these latterday Orthodox fanatics, with no sense of romanticism modifying their laws, to "raise" such a problem where none had ever existed before! No Sir, your facts are as faulty as your opinions. This tragic problem was "raised" neither "now" nor by the Rabbinate in Israel. Ever since Jews from Europe, Bagdad and elsewhere settled in India over a century ago down to the present day, they have refused to inter-marry with the Bene Israel whose status was always considered doubtful. The Israel Rabbinate, far from "raising" the problem, has in fact begun to solve it, by relaxing the hitherto rigid isolation of this community in their own former country.

Another sample of ignorance or fact-twisting is given in your reference to the fight of "non-Orthodox organizations . . . for the right of Orthodox storekeepers to keep their businesses open on Sunday . . ." as proving these organizations' "reserve of sympathy and respect for the genuine believers." It proves nothing of the kind. The organizations fought not *for* the sanctity of the Sabbath, but *against* the public acknowledgment of the Christian Sunday; not for the observant Jewish storekeeper as much as for the wall of separation between Church and State. That is why this fight was lost year after year until Orthodox representatives themselves took up the matter and convinced the authorities in Albany and elsewhere that this was not a secularist attack on religion in public life but a genuine concern for the religious and economic rights of observant Jews (as I know from my personal involvement in this fight). Had you cited the community-wide opposition to anti-*Shechitah* legislation, you would have had a more relevant argument.

You object to the division of Jews into True and False Jews. I have never heard of such a classification, and I would sustain your objection. Instead, they should be divided into law-abiding and law-breaking Jews, a classification with which you should have little cause to quarrel if by law is meant Jewish law.

Finally a comment on your *piece de resistance*. What, I wonder, if not wishful thinking, could possibly substantiate your startling statement: "Even the most insecure secular family structure begins to appear morally superior (to the religious)"? Really?! Had you attended the school principals' conference in Israel not so long ago you would have heard the secularists inquire from their religious colleagues how and why it is that juvenile delinquency and other vices, now so rampant in Israel as elsewhere, are almost completely unknown among the students and graduates of religious schools. You ought to go to the police precinct serving Mea Shearim and ask how many youngsters have ever been arrested there for immoral or criminal acts (I understand none). You ought

to compare the illegitimacy, divorce and dope addiction rates
among the Orthodox and the non-Orthodox in Israel, America
or anywhere else, and you would know better than to put
such a fantastic canard into print.

Your "dismay" and "shock" in suddenly discovering the
renewed "creeping" ascendancy of Orthodox is understandable. That Orthodox Jews have confounded with a vengeance the prophets of doom who not long ago gleefully forecast the speedy extinction of Orthodoxy; that they constitute
today the only segment of our people with a birthrate high
enough and an assimilation- and intermarriage-rate low
enough to ensure survival and growth; that they are now in
control of virtually all Jewish day schools in the Diaspora
and of all organizations of Jewish scientists; that they are
again sufficiently bold to challenge Christian missionaries, and
Jewish opponents of the primacy of religion in the Jewish
national purpose; that they have ceased to submit to the
direction of our future by those who refuse to acknowledge
our past—all this is bound to be most discomfitting to the
secularists and non-conformists who now find confident victory over the faithful snatched from their grasp. In asking
"Whither Orthodoxy?" you really question, as you well may,
the ability of the non-Orthodox to retain their sway over our
destiny and to stem the new tide of religious resurgence manifest all over the world.

In this spiritual revolution—or *Kulturkampf,* as you may
call it,—there are some features of militancy and fanaticism
which may be open to legitimate criticism, though even you
will admit that these features are by no means limited to the
Orthodox. I have not read of religious fanatics hiring trucks
to invade non-religious Kibbutzim to protest the desecration
of the Sabbath with sticks and beatings, as I did read of truck-
loads of non-Orthodox Kibbutznicks invading the Orthodox
quarters of Jerusalem to protest the sanctification of the Sabbath with riotous mobs!

With the fearful blows sustained by Orthodoxy after decades
of spiritual defections and corrosion, culminating in the annihilation of the principal Orthodox bastions during the holo-

caust, there are bound to be occasional manifestations of excessive zeal in the gigantic task of restoring our people's religious integrity. The twin assaults of irreligion and inhumanity on Orthodoxy, combined with a sense of urgency to make good its calamitous losses, have produced a frame of mind which is little amenable to patience and moderation. This is granted; the situation will gradually adjust itself to the degree to which Orthodoxy will regain its strength and self-confidence. Meanwhile it is scarcely right to belabor Orthodox leaders for militantly shouldering the burden of religious reconstruction which should be borne in equal shares by all sections of our people.

(Rabbi Dr.) IMMANUEL JAKOBOVITS

Fifth Avenue Synagogue
New York City

NOTES ON CHAPTER 1

1. See Rashi, Ex. 13:18.
2. Ex. 32:26; and *Yoma* 66b.
3. cf. *Shabbath* 130a; and *SeMaG*, positive com., no. 3.
4. See *Rosh Hashanah* 34b.
5. See *Akedath Yitzchak, Sha'ar* XX.
6. Ps. 14:1.
7. Ps. 92:7.
8. Is. 11:9.
9. See *Even Ha'ezer*, 2:2; and Yechiel M. Epstein, *Arukh Hashulchan*, a.l., no. 14.
10. See *Ba'er Hetev*, a.l., no. 4.
11. *The New York Times*, Oct. 26, 1963.
12. *Universal Perpetual Calendar Reform*, New York, 1957.
13. *Yevamoth* 63a.
14. Ps. 127:1.
15. Ps. 81:14 f.
16. Deut. 11.
17. Rashi, a.l.
18. Nachmanides, a.l.
19. Deut. 17:9.
20. *Rosh Hashanah* 25b.
21. cf. Ps. 14:1; and *Avoth*, 2:5.
22. See *Chullin* 90b.

NOTES ON CHAPTER 3

1. Hence their inclusion in the *Shulchan Arukh* (*Yoreh De'ah*, 267).
2. Lev. 25:40.
3. *Erakhin* 29a; Maim., *Hil. Shemittah*, 10:8-9; *Hil. Avadim*, 1-10; *Yoreh De'ah*, 267:14.
4. Lev. 25:10.
5. *Erakhin* 32b. But according to Tosaphoth (*Gittin* 36a), the institutions of the Jubilee Year and the *eved ivri* were revived and observed at the time of the Second Temple. In the Talmud (*Erakhin* 33a), too, there is an opinion that that the exiled tribes were restored, and the Jubilee Year and *eved ivri* legislations consequently reintroduced, for a short period by Jeremiah. That would explain the reference to these laws in Jer. 34:13-16. Cf. note 16 below.
6. *Antiquities*, xvi, 1:1.
7. Ex. 22:2.
8. *Chinnukh*, 346 and 482. Thus, on the basis of these laws, it is forbidden even today to ask a person to do humiliating work against his will (R. Jonah, *Sha'arei Teshuvah*, 3:60).
9. *Minchath Chinnukh*, 42.
10. Lev. 25:55.
11. Tosaphoth, B. *Bathra* 13a.
12. *Kiddushin* 22b.
13. *Jer. Kiddushin*, 1:2.
14. Maim., *Hil. Matnoth Aniyim*, 10:17.
15. R. Bachaya, on Ex. 21; cf. Nachmanides, on Ex. 21:2.
16. *Echa Rab.*, on Lam. 1:3; *Jer. Rosh Hashanah*, 3:5.
17. *Korban Ha'eda*, a.l.
18. *Jer. R. H.*, loc. cit.
19. R. Bachaya, on Ex. 21.
20. Nachmanides, on Ex. 21:20.
21. Deut. 20:16.

22. Rashi, Ibn Ezra and Malbim, on Lev. 25:44.
23. *Sifra*, on Lev. 25:44.
24. Gen. 9:25; see *Chinnukh*, 347.
25. Lev. 25:39, and *Sifra, a.l.*
26. Ex. 21:7; see also note 28 below.
27. Maim., *Hil. Avadim*, 1:1.
28. *Ib.*, 4:2.
29. *Minchath Chinnukh*, 42.
30. Maim., *Hil. Avadim*, 1:1.
31. Maim., *Hil. Genevah*, 3:11.
32. *Minchath Chinnukh*, 42.
33. Ex. 22:3-8.
34. Maim., *Hil. Genevah*, 3:12.
35. *Ib.*, 3:14.
36. *Ib.*, 3:13.
37. *Ib.*, 3:15.
38. *Ib.*, 3:12-15.
39. *Sifra*, on Lev. 25:46; Maim., *Hil. Avadim*, 1:7. Hence, domestic servants today may be given charges which must not be imposed on an *eved ivri* (*Magen Avraham, Orach Chayim*, 148:1). But cf. note 8 above.
40. *Sifra* and *Rashi*, on Lev. 25:44.
41. *Kiddushin* 20a.
42. *Erakhin*, 8:5; *B. Metzi'a* 99a; *Yevamoth* 70b.
43. *Ma'aser Sheni*, 4:4, and *Bartinura, a.l.* See also note 85 below.
44. Maim., *Hil. Avadim*, 4:6.
45. Ibn Ezra, on Ex. 21:10.
46. RaSHBaM, on Ex. 21:20. The exception is the servant's right to marry a non-Jewish bondwoman (see notes 87 ff. below). But some authorities deduce from this that such a marriage, even by a freeman, can only rabbinically be forbidden, since a Jewish slave—sharing all the religious restrictions imposed by the Torah on other Jews—would not otherwise be permitted to do so. See *Mishneh Le-Melekh, Hil. Avadim*, 3:3 (middle).
47. Maim., *Hil. Avadim*, 2:2; *Hil. Chovel Umazik*, 4:16.
48. See *Mishneh Le-Melekh*, on *Hil. Avadim*, 2:2.
49. Maim., *Hil. Avadim*, 2:3.
50. *Ib.*, 2:4.
51. *Ib.*, 3:15.
52. *SeMaG*, pos. com., 83. See *Mishneh Le-Melekh*, on *Hil. Avadim*, 2:4.
53. *Maim., Hil. Avadim*, 2:5.
54. *Ib.*, 2:12.
55. *Ib.*
56. *Ib.*, 3:6.
57. *Ib.*, 3:13.
58. *Ib.*, 3:9.
59. Ex. 12:7 *ff.*; and Rashi, on Ex. 21:6.
60. Maim., *Hil Avadim*, 3:11.
61. *Ib.*, 3:10.
62. *Ib.*, 3:6. The term used in the Torah is literally "for ever" (Ex. 21:6; Deut. 15:17). But for proofs that this phrase implies a limited time, see RaSHBaM and the Gaon of Vilna, on Ex. 21:6; and David Hoffmann, on Lev. 25:39-41, and Deut. 15:12-18. Cf. also the interesting interpretation by Mecklenburg, *Ha-Kethav Veha-Kabbalah*, on Ex. 21:6. The rabbinic explanation of "for ever" is also confirmed by Josephus, *Antiquities*, iv, 8:28.
63. Maim., *Hil. Avadim*, 3:7.
64. Lev. 25:10, 41.
65. Maim, *Hil. Avadim*, 3:8.

66. See Isaac Breuer, "Die rechtsphilosophischen Grundlagen etc.," in *Jahrbuch der Juedisch-Litterarischen Gesellschaft,* vol. viii, p. 61.
67. *Sifra,* on Lev. 25:39; Maim., *Hil. Avadim,* 1:9.
68. Lev. 25:39, 46-47; Deut. 15:12.
69. Maim., *Hil. Avadim,* 1:5.
70. *Ib.,* 1:7. But a son or a disciple can be expected to do such work; see *Mekhilta,* on Ex. 21:2.
71. Maim., *Hil. Avadim,* 1:7. But see notes 8 and 39 above.
72. *Sifra,* on Lev. 25:43.
73. Maim., *Hil. Avadim,* 1:6.
74. Rashi, on Lev. 25:40. For the source on this remarkable provision of a slave's payment for non-domestic work—not mentioned elsewhere in rabbinic literature—see *Sifra* and *Malbim,* a.l. These sources even apply the law not to delay a hireling's wages overnight but to pay him "on the same day" (Deut. 24:15) to the *eved ivri.*
75. Maim., *Hil. Avadim,* 1:8.
76. Tosaphoth, *Kiddushin* 20a.
77. *Kiddushin* 20a; Maim., *Hil. Avadim,* 1:9.
78. *Kethuboth* 43a.
79. Maim., *Hil Avadim,* 2:12 (end).
80. RITVA (on *Kiddushin* 22a) expressly mentions clothing; the other authorities presumable include it, together with housing, among the master's responsibilities for the maintenance of the slave's family in general under the heading of "alimentation."
81. Maim., *Hil. Avadim,* 3:1.
82. RITVA, *loc. cit.* See also note 85 below.
83. Elijah Mizrachi, on Lev. 25:41.
84. Nachmanides, on Ex. 21:3.
85. Maim., *Hil. Avadim,* 3:1, according to *Mishneh Le-Melekh,* a.l. The master's duty towards the slave's family thus exceeds that legally binding upon a husband towards his own family; we assume that a husband will discharge his responsibilities without the compulsion of the law. See Nachmanides and RITVA, *loci cit.*
86. Maim., *Hil Avadim,* 3:2.
87. Nachmanides and RITVA, *loci. cit.*
88. Maim., *Hil. Avadim,* 3:3.
89. *Ib.,* 3:4.
90. Nachmanides, on Ex. 21:3.
91. Maim., *Hil. Avadim,* 3:3.
92. Jacob Emden, on *Kiddushin* 20a.
93. Maim., *loc. cit.*
94. RITVA, on *Kiddushin* 15a. Cf. *Ha-Kethav Veha-Kabbalah,* on Ex. 21-3.
95. Deut. 15:13.
96. Maim., *Hil. Avadim,* 3:14.
97. Ex. 21:32. Cf. notes 176-178 below.
98. *Mishneh Le-Melekh,* on Maim., *loc. cit.*
99. Maim., *loc. cit.*
100. Maim., *ib.,* 3:15.
101. The highest of the eight graded ranks of "charity" is performed by him who gives his poor fellow-man a gift, loan, partnership or employment to enable him to become financially independent (Maim, *Hil., Matnath Aniyim,* 10:7; *Yoreh De'ah,* 249:6).
102 *Tosephta, Pe'ah,* 4:16; Mordecai, *B. Bathra,* 1:497; *Yoreh De'ah,* 253-12.
103. Rashi, on *Kiddushin* 15a.
104. *Mishneh Le-Melekh,* on *Hil. Avadim,* 3:15.
105. *Kiddushin* 15a.

106. Maimonides (*Hil. Avadim,* 3:12) and most authorities (see *Mishneh Le-Melekh,* a.l.) hold that the self-sold slave is not entitled to the gift; Tosaphoth (*Kiddushin* 15a) adopts the opposite view. See also *Minchath Chinnukh,* 482.
107. Isaac Arama, *Akedath Yitzchak,* chpt. 46 (ed. Frankfurt a/0. ii.32b).
108. See above under sub-heading "The Insolvent Thief and the Self-sold Slave."
109. Maim., *Hil. Genevah,* 2:11.
110. Epstein, *Torah Temimah,* on Deut. 15:14; D. Hoffmann, on Deut. 15:14.
111. Deut: 15:15.
112. *Sifri,* Rashi and RaSHBaM, *a.l.*
113. Maim., *Hil. Avadim,* 1:3.
114. *Ib.,* 1:4.
115. *Ib.,* 2:7.
116. *Ib.,* 2:6.
117. *Ib.,* i:6 (end).
118. *Ib.,* 1:3.
119. *Ib.,* 1:2; *Yoreh De'ah,* 267:19.
120. Maim., *Hil. Avadim,* 1:2.
121. Ib., 1:2; *Hil. Genevah,* 2:12.
122. Nachmanides, on Ex. 21:4 (end).
123. Maim., *Hil. Avadim,* 1:2.
124. See *Mishneh Le-Melekh,* a.l.
125. Maim., *Hil. Avadim,* 4:1.
126. *Ib.,* 1:9.
127. See Rashi, on *Kiddushin* 18a.
128. *Kiddushin* 18a; Maim., *Hil. Avadim,* 4:2.
129. *Ib.*
130. *Ib.,* 4:4.
131. *Ib.*
132. *Ib.,* 4:5.
133. *Ib.,* 3:13.
134. *Mishneh Le-Melekh,* a.l.
135. *Bekhoroth,* 4:7; Maim., *Hil. Avadim,* 1:7.
136. Maim., *Hil. Avadim,* 4:11.
137. Ib., 4:8, and *Keseph Mishneh,* a.l.; against the view of Tosaphoth (*Kiddushin* 5a, bottom).
138. Maim., *Hil. Avadim,* 4:7, 9.
139. Ex. 21:10, and *Mekhilta,* a.l.
140. Lev. 24:12; Nu. 15:32; *Sanhedrin* 78b; Maim., *Hil. Rotze'ach,* 4:3.
141. Maim., *Hil. Rotze'ach,* 4:8.
142. *Ib.,* 7:1.
143. Nu. 35:22-34.
144. *Sanhedrin* 44a; see also *Seder Eliyahu Rabba,* 7 (ed. Friedman, p. 33), on Deut. 33:29.
145. *Kiddushin* 36a; cf. *Midrash Tanna'im,* on Deut. 11:17 (ed. Hoffmann, p. 39, bottom).
146. Cf. Samson Raphael Hirsch, on Ex. 21:2-11.
147. See, e.g., Michael Guttmann, *Das Judentum und seine Umwelt,* 1927.
148. *Avoth,* 6:2.
149. *Esther Rabba,* on 6:6.
150. *Chagigah* 4a; Maim., *Hil. Chagigah,* 2:1; *Yoreh De'ah,* 267:17.
151. *Kiddushin,* 1:7; Maim., *Hil. Avodah Zarah,* 12:3; *Orach Chayim,* 70:1.
152. Maim., *Hil. Milah,* 1:3; *Yoreh De'ah,* 267:1.
153. *Tur, Yoreh De'ah,* 267. Cf. Maim., *Hil. Rotze'ach,* 2:11; *Jer. Avodah Zarah,* 1:1; *Ber. Rabba,* 41:10.
154. *Yoreh De'ah,* 267:3.
155. See ReSHaSH, on *Yevamoth* 99b.

156. Ibn Ezra, on Ex. 22:44. See also next note.
157. *Yevaboth* 48b; Maim., *Hil. Avadim*, 8:12; *Yoreh De'ah*, 267:4.
158. Maim., *ib.*, and *Hil. Milah*, 1:6; *Yoreh De'ah*, 267:4, gloss. But the slave must under all circumstances submit to the Seven Noachidic Laws (Maim., *ib.*).
159. Ex. 20:10; 23:12; Deut. 5:14.
160. Deut. 16:11, 14.
161. Lev. 25:6.
162. Ex. 12:44.
163. Lev. 22:11; Deut. 12:12, 18.
164. Deut. 5:14.
165. Ex. 12:44; 21:21; Lev. 22:11.
166. *Yoreh De'ah*, 267:22. This regulation may be designed to protect the master from otherwise uncontrollable thefts by slaves whose tendency to steal was proverbial (see Rashi, on *Kiddushin* 11a; *Avoth*, 2:8; *Pesachim* 113b; *B. Metzi'a* 86b; *Ber. Rabba*, 86:3.)
167. "His (the slave's) soul is not acquired by him (viz., the master)" (*Sotah* 61a).
168. Ex. 21:26-27.
169. Ex. 21:20-21.
170. Ex. 21:32; cf. 28-30.
171. *Mekhilta*, on Ex. 21:20.
172. Maim., *Hil. Nizkei Mamon*, 8:5; cf. 10:1. See also next note.
173. Maim., *Hil. Rotze'ach*, 2:11.
174. Ex. 21:20-21; Maim., *Hil. Rotze'ach*, 2:12.
175. See *Otzar Yisrael*, vol. vii, p. 293; cf. Ibn Ezra, on Ex. 21:21.
176. Maim., *Hil. Rotze'ach*, 2:14; RaSHBaM, on Ex. 21:21.
177. Maim., *Hil. Rotze'ach*, 2:13; Rashi, on Ex. 21:21.
178. Ex. 21:32; Maim., *Hil. Nizkei Mamon*, 10:1; 11:1.
179. Lev. 27:4.
180. Seforno, on Ex. 21:32.
181. Maim., *Hil. Sanhedrin*, 16:12.
182. *Ib.*, *Choshen Mishpat*, 420:1-3. These regulations expressly include the non-Jewish slave; the cases mentioned later (see following notes) are exceptions from the general rule.
183. Maim., *Hil. Chovel Umazik*, 4:10; *Choshen Mishpat*, 424:3.
184. *Ib.*
185. *Derishah*, on *Tur, Choshen Mishpat*, 420.
186. *Beth Yoseph*, on *Tur, ib.*; *Choshen Mishpat*, 420:2, and *Ba'er Ha-Golah*, a.l.; *Arukh Ha-Shulchan, Choshen Mishpat*, 420:3. But for the opposite view, see Maim., *Hil Rotze'ach*, 2:12; *Me'irath Einayim*, on *Choshen Mishpat, ib.*; *Derishah*, on *Tur, ib.*
187. *B. Kamma* 88a. The equal treatment of the slave is based on his "obligation to submit to the commandments (of the Torah,) " whereby he is included in "the inheritance of the Lord" (Maim., *Hil Rotze'ach*, 2:11; *Choshen Mishpat*, 420:2).
188. See *Arukh Ha-Shulchan, Choshen Mishpat*, 420:6.
189. Maim., *Hil. Avadim*, 9:8; *Yoreh De'ah*, 26:17. Cf. note 40 above.
190. *Niddah* 47a; Maim., *loc. cit.*
191. Maim., *loc. cit.*; *Yoreh De'ah*, 267:17. Cf. *Yevamoth* 79a; Ibn Eza, on Ex. 21:21. For talmudic sources on these directives, see Gaon of Vilna, on *Yoreh De'ah*, 267:17. Cf. also Malbim, on Lev. 25:46.
192. Maim., *Hil. Avadim*, 9:8; *Yoreh De'ah*, 267:20.
193. *Ib.*
194. *Gittin* 12a; *Yoreh De'ah*, 267:20, gloss.
195. Lev. 25:46.
196. Maim., *loc. cit*; *Yoreh De'ah*, 267:79. But in the Talmud this is a matter of dispute, see *Sotah* 38a f.
197. RaN, on *Gittin* 38a.

198. Maim., *loc. cit; Yoreh De'ah*, 267-79. This concession, whereby a biblical commandment gives way to a rabbinical enactment, derives from the fact that the entire legislation aims at securing the maximum "fulfillment of the Law" by the slave; see *Chinnukh*, 347.

199. Maim., *Hil. Avadim*, 5:4 ff.; *Yoreh De'ah*, 267:27. *ff.*

200. Maim., *Hil. Avadim*, 7:7; *Yoreh De'ah*, 267:62.

201. Maim., *Hil. Avadim*, 8:17; *Yoreh De'ah*, 267:70.

202. Maim., *Hil. Avadim*, 9:6; *Yoreh De'ah*, 267:79.

203. Maim., *Hil. Avadim*, 8:5; *Yoreh De'ah*, 267:80.

204. Maim., *Hil. Avadim*, 8:9; *Yoreh De'ah*, 267:84.

205. Maim., *Hil. Avadim*, 8:8; *Yoreh De'ah*, 267:82.

206. Maim., *Hil. Avadim*, 8:10; *Yoreh De'ah*, 267:85. That is the case referred to in Deut. 23:16-17; see Rashi and Nachmanides, *a.l.*

207. Deut. 23:17.

208. *Sifri, a.l.*

209. Ez. 47:22-23. But according to Rashi (*a.l.*), this privilege is granted only after conversion.

210. *Avoth d'Rabbi Nathan*, 35:2; *Tosephta, Nega'im*, 6:2; Maim., *Hil. Beth Ha-Bechirah*, 7:14. See Guttmann, *op. cit.*, p. 45 *f.*

211. Maim., *Hil. Avadim*, 8:11; *Chinnukh*, 569.

212. *B. Kamma* 74b; *Jer. Kethuboth*, 3:10 (end).

213. Deut. 6:7.

214. *Lev. Rabba* 4:6.

215. Job 32:9.

216. *Ikkarim* 3:23.

217. *Ib.* 3:6.

218. The Sanhedrin (seat of supreme court, functioning also as government and parliament) had to be placed next to the altar (religion and morality) see Rashi, Ex. 21:1.

219. The full operation of the Sanhedrin is conditioned by the existence of the Temple. See Ramban, Nu. 35:29.

220. As illustrated by the functions of the members of any Beth Din as well as of the Supreme Court.

221. Ex. 23:2.

222. *Chinnukh*, 78.

223. Maim. *Hil. Sanh.* 2:1ff.

224. See Abarvanel, Deut. 16:18. Cf. *Jerus. Sanh.* II (end).

225. *Berakhot* 55a.

226. Responsa of Adret (RaSHBA) attributed to Nachmanides (RaMBaN), No. 65.

227. MaHaRDaL ibn Chaviv, No. 99; quoted in commentary *"Panim Chadashot"* following *Yoreh De'ah*, 334 (Vilna).

228. Resp. of Adret attr. to Nachm. No. 280.

229. Resp. of Adret, No. 729.

230. Mordecai, *B. Metz.* I. No. 482.

231. See Hastings, *Encycl. of Religion and Ethics*, VI. 362.

232. Nu. 11:29; see S'forno, a.l.

233. *Ruth Rabba* 1:1.

234. Maimonides, *Hil. Ma'aser*, 2:1.

235. Deut. 26:11.

236. Deut. 19:11.

237. Esther 9:22.

238. *Ta'anith*, 4:8.

239. Lev. 23:40.

240. *Sukkah* 29b.

241. Deut. 15:10.

242. Deut. 15:11.

243. *Sepher Hachinnukh*, No. 66.

244. *Yoreh De'ah*, 248:1.

245. Nu. 18:26.
246. Lev. 19:18.
247. Ex. 20:14.
248. Lev. 18:20.
249. Lev. 25:35.
250. Lev. 25:39.
251. Deut. 15:12.
252. Deut. 22:1.
253. Deut. 22:4.
254. Deut. 23:8.
255. Lev. 19:17.

NOTES ON CHAPTER 5

1. "Illegal Abortion as a Public Health Problem," by Mary Steichen Calderone, in a Paper presented at the 87th annual meeting of the Maternal and Child Health Section of the American Public Health Association.
2. Dr. Alan F. Guttmacher, quoted in *Newsweek*, August 15, 1960, p. 51.
3. Deut. 17:11.
4. *Yoreh De'ah*, 335.
5. Eliezer Yehudah Waldenberg, *Sepher Ramat Rachel (Kuntres Bikkur Cholim)*, at the end of responsa *Tzitz Eliezer*, part 5, p. 1 ff., and Yechiel Michel Tuczinsky, *Sepher Gesher Ha-Chayim*, 1960, part 1, p. 27 ff.
6. Jacob Breisch, responsa *Chelkat Ya'akov*, part 2, no. 128.
7. Isaac Jacob Weisz, responsa *Minchat Yitzchak*, part 2, no. 84. See also *No'am*, vol. 6, p. 285 f.; and Mosheh Benjamin Tomashoff, responsa *Avnei Shoham*, part 4, no. 56.
8. responsa *ReMA*, no. 19 (end).
9. See *JME*, p. 108 f.
10. *Nedarim* 39b; *Berakhot* 22b; cf. also Rashi, *Shabbat* 30a.
11. *Hane'eman*, Tel Aviv, Nisan-Iyar 5724, p. 2 f.
11a. Responsa *Bet David*, nos. 22 and 108, cited in *No'am*, vol. 4, p. 6.
12. Shemaryahu Arieli, "*Whether a Kohen May Visit a Hospital*," in *No'am*, vol. 2, p. 55 ff.
13. See *JME*, p. 243.
14. Jacob Meskin, responsa *Even Ya'akov*, nos. 47-51, agreeing with Rabbi J. E. Henkin in exchange of letters.
15. Yechiel Weinberg, responsa *Seridei Esh*, part 2, no. 134.
16. Chayim Yitzchak Abramowitz, *Sepher Vechay Bahem—Piku'ach Nephesh be-Halakkah*, Jerusalem, 1957; see also articles in *No'am* by Israel Aryeh Zalmanowitz (vol. 4, p. 175 ff.), Benjamin Rabinowitz Teumim (vol. 5, p. 281 ff., and vol. 6, p. 240 ff.), and Yitzchak Glickman (vol. 6, p. 220 ff.).
17. Isaac Herzog, responsa *Heichal Yitzchak, Even Ha-Ezer*, no. 8; and Abraham Chaphuta, "*On the Law of Majority Views in Medical Assessments*," in *No'am*, vol. 5, p. 195 ff.
18. Moshe Feinstein, responsa *Igrot Mosheh*, part 1, no. 129. It is, of course, permitted to take the temperature on the Sabbath (ib., no. 128; and *Minchat Yitzchak*, part 3, no. 142).
19. Responsa *Yad Yitzchak*, no. 95, cited in *No'am*, vol. 5, p. 323; and responsa *Shemen Ha-Ma'or, Orach Chayim*, no. 34, cited in *No'am*, loc. cit.
20. *Minchat Yitzchak*, part 3, no. 20.
21. *Seridei Esh*, part 2, no. 30, based on varying interpretations in *Magen Avraham*, 327.
22. *Ib.*, no. 28.
23. See *JME*, p. 62 f.

474   *Notes on Chapter 5*

24. *Minchat Yitzchak*, part 3, no. 20. Cf. *Mishnah Berurah*, 330:8.
24a. *Minchat Yitzchak*, part 1, no. 37; part 2, nos. 17, 18, 112 and 113.
But see also *Chelkat Ya'akov*, part 1, no. 55; part 2, no. 41.
24b. *Igrot Mosheh, Orach Chayim*, no. 22.
24c. *Minchat Yitzchak*, part 2, no. 114.
25. *Seridei Esh*, part 2, no. 59.
26. *Ib.*, no. 63.
27. Mosheh Dov Wollner. "*The Physician's Rights and Qualifications*," in *Ha-Torah Veha-Medinah*, vol. 7-8 (5716/7), p. 320, based on Jacob Emden, *Mor Ukzi'a*, on *Orach Chayim*, 228.
28. *Ib.*, p. 306 f.
29. *Ib.*, p. 314 f.
30. *Ib.*, p. 311 f.
31. See *JME*, p. 96 ff.
32. Iser Judah Unterman, *Shevet Miyehudah*, 1955, p. 313 ff.
33. Myer Steinberg, in *No'am*, vol. 3, p. 87 ff.; Benzion Fierer, in *No'am*, vol. 4, p. 300 ff.; and Issachar Halevi Lewin, "On the Question of Autopsies," in *Ha-Torah Veha-Medinah*, vol. 7-8 (5716-17), p. 325.
34. *Seridei Esh*, part 2, no. 120. But cf. Zvi Pesach Frank, responsa *Har Z'vi, Yoreh De'ah*, no. 277 for a sanction based solely on the minute size of the tissue used.
35. Steinberg, *loc. cit.*
36. *Igrot Mosheh. Yoreh De'ah*, no. 229; and Isaac Arieli, in *No'am*, vol. 6, p. 99 f.
37. Isaac Glickman, in *No'am*, vol. 4, p. 206 f.
38. *Igrot Mosheh, loc. cit.*
39. Arieli, *loc. cit.*
40. Immanuel Jakobovits, in *No'am*, vol. 6, p. 271.
41. See Symposium on "*Religious Views on Cosmetic Surgery*," in *The Eye, Ear, Nose and Throat Monthly*, (New York) February and March 1962, giving Protestant, Catholic and Jewish views (also published as a special reprint and reproduced in this book).
42. Immanuel Jakobovits, "*Plastic Surgery for Cosmetic Purposes*," in *No'am*, vol. 6, p. 273 f.; and in Symposium, *loc. cit.*
43. Lev. 19:16.
44. *Sanhedrin* 73a.
45. Wollner, *op. cit.*, p. 307 ff.
46. *Igrot Mosheh, Choshen Mishpat*, no. 103.
47. See *JME*, p. 116 f.
48. *Sepher Gesher Ha-Chayim, op. cit.*, vol. 2, p. 7 f.
49. Israel Baruch Ness, in *Hapardes*, Iyar 5717, p. 18.
50. See *JME*, p. 357 note 43.
51. *Igrot Mosheh, Yoreh De'ah*, nos. 231 and 232.
52. See *JME*, p. 249 f.
53. *Minchat Yitzchak*, part 3, no. 108; *Igrot Mosheh, Even Ha-Ezer*, nos. 63. 70 and 71, and part 4, *Even Ha-Ezer*, no. 16; also found in Aaron Walkin, responsa *Zekan Aharon*, part 1, nos, 66 and 67.
54. *Igrot Mosheh*, part 4, *Even Ha-Ezer*, no. 3.
55. Nathan Zvi Friedman, responsa *Netzer Mata'ai*, no. 40.
56. See *JME*, p. 249 f.
57. Moshes Findling, "Artificial Insemination," in *Rabbi Breuer Jubilee Volume*, 1962, p. 45 ff., citing Zvi Pesach Frank, *Har Tzevi, on Tur, Even Ha-Ezer*, 61; and J. Baumol, *Sepher Emek Halakhah*, no. 68.
58. See *JME*, p. 360 note 47; and Chaim Leib Zacks, in *Hapardes*, Tishri 5722, p. 23.
59. *Igrot Mosheh*, part 4, *Even Ha-Ezer*, no. 18; and Ness, in *Hapardes*, Tishri 5718, p. 27, and Cheshvan 5718, p. 25.
60. Findling, *loc. cit.*, citing Abraham Isaiah Karelitz (*Chazon Ish*), *Ha-Ish Vechazono*, p. 13.
61. Findling, *loc. cit.*

62. See *JME*, p. 248 f.
63. *Igrot Mosheh, Even Ha-Ezer*, no. 10. The author suggests that it is preferable to use a non-Jewish donor.
64. Findling, *loc. cit.*
65. Findling, *loc. cit.*
66. Doornbos v. Doornbos, no. 54. S. 14981 (Superior Court, Cook Co., Ill., December 13, 1954); and Gursky v. Gursky, 242 N. Y. S. 2nd 406 (Supreme Court of New York, July 26, 1963). In the latter case, interestingly, it was held that "while Section 112 of the New York City Sanitary Code appears to constitute a recognition of the practice of artificial insemination by setting forth measures required to be adopted by physicians engaged in the practice, such provision of law must be read within the framework of the established concept of illegitimacy.... and can in no wise be deemed to sanction the practice of artificial insemination or to render legitimate any issue thereof. . . ."
67. See *JME*, p. 168 f.
68. *Ib.*
69. *Yevamot* 65b, a. fr. See also *JME*, p. 332 notes 63 and 64.
70. *Igrot Mosheh, Even Ha-Ezer*, nos. 62 and 63.
71. *Even Ha-Ezer*, 5:11.
72. For a liberal ruling just published, see Samuel Hibner, in *Ha-Darom*, Tishri 5725.
73. *Igrot Mosheh*, part 4, *Even Ha-Ezer*, no. 17.
74. Ephraim Oshri, responsa *Mima'amakim*, part 1, no. 18.
75. *Even Ha-Ezer*, 5:11.
76. *Igrot Mosheh, Even Ha-Ezer*, no. 13. But for a contrary opinion, see *JME*, p. 326 note 145.
77. See *JME*, p. 323 note 79.
78. *Igrot Mosheh, Even Ha-Ezer*, no. 12.
79. *Minchat Yitzchak*, part 2, no. 123.
80. *Heichal Yitzchak, Even Ha-Ezer*, no. 15.
81. The rate of congenital deformities among live-born babies of women with rubella during the first trimester is now found to be under 10%, and "one can conclude (from various studies) that the incidence of congenital malformations reported by earlier workers are fantastically high and incorrect. The recommendation of therapeutic abortion based on those rates is not medically justified" (Morris Greenburg, Ottavio Pelliteri and Jerome Barton, "Frequency of Defects in Infants Whose Mothers had Rubella during Pregnancy," in *Journal of the American Medical Association*, vol. 165 [1957], p. 675 ff.).
82. Immanuel Jakobovits, "The Deformed Babies Tragedy," in *The Jewish Review*, (London), Nov. 14, 1962; and in *Tradition*, Spring 1963, p. 267 ff.; Iser Judah Unterman, "On Saving the Life of a Foetus," in *No'am*, part 6, p. 1 ff.; and Mosheh Jonah Zweig, "On Abortion," in *No'am*, part 7, p. 36 ff.
83. Unterman, *loc. cit.*
84. Zweig, *loc. cit.*
85. Jakobovits, *loc. cit.*
86. *Igrot Mosheh*, Yoreh De'ah, no. 87.
87. Waldenberg, *op. cit.*, p. 38 f.; Tuczinsky, *op. cit.*, vol. 1, p. 44; and Friedman, *op. cit.*, part 1, no. 30.
88. RI Hazaken, *Gilyon Ha-Shas*, on *Kiddushin* 82a.
89. Friedman, *loc. cit.*
90. Responsa *Besamim Rosh* (wrongly ascribed to Asheri), no. 348.
91. Friedman, *loc. cit.*; and Nisan Telushkin, "A person's Rights over his Life," in *Or Ha-Mizrach*, Nisan 5761, p. 20 ff; based on *Chatam Sopher, Yoreh De'ah*, no. 327.
92. Telushkin, *loc. cit.*
93. Wollner, *op. cit.*, p. 319 f.
94. *Avodah Zarah* 18a; see *JME*, p. 122 f.

476   *Notes on Chapter 5*

95. Wollner, *op. cit.*, 317 ff.
96. Maimonides, *Mishnah Commentary*, on *Nedarim*, 4:4; and *Hil. Nedarim*, 6:8; see *JME*, p. 4.
97. *Yoreh De'ah*, 339:1; gloss; Immanuel Jakobovits "On Euthanasia," in *Hapardes*, October 1956, p. 28 ff.; and December 1956, p. 16 ff.
98. Jakobovits, in *No'am*, vol. 6, p. 271.
99. Friedman, *loc. cit.*
100. Telushkin, *loc cit.*
101. Immanuel Jakobovits, "The Religious Problem of Autopsies in New York Jewish Hospitals," in *Hebrew Medical Journal* (New York), vol. 34:2 (1961), p. 238 ff.
102. *Torah shebe'al Peh*, ed. Yitzchak Raphael, Jerusalem, 5724, p. 40-74.
103. Responsa *Noda Biyehudah*, *Yoreh De'ah*, no. 210. For the place of this important responsum in the history on the Jewish attitude to autopsies, see *JME*, p. 145 ff.
104. *Seridei Esh*, part 2, no. 119.
105. *Netzer Mata'ai*, part 1, no. 31.
106. Yitzchak Arieli, in *No'am*, vol. 6, p. 997 also citing *Chazon Ish*, *Oholot*, no. 22. For earlier statements of this view, see *JME*, p. 317 note 211.
107. Immanuel Jakobovits, "The Problem of Autopsies in Theory and Practice," in *Torah shebe'al Peh*, *op. cit.*, p. 66.
108. Lewin, *op. cit.*, p. 322 ff.
109. Yitzchak Arieli, "The Problem of Autopsies," in *Torah shebe'al Peh*, *op. cit.*, p. 58 f.; Yitzchak Yaakov Wachtvogel, in *No'am*, vol. 5, p. 164.
110. *Ib.*, p. 59; Nachum Shemaryahu Schechter, in *No'am*, vol. 5, p. 171; see also *JME*, p. 151.
111. Immanuel Jakobovits, "The Laws of Mourning and Defilement in Case of Autopsies," in *Ha'Darom*, Nisan 5720, p. 9; Eliezer Silver, in *Hapardes*, Sivan 5720, p. 15; Wachtvogel, *op. cit.*, p. 163; Arieli, *op. cit.*, p. 47, and in *No'am*, vol. 6, p. 88 f.
112. Shemuel Tanchum Rubinstein, "On the Question of Autopsies in Jewish Law," in *Torah shebe'al Peh*, *op. cit.*, p. 72.
113. Jakobovits, in *Torah shebe'al Peh*, *op. cit.*, p. 66.
114. Yechiel Weinberg, in *Hapardes*, Tishri 5723, p. 9, and Cheshvan 5723, p. 5 f.; against the view of responsa *Imrei Yosher*, part 2, no. 140.
115. *Igrot Mosheh*, *Orach Chayim*, no. 11.
116. Leib Grossnass, responsa *Lev Aryeh*, no. 11. Cf. also *Mima'amakim*, *op. cit.*, part 2, no. 15.
117. *Chelkat Ya'akov*, part 2, nos. 21 and 22; *Igrot Mosheh*, *Orach Chayim*, no. 41; and *Lev Aryeh*, no. 41.
118. Cf. *JME*, p. 198.
119. Yechiel Weinberg, "May One Circumcize a Proselyte Endangered by the Operation?," in *Leo Jung Jubilee Volume*, 1962, p. 19 ff., a decision of 1926 endorsed by R. Chaim Ozer Grodzinsky and R. Abraham I. Kook; and *Har Z'vi*, *Yoreh De'ah*, no. 220.
120. Baruch Rakower, "May a Physician Testify on a Patient without his Consent?," in *No'am*, vol. 2, p. 188 f.
121. *Minchat Yitzchak*, part 3, nos. 104 and 105; see also *Ramat Rachel*, *op. cit.*, p. 29 f.
122. *Yoreh De'ah*, 336:1; see *JME*, p. 216 f.
123. *Ramat Rachel*, *op. cit.*, p. 27 f.
124. Abraham Chaphuta, "On the Law of Cruelty to Animals for Medical Needs," in *No'am*, vol. 4, p. 218 ff.; and Nathan Zvi Friedman, "Scientific Experiments in Living Creatures," in *No'am*, vol. 5, p. 188 ff.; see also *JME*, p. 291 note 168.
125. Ed. Irving Ladimer and Roger W. Newman, Boston University Law-Medicine Research Institute.

126. *Ib.,* p. 270, by J. J. Groen.
127. *Horiyot,* 3:7, 8.
128. Iser Judah Unterman, "The Precept of the Saving of Life and its Definition," 5723, p. 3 ff., offprint from *Ha-Torah Veha-Medinah,* vol. 4.
129. See *JME,* p. 242.
130. Samuel Hibner, in *Ha-Darom, Elul,* p. 17 ff.; and Mordecai Hacohen, in *Torah shebe'al Peh, op. cit.,* p. 75 ff.
131. See *JME,* p. 117 f.
132. See *JME,* p. 62.
133. *Yoma* 85b; see *JME,* p. 46 f.
134. *Netzer Mata'ai, op. cit.,* part 1, no. 8.
135. *Igrot Mosheh,* part 4, *Orach Chayim,* no. 88; based on *Chatam Sopher, Orach Chayim,* no. 83.
136. Cf. ' "He shall cause him to be thoroughly healed" (Ex. 21:19) — from here [it is deduced] that permission is given to the physician to heal' (*Berakhot* 60a; *Baba Kamma* 85a).
137. Cf. "I kill, and I make alive; I wound and I heal; and there is none that can deliver out of My hand" (Deut. 32:39). See also commentaries of Rashi and Tosaphot, on *Baba Kamma* 85a; Abraham ibn Ezra on Ex. 21:19 and 15:26; and Nachmanides, on Lev. 26:11.
138. ' "Ye shall therefore keep My statutes . . ., which if a man do, he shall live by them" (Lev. 18:5) —that he shall live by them, and not that he shall die by them' (*Yoma* 85b). See also Maimonides, *Yad, Hil. Shabbat,* 2:3.
139. Cf. "And if a man have committed a sin worthy of death, and he be put to death, and thou hang him on a tree; his body shall not remain all night upon the tree, but thou shalt surely bury him the same day; for he that is hanged is a reproach unto God. . . ." (Deut. 21:22-23).
140. Gen. 1:26, 27.
141. Rabbis and physicians are often governed by identical rules of professional conduct; for several examples, see *Tur and Bet Yoseph, Yoreh De'ah,* 336.
142. See D. Campbell, *Arabian Medicine and its Influence on the Middle Ages,* 1926, vol. i, p. 8.
143. See M. Neuburger, *History of Medicine,* 1910, vol. i, p. 62 f; and A. Castiglioni, *A History of Medicine,* 1947, p. 102.
144. See Th. Puschmann, *A History of Medical Education,* 1891, p. 14.
145. See Neuburger, *op. cit.,* p. 48; and Castiglioni, *op. cit.,* p. 88.
146. See E. A. W. Budge, *Syrian Anatomy, Pathology and Therapeutics;* or "The Book of Medicines", 1913, vol. i, p. clxii f.; and vol. ii, pp. 107 and 129.
147. See Budge, *op. cit.,* vol. i, p. xlvii.
148. See Puschmann, *op cit.,* p. 57.
149. See Th. C. Allbutt, *Greek Medicine in Rome,* 1921, p. 98.
150. See G. Wolff, "Leichenbesichtigung und Untersuchung bis zur Carolina als Vorstufe gerichtilicher Sektion," in *Janus,* vol. xliii (1938), p. 228 f.
151. See Neuburger, *op. cit.,* p. 150.
152. Gen. 1:2.
153. See G. Maspero, *The Dawn of Civilisation: Egypt and Chaldea,* ed. A. H. Sayce, 1910, p. 216; Puschmann, *op. cit.,* p. 23; and Castiglioni, *op. cit.,* p. 59.
154. See C. Singer, "Galen as a Modern," in *Proceedings of the Royal Society of Medicine,* vol. xlii (1949), p. 565.
155. Philo, *De special. leg.,* iii. 117; see translation by F. H. Colson, Loeb Classical Series, vol. vii, p. 549 f.

156. First made by E. Carmoly (*Histoire des médecins juifs*, 1844, p. 12) and later endorsed by R. Landau (*Geschichte der juedischen Aerzte*, 1895, p. 15).

157. The allegation is based on a passage in the Talmud (*Sanhedrin* 47b) in which the use of earth from Rab's grave is justified for curing a fever; ostensibly that indicated the people's desire to avenge Rab's (alleged) dissection of the dead by destroying his grave. In fact, the passage evidently describes some form of homage to a saint; see J. Preuss, *Biblisch-Talmudische Medizin*, 1911, pp. 45 and 184.

158. H. Baas, *Outlines of the History of Medicine*, 1889, pp. 37 and 295 (note 2).

159. A. H. Israels, *Collectanes gynaecologica ex Talmude Babylonico*, 1845; cited by H. H. Ploss and M. Bartels, *Woman*, ed. E. J. Dingwall, 1935, vol. i, p. 380 f; and Puschmann, *op. cit.*, p. 30.

160. *Tosephta, Niddah*, 4:17; cf. *Niddah* 30b, where the account is slightly varied.

161. A similar report is mentioned by the Roman historian Pliny (*Nat. Hist.*, xix. 27); see Preuss, *op. cit.*, p. 44. Cf. J. Needham, *A History of Embryology*, 1934, p. 47.

162. *Bekhorot* 45a.

163. Rabbi Yishmael, though also a physician, probably did not carry out the operation himself because he was of priestly descent; see Preuss, *op. cit.*, p. 46.

164. Hebrew: "*shalak.*" This is translated as "slit," "anatomised," or "dissected" by J. Levy (*Neuhebraeisches und Chaldaeisches Woerterbuch*, vol. iv, p. 566), A. Kohut (*Aruch Completum*, 1926, vol. viii, p. 90) and M. Jastrow (*A Dictionary of the Targumim, etc.*, 1926, p. 1588). But Preuss (*op. cit.*, p. 48), supported in a note by Immanuel Loew, maintains that the word should here, as usual, be rendered "cooked" or "boiled hard." Preuss therefore believes that this may be the only mention of boiling as a method of dissection in antiquity, a method otherwise unknown until Vesalius introduced it.

165. I. L. Katzenelsohn (*Ha-talmud vechokhmat Ha-refu'ah*, 1928, p. 237 f.) regards this experiment as the first return to human anatomy since Herophilus and Erasistratos of Alexandria.

166. *Oholot*, 1:8. See Katzenelsohn, *loc. cit.*

167. Thus I. M. Rabinowitch (*Post-Mortem Examinations and Jewish Law*, 1945, p. 25 [note]) argues that the Talmudic figure—at 248 to 252 bones—approximates more closely the findings of modern anatomy (assigning 270 to the new-born, 350 at the age of 14 years and 206 after middle life) than the number given by Hippocrates (111) or Galen (over 200).

168. In a statement ascribed to King David (*Berakhot* 4a).

169. *Sanhedrin* 82a.

170. *Baba Batra* 116a.

171. *Niddah* 24b.

172. With the exception of the last three statements, which have no bearing on medicine, all the preceding accounts deal with observations for ritual purposes. The formation of the foetus affects the laws of uncleanliness in cases of miscarriages. The number of bones in the body determines the defilement caused by touching an incomplete skeleton. The examination of blood and other discharges is necessary to decide whether a woman is ritually pure or not.

173. See note 139 above.

174. See *Sanhedrin* 46b.

175. *Chullin* 11b.

176. See Rabinowitch, *op. cit.*, p. 28; and Preusss, *op. cit.*, p. 46.

177. *Baba Batra* 154a and b; see R. Gershom, *a.l.*

178. *Sanhedrin* 47a.

179. See Wolff, *op. cit.*, pp. 226 and 285.

180. Vesalius himself attributed the decline of dissection since ancient times to the practice of entrusting manual operations to barbers "who were too ignorant to read the writing of the teachers of anatomy"; see translation by B. Farrington, in *Proceedings of the Royal Society of Medicine*, vol. xxv (1932), p. 1357; cited by B. J. Stern, *Society and Medical Progress*, 1941, p. 13.

181. The charge of human vivisection, repeated by Augustine elsewhere *(De anima,* iv. 3 and 6), was already levelled by the 1st century writer Celsus *(Proem)* against the Alexandrian anatomists; it was also sustained by Tertullian *(De anima,* x). It is probably quite unjustified; See C. Singer, *The Evolution of Anatomy,* 1925, p. 34 f.

182. Augustine, *The City of God,* lib. xxii, cap. xxiv *(A Select Library of the Nicene and Post-Nicene Fathers of the Christian Church,* ed. Ph. Schaff, 1903, vol. ii, p. 503); see Stern, *op. cit.,* p. 179 f.

183. Singer, "Galen as a Modern," *op. cit.,* p. 570.

184. H. E. Sigerist, "Die Geburt der abendlaendischen Medizin," in *Essays on the History of Medicine,* presented to K. Sudhoff, ed., Singer and Sigerist, 1924, p. 196.

185. See Puschmann, *op. cit.,* p. 144.

186. *Ibid.,* p. 202.

187. *Ta'anit* 21b. The belief survived to modern times, though Tyson had dismissed it as a "vulgar error," see F. J. Cole, *A History of Comparative Anatomy,* 1944, p. 49.

188. See D. Riesman, *Medicine in Modern Society,* 1939, p. 94.

189. See Puschmann, *op. cit.,* p. 244.

190. See Mary N. Alston, "Attitude of the Church to Dissection before 1500," in *Bulletin of the History of Medicine,* vol. xvi (1944), p. 225 f.

191. See W. Osler, *The Evolution of Modern Medicine,* 1921, p. 146.

192. See C. Singer, *The Evolution of Anatomy,* 1925, p. 71.

193. *Ibid.,* p. 73; and Puschmann, *op. cit.,* p. 244 f.

194. See Puschmann, *op. cit.,* p. 247.

195. See Sigerist, *op. cit.,* p. 196 f.; and Castiglioni, *op. cit.,* p. 375.

196. See Puschmann, *op. cit.,* p. 249 f.

197. See Osler, *op. cit.,* p. 116.

198. *Ibid.,* p. 148; and H. Rashdall, *The Universities of Europe in the Middle Ages,* 1936, vol. i, p. 148.

199. D. J. Guthrie,ˆ*A History of Medicine,* 1945, p. 159.

200. *Ibid.*

201. See F. H. Garrison, *An Introduction to the History of Medicine,* 1929, p. 282.

202. *Ibid.,* p. 398.

203. For the text of this Bull, see J. J. Walsch, *The Popes and Science,* 1912, p. 32 ff.

204. So H. Haeser (see *Catholic Encyclopedia,* vol. i, p. 458), J. L. Pagel *(ibid.)*, M. Neuburger *(Geschichte der Medizin,* 1906, vol. ii, p. 432), Walsch *(op. cit.,* p. 28 ff.), Garrison *(op. cit.,* p. 161), Rashdall *(op. cit.,* vol. i, 244 f.), and Castiglioni (who omits the reference to the Bull altogether).

205. So R. Virchow ("Morgagni and the Anatomical Concept," in *Bulletin of the History of Medicine,* vol. vii (1939), p. 981), R. Park *(An Epitome of the History of Medicine,* 1903, p. 93), Baas *(op. cit.,* p. 295), Puschmann *(op. cit.,* p. 245), Allbutt *(op. cit.,* p. 476), Stern *(op. cit.,* p. 177 ff.) and Singer *(op. cit.,* p. 85 f.).

206. Thus Mondino declared: "The bones which are below the '*os basilare*' cannot well be seen unless they are removed and boiled, but owing to the sin involved in this I pass them by" (From the *Fasciculo di Medicina,* Venice, 1493, ed. C. Singer, 1925, p. 26).

207. Around 1340 the famous physician Guido de Vigevano expressly stated (in his *Anatomy*) that the Church forbade dissection; see Alston, *op. cit.,* p. 225 f. In 1519 Pope Leo X denied Leonardo da Vinci ad-

mission to the hospital at Rome, where he wished to study anatomy, because he had engaged in dissection; see J. P. McMurrick, "Leonardo da Vinci and Vesalius," in *Medical Library and Historical Journal*, vol. ix (1906), p. 344; cited by Stern, *op. cit.*, p. 177. A little later Vesalius complained that "the ecclesiastical caucus would not countenance the vivisection of the brain" (see Cole, *op. cit.*, p. 57) and that in Madrid he could not lay his hands on as much as a dried skull; see M. Forster, *History of Physiology*, 1901, p. 17.

208. See Rashdall, *loc. cit.*; Puschmann, *op. cit.*, p. 327; and Sigerist, *op. cit.*, p. 197.

209. In 1482 Pope Sixtus IV authorised dissections provided ecclesiastical sanction was first obtained, a practice again confirmed by Pope Clement VII in 1524; see Singer, *The Evolution of Anatomy*, p. 85 f.; and Castiglioni, *op. cit.*, p. 368.

210. See G. Sarton, *Introduction to the History of Science*, 1927, vol. ii, pp. 783 and 1081; and Stern, *loc. cit.*

211. See A. H. Buck, *The Growth of Medicine from the Earliest Times to about 1500*, 1917, p. 346.

212. From the 15th century onwards, experimental anatomy was greatly stimulated by the desire of artists to portray the human body realistically. Among those who engaged in dissection were Verrocchio, Andrea Manegno, Lucio Signorelli, Pollajuolo, Donatello, Leonardo da Vinci, Albrecht Duerer, Michelangelo, and Raphael; see Stern, *op. cit.*, p. 49; and Guthrie, *op. cit.*, p. 135.

213. See Alston, *op. cit.*, p. 221 ff. For the full text of the reply, see Th. Puschmann, *Handbuch der Geschichte der Medizin*, 1902, vol. ii, p. 227; and Walsch, *op. cit.*, p. 58 f.

214. The present-day Code of Canon Law only regards the "dishonouring of the bodies of the dead by theft or other crimes committed on the bodies or graves of the deceased" as a penal offence, but not dissection for medical ends; See S. Woywood, *A Practical Commentary on the Code of Canon Law*, 1926, vol. i, p. 526; and vol. ii, p. 479.

215. Rashdall, *op. cit.*, vol. ii, p. 136.

216. P. L. Burshall, *Ancient History of Medicine*, 1878, p. 18.

217. See Puschmann, *Medical Education*, p. 163; Osler, *op. cit.*, p. 102; Garrison, *op. cit.*, p. 135; E. G. Brown, *Arabian Medicine*, 1921, p. 36 f.; and M. Meyerhof, "Science and Medicine," in *Legacy of Islam*, ed. T. Arnold and A. Guillaume, 1931, p. 344.

218. See Ploss and Bartels, *op. cit.*, vol. iii, p. 8.

219. See B. Stern, *Medizin, Aberglaube und Geschlechtsleben in der Tuerkei*, 1903, vol. i, p. 53.

220. See S. Muntner, "Persian Medicine and Its Relation to Jewish and Other Medical Science," in *The Hebrew Medical Journal*, vol. xxv (1952), p. 202.

221. See Stern, *op. cit.*, p. 54.

222. See Castiglioni, *op. cit.*, p. 284.

223. H. Friedenwald, *The Jews and Medicine*, 1944, vol. i, p. 192.

224. *Ibid.*, p. 251. Astruc (1684-1766) was himself of Jewish descent.

225. The charge occurs, for instance, in *The Healing Art the Right Hand of the Church*, 1859, p. 111 f.; and in *A General Exposition of the General State of the Medical Profession*, by "Alexipharmacus," 1829, p. 12.

226. See Preuss, *op. cit.*, p. 45; and Rabinowitch, *op. cit.*, p. 23 f.

227. For that reason graves should be marked; see *Mo'ed Katan* 5a. Following this law, Jacob Ettlinger (responsa *Shomer Tziyon*, no. 213) ruled that one must not preserve in spirit even a foetus for anatomical studies; See also Moses Shick, responsa *MaHaRaM Shik, Yoreh De'ah*, no. 344.

228. Ardet, responsa *RaSHBA*, no. 369; see H. J. Zimmels, *Magicians, Theologians and Doctors*, 1952, p. 58.

229. *Yoreh De'ah*, 363:2, gloss.
230. So first the questioner in R. Ezekiel Landau's famous responsum (*Noda Bi-yehudah*, part ii, no. 210). See also A. A. Price, *Mishnat Abraham* on *Sefer Chasidim*, 1955, p. 179.
231. Cf. *Shabbat* 152b. Hence also the rule to bury the dead in direct contact with the earth; See *Jer. Kilayim*, ix. 3; and *Yoreh De'ah*, 332:1.
232. Ibn Zimra, responsa *RaDBaZ*, part i, no. 484; See Zimmels, *op. cit.*, p. 58.
233. Isaac Elchanan of Kovno, responsa *Eyn Yitzchak, Yoreh De'ah*, no. 333; see Zimmels, *loc. cit.*
234. So D. Z. Katzburg (in *Tel Talpiyot*, vol. xxi (1924), p. 123), based on assertion by C. J. D. Azulai (*Debash Lefi*, Livorno, 1801, no. 20) that "Maimonides was familiar with all sciences . . . including anatomy." A similar view was already expressed by Isaac ben Sheshet Barfat (responsa *RIBaSH*, no. 447) in the 15th century. Benzion Uziel (responsa *Mishpetei Uziel*, no. 4), too maintained that "without doubt all our early rabbis who were also competent doctors must have examined dead bodies for study purposes" (quoted by S. Muntner, *Ba'ayat Ha-nitu'ach Vechokhmat Ha-bittur Be-yisrael*, 1955, p. 9).
235. Friendenwald, *op. cit.*, vol. i, p. 334; see also pp. 339 (note), 342 and 381 ff.
236. Amatus, *Centuria* i, cur. 52; see I. Muenz, *Die juedischen Aerzte im Mittelalter*, 1922, p. 112 f.; and Friedenwald, *op. cit.*, pp. 338 and 354.
237. See C. Singer, "Science and Judaism," in *The Jews: Their History; Culture and Religion*, ed. L. Finkelstein, 1949, vol. iii, p. 1069.
238. Friedenwald, *op. cit.*, p. 332.
239. J. Zahalon, *Otzar Ha-chayyim*, Venice, 1683; see J. Leibowitz, "On the Plague in the Ghetto at Rome," in reprint from *Dappim Rephu'im*, 1943, p. 3.
240. The illustration is reproduced in *Jewish Encyclopedia*, vol. iii, p. 162; and in *Enclyclopedia Hebraica*, vol. iv, p. 406.
241. *Address to the Public, Drawn from Nature and Religion, against the Unlimited Dissection of Human Bodies*, London, 1829, p. 7.
242. See S. W. Baron, *The Jewish Community*, 1942, vol. ii, p. 151; citing Antonio Ciscato, *Gli Ebrei in Padova*, Padua, 1901; see also *Jewish Encyclopedia*, vol. ix, p. 459. Complaints of "body-snatching" from Jewish cemeteries were also made in London in the 18th century (see *The Jewish Chronicle* [London], March 25, 1955) and in America in the 19th century (see note 233 above).
243. J. Emden, responsa *She'ilat Ya'abetz*, part i, no. 41. As this decision is dated Shevat 15, 5497 (corresponding to January 17, 1737), the enquiry leading to it can hardly have been prompted by the similar question answered in Rome in the same year.
244. E. Landau, responsa *Noda Bi-yehudah*, part ii, no. 210; see Rabinowitch, *op. cit.*, p. 28 f.
245. M. Schreiber, responsa *Chatam Sofer, Yoreh De'ah*, no. 336.
246. Hence, for example, the dead may be clothed in shrouds made of materials Jews must not otherwise wear (*Yoreh De'ah*, 351:1).
247. The question is already raised in the Talmud (*Baba Kamma* 60b). For further sources on the subject, see *Talmudic Encyclopedia*, vol. v, p. 457.
248. J. Ettlinger, responsa *Binyan Tziyon*, no. 170.
249. The Talmud assumes that burial is required to prevent disgrace; hence a person's expressed desire not to be buried must not be fulfilled (*Sanhedrin* 46b).
250. *Pesachim* 25b; cf. *Sanhedrin* 74a.
251. M. Shick, responsa *MaHaRaM Shik, Yoreh De'ah*, no 347.
252. B. H. Auerbach (*Nachal Eshkol*, 1868, part ii, p. 117 ff.); and S. Bamberger (responsa *Zekher Simchah*, no. 158).
253. H. Adler, *Anglo-Jewish Memories*, 1909, 137.

254. A. I. Kook, responsa *Da'at Kohen*, no. 199.
255. B. Uziel, responsa *Mishpetei Uziel, Yoreh De'ah*, nos. 28 and 29.
256. Hillel Posek, in *Ha-posek* (Tel Aviv), vol. xi (1949), no. 111 (Ab 5709).
257. So Joseph Zweig, responsa *Porat Yosef*, no. 17; and Price, *Mishnat Abraham, op. cit.*, p. 180. See also Simon Gruenfeld, in *Tel Talpiyot*, vol. xxxi (1924), pp. 117 and 122.
258. Eliezar Duenner, *Zikhron Abraham Mosheh*, 1945, p. 82 ff.; based on the permission to engage in sorcery for study purposes, though otherwise biblically forbidden (*Sanhedrin* 68a).
259. So Bamberger, *loc. cit.*; D. Z. Katzburg, in *Tel Talpiyot, op. cit.*, p. 130; Hillel Posek, *loc. cit.*, Uziel, *loc. cit.*; and Zweig, *loc. cit.*
260. J. L. Lewin, in *Yagdil Torah*, vol. viii, no. 31; cited by J. D. Eisenstein, *Otzar Dinim Uminhagim*, 1917, p. 453. See also Uziel, *loc. cit.*
·261. So Hillel Posek, *loc. cit.*, Duenner, *loc. cit.*; and Price, *op. cit.*, p. 184. Cf. also Rabinowitch, *op. cit.*, p. 29.
262. Y. J. Greenwald, *Kol Bo*, 1947, vol. i, p. 40 f.
263. *Ibid.*, p. 44 f.
264. Asher Gronis, *Peri Asher*, 1936, no. 3.
265. D. Hoffman, responsa *Melamed Le-ho'il, Yoreh De'ah*, no. 109.
266. See Yehuda Meir Schapira, responsa *Or Ha-me'ir*, part i, no. 74.
267. *Ibid.*; see also David Menahem Babad, responsa *Chabatzelet Ha-sharon, Yoreh De'ah*, no. 95; and authorities cited by Greenwald, *loc. cit.*
268. See Elazar Hayim Schapira, responsa *Minchat Elazar*, part iv, no. 25; cited by Greenwald, *loc. cit.*
269. See *Yagdil Torah*, vol. vii, p. 17; and vol. viii; cited by Greenwald, *loc. cit.*
270. See Moses Jonah Zweig, responsa *Ohel Mosheh*, part i, no. 4. See also Jacob Levy, "Nituchei Metim Be-yisrael," in *Ha-ma'yon*, vol. iii, (1956), p. 26.
271. *Ibid.*, and Babad, *loc. cit.*
272. See M. J. Zweig, *loc. cit.*
273. *Ibid.*, based on Malkiel Tzevi Halevy of Lomza, responsa *Dibrei Malkiel*, part ii, no. 95.
274. See Y. M. Schapira, in *Or Ha-me'ir, loc. cit.* See also Levy, *op. cit.*, p. 29.
275. See M. J. Zweig, *loc. cit.*
276. See following pages.
277. See Katzburg, in *Tel Talpiyot, loc. cit.*; quoting Hayim Hirschson, *Malki Ba-kodesh.*
278. See Ch. LaWall, *Four Thousand Years of Pharmacy*, 1927, p. 133.
279. See M. D. Silberstein, "Ba'ayat Nitu'ach Ha-metim Upitronah," in *Yabneh* (Jerusalem), 1949, p. 214 ff. (Nisan 5709); and in *Dat Yisrael Umedinat Yisrael*, 1951, p. 159 ff.
280. *Ibid.*, p. 161. The terms of the agreement are also given and fully discussed by Eliezer Judah Waldenberg (a member of the Chief Rabinate), responsa *Tzitz Eliezer*, part iv, no. 14.
281. Silberstein, *loc. cit.*
282. By Silberstein, *loc. cit.*
283. The Act still governs the law in England.
284. See Lev. 21:11, and Rashi, *a.l.* This point is emphasized by Levy, *op. cit.*, p. 25.
285. See Levy, *op. cit.*, p. 28 f.
286. *Ibid.*, and *The Jewish Chronicle, loc. cit.*
287. Friedenwald, *op. cit.*, vol. i, p. 126. The articles listed are: C. D. Spivak, "Post-Mortem Examinations Among the Jews," in *New York Medical Journal*, June 13, 1914, p. 11; N. Mosessohn, "Post-Mortem Examinations Among the Jews," in *Jewish Tribune*, December 18, 1914; J. Z. Lauterbach, "The Jewish Attitude Toward Autopsy," in *The Jewish Indicator*, October 30, 1925; M. Robinson, "The Advancement of

Science through Autoposy," in *The Synagogue Light*, Brooklyn, February 1938; and O. Saphir, "Autopsies Among Jews," in *Medical Leaves*, 1939.

288. Apart from the monographs and articles by Rabinowitch, Silberstein, Muntner, and Levy already noted, the following could be added: H. L. Gordon, "Bedikat Metei Yisrael al pi Dinei Yisrael," in *The Hebrew Medical Journal*, 1937, part i, p. 141 ff.; M. Greiber, *Nituach Ha-metim Le-tzorkhei Limmud Vachakirah*, Jerusalem, 1943; and A. Kottler, "The Jewish Attitude on Autopsy," in *New York State Journal of Medicine*, 1957, p. 1649 ff.

289. Muntner, *op. cit.*, p. 3.

290. *Ibid.*, p. 6.

291. Levy, *op. cit.*, p. 30. This trend was also confirmed by Professor H. Baruk of the Sorbonne (as reported in *Ha-aretz*, Elul 7, 1955) ; see Levy, *loc. cit.* (note 25) .

292. *Ibid.*, p. 31. In fact, Prof. Baruk offered to supply Jerusalem with all materials required for a model anatomical institute to dispense with dissection; See Levy, *loc. cit.*

293. *Ibid.*, p. 28 f.

294. *Ibid.*, pp. 21 and 30.

295. Johnson, in *Idler*, no. 17 (August 5, 1758) .

296. A. H. Merzbach, in *Dat Yisrael Umedinat Yisrael*, 1951, p. 150.

297. *Uktzim*, 3:12.

298. Ps. 37:37.

299. R. Isaac Arama, in *Akedath Yitzchak*, Chpt. 20 (ed Frankfurt a/o, 1785, p. 41b) .

300. See Robert Forbes, "The Medico-Legal Aspects of Artificial Insemination," *Medico-Legal Review*, vol. xii (1944), p. 139.

301. The first experiments were carried out on a dog by an Italian physiologist, the Abbate Spallanzani, in 1780. See J. P. Greenhill in Symposium on "Artificial Insemination," *American Practitioner*, vol. i, no. 5 (1947), p. 227.

302. *ib.*

303. By the year 1941, 3649 such children were known to have been born in the United States. See Schatkin, "Artificial Insemination and Illegitimacy," *New York Law Journal*, vol. cxiii, no. 148 (1945) , quoted in *The Report of a Commission appointed by the Archbishop of Canterbury on Artificial Human Insemination*, 1948, p. 38. Other sources claim a much higher frequency of such inseminations; see *The Report etc.*, p. 12.

304. See *The Report etc.*, p. 13.

305. The eminent medical historian H. E. Sigerist, in his book *Civilisation and Disease*, 1944, p. 107, advocates that the practice of euthanasia should be left to the "individual conscience of the physician"; he believes that it is probably carried out "by conscientious physicians much more often than we know."

306. Forbes, *op. cit.*, p. 144.

307. Russel v. Russel, 1924, A.C. 721.

308. *American Practitioner, op. cit.*, pp. 277 ff.

309. April 19th, 1945.

310. See also H. U. Willink, in *The Practitioner*, vol. 158 (1947), p. 349; and *British Encyclopedia of Medical Practice*, Suppl. 1950, p. 287.

311. Forbes, *op. cit.*, p. 144.

312. May 17th, 1897. See A. Bonnar, *The Catholic Doctor*, 1948, p. 87.

313. Gerald Kelly, "Moral Aspects of Sterility Tests and Artificial Insemination," *The Linacre Quarterly*, vol. 16, Nos. 1-2 (1949), p. 35. See also J. C. Heenan, in "Artificial Human Insemination" (The Roman Catholic Church), *Report of a Conference held under the auspices of the Public Morality Council*, 1949, pp. 18 ff.

314. Gerald Kelly, *Medico-Moral Problems*, 2, (published by the Catholic Hospital Association of the U. S. and Canada, 1950) pp. 18 ff.

315. Gerald Kelly, "Moral Aspects etc." *op. cit.*, p. 35.
316. *The Report, etc.*, p. 58.
317. *The Report, etc., ib.* Cf. also G. L. Russell, in *Report of a Conference, etc.* (The Church of England), pp. 50 ff.
318. Leviticus, 21:13.
319. *Chagigah* 15a.
320. H. H. Ploss & M. Bartels, *Woman* (ed. by E. J. Dingwall, 1935), vol. ii. p. 651 consider the famous 12th Century Arabian physician Averroës "of interest" because he was, apart from the Talmud, the first seriously to contemplate a tub-pregnancy. Cf. J. Preuss, *Biblisch-Talmudische Medizin*, 1911, p. 541.
321. See *Midrash Alpha Betha d'ben Sirah*, in J. D. Eisenstein, *Otzar Midrashim*, 1928, p. 43. L. Zunz, *Die gottesdienstl. Vortraege der Juden*, 1909, p. 105, regards this Midrash as a late composition. The source usually quoted by halachic authorities is R. Jacob Molon Segal, (1365-1427) in his *Lekutei MaHaRIL* (end).
322. See J. Landau, in *Noda Biyehudah*, ii, *Choshen Mishpat*, 14. Based on *Jerus. Pe'ah*, ii. 4. But most authorities agree that this rule does not apply unless the law derived from the Midrash is contradicted by the Talmud. See *Yad Malachi*, i, No. 72; R. Akivah Eger's commentary on *Berakhoth* V, 4. Cf., however, *S'dei Chemed*, s.v. *Aleph*, 95, where a contrary opinion is expressed. See also *Noda Biyhudah*, ii, *Yoreh De'ah*, 161.
323. See Preuss, *loc. cit.*; H. Friedenwald, *The Jews and Medicine*, 1944, I, pp. 363, 386.
324. R. Moses Lima, in *Chelkath M'chokek, Even Ha'ezer*, 1:8; so also R. Chaim J. David Azulay, in *Birkei Yoseph, Even Ha'ezer*, 1:14.
325. *Pachad Yitzchak*, ii, 30a.
326. R. David Halevy, in *Turei Zahav, Yoreh De'ah*, 195:7 and *Even Ha'Ezer*, 1:8. So also R. Jacob Emden, in *Sh'ilath Ya'avetz*, ii, 97. These (and other) authorities hold that the duty of procreation can not be fulfilled without the father's active and intimate association. Quoted in *Turei Zahav, Yoreh De'ah, loc. cit.*
327. R. Samuel Uri, in *Beth Sh'muel, Even Ha'Ezer*, 1:10; *Birkei Yoseph, loc. cit.*
328. *Mishneh L'Melekh, Ishuth*, 15:4.
329. E.g. R. Moses *(MaHaRAM)* Schick, in *Taryag Mitzvoth*, 1; R. Solomon Schick, Responsa *RaSHBaN, Even ha'Ezer*, 8. Cf. L. Loew, *Lebensalter*, 1875, pp. 57 ff, where the Talmudic reference to a conception *sine concubito* is construed as a sarcastic allusion to the Christian belief in the Immaculate Conception of Mary. But this view is opposed by Preuss, *op. cit.*, p. 558, since Ben Zoma lived at a time (end 1st Century, C.E.) when the dogma of the Immaculate Conception was still unknown; cf. W. E. H. Leckey, *History of the Rise and Influence of the Spirit of Rationalism in Europe*, 1870, vol. i, p. 213.
330. *Zemach David*, ed. Offenbach 1768, p. 14b.
331. *Birkei Yoseph, loc. cit.*
332. *B'nei Ahuvah, Ishuth* 15:6. so also R. Jacob Ettlinger, in *Arukh L'Ner, Yevamoth* 12b.
333. Responsa *Ma'archei Lev*, 73.
334. Lev. 20:20.
335. On Lev. 20:12.
336. *HaPosek*, Cheshvan-Kislev, 5710.
337. *Mishpetei Uziel, Even Ha'Ezer*, 19.
338. Moreover, the danger of an incestuous marriage between a brother and a sister is not so remote as might appear, if it is borne in mind that—as has been computed (M. Barton, K. Walker & B. P. Wiesner, "Artificial Insemination," in *British Medical Journal*, 1945, 1, p. 40)— one fecund donor submitting two specimens weekly could produce 400 children every week, or 20,000 annually!

339. See *Kiddushin* 75a; Maimonides, *Issurei Bi'ah*, 15:23, 33.
340. *HaPosek*, Adar 5709.
341. *Otzar HaPoskim*, *Even Ha'Ezer*, 1947, vol. 1, pp. 129 ff.
342. Rabbi S. M. Holland, *Ha-Posek*, *Sh'vat*, 5710. R. Malchiel Zvi Halevy of Lomza, in *Divrei Malchiel*, part 3, 107, 108, is likewise inclined to prohibit the practice completely.
343. *Beth Sh'muel*, *op. cit.* 25:2; *Sh'ilath Ya'avetz*, *op. cit.* i, 43; R. Shalom Mordecai HaCohen, Responsa *MaHaRSHaM*, iii, 268; R. Elazar Deitsch, Responsa *Pri HaSade*, iii, No. 53.
344. See *Otzar HaPoskim*, *op. cit.*, p. 11.
345. See J. McCarthy, "A Lawful Method of Procuring Seminal Specimens for Sterility Tests," in *Irish Ecclesiastical Record*, vol. lxx (1948), pp. 533 ff.
346. See Joseph B. Doyle, "The Cervical Spoon: an Aid to Spermigation and Semen Sampling," in *Bulletin of the New England Medical Center*, vol. x (1948), pp. 225 ff. The instrument is a concave lucite spoon which is inserted into the vaginal canal before coitus, and withdrawn an hour later with its contents which can be used for a seminal test or for renewed insemination. See Also Gerald Kelly, "Current Theology," in *Theological Studies*, vol. xi (1949), pp. 105 ff.
347. See *Bereshith Rabbah*, 23:2, 4. Er is also alleged to have given Tamar a contraceptive potion to preserve her beauty; see *Yevamoth* 32b.
348. Such a drink, designed to produce sterility, is frequently mentioned in the Talmud and Rabbinic literature. But already in 1849 Rabbi Dr. J. Horovits (*Matteh Levi*, part 2, 31) satisfied himself by obtaining medical evidence from qualified physicians that such a drink was "no longer known in our time" and that it had "surely been forgotten in the course of time". Such drugs (anaphrodisiacs?) were also known to the ancient Egyptians who prescribed them (about 1550 B.C.F.) in the Ebers Papyrus, sec. 93 (ed. & translated by B. Ebbell, 1937, p. 108). For similar ancient and primitive drugs to prevent conception, see Ploss & Bartels, *op. cit.* vol. 2, pp. 289 ff. Cf. also note 355.
349. Gen. 38: 7-10.
350. Cf. R. Jacob Ettlinger, *Binyan Zion*, 137.
351. See *Dio Cassius*, 56, 5.
352. E.g. Pliny, *Nat. Hist.* 29:27. For numerous other examples, see I. Thorndike, *A History of Magic and Experimental Science during the First 13 Centuries of our Era*, 1923, vol i, p. 656; vol ii, pp. 470, 736, 744, 763. The ancient Greeks and Romans possessed uterine pessaries; see J. S. Milne, *Surgical Instruments in Greek and Roman Times*, 1907, pp. 159 f. Even among the primitive and most ignorant nature-races artificial prevention of pregnancy is frequently practised; see D. McKenzie, *The Infancy of Medicine*, 1927, pp. 294 f. Cf. also note 348.
353. See A.D. Nock, *Conversion, The Old and the New in Religion from Alexander the Great to Augustine of Hippo*, 1933, p. 217. Cf. Martial's condemnation of masturbation "omnia perdiderat" (*Epigrams*, ix. 14).
354. See, e.g. Encyclical on Christian Marriage, "Casti Connubii," by Pope Piux XI, December 31st, 1930; F. J. Connell, *Atlantic Monthly*, 1939, pp. 471 f; Statement of Cardinal Bourne, Archbishop of Westminister, quoted in *Encyclopedia Britannica*, 1950, vol. iii, p. 650.
355. The use of the "safe period" is generally assumed to have been expressly excluded from Pope Pius XI's condemnation of contraceptives in the Encyclical, *op. cit.*; see H. Sutherland, *Control of Life*, 1936, pp. 222 f. The medical and theological (Catholic) aspects of the subject are presented in great detail in P. Ahearne's "The Confessor and the Ogino-Knaus Theory," in *Irish Ecclesiastical Record*, vol. xxi. (1943), pp. 1 ff. See also A. Bonnar, *op. cit.*, p. 73. According to a statement by Pope Pius XII to the Italian Catholic Obstetric Union on October 29, 1951, a married couple could lawfully limit sexual intercourse to the wife's "safe

period" when "grave reasons" demand this; but total abstinence is necessary when maternity would endanger a wife's health, as "safe periods" are not a sufficient guarantee against conception; see report in *The Irish Times*, October 30, 1951.

356. Lambeth Conferences of 1908 and 1920. So also in a "Bishop's Memorandum" of 1914.

357. Lambeth Conference of 1930, resolution 15.

358. E. T. Kerby at Lower House of Northern Convocation, January 1932; quoted by H. Sutherland, *Control of Life*, 1944, p. 56.

359. See *Encyclopedia Britannica*, vol. iii, p. 650; also *International Clinics*, vol. i, New Series 5 (1942), p. 301. Another estimate holds that appr. 375,000,000 condoms were sold in the U.S.A. in 1937; see Norman E. Himes, "Forrunners of the Modern Condom," in *Janus* (Amsterdam), vol. xlii (1938), p. 1.

360. The problem has been discussed in German by Rabbi Dr. H. Klein in an article "Geburtenregelung: Eine halachische Betrachtung," in *Nachalath Zwi*, vol. i (1931), pp. 251 ff; by Dr. J. Levy, in "Geburtenstreik—die Frage der juedischen Ehe," *ib.*, pp. 380 ff. The latter article (p. 391) records a resolution of the "Vereinigung traditionell-gesetzestreuer Rabbiner Deutschlands," according to which "birth-control generally involves a grave religious offence. Such measures can be justified before our conscience only in cases of serious danger to health. In no case, however, can the individual allow personal considerations to determine the issue without seeking the objective, halachic advice of his rabbi."

361. A. M. Carr-Saunders, *World Population*, 1936, p. 104.

362. H. Sutherland, *Control of Life*, op. cit., pp. 188 f.

363. See note 360.

364. Large families are regarded as an unmitigated blessing. The Midrash expresses this in its customary figure of speech by asserting that in messianic days women will give birth every day (*Kallah Rabb.*, 2, begin.); see also L. Wiesner, "Kindersegen and Kinderlosigkeit in altrabbinischen Schrifttume," in *Monatsschrift*, 66 (1922), pp. 34, 138 ff.

365. See R. Aaron Helevi, *Sepher HaChinukh*, *Mitzvah* 1.

366. *Shulchan Arukh*, *Even Ha'ezer*, 1:1; cf. Rashi, Gen. 9:7.

367. Gen. 16:2; 30:1; see also Wiesner, op. cit., pp. 139 ff.

368. For recent Jewish population statistics, see *American Jewish Year Book*, vol. 50, (1949) pp. 691 ff.

369. *Yevamoth*, 6:6.

370. *Shulchan Arukh*, *Even Ha'Ezer*. 1:13.

371. See e.g. Preuss, *op. cit.*, p. 479.

372. Gen. 3:20.

373. *Yevamoth* 12b; and parallel passages.

374. R. Tam in Tosaphoth, *a.l.*; R. Solomon Luria, in *Yam shel Sh'lomo*, *Yevamoth*, 1, 8.

375. Cf. Isaiah's reproof of Hezekiah who had excused his refusal to marry and have children by his fear that his progeny would (as he prophetically saw) be wicked. Isaiah's reply was: "What do you care for the secrets of God? You should perform your duty, the pleasure of God!"; see *Berakhoth* 10a; *Yalkut*, 2 Sam; 242. Yet, Ben Sirah (16:3) considers it better to be childless than to have godless children. R. Solomon Luria, in *Yam shel Sh'lomo*, *Yevamoth*, vi, 44, also admits this consideration in allowing the wife to drink the *poculum sterilitatis*.

376. In times of famine sexual intercourse is prohibited; see *Bereshith Rabbah*, 31:12: *Shulchan Arukh*, *Orach Chayim*, 240; 12, 574: 4. Yet, even in such times of economic stress, childless couples are exempt from this restriction; see *Jerus. Ta'anith*, 1:6; *Shulchan Arukh*, *ib*. It is therefore doubtful if the reason for this regulation can be to prevent overpopulation, as claimed by L. Wiesner, *Monatsschrift*, vol. lxvi, 1922, p. 38. The motive seems rather to be the avoidance of pleasures at such times; cf. also commentaries on *Shulchan Arukh*, *ib*.

337. At the time of the Hadrian persecutions the Rabbis considered banning marriages so as to prevent new births, but the imposition of continence was never contemplated; see *B. Bathra* 60b. A Jewish marriage involving permanent abstinence would be inconceivable; see R. Elijah Mizrachi, on Gen. 4:23.

378. *Shulchan Arukh, Even Ha'Ezer*. 76.

379. *Shulchan Arukh, loc. cit.*, 6. See also R. Joseph Kolon, Responsa *MaHaRIK*, 10:3.

380. See, e.g., *Shulchan Arukh, Yoreh De'ah*, 187:12.

381. See R. Abraham Gumbiner, in *Magen Avraham, Orach Chaim*, 176: 8; 574: 5. H. Sutherland, *Control of Life*, 1944, p. 235, believes that the purity legislation in Leviticus reveals a knowledge of this agenic cycle.

382. As early as 1937 J.G.H. Holt was able to attach a 20-page medical bibliography on the "safe period" to his work *Marriage and Periodic Abstinence*.

383. E.g. in the works of H. Sutherland, *loc. cit.*; see also L. J. Latz, *The Rhythm of Sterility and Fertility in Women*, 1946. The popularity of such books can be gauged from the fact that the latter, which was issued under Catholic ecclesiastical approbation, had nearly 300,000 copies sold by 1946.

384. Rabbi Dr. Jakob Horovits, in a responsum dated 1894 (*Matteh Levi*, ii, 31), advises women whose pregnancy may endanger them to restrict intercourse to the infertile period. They may then also use a tampon to ensure their safety, since conception at that time is in any case unlikely. Cf. note 360. Its application, however, requires rabbinical endorsement in every individual case; see J. Levi, *op. cit.*, pp. 385-389.

385. On *Yevamoth*, i, 8.

386. R. David ibn Zimra, in responsa *RaDBaZ*, part iii, 596. The first of the more recent authorities to favor this lenient view is R. Solomon Zalman of Posen, *Chemdath Sh'lomo, Even Ha'Ezer*, 46 in a responsum first published in 1836. Within the last sixty years the same opinion has been expressed by Rabbi Dr. J. Horovits (see note 384), by R. Chaim Ozer Grodzinsky, responsa *Achi'ezer, Even Ha'Ezer*, 23, and Rabbi Dr. D. Hoffmann, responsa *M'lamed L'ho'il, Even Ha'Ezer*, 18.

387. Responsa, 71, 72. Originally he held that the wife must not render the husband's act ineffective even after coitus, a view put forward in 1864 by R. Jacob Ettlinger, *Binyan Zion*, 137. But he later adopted the attitude expressed by his son-in-law, R. Moses Sopher (see next note), though he doubted the effectiveness of such post-coital action.

388. R. Moses Sopher, Responsa *Chatham Sopher, Yoreh De'ah*, 172.

389. See Rabbi Dr. H. Klein, *Nachalath Zwi, op. cit.*, p. 259.

390. *Ib.*, p. 260. So also Rabbi J. J. H. Horowitz, in *Rosenheim Festschrift*, 1932.

391. Cf. *Yoma*, 8: 6; 83a and 85b (see Rashi, *a.l.*); and corresponding codes.

392. *Sotah* 12a.

NOTES ON CHAPTER 6

1. *Berakhot* 5a; *Jer. Pe'ah* 2:4.
2. *Shemot Rabbah*, 28:4.
3. Deut. 17:11.
4. Sifri, *a.l.*
5. Deut. 17:8-10.
6. *Berakhot* 19b.
7. Maim., *Hil. Berakhot*, 11:3.
8. *Shabbat* 23a.

9. *ib.*

10. Maim., *Sepher HaMitzvot, Shoresh I; Hil. Mamrim,* 1:2.

11. Nachmanides, *Sepher HaMitzvot, loc. cit.*

12. *ib.* For instance, a doubt arising in regard to a biblical law is resolved in accordance with the stricter practice, whereas a similar doubt affecting a rabbinic decree is decided in favor of the lenient practice.

13. Responsa, *TaSHBaTZ,* No. 141.

14. See *Shavuot* 21b; *Yoma* 73b.

15. *Lechem Mishneh,* on Maim., *Hil. Mamrim,* 1:2; *Megilat Esther,* on *Sepher HaMitzvot, loc. cit.*

16. *Megilat Esther, loc. cit.;* Responsa, *Avnei Milu'im,* no. 14.

17. Nachmanides, *loc. cit.*

18. *ib.*

19. *Minchat Chinnukh, Mitzvah* 496; Epstein, *Torah Temimah,* Deut. 11, No. 58.

20. Zvi Hirsch Chajes, *Sepher Eleh HaMitzvot,* Chapter "Lo Tasur."

21. *ib.;* Cf. Epstein, *loc. cit.*

22. *Lechem Mishneh, loc. cit.*

23. Chajes, *loc. cit.*

24. *Rosh Hashanah* 25b and Rashi, *a.l.;* Maim., *Hil. Mamrim,* 2:1.

25. *ReSHaSH,* on *Rosh Hashanah* 25b.

26. *RaDBaZ* and *Kesef Mishneh,* on Maim., *loc. cit.*

27. *Yevamot* 21a.

28. *Yoma* 80a, and Rashi *a.l.*

29. *Yad Mal'akhi,* Rule 216.

30. *Bekhorot* 26b; *Chagigah* 18a.

31. See following notes.

32. *Chagigah* 18a.

33. Rashi on *Kiddushin* 11b.

34. *Yad Mal'akhi,* Rule 216, citing *RITVA* on *Yevamot,* 10.

35. *RaN,* on *Yoma,* 8.

36. *Kesef Mishneh,* on Maim., *Hil. Avodah Zarah,* 11:3.

37. *Kesef Mishneh,* on Maim., *Hil. Chametz U'matzah,* 2:2.

38. Asheri on *Sukkah,* 3 (No. 14).

39. Responsa, *Chakham Zvi,* No. 9.

40. *Korban Nethan'el,* on Asheri, *loc. cit.* (No. 5); *Yad Mal'akhi, loc. cit.*

41. *Gittin* 36b; Maim., *Hil. Sanhedrin,* 4:6.

42. *Beth Yosef, Tur Chosen Mishpat,* 67, citing Nachmanides and *RaSHBA;* Responsa, attributed to Nachmanides, No. 256; Responsa, *RaSHBA,* No. 775. So also Responsa *Chatham Sopher, Orach Chasim,* No. 117.

43. *ReMA, Shulchan Arukh, Choshen Mishpat,* 2 (Gloss). Cf., however, text cited in note 48.

44. Rashi on *Gittin* 36b; *Mishneh L'Melekh,* on Maim., *Hil. Malveh V'loveh,* 14 (beginning).

45. *RaSHBA* on *Gittin* 36b.

46. See authorities cited in *Sedeh Chemed, Ma'ar. HaHei,* Rule 59.

47. Chajes, *op cit.,* chapter *Torat Nevi'im, II* (footnote) ; *Pitchei Teshuvah, Choshen Mishpat,* 2 (No. 2) .

48. Responsa, *MaHaRIK,* Nos. 1, 14; *MaHaRAL,* No. 273. See *M'irat Enaim,* on *ReMA, op. cit.*

49. Maim., *Hil. Sanhedrin,* 24:9.

50. *Kethubot* 3a.

51. Rashi and Tosaphot, *a.l.; ReMA, Shulchan Arukh, Even HaEzer,* 27:1 (gloss)

52. *Baba Bathra* 48b, and Tosaphot, *a.l.*

53. *Shulchan Arukh, Even HaEzer* 42:1.

54. Responsa, *RaSHBA,* No. 1185.

55. *ib.; Tos. Yom Tov* on *Pesachim,* 8:2.

56. Mordechai, *Kiddushin*, 3 (beginning). In case the marriage involves a biblical or rabbinic offense (e.g. between a priest and a woman who has received a divorce or a *Chalitzah*) it is valid, unless the offense committed was of the capital character.
57. Responsa, *RaSHBA*, No. 1162; Cf. Tosaphot on *Baba Bathra* 48b.
58. Responsa, *RaSHBA*, No. 1185.
59. *Pesachim* 30b; *Gittin* 65a.
60. *Bekhorot* 54a.
61. Maim., *Hil. Ishut*, 12:9.
62. *Gittin* 65a.
63. *Yad Mal'akhi*, Rule 331, citing *Yedei Eliyahu, Tikkun* 92.
64. E.g. *RaDBaZ* on Maim., *Til. Terumot*, 10:4.
65. *Baba Metziah* 55b.
66. *Eruvin* 77a; *Yevamot* 36b.
67. Tosaphot on *Zevachim* 101a.
68. *Ta'anit* 17b; *Jer. Yevomot*, 9;4.
69. Maim., *Hil. Terumot*, 10:4. *RaDBaZ* on Maim., *Hil. Nedarim*, 3:9.
70. Maim., *Hil. Nedarim*, 3:9.
71. *RaDBaZ, loc. cit.*
72. Tosaphot on *Baba Bathra* 49b.
73. *Kesef Mishneh*, on Maim., *Hil. Nedarim*, 3:9; *Beth Yosef, Tur Orach Chaim*, 613.
74. *Yad Mal'akhi*, Rule 286.
75. Tosaphot on *Baba Metzia* 55b.
76. Tosaphot on *Yevamot* 36b.
77. *Kesef Mishneh, loc. cit.* For instance, by not blowing the *Shofar* on Rosh Hashanah—a biblical law, if this falls on Sabbath—in consideration of a rabbinic enactment.
78. *Kethubot* 56a; also reference in note 64.
79. *Pesachim* 4b; *Kethubot* 10a. Cf. note 12.
80. *Gilyon MaHaRSHA*, on *Pesachim* 4b, quoting *Megilat Esther* on *Sepher Ha'Mitzvot, Shoresh* I.
81. *Yad Mal'ackhi*, Rule 287, citing *Chut HaShani*, p. 81a. Cf. reference in note 58.
82. *Eruvin* 21b; *Avodah Zarah* 35a; *Jer. Megilah*, 4:1; *Jer. Chagigah*, 2 (end).
83. *Eruvin* 21b; *Shir HaShirim Rabbath* on 1:2; *Jer. Sanhedrin*, 11:4; *Jer. Avodah Zarah* 2:8; *Jer. Berakhot*, 1:4.
84. *ib.; Berakhot* 4b; *Sotah* 4b, and *Rashi, a.l.*
85. Chajes, on *Eruvin* 21b.
86. *Yad Mal'akhi*, Rule 310, citing *Chut HaShani*, p. 21a.
87. Maim., *Hil. Edut*, 10:1-3; *Shulchan Arukh, Choshen Mishpat*, 34:3.
88. ReMA, *ib* (gloss); and *M'irat Enaim, a.l.*
89. *Numbers Rabbah*, 21:6 and *Matnath Kehunnah, a.l.*
90. Responsa, *ReMA*, No. 91.
91. *ib; Levush, Atereth Zahav*, 114.
92. Mordecai, *Chullin*, 8, No. 687; see also *Pithchei Teshuvah, Yoreh De'ah* 116:10.
93. *Rosh Hashanah* 14b.
94. Tosaphot, *Niddah* 36a.
95. On *Kethuboth* 7a.
96. *Betza* 2b.
97. *Yadaim*, 4:3.
98. Responsa, *RIVaSH*, No. 394; cf. *Machazith HaSheckel, Orach Chaim*, 608:3, citing *Shittah Mekubetzeth*.
99. *Tur Orach Chaim*, 635.
100. Zvi Hirsh Chajes, *Sepher Darkei Hora'ah*, chapt. 2.
101. *ib.*
102. Deut. 17:11.
103. *Sifri, a.l.*

104. *Jer. Horayoth*, 1:1; *Torah Temimah*, on Deut. 17:11, No. 62.
105. *Baba Metzia* 59b.
106. *Rosh Hashanah* 2:9.
107. *Chinnukh, Mitzvah* 496.
108. *ib.: RaMBaN* on Deut. 17:11; Responsa, *ReMA*, No. 91.
109. *Rosh Hashanah* 25a, and Glosses of Zvi Hirsh Chajes, *a.l.*
110. See notes 104, 107 and 108.
111. *Torah Temimah, loc. cit.*
112. *Chinnukh, loc. cit.; RaMBaN, loc. cit.*
113. *Chinnukh, loc. cit.*
114. Zvi Hirsh Chajes, *Sepher Eleh HaMitzvoth*, chapter "Lo Tasur."
115. *Minchath Chinnukh, Mitzvah* 78.
116. Maim., *Hil. Shigg.* 12:1.
117. *Chinnukh, Mitzvah* 78.
118. Maim., *Hil. Shigg.,* 12 (end).
119. *ib.* 13:1.
120. *ib.*
121. *ib.*
122. *ib.*
123. *ib.* 1, 2.
124. *ib.* 5.
125. *ib.* 14:3.
126. *ib.* 1, 2.
127. *ib.* 13, 1, 2.
128. *ib.* 5.
129. Tosaphot, *Horayoth* 2a; cf. also references in notes 119 ff.
130. *Sifri* on Deut. 17:9.
131. *Sifri* on Deut. 17:10; cf. *Minchath Chinnukh, Mitzvah* 496.
132. *Zevachim* 101a.
133. *Sanhedrin* 102a; *Makkoth* 12a; *Megillah* 12a.
134. *Shabbath* 63b; *Eruvin* 65b; *Yevamoth* 121a; *Niddah* 68b; see also Responsa, *TaSHBaTZ*, II. No. 9.
135. On Ex. 22:28; Lev. 13:4; Deut. 33:24; Isa. 13:21; Ex. 42:3; Prov. 30:31; *Yevamoth* 92b; *Jer. Kiddushin*, 3:5.
136. Eccl. 7:20; see *Torah Temimah, a.l.* (No. 88).
137. Ps. 116:11; see Rashi, *a.l.*
138. *Hil. Tephillin*, ed. Vilnah. p. 8a; *Hil. Tzitzith*, p. 13b.
139. *Hil. Issurei Bi'ah; Hil. Ma'ach. Assur.*, 10:18.
140. *RaMBaN, Milchamoth HaShem, Baba Bathra* 45b; *Maggid Mishnah, Hil. Chametz U'Matzah*, 5:20.
141. *Kethuboth* 21a; *SHaCH, Yoreh De'ah*, 161:19; *Me'irath Enaim, Choshen Mishpat*, 33:4; cf. references in notes 145 and 146.
142. *Baba Bathra* 138b.
143. *SHaCH, Yoreh De'ah*, 269:13.
144. Maim., *Hil. Eduth*, 6:4; *SHaCH, Choshen Mishpat*, 34:36; *ROSH, Baba Bathra*, 8, No. 54.
145. Yomtov Lipman Heller, *Pilpula Charifta* on *ROSH, loc. cit.*
146. *ReMA, Even HaEzer*, 142:9; and 17:5.
147. *Ture Zahav, Yoreh De'ah*, 1:5.
148. *TaSHBaTZ, loc. cit.*
149. *Baba Bathra* 12a.
150. *Chinnukh, Mitzvoth* 188 and 496.
151. Elijah Mizrachi, on Deut. 17:11.
152. *Kusari*, II.64.
153. Maim., *Hil. Sanhedrin* 2:1, 5.
154. *Shabbath* 75a.
155. *RaMBaN, Sepher HaMitzvoth, Shoresh* I (end); *Sepher Mitzvoth Gadol*, positive Mitzvah 47.
156. *Shabbath* 75a.
157. E.g. *Sanhedrin* 5b; *Chullin* 58b; *Bekhoroth* 8a.

158. E.g. *Niddah* 22b; cf. following note.
159. Maim., *Hil. Kiddush HaChodesh*, 17:24; *Krethi U'Plethi, Yoreh De'ah*, 40.
160. Maim., *loc. cit.; Moreh Nevukhim*, 1.71, II.11; *Kusari*, I.63, II.66: *Kaphtor VaPherach*, chapt. 44 (end).
161. Responsa, *RIVaSH*, No. 45; *Krethi U'Plethi, loc. cit.*
162. *RIVaSH*, No. 447; Maim., *Hil. Shechitah*, 10:12, 13.
163. Moses Chagiz, *Lekach HaKemach, Yoreh De'ah* 16b; *Krethi U'Plethi, loc. cit.*
164. *Tosaphot Yomtov, Kilaim* 5:5.
165. *Tosaphot, Eruvin* 14a.
166. *RaSHBA, Mishmereth HaBayith*, 7:3, ed. Vienna, p. 108b; Responsa, *Chatham Sopher, Even HaEzer*, No. 6.
167. *SHaCH, Yoreh De'ah*, 179:13.
168. *Rosh Hashanah* 15a.
169. Responsa, *Chatham Sopher, Orach Chaim*, No. 14.
170. *Niddah* 38a.
171. *Jer. Nedarim*, 6:8 (end); *Magen Avraham, Orach Chaim*, 55:10.
172. *Sanhedrin* 18b.
173. *RaMBaN*, on Nu. 5:20.
174. *Or HaChaim*, by author of *Tif'ereth Yisrael*, at the end of Mishnah division *Nizakin*.
175. *Ein Ya'acov* on *Berakhoth* 61a; Rashi on *Eruvin* 65a; Rashi on *Ein Ya'akov* version of *Sanhedrin* 103b; Rashi on *Zevachim* 118b; *P'nei Moshe* on *Jer. Sanhedrin*, 4:6; *P'nei Moshe* on *Jer. Baba Bathra*, 6:2; gloss on Maim., *Hil. Matnath Aniyim*, 10:3.
176. *Tosaphot, Baba Bathra* 113a.
177. *Avodah Zarah* 29b; Responsa, *RIVaSH*, No. 284; Responsa of *RaSHBA* attributed to *RaMBaN*, No. 232; D. Hoffmann, *Lekutei bathar lekutei* of *Mechilta* on Deut. 14:2.
178. Akiva Eger, *Gilyon HaShass, Shabbath* 55b.
179. *Tosaphot, Shabbath* 128a; Zvi Hirsh Chajes, Introduction to *Ein Ya'acov*, ed. Vilna, p. 25; *Yad Mal'akhi*, rule 283.
180. Maim., on *Gittin*, 6 (end).
181. *Yad Mal'akhi*, rule 299.
182. Ibn Ezra on Eccl. 5:1; glosses of Ya'acov Emden on *Kiddushin* 18b.
183. Responsa, *TaSHBaTZ*, 1:33; Responsa, *ReMA*, No. 7.
184. Responsa, *Chavath Ya'ir*, No. 124; Chaim ben Betzalel, *Sepher Etz Chaim*, Introduction, cited in *Hamagid* 1869, p. 293.
185. E.g. of *"Totaphoth," Menachoth* 34b, and Rashi on Deut., 6:8; of *"ve'eth-hen,"* Rashi on *Yevamoth* 94b; of *"Sanhedrin,"* Ovadiah of Bartinura on *Sotah*, 9:11.
186. Ibn Ezra, on Ex. 2:22.
187. Maim., *Moreh Nevukhim*, 3:14; cf. quotation of Hai Gaon in *"Perush al Ibn Ezra," loc. cit.*
188. *Akedath Yitzchak*, Sha'ar 37.
189. Azariah di Rossi *Sepher M'or Enaim, Imrei Binah*, chapter 27.
190. *ib.*, chapters 11, 28; Maim., *loc. cit.*
191. di Rossi, *ib.*, chapter 27.
192. *Keseph Mishnah, Hil. Mamrim*, 2:1; Maim., Introduction to *Mishnah Torah;* cf. also references in note 74.
193. *Sanhedrin* 34a.
194. Gen. 1:28.
195. Ex. 2:10; 1 Chron. 4:18.
196. 2 Sam. 21:8.
197. Ruth 4:16, 17.
198. Esth. 2:7.
199. *Megillah* 13a; *Sanhedrin* 19b.
200. *Choshen Mishpat*, 42:15.

201. *Even ha-Ezer*, 129:10.
202. *Chatam Sofer, Even ha-Ezer*, no. 76.
203. *Sha'arei Uziel*, part II, no. 183.
204. Psalms 66:3.
205. Nu. 35:9 ff.; Deut. 19:1 ff.
206. *Makkot* 10a.
207. *ib.* 11b.
208. Maimonides, *Hil. Rotze'ach*, 5:10.
209. Rashi, on Nu. 35:27.
210. Maim., *op. cit.*, 1:2.
211. Deut. 19:12.
212. *Sefer ha-Mitzvot*, additions to positive commandments, no. 13.
213. Gen. 4:14.
214. Ex. 21:14.
215. See Gen. 34:25.
216. *Hil. Melakhim*, 9:14.
217. Obad. 1:21.
218. *Sanhedrin* 49a.
219. *Pesachim* 25b.
220. Maimonides, *Hil. Melakhim*, 10:1.
221. *Kiddushin* 42b.
222. Gen. 9:6.
223. *Ber. Rabba*, 34:19.
224. Resonsa *TaSHBaTZ*, 1:156; *Choshen Mishpat*, 388:15, gloss.
225. *Teshuvot Maimuniyot*, end *Sefer Nezikin*, 14.
226. 2 Sam. 12:9.
227. R. David Kimchi, *a.l.*
228. Prov. 28:17.
229. I. Kings 21:25.
230. *ib.* 21:21.
231. *Sanhedrin* 102a.
232. *Hil. Rotz'ach*, 4:9.
233. *ib.*, 2:4.
234. R. Abraham I. Kook, *Mishpat Kohen*, p. 337.
235. *Choshen Mishpat*, 388:10.
236. Deut. 19:20.
237. *Gilyonei Hashas, Pesachim* 91b.
238. *Yalkut Shemuel*, 121.
239. Ps. 58:11, 12.
240. *Baba Metzia*, 7:1.
241. Prov. 2:20.
242. *Baba Metzia* 83a.
243. "On the Problem of Compensation," in *Techukat Ha-Avoda*, p. 132.
244. Cf. *Choshen Mishpat*, 12:2, gloss.
245. Deut. 15:14.
246. *Yoreh De'ah*, 267:14.
247. *Chinnukh*, no. 482.
248. *loc. cit.*
249. See *Piskei Din*, vol. I p. 330; vol. III, p. 91.
250. See *Hapoel Hatzair*, vol. XLIII, p. 16.
251. Responsa of *Rashba ascribed to Ramban*, no. 20.
252. Deut. 24:15.
253. *Baba Metzia* 112a.
254. *Bet Yosef, Choshen Mishpat*, 188.
255. Mordecai, *Baba Metzia*, 7:367 and gloss.
256. *Choshen Mishpat*, 186:48, gloss.
257. Responsa *Chatam Sofer, Choshen Mishpat*, no. 52.
258. *Mishpetei Uziel, Choshen Mishpat*, no. 43.
259. Deut. 22:8.

260. *Hil. Bet Ha-Bechirah*, 7:14.
261. *Kaftor Vaferach*, ch. 10.
262. *ib.*
263. Responsa *Radvaz*, part II no. 633.
264. *Erakhin* 32b.
265. *Ketuvot*, 13:11.
266. *Even Ha-Ezer*, 75:4.
267. *ib., 5.*
268. Responsa, *Yoreh De'ah*, 234.
269. *Derashot.*
270. *Pe'er Ha-dor*, 372.
271. *Radvaz*, part II, no. 741.
272. *Keilim*, 1:8.
273. *Hil. Bet Ha-Bechirah*, 6:11.
274. *Orach Chayyim*, 561:1, 2.
275. *Bet Yosef, a.l.*
276. *Hil. Ta'aniyot*, 5:12-15.
277. *RIVaSH*, 158.
278. *Darkei Mosheh, Yoreh De'ah*, 393.
279. David Hoffman, *Melamed Leho'il, Orach Chayyim*, 16.
280. *Orach Chayyim*, 55:1.
281. *Chavat Yair*, 222.
282. *Ba'er Hetev, Orach Chayyim*, 132:5.
283. *Keneset Yechezkel*, p. 53.
284. *Shevut Ya'akov*, part 2, *Yoreh De'ah*, 93.
285. *Mattei Ephrayim*, end.
286. *Teshuvah Me-Ahavah*, part 2, *Orach Chayyim* 229.
287. 2:20.
288. *Rosh Hashanah* 20b.
289. See Numbers 33:14.
290. *Ha-Maor ha-Katan*, on *Rosh Hashanah* 20b.
291. 2:17.
292. *Rosh Hashanah* 21a, see Tosaphot, *a.l.*
293. *Jer. Shevi'it*, 6:1, Tosaphot, *Gittin* 2a.
294. *Benei Zion*, 2:10.
295. Lev. 23:3.
296. *Seforno, a.l.*
297. *Shabbat* 69b.
298. *Radvaz*, 1:76.
299. *Mor Uktzi'ah*, 344.
300. *Divrei Yosef.*
301. e.g., *Shoel Umeshiv*, 4:2:154; *Even Yekarah*, 1:11.
302. cf. above.
303. The incidence of abnormalities following German measles, particularly in epidemic form, was first pointed out in an Australian medical journal in 1941, and the right to resort to abortion in such cases has been discussed in medical literature, with mostly negative conclusions, ever since.
304. But the article omits to mention the view that the violation of the Sabbath is sanctioned only because any danger to the embryo is considered as involving a danger to the mother's life, too—a consideration not necessarily applicable here (see RaN and ROSH, on *Yoma* 82a).
305. RaMBaN, *Torat Ha-Adam, Sha'ar Ha-Sakanah.*
306. *Halakhot Gedolot* and others.
307. Maimonides, *Hil. Rotzeach*, 1:9.
308. This deduction is not altogether conclusive, for there is evidence that in certain cases abortions may be permitted even when the threat to the mother's life does not come from the child (see my *Jewish Medical Ethics*, 1962. p. 184 ff.).
309. See Ex. 21:12 and Rashi, *a.l.*

310. Gen. 9:6, see *Sanhedrin* 57b.
311. Ex. 21:12; see Rashi, *a.l.*
312. *Teshuvah Me-Ahavah*, vol. I, no. 53.
313. *Mishneh Berurah, Bi'ur Halakhoah*, 329:4.
314. *Oholot*, 7:6.
315. Israel Meir Mizrachi, *Peri Ha-Aretz, Yoreh De'ah*, no. 21.
316. I. J. Unterman, in *Ha-Torah Veha-Medinah*, vol. IV, pp. 25, 29.

NOTES ON CHAPTER 9

1. *Ethics of the Fathers*, 4:21, 22.
2. Nu. 23:10; cf. *Sanhedrin* 105a.
3. 1. Sam. 25:29.
4. Eccl. 12:7.
5. Ps. 16:10.
6. Eccl. 7:1.
7. Maimonides, *Mishnah Commentary, Sanhedrin*, chapt. X (introduction).
8. *Berakhoth* 17a.
9. Is. 25:8.
10. Amos 36:6-8.
11. Ps. 20:8.
12. Gen. 48:22.
13. E. Munk, *The World of Prayer*, 1954, p. 1.
14. Ps. 34:19.
15. 102:1.
16. *Kitzur Shulchan Arukh*, 128:7.
17. Bezalel Landau, "Prayer in the Teaching of Chasidism," in *Or Hamizrach*, Sept., 1960, p. 57, in the name of the name of the Maggid of Koznitz.
18. *Gen. Rabba*, 45:5.
19. Gen. 30:1.
20. 1. Sam 1:10.
21. *Yevamoth* 64b.
22. *Ta'anith* 8a.
23. Quoted by S. A. Horodetsky, *Leaders of Hasidism*, 1928, p. 94.
24. *Ta'anith* 2a.
25. Ephraim Lencziez, *Amudei Shesh*, 1617, p. 23c.
26. *Or Hamizrach, op. cit.*, p. 55f.
27. *Or Hamizrach, op. cit.*, p. 53f.
28. Quoted by M. Samuel, *Prince of the Ghetto*, 1948, p. 162.
29. Jonah 3:1-10.
30. Deut. 6:5.
31. 19:2.
32. *Shulchan Arukh, Orach Chayim*, 42:1.
33. Alfred North Whitehead, *Science and the Modern World*, 1960, p. 13.
34. J. W. N. Sullivan, *The Limitations of Science*, 1959, p. 94.
35. Gen. 15:5.
36. 19:2.
37. Fred Hoyle, *Frontiers of Astronomy*, 1960, p. 52.
38. *Emunoth Vede'oth*, 3:7.
39. Micah 6:8.
40. Jer. 31:17.
41. Deut. 32:4.
42. Gen. 4:1.
43. Hos. 2:21-22.
44. Is. 58:5-7.

45. *Berakhoth* 6b.
46. *Sanhedrin* 35a.
47. See Rashi, on Gen. 47:29.
48. Max Otto, *Science and the Moral Life*, 1958, p. 37.
49. Nachman of Kasovir, quoted by J. J. Katz, *Toldoth Jakov Joseph*, 1903, p. 39f.
50. Ps. 17:19; *Baba Bathra* 10a.
51. Is. 58:8-9.
52. Zech. 14:7.
53. *Hil. Teshuvah*, 3:4.
54. *Eccl. Rabba*, 9.
55. Eccl. 9:7; *Kitzur Shulchan Arukh*, 133:29.
56. Malachi 2:10.
57. *Sanhedrin* 4:5.
58. Hos. 4:9; *Shabbath* 119b.
58a. *New York Times*, September 9, 1963.
59. Deut. 4:6, *Shabbath* 75a.
60. *Orach Chayim*, 224:7.
61. Ps. 19:2.
62. *Gen. Rab.*, 1:10; *Tanchuma Yashan, Yithro*, 16.
63. Is. 27:13.
64. *Berakhoth* 32b.
65. *Erakhin* 15b.
66. Jer. 6:13.
67. *ib.*, 14.
68. Maim., *Hil. Issurei Bi'ah*, 19:17.
69. Lev. 19:17.
70. *Baba Bathra* 12a.
71. Ps. 49:18.
72. Nu. 11:29.
73. *Yoma*, 2:6.
74. Job. 5:7.
75. Gen. 2:15.
76. *Ethics of the Fathers*, 2:15.
77. *Orach Chayim*, 231.
78. Deut. 7:12-15.
79. Deut. 30:26.
80. Deut. 16:14.
81. *Eccl. Rabba*, 2:23.
82. *Berakhoth* 58a.
83. *Horayoth* 10b.
84. Deut. 1:12.
85. Ps. 82:3.
86. *Yalkut Shimoni*, 2:831.
87. Is. 55:10-11.
88. Ps. 90:3.
89. Is. 66:23.
90. Lev. 23:27.
91. Gen. 3:17-19.
92. Gen. 41:52.
93. Ex. 1:12.
94. *Baba Kamma* 85a.
95. Deut. 16:16.
96. Ps. 126:5.
97. Ps. 128:2.

NOTES ON CHAPTER 10

1. Ex. 12:23.
2. I Kings 18:21.
3. 2 Sam. 5:6.
4. Is. 1:17.
5. Ps. 71:4.
6. *Sepher Ta'amei Haminhagim.*
7. Is. 58:4.
8. Cf. "In the sweat of thy face shalt thou eat bread" (Gen. 3:19).
9. See S. J. Zevin, *Hamo'adim Behalakhah*, p. 244 f.; and Solomon B. Freehof, *The Responsa Literature*, 1955, p. 181 ff. for full details.
10. See S. Gaguine, *Kether Shem Tov*, Vol. III, p. 18; and S. J. Zevin, *Hamo'adim Behalakhah*, p. 252 ff.
11. Cf. *Siddur*—"Order of Service."
12. MaHaRaL of Prague.
13. *Orach Chayim*, 487:2.
14. Ex. 13:8.
15. Ps. 94:21.
16. 2 Sam. 3:22.
17. Deut. 14:1.
18. S. Wiener, *Bibliographie der Oster-Haggada 1500-1900*, Petersburg, 1902.
19. Ex. 13:1-16.
20. *Orach Chayim*, 448:3, and commentaries.
21. Lev. 23:15.
22. See Ibn Ezra, *a.l.*; and *Menachoth*, 10:3.
22a. *Yevamoth* 62b.
23. *MaHaRIL*, ed. Warsaw, p. 21b.
24. *Seder Hadoroth*, 2:306.
25. *Zohar*, 3:296b.
26. *Chatham Sopher, Yoreh De'ah*, 233.
27. See *Sepher Ta'amei Haminhagim*, part 1, p. 73.
28. R. Yitzchak of Gur.
29. Nu. 28:26.
30. Lev. 23:20.
31. Ex. 4:23.
32. Lev. 23:15-16.
33. Ex. 19:1.
34. Rashi, *a.l.*
35. *Orach Chayim*, 494.
36. Songs, 4:1.
37. *Mishnah Brurah*, 494:12, 13.
38. S. J. Zevin, *Hamo'adim Behalakhah*, p. 311.
39. *Orach Chayim*, 494:3 gloss.
40. Ex. 34:3.
41. Mordecai Jaffe, *Levush*, 494:1.
42. *Rosh Hashanah*, 1:1.
43. Abraham Gumbiner, *Magen Avraham*, 494:5.
44. *Chayei Adam*, 131:13.
45. Ex. 2:2-3.
46. *Emor*, 95a.
47. Zevin, *Hamo'adim Behalakhah*, p. 309 f.
48. *Tamid*, 5:1.
49. *Jer. Berakhoth*, 1:5.
50. Maimonides, *Responsa*, ed. Freiman, no. 46.
51. See Ibn. Ezra, on Ex. 20:2.
52. Ex. 23:28.
53. Ps. 18:48; 47:4.

54. On Ex. 24:12.
55. On. Ex. 20:1.
56. R. T. Herford, *Pharisaism*, p. 289.
57. *Jer Berakhoth*, 1:8.
58. Ibn. Ezra, on Lev. 19:2.
59. Abarvanel, introduction to Ex. 21.
60. *Mekhilta*, on Ex. 20:13.
61. Nu. 28:30.
62. *Jer. Rosh Hashanah*, 5:4.
63. Moses Schreiber, *responsa Chatham Sopher, Orach Chayim*, no. 145.
64. *Soferim*, 14.
64a. *Abudarham*.
65. *Bekhor Shor, Baba Bathra* 13b.
66. *Teshu'oth Chen*.
67. *Berakhoth* 7b.
68. *Ruth Rabba*, on 1:4.
69. Rashi, Ex. 18:13; 31:18; and 35:1.
70. *Orach Chayim*, 581:1.
71. Nu. 14:19-20.
72. Ex. 34:9.
73. Ex. 34:6-7, Nu. 14:18.
74. *Mekhilta*, on Ex. 19:5.
75. *Rosh Hashanah*, 1:1.
76. *Avodah Zarah* 9b.
77. Eduard Mahler, *Handbuch der juedischen Chronologie*, 1916, p. 153 ff.
78. *Levush, Orach Chayim*, 582:8.
79. Nu. 10:10.
80. Lev. 25:9.
81. Ex. 19:16; 20:15.
82. Nu. 29:1.
83. *Rosh Hashanah* 26b, and Rashi.
84. R. Akivah Joseph Schlesinger, supported by others.
85. *Rosh Hashanah* 29b.
86. See S. J. Zevin, *Hamo'adim Behalakhah*, p. 53.
87. Simon ben Zemach Duran, *responsa on Prayer*, no. 253.
88. *MaHaRIL*.
89. Micah 7:19.
89a. *Tanchuma, Vayera*, 22.
90. *MaHaRIL*.
91. Eccl. 9:12; *SHeLaH*.
92. *Peri Megadim*.
93. *Orach Chayim*, 603:1, gloss.
94. Maimonides, *Hil. Teshuvah*, 2:1.
95. *Berakhoth* 5b.
96. Rabenu Asher, *Yoma*, 8:22.
97. *MaHaRIT*, 2:8.
98. *Siphsei Tsaddikim, Emor*; see *Sepher Ta'amei Haminhagim*, Lemberg, part 1, p. 86.
99. *Orach Chayim*, 611:1.
100. Lev. 23:27,29.
101. *Orach Chayim*, 618:10.
102. Maimonides, quoted by Karo, *Beth Yoseph, O.C.*, 618.
103. *ib.* 7,8.
104. I.e. *Shacharith* reading from Lev. 16.
105. Deut. 21:8.
106. *Sifri*.
107. Rabbi Jacob Weil, Germany, 15th Century.
108. Lev. 25:9.
109. Ps. 47:6; *Turei Zahav, O.C.*, 623:2.

110. Gen. 33:17.
111. Nachmanides.
112. Gen. 33:17.
113. Ex. 25:20.
114. Lev. 23:33-43.
115. Samson Raphael Hirsch.
116. *RaSHBaM, on Lev.* 23:43.
117. Lev. 23:42.
118. *Ib.,* 43.
119. Ibn Ezra.
120. *RaSHBaM.*
121. Maimonides, *Guide of the Perplexed,* 3:43.
122. Lev. 23:40; Deut. 16:14,15.
123. *Orach Chayim,* 529:1-4.
124. *MaHaRSHaL.*
125. Ps. 84:8.
126. See *Orach Chayim,* 624, end, and commenteries.
127. Lev. 23:43.
128. *Tur, Orach Chayim,* 625.
129. *Orach Chayim,* 639:1,2.
130. Isserles, gloss, *a.l.*
131. Mishnah, *Sukkoth,* 1 and 2.
132. Lev. 23:40.
133. Nachmanides.
134. *Sukkah* 35a.
135. Is. 41:19 and elsewhere.
136. Gesenius, *Dictionary.*
137. *Sukkah* 37b.
138. *Ber. Rabba,* 16:8.
139. Lev. 23:40.
140. Introduction, *Mishnah Commentary.*
141. *Orach Chayim,* 656, end.
142. *Sukkah* 53a.
143. Abudarham.
144. *Sukkah* 34a.
145. *RaVeD, Hil. Kiddush Hachodesh,* 7:7.
146. Nu. 29:35.
147. *Berakhoth,* 5:2.
148. *Mishnah Berurah,* 114:1.
149. *Pesikta Rabbathi,* 193a.
150. *Mishnah Berurah,* 669.
151. Ex. 34:22.
152. *Ta'anith* 7a; based on Jer. 23:29 and Is. 55:1.
153. Lev. 16:12.
154. Neh. 12:27.
155. Nu. 7:10 ff.
156. I Kings 8:63; Ps. 30:1.
157. Deut. 20:5.
158. Pr. 22:6.
159. *Shevilei Haleket,* no. 189.
160. 21:7, 7.
161. Mordecai Joffe, *Levush, Orach Chayim,* 670.
162. 68:32.
163. I. Sam 2:4.
164. 15:27.
165. *Middoth,* 1:6.
166. *Baba Kamma,* 6:6.
167. See sources in *Otzar Yisrael,* Vol. 4, p. 316.
168. Nachmanides, on Nu. 8:1.
169. *Shabbath* 21b.

170. *Beth Yoseph, Orach Chayim,* 670.
171. 2 Kings, 4:1-7.
172. *Turei Zahav, Orach Chayim,* 670.
173. *Chayei Adam,* 154:2.
174. *Shabbath* 104a.
175. Is. 5:26; 11:10, 12.
176. Nu. 21:8, 9.
177. Is. 33:23.
178. Deut. 7:7.
179. *Shabbath* 21h.
180. *ib.*
181. *Menachoth* 28b.
182. *Orach Chayim,* 671 5 ff.
183. *ib.* 671:1.
184. *ib.* 673:2.
185. Deut. 17:11.
186. *ib.* 32:7.
187. *Shabbath* 23a.
188. *Orach Chayim,* 679:1.
189. *Ib.* 679:1.
190. *Shulkhan Aruch, Orach Chayim,* 673:1.
191. *Orach Chayim,* 656.1, gloss.
192. 671:1.
193. See *Mishnah Berurah, Bi'ur Halakhah,* a.l.
194. See *Jewish Encyclopedia,* vol. 8, p. 315 f.
195. *ib.* vol. 5, 564 f.
196. Esth. 3:7.
197. Ibn Ezra.
198. Esth. 3:7; 9:24, 26.
199. 9:26-32.
200. Esth. 9:16-17.
201. M. L. Margolis and A. Marx, *A History of the Jewish People,*
1953, p. 127.
202. *Megillah* 15a.
203. *Sanhedrin* 74b; and Tosaphoth, *a.l.*
204. *Orach Chayim,* 686:2.
205. S. J. Zevin, *Ha-Mo'adim Behalakhah,* 1957, p. 194.
206. See note 166 above.
207. 9:32.
208. 2:7.
209. *Meggilah* 13a; based on Zech. 1:9.
210. *ib.*
211. *Ex. Rab.,* 15.
212. *Megillah* 15b; *Midrash Abba Gurion,* 1.
213. Ibn Ezra, Introduction.
214. Isaac Abrama, *Akedath Yitzchak, Esther,* Introduction.
215. Ex. 1:10.
216. Ex. 14:14.
217. Ex. 17:13.
218. e.g. Jer. 36: 2 ff.; Ex. 3:1; Ps. 40:8.
219. 9:26, 29.
219a. *Orach Chayim,* 690:17.
220. *Yoreh De'ah,* 245:13.
221. *Orach Chayim,* 687:2; and *Arukh Hashulchan, ib.,* 62.
222. *Ba'er Hetev, a.l.,* 5.
223. *Arukh Hashulchan, loc. cit.,* 9.
224. *Orach Chayim,* 690:9.
225. *Arukh Hashulchan, ib.,* 13.
225a. *Orach Chayim., ib.,* 11.
226. *Mishnah Berurah, a.l.,* 37.

227. *Orach Chayim,* 691:9; and *Arukh Hashulchan, a.l.,* 14.
227a. Tosaphoth, *Megillah* 4a, bottom.
228. Esth. 9:28; *Sepher Ha'eshkol,* 1868, part 2, p. 31.
229. *Orach Chayim,* 689:1.
230. Tosaphoth, *Megillah* 4a, middle.
231. *Orach Chayim,* 692:2.
232. *Mishnah Berurah, a.l.*
233. *Megillah* 16b.
234. Deut. 25:19.
235. Aburdarham, 13th century.
236. *Megillah* 14a.
237. Rashi, *Megillah* 21a.
238. *Orach Chayim,* 694:1.
239. *Shekalim,* 1:1.
240. *Ta'amei Haminhagim,* part 1, p. 101.
241. Ex. 25:2-3.
242. *Orach Chayim,* 694:1, gloss.
243. Esth. 9:22.
244. *Ba'er Hetev, a.l.,* 2.
245. *Orach Chayim,* 695:1.
246. *ib.,* 2.
247. Abudarham.
248. Esther 9:18-19.
249. See *Megillah* 5b.

NOTES ON CHAPTER 11

1. Is. 13:11.
2. Lam. 1:8.
3. *Yoma* 9b.
4. Cf. Nachmanides and Abarvanel on Lev. 26:11; Nachm. on Deut. 11:13; Ibn Ezra on Ex. 20:12 and Deut. 25:15; *Ikkarim,* IV, 40.
5. Jer. 5:25.
6. Maimonides, *Hil. Ta'anith,* 1:2,3.
7. Ex. 9:9-11.
8. e.g. Lev. 26, 16; Deut. 28,22.
9. e.g. Ex. 15,26; Deut. 7, 15.
10. *Rosh Hashanah* 25b.
11. Deut. 17:9.
12. *Sanhedrin* 4:5.
13. *Yoreh De'ah,* 157:1, gloss.
14. ib., 339:1; and Maimonides, *Hil. Rotze'ach,* 2:7.
15. Ex. 22:1.
16. Rashi, *Sanhedrin* 72a.
17. Maimonides, *Hil. Rotze'ach,* 1:10-12.
18. *Hil. Yesodei Hatorah,* 5:1-2.
19. ib., and Lev. 22:32.
20. Ps. 118:18.
21. Ps. 81:14-16.
22. Gen. 17:24-27.
23. 21:4.

SUBJECT INDEX

(Major references appear in bold type)

Subject Index